California

THIRD EDITION

California

A Remarkable State's Life History

John W. Caughey

Prentice-Hall, Inc.,   Englewood Cliffs, New Jersey

13–112482–x

Library of Congress Catalog Card No. 73–118334

Printed in the United States of America

Current printing (last digit):
10   9   8   7   6

PRENTICE-HALL INTERNATIONAL, INC., London
PRENTICE-HALL OF AUSTRALIA, PTY. LTD., Sydney
PRENTICE-HALL OF CANADA, LTD., Toronto
PRENTICE-HALL OF INDIA PRIVATE LIMITED, New Delhi
PRENTICE-HALL OF JAPAN, INC., Tokyo

To LaRee

Overview

California's history is a bundle of contradictions. It is long, with the first recorded entry just 50 years after Columbus' voyage of discovery, but with a great part of the action crowded into the period after the Second World War.

California began as a faraway land and still is "an island on the land," set off by desert and mountain wilderness and the Pacific Ocean. Provincialism resulted and continues in spite of instant communication by telephone, teletype, and television, and half-day flights to and from Washington and New York. Yet from Spanish days on, much of the most important decision making about California occurred at the political capitals in Madrid, Mexico City, and Washington, and at the economic headquarters in Boston and New York.

The center of gravity was first at Monterey. Gold moved the focus of attention to San Francisco and Sacramento, and eventually a combination of attractions drew the center to Los Angeles. Throughout, the populated area has been the coastal belt chosen by the Spaniards between San Diego and San Francisco Bay, with later addition of a secondary concentration in the Central Valley.

Sharp periodization characterizes California's history. On the base of an Indian society of thousands of years duration, Spanish soldiers and missionaries erected an outpost of empire, which after 50 years phased into a Mexican pastoral province of about half that duration. Gold dominated the early American decades. A railroad and ranching period followed. Then came emphasis on oranges, oil, health seekers, and real-estate promotion. Shortly thereafter the automobile claimed the state, helping to create a burst of prosperity which was followed by deep depression. Seven years of crash programs for building ships and airplanes, training troops, and helping to fashion the atomic bombs led into the postwar era in which Californians became heavily engaged in the most advanced science and technology and their applications in the space and armaments programs.

The bold changes from period to period have been paralleled by tremendous waves of immigration from foreign lands and in much larger volume from other parts of the United States. In the gold rush the newcomers almost completely engulfed the older Californians. In the boom of the eighties, Los Angeles was swamped by a fivefold or sixfold reinforcement. In later decades literally millions of new residents came, many of them in the prime of life, educated, trained, and experienced people ready to plunge immediately into work, business, and politics. They contributed vitality to the society and the economy. Because they were unacquainted with the land and the climate and knew none of its history, their coming sharpened the breaks with the past.

The exponential rate of population growth accentuated this trend. Through the Spanish and Mexican periods the population curve was almost flat. After 79 years the effective population, not counting the uncontrolled and nonparticipating Indians in the hinterland, numbered only about 15,000. Twenty years later, in 1868, there were half a million Californians; another twenty years later a million; by 1908, 2 million; by 1928, 5 million; by 1948, 10 million; and by 1968, 20 million. This heady spiraling of the population force-fed the changes in each of the superimposed periods and with steadily increasing impact.

Nevertheless, there have been continuities, some of them enforced by the land and climate, the apartness of the state, the rooted laws, and by examples, institutions, and precedents set by earlier generations.

One other change must be noted. Throughout most of its transformations California impressed as strange and exotic. In its most recent manifestations it is coming to be regarded as a pioneer testing new technologies and behavior, a portent of the future, and a leader into a new American or Western culture.

This book surveys this remarkable life history. The flow is chronological but allowed to spread as the complexity of the subject matter dictates. One chapter is allotted to the Indian eon, with primary attention to the way of life at the time of white contact. For the Mexican period there are three topical chapters; for the age of gold two or three times that many. After the

First World War, separate chapters on the twenties, the thirties, and the Second World War were natural. A dozen chapters are devoted to the 20th century, half of them to topical discussion of the throbbing postwar years.

I am deeply indebted to a host of scholars who have worked in this rich field and to students and colleagues who have helped my understanding. Great photographers made selections of their work available, James F. Beggs designed the book, and Sandra Mangurian masterminded its production. My wife deserves far more thanks than the two words on page v.

J.W.C.

May, 1970

Contents

Maps

Illustrations

California

chapter one

The First Californians

Inside a cave in a narrow canyon near Tassajara
The vault of rock is painted with hands,
A multitude of hands in the twilight, a cloud of men's
                    palms, no more,
No other picture. There's no one to say
Whether the brown shy quiet people who are dead intended
Religion or magic, or made their tracings
In the idleness of art; but over the division of years these careful
Signs-manual are now like a sealed message
Saying: "Look: we also were human; we had hands, not paws.
            All hail
You people with the cleverer hands, our supplanters
In the beautiful country; enjoy her a season, her beauty, and
            come down
And be supplanted; for you also are human."

                                    Robinson Jeffers, "Hands"

Before 1769 The history of California has a tentative beginning in 1542 with a Spanish discovery voyage and a more solid start in 1769 when the Spaniards established an outpost of settlement that endured. The United States took over in 1846–48. A year later the gold rush brought enough new residents to warrant launching a state government which was approved by Congress in 1850. In retrospect these dates bear some resemblance to the 1492 of Columbus, the 1607 of Jamestown, and the 1775–83 of the winning of independence; but for California, even more than for the nation, growth and development came in ever-expanding pulsations over the decades since political majority was attained.

Study of California history inevitably concentrates on the circumstances and consequences of the feverish activities of the gold

Cave Painting, Tassajara

L. S. Slevin

2

rush, the broadening development in the era of emphasis on railroads and agriculture, a subsequent time in which oil, tourists, movie making, and the automobile stood out, and then the mid-decades of the twentieth century, in which far more sophisticated applications of science and technology raised the dimensions fantastically.

From the outset the personnel in this history making was cosmopolitan, with Portuguese, Englishmen, Filipinos, and natives of southern Mexico participating in the early voyages, and the gold rush drawing men from every quarter of the globe. Throughout, the participants named in the records and visible in the leadership have been almost without exception of European extraction, participants in the vast expansion of Europe which dominated the post-Columbian centuries.

In contrast to history, the story of man in California would have very different proportions. Although also emphasizing the recent past and the present because of the vast numbers of people on hand and the range of activities, this story of man would take a longer view and recognize the Indians as the largest minority for a generation after 1849, heavily in the majority through the preceding 80 years, and the only residents for centuries and millenia prior to 1769. In other words, from man's first appearance in this area the Indian monopolized the scene for at least 97 per cent of the time span, continued as the numerical majority for another 2 per cent, and has had a continuing role of some interest ever since.

Prehistory

In archeological excavations at Agoura and Mugu in southern California skeletal remains have been found which are dated 6,000 or 7,000 years old. The most ancient mementos thus far authenticated are carved bones of animals long extinct, part of the salvage from La Brea tar pits in Los Angeles. Microscopic tests have established that this carving was done when the bones were "green" (that is to say, fresh); and their radiocarbon dating reads 15,500 years. Other findings may push the horizon back even a little farther.

Taking into account a great mass of nonverbal evidence—archeological remains, anatomical characteristics, culture traits and complexes—anthropologists convincingly ascribe pre-Columbian populating of America to migration from the Old World by way of Alaska. In fairly short order the descendants of these pioneers spread into all parts of North and South America, where processes of isolation and adaptation to contrasting environments began to bring about physical types and ways of life that were readily distinguishable one from another. The California Indians and their way of life at the time of white contact were products of this background. Clearly also there had been several waves of migration into California from other parts of Indian America.

Piecing together what they have learned from Indian artifacts and remains, testimony of surviving Indians, recorded descriptions from earliest contacts to the present, and analysis of Indian adaptations to the way of life imposed by the whites, anthropologists have little to report on year-to-year or even millenium-to-millenium development in Indian California. Anthropologists cannot offer a prehistory at all approaching the sequential beauty and complexity of history, but they can describe, with great richness of detail, Indian life as it was at the coming of the white man. And that is precisely the information most useful to an understanding of the events and processes of history that then ensued.

As the Spaniards saw at once, these Californians were rustics compared to the Aztecs. Nowhere in California were there palisaded towns and vast cornfields such as De Soto saw in Alabama or multistory apartment houses such as Coronado found in New Mexico. The Spanish missionaries, when they began their work, complained that they had to teach the California natives almost everything. The overland pioneers from the United States saw these Indians as many steps below the Iroquois or the Civilized Tribes of the Southeast and much less formidable than the horsemen of the Plains.

Scientific study confirms that these Indians, with the exception of some along the lower Colorado, did not practice agriculture or make pottery. They had no metallurgy, no domesticated animals except dogs, no reading or writing, little emphasis on warfare or government, and no full-time priesthood. Yet they were more numerous than the occupants of any comparable area north of Mexico. They excelled in certain skills, had an oral literature of interest and wisdom, and followed social customs yielding substantial satisfactions. Thus seen, they are promoted several grades above the level assigned to them by the Spanish and American pioneers.

Numbers and Grouping

Before the Spaniards penetrated beyond the southwestern third of present California, the missionized coastal Indians were much reduced in number. In spite of many Spanish assertions that the population was large, a tendency developed to discount the Spanish figures. Then in the 1870's an enthusiastic amateur ethnologist, Stephen Powers, boosted the estimate to 700,000, which is just a trifle short of today's best guess for the pre-Columbian population of the 48-state area of the United States. The most careful judgment, A. L. Kroeber's, gives California about 130,000, a number not much in excess of the capacity of the Rose Bowl and very small compared to the present population of California or to the several million Indians of Mexico. As of the late 1960's, when Californians rose to 10 per cent of the population of the United States, the universal feeling was that theirs was a highly populous state. In Indian America the preference for California had been even greater; 130,000 was about 17 per cent of the nationwide population.

Indian California had some 135 different Indian languages, each on the average serving 1,000 persons. For many years these tongues defied re-

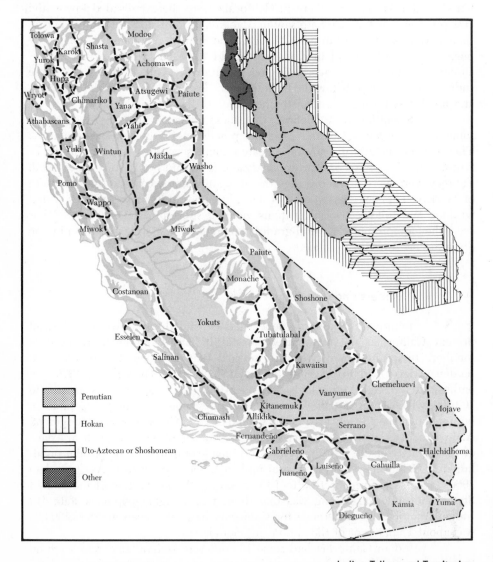

Indian Tribes and Territories

duction to less than 21 or 22 linguistic families. Additional relationships have been discovered, but half a dozen distinct groups remain, indicating that diversity of speech was of long standing.

Villages, usually called rancherías as in Spanish, numbered approximately 1,000. Arithmetically, this figure yields 130 as the average village population. Some, to be sure, were smaller, others larger, but few communities exceeded twice this size. For political units, the individual ranchería is about as high as one can go. A number of tribal groupings, however, reflect cultural, if not political, entities.

When shown on a map, Indian California appears to have been split into very small linguistic and governmental units. In a sense, however, this is an optical illusion, for the average number of persons speaking an idiom or constituting a village or tribal group was not excessively small. Had the Great Basin Indians or the Plains Indians been compressed into smaller areas of the same population density, the effect would have been very similar. Viewed thus, the distinctive feature about the California natives was not the smallness of the units but the smallness of the area occupied by each unit or, in other words, the density of population. The latter rested, of course, upon the distinctive economy that had grown up in California.

Perhaps the most convenient method of tracing the linguistic and tribal groupings is to start at San Francisco Bay and circle out. Just north of the Golden Gate and up the west side of the Sacramento Valley from Suisun Bay to Mt. Shasta resided the Wintun. Across the Sacramento River were the Maidu, and in the Sierra foothills from the Cosumnes to the Merced lived the Miwok. The southern half of the Central Valley belonged to the Yokuts, while in the Coast Ranges from Soledad and Carmel to San Francisco were the villages of the Costaño, or coast men. These tribal groups constituted the Penutian speech family and are estimated to have numbered 57,000.

The second largest linguistic family, the Hokan, was made up of tribal groups roughly encircling the Penutian speakers. In modern Sonoma, Lake, and Mendocino counties were the Pomo, renowned for their excellent basketry. Capping the northern end of the Central Valley were the Chimariko, Karok, Shastan, and Yana. Of these, the Karok were the most advanced in culture and the Yana the most warlike. The Washo, a Nevada group, intruded as far as Lake Tahoe and flanked the eastern Sierra from the lake northward. In the southern Coast Ranges and along the Santa Barbara Channel lived the numerous and prosperous Chumash, and beyond them the Salinan and the Esselen. Fringing the state at the south and southeast were still other members of the Hokan Family: the Diegueño (their name derived from Mission San Diego), and the Cocopa, Yuma, and Mojave along the Colorado River. These tribes were noted for their warlike disposition. Because it included the Pomo and the Chumash, the Hokan family was important out of proportion to its number, estimated at 37,500.

Some 23,500 Californians used languages belonging to the Shoshoean family, which also included such distant tribes as the Comanche of the Plains and the Aztec of Mexico. The Paiutes in the northeast corner of the state belong to this speech family, but most of its representatives were in the Great Basin and southern California, among them the Mono in the valley that bears their name, the Tübatulabal of Kern River, the Chemehuevi and others in the Mojave Desert, the Cahuilla in the Colorado Desert, the Serrano, or mountaineers, in the San Bernardino Mountains, and several groups so effectively missionized by the Spaniards that they are known by mission names, such as Luiseño, Juaneño, Gabrielino.

The remaining groups were comparatively small and confined to northern California. North and inland from the Pomo were the ruder Yuki, who had not only a speech of their own but distinctive physical traits as well. To the north were several groups that, like the Dene of Alaska and the Apaches of the Southwest, belonged to the Athabascan family. Interspersed among them in Humboldt County were the Algonkin-speaking Wiyot and Yurok, whose superior culture was similar to that of the Hokan-speaking Karok. Finally, among the lava beds of the Tule Lake region was a small group of Modocs, having linguistic and cultural connections with the Indians of Oregon.

Material Culture

Throughout California the fundamental garment was a two-piece apron of buckskin, shredded bark, or other plant fibers, worn with the smaller apron in front. The back piece extended to the thighs and might meet the front apron at the sides. For females this double apron was universal; even girl babies only a few days old were so attired. The manly fashion was to go naked. In cold weather men and women wrapped themselves in blankets, preferably of otter skins though more often of rabbitskins or deerskin. The central and northern Californians had moccasins but normally went barefoot. Skin leggings and oval snowshoes had more restricted distribution. South of the Tehachapi sandals replaced moccasins but again were not worn constantly. Basketry caps occurred in the north and south but not in central California. Southern women used them as a comfortable pad for the packstraps; in the north they were fashionable as a constant item of female attire.

Buildings varied widely. Some were covered with brush, others with thatch, bark, or earth. Conical and dome shapes were favored except in the northwest where the rectangular pattern of the neighboring woodworking experts was followed. Some houses were partly dug out. Most were one-family dwellings, and, except in the northwest where a non-California idea had penetrated, all were rude huts.

Sweat houses rather than residences were the most characteristic structures. Throughout central California sweat houses were small and conical, covered with earth to conserve heat, and reserved for men. After kindling an open fire inside the sweat house (temescal), three or four men would enter and lounge on the floor to escape the smoke. When a free perspiration had been produced, they rushed out and plunged into a nearby stream or lake. For certain disorders, such as rheumatic complaints, this treatment was beneficial, but when applied to new maladies such as measles and smallpox, introduced by the whites, it was disastrous. Yet therapeutic use was at most incidental; the sweat house was really a daily masculine social habit. In northwestern California the temescales were larger and served as clubs where the men assembled to discuss affairs of state. In some villages it was customary for the men to spend the night at the temescal club and only the women and children slept in the ordinary houses.

Most of the Californians had no better boats than tule balsas, bundles of reeds hurriedly tied together for ferrying a river or made with greater care and propelled by poles or paddles on lakes and bays. Dugouts, nicely fashioned from cedar logs, were employed in the northwestern rivers and bays and on the ocean. By sewing planks together the Chumash of the Santa Barbara Channel made seaworthy boats described as trim, light, and capacious. The Chumash used these boats to paddle back and forth to the Channel Islands.

The commonest archeological specimen in California is the stone grinding bowl, or mortar. The Indians had many other implements of stone, bone, shell, and wood, many of them less enduring. These implements included simple bows and arrows in the south and sinew-backed bows in the north, arrows with flint or obsidian points, harpoons, and spears, in the south a throwing stick for rabbit hunting, awls and arrow straighteners, rattles and whistles, bull roarers, crude flutes, and Jew's harps. Pottery was much less emphasized and limited to the region of strongest Southwestern influence.

Shields and protective armor were almost unknown. Bows and arrows, spears, and clubs were used, but in actual fighting the Californians exhibited a more primitive tendency to let fly any stones that might be lying about. Warfare was uncommon. One village might attack a neighboring one to avenge a visitation of disease supposedly caused by the neighbors, but the fighting usually stopped before many lives were lost. There was very little discipline or strategy, though Stanislau and Modoc Jack later won recognition as highly capable leaders. Although scalps were sometimes taken, scalping as a means of winning renown and scalp dances to claim public honors were not California traits.

Hunting and fishing were done mainly with nets and traps. Although fish and game were sometimes speared, the Channel Indians did most of their fishing with hook and line. Large game was generally avoided. Coyotes and eagles had mythological connections that secured them a reverent regard. Bears were looked upon as semihuman, and the flesh of the dog was abhorred as poisonous. Along with the total lack of agriculture these taboos seriously restricted the food list. Yet an adequate food supply was characteristic rather than exceptional. Acorns were the staple, and herbs and grass seeds were next in importance, followed by fish, shellfish, rabbits, and other small game. Snakes, angleworms, grasshoppers, honey, snails, and grubs were relished, but their use was by no means universal.

Indian Mortar Holes, Pine Needles, Yosemite National Park

Throughout most of the area oak groves dotted the landscape and provided large and regular crops ot acorns. Acorns could readily be stored and, being richly nutritious, were eminently suitable for human consumption, provided that the tannic acid could be removed.

The clever extraction process represents one of the greatest California achievements. Since food preparation was women's work, the leaching procedure almost certainly was a woman's invention, as were other refinements and improvements. Taking a few handfuls of acorns from the basketry granary, the squaw removed the husks and pulverized the nut meats, using a stone pestle on a bedrock mortar or in a bottomless basket on a rock slab or stone bowl. The flour was then winnowed by tossing in a shallow basket. Meanwhile, water had been heated by dropping hot stones into a basket of water. The meal was spread out on a sand pile and leached with eight or ten doses of water. When the water ran off clear, revealing that the tannic acid was gone, the meal was gathered up and cooked in water, again heated by plunging hot stones into the basket. Acorn meal swelled up like cornstarch, forming a gruel or pudding, which was eaten either plain or flavored with berries, nuts, rabbit meat, grasshoppers, or insects.

Although ingenious, the acorn process was most laborious and time consuming. Like manna, prepared acorn meal would keep only a short time; the California women therefore were almost constantly employed in some part of the process. Once developed, the process became firmly established. Grinding was extended to other foods, such as buckeye berries and rabbit meat, which many toothless old people prepared similarly.

Basketry was the handicraft in which the Californians excelled. They used baskets for all conceivable purposes—for hats, for storage granaries, for containers of all sorts, and for cooking vessels. In some instances cooking baskets were caulked with pitch or tar, but others were woven so compactly as to be watertight. These baskets could withstand stone boiling provided the cook stirred and kept the hot stone from resting too long against the side or bottom. These basketmakers had command of several techniques of weaving and of many methods of decorating in geometric or pictorial designs or by application of shell mosaics, beads, or feathers. Museum collections provide vivid exhibits of this California skill. The most skilled weavers enjoyed proving their craftsmanship by fabricating tiny thimble-sized baskets, perfect in almost microscopic detail, jewel-like demonstrations of virtuosity.

Social and Religious Practices

Except that the Yuma and Mojave were better organized and the Yokuts had a semblance of a tribal system, the largest political unit was the ranchería. In the northwest the essential groups were even smaller. In most villages the chieftainship was hereditary and strictly civil. Some chiefs were women, some had an assistant chief, some had specified assistants to act as messengers, some were accorded deference, but all lacked real power.

Most of the tribes south of San Francisco were split into moieties with descent traced along the father's side and with marriage partners to be selected from the other moiety. Marriage was characteristically arranged by purchase, though in the south often only by token purchase. Several tribes had kinship taboos, such as against conversing with one's mother-in-law. The Yana had separate dialects for men and women. Cremation was standard in most of California. In the northwest the Indians held slaves and placed great emphasis on wealth, though they lacked the associated symbolism of the property-minded Kwakiutl and Haida. Other Californians were less mercenary but set store by strings of dentalium shells or clamshell beads and cylinders of magnesite or shell.

From the pioneers, both Spanish and American, later Californians inherited a low appraisal of the California Indians, often spoken of in contempt as Digger Indians, a canard that anthropologists protested as inappropriate and uncalled for. Certain modern writers lapse into the old attitude and, in addition, picture those Indians as wallowing in vermin, filth, and stench. To these writers it seems irrelevant that the Spanish and American frontiersmen went a long time between baths and changes of clothes. Allowance should be made for liberal exposure of the Indians to one cleansing element, the air. The temescal also was a great cleanser. Visitors report many rancherías where everyone bathed daily and speak of fastidiousness and cleanliness.

The Californians had a variety of games calling for strength or dexterity, among them contests roughly similar to shinny, lacrosse, football, double ball, and the hoop and pole game. They were more addicted to gambling, betting heavily on athletic contests and on guessing games such as the hand game (similar to up-jinks) and the throwing of marked sticks (similar to dice). The Californians by all accounts played the hand game zealously and passionately, appointing someone to keep up the fire and to sing, an accompaniment that doubtless helped the players to keep poker faces. Psychologically, poker and the hand game are very similar. In Indian California there was no frowning on their game or on the betting that went with it.

In California the foremost men of religion were the shamans, or doctors, who cured through songs or, more often, by removing the "disease object," usually by pretended sucking. In much of California, the shaman's power to cure was believed to rest upon his having within his own body disease objects which would have caused a nonshaman immense pain. There also were specialists: weather shamans who engaged in rainmaking, rattlesnake shamans who handled snakebite cases, and grizzly-bear shamans who either changed into bears or masqueraded in bearskins, thereby gaining extraordinary powers, which, it was hoped, they would use for the good of the tribe rather than against their fellow tribesmen.

Ceremonials were few but some were highly developed. A girls' adolescence ceremony was universal and was taken as the occasion for liberal preachments on the advisability of good behavior for the benefit of the entire community. Southern and Sierra tribes also had an annual mourning ceremony. Other ceremonies occasionally encountered included semiconfinement of the father at time of childbirth, New Year observances, boys' puberty rites, the first salmon rites, and the ant ordeal.

More distinctive were the initiation rituals of the Kuksu cult in central California and of the toloache, or Jimsonweed, cult in the south. Embracing every man in the villages involved, these societies had developed complicated and impressive ceremonies of initiation. The Kuksu rituals were built around impersonated spirits, with elaborate costumes, regalia, and disguises representing the mythical characters. In the toloache cult the ceremonial began with the administration of the powerful drug, which stupefied for one or more nights and, in some instances, killed. The visions seen during this period of narcosis were of lifelong sanctity. Then followed several nights of dancing and a period of fasting. Much instruction was included, partly by song and partly by means of ground painting.

These Indians had a profusion of legendary stories, many of which represented high achievement in speculation on fundamental philosophical problems: explanations of the creation, the origin of death, and the problem of good and evil. The characters were animals. The coyote was a favorite, an arrogant, mischievous trickster, sometimes a benefactor of mankind, at other times bringing disaster or embarrassment. Apart from their mythology these often humorous tales make good reading or good listening, and, like the Old Testament of the Hebrews, they shed much light on the mundane habits of the people who passed them on to posterity.

Adjustment to Environment

In California nature gave the Indians a great variety of environments. It is a land of many and great contrasts, often in close juxtaposition. First there are the mountains, beginning with the mighty Sierra Nevada, the longest and boldest range in the United States, more than 400 miles long, including Mt. Whitney (14,496 feet in elevation) and fifty others towering over 13,000 feet. This range was created by the raising of a great block of the earth's crust, with faults and subsidence at the eastern edge and tilting toward the west. There are passes, but of some difficulty and elevated 7,000 to 10,000 feet.

The Cascades to the north are more recent and volcanic in origin. Mt. Shasta (14,161) has the classic beauty of a volcanic cone, and Mt. Lassen was an active volcano as recently as 1914. The northwestern corner of the state is a jumble of nonvolcanic mountains, the Klamaths, with some peaks approaching 10,000 feet. The Coast Ranges reach southward as parallel fingers set at a slight eastward angle from the coast. Along the Eel there are peaks of 7,000 to 8,000 feet; near San Francisco Bay the mountains are not above 3,000 to 4,000 feet; the Santa Lucia range is higher; and Mt. Pinos is elevated 9,214 feet.

From Mt. Pinos the Tehachapis extend east and northeast to meet the Sierra, while the mountain axis of southern California, culminating in the San Gabriel and San Bernardino Mountains, stretches eastward. From the San Bernardinos one short jump southward is Mount San Jacinto, outpost of the Peninsular Range, which extends into Lower California.

These mountains and other stray peaks and ranges in the deserts occupy a good half of the surface area of the state. By intercepting and storing moisture carried in by winds from the Pacific, the mountains perform an inestimable service. They have other uses, but they never have supported anything like half of California's residents.

Another third of the state—the Colorado and Mojave deserts, the arid Carrisa Plain, the overwet valley of the Eel, and the frosty and thin-soiled volcanic Plateau in the northeast—has obvious drawbacks. The Indians shunned the highest mountains, the thickest forests, and the deserts except where there were oases. They much preferred the flat land of plains and valleys, the rolling hills where grass and trees interspersed, and the coastal spots where fish could be had.

In order to make the most of the foods to be gathered, many of the Indians shifted their base with the seasons, camping on the plain in the spring when grass and certain bulbs were tender, pursuing game into the hills or mountains in summer, coming down to the oak groves for the acorn harvest, and going to another site for the winter camp. Other Indians were on the coast for a season of fishing, elsewhere when grass seeds were most abundant, and in the desert at harvest time for mesquite beans and agave.

Despite such shifting about, the California Indians seem not to have been great travelers. Few if any, one gathers, could have passed an examination on the geography from one end of the state to the other and from the mountains to the sea. Yet from most localities, it is possible without traveling far to reach a place that is much warmer or cooler, wetter or drier, with more fog or more sunshine. In general the Indians chose the sites where the climate is benign. They paid the climate the further compliment of wearing little or no unnecessary clothing and chose to live where light shelter was enough.

Along the American Nile (the Colorado), where all they had to do was scatter seeds where the river overflowed, the Yumas and their neighbors had crops to harvest. Since they merely planted and harvested but did not cultivate, perhaps that was not real farming, yet the concept of agriculture came that close to the rest of the California tribesmen. They resisted it, in part because their gathering techniques and the acorn process were satisfactory, and in part because to have tied themselves down to localized planting and cultivating would have interfered with the larger harvesting of the natural crops.

Oak-dotted Grassland, near Clements, California

Philip Hyde

These Indians lacked the technological means that would have permitted them to use many resources that the land had in store: gold, silver, tungsten, the power of falling water, oil (except in the brea used to caulk boats and baskets), San Francisco Bay (except as a clam and oyster flat), the climate as an inducement to tourists, and real estate as a medium of speculation. In terms of the technology available to them they had a most satisfactory inventory of what was edible or poisonous, what fibers were suitable for basket making, what stones would chip sharp for knives and arrowheads, how to outwit fish and game, and where to be in each of the many harvest seasons.

Short of what we call science they had rich knowledge as naturalists. Their mode of life, furthermore, put little or no strain on the natural resources. A. L. Kroeber's population estimates have as one base his calculation of the carrying power of a given area with its foodstuffs and other necessities. He assumes that population would tend to rise to this carrying power. He says, however, that the Californians seldom experienced famine or starvation, another way of saying that they did not overtax the natural supply. A conservationist would say that their behavior was exemplary.

Appraisal

Such, in brief, was the culture of the California Indians when the white man arrived. Their subsequent experiences at mission and rancho, in the gold fields, on the reservation and off, as early town and farm laborers, and as participants on the modern scene are threads in the general history of the state since 1769 and are handled in that fashion in the chapters that follow.

Since modern California has moved so rapidly, the question arises why the Indian life was so static as well as primitive. If this criticism implies that these Indians should have invented a printing press, steam engine, or atomic bomb, it asks the impossible. Such achievements could come only after certain plateaus in science had been reached. The first Californians were far from that eligibility, and they were a conservative people with built-in resistance to change. As they saw it, their way of life had many good points. Later, many Indians looked back on the pre-white period as a happier day of peace, leisure, enough to eat, and lots of fun.

Whatever else it may signify, this conservatism does not mean that these Indians were innately stupid as some have alleged. The life of Ishi of the Yahi, "the last wild Indian," exemplifies a high capacity to adjust to radically different circumstances.

Ishi grew to manhood in an enclave of wild hill country east of Marysville. With an old uncle, his mother, and his sister, the last remnant of their tribe, he followed the ancient practices near ranches and towns and the railroad but with almost complete avoidance of the new California. Fleeing from a party of surveyors, his little group split. He never saw the old man or his sister again, and his mother soon died. In 1911, almost starving, he came down to Marysville

Ishi Fashioning a Harpoon

where, for safekeeping, he was put in jail. A newspaper story alerted University of California anthropologists, one of whom came to see this derelict. After reading off a long list of Indian words the visitor came at last to a word Ishi recognized. Gradually he won Ishi's confidence. He took him to live at the anthropological museum in San Francisco where he was initiated into the intricacies of the white man's way of life.

Ishi responded by becoming a most valuable informant on the Yahi language and on many elements of Indian culture. One of his new associates, T. T. Waterman, rated him the man of all others he most admired. His story has been told and retold, most effectively by Theodora Kroeber in *Ishi in Two Worlds* and *Ishi, Last of His Tribe*.

Other Indians, less dramatically, have demonstrated similar capacity to adapt to what we consider a much more sophisticated civilization. The clear implication is that their native capacity is substantially the same as that claimed by other Californians. The twentieth century instance of Ishi cuts shorter the time gap between today's most modern culture and that of the Stone Age people who were the only Californians as recently as 1768. Expanding knowledge of the full picture of life in prehistoric California also suggests that in many particulars the arrangements then achieved were much to be admired. Not least was the continence in handing the land on to each succeeding generation as beautiful and habitable as before.

For Further Reading

R. F. HEIZER and M. A. WHIPPLE, *The California Indians* (1951), a selection of essays and original sources.
C. HART MERRIAM, *Studies of California Indians* (1955), field work reports.
E. W. GIFFORD and G. H. BLOCK, *Californian Indian Nights Entertainments* (1930).
JAIME DE ANGULO, *Indian Tales* (1953).
THEODORA KROEBER, *The Inland Whale* (1959), stories about Indian women and girls.
C. L. McNICHOLS, *Crazy Weather* (1944, 1967), about a Mojave boy.
THEODORA KROEBER, *Ishi in Two Worlds* (1961).
THEODORA KROEBER, *Ishi, Last of His Tribe* (1964).
The Autobiography of Delfina Cuero (1968).
JOHN and LaREE CAUGHEY, *California Heritage* (1971), 2–43.

The following are abbreviations used in the chapter reading lists and in the bibliographical essay at the end of the book.
CHSQ   *California Historical Society Quarterly*
HLQ   *Huntington Library Quarterly*
JAH   *Journal of American History*
MVHR   *Mississippi Valley Historical Review*
PHR   *Pacific Historical Review*
SCQ   *Southern California Quarterly* (earlier known as *Historical Society of Southern California Quarterly*)

chapter two

Explorers

Know ye that on the right hand of the Indies
there is an island called California. . . .

Garci Ordóñez de Montalvo,
Las sergas de Esplandián (about 1510)

Spanish Beginnings

**1492
to
1603**

Columbus' point of discovery in America fell short of California by about 3,000 miles. As the crow flies, he had come only about half the distance from Spain; it took other Spaniards another 50 years to reach California.

From his first voyage Columbus carried home tantalizing word of islands 33 days' sail out into the western ocean. Believing he had reached the vicinity of the Spice Islands and the Indies, he identified the people of these islands as Indians. The king and queen of Spain sent him back to learn more and to claim more lands in their names. On that and two other voyages Columbus made other landfalls and ran other coasts bordering the Caribbean Sea. This part of

Drake's Beach, Point Reyes National Seashore, California,
in the vicinity of Drake and Cermeño landings

Philip Hyde

the New World soon was accurately charted. A little later Balboa crossed a narrow isthmus to the South Sea, subsequently called the Pacific. Other Spaniards sailed around the Gulf of Mexico, while still others probed the Florida coast all the way to Maine and the South American coast to the Straits of Magellan.

The explorations of these first 25 or 30 years brought the discouraging news that for 50 degrees on each side of the equator a continuous landmass blocked the westward route to the Orient. A little gold was found on the island of Haiti and pearls on the north coast of South America, but thus far the New World was not making anyone rich. Spain administered it rather nonchalantly.

In 1521 a ship of Magellan's fleet completed the first voyage around the world, demonstrating the existence of a westward water route to the Orient. Spain took little pleasure in the news. The Straits of Magellan, besides being tortuous, lay much too far south, and Magellan's Pacific, reaching almost halfway around the earth, was far too wide. Besides, Portugal had already opened an easier route around Africa, and Spain and Portugal in the Treaty of Tordesillas had marked off the non-European world into spheres of interest, Portugal getting the bulge of Brazil and eastward to the East Indies, and Spain the bulk of America and the Pacific.

Cortés' conquest of the Aztecs, also completed in 1521, forced a reevaluation of America. The Aztec capital was a city as large as any in Spain. Its public buildings were impressive; its people, skilled in many crafts. It was, furthermore, a city abounding in gold and silver. In the light of these new facts, the king began to pay more attention to his overseas domain and property. To the Casa de Contratación, which already controlled commerce and navigation, he soon added the Consejo de las Indias, or Council of the Indies. This action amounted to the creation of a cabinet-rank department with jurisdiction over Spain's colonies in America. In 1535 the king sent to Mexico a viceroy, a higher-ranking official than England ever saw fit to assign to an American station.

Through these and other agencies the Spanish monarchy imposed a centralized administration. Its fundamentals can be simply stated. The king was supreme. The religion would be Roman Catholic, with the church more controlled by the king than was true in Spain. In all things economic the king's interest would come first. Taxes, trade, and the channeling of production would be specified by the monarch. The king would also stand as protector of the Indians, who must be Christianized, civilized, and preserved to do their part for the improvement of the Indies as the possession of the king.

Even before imperial control was galvanized in this fashion, Spaniards from the Caribbean islands and from Spain responded to the news from Mexico by rushing to help Cortés and his men seize the Indian riches. They were ready to follow any lead that might point to another Mexico. Under Jiménez de Quesada some found almost as much wealth in the high country around Bogotá, located in present-day Colombia. Under Francisco Pizarro the conquest of the Incas yielded even greater booty. These were the great conquistadores.

Other parties of as few as 100 or as many as 600 men marched off to try to match these successes. They moved from Peru to Charcas (Bolivia) and

Chile, across the Andes and down the Amazon, up the Plata and into the interior, from the Caribbean into the valley of the Orinoco and on to the Amazon, into Central America, into Florida and ranging far into the continent, northward from Mexico thousands of miles into the interior, and by sea along the untracked Pacific coast. Some of these adventurers laid the basis for new provinces and modern nations, though their rewards were less than those of Cortés or Pizarro and they rank only as minor conquistadores. Those who operated east of the Andes or north of Mexico and the Gulf of Mexico were dismal failures, except for their contributions to the greatest expansion of geographical knowledge any generation has ever carried out. As part of this penetration of the hemisphere Spanish exploration of California began.

California as an Island

Section of a map by Joannes Blaeu, 1648

The Lure of the Northwest

The pioneer in exploration northwestward was Cortés. While the work of building a Spanish city on the Aztec ruins was still in its early stages, he led an expedition south to Honduras. Shortly, however, his interest turned to the west coast, which in this latitude led off more to the west than to the north, and that meant toward the Orient.

To sail this coast Cortés first had to build ships, a discouraging assignment. The west coast could provide timber, but nails, ropes, and everything else had to be packed across from Veracruz. Skilled workmen were hard to find. A fire in the warehouse set the project back a year, and by royal order the first four ships launched were diverted to a different use, after which Cortés had to go to Spain to answer charges by his enemies.

At last in 1532 he sent out two ships. They did not return; word trickled in through the Indians that a rival leader, Nuño de Guzmán, had intercepted them at some point up the coast. Another pair of ships sailed in 1533. In one Hernando de Grijalva deserted and discovered the Revilla Gigedo Islands. On the other Fortún Jiménez led a mutiny in which the commander was killed. Jiménez went on to a bay which he named La Paz on what he took to be an island. On the way back he was killed by Indians of the mainland, but the survivors reached Cortés with reports of the island visited.

Because they said the island was rich in pearls, Cortés announced he would go there personally. So great was his reputation as a treasure finder that this announcement produced a rush of volunteers. Ship space was available for only half the men eager to go, and, when Cortés sailed in 1535, he could only promise to send back for the others. At Santa Cruz, his name for the island, he found few pearls. He also discovered that the voyage from the mainland was most difficult. A ship sent back for more men and supplies could not make the island again, and, when Cortés attempted it personally, he got back to Santa Cruz only after much trouble. In the meantime, 23 men had died of starvation. The barrenness of the land, the backwardness and hostility of the natives, and the adverse sailing conditions impelled him to abandon this pearl fishery. The last of his men were taken off in 1536.

Flagging interest in the northwest was revived almost at once by the arrival at Culiacán, the northwest outpost of New Spain, of Alvar Núñez Cabeza de Vaca. He told a marvelous tale of shipwreck on the Texas coast, six years as slave, trader, and medicine man among the Indians, and a transcontinental hike with black Estevanico through western Texas and northern Mexico. His story was the more exciting because he had heard mention of seven wondrous cities farther north. These, the Spaniards assumed, must be the Seven Cities famous in European legend as Christian oases stranded far out in heathendom.

As the chief activist in northwestward exploration, Cortés considered himself the proper person to investigate this new attraction. Antonio de Mendoza, however, the newly arrived Viceroy of New Spain, was under instructions to reduce Cortés' power. To allow the great conquistador to lead an expedition which might surpass the conquest of the Aztecs would make him an untouchable hero. Without hesitation Mendoza named Francisco Vázquez de Coronado to this command. Friar Marcos and Estevanico were sent to reconnoiter. When Marcos on his return reported seeing one of these cities from a distant hill, compared it in size to the city of Mexico, and said its buildings were of silver, the viceroy was ready to invest heavily in the Coronado expedition.

Blocked on land, Cortés was still able to operate by sea. In 1539, as his final gesture toward the northwest, he sent Francisco de Ulloa with three vessels to sail up the coast of the mainland, on the chance that the Seven Cities might be within striking distance of the sea.

Performing this task with thoroughness, Ulloa sailed up the strait between the mainland and Cortés' Santa Cruz. He went far enough to be convinced that the strait was a gulf and the island a peninsula. Rounding the tip of the peninsula, he ran its outer shore as far as Cedros Island, at about the twenty-eighth parallel. From this point he sent back his larger vessel to report the discoveries made, while with the 35-ton vessel he continued to explore.

Except that maps of the time soon showed the coast another degree to the north, quite possibly reflecting discovery by Ulloa, no further record of his work has been preserved. Historians wrote him off as lost, but a court record revealing his appearance years later as a witness proves that he returned safely. He may have seen more of this outer coast, but his fame properly rests on his voyage up the gulf and along both sides of the peninsula and on his proof that it was a peninsula. In another year or two his gulf and peninsula would have the name California.

The Ulloa enterprise marked Cortés' last connection with Pacific coast exploration. He went to Spain in 1540 to seek compensation for his losses and to insist on his rights to explore. Legal complications engulfed him, and he spent the rest of his days in Spain.

Coronado, meanwhile, was gathering a force of 300 Spaniards and several hundred Indians, besides thousands of animals for remounts and provisions. After parading in review before the viceroy at Compostela, they took the trail to what became a bitter disappointment. Marcos' silver buildings proved to be whitewashed adobe glistening in the sun. The Seven Cities increased in number but dwindled in splendor to the humble status of the Pueblo towns. Coronado called the region New Mexico, but it fell far short of being another Mexico.

Hope revived when an Indian told of a richer land, Gran Quivira. Coronado plunged into the Great Plains in the spring of 1541 in search of this new wonder, but of course it was not there. The guide had fabricated it, as he later confessed, to lure the Spaniards onto the trackless plains, hoping they would not return. Coronado came back to the Rio Grande but did not tarry long. The next spring his tattered followers were on their way to Mexico. Because of the high expectations with which he had set out and the lavishness of the equipment, he was regarded a failure.

With occupation of the upper Rio Grande postponed half a century,

Coronado's expedition was rich only in explorations and these turned north-eastward, away from California. One small party of his men, it is true, had an assignment that took them toward California. In 1540, shortly after Coronado's departure for the north, Hernando de Alarcón was sent on a voyage up the gulf. He reached its head, took his ships across the bar and into the river later named the Colorado, and ascended it several days' journey, how far it is impossible to say. Finding no sign of Coronado, he turned back to Mexico.

The detachment sent by Coronado arrived too late. Its leader, Melchor Díaz, crossed the Colorado and turned south hoping to find Alarcón. Severely injured in an accident, Díaz died, whereupon his men retraced their steps. Both parties were close enough to glimpse the southeastern corner of the present state of California, but the record does not show that either set foot on this soil.

California Named and Discovered

Meanwhile, one of the heroes of the conquest of the Aztecs, Pedro de Alvarado, was assembling a fleet of 11 ships for further efforts northwestward. Volunteering to help put down an Indian rebellion, he was killed in the fighting. His ships were then used by the viceroy in the Villalobos, Bolaños, and Cabrillo voyages.

Ruy López de Villalobos was to sail across the Pacific to the Spice Islands. His westward track took him to the archipelago where Magellan had been killed. Villalobos named the islands the Philippines in honor of the Spanish Prince and claimed them for Spain. When he attempted to make the return voyage to New Spain, however, he found the winds consistently contrary.

On his voyage Francisco de Bolaños was to try to make contact with Coronado and the Seven Cities. Setting out in 1541, he confined his work to the area near the tip of Ulloa's peninsula. He is, nevertheless, the most likely candidate for the honor of having named California.

In 1542 in the narrative of the Cabrillo expedition, Cortés' island of Santa Cruz, which Ulloa had demonstrated to be a peninsula, is referred to as California. The usage is casual, as though it were a name already established and familiar. The time of christening must have been after Ulloa in 1539 and before Cabrillo in 1542. Bolaños was the principal leader then in the field, and other place names such as Cabo de San Lucas are his.

For a long time the derivation of the name was a matter of wildest speculation. Now it is convincingly traced to one of the most popular pieces of early sixteenth century fiction, *Las sergas de Esplandián* (*The Deeds of Esplandián*), by Ordóñez de Montalvo. *Esplandián* was a fantastic thriller, written as a sequel to the more famous *Amadís de Gaula*. Among other wild adventures it relates how the Christians at Constantinople were opposed by a force of Amazons led by Queen Calafía of the island of California. The island of California was described as being "at the right hand of the Indies" and very close to the Terrestrial Paradise, an Amazon island abounding in gold and infested with many griffins. Cortés as early as 1524 and Guzmán in 1530 expressed their expectations of finding an Amazon island 10 days' sail off the coast. This fact, together with the certain familiarity of Cortés' men with the Montalvo romance, establishes the derivation of the name almost beyond doubt.

The state of California not only has this literary derivation for its name, it also has the distinction of having been named before it was discovered.

First Visit to the Coast of California

By the time of Bolaños' return, the viceroy was disillusioned about the Seven Cities. He charged Juan Rodríguez Cabrillo, a Portuguese in the Spanish service, to sail along the coast toward Cathay and also to look for the western entrance to the Strait of Anian, the much talked-about water route from North Atlantic to Pacific.

Cabrillo gave the coast only a cursory examination up to Cabo del Engaño, apparently because Ulloa had explored that far. When he landed and took possession for the king, he heard from the Indians of other whites to the east, presumably the men of Coronado. Continuing northward, he passed the later boundary and became the first authenticated visitor to Alta California. On September 28, 1542, he discovered San Diego Bay, which he named San Miguel, and behind Point Loma his two tiny ships lay sheltered during a three-day storm. "They discovered a port, enclosed and very good," reads the account of this voyage.

They were at Santa Catalina and San Clemente islands on October 7 and 8, named San Pedro Bay the Bay of Smokes, and journeyed on to Town of Canoes, where possession was again taken in the name of the king. Repeatedly, the Indians made mention of other Spaniards to the east. Cabrillo followed the coast very closely as far as Point Concepción, stopping at several places.

Encountering stiff northwest winds beyond the point, he returned temporarily to San Miguel Island and there had the misfortune to break an arm, or, as other accounts have it, a leg. Although the break was most painful and did not heal properly, Cabrillo shortly took advantage of a southwester to explore more of the coast. Just how far north he went is not clear. He made no landings and much of the time had to stand well out to sea. He did, however, become well acquainted with a Baia de Los Pinos (according to the description, Monterey Bay), and he observed some other parts of the coast both north and south of this bay. Stormy weather finally forced him back to San Miguel Island, where the old injury brought death on January 3, 1543.

On his deathbed Cabrillo instructed his second in command to continue the northward exploration. Bartolomé Ferrelo made a sincere effort, but stormy weather still interfered, and, like his master, he was unable to land anywhere north of Point Concepción. His northernmost glimpse of the coast was not far from Point Reyes. Either out at sea off the mouth of Rogue River in Oregon or, more probably, off Eel River or Mad River, at about the forty-first parallel, signs seemed to point to a great river in the locality. This was interpreted to mean the western mouth of the Strait of Anian. Except for this conjecture Ferrelo got little information about this part of the coast. He gave up the battle against the storms and took the survivors back to Navidad, submitting from there his and Cabrillo's reports to the viceroy.

In Alta California they had found no more wealth than Coronado had in New Mexico and Kansas. Although the Indians of southern California were numerous and friendly, they were not advanced or wealthy enough to invite Spanish exploitation. The bay at San Diego, though admittedly excellent, was of little or no practical use until some excuse for occupying Alta California should arise. Even the recognition of southern California as a "land of endless summers" did not rouse Spanish interest in this distant region. The best news, perhaps, was that the Strait of Anian, if it existed at all, must strike the Pacific so far north that its discovery by other Europeans would not seriously menace Spain's hold upon Mexico and South America.

Silver Mines and the Manila Galleon

For a score of years after Cabrillo interest in California lagged. Negative findings from the field were reason enough; attention was also monopolized by the great silver discoveries at Zacatecas, Guanajuato, and elsewhere in Nueva Galicia. What ensued was the prototype for the whole series of mining rushes in western North America; indeed, the "days of '48" at Zacatecas, though three centuries removed, are compared with the "days of '49" in California. There was one difference: some of the ore deposits, that of the Veta Madre at Guanajuato, for instance, were extensive enough to support mining for generations, in fact, for centuries. Booming mining activity stimulated stock raising and farming throughout the adjacent regions. Silver mining satisfied most of the demands for profit and adventure that had impelled the earlier explorations. In the 1560's, however, Francisco de Ibarra drew on a family fortune made in the mines to support a program of exploring, prospecting, and conquest that added another northwestern province, Neuva Vizcaya, with its own mines and ranchos.

At the same time Philip II ordered renewed efforts on two unsecured frontiers of New Spain. To Florida he sent a large naval force to break up a settlement of French heretics, potential raiders of Spanish treasure ships. A fortified outpost at San Agustín was the result. Far off on the western flank he ordered a new effort to establish an outpost in the Philippine Islands. Because of Portugal's exclusive right to the route around Africa, Spain had to depend on access to these islands by way of New Spain.

Carried westward by the trade winds, the little fleet sent out for the purpose in 1564 had an easy time reaching the archipelago. Commander Miguel López de Legazpi established a foothold at Manila. The task remained to find a return route to the west coast of Mexico. How to do it had been figured out theoretically many years earlier. It would be by the formula used in the Atlantic

—making a northing to the latitude of the prevailing westerlies, riding them eastward across the ocean, then sailing down the coast to the home port.

Fray Andrés Urdaneta accompanied the expedition to the Philippines for the express purpose of testing this theory and discovering such a route. Early in 1565 he set sail in a 500-ton ship on this slightly modified great-circle course. It was favored by ocean currents as well as winds, but the distance was great. The voyage took 129 days; 16 of the crew died before reaching port and four after, in addition to four Filipinos.

Urdaneta's feat is somewhat eclipsed by the fact that he was preceded across the Pacific by a deserter from Legazpi's fleet, Alonso de Arellano, in the 40-ton patache *San Lucas*. Deserting on the voyage out, Arellano hurried on to the Philippines and began the return voyage in April. His account bristles with extravagances about pelicans the size of ostriches, porpoises as large as cows, barking sea dogs with hands and feet and foxes' ears. These inaccuracies make it easy to doubt his claim that he reached latitude 43, but there seems to be no question that he sailed into Navidad before Urdaneta arrived and that he sought, though unsuccessfully, to get recognition and rewards as the real pioneer of the route from the Orient. The Spanish government continued to regard him as a deserter from the Legazpi–Urdaneta expedition, and his only consolation was that cartographers adopted some of his names for islands in the Pacific.

Urdaneta's sailing course became popular at once. Trade at first was unrestricted and many merchants engaged in it. Silks, wax, chinaware, spices, and other eastern staples were the principal items involved. The trade assumed such great proportions that merchants in Spain protested to the court that they were losing the market of New Spain. The king obliged them in 1593 by restricting the Mexican-Philippine trade to a single 500-ton vessel each year, with a cargo not to exceed 250,000 pesos in value and not to include any silks, and with the privilege of exporting reserved to citizens of Manila. The restrictions lessened the volume of the trade—though there were evasions, as by undervaluation of cargoes really worth a million pesos or more—but the restrictions enlarged the profits for those who could participate.

Annually, until almost the very end of the Spanish colonial period, the Manila galleon in making its eastward trip skirted the California coast from Cape Mendocino or Monterey to the tip of Baja California. Landings were infrequent, and the shore usually was not sighted north of Cenizas Island; but for almost two centuries this was the one regular coming of Spaniards into the vicinity of California. Some of the galleons were utilized for exploration of the California coast. The advisability of having a port along the coast at which the galleon could inquire for news of pirate activities and perhaps secure an escort for the remainder of the voyage to Acapulco came to be a basis for recurrent suggestions to occupy California.

A California port of call would also have lessened the ravages of the scurvy always present on the galleons. The trade restrictions made every bit of cargo space exceedingly valuable. Profits were supposedly limited to 100 per cent but usually ran higher, sometimes to 400 per cent. Consequently, it was perfectly natural to ship an additional bale or two of silk instead of an extra barrel of water or foodstuff. Only the bare necessities were provided and, if the voyage was at all prolonged, suffering was certain. Since fresh foods were out of the question for a trip of five to eight months, scurvy afflicted every galleon. Those who advocated a California station emphasized, therefore, the boon that a cabbage patch would be to crew and passengers aboard the galleons.

Drake at Nova Albion

Throughout the English-speaking world the 200-odd sailings of the Manila galleon have been eclipsed by a single voyage of Sir Francis Drake. His was the first English circumnavigation of the globe. By plundering the Spaniards and Portuguese, and above all by capturing the Panama-bound treasure galleon from Peru, he acquired literally tons of silver and gold and ranks as the most successful freebooter save only Piet Heyn, the Dutchman, who managed to capture a whole silver fleet.

In the course of his voyage Drake spent a month along the northern California coast, repairing and provisioning the *Golden Hind*, exchanging presents with the Indians, taking possession in the name of his queen, and conferring upon the entire region the name Nova Albion (New England). Undoubtedly these actions had some significance, yet Californians have magnified them out of all due proportion. In the 1890's there was need for an attack on the popular supposition that Drake discovered San Francisco Bay. Another bay, provisionally but not certainly identified as his anchorage, bears his name, as do hotels, streets, and a highway, while popular writing has made much of his alleged dream of founding an English colony on this coast.

In 1937 a plate of brass discovered in Marin County was promptly asserted to be the one Drake nailed to a post when he took possession of Nova Albion. Certain experts on history, language, and hieroglyphics expressed doubt. An electrochemist, asked to examine the plate, pronounced it not only sixteenth century brass but Drake's very own, perhaps more certitude than can rightfully be expected of his science. Unfairly compared with Minnesota's Kensington Stone, which has all the stigmata of a hoax, Drake's plate has now weathered practically all skepticism. It is a prized exhibit in the Bancroft Library in Berkeley.

The location of Drake's anchorage is more arguable. Some insist it was inside the Golden Gate, though it strains credulity that Drake and his men would have made no mention of such a magnificent closed bay. Henry Raup Wagner, chief historian of the early voyages to this coast, opts for several places well to the north of Point Reyes and doubts that Drake was ever in Drake's Bay just south of that point. An argument against that location is that Cermeño was there a few years later and saw or heard no hint of any ship before his.

By comparison, the purposes of Drake's voyage are crystal clear—to develop new trade, particularly in the Moluccas, and to engage in freebooting.

The Plate of Brass, claiming California for England

Ansel Adams, from Fiat Lux

After passing through the Straits of Magellan into the Pacific, until then a Spanish lake, Drake had golden opportunity to plunder. He pillaged defenseless towns and ships all the way from Chile to Mexico, his biggest haul being the treasure galleon *Cacafuego* on its way from Callao to Panama.

After this capture, with his ship bulging with silver, Drake's prime consideration was to get the fortune safely to England. Rather than risk interception at the Straits of Magellan, he resolved to go on around the world. Informed by captured sailing instructions that the season was a little early for crossing the Pacific, he decided to seek an out-of-the-way harbor where he could repair and provision his ship and await the season. That is how Drake happened to come to California. He took possession and looked, although only incidentally, for a Northwest Passage. Nothing suggests that he expected to find such a passage or that he looked forward to English colonization of California.

29

Spain was tremendously concerned about Drake's freebooting in the Pacific. To prevent a recurrence, the galleons were armed, larger naval forces were maintained, and some of the coastal towns were better garrisoned. These precautions were partly but not completely effective. Cavendish, Anson, and others followed Drake's example with varying fortunes. The menace to the Manila ships, which Drake and more especially Cavendish represented, was one of the factors inviting renewed attention to the California coast. Establishment of a California station where warnings of pirate danger could be given the Manila ships was the primary motive for the Spanish explorations which followed.

Drake's excursion to California, on the other hand, aroused no Spanish concern. It is difficult to say just when the Spaniards learned that he had been there, but they seem to have estimated correctly that he had found no compelling attraction for English colonization. Subsequent Spanish activity on the coast apparently had no connection with his visit.

Seeking a Port of Call for the Galleon

In 1584 a Manila galleon commander forwarded reports of a cluster of islands east of Japan—the Armenian Islands, according to one version; Rica de Oro and Rica de Plata, according to another. Islands so located would be a most useful way station for the galleon. The viceroy ordered a search, and in 1587 galleon commander Pedro de Unamuno faithfully complied but to no avail. In accordance with further instructions Unamuno put in at the first bay he sighted on the California coast, probably Morro Bay, to see whether it would qualify as a station for the galleon. Landing with 12 soldiers and some Filipinos, he made a short reconnaissance inland. They saw many trails and a few Indians, who were timid and fled precipitately. Unamuno erected a cross and took possession.

For the next two days they went farther inland where, off guard, they were surprised by an Indian attack. One of the Spaniards, who had taken off his coat of mail, was killed, as was one of the Filipinos; others were wounded. In view of the number of men wounded and the scant supply of powder, Unamuno refrained from punishing the Indians and set sail for Mexico the following day. Unamuno's experience with hostile Californians impressed the authorities; they instructed subsequent explorers of the coast not to venture inland.

Sebastián Rodríguez Cermeño made the next reconnaissance. He set out from Manila on July 4, 1595, in the 200-ton San Agustín. The vessel sailed at the king's order, but the expenses were borne by the owner, by Cermeño, and by others, whose profits would derive from the sale of the 130-ton cargo. The San Agustín also carried a knocked-down launch to be assembled when the exploration of the coast began.

Crossing the Pacific in the usual fashion, Cermeño made his first landfall at what he called Cape Mendocino, apparently somewhat south of the cape so called today. Unable to land on the bold and dangerous coast because of the heavy sea and the boisterous weather, he sailed slowly southward. Appreciating the risk to the ship, the pilot, master, and boatswain presented a written demand to Cermeño that he abandon the examination of the coast and run forthwith to Mexico, but the captain persisted in his explorations. A day or two later he brought the ship to anchor in a great ensenada which he named La Baya de San Francisco. He was at Drake's Bay under Point Reyes.

Many Indians appeared on the beach. One paddled out in a balsa and was rewarded with some cotton and silk cloth and a red cap. The next morning four natives came out and received presents, whereupon the captain and 22 men went ashore. They described the Indians as friendly and hospitable, well built, and more robust than the Spaniards. Cermeño thought their culture roughly comparable to that of the Chichimecos of northern Mexico. Farther inland the Spaniards met a more warlike band, which deployed around them in a circle and howled loudly. When the Indians who had already received gifts reassured these others, they laid down their bows and arrows and exchanged embraces with Cermeño's men. Silk sashes were presented to them.

The Spaniards stayed a month, assembling the knocked-down launch. During this time there was opportunity for a journey or two inland. The estuary of Drake's Bay was visited, and Cermeño's exact description of it confirms identification of the anchorage, also established by archeological finds. These Spaniards recorded far more accurate descriptions of the topography and of the friendly Indians than Drake had done 16 years earlier.

On November 30 a storm arose and drove the *San Agustín* ashore. She was a total wreck; the cargo and all the provisions were lost, along with at least two of the crew. The only thing left for the survivors to do was to complete the open launch, get what supplies they could from the natives, and set sail. They made another journey inland and acquired a quantity of acorns, though only after a sharp skirmish with the natives. On December 8, Cermeño and his 70 men sailed across toward the other point of the great bay, passing inside the Farallones.

The men seem to have taken for granted, after the disaster to the *San Agustín*, that their commander would abandon further examination of the coast and proceed with all possible haste to Mexico. Some stops, of course, were essential so that they might go ashore to seek water and food, but Cermeño had the launch heave to on dark nights and imposed other delays so that the work of exploration might be accomplished.

He acquired a knowledge of the coast from 41 to about 30 degrees latitude that was surprisingly accurate, considering the difficulties under which he was operating. As a thorough survey of the coast his compares favorably, in fact, with any other prior to the late eighteenth century. He crossed Monterey Bay from point to point and ran down the coast to San Luis Obispo. Much of the time the launch was within a musket shot of the shore. At San Luis Obispo the natives surprised them with shouts of "Christianos" and "Mexico," which were taken as echoes of Unamuno's visit in 1587. In response to signs that the Spaniards were hungry, these natives obliged them with a few acorns and some acorn mush. The Indians here exhibited an avarice such as was later attributed to the Santa Barbara tribes. Cermeño wrote, "After we gave them pieces of taffeta and satin and woolen blankets, they asked for more." Cermeño's men fished and traded at San Miguel and Santa Rosa islands. They passed across Santa Monica Bay, continued down the coast, and landed at San Martín Island.

The story of the voyage of these 70 men in their open sailboat is one of incredible hardships and privations. Their one stroke of good fortune was finding a large fish, probably a tuna, stranded in the rocks on San Martín Island. "We went on shore and found many wild onions and prickly pear trees," runs Cermeño's account, "and likewise God willed that we should find a dead fish among the rocks with two mortal wounds, and it was so large that the 70 of us sustained ourselves on it for more than a week, and if it had not been so large we would have perished there of hunger." Finally the men reached such desperate straits that Cermeño gave in and abandoned efforts at further discovery. Making no more stops, he sailed to Chacala, where his weary, half-starved, and half-sick crew disembarked. A few men took the launch on to Acapulco, while he and the ship's officers journeyed inland to report their achievements and their misfortunes.

Cermeño's remarkable survey of the coast was overshadowed by the loss of the galleon and its valuable cargo. Even his explorations were discounted. After much taking of testimony the viceroy held that there seemed to be "convincing proof, resting on clear inference, that some of the principal bays, where with greater reason it might be expected harbors would be found, they crossed from point to point and by night, while others they entered but a little way. For all this a strong incentive must have existed, because of the hunger and illness they say they experienced, which would cause them to hasten on their voyage." He concluded, therefore, that the king's plans for surveying the California coast had not been entirely carried out. That Cermeño was Portuguese may have contributed to the bitterness of the criticism, but the wreck of the *San Agustín* was the main thing held against him. As the moral of this costly lesson came the decision to conduct future explorations of the coast with smaller vessels sent out from Mexico expressly for that purpose rather than subjecting the Manila galleons with their rich cargo to so great a risk.

Vizcaíno and the Port of Monterey

In the meantime interest in New Mexico rekindled, and in 1595 the viceroy contracted with Juan de Oñate to establish a colony. Preparations took three years. In 1598 Oñate moved north, not by Coronado's western corridor but by cutting across from the Conchos to the Rio Grande in the El Paso vicinity and up to San Juan (formerly Caypa), which he made his headquarters. The Pueblo Indians seemed pleased to have the Spaniards come, though those at Acoma resisted. Oñate made two forays far out on the Plains and another all the way to the mouth of the Colorado. He might have done better had he consolidated his hold on the Pueblos. Yet his colony was a Spanish island hundreds of miles beyond the continuous frontier, and it was natural to want to establish connections. After some years he was relieved and subjected to long investigation as to why he had not accomplished more.

The west coast counterpart to Oñate's work was a voyage by a merchant contractor, Sebastián Vizcaíno. In 1596, armed with a concession from the viceroy, he sailed to Baja California to fish for pearls. The voyage was a fiasco, but Vizcaíno argued strenuously for another chance, which came in 1602 in another expedition partly supported by the viceroy. This time the viceroy set the firm condition that Vizcaíno was to proceed at once to the exploration of the outer coast. On the way back he could fish for pearls but not on the way out on pain of death.

Vizcaíno's little fleet had an easy voyage to Navidad, the Mazatlán Islands, and across to the tip of the peninsula. On the beach at San Bernabé there were so many pearl oyster shells catching the rays of the sun that Father Ascensión likened it to a starry heaven. Four times the fleet set out, only to be forced back; consequently, it was more than two months later when the vessels reached Cedros Island. Aside from adverse winds, the major difficulty was getting an adequate supply of water. The equipment for carrying water was unsatisfactory, and search for springs or streams along the arid coast was frequently unsuccessful.

Beating back and forth along these few hundred miles of shore line, the explorers came to know it intimately. The cosmographer's map took on a wealth of detail, and Ascensión's diary was enlivened with snatches of interesting minutiae, such as that about the Indians who "fished with dry feet" by tying a pelican with a broken wing and then helping themselves to the fish contributed by its concerned and devoted pelican friends.

Along the peninsula Vizcaíno made free with the geographic names given by earlier explorers. His San Bernabé, Magdalena, San Hipólito, San Roque, and San Bartolomé, for example, permanently displaced earlier names. After he reached Upper California, the same process continued. He rechristened with their present names San Diego, Santa Catalina, most of the Channel Islands, Buenaventura, Santa Barbara, Point Concepción, Point of Pines, Carmel, and Monterey.

From San Diego to Point Concepción, Vizcaíno's journey was more pleasant. Compared with the barren peninsula, southern California seemed a very rich land. In his enthusiasm, Father Ascensión mentions "golden pyrites . . . , a sure sign that there must be gold in the mountains," and quantities of another substance which the Spaniards called amber. The Indians were numerous and friendly and offered the Spaniards water, fish, and jicama roots. Their petty thievery led the good father to insist that "they beat the gypsies in cunning and dexterity."

The Port of Monterey

North of Point Concepción, Vizcaíno ran the coast somewhat more hurriedly. He charted one bay, probably San Luis Obispo, but the next stop was at Monterey. The Port of Monterey was the prize discovery of the voyage. Vizcaíno called it "the best port that could be desired, for besides being sheltered from all the winds, it has many pines for masts and yards, and live oaks and

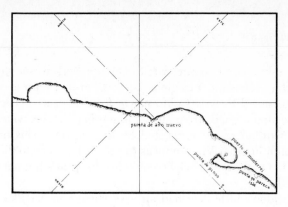

The Port of Monterey

As drawn and reported by the Vizcaino Expedition, 1602-03

white oaks, and water in great quantity, all near the shore." He spoke of the land as being thick with Indians and very fertile, the "climate and the quality of the soil resembling Castile," and the port commodious, "sheltered from all winds," and at the ideal latitude to provide "protection and security for the ships coming from the Philippines."

Since Vizcaíno had been sent to explore the California coast largely to select a port for the use of the Manila galleons, his enthusiastic description of Monterey was the most impressive feature of his report. In fact, until more than a century and a half later, the excellence of Monterey was accepted as the central fact about Alta California and was the chief motivating force attracting Spanish interest in the region.

From Monterey, Vizcaíno sent back one ship bearing the sick and disabled. With the other two he started north on January 3, 1603. He entered Drake's Bay, which to all these Spaniards was Puerto de San Francisco and which his chief pilot Bolaños, who had been with Cermeño, recognized. They planned to go ashore to look for the silk and wax left there after the wreck of the *San Agustín* but did not do so. Instead, they rounded Point Reyes—again the name is Vizcaíno's—and bore on up the coast. They sighted a cape near snowy mountains, which Bolaños thought was Cape Mendocino. Then fog, heavy seas, and stormy weather beset them. The two boats were already separated. Although Vizcaíno's pilot thought his farthest point north was 41 or 42 degrees, and the other vessel was said to have reached 43 degrees, neither gained much information about the coast north of Point Reyes.

Vizcaíno's decision to turn back was prompted by the unfavorable weather and the sickness of his men. "There were only two sailors," he reported, "who could climb the maintopsail." He had complied with his instructions to explore as far as Cape Mendocino. The voyage had stretched out over eight months and supplies were running short. Finally, off the northern California coast, "the pitching was so violent that it threw both sick and well from their bunks and the general [Vizcaíno] from his. He struck upon some boxes and broke his ribs."

The voyage south was rapid. Vizcaíno made some additional observations of the coast but did not anchor, doubting the ability of his men to lift the anchor again. Another search for pearls in the Gulf of California had been contemplated, but it was obvious that the men were not equal to it. Vizcaíno hurried to the mainland. With the five men who were still fit, he went ashore at Mazatlán to get aid and supplies, then continued to Acapulco. The men on the other vessel had equally harrowing experiences.

Viceroy Monterey was highly pleased with what Vizcaíno had done and appointed him commander of the next Manila galleon, a position highly lucrative as well as honorable. Unfortunately for Vizcaíno, the Conde de Monterey was promoted to the viceroyalty of Peru, and his successor at Mexico City reversed many decisions and appointments. The new viceroy, Montesclaros, took the galleon away from Vizcaíno and had the cosmographer Martínez Palacios tried for forgery, condemned, and hanged. Even when the king ordered that Vizcaíno be suitably rewarded for his efficient survey of the difficult California coast, Montesclaros found a way to evade the command.

The viceroy correctly insisted that a California port of call would not greatly benefit the galleon. The galleons seldom sighted the coast north of Cenizas Island, and by the time they were opposite Monterey the voyage was practically over. That they hardly ever stopped in California after it was finally settled substantiates Montesclaros' reasoning. His advocacy of further search for the Armenian Islands was less defensible, even though a station in that location would have been worth much more to the galleons. Unamuno's negative findings had not counteracted all the alluring fabrications about these islands. Consequently, the expedition which Vizcaíno wanted to lead to occupy Monterey was diverted to a useless search for these phantom islands.

Denied thus the opportunity to establish the first settlement of Alta California, Vizcaíno nevertheless deserves full recognition for his exhaustive survey of the coast from the tip of the peninsula to beyond Monterey, for his permanent contributions to the nomenclature of the coast, and for the glamor he bestowed upon California through his praise of the Port of Monterey. His work was a fitting climax to the revival of interest in exploration which had characterized the latter part of the sixteenth century.

For Further Reading

H. E. BOLTON, *The Spanish Borderlands* (1921), 1–119.

MORRIS BISHOP, *The Odyssey of Cabeza de Vaca* (1933).

H. E. BOLTON, *Coronado, Knight of Pueblos and Plains* (1964).

H. R. WAGNER, *Spanish Voyages to the Northwest Coast* (1929).

H. R. WAGNER, *Sir Francis Drake's Voyage Around the World* (1926).

W. L. SCHURZ, *The Manila Galleon* (1959).

R. F. HEIZER, "Archaeological Evidence of Sebastián Rodrígues Cermenho's California Visit," *CHSQ* (1941), 315–28.

W. MICHAEL MATHES, *Vizcaíno and Spanish Exploration in the Pacific Ocean* (1968).

CAUGHEY, *California Heritage*, 44–57.

chapter three

Spanish Approaches

River by river, valley by valley, canyon by canyon,
tribe by tribe, these harbingers of Christian civilization
advanced into the realm of heathendom.

Herbert Eugene Bolton,
Rim of Christendom

Imperial Method

1565
to
1768

In the sixteenth century Spain acquired a vast and rich empire in the
Caribbean and on the American mainland from central Mexico
through Peru to Chile and the mouth of the Plata. Much of the land
abounded in pearls, gold, and silver. It was also rich in its natives,
many of whom were skilled artisans and farmers capable of producing valuable commodities. Wealth-seeking Spaniards eagerly volunteered to go and seize such choice districts. Imperial growth thus was
accomplished at no cost to the royal treasury.

The latter part of the century, when Philip II was king, was
something of a transition period. His emphasis and his forte were in
administration of the empire rather than in additional conquest.
There were volunteers aplenty for the silver rushes into north-central
Mexico and upper Peru, later called Boliva. But for the occupation

Facade of Mission San Francisco de Borja, Baja California

Eliot Porter, Sierra Club

37

of Florida and the Philippine Islands, Philip relied on garrison outposts staffed and financed by the government.

At the end of the century Oñate and Vizcaíno invested substantially in expeditions. With them the epoch of frontier expansion by adventures of the conquistador-adelantado type came to an end. Thereafter such private contributions appeared only rarely.

There were good reasons for the change to government direction and backing. The royal preference was for more centralized control of the empire. More compelling, the lands lying ahead seemed barren of ready wealth, and their Indians were fewer, ruder, and wilder. Although some of these Indians planted, their farming and hunting yielded little more than a bare living. Even if brought under control, their potential as a useful labor force was uncertain.

Important continuities carried on into the seventeenth and eighteenth centuries. Then as earlier everything was done in the name of God and the king. The Spanish empire was to be made Catholic as rapidly and thoroughly as possible, and the dominion of the king was never challenged. A fundamental purpose continued to be to make the Indians over in the Spanish image, in religion, language, work habits, and behavior, and to perpetuate them as the backbone of the colonial population.

The mechanical means of carrying out expansion into new territories also continued much the same as before. Eighteenth century ships were little improved over those of Columbus. The pack train, a primary means for overland freighting, was an almost exact replica of what had been available earlier. The guns, lances, and swords issued to eighteenth century troops and the occasionally used field pieces were much like those of Cortés' day. The leather shields and armor of the late frontier were superior to the chain and plate armor worn by some of the conquistadores. Although affording about the same protection against Indian arrows, leather armor was much less burdensome. As to equipment, the two eras differed little.

Spanish Frontier Institutions

As to institutions, however, the contrast is marked. Three institutions characterized the later frontier. In the order of their appearance in Spanish America, they were the pueblo, representing the civilian; the presidio, representing the military; and the mission, representing the religious. The three were linked together as agencies of the state. Indeed, the cardinal change after the sixteenth century was that government direction, control, and financing pervaded the entire operation.

In Spain medieval habit had ingrained a preference for living in towns. The characteristic pattern of farm life was a town surrounded by individual fields rather than residence on single-family farms. The long struggle against the Moorish invaders put another premium on the town, walled and able to defend itself. When Ferdinand and Isabella unified Spain, they did so at the expense of the rival Spanish kingdoms, the Moors, and the feudal orders. Seeing the towns as necessary agencies in local government, they intruded on them much less.

The earliest Spaniards in America promptly founded towns in the Spanish pattern. Columbus and his companions did so in the islands, Balboa at Panamá, and Cortés at Veracruz and then on the ruins of the Aztec capital, where the Spaniards built a Spanish city, Mexico. The late sixteenth century found most Spaniards in America living in organized, functioning towns and cities, the predominant unit of local government throughout the empire.

Later, whenever civilian settlers went or were sent to the frontier, the most common practice was to cluster them in pueblos in the model of the towns in Spain. Spanish law required clustering in this fashion. Here is a substantial contrast to the individualism of the westward-expanding frontiers of settlement in the United States.

The second institution of the Spanish frontier, the presidio, is easier to understand because of its similarity to the forts maintained by the army in frontier days in the American West. The presidio was a walled fort, garrisoned by one or two officers and from 20 or 30 to as many as 100 or more soldiers. Characteristically these soldiers were mounted men rather than foot soldiers and, for effectiveness, needed several remounts apiece. Therefore, each presidio also needed a range for maintaining these animals. Although soldiers' families and a few other civilians might also cluster at a presidio, its prime function was military.

The contrast to the armies of Cortés and Pizarro is clear. Those forces had been bands of private adventurers, often operating under royal permit but campaigning at their own expense and on their own initiative. The presidial troopers were regular soldiers at assigned stations and under official orders. Commanders, furthermore, were regularly commissioned career officers on regular duty.

In the earlier conquests, men of religion were often present, spreading the faith among the many Indians subjugated. They made some contributions to educational advancement, and on occasion churchmen were involved in actual governing. Notable churchmen of the early period included Bartolomé de las Casas, champion of the Indians and chief advocate of the New Laws designed for the protection of the natives; Pedro de Gante, first schoolmaster in Mexico; and Pedro Sánchez, first provincial of the Jesuits in New Spain. Throughout this period, however, the religious were secondary rather than primary agents in frontier advance. To rely on the mission as a principal means of extending Spanish control into new areas was a new policy.

The mission, though not duplicated or even approximated on the Anglo-American frontier, has been much written about and, in the United States, is doubtless the best-known institution of Spanish America. It was essentially a place where, under clerical discipline, Indians were persuaded to come and live together and be taught the Catholic religion, the Spanish language, and the rudiments of the white man's way of life. These fundamentals are reminiscent of the encomienda system under which Indians had been assigned to individual Spaniards who were to protect, Christianize, instruct, and put them to work.

A mission was staffed by one or perhaps two padres of the Jesuit, Franciscan, or some other order. The first task was to persuade Indians to come and live at the mission. Ideally, the population would rise to a few thousand men, women, and children as permanent residents. The missionary had charge of them 24 hours a day, every day of the year. In addition to indoctrination and instruction, he supervised everything that went on—building the church, residences, granaries, and workrooms; tilling the fields; caring for stock; making clothes, furniture, and other necessities; and preparing meals. Besides being priest and teacher, he was responsible for every other activity in the self-sufficient community that his mission must be. To this multiple challenge some missionaries measured up better than others. It is remarkable that so many did so well.

"Their Most Catholic Majesties," the monarchs of Spain, devout sons of the church, had a genuine interest in the conversion of the heathen, yet even churchmen admit that royal support of missions was because of the practical services rendered the empire by the missions. For these services the government paid. In the royal bookkeeping, under the general heading of frontier expense, expenditures for missions were lumped together with those for presidial upkeep and for the establishment of new pueblos. That was appropriate, for the mission was a most useful agency in the mundane as well as the religious work of frontier advance.

Theoretically the mission was temporary. It was to continue in a given locality only long enough to start the Indians on the road to Christianity and civilization. Then it would be secularized and pass from the control of the regular clergy of the Jesuit, Dominican, or Franciscan order and be staffed henceforth by a parish priest of the secular clergy. When the mission church became a parish church, the Indians would be released from mission discipline, given their initial necessities from the mission property, and launched as full-fledged members of colonial society. Ten years was designated as the proper duration for a mission, but that schedule seldom was met. Usually the Indians needed a longer period of tutelage, and often the lay settlers among whom the secularized Indians were supposed to be assimilated had lagged behind. Many missions operated for 40 or 50 years, and others passed well beyond the century mark.

Black Robes at Work

From the late sixteenth century on, Spain employed missions, presidios, and pueblos on many frontiers and with many variations. The system entered the history of southern Chile, the Plata basin, portions of present-day Colombia and Venezuela, and Florida, Texas, New Mexico, and many other areas. A frontier of particular emphasis was northwestern Mexico, where the Jesuits labored.

The work in this quarter began in 1591 when two Black Robes, Gonzalo de Tapia and Martín Pérez, opened a mission at San Felipe on the

The Northwestern Frontier of New Spain

Section of a map by Eman. Bowen, 1747

Sinaloa River. The Indians were willing converts, some 2,000 being baptized the first year. Other Jesuits came and the work expanded, but in 1594 an Indian shaman led a revolt in which Tapia was killed, thus becoming the first Jesuit martyr in New Spain.

Spain responded by sending 25 soldiers to establish a presidio at San Felipe. Tapia's remains were recovered—the Indians, it was reported, had tried to roast one of the martyr's arms, but fire had had no effect. The Jesuits redoubled their missionary efforts and by the end of the decade had 60 temporary structures in use, eight modest but well-built churches, and 10,000 baptisms to their credit.

Meanwhile other Jesuits opened missions on the east side of the Sierra Madre and as far afield as the Laguna district in modern Coahuila. Here too were uprisings by the neophytes and reported miracles. In 1608 the Laguna missions lost 400 neophytes by smallpox.

On the west coast the missionary advance north of the Sinaloa was greatly assisted over a period of 30 years by presidial captain Diego Martínez Hurdaide. By ruse, boldness, and remorseless pressure, he discouraged half a dozen tribes from resisting the advance of the Black Robes. By 1620 the provinces of Sinaloa and Durango were under permanent Spanish control. By 1624 the west coast branch of this mission frontier claimed 100,000 converts. Less rapidly, over the next 50 or 60 years, the field advanced into Chihuahua and Sonora.

From 1687 to 1711, this northwestern frontier had the services of a remarkable missionary, Italian-born and German-educated Eusebio Francisco Kino. Sent to Mexico in 1681, he had his first field experience in Lower California with an unsuccessful colonization attempt in 1685. After that he was sent to Pimería Alta (Upper Pima Land) in northern Sonora. He spent the rest of his life there, as his biographer puts it, as Apostle to the Pimas.

Using the Mission Dolores on the San Miguel River as his base, Kino added a score of other missions on the Altar, Magdalena, and Santa Cruz. Besides ministering to three of these stations and supervising the rest, he explored beyond to the Gila and the Colorado and across into Lower California. He added to and corrected geographical knowledge and made a map of Pimería which was not improved on for a century and a half. He wrote a history of his work, modestly entitling it *Celestial Favors*. In addition to his work as explorer, geographer, and historian, his assignment required that he be preacher, teacher, builder, cattleman, planter, irrigator, ruler, and guardian of many thousands of Indians. He is an outstanding figure among many brave, devoted, and hardworking missionary frontiersmen.

Pearl Fishers in Baja California

While the Jesuits, assisted by presidial soldiers and pueblo settlers, were advancing the frontier from Durango and San Felipe de Sinaloa to the Gila, a quite different and more sporadic interest was shown in the peninsula of California. In the 1530's and in 1601 Cortés and Vizcaíno had identified the chief attraction, pearls.

In 1611 the king granted Tomás de Cardona a monopoly on pearl fishing in the New World. His agents began in the West Indies and reached Acapulco in 1614 but were diverted to patrols against Dutch pirates, who, guttural-voiced or chest speakers, were therefore called Pichilingues. In 1615 a Cardona-sponsored expedition sailed north, commanded by Juan de Iturbe. He found pearls, but on the return voyage the one ship with most of the pearls was captured by the Pichilingues.

Iturbe's most spectacular achievement was upsetting the prevailing cartographical theory concerning California. Returning from his voyage up the gulf, he claimed to have reached latitude 34 degrees and reported that it was not a gulf but a strait extending still farther north, which meant that California was an island. The mapmakers fell in line, showing the "Strait of California" opening again into the Pacific, usually north of Cape Mendocino.

Nicolás Cardona, nephew of Tomás, kept memorializing the court until as late as 1643 on the subject of pearl fishing and settlements, but whether he sent any pearl fishers to the "Island of California" is uncertain.

In 1627 Martín de Lezama began to build a pearl-fishing ship at San Blas. He was discouraged by swarms of mosquitoes. In the early 1630's Francisco de Ortega made three voyages and found many pearls. A certain Esteban Carbonel applied to the king in 1636, but when it was revealed that he was a Frenchman he was charged with plotting against Spanish interests.

In 1644 a ship belonging to Pedro Porter y Casanate went out to warn the Manila galleon of Pichilingues and on the return picked up a few pearls. He made another try in 1648. The next pearl fisher on record is Bernardo Bernal de Pynadero in 1664. On his return to Spain, he was investigated on charges of gross cruelties to the natives.

That pearl fishing at the "Island of California" far exceeded the revealed record is likely. Known facts include use of Negro as well as Indian divers; trade with the Indians, though most of their pearls had been spoiled by fire; some finds of excellent pearls, including one valued at 4,500 pesos; interference by Pichilingues and rumors of Pichilingues. The pearlers accomplished no more than temporary and interrupted residence on the scene.

Atondo and Kino

In 1679 Governor Isidro Atondo y Antillón of Sinaloa was given a California contract different from all the earlier ones in that partial support from the royal treasury was promised. Early in 1683 he landed at La Paz. The parched and barren lands, the backwardness of the Indians, and the small haul of pearls were a discouragement. Atondo returned to the mainland for supplies and in October made a fresh start farther north at San Bruno. With Indian labor paid for by rations of pozole (cornmeal mush), Atondo built a fortified town and church. He scouted inland; in fact, he went all the way to the Pacific. At San Bruno, he diverted water from a stream to irrigate plantings of maize, frijoles, garbanzos, and melons. But the rains stopped, the river dried up, and all the crops failed. In May of 1685, Atondo abandoned San Bruno. Sending again to the mainland for supplies, he spent the summer months pearl fishing, with little success. He was preparing one more try when orders came to warn the galleon of pirates who had raided Panama. By that time the cost of his expeditions to the royal treasury had mounted to 250,000 pesos.

History is much richer because Padre Eusebio Kino had his first missionary assignment as cosmographer for the Atondo expedition. For the first time Kino encountered Indians untouched by any Christian influence, although for a century and a half, it is true, they had been exposed to the visits of pearl fishers from Cortés to Pynadero. The depth of the ignorance of these Californians impressed Kino. He also saw them as a kindly, trusting, simple people, profoundly in need of what missionaries could do for them. Practical considerations forced Atondo to give up the project of occupying the "Island of California." Kino returned with him to mainland Mexico and went on to 25 years of work in Pimería Alta. He became, however, the foremost advocate of renewed missionary effort with and for the Californians. Kino's first convert to his California enthusiasm was another Jesuit, Juan María de Salvatierra. Later they persuaded their superior in the Jesuit Order that this mission field should no longer be neglected.

The Jesuits Enter Baja California

Having had such little success in colonizing California by government expeditions, merchant adventurers, and pearl-fishing companies, the Spanish crown was willing to grant unusual powers and inducements to the Jesuit Order to undertake the task. This policy well illustrates the elasticity of frontier technique that Spain was able to attain. The Jesuits were to be in full control. On most missionary frontiers regular army officers controlled the presidios, but for Baja California the Jesuits were to command all soldiers and civilians as well as the missionaries. Because of the strategic usefulness of an occupied California as a defense against Dutch, English, and French freebooters who might lurk in California waters, the government agreed to subsidize the Jesuit colony. Spain also departed from customary procedure in permitting the Jesuits to solicit an endowment fund to support the missions. The faithful in New Spain, Central America, and elsewhere responded in most generous fashion to this campaign. The solicitors, of whom Father Juan de Ugarte was one of the most successful, built up the Pious Fund to more than a million pesos, thus creating a handsome income for the California missions.

Yet the actual start in 1697 was humble enough. Because Kino could not go and another padre was detained temporarily, Salvatierra went as the lone missionary. At his command was an army of six soldiers with one swivel gun constituting their artillery. Salvatierra's boat crossed the gulf in a single day, but the accompanying vessel was more than a month making the voyage. A tiny fort was built a few miles south of Atondo's San Bruno, and the natives who assisted were rewarded with gifts of maize and porridge. To stimulate interest in his religious teaching, Salvatierra withheld presents from those Indians who failed to attend. Resenting this discrimination, they staged California's first student protest, demanded a share in the material benefits of Christianity, and became so obstreperous that Salvatierra had to call out the guard.

Salvatierra held his fire as long as seemed prudent and then ordered a shot from the swivel gun. The result surprised the Spaniards more than the Indians. The gun burst; two soldiers were killed, and the Indians would have wiped out the rest had not the muskets proved far more effective. The next day the Indians were willing to make peace.

Before the end of November the second boat arrived, and the first returned again, bringing Padre Francisco María Pícolo, additional men, and supplies. The force now totaled seven soldiers, five sailors, four Christian Indians from the mainland, and two padres. Salvatierra founded Loreto, which was to be the capital and mother mission. San Javier followed two years later. Padre Juan de Ugarte joined the force in 1701, and Padre Jayme Bravo, four years later. These four—Salvatierra, Pícolo, Ugarte, and Bravo—were the principal missionaries until Salvatierra's death in 1717, by which time five other missions had been established.

The narrative of these 20 years is full of stirring events. More than once Salvatierra showed his fortitude and proved the support of Providence. Once when the Indians attacked he went out to reason with them. Three arrows were shot at him but lodged harmlessly in the folds of his robe. On another occasion he and his companions escaped injury when most of the Indian arrows struck the pavilion housing the image of Our Lady of Loreto, sainted patroness of the Baja California missions. Again, losing his way after being summoned to baptize a dying Indian, he gave free rein to his mule and was miraculously guided to the ranchería of the stricken Indian. His official biographer does not record the incident, but tradition has it that Salvatierra saved the pitahaya crop on the peninsula by praying for gulls to come and devour a plague of locusts.

Conversions, however, were few; the natives were more interested in porridge than in religion, and the mission field was by no means self-supporting. Except for the Pious Fund, the government subventions, and the herculean work of the missionaries, the colony could not have endured.

A major difficulty was the isolation of Baja California. Even after Kino proved that a land connection existed, a land route from the mainland was never opened. Dependence was on navigation across the gulf, which was notoriously hazardous. Many boats were lost. The barren nature of the land hindered development in farming and stock raising, such as Kino achieved in Pimería Alta, and the Indians did not have the ability demonstrated by Kino's wards. Unlicensed pearl fishers persisted in coming to the peninsula despite the monopoly granted the Jesuits. Their influence upon the Indians was usually bad and served to counteract the work of the missionaries. Although Salvatierra refused to sell them supplies, the secular authorities on the mainland did little or nothing to

A Baja California Scene Typical of the Sonora Desert

Eliot Porter, Sierra Club

stop their coming. Sometimes, the soldiers also proved more of a handicap than a protection. On one occasion Salvatierra courageously discharged 18 of his army of 30.

In 1717 robust Juan de Ugarte, already notable as the prize solicitor for the Pious Fund, succeeded Salvatierra. Since 1701 he had been in charge of Mission San Javier, where, despite a tradition of failure, he had succeeded in raising crops. This first successful farming in the peninsula expanded to include stock raising and spread in limited degree to other sites. Ugarte staved off abandonment once by announcing that he would remain even though all others left. On another occasion he used his great physical strength to quell an Indian uprising by seizing two ringleaders by the hair and cracking their heads together. Largely by personal bravery he and Padre Bravo overawed the Guaicuros, who had caused Atondo so much trouble, and forced them to submit to mission discipline. Another of Ugarte's feats was to cajole the Indians to work with him in cutting timber and packing it a hundred miles to the coast, where it was used to build a ship, *Triunfo de la Cruz,* for exploration of the gulf. By the time of his death in 1730 the mission staff had been increased and the number of missions doubled.

Turmoil and Decline

In the 1730's uprisings and rebellions set back the mission program. In the southern missions in 1733, after the padres tried to stamp out polygamy, a mulatto and a mulatto Indian led a rebellion. Although this revolt was quickly suppressed, the next year these same malcontents were more successful. They killed Padres Lorenzo Carranco and Nicolas Tamaral and three of the six soldiers of the mission guard. Padre Sigismundo Taraval and the other three soldiers fled by night to La Paz and from there to the island of Espíritu Santo. The rebels massacred 27 of Taraval's neophytes.

Estevan Rodríguez Lorenzo, captain of the Jesuit-directed soldiers on the peninsula, undertook a retaliatory campaign. With 20 soldiers and a few Indian allies he came to La Paz, where he tried unsuccessfully to enlist the supposedly friendly Callejues. In his journal Taraval vividly depicts the uncertainties afflicting Rodríguez' little band. Finally the timorous Callejues agreed to help. Rodríguez marched into hostile territory but was not able to punish the rebels. Rumors that the rebellion was spreading north led to recall of Rodríguez and concentration of the missionaries at Loreto.

Meanwhile, the emboldened Indians threatened the Manila galleon. The galleon of 1735 put in at Rio San José near Cabo San Lucas to provision and to recruit the sufferers from scurvy. Led by a certain Gerónimo, the Indians killed 12 men who had been sent ashore and tried to lure the other Spaniards to land. Finally the captain became suspicious. Seizing Gerónimo and a few others, he beat off the attack of some 600 Indians and sailed away. With a little better luck Gerónimo and his followers might have captured the galleon.

Arrival of 60 Yaqui warriors ended the threat of an uprising in the northern missions. With 40 soldiers and another 100 Yaquis, Manuel Huidobro came over from the mainland to put down the rebellion in the south. The hostiles were evasive. Huidobro marched up and down and after months of campaigning had not come to grips with them. Finally the Jesuits helped maneuver the insurgents into two pitched battles which ended the resistance. The Jesuit chronicles contend, however, that Huidobro let the ringleaders off with inadequate punishment.

Mission work was resumed but the pacification was imperfect. New uprisings necessitated more troops and new campaigns. Not until a decade later was the region quieted, and then it was mainly because epidemics had carried off most of these turbulent natives.

The remaining annals of Jesuit activities are more humdrum. On the northern frontier new stations were established, notably Santa Gertrudis, San Francisco de Borja, and Santa María de Calamajue. But as the population declined, some of the older missions were consolidated. In the south the women died off more rapidly than did the men. Attempts to import wives from the mainland were unsuccessful.

Toward the last the Jesuits adopted a less exclusive policy. Pearl fishing was encouraged, the galleons stopped regularly, a few settlers and miners were welcomed to the peninsula, and the southernmost missions were secularized. Yet, at best, Baja California was barely self-supporting and no real encouragement to northwestward expansion.

The End of the Jesuit Epoch

In 1767 the Spanish court decided to follow the lead of Portugal and France and expel the Jesuits. The reasons stemmed but slightly from the conduct of the missionaries in Baja California or on the Mexican mainland, though there were some complaints and also wild rumors that the missionaries were hoarding vast treasures from secret mines, pearl fisheries, and exactions from the natives.

The expulsion of some 678 Jesuits from New Spain was thought too delicate a task for the viceroy and his staff. Instead it was entrusted to Visitador-general José de Gálvez, who was on the scene conducting an inspection and overhaul of imperial administration in the viceroyalty. So that the neophytes would not dispute the removal and the missionaries would not have time to hide or dispose of their mythical treasures, Gálvez moved secretly. For the task in Baja California, where there were 16 Jesuits to be sent toward the Vatican, he delegated the responsibility to Captain Gaspar de Portolá.

Reaching Loreto on December 17, 1767, Portolá notified the missionaries to be prepared to board ship on January 25, 1768. Although they and their charges were grief-stricken, there was no resistance. The Black Robes sailed on February 3, leaving the Indians with no guardians other than Portolá's soldiers. Fray Junípero Serra and his brother Franciscans of the College of San Fernando did not arrive until April. Meanwhile, Portolá carefully inventoried the mission property, which fell far short of expectations. Some of this property was dissipated before April, and there were further losses during a transition period in which the Franciscans had merely spiritual authority. On August 12 Gálvez placed them in full charge of the missions.

Gálvez saw need of other reforms in Baja California. He came with an optimism that mining could be developed, and he tried to encourage the coming of miners and agricultural settlers. He soon realized that regeneration of the missions was the real hope of the colony. He had several missions consolidated, others abandoned, and the neophytes transferred to better situated missions. Some of his more radical proposals, such as transferring northern Indians far to the south, were not carried out. Nor were the Franciscans able to accomplish much in their five-year tenure on the peninsula. They established only one new mission, San Fernando de Velicatá.

On the northeastern exposure of New Spain an advance into Texas balanced the expansion into Baja California. There the agencies used were the full complement of missions, presidios, and pueblos, rather than a near monopoly granted to the missionaries. Possession of Texas gave Spain certain advantages of position in the rivalry for North America, but Texas was little more flourishing than the Jesuit preserve in Baja California.

During the first two thirds of the eighteenth century the intervening frontier was not appreciably advanced. Sinaloa, Durango, and parts of Sonora and Chihuahua had long since passed out of the frontier stage and no longer required missions or the protection of presidial troops. Well to the north, however, was the province of New Mexico, suspended like an island among the as yet unsubdued Apaches, Navajos, and Utes. Aside from New Mexico, El Paso del Norte and San Xavier del Bac were the northernmost outposts in a frontier zone where missions, presidios, and pueblos were in uneasy equilibrium with the uncontrolled Indians.

Over the years since 1603, when Vizcaíno reported with such enthusiasm on the Port of Monterey, the idea of occupying Alta California was occasionally advanced. The Bolas de Plata mining flurry renewed optimism about the northwest, and the Fernando Sánchez memorials of 1751, reviving the bogey of French discovery of the Strait of Anian, urged Spanish occupation of Alta California as a means of forestalling such a disaster.

Spanish imperial policy, however, was not that aggressive. And the mission frontier in Baja California, except on a purely religious basis, was not successful enough to stimulate a further advance.

For Further Reading

H. I. PRIESTLEY, *The Coming of the White Man* (1929).

H. E. BOLTON, *The Spanish Borderlands* (1919, 1960), 120–295.

H. E. BOLTON, *Wider Horizons of American History* (1939, 1967).

P. M. DUNNE, *Pioneer Black Robes on the West Coast* (1940).

H. E. BOLTON, *Rim of Christendom* (1936).

P. M. DUNNE, *Black Robes in Lower California* (1952, 1968).

PEVERIL MEIGS, *The Dominican Mission Frontier of Lower California* (1935).

ANTONIO DE FIERRO BLANCO [Walter Nordhoff], *The Journey of the Flame* (1933, 1955).

CAUGHEY, *California Heritage*, 90–101.

chapter four

Outpost of Spain

> The departure [from San Diego] having been fixed for the 14th of July [1769], the governor ordered out six soldiers and a corporal to explore the country for the distance of the first two days' marches. These soldiers left on the morning of the 12th, and returned on the afternoon of the following day with the information that they had found a watering-place sufficient for the men and horses at a distance of six or seven leagues.
>
> Miguel Costansó,
> *Diary*

Imperial Change

1768
to
1773

On the eve of the expulsion of the Jesuits from New Spain there was little reason to suspect that the frontier would suddenly leap-frog to San Diego and Monterey. Two centuries and a quarter had gone by since receipt of the reports of Cabrillo's discovery and one century and two thirds since Vizcaíno gave his more enthusiastic description. Meanwhile, the frontier had advanced to Sinaloa and Sonora, Pimería Alta, and Baja California but without generating enough momentum to carry on into Alta California.

Nevertheless, much of imperial policy was in flux. The decisive outcome of the Seven Years War led to the partition of French America along the Mississippi. Britain gained the St. Lawrence Valley, west to the Canadian Rockies, and the eastern half of the

Opening Page of Portolá's Diary

Diario del Viage que haze por tierra Dn Gaspar de Sorrola Capitan de Dragones del Regim.
de España Governador de Californias á los Puer-
tos de San Diego y Monterrey situados en 33 y 37
grados haviendo sido nombrado Comandante en Ge-
fe de esta expedicion por el Illmo Señor Dn Joseph de
Galbez en virtud de las facultades Vice-Regias que le
há concedido su Excel. Dicha expedicion se componia
de 51 Soldados de Cuera con su Capitan Dn
Fernando de Rivera deviendo este adelan-
tarse con Veinte y siete Soldados, y el
Governador con diez, y un
Sargento

Horas

El dia 11 de Mayo sali de Sancta Maria vltima mision
del Norte, escoltado de quatro Soldados en compañia del Padre
Junipero Serra Presidente de las Misiones y el R. P. Dr.
6 | Miguel Campa; en este dia se handuvo como quatro horas con
poquisima agua para las Bestias, nada se paró por lo que
obligó á marchar por la tarde para lograr lo aunque sin
agua.

El dia 12 handuvimos por buen camino as co horas
5 | paramos en el parage que llaman la Poza de agua dulce
sin paro.

Mississippi Basin. Spain was forced to relinquish the Floridas to Britain but acquired New Orleans and the western half of the Mississippi Basin. The new map necessitated administrative changes and other modifications with regard to Cuba, Louisiana, and Texas, an area distant half a continent or more from California. The same period saw a revival of British voyages to the Pacific, but again with focus on the South Pacific, half an ocean removed from California.

After the war each imperial power in America undertook vigorous reforms. Portugal expelled the Jesuits and liberalized trade for Portuguese America. In Britain George III and his ministers aimed at increased revenue to the royal treasury and more effective royal control. Their steps, such as the Proclamation of 1763, the Stamp Act, and the tax on tea, are remembered less as reform measures than as irritations contributing to the American Revolution.

In Spain a much more able monarch, Charles III, carried out similar, more extensive, and much more fruitful reforms. He redeployed garrisons, set up Buenos Aires as capital of a new viceroyalty, appointed a commandant general for the northern frontier, and overhauled the revenue system of the empire. Adapting a French device, he appointed intendants, new officials specifically charged with stimulating economic development. He also opened additional ports to trade with Spain and France. In the epoch of these reforms Spanish America prospered.

As part of his program of strengthening the empire, Charles sent José de Gálvez to inspect the viceroyalty of New Spain. As visitador-general he could proceed independent of the viceroy and other regular officials. He also was empowered to carry out such changes as he deemed advisable.

Gálvez began at the customhouse in Veracruz, the one authorized port of entry from Spain. By striking at graft he much improved the revenue. He established the tobacco monopoly for the benefit of the royal treasury and improved collections in the powder, quicksilver, and playing-card monopolies. In several areas where it had not been operating, he installed Indian tribute, a head tax to the royal treasury. As indicated in the preceding chapter, he was also entrusted with expelling the Jesuits from New Spain.

In San Juan Potosí, Guanajuato, and several other mining centers, rioting broke out in protest against these reforms. With 500 soldiers Gálvez marched against the rioters, most of whom were Indians. He made wholesale arrests, held quick trials, and handed down harsh sentences. Of 3,000 brought to trial, 85 were executed, 73 were lashed, 674 were imprisoned, and 117 were banished. Though enlightened in other respects, the late eighteenth century was an age when cruel punishment was commonplace. Even so, Gálvez has been criticized for his excesses. The crown, however, looked with favor on his pacification of this important silver-mining district.

Gálvez Decides

With the viceroy, early in 1768, Gálvez outlined a plan for pacifying the entire northwestern frontier. He proposed a united command over Nueva

José de Gálvez, Visitador-General

L. Alamán, Disertaciones sobre la historia de la República mexicana

Vizcaya, Sinaloa, Sonora, and the Californias, roughly the area missionized by the Jesuits. He recommended that the command center be well to the north, at Caborca or perhaps where the Gila River joins the Colorado. His plan called for a concentration of troops in place of some of the scattered presidios, new settlements to bolster the frontier, and an outpost up the coast at Monterey. Nothing could be done, however, until the rebellion of the Pimas and Seris was put down, a task assigned to Colonel Domingo Elizondo.

Meanwhile, Gálvez started for San Blas, a west coast port he had ordered developed to support Elizondo's Sonora campaign and the Californias. En route, on May 5, 1768, he received a letter from the viceroy telling of a dispatch from the ambassador to the court of the Empress Catharine reporting Russian penetrations along the northwest coast of America. The news was imprecise and geographically indistinct—as of the 1760's the Russians were exploiting only the Aleutian Islands area. On the chance that the Russians might intend to occupy the Port of Monterey, the viceroy recommended a voyage of reconnaissance.

Gálvez seized on this communication as justification for going ahead with a plan already of much interest to him. In his reply he adroitly magnified Viceroy Croix's request into an order to occupy Alta California, at the same time making Croix appear responsible for the step. In reality, the Russian danger was only an excuse; the reason for the occupation was José de Gálvez.

On to California

In May, 1768, Gálvez sailed for Baja California, intending to send a force to occupy Monterey. He found only a skeleton group of Spaniards and fewer than 8,000 Indians at the missions. He instituted certain reforms and for a time was optimistic about mining and pearl fishing, but little was achieved. Organizing the expeditions for Alta California was his major preoccupation in the months that followed. Not until the following May did he return to the mainland. That he devoted a year of his time as visitador-general to marshaling men and materials for the expeditions to California indicates the importance he attached to this advance of the frontier.

Although there had been many complaints about the poverty of Baja California, Gálvez did not hesitate to draw upon its meager resources. He drafted the Franciscans for missionaries in the new field and requisitioned altar furniture, vestments, implements, foodstuffs, and livestock from the peninsula missions. In spite of a few complaints, the propriety of calling on older missions for assistance in starting new ones was generally accepted. Gálvez commandeered the *San Carlos* and the *San Antonio*, which had been built to assist in Elizondo's Sonora war. From the mainland he recruited additional officers and soldiers. Things hummed because the visitador had both authority and enthusiasm.

When the *San Carlos* arrived, it was unseaworthy and had to be unloaded, careened, and reloaded. Gálvez directed the work personally, frequently lending a hand, and by January 9, 1769, this 200-ton ship, with Vicente Vilá as captain, was ready to sail. Lieutenant Pedro Fages and 25 Catalan soldiers brought over from Sonora were on board, along with cosmographer Miguel Costansó, the sailors, a baker, two blacksmiths, seed, agricultural implements, altar furniture, and other materials for the new settlements. Gálvez "went a piece" with the *San Carlos*, sailing down from La Paz to see it round the cape at San Lucas. Although the *San Antonio* was in better shape, Gálvez had it thoroughly overhauled also before sending it out under Juan Pérez on February 15. Less is known about the personnel and cargo aboard the *San Antonio*, but Pérez came to be the ranking mariner along the California coast.

Captain Fernando de Rivera y Moncada was put in charge of the first division of the land party. He had 25 "leather-jacket soldiers," so called because of their sleeveless jackets of tough leather, protection against most Indian missiles. They also carried bullhide shields and wore heavy leather chaps fastened to the pommels of their saddles. They were as much cowboys as soldiers, and Fray Juan Crespi called them "the finest horsemen in the world." This party included three muleteers and 40 mission Indians from Baja California with tools for roadwork, who were counted on to help pacify the Indians farther north. Crespi was chaplain and diarist. Encountering difficulty in finding pasturage for his 400 animals, Rivera moved up to Velicatá, at that time the limit of Spanish control. He set out for San Diego on March 24.

The second land expedition consisted of Captain Gaspar de Portolá as officer in charge of the entire project, Fray Junípero Serra as head of the missionaries, Sergeant José Francisco de Ortega, 10 or 12 soldiers and servants, and 44 Christian Indians. Starting from Loreto on March 9, they proceeded to Velicatá where, on May 14, with due formalities, the mission of San Fernando de Velicatá was founded. It was designed as a way station between Baja and

Alta California. On May 15 Portolá and his men took the trail for San Diego, the appointed rendezvous with Rivera and the ships. Gálvez equipped a third vessel, the *San José*, which sailed on June 16, but it was lost with all on board.

Having sent five detachments to Alta California, Gálvez went to Sonora where Elizondo was meeting only frustration in his attempts to subdue the rebel Seris and Pimas. Gálvez tried offers of amnesty, a campaign in force into the mountain stronghold of the rebels, and then a shift to guerrilla operations, none of which succeeded. In the midst of these efforts, he suffered chills and fevers and a mental breakdown during which his staff had trouble restraining him from foolish acts. Only when he returned to Mexico did he recover his reason.

These difficulties prevented the carrying out of his plans for a general frontier commandancy, occupation of the Gila-Colorado district, and opening a land route to Monterey. Yet Gálvez had improved conditions in Sonora by secularizing certain missions, defining Franciscan powers, and encouraging mining. Just after he left, a gold rush to Cieneguilla and Huerta brought thousands of miners to the frontier. This addition to the civilized population did more than all the military campaigns to stabilize control of the province.

While Gálvez and Elizondo were wrestling with the Sonora problem, the expeditions advanced to San Diego. Because the latitude of the bay had not been accurately charted by previous explorers, Pérez sailed too far north. He first took the *San Antonio* to the Santa Barbara Channel and then dropped down to San Diego, where he anchored after 54 days' sail. The *San Carlos*, which had started a month earlier and was 110 days on the way, did not arrive until April 29. Her crew was so wracked by scurvy that Pérez' men had to come to lower the boats. For a fortnight the chief work was caring for the sick and burying the dead.

The land parties fared much better. Rivera's men had to make a number of dry camps along the arid peninsula, and the water they found for their skin-bag canteens was not always agreeable. By contrast, they were thoroughly drenched in a couple of rainstorms. For most of the distance they were breaking a new trail over rough and mountainous terrain. The savages along the way gave numerous demonstrations of hostility, frightening some of the Christian Indians into deserting and running back to their homes, but Rivera's men had no fighting to do. Any self-pity they may have felt over the rigors of this journey vanished on May 14 with their arrival at San Diego and the sight of the sad plight of the sea parties. Portolá and Serra had fewer cattle to bring over the trail, traveled during better weather, and much of the way followed the route Rivera had tested. Thus, they reached San Diego in six weeks.

By July 1 these four divisions were united. Possession was formally taken in a ceremony in which Serra said Mass, all joined in singing the *Te Deum*, and salutes were fired. Shortly thereafter the presidio was founded, and on July 16 Serra founded the mission of San Diego de Alcalá.

Of perhaps 300 men who had set out from La Paz and Velicatá, only 126 now remained. In addition to those lost on the *San José*, 93 had perished on the other two vessels. Only a score of the Indian auxiliaries were left; a few had died en route, the rest had deserted. Almost half of the 126 survivors were unfit for service. Such was the physical toll upon this first band of California pioneers.

Portolá's March through the Land

Because the Port of Monterey, the real objective, was still to be attained, Portolá prepared to march north. He sent Pérez and eight men in the *San Antonio* to get supplies and reinforcements from San Blas. The *San Carlos* was left at anchor in the bay for want of a crew, and Serra and a few others were left to care for the half hundred invalids. As Portolá worded it, he then "went on by land to Monterey with that small company of persons, or rather say skeletons, who had been spared by scurvy, hunger, and thirst."

Sergeant Ortega and the scouts constituted the vanguard. Next rode Portolá, Fages, the six Catalans who were fit for service, Costansó, missionaries Crespi and Gómez, and the Indian auxiliaries. The 100-mule pack train followed, and Rivera and the remaining soldier–cowboys, driving the *caballada*, brought up the rear. Through southern California travel was easy and pleasant. The numerous natives encountered were friendly, though often embarrassingly inquisitive. Pasture was abundant and water easily obtained. A sharp earthquake at the Santa Ana River crossing suggested the name Río de los Temblores. According to Crespi, the earthquake "lasted about half as long as an Ave María, and about ten minutes later it was repeated, though not violently." Other shocks were noticed until the Los Angeles River was crossed.

Along the coast, past San Luis Obispo, they traveled with little difficulty, but the Sierra de Santa Lucía was a real obstacle. For a week they tarried at its base while Ortega and his scouts sought a pass. "The mountains," wrote Crespi, "are inaccessible not only for men but also for goats and deer." Finally, a way was found, and men and mules scrambled up only to be greeted at the summit by the sad prospect of mountainous country as far as the eye could see. Through this rough terrain they laboriously threaded their way. The fatigue of the long journey was particularly felt at this stage, and scurvy broke out. Yet they worked cheerfully, says Crespi, "for the greater glory of God through the conversion of souls, and for the service of the king, whose dominions were being enlarged by this expedition."

After the mountains the Salinas Valley was a real relief. The company descended this valley for six days and approached Monterey eagerly. Ever since Vizcaíno had sung its praises, the Port of Monterey had been California's chief attraction. Portolá recognized Vizcaíno's landmarks—the Point of Pines, the Carmel River, the magnificent sweep of the bay shore—but he was bewildered not to see the fine harbor. He expected the whole bay to be landlocked. Actually, its mouth is more than 20 miles wide. As Robert Louis Stevenson described it, the bay is like a giant fishhook, curving down from the north with the Point of

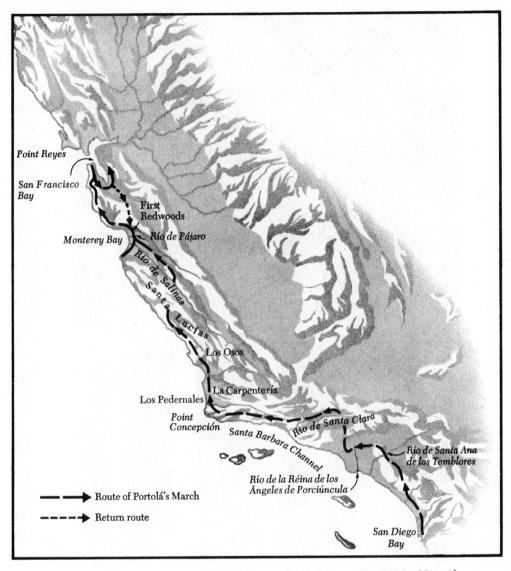

Point Reyes

San Francisco
Bay

First
Redwoods

Monterey Bay — Río de Pájaro

Río de Salinas

Santa Lucías

Los Osos

La Carpentería

Los Pedernales

Point
Concepción   Santa Barbara Channel   Río de Santa Clara

Río de Santa Ana
de los Temblores

Río de la Réina de los
Ángeles de Porciúncula

San Diego
Bay

——➤ Route of Portolá's March

- - -➤ Return route

The March of Portolá

Pines as the barb and the port the small area behind this barb. When later put
to use, this anchorage proved safe and reliable. Reconnoitering it on horseback,
Portolá could not see its full merits; in fact, he did not recognize it. Nonplused,
he concluded that the real Port of Monterey must be farther on and that this
spot merely happened to coincide as to landmarks.

Portolá resumed the northward march and consequently achieved the
honor of discovering the giant redwoods, to which he gave the name palo

Redwoods

Philip Hyde, from The Last Redwoods, Sierra Club

colorado. From Half Moon Bay, a few days later, he could see the Farallones, Point Reyes, and Drake's Bay (to the Spaniards, Bahía del San Francisco, or Cermeño's Bay). These places he recognized unmistakably, for they had been often and well described. Obviously, he had passed Monterey but before turning back to confirm its identification, he determined to explore a little farther. Gálvez had ordered that the third Alta California mission, that in St. Francis' honor, should be established at the Bay of San Francisco (Drake's Bay). Since they were only a few miles from the spot, Portolá decided to visit it before retracing his steps.

Ortega was sent to blaze a trail to Point Reyes. Meanwhile, hunters, climbing the hills east of Half Moon Bay, were the first white men to see San Francisco Bay. They returned to camp to describe the great quiet harbor just over the hills. Hot upon their heels came Ortega with word that the trail to Point Reyes was blocked by the entrance to this bay. Crespi wrote in his diary: "It is a very large and fine harbor, such that not only all the navy of our most Catholic Majesty but those of all Europe could take shelter in it." Portolá, however, entered in his journal on the day of the discovery that "they had found nothing," and his attitude was really that the bay was an obstacle to further advance northward.

Being advised by the Indians that a large ship, perhaps the *San José* or *San Antonio,* was anchored two days' march to the north, Portolá endeavored to get around the arms of the bay. His farthest point north, however, was in the neighborhood of Hayward. On the way south, Monterey was definitely identified and Vizcaíno's Port branded a hallucination. Portolá's band plodded wearily to San Diego, during the final 12 days butchering and roasting one of the weak old mules each evening, and at last entered Serra's camp "smelling frightfully of mules."

Talk of Abandonment

The outlook for California was now most discouraging. The "Estuary of San Francisco Bay" (now known as San Francisco Bay) blocked the way to the site for St. Francis' mission. Monterey apparently had no harbor. The San Diego Indians, repulsing the overtures of the missionaries, had attacked the camp and had stripped garments from some of the invalids. More men had succumbed to scurvy. Portolá's men returned exhausted from their journey. Supplies were very low; for several months, the colony subsisted chiefly on geese, fish, and such food as the Indians would trade for the soldiers' clothing. So acute was the crisis that on February 10, 1770, Portolá sent Rivera and 40 men back to Baja California with instructions to get all the supplies the peninsula missions could spare and to drive up the cattle that had been left at Velicatá. In the meantime their absence would be an asset since it would reduce the number to be fed at San Diego.

For another six weeks privations were severe and abandonment of the colony hung in the balance. Contemporary records do not mention it but in his *Life of Serra,* published 17 years later, Fray Francisco Paloú states that in spite of Serra's intercessions Portolá set March 20 as the date for leaving unless a supply ship should appear sooner. Serra and Crespi announced that they would stay and hold out to the last breath. Vilá agreed to sail the *San Carlos* to Monterey if Portolá should order abandonment. The friars sought heavenly assistance through a novena (a nine-day season of prayer), and their prayers were answered by the appearance of the *San Antonio* one day before the fateful twentieth. The critical situation is not exaggerated; San Diego could not have been held much longer except for the supplies on the *San Antonio.* Portolá's men "got very particular consolation out of the corn, flour, and rice which it brought."

No one could accuse Paloú of praising Serra beyond his deserts. It does appear, however, that in eulogizing his brother Franciscan, whose place as California's hero par excellence is secure for all time, Paloú cast unwarranted reflections upon Portolá. The captain doubtless was less entranced with California than was Fray Junípero, but he had not given up. To his wise and courageous leadership in this initial crisis is due much of the credit for preserving the Spanish hold on Alta California.

Over Pérez' protests Portolá sent the *San Antonio* on to Monterey, while he marched north again with the remaining 16 able soldiers. He repeated the ceremony of taking possession and on June 3, 1770, formally established a presidio and the mission of San Carlos. Then, in accordance with his instructions, he invested Fages with the government of Alta California and sailed with Costansó and Pérez for Mexico.

News of the occupation of Monterey was hurried to Viceroy Croix, who in special compliment to Gálvez ordered the church bells rung and flags flown to signalize the 300-league advance of the frontier to the famed Monterey. Moreover, he ordered the celebration of a special High Mass of thanksgiving, which he attended with his viceregal court.

A Precarious Start

In Alta California celebration of victory seemed premature. In the summer of 1770 the only stations held were San Diego, a long jump from Velicatá, and Monterey, another long jump northwestward. Each had a presidio and a mission, but both were in the early stages of development. They were surrounded by many thousands of Indians, some of whom had already shown hostility. For the presidial garrisons and the mission guards there were, all told, 43 soldiers.

The return of Rivera and his pack train from the peninsula was a valuable reinforcement, but that was partly nullified by his pique at having been passed over for the California command. Hearing that Fages had been given this office, Rivera refused to budge beyond San Diego.

The most crucial problem was that of supply. At Jamestown, Quebec, Plymouth, and elsewhere on the Atlantic seaboard, the early colonists characteristically faced a starving period. Because modern California is so phenomenally productive, it may appear that the Spanish pioneers should have had no worries. Living off the country had proved difficult, however, for Portolá and his men as they made the return journey from Monterey, and at San Diego early in 1770 starvation was imminent. Living off the Indians was difficult too. Although they are praised by anthropologists for the adequacy of their food getting, their food list was one that the Spaniards could not readily adopt, assuming there was an actual surplus.

As soon as they could, the missionaries made small plantings of corn, beans, and wheat. In 1770 and 1771 late spring rains were sufficient to produce a yield. In 1772 more normal conditions prevailed, and it became clear that fields and gardens would have to be irrigated.

Meanwhile, food had to be imported. By 1770 no further exactions

The First Published Picture of a Grizzly

Louis Choris, Voyage pittoresque autour du monde, 1822

"He can take one sniff of you half a mile downwind and tell you the color of your grandmother's wedding dress."
F. H. Riggall

could be made on Baja California. Sustenance had to come by the sea route from Mexico. In 1772 the ships were late and came only as far as San Diego. To relieve what otherwise would have been a famine, Fages organized a famous bear hunt in the San Luis Obispo vicinity. Bear meat was the staple until a pack train came north with beans and flour.

The food shipments from Mexico had additional significance to the program of the missions. Beyond what was required for sustaining the soldiers and missionaries, food was fundamental in attracting Indians to come and live at the missions. Any shortage in supply translated itself into a dearth of new converts as well as a departure of disillusioned neophytes.

The military were plagued by desertions. Soldiers, wearied or bored by their duties, often decamped. Fleeing all the way to Mexico was out of the question, and maintaining themselves in the Indian country was dangerous as well as difficult. Deserters usually were recaptured or came back, but this kind of absenteeism reduced the effectiveness of the troops.

Misconduct of the soldiers, especially toward the Indian women, was another complaint. An Indian uprising at San Gabriel in 1771 was the direct result of the lassoing and mistreatment of the wife of a chief. Elsewhere, Indian resistance was similarly invited. The missionaries could protest, but only the military could punish.

A sharper discord arose over the founding of new missions. In 1771 the *San Antonio* brought 10 Franciscans, two as replacements for their brothers at San Diego who had asked to be retired, the other eight available for assignment at new missions. Serra had the approximate locations in mind. On July 14 he had the pleasure of launching Mission San Antonio de Padua in an oak-dotted valley in the Santa Lucias, some 25 leagues south of Monterey. On November 8 missionaries and soldiers moved up from San Diego to the base of the Sierra Madre and founded Mission San Gabriel Arcangel. On September 1, 1772, Serra added a fifth mission, San Luís Obispo de Tolosa.

Serra had missionaries available for still another mission which he proposed to locate among the Chumash on the Santa Barbara Channel. No step could be taken without Fages' approval and assignment of a military guard. As to the proposed Mission San Buenaventura, Fages demurred on the sound ground that soldiers were not available. Serra also had urged missions in the San Francisco Bay area but had met with the same rebuff. The plain fact was that Spain had provided missionaries enough for six or eight missions but not enough soldiers. By 1773 Fages had 61 for the two presidios and five missions.

Meanwhile, there was work to be done in moving Mission San Diego to a more favorable site and Mission San Carlos from Monterey to the alluvial lands on the Carmel River. In each instance the prime consideration was the better prospects for crop production.

In pleading for additional missions, Serra could not cite much progress at the existing stations. Mission San Gabriel operated more than a year before a single conversion was accomplished, and the first baptism at Mission San Carlos had to compensate for six months' labor. By the end of 1773 not quite 500 Indians had been baptized, not a very large number in comparison with other missionary fields; and of these converts almost all were women and children. The record was so uninspiring that Rafael Verger, father-superior of the College of San Fernando, from which the California Franciscans were drawn, seriously considered recommending closing these missions. The viceroy, late in 1772, warned the authorities in Spain that abandonment of Alta California might be necessary. Planned improvements at San Blas were canceled, and less of an effort was made to send supplies.

The Coast Near Point Lobos

Edward Weston

Serra Intercedes for California

At San Diego in September of 1772 Serra did his best to persuade Fages to cooperate in the establishment of Mission San Buenaventura. When Fages refused, Serra took the extraordinary course of going to Mexico to appeal over Fages' head to the viceroy. For one of his frail health, this action was heroic.

Serra sailed on October 20, arrived at San Blas on November 4, and, although waylaid by illness, reached Mexico on February 6, 1773. Early in March he was granted an audience by Viceroy Antonio María Bucareli y Ursúa. Particulars of their conversation are not recorded, but Serra undoubtedly pled eloquently and passionately for vigorous support of this northwesternmost mission frontier. His arrival was timely. Just a few weeks earlier Bucareli had received royal instructions relative to the frontier provinces. The king directed that the Californias be given "special attention."

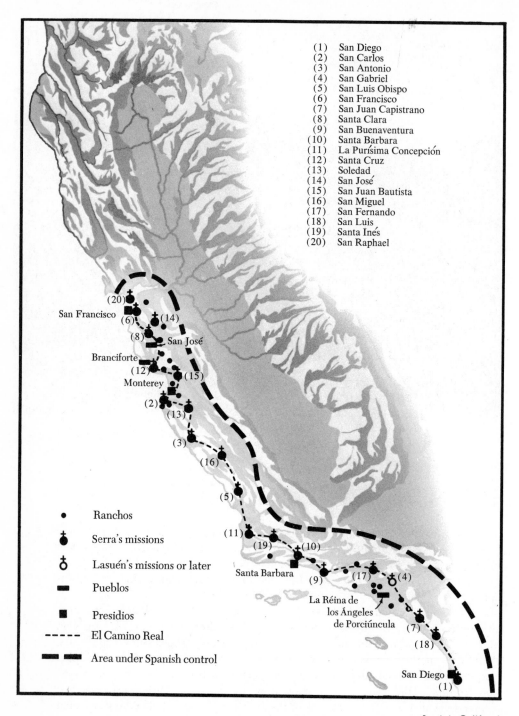

(1)   San Diego
(2)   San Carlos
(3)   San Antonio
(4)   San Gabriel
(5)   San Luis Obispo
(6)   San Francisco
(7)   San Juan Capistrano
(8)   Santa Clara
(9)   San Buenaventura
(10) Santa Barbara
(11) La Purísima Concepción
(12) Santa Cruz
(13) Soledad
(14) San José
(15) San Juan Bautista
(16) San Miguel
(17) San Fernando
(18) San Luis
(19) Santa Inés
(20) San Raphael

San Francisco
(20)
(6)   (14)
(8)
San José
Branciforte
(12)
Monterey
(2)
(15)
(13)
(3)
(16)
(5)
(11)
(19)   (10)
Santa Barbara
(9)   (17)   (4)
La Réina de
los Ángeles
de Porciúncula
(7)
(18)
San Diego
(1)

•   Ranchos

♂   Serra's missions

♀   Lasuén's missions or later

▬   Pueblos

■   Presidios

-----   El Camino Real

▬▬▬▬   Area under Spanish control

Spain's California

On March 13 in a petition with 32 numbered points, Serra put in writing his detailed recommendations. He itemized improvements needed in allowances and delivery of supplies, urged that a land route be opened from Sonora, requested blacksmiths and carpenters and the assignment to each mission of six peons (non-Indian laborers). He proposed enlarging the mission escorts to 10 soldiers, and, for two projected missions, to 20 and 15 respectively. Protesting past interferences with the mission programs, he asked that certain specified powers of decision be given the missionaries. He even went so far as to ask that Fages be removed and nominated as his replacement Sergeant Ortega, who had served ably as Portolá's scout.

After consulting his council, Bucareli acted but did not grant Serra's every wish. The mission guards, for instance, were not expanded, nor was a complement of six peons provided. The viceroy did move to improve the service of supply, order the opening of an overland trail, provide for reinforcements, issue a Reglamento, or governing code, for the province, and recall Commandant Fages. Early in 1774, Serra returned to California much encouraged.

In 1773, during Serra's absence in Mexico, another eight Franciscans came to California.. At the time of the expulsion of the Jesuits, the Dominicans had applied for a share in the California mission field. After the expansion northward, when they renewed this application, the superior of the College of San Fernando readily agreed to surrender the seven declining missions in the southern part of the peninsula. The Dominicans insisted they should have part of the pagan area where new missions could be opened. Therefore, the dividing line was moved up past Velicatá to the arroyo of San Juan Bautista, the northernmost of the potential mission sites on the road to San Diego.

This agreement opened the third mission period in Baja California, during which seven missions were added to the older Jesuit–Franciscan chain. It also released a noteworthy group of eight Franciscans, who in 1773 transferred from Baja to Alta California. Among them were Francisco Palou, Serra's particular friend and biographer and the major historian of this frontier, and Fermín Francisco de Lasuén, later to have charge of the California missions.

For Further Reading

C. E. Chapman, The Founding of Spanish California (1946).

H. I. Priestley, José de Gálvez, Visitador-General (1916).

F. J. Teggert, Diary of Miguel Costansó (1911).

H. E. Bolton, Fray Juan Crespi (1927).

Francisco Palou, Junípero Serra (1784), trans. C. S. Williams (1913) and M. J. Geiger (1955).

M. J. Geiger, The Life and Times of Fray Junípero Serra (1959).

Jeanne Van Nostrand, Monterey, Adobe Capital of California (1969).

T. E. Treutlein, San Francisco Bay, Discovery and Colonization (1969).

Caughey, California Heritage, 58–68.

chapter five

Strengthening the Colony

> No other service could be so important as the encouragement of sowing, planting, and stockraising at the three presidios and also to give the settlers all possible assistance in their farming and stockraising so that a few sites may produce what is necessary to make these new establishments self-supporting

Governor Felipe de Neve to the viceroy,
June 7, 1777

Bucareli Gives Support

1774 to 1782

When Serra returned to California in the fifth year of its existence as a Spanish outpost, the omens seemed favorable. The missionary contingent numbered a score or more. Missions San Carlos and San Antonio were beginning to prosper. A new commandant, Rivera, would govern, and, most encouraging, Viceroy Bucareli was now actively supporting the province.

Mindful of Bucareli's contributions in the mid-1770's, one historian has acclaimed him "the greatest hero who has ever appeared in the field of California history." Mexican historians see him as an outstanding viceroy, and students of the empire in the time of Charles III praise his service. His principal biographer is more restrained,

Medicine Wall

Lee Mullican

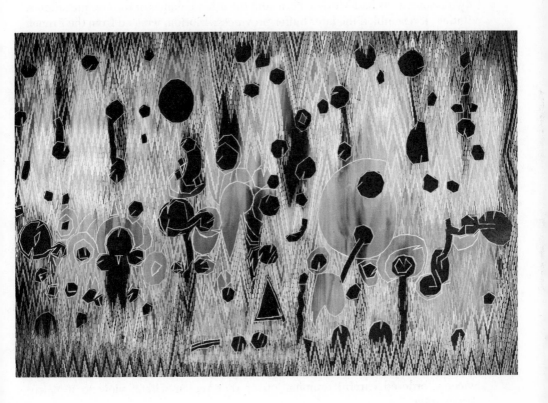

crediting him with being diligent, cautious, and meticulous, efficient in carrying out a policy but not bold or an innovator. Be that as it may, within the next few years California, which had been a precariously held outpost, was put on a much more stable footing.

The map and the day-to-day experiences of the time may suggest that California was a simple open frontier on which the Spanish advance had the land and the Indians to contend with but little else. Its place in the empire, however, was essentially that of a borderland colony. It had not been occupied for its own resources as had Mexico, Peru, and the other colonies of the conquistadores. Rather, it resembled the later buffer provinces: Florida, wrested from the French and garrisoned to guard the passage of the Silver Fleets; Texas, planted in the early eighteenth century to counter French activities in the Alabama and lower Mississippi basins; and Louisiana, accepted from France in the 1760's to shield New Spain from Britain's expanding empire.

As Gálvez had emphasized, the danger on the northwest coast was partly Russian, but in Europe Spain's most formidable adversary was Britain. In North America, too, Britain was the principal power to be feared. The Anglo-Spanish boundary ran through the Gulf of Mexico and up the Mississippi, some distance from California. British explorers were pressing westward in Canada and were active again in voyages to the Pacific. These two expansions might unite. Bucareli saw California not merely as a field for missionary undertakings, as a step toward straightening out the Indian frontier, or as a barrier to Russian expansion. It was also a check on the growing British power in North America.

In July, 1773, Bucareli issued a Reglamento, or frame of government and administration, for Alta California. In August it was amplified in a letter of instruction to the new governor, Rivera. Among other matters Rivera was told to promote the conversion of the natives and their civilization at the missions. These stations, Bucareli predicted, would become great cities; Rivera should plan accordingly in selecting sites, laying out streets, and parceling the land. Other paragraphs dealt with records, reports to Loreto and Mexico City, Indian policy, supply ships from San Blas, and the eventual secularization of the missions. Aware of the strategic importance of San Francisco Bay, the viceroy ordered careful examination of that region with a view to its early occupation.

With the change in governors Bucareli reinforced California. Since Fages would bring his Catalan troops back to Baja California, Rivera was instructed to enlist married recruits in Sinaloa and take them and their families to the new province. Rivera collected a party of 51 persons, whom he transported across to Loreto. By way of Velicatá they reached their destination. Earlier in 1774 Serra had sailed for California accompanied by a new missionary, Fray Pablo Mugártegui, a new commissary, three blacksmiths, and three carpenters, not to mention four reams of fine paper, five bales of cloth for Indian presents, 16 boxes of panocha and six of chocolate, four boxes of beads, and sundry other articles to be used in converting the heathen. These reinforcements were perhaps more encouraging than reassuring. Although not enough to put the province securely on its feet, they were valuable because California was in such a state that every bit helped.

Bucareli also greatly improved the service of the supply ships. Notwithstanding optimistic reports from California, he sent out an extra vessel in 1774, which arrived just in time to avert a serious famine. Every year he was careful to see that the supplies were in good condition and that the ships left San Blas promptly. Merely to keep the service in operation was difficult. The harbor at San Blas silted in, and work on the port was necessary almost constantly. Because of the climate most supplies could not be stored at San Blas but had to be shipped at once. Consequently, perfect timing was necessary in the arrival and loading of the stores and the sailing of ships. Ships were scarce. The voyage was always long and arduous and bore such an evil reputation that sailors commonly had to be shanghaied into service. Yet Bucareli not only maintained but improved the supply service by sea.

Further exploration of the coast was a companion task. In 1773–74 Pérez went as far north as 55 latitude. Three more vessels were sent out in 1775. In the *San Carlos*, Juan Manuel de Ayala made the first entrance into San Francisco Bay. In another ship, Bruno de Hezeta discovered the Columbia River. Juan Francisco de Bodega took the third as far as 58 degrees latitude. In 1779 Bodega again went to Alaskan waters but saw nothing of the Russians. Although these voyages were the sort of investigation the court had ordered Gálvez to make in 1769, they were motivated more by concern about British as well as Russian activities in the North Pacific. In fact, renewed English interest in discovering the Northwest Passage, represented by Cook's voyage, was Bucareli's primary reason for sending out these ships. Because he did so, Spain can claim priority in the exploration of most of the coast from the Columbia to Alaska.

Anza Opens an Overland Route

Experience with the sea and peninsula routes to Alta California had fully corroborated Gálvez' original opinion that the province could not flourish unless a land route was opened from Sonora. The supply ships faced too long and uncertain a voyage to carry families of settlers or herds of livestock to California. The first missionaries, soldiers, mules, and cattle came up the peninsula trails, yet Serra estimated that to supply the province by this route would require the constant services of a train of 1,500 mules, many times more than could be fed and watered along the trail. Bucareli's greatest contribution to California unquestionably was in bringing about the opening of the land route from Sonora, over which came the reinforcements that made Spanish California self-perpetuating and measurably self-supporting. The land route also made possible the founding of San Francisco as the northernmost outpost of Spain's empire.

In choosing leaders to open the trail to California the viceroy made a most happy selection. His principal agent in the land advance was Captain Juan Bautista de Anza, whose father and grandfather before him had served as frontier captains on the rim of civilization at Frónteras and Janos. For two decades Anza had seen similar service at Frónteras and Tubac. Though only 37, he was experienced in Indian control, seasoned through Apache fighting, and expert in campaigning in a half-desert land. Anza led two expeditions to California, one to explore the trail and the other to bring supplies, livestock, and families of settlers, the lifeblood of Spanish Alta California. He did his work brilliantly, getting his parties through expeditiously and almost without loss of life. In length and in difficulties with terrain and hostile natives, Anza's first expedition has been compared with that of Lewis and Clark. His second journey corresponds to that of the first pioneer settlers to Oregon.

Francisco Garcés, a young Franciscan sent to San Xavier del Bac in 1768 when the Jesuits were expelled, shared honors with Anza in advancing land exploration. He made three journeys inland, traveling, as Governor Sastre wrote, "with no other provisions than a little pinole, a little chocolate, and a few strips of jerked beef, and with no other escort than his guardian angel." Twice he traveled El Camino del Diablo to the Pimas on the Gila, and once he crossed the Colorado, going as far as Signal Mountain near Calexico. Intrepid, dynamic, fearless, and trusted by the Indians, Garcés was another Kino, though even more of a wanderer.

Fray Pedro Font is memorable as the diarist of the colonist group. His book-length journal of the day-by-day experience of this party is a most graphic description of western travel. It is so accurate a record of distances and landmarks that its modern translator could make positive identification of every camping place and almost every footstep along the way. At the same time, with a wealth of intimate detail, this diary creates a vivid picture of the experiences of these pioneers.

Take, for example, Font's description of how Garcés assembled a mob of Indians at Santa Olaya, won their attention by distributing a few beads and a little tobacco, and then drew forth from his pack a banner depicting the Child Jesus in the Virgin Mary's arms. The natives were pleased and gladly offered to be baptized. Then Garcés turned his picture around. The reverse side showed a lost soul suffering eternal punishment, at the sight of which the Indians raised a great outcry. The Gileños, the Opas, and the Yumas, as Font remarks, "all replied in the same way, without manifesting any repugnance to Christianity." In Font's opinion Garcés was ideally suited to missionary work among these Indians. Like them he was phlegmatic, content to sit musing by a fire for hours at a time. Nor was he squeamish about eating the Indian foods, which Font considered "nasty and dirty." "In short," Font said, "God has created him, as I see it, solely for the purpose of seeking out these unhappy, ignorant, and rustic people."

The project of opening a land route to Monterey had a long but futile history up to 1773, going back clearly to Kino and rather vaguely to Oñate. Anza's father had urged it vigorously in the 1750's and the plan was more than implicit in Gálvez' labors for the pacification of Sonora. The immediate inspiration, however, occurred in 1769 when Anza's Pima neighbors learned through the Yumas of white men going up and down the west coast. The prompt arrival of this news of Portolá argued the existence of a convenient land route; consequently, Anza sent an offer to Gálvez to seek it out. Encouraged still further by Garcés' report of his journey across the Colorado and of his sight of a great blue sierra not far to the northwest, Anza renewed and expanded the offer.

Bucareli consulted whoever might possess pertinent information. Costansó, Portolá's cosmographer, gave his expert approval of the plan, praising it because it would release the California soldiers from "perpetual and involuntary celibacy." A junta at Mexico City called on Anza and Garcés for more information. Serra, then in Mexico, added his endorsement. Bucareli made his decision and a junta unanimously approved.

An Apache raid on Anza's horse herd delayed the start, but by late December, 1773, he set out with some 20 soldiers, a dozen helpers, and 200 animals. At Caborca he picked up as guide Sebastián Tarabal, a runaway from Mission San Gabriel in California. As far as Caborca they moved through settled country. Beyond came the Camino del Diablo, a 200-mile stretch where they had to depend on water holes or tanks, and where several dry camps had to be made.

Realizing that the Colorado crossing was the crucial point, Anza took pains to win the friendship of the Yumas. He greeted their chief Salvador Palma with appropriate formality. Climaxing an exchange of speeches, around Palma's neck Anza put a red ribbon with a medal, on which was a likeness of Charles III, symbol of his authority under that great monarch. All night the friendly and inquisitive Indians stayed around the camp, "making sleep impossible, and life generally miserable."

In the morning Anza forded the Gila, the tall Yumas carrying his baggage across on their heads. The next day they assisted again in the crossing of the Colorado, celebrated by a salute of musketry that startled and pleased the Indians. All crossed in orthodox fashion except Garcés, who could not swim and did not trust his horse. He crossed on the shoulders of his newly found Indian friends.

Beyond the Colorado, Anza's problem was trail breaking. Garcés had been somewhat farther, and Tarabal had wandered across the sand dunes from the California side, but neither proved a reliable guide. Indian advice was more to the point. The Yumas warned against a northwest or west course, which would have led more directly toward Monterey. On their advice Anza descended the Colorado to Santa Olaya, intending to strike westward from there toward the blue sierra. This three-day journey was as picturesque and bizarre as can be imagined. Some 600 Yumas of all sizes, ages, and descriptions made a holiday outing of this jaunt down the river. They swarmed around the soldiers and cattle and performed a number of small services for the white men, pestering them meanwhile with their prying curiosity and even with the theft of an axe.

From the Cajuenche village at Santa Olaya, Anza struck out into the sand dunes. The first day they made 20 miles. The next, the guides turned back. On the third day, they lost the trail in drifting sand, and horses and mules began to give out. Garcés tried to lead them south to an old camp but could not find it. The only thing to do was to retreat to Santa Olaya. A dozen animals died, and the rest were so worn down by the 10-day battle with the sand dunes that Anza despaired of moving everything to California.

Summoning Palma, he left much of the baggage, the cattle, and the jaded pack and saddle animals in his care. The head muleteer and two soldiers volunteered to remain and watch over this property. While the horses and mules recuperated, the soldiers relaxed by dancing with the Cajuenches to the tune of

Desert Scene, Borrego Springs

Philip Hyde

a soldier's violin. "They seemed so attached to it," wrote Anza, "that they gave up their own pastimes, and in their stead learned the customs of our men, particularly the women, who constantly wished to be dancing the seguidillas which the soldiers taught them, and in whose steps they became proficient."

On March 2 Anza set out again, this time with only 10 pack mules and with his men mounted on the "least bad" horses. To get around the sand dunes they circled farther south, made a dry camp and a 40-mile march to water and pasture, went on to another dry camp, and came to more hard going. Finally they reached a camp that Tarabal recognized.

Their route now led through Borrego Valley to good forage at San Gregorio, up Coyote Canyon to the Royal Pass of San Carlos, to Cahuilla Valley, "most beautiful green and flower-strewn prairies, and snow-covered mountains with pines, oaks, and other trees which grow in cold countries." By way of San Jacinto and Alessandro valleys they had easy going to the Santa Ana, and two more pleasant days brought them to civilization again at San Gabriel. They had broken trail from Sonora to California.

In the spring of 1774 Spanish Alta California could not take care of 25 visitors. Anza sent to San Diego for supplies and mounts so that he could go on to Monterey. From there he intended to return by a more inland route. Neither sort of help was forthcoming. Consequently he had to send Garcés and most of the soldiers back to the Yumas to wait for him there.

Anza made his way to Monterey, where he consulted with Palóu about a chain of missions along the Anza trail and about mail service over it from Mexico to Monterey. Returning to San Gabriel in a nine-day ride, Anza hurried on to Santa Olaya. Palma's Yumas rafted him across the Colorado. He continued by way of the Gila to Tubac and, after a time, was allowed to go to Mexico to report to Bucareli.

Anza's Second Expedition

Along with authorizing the Hezeta-Ayala-Bodega voyages of 1775, the viceroy ordered Anza to go a second time over the trail to California, this time with soldiers and settlers destined for San Francisco Bay. The settlers were to be recruited in Sinaloa where there were many families "submerged in poverty." Colonists were to be outfitted at government expense, each man's outfit costing 42 pesos, one real, each woman's outfit six reales less. Equipment included carbines, cartridge belts, leather jackets, saddles, bridles, pack saddles, blankets, and all the necessary provisions for the journey.

Leaving Horcasitas the expedition numbered 177 persons. Others joined at Tubac, bringing the total to 240. There were 3 missionaries; 3 officers; 20 veteran soldiers; 20 recruits; wives, children, and relatives totaling 165; and some 30 muleteers and other helpers. They moved out with 695 horses and mules and 355 cattle. The cavalcade was equivalent to a ranch on the move, and every night the camp looked like a good-sized town.

Through the diarists of the expedition and their translator, Herbert

Eugene Bolton, we have knowledge of innumerable episodes of the trek. A woman died in childbirth at the first camp beyond Tubac. The infant and two others born along the way came over the trail safely. At the Gila, Pimas presented Anza with two fresh Apache scalps. At one town on the Gila, Anza shook hands with 1,100 Indians. On the king's birthday he issued each soldier a pint of aguardiente.

For Chief Palma, Bucareli had sent a gorgeous outfit consisting of shirt and trousers, a jacket with a yellow front, blue cape with gold braid, and a black velvet cap. Yuma hospitality featured a gift of 3,000 melons. Getting 241 persons across the Colorado was a problem. One rider floundered off course and a little girl riding with him was swept away. Men stationed below the ford for just such an emergency rescued the little girl. Font, suffering from ague, crossed with a Yuma on each side holding him on his horse. Garcés, putting his trust in Indians rather than in horses, crossed on the shoulders of three braves, "two at his head and one at his feet, he lying stretched out face up as though he were dead."

A cabin was prepared and supplies set aside for Garcés and Eixarch and the seven Indian servants who were to tarry with the Yumas. As four months' supply for these nine persons Anza left an arroba (25 pounds) each of chocolate, sugar, and tallow, five beeves, three tierces (small casks) of dried meat, a packload of beans, one of flour, an almud (a little over a bushel) of chick-peas, a box of biscuits, three hams, and six cheeses. For presents and barter, there was a bale of tobacco and two boxes of beads; for holy services, 12 wax candles and a bottle of wine, though the latter proved to be spurious; and for more mundane uses, a frying pan, a griddle, an axe, and two cakes of soap.

At Santa Olaya, Anza split the expedition into three divisions to travel at 24-hour intervals so that the water holes could refill. They had to endure dry camps and camps without firewood, a hardship because they struck the desert when it was unusually cold. Snow and cold continued in the Borrego Valley and at the Royal Pass of San Carlos.

On Christmas Eve, just below Coyote Canyon, another child was born. On New Year's Day they crossed the Santa Ana, and a few nights later were at San Gabriel with the entire complement of people but a substantial shrinkage in the number of horses and cattle.

They arrived at a time of crisis. The mission Indians at San Diego had just risen in rebellion, killing one of the missionaries and two soldiers. Anza and Font and 17 soldiers joined Governor Rivera in a journey to San Diego to punish the offenders. In their absence five muleteers deserted and headed for Sonora with 25 horses. Lieutenant José Moraga pursued, overtook them just short of Santa Olaya, and brought them back with most of the horses and a few head of cattle lost in a stampede in their earlier crossing.

The Founding of San Francisco

On February 21, 1776, Anza and half the party started for Monterey; the rest would follow with the cattle. Four weeks later they reunited at Monterey. Anza's orders were to take them on to San Francisco but, contrary to expectations, a precise site had not been selected. In the seven years since the Portolá discovery there had been several visits: by Fages in 1772, by Rivera and Palóu in 1774, and by Ayala in 1775. Ayala spent a month exploring the various arms of the bay and another 11 days trying to sail out its mouth. He also made a good map of the bay, which he described as the best anywhere along the west coast and as "not one port, but many with a single entrance."

Encouraged by the padres, Anza went north to reconnoiter. He and Font were most enthusiastic about the setting. "The port of San Francisco," wrote Font, "is a marvel of nature, and might well be called the harbor of harbors." In all his travels he had seen no site that pleased him as much. Anza chose Fort Point as the site for the presidio and Arroyo de los Dolores for the mission. He also rounded the southern arm of the bay and followed the east bay all the way to Carquinez Straits and Antioch.

Anza had hoped to conduct the colonists personally to San Francisco, but Rivera's obstructions made that impossible. In mid-April, after turning the settlers over to Moraga's command, he started for Sonora. As one further service to California, he carried two pairs of cats destined for mousing at San Gabriel and San Diego. Below Monterey he met Rivera, half-crazed with anger that the San Francisco project was moving forward despite his disapproval. Rivera had ridden all the way from San Diego to confer with Anza, but he was in such a rage that he rode on to Monterey after only the most perfunctory salutations. Almost immediately he was riding south again to overtake Anza at San Luis Obispo, but the captain declined to have any discussion with him except in writing. In a smouldering rage Rivera waited for an hour and then posted off to San Gabriel, where it became his turn to deny Anza an audience.

Anza camped near the mission. Some letters but no spoken words passed back and forth, and after three days he departed for Mexico without having come to any agreement with the governor about the move to San Francisco. An order from the viceroy, however, reached California soon after Anza left, and Rivera had no alternative but to comply. Lieutenant Moraga, Palóu, and Cambón led the settlers to the chosen site, founded the presidio on September 17, 1776, and dedicated the mission on October 9. But this outpost of empire clearly owed most to Bucareli, who had sponsored the entire project, and to Anza, who had opened the trail and conducted the colonists to California.

Pueblos Recommended; San José Founded

Although Portolá, Fages, and Rivera are customarily thought of as governors, technically they were commandants, subordinate to the governor stationed at Loreto and with jurisdiction over both Californias. In 1776 in recognition of the increased importance of Alta California, Bucareli instructed Felipe de Neve to transfer the governing authority to Monterey.

Neve traveled north in 1777. He rode up the Portolá trail to Monterey and, for good measure, on to San Francisco and back to Monterey. He thus began his governorship with a careful inspection of the entire province, seeing the three existing presidios and the eight missions. Mission San Juan Capistrano, opened temporarily on October 30, 1775, had been reestablished on November 1, 1776, and Mission Santa Clara de Asís had been founded on January 12, 1777.

The new governor realized that what California most needed was adequate food production on the scene. As he traveled the 600-mile length of the province, he took stock of the achievements at the occupied places and carefully examined the agricultural potential at other localities along the way. His residence in Baja California had prepared him to understand that, with rainless summers, irrigation was a necessity. In appraising crop-raising capacity, he therefore looked for two requisites: an adequate year-round flow of water and arable land to which this water could be brought by gravity flow.

On June 6, 1777, Neve wrote to Bucareli on this subject. For background he described the seasonal pattern of rainfall and reviewed the meager and uncertain harvests since 1770. Whenever a soldier or a civilian had attempted a planting, Neve mentioned it, but, because of the presidial locations and the military duties, he saw little prospect that farming would flourish at the presidios. As of 1777 the missions still produced less than their own requirements.

What the province needed, wrote Neve, was a few pueblos—country towns, communities of farmers and stock raisers. Prior to Neve's time Alta California had no pueblos. Baja California had none and, for that matter, no presidios either. But in Sonora, New Mexico, Texas, and most other Spanish frontier provinces, the town was present alongside the mission and the military post.

Explicitly Neve asked for 50 or 60 farmer families to establish two pueblos. As the most advantageous locations he recommended sites on the Porciúncula River (Los Angeles) near Mission San Gabriel and on the Guadalupe near Mission Santa Clara.

Each settler, he advised, should be paid 12 pesos a month and rations and should be assigned two cows, two oxen, two mares, two she-goats, two ewes, and equipment such as plows, spades, colters, field knife, hatchet, sword, and lance. Each pueblo would be provided bulls, stallions, rams, boars, asses and jacks, and tools for community use such as levers, saws, chisels, augurs, and a forge and its accouterments. Each pueblo should have a couple of skilled artisans.

In the established Spanish tradition each pueblo was to be assigned an alcalde to see that each settler planted and cultivated his land. The alcalde would head the pueblo government and direct the community work on projects such as the dam and zanja (irrigation ditch) and the public granary.

Neve proposed that initially each pueblo have a guard of three or four soldiers, that for 10 years they be excused from tithes and tributes, and that none be called away for assignment to a mission.

At the presidio of San Francisco, Neve found four soldier–settlers brought by Anza, the widow of another soldier, and a vaquero; at Monterey he found nine other soldiers, practiced farmers, who could be spared for the establishment of the northern pueblo. Without waiting for specific approval, Neve took the responsibility of moving these 15 and their families, a total of 68 persons, to the bank of the Guadalupe, three quarters of a league from Mission Santa Clara. There on November 29 the pueblo San José de Guadalupe was founded.

Near the plaza, future center of the pueblo, each settler was assigned a building site, lands for cultivation, and cattle. Because the dam and zanja would be adequate to irrigate a spacious meadow, an extra apportionment of lands for cultivation was made, with still other lots reserved for new residents. The pueblo would have ejidos (commons), grazing land, and woods.

It was April, 1778, before Neve could forward a report of this action. He then had to report that for lack of oxen to pull the plows it had been possible to plant no more than six fanegas (hundredweights) of maize and the same amount of beans. Also, a freshet washed out the dam. Within a few years, however, he hoped that the pueblo would supply grain to the presidios of Monterey and San Francisco. On July 15 Bucareli approved Neve's action in founding California's first pueblo.

Shortly thereafter Bucareli was notified that jurisdiction over the northern frontier, California included, was transferred to another official. No letter of Bucareli's carries so much as a hint of regret at the transfer of authority. On the contrary, he seems to have been well pleased that the problems of the frontier now belonged to someone else.

Bucareli could look back on five years of significant strengthening of California by improved shipments of supplies, the opening of an overland trail, the great reinforcement through the second Anza expedition, the advance to San Francisco, and Neve's good start as governor.

Neve Asks for More Settlers

When Gálvez, as the newly appointed Minister of the Indies, persuaded Charles III to set up the frontier commandancy, he nominated Teodoro de Croix for the appointment. California-oriented historians criticize Croix for devoting most of his energies to the eastern sector. However, that was where Croix was experienced, and it can also be argued that the Apache menace was more alarming than anything relating to California. Croix's postponement of personal attention to the western extremity of his far-flung command also meant that Governor Neve could continue to exercise initiative. Croix supported his decisions.

On July 1, 1779, Neve issued a Reglamento amplifying and replacing Bucareli's of 1773. This document became the fundamental code of the province for the rest of the Spanish period. To think of it as a constitution is somewhat misleading because, along with rules of administration, it contained plans and itemized expenditures for the existing presidios, for a new presidio, for a second pueblo, and for additional missions. Neve put his Reglamento into effect. The viceroy approved it in 1780; the king, in 1781. In 1782, the viceroy ordered it printed, and in 1784 his order was carried out.

Although Neve urged and worked for the establishment of three new missions for the Chumash of the Santa Barbara Channel, he was sharply critical of the mission program. The missionaries, he thought, were too intent on subordinating all else to their programs and decision making. He acted several times to protest against what he considered over-reaching by the padres.

One such action concerned Serra's right to confirm. In 1777 Fray Junípero's college had delegated this power to him, and he had proceeded to exercise it. Two years later, Neve notified him to cease confirming and surrender his patent to Croix for inspection. Though "pretending obedience"—the phrase is Neve's—Serra went right on confirming. Only after prolonged correspondence with his college and the viceroy did he submit his patent to Croix, who, finding it in regular form, authorized him to continue.

In his Reglamento and other orders Neve restricted the missionaries in numerous ways. He reduced their privilege of franking letters, curbed their practice of using Indians as messengers and vaqueros, and insisted they apply for a permit from the governor before retiring from the province. Most serious, he forbade the use of military escorts by the friars except when called from their stations to hear confessions. In the regulations for pueblos, he specified that the townsmen were not to be drawn away to work at the missions. When the pueblo of San José was accused of encroaching on the land and water supply of Mission Santa Clara, Neve rejected the charge. He also urged single-friar missions. All these recommendations were in step with the trend toward reduction of control over the temporalities by the religious. With the conditions prevailing in California, however, it was beneficial that Neve did not prevail on the issue of single-friar missions.

Meanwhile, Neve continued his advocacy of the second pueblo and of a presidio and three missions for the Santa Barbara Channel. Croix wrote encouragingly and in December, 1779, commissioned Rivera to recruit settlers and soldiers. Inasmuch as Rivera had led expeditions to California in 1769 and 1770, had raised a party of 51 persons for the province in 1774, and had been governor at the time of the Anza expedition, the task was not entirely novel to him.

Rivera was authorized to enlist 24 married settlers and their families; 34 married soldiers, whose families were to be brought with them to California; and 25 unmarried soldiers, to take the place in Sonora of a like number of Anza's veterans who would thus be released for California service. Rivera could hold out liberal inducements. The settlers would not only be granted lands in California but could count on 10 pesos a month for three years plus a daily allowance for rations. Complete outfits, including everything from saddles and shoes to hair ribbons, would be issued to them in advance. Pack and riding animals would be provided, and at the new pueblo each colonist would be started off with two cows, two oxen, two horses, three mares, one mule, two ewes, and two she-goats, in addition to the necessary tools and implements. Repayment for this advance was to be made out of future production. Rivera, although cautioned not to exaggerate the attractions of California, was authorized to go all the way to Guadalajara if the quota could not be filled in Sonora and Sinaloa.

Despite the generous subsidy offered, recruiting proved difficult. Rivera began his canvassing in February, 1780. Not till May 30 did he enlist the first poblador, or settler, and by August 1 he had only seven. Soldiers were easier to persuade, 45 having enlisted by the latter date. By the end of the year, the full quota of 59 soldiers had been reached, but only 14 settlers were enrolled, and they not of the best. With this number Rivera decided to stop.

Throughout these months of recruiting Rivera had been contracting for horses, mules, and cattle (some 960 head) and for other necessary supplies. Escorted by 17 soldiers, the pobladores—now only 12 because two had deserted—set out for Guaymas, to be ferried across to Loreto. On the peninsula, smallpox eliminated another poblador; thus only 11 families, totaling 44 persons, actually arrived. With the other 42 soldiers, some 30 of whom were accompanied by their families, Rivera set out for the Yuma crossing.

The Yuma Massacre

In the autumn of 1780 Croix ordered an advance to this crossing of the Colorado, a key point on the overland route to California. Gálvez' plan of 1768 had called for it; the Yumas had requested it in 1773; and Anza had prepared for it in 1776 by conducting Palma and a delegation of other chiefs all the way to Mexico City. But in 1780, when Croix finally acted, it was by an unorthodox and parsimonious method. He sent missionaries, soldiers, and soldiers' families but, instead of establishing missions or presidio or pueblo, he substituted two military towns with churches to which the Indians hopefully would come to be made Christians. It was a setup that did much less for the Indians and in which the customary missionary control of the Indians was lacking.

Without the preservation of a diary, the details of Rivera's march are not known. Apparently he reached the Colorado without undue difficulty. There he was met by Sergeant Juan José Robles and five or six soldiers of the Monterey company. For the desert crossing, the California-bound company would have guides.

Because many of the animals were jaded, Rivera decided to tarry among the Yumas with part of the stock and with the unmarried soldiers. Those who had their families with them he sent on. Although it was midsummer, they made their way over this more difficult part of the Anza trail and on to Mission San Gabriel.

Although the Yumas had urged Anza to stay with them, they were restive under the kind of colonization Croix provided. Neither the missionaries nor the soldiers achieved effective control, while the Spaniards and their stock interfered with Yuma food gathering. In such matters as grazing on mesquite beans, Rivera's presence brought further inroads. Conjecture suggests other provocations. The Spaniards, however, entertained no suspicions.

On July 17, in almost simultaneous attacks, the Yumas fell on Croix's two outposts on the west side of the river. The next day they surprised Rivera and his soldiers. Women and children were spared, but every man was killed— four missionaries, Rivera, and more than 30 soldiers.

Governor Neve sent a small force to investigate. It was driven off. Other expeditions from Sonora rescued or ransomed the captured women and children but did not reestablish the outposts or punish the Yumas. With sufficient escort it was still possible to travel the Anza trail, but in actuality this supply route to California was a casualty.

Founding the Pueblo of Los Angeles

On August 18 the band of Los Angeles settlers came in from Baja California. Because they had been exposed to smallpox, they were encamped in quarantine some distance from the others. On September 4, with the assigned guard of four soldiers, they were sent to the site selected, a short distance below where the river Nuestra Señora La Reina de Los Angeles de Porciúncula emerges from the pass separating the Santa Monica and San Gabriel Mountains and flows on to the Los Angeles Plain.

With the damsite and the projected course of the zanja (ditch) in mind, a plaza was laid out and each settler drew a solare (building lot) fronting it and four irrigable suertes (planting lots) in a tract between the plaza and the river. Additional solares and suertes were available for later arrivals. The pueblo as such would have propios (lands which it could use for revenue), ejidos (lands for various common and community uses), pasture lands both nearby and more distant, and montes (woodlands).

The combination of water readily available for irrigation, lands convenient for such development, and ample grazing lands had determined the choice of the site. On the day of the founding the designation of these various elements of the pueblo was of some importance, but the more pressing tasks were to make camp and prepare the evening meal.

Although modern writers have panoplied the founding with the pomp and ceremony befitting the start of the largest city in western America, the basis for their assertions is neither documented nor rational. The beginnings no doubt were as unpretentious as those at San Jose, and the first ceremony was held five years later, on September 4, 1786, when Sergeant José Dario Argüello came over from the neighboring presidio of Santa Barbara to confirm titles to solares and suertes, to record each poblador's brand, and to indicate propios, ejidos, and montes.

Much more effectively than the missions and the presidios, the pueblos were a step forward in the civilian settlement of California. Yet judging from the comments made about them, these pueblos were not an immediate or an unmixed blessing to the colony. The Los Angeles pobladores had been recruited from the most poverty-stricken classes in Sinaloa. Only two could claim to be Spaniards, the rest being of Indian, Negro, and mixed blood. None was literate. Presidial society looked down upon these rustic villagers, and the missionaries regarded them as likely to corrupt the neophytes. Two decades later one of the missionaries complained that the townsfolk were a set of idlers, addicted to cards, song, and seduction of the Indian women, and that all labor at the pueblos was performed by Indians. By 1800, however, Los Angeles was second only to the mission San Gabriel in agricultural production.

In the spring of 1782 Neve ordered the advance to the Santa Barbara Channel. Mission San Buenaventura was launched on March 31 and the presidio of Santa Barbara, three weeks later. Neve was ready to proceed with two more missions. Word came, however, that the viceroy and the College of San Fernando in Mexico had disagreed on whether the missionaries should have the customary control of the temporalities or should operate on Croix's Colorado pattern. News of this deadlock did not reach California in time to prevent the establishment of San Buenaventura and the presidio, but the other two missions were not added until four and five years later—Santa Barbara on December 4, 1786, and La Purísima Concepción on December 8, 1787.

Late in 1782, Teodoro de Croix having been promoted to viceroy of Peru, Neve was named commandant general of the frontier provinces. He left California the better by his Reglamento, two pueblos, a ninth mission, and a fourth presidio. The reinforcements he had urged had consolidated the Spanish hold, and the farming and stock raising which he promoted were on the verge of ending any further dependence on food shipments from Mexico.

For Further Reading

H. E. BOLTON, *Outpost of Empire* (1930), the Anza expeditions and the founding of San Francisco.

PEDRO FONT, *Complete Diary*, volume IV of Bolton's *Anza's California Expeditions* (1930).

BERNARD E. BOBB, *The Viceregency of Antonio María Bucareli y Ursúa* (1962).

H. I. PRIESTLEY, *A Historical . . . Description of California by Pedro Fages* (1937).

Historical Society of Southern California, *Annual Publication* (1931), the founding of Los Angeles.

CAUGHEY, *California Heritage*, 68–77.

chapter six

Local Annals

The Spaniards have, at a great expence and considerable industry,
removed every obstacle out of the way of an invading enemy; they have
stocked the country with such multitudes of cattle, horses, and other useful
animals, that they have no longer the power to remove or destroy them;
they have taught the Indians many of the useful arts, and accustomed
them to agriculture and civilization; and they have spread a number of
defenceless inhabitants over the country, whom they never could induce to act
as enemies to those who should treat them well, by securing to them the
enjoyments of liberty, property, and a free trade, which would almost
instantaneously quadruple the value of their actual possessions: in a word,
they have done everything that could be done to render California an object
worthy the attention of the great maritime powers: they have placed it
in a situation to want nothing but a good government to rise rapidly
to wealth and importance.

William Shaler,
Journal (1804)

A Holding Operation

1782
to
1821

Through the first dozen years of the Spanish period California faced
an endless succession of crises. Whether by sea, up the peninsula, or
over the Anza trail, the road to California was hard. Especially at the
outset the toll of lives was high. The Indians, though not aggressively
warlike, showed meager interest in conversion and on occasion rose
in rebellion. The land itself was refractory, resisting through these
dozen years the efforts of presidios, missions, and pueblos to make it
yield crops sufficient to sustain the few hundred agents of empire, the
soldiers, missionaries, settlers, and mission neophytes.

That the Spanish foothold was maintained in spite of
shipwreck, high death rate, Indian danger, and threat of starvation is

Indians in Reed Balsa, San Francisco Bay

Engraving in Georg Heinrich Langsdorff,
Bemerkungen auf einer Reise um die Welt, 1812

properly credited to the good work of Gálvez, Bucareli, and, though less consistently, Teodoro de Croix, and to the heroism of those in the field, such as Portolá, Serra, Anza, and Neve.

The remaining 40 years of the Spanish period have a quite different character. As livestock multiplied and the people at missions and pueblos learned how to make their plantings productive, the threat of food shortage disappeared. The royal treasury continued to pay wages, salaries, and stipends but seldom made a special outlay. No imperial officer exerted himself particularly on behalf of the province. When the Franciscans on the scene proposed a second chain of missions in the interior, authorization was not given, and the contour of Spanish California continued to be the coastal belt from San Diego to San Francisco. For imperial defense, as in the time of Gálvez and Bucareli, Spain wanted her flag flown over California yet now was content with a holding operation, seeing no profit in any active effort to build up the colony.

California thus was destined for a placid and unprogressive epoch, rustic, untroubled, and, as some see it in retrospect, idyllic and romantic.

Serra and Lasuén

At this stage the annals record the departure of many who had been conspicuous in the earlier work. Several, of course, were already gone. Portolá left in 1770. Gálvez' direct connection terminated at about the same time. Pérez, dean of the ship captains, died in 1775, Anza left in 1776, and Bucareli died three years later. Garcés and Rivera fell in the Yuma Massacre. Crespi, diarist of so much of the early exploration, died in 1782. Later in that year Neve was promoted to the commandancy of the Provincias Internas, in which he died in 1784.

On August 28, 1784, death had overtaken the first father-president of the California missions. Serra's closest companion, Francisco Palóu, had already applied for retirement because of his infirmities. Temporarily, Palóu assumed charge of the mission work, but in 1785 he left for the College of San Fernando, where two years later he issued the first California biography, *Relación histórica de la vida...del venerable Padre Fray Junípero Serra*.

Palóu's *Life of Serra* is from the pen of a confessedly enthusiastic admirer. Its imputations of miracles and its appropriation for Serra of credit partly due Portolá and others are defects, but out of Palóu's love and zeal emerges a portrayal which has beautified this brave and unselfish man in the hearts of Californians, if not in the official list of the church.

A native of Mallorca, Serra entered the Franciscan order at 16 and, after schooling, gained a reputation as an effective preacher. In 1749, at 36, he was sent to America. For 10 years he labored in the Sierra Gorda missions of what is now Tamaulipas and then was attached to the College of San Fernando in Mexico. In 1768 he was put in charge of the missions of Baja California. The last 15 years of his life were devoted to Alta California.

Such is Serra's fame that many have assumed he had full charge of Alta California, as Salvatierra had of the peninsula. In fact, his authority was over only the missionaries. In personal matters he was as humble, meek, and self-effacing as the founder of his order, the gentle St. Francis of Assisi. Yet when mission welfare was at stake, he was spirited and stubborn, quick to make vigorous protest to the viceroy and the court, where often though not always he, rather than the governor, was upheld. Although his combativeness is a principal basis for his recognition, many historians assert that he was a more tempestuous and pugnacious champion of the missions than was necessary.

Another basis for his fame was his willingness to exhaust himself in the service to which he was committed. He was most constant in his devotions; for instance, during his trip to Mexico, in spite of grave illness, he insisted on spending hours on his knees in the cold chapels. Like many of his contemporaries, he believed that pain and discomfort purified the spirit. Besides refusing comforts, he inflicted self-torture. While journeying from Veracruz to Mexico at the outset of his missionary career, he deliberately exposed himself to insects, with the result that he was lame forever after. On the expedition up the peninsula with Portolá, Serra's sore leg plagued him, at length so seriously as to threaten holding up the expedition. Serra steadfastly refused any treatment but finally relented to the extent of allowing one of the muleteers to apply a salve of herbs and tallow intended for use on the animals. His insistence on going about his regular tasks, notwithstanding illness and despite the solicitude of his brother missionaries, expressed the same attitude.

Junípero Serra

Statue in the Capitol, Washington, D.C.

Convento, Yglesia, y Rancherias de la Mision del Carmelo

Drawn by José Cardero of the Malaspina Expedition, Museo Naval, Madrid

Serra's most distinguished successor, Fray Fermín Francisco de Lasuén, is by comparison most obscure. Yet in solid achievement his presidency compares favorably. During his 18 years of control, from 1785 to 1803, the number of missions doubled and the number of Christian Indians approached 20,000.

Lasuén's mission founding began with the second and third that Neve and Serra had planned for the Chumash, Santa Barbara, which opened on December 4, 1796, and Purísima Concepción, which opened on December 8, 1787. In 1791 he added two others in the vicinity of Monterey—Santa Cruz on August 28 and Soledad on October 9. Then in 1797–98 came five others: San José de Guadalupe, June 11, 1797; San Juan Bautista, June 24, 1797; San Miguel Arcángel, July 25, 1797; San Fernando Rey de España, September 8, 1797; and San Luís Rey de Francia, June 13, 1798. Some of these came to be among the most noteworthy. Each was at a site favorable for agriculture and among Indians not yet touched by earlier missions.

Along with numerical growth Lasuén brought about an economic transformation. In Serra's time a rather slender beginning had been made in stock raising and farming. Under Lasuén these activities were furthered, and the introduction of a number of mission industries made the missions diversified establishments rather than mere agricultural centers. Lasuén brought in a score of artisans from Mexico and set them working at their trades and helping instruct the Indians in the work of carpenters, masons, smiths, and the like. The new style in mission architecture exemplifies the change; hitherto the buildings had been unpretentious, thatch-covered structures, now tile and stone came into general use along with timber and adobe. New missions were constructed, and Serra's nine were rebuilt, all in what is now known as the mission style.

Like his predecessor, Lasuén had difficulties with the governors. When it was proposed that new missions be established with only a single missionary, Lasuén, who had had five years of such experience at Borja in Baja California, was adamant that no such unsatisfactory stations should be opened. Nor would he agree that the missionaries should relinquish all temporal control over the neophytes, allow them to live in their own villages, and have them come to the missions merely for religious instruction. Lasuén was as firm in this stand as Serra had been, but he conducted his disputes amiably.

Although an older man, Lasuén was more robust and enjoyed the vigorous longevity for which Californians are noted. He traveled widely and frequently from his headquarters at San Carlos, most notably in 1797 when, at 76, he presided over the inauguration of four new missions and visited all the others in the province.

Fages' Second Term

Of the later Spanish governors, Fages was the most colorful. The central feature of his second administration was the continuation of the contest with the missionaries. In 1785 he entered a formal protest with the viceroy who, through the Audiencia of Mexico City, laid it before the College of San Fernando. The guardian of the college, none other than Francisco Palóu, responded with an elaborate defense of the actions of the friars and preferred countercharges against Fages. The case was then laid before the commandant-general of the Provincias Internas, Jacobo Ugarte y Loyola. The latter asked Lasuén for a detailed opinion on the issues involved, but, because the Provincias Internas had been returned to the direct supervision of the viceroy, Ugarte contented himself with ordering the agents of state and church in California each to observe the proper limits of his jurisdiction and to work in harmony. The temperaments of Lasuén and Fages made this accommodation possible.

Fages' second administration was enlivened by the presence of his spirited wife, Doña Eulalia de Callis. Only by enlisting the aid of Neve did Fages persuade Doña Eulalia to join him in California; but she finally came to Loreto, where her husband met her and escorted her to Monterey. The journey has been likened to a royal progress because of the enthusiastic receptions en route by friars, soldiers, settlers, and Indians for the first lady of California, a pageant which provided the frame for Walter Nordhoff's novel *The Journey of the Flame*. Traveling through the Californias, Doña Eulalia made presents from her own and her husband's wardrobe, especially to the naked Indians, until Don Pedro made clear that there would be no opportunity to purchase such things in Alta California.

After a short residence at Monterey, Doña Eulalia had had enough of California. She tried to persuade her husband to send her and their two children back to Mexico. When he refused she exerted pressures, first excluding him from her rooms and then denouncing him for infidelity, broadcasting threats that she would sue for divorce. After a sojourn at Mission San Carlos, during which the friars were scandalized by her tantrums, Doña Eulalia began divorce proceedings, which were heard before the acting commandant-general at Chihuahua and then transferred to the Bishop of Sonora. Before a decision was reached, Don Pedro effected a reconciliation. A month later, in October, 1785, he had the embarrassing task of trying to intercept a letter in which his wife had petitioned the audiencia to remove her husband from office because of ill health. In 1790 Doña Eulalia won her point by less direct action. She persuaded her husband to ask to be retired, and, when a favorable answer was received late in the year, she and the children sailed at once for San Blas.

Rancho Grants

In 1773 Bucareli authorized grants of land to persons living at a mission or presidio. One such grant was made to Manuel Butron of the Monterey garrison in 1775. It was for a small plot of 140 varas (Spanish yards) and, for lack of use, it reverted. Without land assignments some of the soldiers ran a few cattle.

In 1784 Juan José Domínguez, a retired soldier at San Diego, Corporal José María Verdugo of the military escort at Mission San Gabriel, and Manuel Pérez Nieto, another soldier at San Diego, applied for grants. Each had horses and cattle. Domínguez asked for a tract on the coastal plain south of the pueblo of Los Angeles; Verdugo, for a pie-shaped area rising from a point near the pueblo's *saca de agua* (the dam for drawing off water to be used at lower levels); and Nieto, for a tract on the San Gabriel southward from Mission San Gabriel.

Fages responded favorably, with the proviso that there be no encroachment on the pueblo or the mission. The grant to Nieto specified that he was "to sleep at the Pueblo," that is, to maintain his residence there rather than on the land granted. Presumably that was expected also of Domínguez, while Verdugo would continue at San Gabriel.

None of these grants contained even an estimate of its size, land being in superabundant supply. The Domínguez Rancho, later regranted as Rancho San Pedro and Rancho Palos Verdes, amounted to 74,000 acres in all. Verdugo's San Rafael was later measured at 36,000 acres. Nieto's grant had an extent of 33 square leagues, or more than 150,000 acres.

Domínguez immediately put 200 head of cattle on his grant but did not go to live there until 1800. He was under some criticism for neglecting his stock and letting his horses multiply to the point of being a nuisance. Verdugo stocked his rancho but did not retire to it until 1797. Nieto made the transition somewhat sooner, and by 1800 his headquarters was a small satellite of the pueblo of Los Angeles.

Inasmuch as these were the first grants of their kind in California, Fages' action was taken under review by the legal adviser of the commandant-general, Pablo Galindo y Navarro. Turning to the *Laws of the Indies,* Galindo found permission for grants of land, provided certain conditions were observed: They must not encroach on lands belonging to a pueblo, and their use must not result in any injury to mission, pueblo, or Indian village. The grantee must build a house and stock his rancho with at least 2,000 head of cattle. Grazing lands, though included in such a grant, must continue to be enjoyed in common rather than exclusively. The rights thus assigned were contingent on use rather than having the quality of title in fee simple.

Fages' action did not start a rush. In the rest of the Spanish period, some 30 grants were made, some small, others baronial in extent. Among the more significant were Luís Peralta's San Antonio (1820), covering most of present-day Berkeley, Oakland, and Alameda; José María Soberantes' Buena Vista (1795) near Monterey; the Ortegas' El Refugio (1795), west of Santa Barbara; the Picos' Simi (1795); and José Antonio Yorba's Santiago de Santa Ana (1810). Half the Spanish rancho grants were in the vicinity of the pueblo of Los Angeles. At the close of the Spanish period half the rancho grants had reverted because they were not put or kept in use. At that date also, the number of residents on all the ranchos did not equal the population of the pueblo of Los Angeles. Nevertheless, the device of land grants as encouragement for rancho development was a useful precedent.

Famous Visitors

In 1786 California was visited by the first non-Spanish ship since Drake's *Golden Hind* more than two centuries earlier. The following decades witnessed an increasing international interest in the North Pacific, one consequence of which was a whole series of English, American, Russian, and French contacts with California. Of these nations, France gained the least advantage in the North Pacific, but it was a Frenchman, Comte de Lapérouse, who first visited Spanish California. In the course of a round-the-world reconnaissance for his government, he stopped for 10 days (September 14–24, 1786) at Monterey, where he was entertained by Fages, Lasuén, and the provincials as lavishly as circumstances permitted.

The expedition went on to the Philippines, Kamchatka, and Australia and then disappeared. Fortunately for the historical record, the earlier records of the expedition, including the stay in California, had been sent home and were published in four volumes in Paris in 1797. The unknown fate of the gallant explorers enhanced interest in the Lapérouse account. Years later wreckage discovered on a reef of Vanikoro in the Santa Cruz Islands confirmed the disastrous end of this French voyage.

Lapérouse's observations on California, as printed in his posthumous *Voyage autour du monde,* were perspicacious and, for the most part, sympathetic. The Spaniards, he thought, would not develop the province rapidly; and indeed, except for furs, he did not detect any promising source of wealth. The persons whom Lapérouse met, Lasuén in particular, fare well in his book, but the mission system does not. His verdict was that the missions were making only slight progress toward converting the Indians into civilized, industrious, profit-minded persons.

Some five years later, almost to the day, a Spanish round-the-world scientific expedition put in at Monterey for a 12-day stay, September 13–25, 1791. Fages having retired and his successor not yet having arrived, a subordinate and Lasuén did the honors. This visit by Alejandro Malaspina and company has had small place in California's written history. Its auspices being Spanish, it lacked the cosmopolitan piquancy of the visit by Lapérouse. Nor did its ships sail out into mystery and tragedy. Completing his mission, Malaspina reported at court, was promoted, and began arranging and editing the findings of his voyage. But, on the objection that he was becoming too friendly with ladies of the court, he was soon banished. The result was a 90-year delay in the publication of any account of the voyage. The book issued in 1885, although a weighty tome, was fragmentary on the California interlude.

Recent research has located voluminous scattered records of the Malaspina visit. These visitors were lyrical about the beauty and the varied resources of Monterey. On the age-old question of the suitability of Monterey as a port for the Manila galleon, Malaspina was emphatically negative. He saw it fog-shrouded, rock-girt, and exposed. His ships needed cannon fire from the presidio to guide them in. They lost three anchors in the process and spent several days in laborious and fruitless dragging for them. Relying mostly on what he was told by Lasuén, Malaspina reported favorably on the missionary effort.

The scientists and naturalists of the expedition busied themselves making observations to determine latitude and longitude, gathering information on Indian culture, collecting descriptions and specimens of flora and fauna, fish and birds. Artists sketched or painted scenes and specimens. A complete inventory of all that was done does not exist, but clearly it was a more thorough cataloguing than Lapérouse and his men achieved. Donald Cutter's *Malaspina in California* (1960) for the first time gives due credit to this inspection and reproduces highly informative drawings, paintings, and maps.

In 1778–79 the famous British navigator, James Cook, sailed into the North Pacific, discovered the Hawaiian Islands, reconnoitered the northwest coast of America, and, for the furs that were plentiful on that coast, discovered a most rewarding market in China. A detailed report of this voyage was published in 1784 and circulated widely. Its information about the transactions in furs led to a flurry of commercial voyages under many flags. Spain, alert to protect her northwestern claims, sent a naval officer in 1789 to check on the British, Russian, and American activity in this northern extension of California.

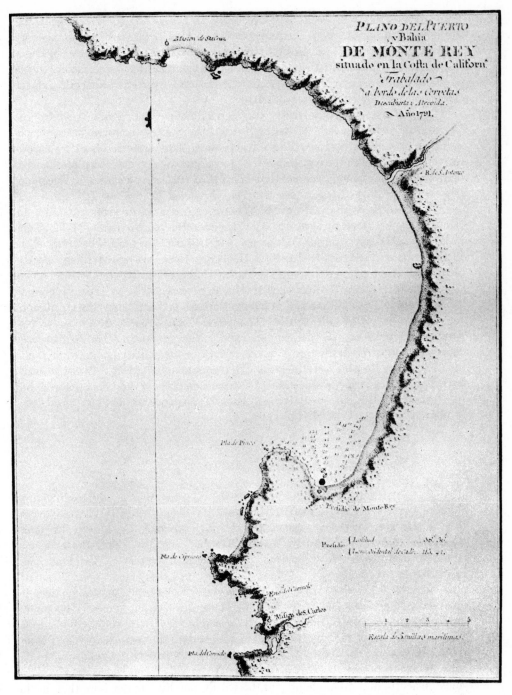

Plano del Puerto y Bahía de Monterey

Atlas para el viage de las goletas Sutil y Mexicana, 1802

This officer acted with what may have been an excess of zeal. While not interfering with American ships, he took possession of a British trading post, or fort, at Nootka on present Vancouver Island, seized two British vessels, and held one ship's captain prisoner. Britain demanded satisfaction for these insults to her flag and compensation for damages due her traders. Spain had to accede, and in 1790 the first Nootka treaty took shape.

To see that the treaty was carried into effect, Britain sent George Vancouver to the Pacific. At Nootka he and the Spanish commander could not agree upon an interpretation of the treaty, which they referred back to Europe for clarification. Vancouver proceeded to engage in entensive exploration and mapmaking, adequately represented in his three-volume narrative, *A Voyage of Discovery*, published in London in 1798.

In the course of his work Vancouver made three visits to California. He was the first foreign visitor to San Francisco Bay, in November, 1792. Then followed a 50-day sojourn at Monterey. After a trip to Hawaii, he returned to San Francisco on October 19, 1793. Governor José Joaquín Arrillaga, in the meantime, had ordered the regulations with regard to foreign visitors to be strictly enforced, and Vancouver got what he considered a very cool reception at San Francisco and Monterey. At Santa Barbara and San Diego the regulations were more hospitably disregarded. Vancouver's final visit to Monterey, in November, 1794, coincided with the arrival of a new governor. The British were welcomed into the festivities. Vancouver had much greater opportunity than did Lapérouse to observe California. His comments are prolix. Except toward Arrillaga he was generous in praise of the personalities he had encountered, but he agreed with Lapérouse's judgment that the province did not hold promise of rapid development under Spanish rule.

Borica and Branciforte

Apart from the Vancouver visits, the governorships of José Antonio Romeu (April 16, 1791, to April 9, 1792) and Arrillaga (April 9, 1792, to November, 1794) were relatively uneventful. Under Arrillaga an abortive attempt was made to occupy and fortify Bodega Bay, but, because of difficulty of access, the Spaniards contented themselves with erecting a battery at Fort Point, San Francisco.

In November, 1794, the government of California was taken over by an urbane, convivial, and witty Basque, Diego de Borica. Quickly becoming enamored of California, Borica liberally sprinkled his letters with tributes to its pleasant and healthful climate, the good provender that was available at Monterey, the good spirits that life in the province seemed to engender, and the "astounding fecundity" of Spaniards and natives. California, he asserted, "is the most peaceful and quiet country in the world; one lives better here than in the most cultured court of Europe."

Borica became governor when, for the first time, California seemed exposed to invasion. The controversy with Britain over Nootka flared again, and the increased activity of British fur hunters along the northwest coast compounded the exposure. In addition, a state of war existed between Spain and France. The California presidios had not been geared to meet anything more powerful than Indian attack. A first step was to bring up reinforcements and more respectable artillery. These were requested and, early in 1796, some 75 Catalan volunteers, commanded by Pedro de Alberni, arrived and were portioned out to the presidios. Repairs were made and additional guns were mounted.

Rumors of an imminent British attack followed the French scare, and Borica issued elaborate instructions on how the Californians should flee inland. In 1800 rumor of a forthcoming Russian attack occasioned the usual precautionary orders, but the provincials refused to be alarmed. "An invasion from Kamchatka," Bancroft observes, "seems to have had no terrors for the Californians after their success escaping from the fleets of Great Britain."

As governor, Borica took a personal interest in development of irrigation, encouragement of hemp and flax culture, a rather futile effort to stimulate sheep raising, and launching of the mission industries. Thanks to his active interest, schools were opened for the children of the soldiers and the settlers. Borica not only arranged for teachers and schoolrooms, as in the public granary at San José, but also planned the curriculum and required that reports and copybooks be sent to him frequently for inspection.

As early as 1794 engineer Miguel Costansó had advised that in addition to better presidios, California needed a second line of defense to which the presidials could fall back if an attack came. From such a base, by harassment, they then could make the invaders' position untenable. Viceroy Branciforte endorsed this proposal and authorized recruitment of settlers to found another town in the neighborhood of San Francisco.

On receipt of this word, Borica sent engineer Alberto de Córdoba and Alberni to select a proper site for the new town. Their reports stated emphatically that the Alameda was impossible because of a meager supply of water which, in addition, lay in a bed far below the land to be irrigated. San Francisco was worse. They saw no land suitable for cultivation within seven or eight leagues of the presidio. Wood was scarce, pasture lacking, and water in very poor supply. Besides, the locale (shades of Candlestick Park) was plagued by unruly winds.

The place to establish an agricultural town, Córdoba and Alberni agreed, was near Mission Santa Cruz, 30 leagues from San Francisco and from Monterey, 22 if by land and 12 if by sea. Borica adopted their recommendations and accepted their justifications. The site, he reported, was wonderfully favored with fertile soil, water for irrigation, abundant pasture, wood and timber, extraordinary opportunity for fishing, and a good landing. So that these settlers might start farming immediately, Borica proposed that the government construct their houses for them.

The settlers recruited for this town, Villa de Branciforte, fell far short of Borica's hopes. He had requested "poor but honorable colonists...of pure blood." Most of those who came were convicts. A few proved vicious and incorrigible; many of the others, though more unfortunate than hardened in crime, were feeble, diseased, or unskilled. On July 17, 1797, Gabriel Moraga supervised the launching of the villa with nine convict colonists and eight others. They were joined by four retired soldiers who brought some 200 head of horses and cattle. Another 19 convicts arrived at Monterey early in 1798. Although most were assigned elsewhere, six eventually came to Branciforte.

The start was inauspicious. A report in 1801 says that the colonists were poor workers. The Franciscans objected strenuously to the settlement as an encroachment and a disturbance to the mission. In part because of these protests, the government financing was cut back, and the town was not granted enough arable land. Borica proposed a radical remedy: let Mission Santa Cruz be closed and its Indians transferred to Missions San Juan Bautista and Santa Clara. That might have saved Branciforte, but it did not happen. Population reached a peak of 16 families and 101 persons in 1802 but declined to 31 persons in 1804. In 1815 there were 53, but the villa disintegrated and did not survive even in name.

Sea-Otter Hunting

By the 1790's an international competition in trade was developing in the North Pacific. The Russians, after a centuries-long advance eastward across Siberia, were as far as southern Alaska. British fur trappers had crossed Canada to the shores of the Pacific. British and American ships were beginning feverish activity in the China trade and were beginning to scour the Pacific for goods in demand in China. On the northwest coast the Americans prevailed in this rivalry and soon were in close collaboration with the Russians in extending this fur gathering southward into the most favored habitat of the sea otter, the California coast down as far as the twenty-eighth parallel.

The first American ship to enter a California port was the *Otter*, captained by Ebenezer Dorr, which put in at Monterey in 1796 for wood and water. The *Eliza* made a similar stop at San Francisco in 1799 and the *Betsey* at San Diego in 1800. Dorr took advantage of the hospitality to put ashore 10 men and a woman, fugitives from Botany Bay. Although these former convicts proved good workmen, Governor Borica, as the law required, forwarded them to New Spain.

These ships were representative of a larger number engaged in sea-otter hunting at the Santa Barbara Channel Islands and along the rockier parts of the California coast. Occasionally an otter might be clubbed on shore. Furs could also be had from the Indians. The standard technique was to go first to Russian America, take on board a number of Aleut hunters with their kayaks, and have them do the hunting with harpoon and line off the California coast. The otter hunters began to use some of California's unoccupied bays as places to career their ships, remove barnacles, and repair before going on to Alaska,

Sea Otter

Allan Brooks, from Grinnell, Dixon, and Linsdale, Fur-Bearing
Mammals of California, *University of California Press, 1937*

China, or New England. Avalon Bay at Catalina was much favored for these purposes. They also opened a small-scale trade with the Californians, bartering New England goods for beef, grain, and furs. Since Spanish law forbade such trade, California officials had to take a stand against it, but it was such a boon to the isolated province that many officials closed their eyes or even connived in the trade.

Occasionally a Yankee captain fell afoul of the California authorities. In 1803 the commandant at San Diego confiscated several hundred otter skins and part of the cargo of the *Alexander*. A few days later the *Lelia Byrd* (so named in the literature but probably a misreading of *Delia Byrd*), with William Shaler as captain, entered port. Its mate, Richard Cleveland, recorded an opinion that the commandant would have liked to sell his stock of a thousand otter skins but, having just penalized the captain of the *Alexander*, could not do so. Three men sent ashore at night to buy furs were arrested. Captain Shaler promptly sent another detachment ashore with drawn pistols to rescue these men. He then raised sail, unlimbered his six three-pounders on the starboard side, and sailed out within musket shot of the battery of eight nine-pounders at the entrance to the bay. For three quarters of an hour the engagement was brisk, but with no serious damage on either side.

Less fortunate was George Washington Eayrs of the *Mercury*. In 1812 he was near Point Concepción, taking on water and getting oak timbers for repairs, when an armed longboat from the *Flora*, one of the Peruvian ships that had come to California that year, demanded his surrender. When Eayrs complied, the *Flora* took the *Mercury* to Santa Barbara. There its cargo was confiscated, and for the next two years Eayrs was detained at Santa Barbara and San Diego. His protests, models of forceful rhetoric and irregular spelling, availed him little. It is significant that he was put out of business by a Peruvian competitor rather than by a California official, for most of the latter were sympathetic toward commerce with the fur ships.

In the period of the Wars of Independence after 1810, with the suspension of regular shipments from San Blas and prolonged failure to meet payrolls, trade with the Boston ships found a new excuse. It increased in volume and in openness and came to be highly convenient for the Californians.

Sea-otter pelts were the first California commodity to find its way to market outside the state. Most of these furs were taken by what the Spanish officials regarded as poaching and without any economic benefit to the province. The rest went out as contraband, in exchange for goods much wanted by the Californians and for which after 1810 there was no real substitute.

To calculate the volume of this trade is not much easier than to compile figures for the number of otter and seal pelts taken. Some estimates are available. In 1801, 18,000 otter furs are said to have been marketed in China. Within half a dozen years the annual average was nearer 15,000, and at the end of the decade it was about 10,000. Of course many of these furs came from the northwest coast. Otter hunting was pursued so relentlessly that after 1820 not enough of these remarkable animals were left to justify further hunting voyages. A few pelts were occasionally obtained in the next two or three decades, but that was all. Thereafter the sea otter became exceedingly scarce. In recent years, under protection, sea otters have staged a comeback and can be seen again, playing in the water, swimming incredible distances under water, and surfacing to recline at ease and dine on mussels or sea urchins.

The fur seal was present in much larger numbers. Furs of this animal bulked large in the cargoes carried to China. The islands of southern Chile yielded millions of these furs, and California was not far behind. Particularly at the Farallones the sealing was excellent. This business was also carried on without any thought of conservation, with the result that by about 1820 the fur seal was almost exterminated from southern waters. Thus an end came to the voyages of the Boston fur ships to California. Their epoch was brief, but it had given to the Californians their first taste of foreign commerce and to Americans their first contact with the inviting land of California.

The Coming of the Russians

In the winter of 1805–06 scurvy and starvation threatened the Russian trading post at Sitka. Nikolai Rezanov arranged temporary relief by purchasing the American ship *Juno* and its cargo. To develop a more permanent source of supplies he decided on a voyage to Spanish California. The Hawaiian Islands might have been a more logical choice had supplies been the only objective, but Rezanov was also interested in developing fur trade along the California coast.

Sailing from Sitka on March 8, 1806, he reached San Francisco on April 5. At first the Russians and Spaniards had great difficulty in communicating. The first conversations were between engineer Langsdorff and Father Uría in Latin. Later, a priest who could speak French came up from Santa Clara.

Rezanov soon discovered that Spanish law forbade any traffic with foreigners and that the California officials were not inclined to permit trade. A battle of wits ensued in which he tried to conceal the dire straits at Sitka, apparently on the assumption that the Californians would be more apt to permit a nonessential commerce than one which would be the salvation of Russian America and the guaranty of its permanence. Both Luís Argüello, the commander at San Francisco, and Governor Arrillaga came to realize, however, that the Russians were in a critical situation.

Rezanov did not prevail until he enlisted the aid of Concepción Argüello, the fair daughter of the San Francisco commander. Their romance is one of the most famous and most touching in all California history. She was the acknowledged belle of the province; he, as dashing and polished a gentleman as had ever visited California. "I imperceptibly," Rezanov says, "created in her an impatience to hear something serious from me on the subject." She quickly accepted his proposal; her father and the padres, though more obdurate because Rezanov was of the Greek Orthodox faith, finally gave in.

Because of his obvious ulterior motives, the genuineness of Rezanov's love has been questioned. His fiancée's influence upon her father and, through him, upon the governor won permission for the desired trade. From the missions Rezanov secured a full cargo of foodstuffs and on May 21 sailed to relieve Sitka. The trade permit, however, was for this one occasion only.

From Sitka, Rezanov returned to Kamchatka and started across Siberia to report to the czar and, presumably, to seek permission to marry his California love. But at Yakutsk he was stricken with what proved to be a fatal illness and consequently did not have the opportunity to prove that his intentions were honorable. Of Doña Concepción's sincerity there is not the slightest doubt. Year upon year she remained true to her lover, at first confidently anticipating his return, then taking refuge in the robes of a nun. Not until 35 years later, when Sir George Simpson visited California, did she learn of her lover's fate. Her faithfulness has been extolled in poem, novel, and story. To the Californians of her day the tragic sadness of her blighted romance was somewhat eclipsed by her kindliness, and it may be that she found consolation in the cherished memory of that spring when she was 16.

During the Wars of Independence

In the Spanish-American Wars of Independence, which raged from 1808 into the 1820's, California, as might have been expected, played the role of innocent bystander. The newest English colonies, Canada and the Floridas,

Maison des colonies de l'Amerique Russe

Duflot de Mofras, Exploration, 1844

had not joined the American Revolution. California, the youngest Spanish colony, was so effectively isolated from Mexico that Hidalgo's Grito de Dolores, which reverberated through most of Mexico, did not find an echo in this province.

Breakdown of supply service and lack of remittances from Mexico made Californians aware of the war. In Bucareli's day such a stoppage would have meant starvation; now it merely meant inconvenience. Missions and pueblos had large enough herds and crops to supply the entire population adequately. Even though the missions were induced to enter upon the unprofitable business of cashing presidial requisitions, the presidial soldiers were the worst off. Except to the soldiers, however, the deprivation was chiefly in luxury goods, and several expedients minimized this distress.

Two Peruvian ships, the *Flora* and the *Tagle*, arrived in 1813 with cloth and other goods which were bartered for tallow and hides. In the cargo of the *Mercury* was $16,000 in coin, which was confiscated for the royal treasury. The governor prudently retained this coin in the provincial treasury and sent a draft to Mexico.

Another trade possibility was with the new Russian establishment at Fort Ross, just north of Bodega Bay. In 1812 Ivan Kuskoff arrived there with 80 Russians and 50 Aleuts to set up a base for fur gathering. Governor Arrillaga was meticulous in refusing official approval to trade with these interlopers, but

Argüello admitted $14,000 worth of Russian goods at San Francisco in 1813, and trade continued. In 1815 when Pablo Vicente de Solá arrived as governor, he interrupted the trade with Fort Ross. He had Eliot de Castro and Boris Tarak-anof arrested and sent to Mexico on the very ship that had brought him north. It did not take him long, however, to see that California must have some sort of foreign trade, and in the following month he authorized barter for $7,000 worth of goods from a British vessel.

The main relief was provided by American ships. These Boston fur ships offered no facilities for the transmission of reports and orders to and from New Spain, and consequently a degree of autonomy was thrust upon Cali-fornians. Officials had to make decisions that once would have been referred to Mexico City.

In 1818 the war was brought home to the Californians by the appear-ance at Monterey of two Buenos Aires privateers operating in the revolutionary cause. An American ship had brought a few weeks' warning that these ships

Asistencia de Pala

David Packwood, Automobile Club of Southern California

*A recent picture; the pews, lights, and rafter
reinforcements are modern.*

were en route from Hawaii, and Solá took energetic though none too effective measures to stiffen the defenses.

On November 21 an improvised shore battery embarrassed the *Santa Rosa* and prevented a direct landing at Monterey. From the *Argentina,* however, Commander Hippolyte de Bouchard landed at Point Pinos, forcing Solá to retreat as far as present-day Salinas, carrying with him the provincial archives.

Bouchard's men, under the loosest sort of discipline, spent a busy week provisioning their ships and plundering the town. They ranged the streets and broke into dwellings as well as storehouses in search of money or other valuables. In their looting they did malicious damage, wantonly destroyed much that they found, laid waste gardens and orchards, and fired the town.

Their next stop was at Refugio, where they burned Ortega's ranch building. The Californians, under Sergeant Carlos Antonio Carrillo, lassoed three of Bouchard's men and carried them off to Santa Barbara. Possession of the prisoners saved that town, because Bouchard agreed to do no harm if the men were given up. Anticipating a descent upon their mission, the San Buenaventurans retreated inland, while the Angeleños for once rejoiced that their pueblo was 20 miles from the coast. San Juan Capistrano bore the brunt for southern California, partly because the commander defied the pirate–patriots. Bouchard's men came ashore, pillaged and burned, got drunk, and sailed away the next morning. San Diego polished its defenses and packed its women and children off to Pala, but Bouchard passed on by, and the War of Independence was over as far as California was concerned.

When news of Bouchard's attack reached Mexico, the viceroy was much alarmed. He immediately ordered two transports sent to California with reinforcements and, even after receiving Solá's report of the departure of the insurgents, he allowed the order to stand. In the late summer of 1819, 100 good cavalrymen arrived from Mazatlán under Captain Pablo de Portilla and an equal number of infantrymen from San Blas under Captain José Antonio de Navarrete. These infantrymen Solá described as vicious, quarrelsome vagabonds, without religion, drunkards, gamblers, thieves, leperos—in short, to sum it up in a vigorous California phrase, cholos. Solá complained very bitterly that they only added to his troubles. Yet each of the presidios had a larger garrison by approximately 50 men.

Two years later the Mexican revolutionaries finally won independence from Spain. The news would not reach California until early in 1822, but by this remote action the province had ceased to be a possession of the king of Spain.

The province at the time included some 20,000 Indians at the 20 missions strung out in a meandering line from San Diego to San Rafael. In the interior were several times that many uncontrolled Indians. The gente de razón are estimated at 3,300, of whom perhaps a fourth were men.

Some of these people lived on the 15 or 20 ranchos. A few lived at or near the missions. A larger number is accounted for at the four presidios. The population of San José is put at 240, and that of Los Angeles at 650, second only to Monterey with 700.

This all adds up to a Spanish occupation which, according to plan, was token but which had preserved Spanish title to the region and which had implanted Spanish institutions and ways that would continue and expand.

For Further Reading

H. H. BANCROFT, *History of California*, volumes I and II (1884, 1885).

GEORGE WHARTON JAMES, *In and Out of the Old Missions of California* (1916).

J. A. BERGER, *The Franciscan Missions of California* (1948).

W. W. ROBINSON, *Land in California* (1948).

GILBERT CHINARD, *Le voyage de Lapérouse sur les côtes de l'Alaska et de la Californie* (1937).

DONALD CUTTER, *Malaspina in California* (1960).

MARGUERITE E. WILBUR, *Vancouver in California* (1954).

FLORIAN GUEST, "The Establishment of the Villa de Branciforte," *CHSQ* (1962), pp. 29–50.

WILLIAM SHALER, *Journal of a Voyage*, ed. Lindley Bynum (1935).

T. C. RUSSELL, *The Rezanov Voyage to Nueva California* (1926).

HECTOR CHEVIGNY, *Lost Empire* (1937), Rezanov's visit.

A. C. MAHR, *The Visit of the* Rurik *to San Francisco in 1816* (1932).

ADELE OGDEN, *The California Sea Otter Trade* (1941).

CAUGHEY, *California Heritage*, 77–118.

chapter seven

A Mexican Province

Now all is gone. These Southern California Missions, built of adobe,
when once unroofed melt away in the rains as quickly as
Christianized Indians also disappear.

Walter Nordhoff,
Journey of the Flame

Introducing the Mexican Period

**1822
to
1846**

Early in 1822 California was notified of the success of the Mexican
revolutionists under Agustín Iturbide. Governor Solá convoked a
junta to advise him in this unexpected emergency. Its counsel, inevitably, was that California accept the accomplished fact, declare
itself a part of the Mexican empire, and pledge obedience to the
regency. Solá, the members of the junta, and the troops at Monterey
swore allegiance on April 11, 1822. Throughout the province an
oath of allegiance to the new government was required. It seems
to have been given with no more hesitation, even on the part of the
missionaries, than had been the case two years earlier when the
Californians had acknowledged Spain's liberal constitution of 1812.

Arcade, Mission San Antonio

UCLA Library

103

The junta defined the procedure for electing a deputy to the Mexican Cortes (congress). Electors were chosen in the four presidial districts and at the pueblo of Los Angeles, with the mission Indians seemingly having some voice in the matter. The five electors sat at Monterey with Solá and three army officers and chose Solá as delegate and Luís Argüello as alternate.

Before Solá set out for Mexico City, an American ship arrived from San Blas with a pattern of the new Mexican flag and news of Iturbide's accession as emperor and of an impending mission to California by an agent of the new government, Agustín Fernández de San Vicente, canon of the cathedral at Durango. Solá waited to welcome this distinguished commissioner. Upon Fernández' arrival at Monterey in September, 1822, the banner of Spain was lowered and the Mexican imperial flag unfurled. The Indians, it is said, exulted over the change from lion to eagle. No record indicates any requirement of new oaths of allegiance to Iturbide as Agustín I.

Commissioner Fernández got down to business quickly, calling on the missionaries for full reports and summoning the governor and his staff to a conference. At this meeting Fernández insisted that the governor's commissioners be recalled from the pueblos and that the ayuntamientos be placed in full control and that a *diputación*, or provincial legislature, be organized. Later in the fall, when he saw that Solá was about to surrender the governorship to a Spaniard, José de la Guerra, Fernández insisted that the choice be made by the diputación and the army officers. Exerting his utmost influence, he was able to gain a bare majority for Luís Argüello, who as an American-born Spaniard was thought more acceptable to the central government. Argüello took office as *jefe político* on the departure of Solá and Fernández at the close of the year.

The most controversial issue during Argüello's first year in office concerned the proposed removal of Mission San Francisco to a more salubrious and promising location in the Sonoma Valley. The success of San Rafael, founded in 1817, encouraged the idea of a transfer. Commissioner Fernández having approved, Argüello encouraged Fray José Altimira to petition the diputación to order the move. The diputación voted in favor, and Altimira reconnoitered the north bay shore, selected a site, and began construction of the new San Francisco. His Franciscan superior now objected; Altimira, with Argüello's support, responded heatedly, but eventually a compromise was effected whereby Altimira was allowed to found a new mission, San Francisco Solano, the final link in the chain, but not to abandon the old Mission San Francisco de Asís. The scant attention paid to the wishes of the father-president illustrates how much California had changed since the founding of the first missions.

In the spring of 1824, a major Indian revolt erupted at Missions Santa Inés, Santa Barbara, and Purísima Concepción. The Santa Inés disturbance was quickly suppressed, though the mission buildings were damaged by fire. At Santa Barbara a force from the presidio came to put down the uprising. The Indians fought back for several hours, wounding a number of the soldiers, and then decamped to the hills. Purísima was in Indian hands for almost a month. It was then attacked by an army of 100 men from the Monterey presidio; 16 of the Indians were killed, and the rest forced to surrender. There followed a number of expeditions in pursuit of the fugitives from Santa Barbara, and most of them were rounded up and brought back.

In November, 1823, California heard of Iturbide's abdication and banishment, which had taken place half a year earlier. Argüello immediately gave notice that California accepted the new national government and rejected all that pertained to the old imperial regime. The overthrow of Iturbide had repercussions at an Indian village near San Diego, where the natives followed the Mexican example, as they understood it, by killing their old chief and installing a new one, whom they warned to expect the same fate if he did not please them. By the California gente de razón the change to republic seems to have been accepted with placid indifference, and there is no record of an oath of allegiance to the new government.

In the following January a local government was drafted and put into operation, only to be discarded a year later when governmental instructions were received from Mexico. The final break with the old order came in the spring of 1825, when the Mexican constitution of 1824, with its provisions for a federal republic, was received and ratified at the presidios and pueblos. The conservatives, particularly the friars, were none too pleased at the change, but, since it had come by gradual transition through the regency, Iturbide's empire, the Congress, and finally the federal republic, the opportunity to resist was negligible.

These details illustrate the uncertainties with which California's Mexican period began. To the very end Mexico's grip on the province was insecure and her voice in its affairs was slight. Separation became something of an ambition and even more of a fact. Although American trade and immigration, foreshadowing acquisition by the United States, may appear as the most momentous development of the quarter century, other changes of genuine significance were also taking place.

Politics by Revolution

The Mexican period began with considerable uncertainty as to how California should function politically. Turbulent politics were characteristic throughout the Mexican period. In all parts of Spanish America the first years of national independence were troublesome times for which the colonial experience had been inadequate preparation. Spain had allowed such little self-government that her colonial subjects were rank novices in the political arts. What the Spanish Americans lacked in experience, however, they made up in the enthusiasm with which they seized upon the opportunity to enjoy public office. Aspiration to office agitated many an ambitious spirit, and, although there was much talk about such abstractions as democracy, class equality, and

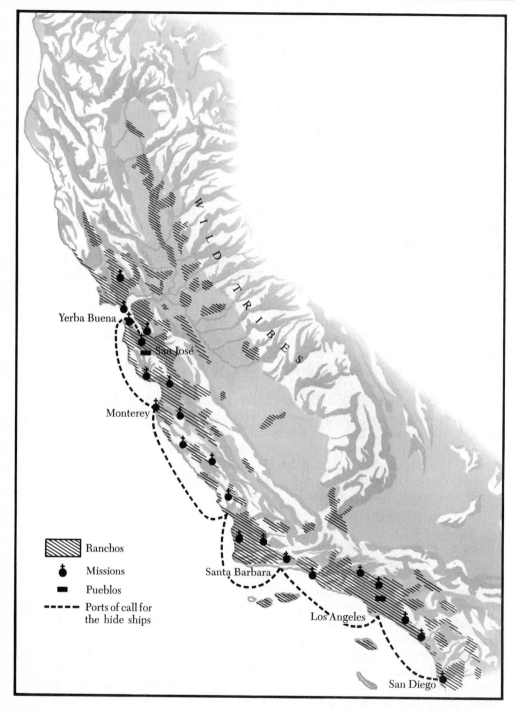

Yerba Buena

San José

Monterey

WILD TRIBES

Ranchos

Missions

Pueblos

Ports of call for
the hide ships

Santa Barbara

Los Angeles

San Diego

Mexican Province

constitutionality, the dominating factors were particularism, personalism, and militarism.

The situation in California was only slightly different in that her position outside the theater of combat during the struggle for independence gave militarism a more rudimentary development. But revolutionary unrest of two sorts was present. One concerned rivalries of individuals for political advantage and of southern California for part of the privileges hitherto monopolized by the north. The other was the emerging conviction that the empty gain of independence from Spain should be followed by some measure, at least, of independence from Mexico.

The Californians of this epoch have been ridiculed because their revolutions consisted of much more parading, military maneuvering, and bombastic proclaiming and fulminating than actual fighting and bloodshed. Yet more carnage would not have made this turmoil more commendable. It was, after all, a political method rather than an attempt to exterminate, and the comic-opera atmosphere had elements of appropriateness. The technique was admittedly more dangerous than the electoral method. Occasionally, a fire-eater overstepped the customary limits, as in the Battle of Cahuenga in 1831 when José María Avila accepted the probably unintentional challenge of Governor Victoria and his henchman Romualdo Pacheco to personal combat. Pacheco and Avila paid with their lives, and the wounded Victoria was sufficiently chastened to turn the province over to the Californians and retire to Mexico. Enlistment of more literal-minded Americans also complicated matters. Their inclination was to shoot to kill, but generally the procedure was political rather than martial.

Whether one starts with Solá, the holdover from the Spanish regime, Argüello, the provisional executive, or José María Echeandía, the first Mexican appointee, the Mexican governors are generally considered to have been of lesser caliber than their Spanish predecessors. Echeandía, for example, arbitrarily moved the capital to San Diego so that his fragile health would not be endangered by the fogs of Monterey. He mismanaged the mission problem, and his measures against the revolt engineered by Commissioner Herrera and ex-convict Joaquín Solís were half-hearted, though ultimately effective.

In 1831 Echeandía led a southern revolt against his successor, Manuel Victoria, and, though this revolt succeeded because of the exciting victory at Cahuenga, little credit redounds to Echeandía. Against him, a new rebellion was raised in the name of Agustín Zamorano, better known as California's first printer, and the end result was a temporary division of California, with Echeandía ruling from San Diego to San Gabriel and Zamorano from Santa Barbara north.

For two and a half years beginning in January, 1833, California was blessed with a governor far above the Mexican average. This man was José Figueroa, a swarthy Aztecan mestizo, a veteran of the Sonora frontier, and a competent executive. After granting amnesty to all concerned in the Zamorano revolt, Figueroa took up the problem of California's northern defenses. Mariano

Guadalupe Vallejo was sent to the north bay region to locate sites for settlements to serve as buffers against the Russians of Fort Ross and the British on the Columbia. After visiting Fort Ross, Vallejo reported that it was a fur-gathering base rather than a fortification, had a personnel of 300, of whom 70 were Russians, was engaged in the fur business, and was having moderate success in farming and stock raising. Vallejo chose sites for countercolonization but warned that the Indians had been antagonized by the attempts to compel them to come and live at the missions. With a handful of colonists Vallejo established settlements at Petaluma and Santa Rosa.

Figueroa's attention was soon engrossed in the assigned task of secularizing the missions and in dealing with an ambitious colonization project.

Secularization

Secularization meant converting the missions into parish churches, releasing the neophytes from complete supervision by the friars, and releasing much of the mission lands for other use. Secularization had long been contemplated. Spain's original plan had been to secularize after 10 years of mission operation, but, because the instruction of the natives and the build-up of a body of settlers to assist in the second stage of civilizing and assimilating the natives went slower than expected, the mission period was prolonged.

When a secularization law passed by the liberal Spanish Cortes in 1813 was promulgated in Mexico eight years later, the guardian of the College of San Fernando expressed complete willingness to relieve the Franciscans immediately of their responsibilities in California, though with no expectation that the step would be taken.

Independent Mexico promptly approved secularization, in theory, and a gradual process began in California. No one claimed the Indians were adequately prepared to be on their own. But pressure was brought to bear because of a desire on the part of certain individuals for the mission lands, admittedly the best in the province. As white population increased and the number of neophytes declined, the argument that the friars should not be left in control of such large tracts strengthened. Nor was the mission system, with its land monopoly and its virtual enslavement of the Indians, in tune with Mexican republicanism.

The first actual steps were taken by Echeandía. He had come to California a reputed anticleric. Then he had become embroiled in a dispute with the friars over the question of an oath of allegiance. This controversy inclined Echeandía even more toward secularization. On July 25, 1826, he issued the first California decree on the subject, authorizing married Indians of long standing in Christianity to leave the missions. Only a very few took advantage of the offer, and they gave quick proof of incompetence to manage their own affairs. An English visitor reports that many of these former neophytes, "having gambled away their clothing, implements, and even their land, were compelled to beg or to plunder in order to support life" and that they became so obnoxious that the friars were asked to take them back.

In the summer of 1829 Echeandía published a Mexican law calling for the expulsion of all Spaniards, but he made no attempt to enforce it. Several friars seized the excuse to demand passports, which of course were not granted. A year later Echeandía formulated a more drastic secularization measure, which he sent to Mexico for approval. No answer was forthcoming, but on January 6, 1831, he nevertheless promulgated it, a step which Bancroft characterizes as "wholly illegal, uncalled for, and unwise." About all this law accomplished was the stimulation of Indian hopes of luxurious freedom and the reduction of their obedience to the Franciscans.

When Figueroa arrived, the intention was to continue the missions. Indeed, he brought 10 Franciscans of the College of Zacatecas to reinforce the Fernandinos. Figueroa outlined a method whereby capable Indians might be released from the missions, but again only a negligible number took advantage of the opportunity. Having observed conditions in California, Figueroa wrote to Mexico advising against any acceleration of secularization and citing the opinions of Friars Durán and García Diego. By the time his protest arrived, plans were far advanced for a colonization project accompanied by secularization. Shortly thereafter the Mexican Congress ordered immediate secularization.

Figueroa had no choice. On August 9, 1834, he ordered 10 missions secularized. Half the property was to be distributed to the Indians, but they were not empowered to dispose of it and were still required to work on essential community enterprises. Secular administrators were to take charge of the rest of the property, and cattle were to be killed only as necessary. Since curates were not available, the friars were to continue their religious functions. The process was extended to six other missions in 1835 and to the remaining five in 1836.

Unfortunately, Figueroa died before the work was well begun, and at the same time revolutionary disorder removed another possible restraint upon the administrators. Only a few of these men were both conscientious and capable, and none was as sympathetic as Figueroa. The mission property slithered rapidly through their fingers into private hands. Notwithstanding the law, the Indians were still more prompt in disposing of their individual shares. Having lost their property, a few returned to the secularized missions, and another few found employment on the ranchos or in the pueblos, but the majority relapsed to barbarism among the inland peoples or sank to a degradation still worse.

As for the missions, the final blow came in 1844 when Governor Manuel Micheltorena found in the threatened war with the United States an excuse to order the disposal of the remaining mission properties. Only two years elapsed before control of the province passed to the United States, but in that period the Franciscans lost all the missions except Santa Barbara. The church buildings and a small amount of land were subsequently recovered through the American courts, but operation as missions was a thing of the past. The death of Narciso Durán on June 1, 1846, was another indication of the end of the missions. In his 40 years of service in California, Durán had proved himself "perhaps the ablest of the Franciscan prelates," yet it was a service of staving off decline rather than of striding progress such as that under Serra and Lasuén.

The Padrés-Híjar Colonists

About the time Figueroa began his governorship, events in Mexico took a peculiar turn. The elected president, Antonio López de Santa Anna, chose to retire to his estate and turn the governing over to Vice President Valentín Gómez Farías. In concert with a reform-minded Congress, Gómez Farías evolved a broad plan designed to bolster California against the Russians, break the mission land monopoly, open for the Indians an opportunity to be integrated into the provincial populace, and, at the same time, stimulate colonization from Mexico and by foreigners. After careful consideration of a bill elaborating such a program, the Congress enacted a much less detailed measure authorizing the executive branch to act, with key expenses to be drawn from the Pious Fund.

Gómez Farías selected José María Padrés, a soldier of some experience in California, and José María Híjar to head the operation, Padrés as military commandant in Alta California and Híjar as governor of Alta California and director of colonization in both Californias. Some 300 colonists were recruited in Mexico City with promise that they would be outfitted, conducted to California, and provided with land and all that was necessary to set them up as colonists. The colonists left the capital in April, 1834, and on August 1 sailed from San Blas on the *Natalia* and the *Morelos*. They went, however, under a cloud. Santa Anna had come out of retirement, issued an antireformist pronunciamento, placed the vice president under arrest, and barred the members of Congress from their meeting place. By special courier over the Anza trail, he sent word to Figueroa that Híjar's appointment as governor was revoked.

In normal circumstances Californians would have welcomed this largest of all contingents of colonizers, among whom were a score of qualified teachers and many skilled artisans. But old California hands saw them as rivals for the mission stock and the Indian labor and as encroachers on the mission lands about to be distributed. Figueroa, though concerned about the Indians and the productivity of the mission properties, resented the threat to his authority and was morbidly suspicious of the whole Padrés-Híjar project. He sent Padrés and half the colonists to a site near Santa Rosa but left the *Morelos* passengers stranded in southern California. He quarreled peevishly with Híjar over the colonization program and, when excuse offered, arrested the leaders and several others on charges of conspiracy to revolt and shipped them off to Mexico. Figueroa then spent several weeks writing a polemic attacking Padrés and Híjar and, their, as he charged, nefarious scheme. He had this printed under the title *Manifesto*.

Except for Bancroft, California historians have been uniformly critical of the Padrés-Híjar colonization project seeing it as a grab for mission land, Indian labor, and power and criticizing the colonists as too effete, possessed of the wrong skills, and unsuited for the rough frontier. In 1969, in *Frontier Settlement in Mexican California*, C. Alan Hutchinson goes to the other extreme, saying that the colonists were of precisely the sort that California officials had been asking for and would continue to request and that the plan had merit in the transition it offered for the mission lands and the Indians released from mission protection. Hutchinson sees Híjar as deserving of a more cordial reception than Figueroa gave him and Figueroa's *Manifesto* as a piece of special pleading unworthy of "the most capable governor" of the Mexican period. The reformist plan failed, but Mexican California was considerably strengthened by the additional colonists.

Further Political Turmoil

Political annals for the province after the death of Figueroa are a compound of vacillation between home rule and government from Mexico and of neighborly quarreling among the Californians, mingled with general resentment against the governors from Mexico. Figueroa's ad interim successor, José de Castro, was followed shortly by Nicolás Gutiérrez, who proclaimed a Mexican decree elevating Los Angeles to the rank of city and designating it the official capital of California. This legislation, however, was contingent on the finding of free quarters for the seat of government. Although Los Angeles had two or three appropriate buildings, their owners did not volunteer to make them available, and no group of citizens rallied to force them to do so. The capital, therefore, remained at Monterey.

Gutiérrez, in turn, was replaced by Mariano Chico, a Mexican appointee who was thus rewarded for his support of the reactionary movement calling itself Centralism. Chico held the office only three months but in that time came to be the most unpopular governor of the Mexican period and perhaps longer. His official actions and pronouncements as recorded do not justify such a rating, but the record is clear that the Californians turned against him, forcing his abdication and departure.

When Chico landed at Santa Barbara en route to Monterey to begin his governorship, the principal news reported to him was from Los Angeles and concerned the work of California's first vigilance committee. A vaquero, Gervasio Alipas, had alienated the affections of the wife of a well-liked citizen, Domingo Felix. Felix asked the alcalde to bring about a reconciliation, which was done. It seemed successful, but as the Felixes rode home to their rancho, Alipas intercepted them, stabbed the husband, and then he and Doña María with a reata dragged the body to a ravine and hastily covered it with earth and leaves. The body was soon discovered and the two brazen suspects were arrested.

Popular indignation led some 50 citizens to take action. As they alleged, several other killings had gone unpunished and the law itself authorized no civil court in the province to assign the death penalty. Organizing as a *junta defensora de la seguridad pública*, these citizens called on the ayuntamiento to surrender the prisoners, sent to San Fernando asking the padre to come and minister "to a dying Indian," seized the prisoners, and with due formality shot them. The regular authorities had protested every step by this vigilance committee, but now accepted the proposal that the committee assist for a few more days in the maintaining of order.

Chico vigorously rebuked these vigilantes, only to find that it was difficult, if not impossible, to prevail against the nearly unanimous community sanction. Chico also quarreled with Durán, the father-president of the Franciscans, and ordered one prominent citizen, Abel Stearns, into exile. The more direct causes of his downfall were the confirmation of a suspicion that the young woman he introduced as his niece was, in reality, his mistress and the introduction at a gala occasion in Monterey of this young woman and a friend under prosecution for adultery. Fifty years later historian Bancroft found that the old Californians to a man denounced Chico as a reprobate.

Against the provisional government of Gutiérrez, whom Chico left in charge, a revolt was raised by a dashing young Californian, Juan Bautista Alvarado. A native of Monterey, a protégé of Solá, a product of California's schooling, and a friend or relative of every prominent paisano of northern California, Alvarado had no dearth of followers. He also enlisted the help of Isaac Graham and his American rifleman. Gutiérrez' surrender was easily secured. Southern California's recognition of the new government proved a more difficult prize, but through show of force, skillful maneuvering, and judicious compromise Alvarado at last got the nominal support of the southern Californians.

At the outset of his administration Alvarado had the diputación declare California "a free and sovereign state," so to remain until Mexico returned to the liberal federal constitution of 1824. The capital was also restored to Monterey, though, in deference to the feelings of southern Californians, the south was organized as a canton under a local jefe político, virtually a subgovernor. As governor, Alvarado also promised, if not open toleration, at least noninterference with private religious practices. In the maneuvering for general support of his government, these plans were greatly modified. The assertion of independence became merely a claim for self-government, and the absolute orthodoxy of the province was reaffirmed.

By 1842 Alvarado had tired of politics. His earlier troubles with the southern Californians had been followed by a difference of opinion with his uncle, Mariano Guadalupe Vallejo, the military commandant. Consequently Alvarado welcomed the arrival of a Mexican appointee, Manuel Micheltorena, who was to take over the reins of government, both political and military. Micheltorena's stay was brief. The 300 cholos who had come with him were an insufferable nuisance. Although Sutter and some other foreigners rallied to his support, a revolution engineered by Alvarado and Castro culminated in another famous battle at Cahuenga Pass, on February 20 and 21, 1845, in which a horse was killed on one side and a mule wounded on the other. The battle proved decisive. Micheltorena agreed to take his cholos out of the province, and

Diseño accompanying the application for the grant of
Rancho San Miguelito de Trinidad, near Monterey

political and military government passed to the Californians Pío Pico and José Castro. Thereafter, Mexico's hold on California was most nebulous.

Pastoral California

In the economic and social realm this period of political turmoil witnessed not only the decline of the missions but also the rise of the ranchos. In the earliest years Spain, although preferring that settlers reside in the pueblos or near the presidios, made generous grants to prospective rancheros. Two features of these land grants contrast sharply with the system of American California: they conveyed a right conditional on use rather than an absolute title and they involved very extensive acreage. Both features, however, were in accord with Spanish custom, and the second represented a far better understanding of a cattleman's needs in a semiarid land than the United States government has yet achieved. A homestead comprising a quarter section or even a full section makes a ridiculous ranch holding.

Although a few earlier grants had enduring importance, the great majority of Spanish grants date from the Mexican period. A score or so were made in the first decade of independence, but applicants were few. A boom came with secularization of the missions, which opened some of the best land for private use and provided cattle for stocking new ranchos. The hide trade, then in full swing, stimulated cattle raising, and the gradual increase in population meant additional manpower.

By 1845 still another incentive appeared. As Mexican control of California came increasingly into jeopardy, the governors were authorized to use land grants as compensation for services rendered or bills owed and to sell lands to raise money for defense of the province. Such purchases were only a small fraction of the total. To the end of the Mexican period, land was super-abundant and private holdings came by application to pueblo authorities for town lots and fields or to the governor for rancho lands. In all, more than 800 grants were made, adding up to approximately 10 million acres. They were spread along the coastal belt from San Diego to Sonoma, with the exception of the Big Sur, and included a much lighter sprinkling in the Delta and Sacramento Valley.

With the rise of the ranchos, pastoral California reached its romantic zenith. Cattle roamed over a thousand hills. Horses became so numerous that they were hunted down to save pasturage for the cattle. Hides and tallow were bartered to Yankee and British traders for all the attractive gewgaws of a more sophisticated civilization. And the outlanders—English and Yankee traders, Russian fur hunters, Hawaiian hide droghers, Rocky Mountain trappers, and American settlers—though they presaged the end of Mexican control, lent a cosmopolitan touch. Even those two inescapables, death and taxes, seemed to have been stayed, the latter being indirect and therefore unnoticed, while the former at least was long postponed.

The Grizzly and His Captors

From an illustrated lettersheet of the fifties

Early California Fiesta

A. F. Harmer, Los Angeles County Museum of Natural History

The bizarre amusements are an index to the spirit of the times. Grizzly-bear hunting with lasso and mustang was a royal sport, demanded, prosaically enough, by the necessity of protecting the cattle herds against these marauders. Similarly, wild-horse hunting was both a diversion and a necessary task, especially in seasons of drought when the grass had to be preserved for the cattle and sheep. Likewise, the rodeo, in addition to being a gala occasion when the men of an entire district convened, was essential to the adjustment of individual ownership of livestock and the unfenced and communal range. Bull and bear fights, with the odds approximately even, had no utilitarian value but were natural in view of the frequency with which the vaqueros had to measure the mettle of these ferocious beasts.

Vaqueros escaped much of the drudgery faced by the cowboys of the American West. They had no fences to ride. Cattle were raised chiefly for their hides and tallow, and consequently there was less concern about their condition. Because California cattle were turned loose and received practically no attention except at branding and butchering time, the vaqueros were spared most of the doctoring and the veterinary work of the cowboy's routine. Even the butchering (matanzas) was done from horseback, by means of dexterous thrusts of the knife. Removal of the hides and rendering of the tallow remained about the only unadulterated toil.

The ranchero's resplendent attire gives a clue to the desultory nature of his labor—gold or silver embroidered deerskin shoes; velvet or satin breeches, slashed at the knee, gold-braided and silver-buttoned; velvet or silk vest, with wide sash of red satin; dark cloth jacket embroidered in gold and silver; wide, flat-topped sombrero, with cord of silver or gold. The ordinary vaquero was less gaudily outfitted, but this was his pattern. The women not only dressed in more sedate fashion but are credited with being more industrious. Since large families were the rule, cooking and housework were substantial tasks. In addition, these matrons indulged in a prodigious amount of lace making and embroidery. Many women rode and hunted, but picnics and dances were the favorite diversions. Dances celebrated every event—weddings, births, political changes, and religious festivals. The elders were privileged to open the festivities; later on the younger people had their turn at the contradanza, jarrabe, and fandango.

These romantic Californians are also renowned for their openhandedness, especially in the matter of meals, lodgings, and provision of riding animals. These three were available without stint to any wayfarer. The mission fathers, as Alfred Robinson relates, might permit a contribution to the saints; rancheros were above accepting pay for their hospitality, and some of them even placed a supply of money in their guest rooms into which visitors might dip as they needed.

Spanish and Mexican Heritage

Although it may appear to the casual observer that the brusk Americans wiped the slate clean and supplanted the older manner of life with a civilization in which Spanish, Mexican, and California elements found no place, this judgment is superficial. Land titles are merely one factor resting on an older base. Place names by the hundreds have survived; highways such as El Camino Real follow the old trails; the modern vocabulary is enriched by scores of words carried over from the Spanish; numerous celebrations, fiestas, rodeos, and the like hark back to the days of romance. Certain modern trends in architecture and furniture, especially in southern California, modify and embellish but also perpetuate features of the Mexican period. Descendants of the old families have been outnumbered by sons of the gold rush, and they in turn by the more recent avalanche of midwesterners, yet these scions of the Arcadian age have attained a position of respect far out of proportion to their small number.

Not the least important part of this heritage has been in history, folklore, and appeal to the imagination. The historical record is rich in nondocumentary materials, of which the chain of missions is the best known but by no means the sole example. Besides the still unpublished treasures with which the archives of Spain, Mexico, and California abound, there is a vast literature of which the Cabrillo and Vizcaíno diaries, the Costansó and Font journals, the Venegas and Palóu histories, and the descriptions by Dana, Robinson, and Colton are merely the outstanding examples. Authoritative historical studies have followed, and a legion of more popular interpreters, including Bret Harte, Lummis, Atherton, Jackson, James, Austin, and White, have found themes and settings for medleys of fact and fiction in the glamorous pre-American period. These writers, along with the Mission Play and the Serra legend, are carried away by the charm of the days of the dons.

Nevertheless, the significance of the Mexican period often goes unnoticed. Certain writers dismiss it as nothing more than an interregnum between the Spanish and American regimes. The old Californians are partly responsible, for out of their dislike for the Mexican governors and their cholo troops came a tendency to shun the very word "Mexican." Yet without the transition provided by the Mexican period, the change from Spanish colony to American state would have been uncomfortably abrupt. It was most fortunate that the work of secularization, the introduction of such concepts as republicanism, constitutionalism, and representation, and the initial contacts with non-Spaniards could take place while California was a Mexican province.

For Further Reading

H. H. BANCROFT, *California Pastoral* (1888).

NELLIE V. SANCHEZ, *Spanish Arcadia* (1929).

C. ALAN HUTCHINSON, *Frontier Settlement in Mexican California* (1969).

GEORGE TAYS, "Mariano Guadalupe Vallejo and Sonoma," *CHSQ* (1937–38), in six installments.

W. J. HANSEN, *The Search for Authority in California* (1960).

G. J. GEARY, *The Secularization of the California Missions* (1934).

MANUEL P. SERVIN, "The Secularization of the California Missions; a Reappraisal," *SHQ* (1965), 133–50.

SUSANNA DAKIN, *The Lives of William Hartnell* (1949).

MARGUERITE EYER WILBUR, *Duflot de Mofras' Travels on the Pacific Coast* (1937).

R. G. CLELAND, *The Cattle on a Thousand Hills* (1951).

CAUGHEY, *California Heritage*, 131–40, 149–55.

chapter eight

Hide Traders
and Mountain Men

Our cargo was an assorted one; that is, it consisted of everything under the
sun. We had spirits of all kinds (sold by the cask), teas, coffee, sugar,
spices, raisins, molasses, hardware, crockery-ware, tin-ware, cutlery, clothing
of all kinds, boots and shoes from Lynn, calicoes and cottons from Lowell,
crapes, silks; also, shawls, scarfs, necklaces, jewelry, and combs for the
ladies; furnityre; and in fact, everything that can be imagined, from
Chinese fire-works to English cart-wheels—of which we had a dozen pairs
with their iron rims on.

Richard Henry Dana,
Two Years Before the Mast

Traders for Hides and Tallow

1822
to
1846

About the time Boston fur ships stopped coming to California, whalers
pushed their search into the North Pacific. Since the voyages from
New England ordinarily were three-year ventures, these whalers
needed ports where they could refit and reprovision before starting
the long voyage home. Hawaii was the favorite resort, with as many
as 400 whaling vessels visiting these islands in a single year. California was next in popularity, with Monterey or, more often, San
Francisco Bay as the port of call. Upon payment of a nominal duty
to the Mexican officials, whalers were allowed to barter for supplies
and to take on wood and water. Evasion of duty payment was not
uncommon, but this was no great loss to the provincial treasury
because the whalers were stocked for only a small trade.

Hide Houses at San Diego

William Meyers, 1843, The Bancroft Library

Later in the century California would have a small whaling industry of its own, operated from shore stations with whaleboats rowed out to intercept California grays in their seasonal migration and with the trying out done on shore. In that later time San Francisco also became a major base for whaling in Alaskan waters. The whalers of the Mexican period took some whales in sight of shore or right in Monterey Bay. Their provisioning stops in California were incidental to their main purpose of filling their holds with oil and bone.

Another set of ships, those sent to load cowhides, was far more important to California. These ships came expressly to California, brought goods to exchange for a full cargo, and constituted Mexican California's chief contact with the outside world.

Cattle raising had flourished mightily in the half century since Rivera and Anza introduced the first herds. These herds were typical Mexican range cattle, wide-horned, long-legged, small-bodied, wild, and well able to forage and fend for themselves. The tough beef they afforded was the staple food in the province. It was often given the credit for the longevity of the provincials and nowadays would at least be cited as the explanation for their excellent teeth. At the end of the Spanish period Californians could not begin to consume all the beef produced; they used only the choicest cuts. At the missions and at a few ranchos a small amount of leather was tanned and a larger quantity of hides was worked up into rawhide, which had many local uses. Tallow was also tried out from the carcasses for candle and soap making, but here as with the hides supply far exceeded demand.

Small quantities of tallow had gone to San Blas before 1810. The Lima ships, beginning with the *Flora* and the *Tagle* in 1813, had taken larger amounts, as well as soap and a few hides, but the real start of the hide and tallow trade came with the opening of the Mexican period. First to arrive were two representatives of the English house of John Begg and Company. These men, Hugh McCulloch and William E. P. Hartnell, operated subsequently as a California partnership which, in Spanish transliteration as "Macala and Arnel," is often mentioned in the early annals. Bringing a small stock of goods from Lima, they opened negotiations for a long-term monopoly of California trade. Father Payeras, prefect of the missions which would supply the bulk of provincial products, proved a canny bargainer. He warned in advance that "the day was long past when hides and tallow could be had for nothing." By the contract as finally drafted, the English firm agreed for three years to take all hides offered at $1 each and at least 25,000 arrobas of tallow at $2 an arroba (25 pounds). Prices of suet, lard, and soap were set at $3, $4, and $16 a hundred, pickled beef at $4, and wheat at $3 a fanega (1.6 bushels). Horns, wine, furs, and other products were listed, but without a fixed price. The English thus had an early advantage in the conduct of California trade. Hartnell remained as resident agent and became a California patriarch.

Within a month after the coming of McCulloch and Hartnell, the first American hide trader appeared. This was William A. Gale, a veteran

dealer in seal and otter furs, who had persuaded a number of Boston merchants
to join him in sending the *Sachem* to California with a cargo of goods. Gale
came on the vessel as supercargo. The McCulloch-Hartnell contract made it
impossible to get a full cargo of hides, yet some of the missions evaded the
contract and thus the voyage was moderately successful. The *Sachem* returned,
other vessels were sent out, and Gale was soon, to all intents and purposes,
resident agent for the Boston firm of Bryant and Sturgis. At the expiration of the
Hartnell contract the English advantage disappeared, and thereafter somewhat
more than half of the trade was carried on by New Englanders.

From the early twenties until the gold rush the trading methods were
the same, the most important exception being that, when the missions were secularized, most though not all of the business was transferred to the ranchos. The
trade has been often and brilliantly described. The ships came stocked with
every conceivable commodity that the Californians might want, from tooth-
brushes to millstones. They were, as Dana described them, floating department
stores. Mexican law regularized the trade. Upon payment of port duties at
Monterey, ranging usually from 5,000 to 15,000 pesos depending on the amount
of cargo, a ship was authorized to trade anywhere in California until its cargo
of hides and tallow was completed. Some captains carried on their trade entirely
within the law. Others resorted to bribery of port officials and still others to
transferring of goods from a non-duty-paying vessel or to caching part of a
cargo at one of the islands before putting the ship through customs at Monterey.
Just how much smuggling went on is not easily determined but, although there
were frequently 20 or 30 ships engaged in the trade, the annual revenue from
port duties seldom exceeded $75,000.

Ship agents went ashore and visited missions and ranchos to arrange
for the purchase of hides and tallow. As the sole purveyors of "civilized" articles
they were welcome visitors and received a special measure of the hospitality for
which friar and ranchero were famous. There was a strong element of incon-
gruity, however, in the picture of these enterprising Yankees transacting the
business of the Californians. Creaking carretas dumped the hides at the beach
or sometimes on the mesa above the beach. It was up to the hide droghers (the
sailors and their Kanaka helpers) to get them aboard. Unfortunately for the
sailors, where the hides were the most abundant the harbor was the worst; the
ships frequently anchored three miles offshore at San Pedro and the sailors had
a long row in addition to the customary work of wading through the surf with
hides balanced on their heads.

Thanks to the twin advantages that subsequently found expression
in the nickname "Baynclimate," San Diego became the principal depot for the
hide business. It had the one good port in southern California, and the weather
was ideal for the curing that the hides required prior to the long voyage around
the Horn. Some of the sailors, together with the ubiquitous Kanakas, were detailed to complete the cleaning of the hides, the Californians being none too
meticulous in scraping off all the flesh. Salt and sunshine had their roles in the

Richard Henry Dana

Title Insurance and Trust Company, Los Angeles

process, after which the hides were stored in warehouses until the time came to load a ship for the return voyage. Usually captains were two or three years in making up their cargoes.

Some of the hide and tallow men remained in California. Alfred Robinson, for example, came in the course of an ordinary voyage, stayed an extra year to act as resident agent for his company, then married into the Noriega de la Guerra family and became a permanent resident of Santa Barbara. A few of the sailors did likewise. A far more significant consequence lay in the dissemination of information about California throughout the United States. Ship captains, supercargoes, and sailors brought back reports of the life in California and of the resources of the province. Robinson's *Life in California* ranks first among the descriptions of the land, the people, the times, and the trade; but it was far surpassed in popularity by Dana's *Two Years Before the Mast,* which gained recognition almost overnight as a literary classic, an outstanding travel book (it was the first sea tale written from the viewpoint of the ordinary seaman), and a vivid description of Mexican California. It is still the most widely read book pertaining to California.

Any account which mentioned merely the immediate satisfaction of California wants, the revenue to the provincial treasury, the marketing of tallow in Mexico, Peru, and Chile, the supplying of leather for the New England boot and shoe industry, and the foreign market for New England manufactures would underestimate the significance of the hide and tallow trade. The transparent consequence of the hide trade was the economic annexation of Mexican California to the United States.

Along with that businesslike impact the hide trade took up where Shaler and the other Boston fur men had left off and familiarized New Englanders with California and its potentialities. This new awareness, in large degree, is why New Englanders helped to swell the American colony in this Mexican province, why they were ready to endorse the annexation program of the Tennessean James K. Polk, and why they participated in such numbers in the gold rush. The hide trade had made California an outpost of New England.

Entrance of the Hudson's Bay Company

Mexican California enjoyed two other trade outlets. One was supplied by the Hudson's Bay Company, which established a trading post at San Francisco in the early forties. Carried westward in the British advance across Canada, the company centered its interests on the Pacific slope to the north of California in the princely domain of Old Oregon. But from Fort Vancouver, on the Columbia, brigades of beaver trappers set out in all directions, and one of these, the Umpqua brigade, came regularly into the California hinterland, the Sacramento–San Joaquin Valley. When Sir George Simpson visited California in 1841, he saw in the turbulence and disorder of the Mexican province a possibility of advantage for his company. He was too late to buy Fort Ross, but he did arrange to purchase a store at Yerba Buena (San Francisco) from an American merchant, Jacob Leese. To this station he sent Glen Rae, son-in-law of the majestic Dr. John McLoughlin, chief factor at Fort Vancouver and King of Old Oregon. Rae was to conduct trade and also to plot toward the possible acquisition of California for the British company and empire. In the intrigue he failed. The prosaic explanation is that he backed the wrong revolutionary faction, one that did not even come out second best. A more romantic explanation is that he fell in love with a certain Carmencita and squandered the company's money on her. At any rate, the funds were lost, and, rather than return to Oregon to face his implacable father-in-law, Rae shot himself. Though thwarted in this intrigue, the company continued its fur trapping and its San Francisco commerce. The latter, however, was not large in volume.

The Santa Fé–Los Angeles Caravans

The other trade outlet likewise involved a transcontinental approach. Its route was an extension of the Santa Fé Trail from Missouri, running by a circuitous route north of the Grand Canyon, through southern Utah and Nevada, across the Mojave Desert and Cajón Pass, and thus to Los Angeles. A California–New Mexico connection had been advocated in the time of Anza, and long stretches of the eventual route had been explored in the 1770's by Garcés in his travels from Yuma and by Escalante in his expeditions from New Mexico. It remained, however, for polyglot traders in 1829 and 1830 to piece these old routes together into what came to be called the Old Spanish Trail. Over this route from Santa Fé to Los Angeles a regular caravan trade developed. Westward, the pack trains brought silver, blankets, and American goods that had reached New Mexico over the more famous Santa Fé Trail from Missouri. Horses and mules for use on that route were the principal California products taken eastward, but China silks were also important.

All too frequently, the Americans and New Mexicans who utilized this route collected horses for the return trip by wholesale theft rather than by honest trade. In this practice they were only emulating the example of the valley and desert Indians, who had developed a passionate liking for horse meat. The white horse thieves were better organized and more ruthless. They scourged the ranchos from Los Angeles to San José and made off with hundreds of animals, thus giving a bad name to the only trade of importance between California and her sister provinces in the Mexican republic.

The Quest for Beaver Pelts

Whereas the earliest American voyages to California were in search of the sea otter, the earliest American overland expeditions, complementing the approach by fur ships, whalers, and hide traders, were after another very remarkable animal, the beaver. Long extolled as a model of industry and recently praised as an engineer of no mean value in flood prevention and erosion control, the beaver has not had full recognition for his role in North American history. Beaver pelts were the first marketable product of the French, Dutch, and English colonies. Exploration of the northern two thirds of the interior of the continent was carried on primarily by beaver trappers who were the vanguard of the westward movement in both Canada and the United States.

Throughout most of the colonial period, the French dominated the fur trade in the Great Lakes area, the Ohio Valley, the Mississippi Valley, and on the Canadian plains. Abruptly in 1763 they lost this rich trade area by defeat in the Seven Years War. The British were the principal gainers, but they were challenged by the Russians on the northwest coast, John Jacob Astor's efforts on the Columbia, and smaller-scale American activity on the Missouri. In the 1820's and 1830's American trappers suddenly swarmed out of St. Louis onto the plains, into the Rockies, and into the Southwest.

Although they sometimes grouped themselves in organized companies, these Americans were rugged individualists. Their method was the antithesis of the old Hudson's Bay habit of sitting down in a factory and waiting for the Indians to come in and trade. It resembled more the French technique of going out among the Indians. Much of their vocabulary and many of their number were French. But whereas the French had gone out to trade, the American mountain men emphasized trapping. Their dealings with the Indians were at times on a friendly basis, and many a fur trapper was a squaw man, yet more frequently their attitude was that the Indian was a "varmint" and, as such, worthy of no trust or consideration.

These beaver trappers were equally unimpressed by Mexico's claims to the Southwest. By the Treaty of 1819 the United States had accepted a southwestern limit along Texas' eastern and northern boundary, by the Red and the Arkansas rivers to the Rockies, and north along their crest to the forty-second parallel. The fur men crossed this boundary with lordly disdain. A large fraction of their trapping was outside the limits of the United States. From Taos in New Mexico, which became one of their favorite haunts, they trapped in the Great Basin, the Gila Valley, and Sonora. Nor did they have any compunction about entering Mexican California.

In this opening of the transcontinental routes to California, the mountain men were carrying on the tradition established by Champlain, La Salle, Verendrye, Mackenzie, and a host of others that fur men should be the vanguard in the opening of the West. These particular trappers broke trails later to be followed by pioneer settlers, government explorers, and gold seekers. For many of these later parties, mountain men served as guides. They were the true pathfinders.

Jedediah Smith, Pathfinder

First of the mountain men to reach California was Jedediah Strong Smith. In 1822, at the age of 23, he had entered upon fur trapping as a member of the expedition of 100 men which William Ashley and Andrew Henry recruited at St. Louis. After spending the winter with Henry on the upper Missouri in what is now Montana, Smith hurried south to meet the new party that Ashley was bringing up. He was on hand at the famous battle with the Aricaras and was chosen to carry the news of this reverse to Henry and bring his men to Ashley's assistance. This exploit was followed by many others in the course of the next few years. His feats of daring and bravery in conflict with Indian and grizzly bear won him a reputation for the traits dearest to the mountain men.

In these years the fur business was changing rapidly. Smith's own explorations were largely responsible for shifting the center of activities southwestward into the Rockies and into the vicinity of Great Salt Lake. This transfer made necessary a local base, a rendezvous, at which the trappers could make delivery of a season's catch of furs without having to go all the way to St. Louis. It became increasingly common for men to remain in the beaver country for three or four years.

Another change came in 1826, when Ashley sold the Rocky Mountain Fur Company to Smith, David Jackson, and William Sublette. At the Jackson's Hole rendezvous that same year these men determined to attempt a further expansion southwestward in search of virgin beaver streams and if possible to open a new marketing outlet through California. Smith, then 27, was the logical choice for leader. The territory into which he was about to plunge was very nearly the least known part of North America. Exploration had swirled all around it—the Spaniards far to the south and on the California coast; Zebulon Pike on the eastern flank of the southern Rockies; Lewis and Clark, the Astorians, the Nor'westers, and Ashley's men in the Northwest—but from Great Salt Lake west and southwest to the Sierra Nevada no one had traveled. Such exploration was prerequisite to the opening of the most convenient land routes from the United States to California.

Accompanied by 17 men Smith left Salt Lake in August, 1826. He went southward past Utah Lake and up the east side of Sevier River, to which he gave the name Ashley. From here he turned southwestward into a range of mountains which he called the Adams in honor of President John Quincy, then south again across the Beaver to the lower course of the Virgin River, in his terminology also the Adams. Smith's whereabouts are not absolutely identifiable for this portion of his trip. One writer is of the opinion that he reached the Virgin by way of the Escalante Desert, Meadow Valley Wash, and the Muddy.

Smith's course down the Virgin is clear enough, though for his little party it was difficult terrain. Arriving at the Colorado or, as he called it, the Seedskeeder, he crossed over and followed it down to the Mojave villages. Here he remained 15 days, recruiting men and horses. Then with two Indian guides and fresh horses obtained from the Mojaves he recrossed the river and traversed the desert to the Mojave River, for which he had a more appropriate name, the Inconstant. Following this stream into the San Bernardino Mountains, he crossed the latter, presumably by Cajón Pass, and in November arrived at the mission of San Gabriel.

The friars extended a generous welcome, supplying the Americans with beef, cornmeal, wine, and 64 yards of cloth with which to replace their tattered shirts. In 1774 the arrival of Anza's party had taxed the province's food supply so severely that half the soldiers had to be sent back forthwith to the Yumas. A half century later there was no such shortage of foodstuffs. A single mission could set an abundant table for a score of unexpected guests even though they tarried six weeks.

Harrison G. Rogers, Smith's lieutenant and the principal chronicler of the expedition, paid his respects to the prosperity of the mission. It had more than 1,000 Indians employed in a variety of tasks. Some 30,000 head of cattle bore the mission brand, with horses, sheep, and swine by the thousands. There were grain fields, vineyards, and orchards of apples, peaches, oranges, and figs. In workshops lining two sides of the quadrangle, skilled workers produced cloth, blankets, and soap, while a water-driven gristmill and a distillery were also in operation. Rogers mentioned all this and more; he was captivated, too, by the favorable location and the attractive appearance of this mission community. His highest praise, however, was reserved for the jovial, friendly friars who were gracious and generous hosts to the Smith party. He was particularly drawn to José Bernardo Sánchez. "Old Father Sanchus," in fact, he was prepared to list as his "greatest friend" and in every respect "worthy of being called a Christian."

Six weeks was a long time for these mountain men to remain inactive. The first week made them forget the difficult three months' journey to California. A wedding, the Epiphany celebration at the mission, the setting of a bear trap among the priest's orange trees "to catch the Ind[ian]s in when they came up at night to rob his orchard"—these were divertissements. Several of the Americans were employed to cut wood for the charcoal pit, and a few others found temporary employment with a hide and tallow ship at San Pedro. But restlessness increased, and overindulgence in the wine and aguardiente so bounteously provided by the padres led to a disturbance that might easily have ended in trouble had it not been for Rogers' restraining influence and the friars' tolerant attitude.

Smith's plans for a trade outlet in California were balked by the

Mexican restrictions upon foreigners. Following the advice of Father Sánchez, Smith wrote to Governor Echeandía petitioning permission to institute this commerce. When 10 days passed without a reply, he went to San Diego to intercede in person. The governor was not inclined to set aside law and custom but finally acceded partially to the joint persuasions of Smith and the captain of one of the hide ships and issued passports permitting the Americans to leave California by the route over which they had come. Despite a present of eight fine beaver skins Smith could not secure permission to traverse California to the Russian post at Bodega.

Having purchased the necessary horses and supplies, Smith left San Gabriel on January 18, 1827, in apparent compliance with the governor's conditions. But after crossing Cajón Pass he turned northward instead of eastward and by Tejón Pass or the Tehachapi entered the southern part of the San Joaquin Valley. The journal describing his next activities is too sketchy to make possible exact identification of the places visited. Smith traveled leisurely down the valley and turned up one of the eastern tributaries, perhaps the Stanislaus.

An attempt to take his whole party across "Mount Joseph," apparently his name for the entire Sierra, failed because there was no pasturage in the deep snow at the higher levels. After five horses died, Smith retreated to the valley, where he left most of his men to trap beaver. On May 20, in company with Robert Evans and Silas Gobel, he tackled the Sierra crossing again, this time with seven horses and two mules loaded with hay, as well as with provisions for the men. They encountered snowfields packed four to eight feet deep, but within eight days managed to struggle across. Theirs is the first recorded crossing of the Sierra Nevada.

Beyond the Sierra the three men struggled for 20 days across a parched and barren desert. At approximately the Nevada–Utah line Smith's journal resumes. Finding water was the major problem. They saw many antelope but, except for two rabbits that Smith killed, subsisted chiefly on the flesh of the played-out horses. A little farther on, Smith climbed a hill to scout the course ahead, but the prospect was so discouraging that he dared not tell the whole truth to his followers. They lurched on through the soft sand, halting occasionally to search fruitlessly for water, and that night made a dry camp. The next morning at ten o'clock Evans gave out. Smith and Gobel luckily found good water some three miles farther on and rushed back to Evans with a kettleful. And Evans, so Smith reports, downed four or five quarts and asked for more. Their hunger was alleviated the next day by a present of antelope meat from some friendly Indians, but two days later it seemed a real tragedy when a deer that Smith shot got away. Fortunately, Smith was able to track the animal down and hamstring it. No time was lost in building a fire and cooking some of this venison. In his journal, Smith records that they then employed themselves "most pleasantly" in eating for about two hours and for the time being forgot that they "were not the happiest people in the world."

To their further relief they had sighted Great Salt Lake, "a most cheering view," and from a band of Snake Indians they soon learned that their fellow trappers were in camp on Bear Lake. Hiring a horse and an Indian guide,

Smith hurried on to the rendezvous, which he reached on July 3. His arrival, he says, caused considerable bustle, for his party had been given up for lost. A small cannon was loaded and fired in salute.

Ten days later Smith was off for California again with 18 companions. His route was approximately that of the preceding year, though somewhat improved by going over to the Santa Clara and Beaver Dam Wash instead of trying to follow the lower course of the Virgin. In this region and from the Mojaves he learned of another party of whites that had come up from the Gila Valley and moved northeastward along the Colorado toward the Sevier. This probably was the party described later in the account of the career of James Ohio Pattie.

As far as the Mojave villages Smith's course was uneventful. Again he traded with these Indians for horses and supplies. But after three days of friendly trade, as the Americans were rafting their goods across the Colorado, the Mojaves suddenly fell upon them, killing 10 of their number. Smith and the eight survivors threw their heavier goods into the river and left most of their trappings on a sand bar in hopes of distracting the Mojaves from pursuit. This ruse gave Smith time enough to get his men to the west bank, where they made a crude breastwork of cottonwood saplings. Four or five hundred Mojaves threatened them there, but, when two braves were killed at a long distance by the American marksmen, the rest ran off. Traveling by night Smith managed to get his party across the desert to the California settlements.

This time his reception was less cordial. He obtained some supplies at San Gabriel, left the injured Thomas Virgin and the free trapper Isaac Galbraith, who preferred to remain, and hurriedly rejoined the men of his first expedition in the San Joaquin Valley. At Mission San José, where he went in search of assistance, Smith was lodged in a most uncomfortable jail by Father Durán, whose displeasure was occasioned by the belief that the trappers had enticed away some of his neophytes. After a time Smith got to Monterey, where he found Governor Echeandía incensed over the breach of the January promise. The governor talked of sending him to Mexico to stand trial, but hide and tallow men again came to the rescue and persuaded Echeandía to allow the trappers to depart.

Early in 1828 they were on their way into the valley of the "Bonadventure" (Sacramento), seeking unsuccessfully a pass through the Sierra. In April they gave up this endeavor and, turning northwestward toward the coast, struggled through very rough and broken country to the mouth of the Klamath, then along the coast and sometimes on the beach itself to the Umpqua River. Game was scarce and travel difficult, but beaver hunting and trade proved excellent.

After breakfast on July 14 Smith left camp to blaze a trail for the day's march. The Umpqua Indians, hitherto friendly, attacked the camp during his absence and killed most of the men. John Turner and Arthur Black fought their way out and, with Smith, were the only ones who managed to reach Fort Vancouver. Dr. John McLoughlin offered Smith men with whom to recover his lost property, and, when the American shrugged his shoulders over the uselessness of the effort, he sent his stepson, Tom Mackay, to put the Umpquas in their place.

The party returned shortly with nearly all the furs. Charging Smith $4 a head for horses lost on the journey and $5 a month for his men's services, McLoughlin gave him a draft on a London bank for the balance of the value of the peltries, about $3,200. Furthermore, he assisted Smith to rejoin his partners in the Rockies.

Smith's subsequent experiences did not concern California directly. After trapping for a while in the Rockies, he returned to St. Louis and in 1831 started west over the Santa Fé Trail. Traveling with a large party on such a well-beaten trail an experienced man like Smith might be considered perfectly safe. Carelessness, however, led him into an Indian ambush near the Cimarron River, and, as he knelt down to drink, he was shot in the back by Comanche arrows and killed.

Jedediah Smith's contact with California was brief. It was marked by imprisonment at San Diego, Mission San José, and Monterey. But it was he who opened the route from Great Salt Lake to southern California; it was he who first crossed the Sierra and first traveled between the Sierra and Salt Lake; it was he who opened a trail to Oregon, a route improved by the Hudson's Bay Company brigades and utilized thereafter as an Oregon–California link. On all these routes he was the forerunner of the American pioneers.

James Ohio Pattie

Smith was one of the Rocky Mountain group of American fur men. Another group fully as influential in California's development operated from Taos and Santa Fé in New Mexico. Of these James Ohio Pattie deserves chief mention. With his father he had come out over the Santa Fé Trail to try his hand at silver mining or trade or whatever the Mexican province beyond the southwestern frontier might offer. Mining was his first venture, but trapping proved more attractive, and in 1825 Pattie set out with a group of Americans to trap in the Gila Valley, the Helay in his orthography.

Since the Gila Valley was virgin territory for trapping, these men found beaver very plentiful and accumulated a good quantity of furs. An Indian attack, however, resulted in the loss of most of the pelts, and they returned to Santa Fé almost empty-handed.

Pattie returned with another group of trappers the next year. The Pápagos attacked again, killing many of the fur men, but the survivors continued down the Gila Valley, trapping as they went. The Yumas proved friendly and a brisk trade went on with them, after which the Americans moved north into the land of the Mojaves. One night at about eleven o'clock these Indians surprised the trapper camp with a shower of arrows which killed two men and wounded two others. Pattie's bedfellow was one of those killed; two arrows struck his own hunting shirt, and 16 pinned his blanket to the ground. The most provoking thing about the attack, to judge from Pattie's laconic account, was that the Mojaves fled before the trappers could fire a shot in return, but he concluded, "We extinguished our fires and slept no more that night."

Shaking off the dust of the Mojave country, the trappers moved eastward along the Colorado. They skirted the Grand Canyon, whose magnificence evoked no exclamations from Pattie. Instead, he complained about the foot of snow through which they had to struggle. East of the canyon they veered northward again, going as far as the Yellowstone, where they crossed over east of the Rockies and returned to Santa Fé by way of the upper branches of the Platte and the Arkansas. At Santa Fé the Mexican governor welcomed them rudely by confiscating their furs on the excuse that they had been trapping in Mexican territory without the proper passports or official permission. The ruling was harsh considering all the hardships and dangers these men had endured, but it was legitimate enough—practically all their trapping had been on Mexican soil.

Quite undaunted, Pattie joined a third party in September, 1827, which also headed for the Gila. This time the Pápagos were circumspect and the beaver abundant, and trouble was not encountered until the Yumas ran off all their horses. Left stranded on the bank of the Colorado with more beaver pelts than they could carry back to Santa Fé, they decided to fashion cottonwood dugouts in which to carry them down the Colorado to the Mexican town at the head of the gulf. As they approached the mouth of the river, their geographical notions were roughly corrected. They had gone far enough, also, to find that navigation was most hazardous, though they did not experience one of the bore tides for which the locality used to be famous.

Turning about, they made their way laboriously upstream for a short distance. Then, because the current was too strong and because many of them knew how long, if not how impossible, a voyage it would be to Santa Fé, they decided to cache their furs in the bank of the river and go overland to California.

The desert crossing was reminiscent of Anza's battle with the sand dunes a half century earlier. Their route lay somewhat farther south, but they were miserably equipped, having no animals and not much to eat except dried beaver meat. In desperate straits they emerged from the desert at an Indian village on the San Quentin River, near the mission of Santa Catalina in Lower California. The Dominican fathers gave some relief but sent them under guard to San Diego, where Governor Echeandía, scarcely recovered from the alarm occasioned by the recent intrusion of Jedediah Smith, lodged them in the calabozo.

What Pattie recorded of his experiences substantiates the usual impression of Mexican gaols and gaolers. So harsh was the treatment and so poor the fare that Pattie's father, Sylvester, pined away and lapsed into a fatal illness. The fatigue and sufferings of the desert crossing were partly responsible, but the jail life was the final cause. As a particular refinement of cruelty, Pattie was not allowed to be with his father during this last illness.

Thereafter some improvement in the treatment of the Americans came about. Pattie was even employed occasionally by the governor in the capacity of interpreter. But the hide and tallow men were not as successful in securing release for this group as they had been in the case of Smith a few months earlier. Permission finally was granted for the trappers to go to the Colorado cache and bring in the furs, Pattie remaining in jail to ensure their return.

Unfortunately, the Colorado overflow had ruined the pelts. Two of the trappers went on toward Santa Fé; the others returned to San Diego and further imprisonment.

Release came finally in most novel fashion. A smallpox epidemic struck northern California. Pattie let it be known that he had a supply of vaccine, and the governor contracted with him to vaccinate the Californians—officials, soldiers, settlers, padres, and mission Indians. In the capacity of "Surgeon Extraordinary to his Excellency, the Governor of California," he toured California, inoculating 1,000 at San Diego, 4,000 at San Juan Capistrano, 2,500 at Los Angeles, and lesser numbers elsewhere, to make a grand total of 22,000. The Russians at Fort Ross paid him $100 for similar medical services.

Besides the liberation of his party, Dr. Pattie expected additional payment for his professional services. Echeandía offered the remuneration in land and cattle but added the condition that Pattie profess Catholicism. Though willing to assume Mexican citizenship, Pattie categorically refused to meet the religious requirement. Even after he had assisted in the suppression of the Solís revolt, he still could not get payment from the governor. Consequently, he decided to go to Mexico to press his claim. President Bustamente listened to him but gave him no tangible satisfaction. Discouraged and impoverished, Pattie went back to his native Tennessee, there to remain until 1849. He is said to have come to California again during the gold rush, but history has no record of his experiences then. Pattie's fame rests on his fur trapping, his opening of the Gila route, his incarceration, and his prophylactic peregrination.

The California visits of Smith and Pattie have an intrinsic interest; their significance expands with the similar journeys to California by other overland fur men, which in turn led to the coming of the pioneer settlers in 1841. These immediate successors of Smith and Pattie left only fragmentary records. The fur trade now featured the Indian pony rather than the canoe; French voyageurs became less numerous than men from Kentucky and Tennessee, and company engagés less characteristic than free trappers. Beaver continued, however, as the central and dominating factor.

Ewing Young

Meanwhile, two other parties had ventured from New Mexico to California. One, consisting of Mexican traders and led by Antonio Armijo, left New Mexico in November, 1829, by way of the San Juan Valley. Crossing the Colorado, they moved on to the Sevier from where their route to Los Angeles was not unlike Smith's. The following year a party of American trappers under William Wolfskill struck out northwestward from Taos, crossing the Grand and the Green. From the Sevier they went westward into mountainous country where they suffered severely in a heavy snowstorm which forced them south toward the regular route. In the development of this "great circle" course Armijo and Wolfskill had a part along with Garcés, Escalante and Domínguez, and our good friend Smith. It came to be called the Old Spanish Trail. Used almost

Kit Carson

every year thereafter by trading caravans, it was for a decade the most important land route to California and was still popular at the time of the gold rush.

In 1831 Ewing Young entered into partnership with David Jackson, former associate of Jedediah Smith. While Young trapped along the Gila and the Colorado, Jackson was to go to Los Angeles with five packloads of silver pesos to buy 2,000 mules and horses for the Santa Fé Trail caravans. The plans went awry. Young took very few beaver pelts and Jackson could purchase only 700 animals. It was agreed, therefore, that Jackson should take the mule herd back to Santa Fé while Young continued trapping. Just beyond the Colorado a Mojave attack relieved Jackson of more than half his animals, and he reached Santa Fé with only about 200 head.

Meanwhile, Young went on to Los Angeles, and throughout the summer of 1832 his men hunted sea otter along the coast. In the fall he crossed Tejón Pass into the San Joaquin Valley and advanced slowly toward the north until he met a Hudson's Bay Company party on the Sacramento. Then he swung in a wide circle to the coast, the Umpqua Valley, Klamath Lake, the Rogue and Pit rivers, and back to the upper Sacramento. His route next lay southward, through the San Joaquin Valley, across Tejón and Cajón passes, by Temecula to the Colorado, and over into the Gila Valley. Early in 1834 he returned to Los Angeles, where he secured a herd of horses. Accompanied by the self-appointed advocate of Oregon, Hall J. Kelley, he drove these horses north to the Columbia. McLoughlin received these Americans with less than his customary hospitality because Governor Figueroa had sent a warning that there were horse thieves in the party. Although Kelley never forgave McLoughlin, Young adopted Oregon as his home. He returned to California in 1837 to purchase 500 or 600 head of California cattle to drive to the Willamette Valley. Four years later he died in Oregon, a well-to-do and respected settler. But before forsaking the Southwest, he had gone far toward perfecting the route between New Mexico and California. After Smith he was the pioneer of the Oregon–California trail and was considerably more instrumental than Smith in bringing that trail into practical use.

Joseph Reddeford Walker

Fur trappers blazed still another trail to California, the central route down the Humboldt Valley and across the Sierra. The prime agent was Joseph Reddeford Walker, whom Washington Irving characterized as "one of the bravest and most skillful of the mountain men." In the summer of 1833 Captain Benjamin Bonneville placed Walker in charge of about 60 trappers and instructed him to reconnoiter west of Great Salt Lake. Walker put a very liberal construction upon this order. Beyond the lake he traveled to a river which he called the Barren and which was successively christened the Mary's, the Ogden, and the Humboldt. In expressive accuracy the first name was very much the best. But barren though the Humboldt Valley was, it proved a godsend to California-bound travelers. Walker followed the river to its sink, crossed the 40 miles of desert that lay beyond, came to the lake which bears his name, and made his way with great difficulty across the Sierra and into the San Joaquin Valley. It was the first entrance into California over the Sierra. Irving and subsequent writers have been in some doubt as to the exact route followed. The best surmise is that from the headwaters of the East Walker he crossed over to those of the Tuolumne. It is clear that Walker's men looked down upon Yosemite Valley from the precipitous heights surrounding it, the first white men to gaze upon its majestic grandeur. In their writings these fur men gave but slight indication that they were affected by the beauty of this wonderland. They were more concerned about finding a place to get down with their horses to the game-filled San Joaquin Valley that lay ahead of them. As a wonder of nature the giant sequoias of the Tuolumne or Merced grove brought more of a response. Zenas Leonard commented on them as "incredibly large," 16 to 18 fathoms around at the height of a man's head.

Walker proceeded to San Francisco Bay and on to Mission San Juan Bautista, where he left most of his men. He went on to Monterey and got permission to winter in California. Half a dozen of his men preferred to stay in California, including George Nidever, of subsequent fame as a grizzly-bear hunter, a crack shot, and a long-time resident of Santa Barbara. With the remaining 52, Walker started up the San Joaquin Valley in the spring of 1834. Crossing the Sierra by the wide and easy pass that has carried his name ever since, he came to Owens Valley, which he followed northward for practically its entire length. Then the route turned northeastward into the Nevada desert where the worst suffering of the entire journey was encountered, north to the Humboldt, across that shallow rivulet, and on to join Bonneville once more on the Snake. Of Walker's numerous discoveries on this expedition, including the Yosemite, the sequoias, Walker Pass, and Owens Valley, the greatest historical significance attaches to the route to California, which he had pioneered by way of the Humboldt Valley and a central Sierra crossing. With certain modifications this trail was to prove the most popular for the pioneer settlers, the forty-niners, and the first railroad builders.

No pretense has been made of calling the entire roll of the mountain men who penetrated California. Many a name has slipped from remembrance,

Mariposa Grove of Giant Sequoias,
"Yosemite and the Sierra Nevada"

Ansel Adams

and men who constituted the rank and file of most expeditions are lost in anonymity. Again, the fur trapping of many of the ordinary members of these parties
is so overshadowed by their later activities that they are seldom thought of as
trappers. J. J. Warner and Isaac Williams, for example, are better known as
California ranchers, Thomas Fitzpatrick and James Clyman as guides for the
pioneer settlers, and Fitzpatrick and Kit Carson as guides for Frémont and for
the United States Army in the war with Mexico and in the subsequent Indian
campaigns. Other mountain men, such as Jim Bridger, were of great assistance
to the overland forty-niners, and Antoine Robidoux is an often quoted advertiser
of California.

These functions may seem diverse, but upon analysis they are seen to
rest on the superior knowledge of the West acquired by the mountain men. In
the search for beaver they penetrated every park and valley in the Rocky Mountain area, every potential trapping spot in the Great Basin, and all the beaver
streams in the California mountains and foothills. In so doing they blazed and
mastered the major transcontinental routes to California; they became the experts on the Rocky Mountain and Intermountain West, the most competent
guides for all others who wished to venture into this vast area, and the dissemi-
nators of information about it and about the Mexican province of California
which lay beyond. Thus, they were stimulators of interest as well as invaluable
guides for the westward migrations which followed.

For Further Reading

RICHARD HENRY DANA, *Two Years Before the Mast* (1840).

ALFRED ROBINSON, *Life in California* (1846).

W. D. PHELPS, *Fore and Aft* (1871), a ship captain's account.

RAYMOND A. RYDELL, *Cape Horn to the Pacific* (1952).

SAMUEL ELIOT MORISON, *The Maritime History of Massachusetts* (1921).

DALE MORGAN, *Jedediah Smith and the Opening of the West* (1953).

MAURICE S. SULLIVAN, *The Travels of Jedediah Smith* (1934).

The Personal Narrative of James O. Pattie (1831).

W. H. ELLISON, *The Life and Adventures of George Nidever* (1937).

DOUGLAS S. WATSON, *West Wind, The Life Story of Joseph Reddeford Walker* (1934).

STANLEY VESTAL, *Kit Carson* (1928).

R. G. CLELAND, *This Reckless Breed of Men* (1950), the fur trappers in the American
          Southwest.

CAUGHEY, *California Heritage*, 118–31.

chapter nine

Pioneer Settlers

You have undoubtedly heard that there are English and American
settlements in California; but it is not the case. There are from 3 to 600
foreigners here, principally English and American, but they do not live in
settlements by themselves; they are scattered throughout the whole Spanish
population, and most of them have Spanish wives, and in fine they live
in every respect like the Spaniards.

John Bidwell,
A Journey to California, 1841

The Prepioneer Settlers

1841 to 1846 The year 1841 is memorable because of the arrival of the first parties of pioneer settlers. By local definition, the term *pioneer settlers* applies to the overland emigrants from the United States who, prior to the gold rush, set out for California with the avowed intention of making it their home. Most of them were farmers and many were accompanied by their families. The coming of such persons was indeed significant. It represented a more intense and perhaps a more acquisitive American interest than had been evident in the earlier day of commercial contacts. It led to a more rapid influx of Americans and presaged annexation to the United States.

The Californians were not immediately aware of the portentousness of the new migration. The emigrants of 1841 were not

Covered Wagon Train

Andrew P. Hill, California State Library

numerous or imposing. They came over trails which mountain men and Santa Fé traders had been using for 10 or 15 years. Throughout the 30 years preceding their arrival, the trade of the province had been almost entirely in the hands of English-speaking aliens, and for a round half century California had been visited first occasionally and then frequently by foreigners. The novelty of the pioneer settlers was further reduced because many other visitors and traders of earlier days had also taken up permanent residence among the Californians. These foreign residents, the real old-timers, or "prepioneer settlers," deserve more attention than has been accorded them.

Thanks to the prodigies performed by Hubert Howe Bancroft in accumulating information about the early Californians, it is possible to compile trustworthy statistics on the number of foreign residents year by year throughout this period, to identify a surprisingly large number by name, and to trace the career of practically every individual who figured at all prominently in the affairs of the province. Bancroft's disclosures are supplemented here and there by other writers on early California.

The first entry in the record is more macabre than significant. A certain Bostonian, John Groem or Graham, a gunner on Malaspina's ship, died as the expedition reached California, and on September 13, 1791, his body was landed for interment at Monterey. To list him as the first foreign resident is unrealistic. That distinction belongs to John Gilroy, Scotch by birth, English by residence, and a sailor by profession. In 1814, as a lad of 20, Gilroy was set ashore from an English vessel because of sickness. Baptized in 1814, seven years later he married a daughter of Ignacio Ortega and in 1833 was naturalized and became a ranchero. A town on the ranch site still bears his name, but Gilroy lost out to the land lawyers as did so many of the natives early in the American period. Gilroy has something of a reputation as a happy-go-lucky fellow and a hard drinker. As to the latter he must yield the palm to an Irishman, John Mulligan or Milligan, who came about the same time and perhaps on the same vessel. Mulligan taught weaving to the neophytes at several missions and drank himself to death in 1834.

In 1816 two Americans arrived. From the *Albatross* a 27-year-old Bostonian named Thomas Doak landed at Monterey, and Daniel Call, aged 17, came on the *Atala* to Santa Barbara. Both married in California and settled down to ply their trade as carpenters, but neither was prominent. Joseph Chapman, who arrived two years later, is often mentioned as the first American. Chapman, who came with the Bouchard expedition and was one of those captured at Monterey, quickly adapted to California and proved his usefulness by building gristmills at several of the missions and even a schooner. He was married and baptized in 1822 and naturalized in 1831. He was a great favorite in the province, particularly with Father Sánchez of San Gabriel, and a most resourceful craftsman. Other foreigners to the number of perhaps a score took up their residence in California before the end of the Spanish period. Their coming, as in the case of Gilroy and Chapman, was usually accidental, and the part they played in provincial affairs was very minor.

With the start of the Mexican period and the simultaneous launching of the hide trade and the visits of the whalers, the entrance of foreign residents greatly accelerated. The coming of William E. P. Hartnell and William A. Gale as resident agents for the hide trade has been noted. Bancroft lists 15 other new arrivals, including William Anthony Richardson, mate on the whaler *Orion* and renowned as the father of Yerba Buena, from which the city of San Francisco evolved. Robert Livermore, later a noted ranchero in the beautiful valley that bears his name, was another Britisher of the class of '22.

For 1823 only eight additions are recorded, the most notable being Captain John R. Cooper of the *Rover*, who sold this schooner to Luís Argüello but continued as its master. Thereafter new foreign residents were added at the rate of 15 or 20 in 1824, a half dozen in 1825, and 25, 12, 18, 17, and 24 in the remaining years of the decade. For the early thirties, Bancroft's figures are 27, 45, 37, 36, and 16; for 1836 to 1840, they are 31, 25, 20, 25, and 46.

Space does not permit the introduction of each of these men. Many of them were not of sufficient importance to justify such attention, and the rest have similarities which make possible classification and generalization. For several of them the remarks made in connection with Gilroy and Chapman are apposite; that is, because of sickness or other circumstances beyond their control they left ship and took up residence in California.

Beginning with Hartnell and Gale in 1822 and continuing with Cooper in 1823, David Spence the following year, William G. Dana and Henry Delano Fitch in 1826, and Alfred Robinson and Abel Stearns in 1829, we meet a different type. Coming with their eyes open, they were alert to the commercial advantage that might be gained. They quickly took over the trade of the province, and, with a few later recruits, notably Thomas O. Larkin, who arrived in 1832, they transacted most of California's business to the end of the Mexican period. Most of these men found it advantageous and pleasant to become Californians. With few exceptions they professed the Catholic faith, took California wives, learned and used the Spanish language, adopted California dress, Hispanicized their names, applied for naturalization as Mexican citizens, and conformed to the mores of their adopted land. Many of them retained a certain quality, a superior energy or a more astute business sense, which made them outstanding among the native residents, but as a class these were the men who became most thoroughly naturalized, altogether Californians.

Representative Californians

Hartnell is a good example of thorough adaptation to California, a process made easier by his previous residence on the west coast of South America. Two years after his arrival he was baptized, and a year later he married María Teresa de la Guerra, who, in the course of the years, presented him with 20 sons and five daughters. After a trip to South America to terminate his partnership he returned and was naturalized in 1830 as a Mexican citizen. The next year he became a ranchero and in 1834 received patent to Rancho Patrocinio del Alisal, about 20 miles inland from Monterey. As a ranchero he had average success. By 1849 he had some 8,000 head of cattle and several thousand horses and sheep. His cultivated fields, or milpas, were tilled indifferently, and the vineyard was also the victim of neglect, but the vegetable garden, with a year-round production of vegetables and berries of many kinds, left nothing to be desired.

Hartnell held various governmental posts: regidor, collector of taxes and customs, court clerk, interpreter (he used Spanish, French, and German as freely as his native English), surveyor, and county assessor. From 1833 to 1836 he was agent for the Russian American Fur Company. At about the same time he opened a school known as the Seminario de San José in which his own children were often in the majority. His most important commission was as visitador-general of the secularized missions in 1839–40. On this hopeless task he worked faithfully and heroically, only to find the forces of spoliation and disintegration inexorable. Notwithstanding his several official capacities, Hartnell is best remembered as a genial, liberal, hospitable ranchero, honest and loyal, too easy-going to prosper greatly in business but a boon companion and a most estimable friend and neighbor.

Another of California's adopted sons famous for his large family was William Goodwin Dana. Almost immediately upon his arrival from Boston in 1826, he fell in love with Josefa Carrillo, daughter of the prominent Santa Barbaran, Don Carlos. To Dana's great disgust he was not allowed to contract the marriage until the preliminaries of his baptism and naturalization were fulfilled, processes which wasted the better part of two years and delayed the wedding until his intended bride's sixteenth year. Besides his 21 children, Dana's achievements included service as appraiser, captain of the port, and alcalde of Santa Barbara, and in the American period as prefect and county treasurer. He is listed as a trader, soapmaker, physician, and architect, and for a time as the holder of a special license for sea-otter hunting, but his livelihood was drawn principally from Rancho Nipomo, near San Luís Obispo, granted him in 1837.

Abel Stearns

Title Insurance and Trust Company, Los Angeles

Don Abel Stearns, though childless, became the patriarch of southern California. After three years of residence in Mexico he came to Monterey in 1829 and played with the idea of a rancho in the great central valley. Instead, he moved to Los Angeles, where he became the leading trader and also distinguished himself by the frequency with which he fell afoul of the authorities. Smuggling was the usual charge, but in 1836 Governor Chico added that of being implicated in a lynching. Stearns quarreled also with a certain William Day and in the broil that ensued suffered a facial wound which so enhanced the ugliness with which nature had endowed him that his nickname Cara de Caballo, or Horseface, was most apt. In matrimony and in business he was conspicuously successful. He won the hand of the beauteous Doña Arcadia Bandini and, from modest beginnings in hides and wines at Los Angeles and San Pedro, became the wealthiest man in southern California. He acquired several ranchos, including the Laguna and the Alamitos, and, in spite of a setback in the drought of 1863–64, he left holdings of more than 200 square miles of land to his widow in 1871. In the forties he held a number of minor offices and in 1849 was a member of the constitutional convention, but his reputation is properly that of a hardheaded businessman.

Thomas O. Larkin, who began in 1832 to make himself the foremost merchant at Monterey, was in many respects unlike his fellows. Instead of marrying a Californian, he chose as his bride an American widow who had come to California on the ship that brought him. He mastered Spanish and gained the confidence of the provincial officials but did not become a ranchero and was far from simpático with the Mexican regime. Aside from the rapid increase in his wealth, to which his closefistedness was a contributing factor, Larken is best known as the first United States consul, as Polk's secret agent looking toward American acquisition of the province, as a check upon Frémont, and as a prisoner of Castro's during the war. Except for his membership in the constitutional convention in 1849, the remaining decade of his life was spent managing his extensive property holdings.

After 1826 the annual increments included beaver trappers from the overland trails. Few if any of these men had set out with the express intention of settling in California. That they did so was as accidental as in the earlier years when sailors had begun to drop off the visiting ships. There was no uniform way in which the mountain men fitted into California society. Some of them preferred the back country where trapping could be carried on, others shifted to otter hunting along the coast. Isaac Graham, though best known as a fighting man and a revolutionist, ran a distillery in the Pájaro Valley near Monterey. J. J. Warner served an apprenticeship in Stearns' store and then went into business for himself before turning to ranching. On the whole, ranch life, rather than commercial activities in the coastal towns, seemed to be the preference of the mountain men. Although a trifle less exposed to assimilating influences, many married daughters of the country and became dons in habit as well as in name.

Because of their expertness with rifle and knife, the mountain men had greater military potentialities for good or ill than their compatriots who had come by ship. The Americanos who were sometimes enlisted on one or both sides of a revolution were mostly former fur trappers, and the most celebrated instance of friction between the provincial authorities and resident foreigners also centered around a group of former mountain men. In his successful revolution of 1836 Alvarado had been supported by a group of Mexicans, Indians, ex-sailors, and trappers under the celebrated rifleman Isaac Graham. Four years later Alvarado found this "foreign legion" more dangerous than useful. He brought about the arrest of Graham and some 38 of his followers and shipped them off to Mexico. Through the intervention of British diplomacy they were released and permitted to return to California, Graham and about half his men actually doing so. The incident illustrates distrust of the wild and reckless Americans whom the fur trade brought to California. On the other hand, by no means was every mountain man suspect. The majority fitted very smoothly into provincial society.

Mention must also be made of one or two individuals who had come to California prior to 1841, but who do not fit into any of the classifications suggested above, of ex-sailors, commercial agents and businessmen, and ex-beaver trappers. John Marsh, for example, came in 1836 with the intention of settling, a purpose that perhaps should not be taken very seriously, since he had gone to Missouri and then to New Mexico with like intent. With his Harvard Bachelor of Arts diploma as a certificate he practiced medicine at Los Angeles. Later he moved to northern California and a rancho near Mt. Diablo, where he availed himself of Indian labor at a mere pittance, continued his practice of medicine for fees paid in cattle and produce, and spent his spare time urging acquaintances in the States to come to California. Far better educated than most Californians, Marsh was notoriously disagreeable and parsimonious. At times, however, he was an important influence in local politics, and his biographer gives him much of the credit for the Americanization of the province.

John A. Sutter was another who came with the intention of staying and of building up a fortune by pursuits more agricultural than commercial. Swiss by birth and American by adoption, Sutter came to California by way of Indiana, St. Louis, the Santa Fé Trail, the Rocky Mountains (where he joined a trapping party), the Columbia, the Sandwich Islands, and Alaska. From Oregon on, his travels had been motivated by the ambition to develop a feudal colony in California. He secured the necessary permission from Governor Alvarado in 1840 and selected a site in the unoccupied Sacramento Valley. His establishment began as a rancho, differing from other California ranchos only in that Sutter employed Kanakas and foreigners as well as Indians and Californians. In 1841, however, he bought out the Russians at Fort Ross, securing among other things horses, cattle, a launch, and 40-odd assorted cannon.

With this artillery he was able to fortify his New Helvetia. An adobe fortress was erected, 12 guns were mounted, an armed garrison was maintained, and sentries were posted. Sutter was secure not only against Indian attack but also against any interference by the Mexican authorities in California, yet for the most part he was on the best of terms with the provincial officials.

Sutter's Fort

Joseph Revere, A Tour of Duty, *1849*

Many different economic pursuits characterized New Helvetia. In addition to the cattle ranch Sutter engaged in extensive fur trade and trapping, planted a large acreage in wheat, constructed an irrigation system, built a mill, a distillery, and a tannery, set some of his Indian employees to blanket weaving, and ran his launch regularly to San Francisco Bay. The debt to the Russian American Fur Company was one incentive for this feverish activity; another was his feeling of obligation to find or make work for any foreigners who came and asked it. "Hospitable, visionary, improvident land baron of the Sacramento," Sutter has been well called. The unbounded hospitality that he extended to American immigrants is the real key to his greatness. It made his fort the mecca of the overland pilgrimages. He set weary travelers on their feet as McLoughlin did in Oregon. He sent relief parties as far east as Reno to assist the faltering steps of the less sturdy pioneers. The military accouterments and strategic location of his fort made impossible any Mexican exclusion of American immigrants.

By 1840 the number of foreign residents in California had grown, according to Bancroft's estimates, to something like 380. Of these, about 50 had come by the overland routes; the rest, in connection with the various forms of seaborne commerce. Because of old age, infirmities, or inaction many were inconspicuous, but others constituted "an influential and highly respected element of the population, largely controlling the commercial industry of the country." The more thoughtful expected to see the day when California would cease to be Mexican, but few were ready to take active steps to turn the province over to Great Britain or the United States. In fact, the majority of these foreign residents, while more aggressive in business, were as conservative in politics as the native Californians, and, except in the Graham incident (and there the fear was largely feigned), they were not a cause of apprehension to Mexico's California officials. In the stirring events of the next decade, the attitude of these old-timers continued to be conservative.

The Migration of 1841

The pioneer settlers of 1841 and thereafter are distinguished from earlier residents by their greater utilization of the overland trails; their coming almost unanimously from the Midwest; their preference for the inland, unsettled, and agricultural portions of California; and their lesser mingling with the native Californians. Relatively few took California wives, and cultural assimilation did not progress rapidly. In view of what had happened in Texas, the presence of such an alien group was disquieting. Even without looking ahead to American annexation, it is obvious that these pioneers were a jarring note in the California scene. The pioneer settlers, furthermore, were competitors of the Californians in land ownership and crop production, without performing a useful economic service such as that of the resident foreign merchants along the coast.

Their coming was a predictable extension of the American westward movement. By 1841 the frontier of settlement had been pushed to the edge of the treeless and poorly watered plains area, a land regarded as unsuitable for white habitation and therefore called the Great American Desert. The panic of 1837 was a propulsive force, and beckoning to the Far West were the trails broken by the mountain men, the trade route southwest to Santa Fé, and the path of fur men and missionaries to Oregon. Because the government laid claim to Oregon, the interest aroused by explorers, fur men, and missionaries was fanned by flag-waving editors and congressional debates. California could not compete with Oregon in its hold on the attention of the United States—the migration figures for the early forties are in the ratio of eight or ten to one—but she did gain a secondary advantage from the Oregon publicity.

California was also the beneficiary of direct advertising. The overland fur men, in particular, supplemented the reports of the Boston ship captains, and what they had to say of California's climate, wild game, fertility, resources, accessibility, and openness led directly to the coming of the pioneer settlers. Pattie, for example, after praising the province as "beautiful and sublime in scenery," added that it was "no less remarkable for uniting the advantage of healthfulness, a good soil, temperate climate and yet one of exceeding mildness, a happy mixture of level and elevated ground and vicinity to the sea." Dana, Kelley, and Thomas Jefferson Farnham were even more fulsome in their praise. More seductive than the written word were the dulcet voices of some of these men who had tasted the wonders of California. The trapper Robidoux, for example, addressing a meeting in Platte County, Missouri, in the fall of 1840,

John Bidwell in 1850

California State Library

climaxed his rhapsody on California by extolling the salubrious climate. In answer to an ague-racked inquirer, he asserted that the chills were unknown in California except for one fellow who had carried the disease in his system from Missouri. His shaking, Robidoux affirmed, was such a curiosity that "the people of Monterey went 18 miles into the country to see him."

As a result of Robidoux's speech and his roseate answers to all the questions asked him, the Western Emigration Society was organized, and more than 500 persons signed a pledge to meet the next spring at Sapling Grove, just beyond Independence on the Missouri, prepared to journey to California. During the winter the Platte County merchants, fearful of losing so many customers, circulated discouraging reports about California. They made particularly good use of a clipping from the New York press in which Thomas Jefferson Farnham recanted all the praise of California that had gone into his volume on western travels. His first impression had been good, but, when he visited Monterey a second time and without cause was lodged in jail, he had a complete reversal. Sabotaged thus, the Western Emigration Society dwindled from 500 would-be emigrants to a single person, young John Bidwell, erstwhile schoolmaster. At Sapling Grove he was soon joined, however, by 68 others who had not promised but now proposed to go.

The group organized and selected as captain John Bartleson, perhaps the least qualified member of the entire party. He is remembered chiefly for his blunders, selfishness, and ineffectual leadership, especially over the latter part of the journey. Bidwell looms far more important, partly because he was the one member who had signed the original agreement, partly because he subsequently became one of California's leading men, partly because the best contemporary description of the journey is from his pen, but mostly because of his informal assumption of command when the real difficulties were encountered. Historians speak of the Bidwell–Bartleson party or, more simply, of the Bidwell party.

Although many of the group had resided near the frontier of settlement in Missouri and all had heard a great deal about California, none had an accurate understanding of the intervening country through which they proposed to pass. Bidwell tells how "an intelligent man" with whom he had boarded showed him a standard map on which was shown a large lake in the vicinity of Great Salt Lake having two outlets, each appearing as large as the Mississippi and emptying into the Pacific. Bidwell's friend advised him to take along tools for canoe making so that, if the country proved too rough for their wagons, they could reach California by water. Since this is a fair example of the Bidwell party's advance knowledge of the West, their great good fortune in falling in with a small band of fur trappers and missionaries who were bound for Oregon is apparent. Father De Smet of the latter group was a regular globe-trotter and well versed in northwestern travel. Thomas Fitzpatrick, leader of the trappers, was one of the best of the mountain men. From Sapling Grove to Soda Springs in the southern part of present Idaho, these expert guides smoothed the way for the California-bound emigrants. The route followed was the one that was soon to crystallize as the Oregon Trail. From Sapling Grove it led northwestward across a rolling prairie to the Platte, along this stream to the Forks, past Fort Laramie on the North Platte to Independence Rock and the Sweetwater, through South Pass to the Sandy and the Green, and across a divide to Bear Valley with its Steamboat and Soda Springs.

Thus far the pioneers had smooth sailing, though enlivened with many a stirring incident. Young Nicholas Dawson acquired the nickname "Cheyenne" by venturing out to hunt and shortly rejoining the train "without mule, gun or pistol and lacking most of his clothes." He reported that thousands of Indians had despoiled him and were about to attack the train. Forty or fifty Cheyennes returned Dawson's belongings, professed friendship, and explained that they had disarmed the frightened hunter to prevent his shooting at them in his excitement. Another member of the party died of an accidentally self-inflicted gunshot wound. Four others turned back. But there was nothing particularly hazardous or difficult in this much of the journey. Later parties likewise found it comparatively easy to negotiate this first half of the trail to Oregon or California.

Beyond Soda Springs the Bidwell party faced an unknown trail. Half the group decided to forego the joys of California and continue with their guides to Oregon. The other 32 struck out southwestward to open their own trail to California. They asked directions from the Hudson's Bay Company men at Fort Hall, but none of these had traveled the route. All that they learned was not to go too far to the north, lest they get into rough terrain where many fur men had died, and not to go too far to the south, lest they get into a very arid country where they probably would die—sound advice but not very illuminating. Undaunted, the 32 pioneers moved out.

Soon after leaving Bear Valley, they found it necessary to abandon their wagons and much of their baggage and pack the base essentials on their horses, mules, and oxen. At making and fastening packs they were greenhorns. The result was great confusion, though soon they and their animals came to a

Contra Costa Hills

Rondal Partridge

working understanding. Eventually they got across to the south branch of the Humboldt. Over alkaline flats, finding little grass or game, they went on to Humboldt Sink. Bartleson and eight of the best mounted men deserted the rest and pushed on ahead toward California. Bidwell and the others struggled across the desert to Carson River and the Balm, which was their grateful name for the Walker. Here the Bartleson deserters straggled into camp, none the better off for having gone ahead so selfishly.

After the last oxen had been killed and the meat jerked, the men began the ascent of the Sierra. They were three weeks in finding a pass and making their way across by the Walker and Stanislaus. Fortunately for them the winter set in late, and, though they did not get over the divide until the very last of October, they escaped being snowed in. Their supplies, however, were virtually exhausted, and the grass and game of the San Joaquin Valley were most welcome. Bidwell wrote with great feeling about their first California feast, a fat coyote of which his share was only "the lights and the windpipe." Unappetizing as this may sound, Bidwell thought it a welcome change from mule meat. He cooked the morsel on the coals and "greedily devoured it."

A little farther on they came to better hunting, "elk tracks by the thousands" and "hundreds of antelope in view." Many of the party despondently reckoned 500 miles still to go and another mountain range (the Coast Ranges loomed to westward) to cross before reaching California. But the end of their six-month journey was at hand. They soon reached the ranch of Dr. John Marsh near Mt. Diablo and had their California geography set straight.

147

In the reminiscences of his mellower years "Cheyenne" Dawson wrote very warmly of Marsh and the hospitality he extended to these wayfarers. Bidwell concurred in the more general opinion that their host was a skinflint. Marsh charged what Bidwell considered an exorbitant price for a bullock and a small hog, the emigrants paying in lead, powder, and knives. To this price was added a fee of $3 apiece for getting them passports from the provincial authorities. Worst of all, Marsh complained bitterly about the heavy expense these emigrants were occasioning him, whereupon Bidwell was convinced that they had fallen in with "the meanest man in California."

In fairness it should be pointed out that the emigrants had made the mistake of butchering a bullock that had been broken to the yoke. And since the California authorities had repeatedly taken a stand against the entrance of Americans by the overland route and more recently had shown an anti-American spirit in the Graham affair, it was not easy for Marsh to persuade Vallejo to issue passports for the party. Furthermore, it was merely by oversight that a passport was not secured for Bidwell. His three days without food in the flea-infested jail at San José undoubtedly sharpened his pen against Marsh.

Nevertheless, the significance of the Bidwell party does not lie in these personal issues or even in the trying difficulties encountered along the way. It lies rather in the fact that the party was the entering wedge for the new type of migration to California. The group soon scattered. A number of the men went to work for Sutter at New Helvetia; most of the others, including Benjamin Kelsey's wife and daughter, the first American woman and child to come overland, settled in the northern part of the province. Flood tide in the flow of Americans into California was not to come until the gold rush and the boom of the eighties, but the arrival of these pioneers marked the start of a steady current of migration.

A second party of 25 reached southern California that same season. Included were Isaac Given and Albert Toomes, who, missing connections with the Bidwell party near Sapling Grove, had elected to follow the Santa Fé Trail with one of the trading caravans. Because New Mexico at that time was in a state of alarm over an expected invasion from Texas, a number of American residents decided that the prudent thing to do was to move on to California. Given and Toomes joined this party under the leadership of William Workman and John Rowland. They left Abiquiu in September, followed the usual trade route, the Old Spanish Trail, across the Colorado, through southern Utah and Nevada, and over the Mojave Desert and Cajón Pass to Los Angeles, where they arrived some two months later. The party drove along a flock of sheep for food and traveled much of the distance in company with the annual band of traders from New Mexico. A dozen of these Americans intended to settle in California, and a few others actually did so, including Benjamin D. Wilson, who wanted to go on to China but could not make connections with a ship. Workman, Rowland, and Wilson became rancheros and prominent figures in southern California.

From Oregon a few other Americans moved to California in 1841, among them Joel P. Walker, brother of the famous fur trapper, Joseph Reddeford. Joel Walker came with the land party of Wilkes' United States exploring expedition. He brought with him his wife and five children. Two other Oregonians brought their families. Their coming, though less spectacular than that of the Bidwell and Workman–Rowland parties, was not necessarily less significant.

Other Pioneers

In 1842 there was a temporary backwash in the tide of American migration to California. No parties came westward; instead, nine or ten men of the Bidwell party, led by Joseph B. Chiles and Charles Hopper, ascended the San Joaquin Valley, crossed Walker Pass, and by way of the Old Spanish Trail went on to Santa Fé and Missouri. Nevertheless, these men contributed to the advertisement of California as a land highly suitable for American settlement. Many others joined in the same work. John Marsh's correspondence included a 19-page letter to Commodore Jones expounding "some of the most interesting facts relative to California." Captain Henry A. Pierce dispatched a similar letter to Honolulu, and eastern papers printed his comments on the designs on California of the Hudson's Bay Company. John Rowland went back to New Mexico to get his family, while Bidwell forwarded to a printer friend in Missouri copy for a 32-page pamphlet on his journey to California. Publicity of this sort, coupled with increasing volume of migration to Oregon and continued hard times in the Midwest, led to more migration in succeeding years.

The first immigrants of 1843 were recruited by Lansford W. Hastings, mostly from a party of 160 persons which he had led to Oregon the year before. Late in May he started south with some 25 armed men and their families, a total of 53 persons. Beyond Rogue River they met a band of cattle drivers, accompanied by a few disillusioned California settlers. A third of Hastings' party turned back; the remaining 35 proceeded by way of Shasta River to California. On the way they had much unnecessary trouble with Indians. According to one informant, two or three of the party were continually taking potshots at Indians. Hastings tells of one occasion when he did the same thing. Between Stony Creek and Colusa, on the upper Sacramento, a pitched battle took place and 20 or 30 natives were killed. In the lower Sacramento Valley and the north bay region these Indian fighters settled down, but first, two of the party, George Davis and a certain Miss Sumner, crossed over to New Helvetia and had Sutter marry them.

Joseph B. Chiles, veteran of the Bidwell expedition, organized the second party of 1843. In Missouri he gathered about 50 persons and led them over the standard trail to Fort Hall. There, because of shortness of provisions, it was decided that Chiles should go on with about 10 men to Fort Boise and strike directly for California. He did so, getting in safely by a new route along the Malheur and Pit rivers, though there are intimations of fighting with the Indians and of one of his men having to be extricated from a bear trap.

The rest of Chiles' party was conducted by Joseph Reddeford Walker

Camp at Donner Lake, November, 1846,
based on a description by one who was there.

Thompson and West, History of Nevada County

over the route he had explored a decade earlier. With comparatively little difficulty they took their wagons down the Humboldt Valley, across the desert to
Walker Lake, and then "with infinite hardships" across the divide to Owens
Valley. There they buried some of their belongings, burned the wagons, and
packed into the California settlements by way of Walker Pass. Chiles had been
expected to come to their relief in the upper San Joaquin Valley. He did not
come or, at least, did not meet them, and their worst hardships were in getting
across the valley and over the next range of mountains to the Salinas Valley
and Gilroy's rancho.

In 1844 a party of 36 persons put in its appearance from Oregon.
Included were several members of the Kelsey family who had been shuttling
back and forth between California and Oregon. More notable was the Stevens–
Murphy party from Missouri by the regular route along the Platte and the
Humboldt. At the foot of the Sierra this party split. The Murphys and a few
others crossed by way of Lake Tahoe and the headwaters of the American
River. Three men attempted to winter at Donner Lake, and one, Moses Schal-
lenberger, stayed there till spring. The main body of the party pushed on into
California by Truckee River and Pass, the first to utilize this subsequently fav-
orite route and the first to get their wagons into California.

At least 250 persons came over the trails in 1845, the movement to California having been stimulated by reports carried back by the earlier settlers, by the showmanship of the government explorer John Charles Frémont, and by the strenuous efforts of Lansford W. Hastings, who returned to the States in 1844 to foment American migration to California. Green McMahon and James Clyman brought in 43 persons from Oregon, among them James Marshall, who was to be the discoverer of California's gold. The Swasey–Todd train came by the Truckee route. From St. Louis, Solomon Sublette brought 15 men, described as the best equipped of any who made the journey. The Grigsby–Ide party, also by Truckee, numbered more than 100 members, and Hastings conducted a much smaller party across the Sierra just before the winter snows closed the passes. There may have been still another party not recorded.

The Donner Tragedy

In 1846 Elder Sam Brannan headed a party of 200 Mormons who moved to California by the sea route around Cape Horn. Overland pioneers that same year considerably exceeded that figure. The majority reached California safely. Notwithstanding such excellent trail records as Edwin Bryant's *What I Saw in California* and J. Q. Thornton's *Oregon and California in 1848*, these parties are usually lost sight of in the stark tragedy that overtook the Donner party.

In the vicinity of Fort Bridger, Lansford W. Hastings met the westward caravan in 1846 and tried to induce those California-bound to take a cutoff south of Great Salt Lake. Guided by James M. Hudspeth, Bryant's pack-train party followed this route without accident. Hastings personally guided a wagon party which reached the Humboldt after considerable difficulty. The Donner party, coming a trifle later, attempted the cutoff, got lost, and wasted valuable time and strength clearing a road for their wagons. Loss of oxen here and in crossing the Great Salt Desert necessitated abandonment of essential supplies, and, when finally they reached the Humboldt, they were both destitute and far behind schedule. William McCutcheon and Charles Stanton were sent ahead for supplies, and Stanton returned with two California Indians and five muleloads of beef and flour sent by Sutter.

An unusually early snow plunged the distraught group into panic. No leader rose in this crisis to insist on energetic cooperation to get over the Divide or on careful preparations for a winter in camp. Instead, the party strung out along the trail and was thoroughly snowed in early in November by 10 feet of snow. Shelter was inadequate, firewood had not been gathered, and most of the cattle had been lost in the storm. Inevitable tragedy ensued, with starvation and cold and death at Donner Lake. The "forlorn-hope" party sought to escape on makeshift snowshoes to Sutter's Fort, but only seven of the 15 got through, and they had subsisted upon the flesh of their dead companions and had shot their two Indian guides for the same purpose. Four rescue parties were necessary to extricate the others. Only 45 of the 79 who had been snowed in escaped and their sufferings beggar description, even though some of the shocking things said about their actions are probably untrue. The ordeal also called forth many acts of high courage and unselfishness by, among others, Tamsen Donner, Virginia Reed, William Eddy, William McCutcheon, and James F. Reed. It was the worst western tragedy since the Yuma Massacre.

Although the pioneers of 1846 and the smaller parties which came over the trails in the next two years shared many of the experiences of those who had come earlier, in one respect they belong in a different category. They found the American flag waving over California, for the outbreak of the War with Mexico had afforded the opportunity to terminate the Mexican regime and to claim the province for the United States. The military completed this step, yet the pioneer settlers of the early forties had laid the foundation, and there is good reason to believe that, without any assistance from the military, the infiltration of settlers—the process whereby Texas and Oregon had been acquired—would soon have achieved the same result in California. Viewed in this light the pioneers of 1841 through 1845 appear not as mere curiosities, objects of interest because of their early appearance in California, but as effective agents in the epic of American expansion.

Diary of Patrick Breen, February 25 and 26, 1847,
a member of the ill-fated Donner Party

The Bancroft Library

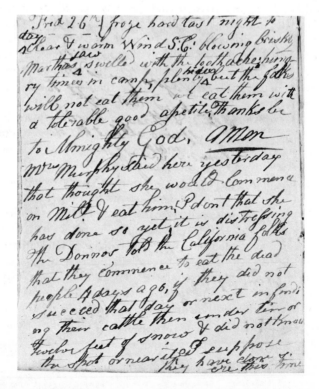

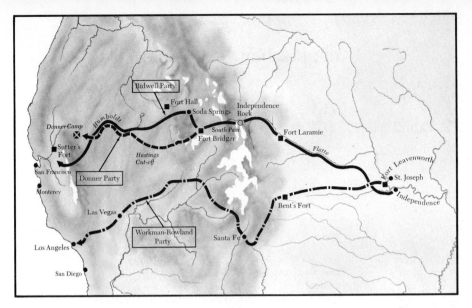

Covered Wagon Trails

Nevertheless, the vast majority of the pioneer settlers came to California because they envisioned an opportunity for a better livelihood, not to acquire the province for the United States. The majority did not scruple about professing the Catholic religion or applying for Mexican citizenship. Paradoxically, a large number of the pioneer settlers did not settle but drifted on to Oregon or returned to the States, and consequently the "foreign colony" in the province was only increased from 380 in 1840 to about 680 at the end of 1845, a fact which would imply that much significance still attached to the older settlers who antedated the covered wagon. To these pioneers, however, goes the credit for setting in motion the first conscious migration to California and for bringing the province within the scope of the westward-moving American frontier.

For Further Reading

SUSANNA DAKIN, *The Lives of William Hartnell* (1949).

SUSANNA DAKIN, *Scotch Paisano, Hugo Reid's Life in California* (1939).

ANDREW F. ROLLE, *An American in California: The Biography of William Heath Davis* (1956).

ROBERT L. UNDERHILL, *From Cowhides to Golden Fleece* (1939), a biography of Thomas O. Larkin.

GEORGE D. LYMAN, *John Marsh, Pioneer* (1930).

J. P. ZOLLINGER, *Sutter: The Man and His Empire* (1939).

JOHN BIDWELL, *A Journey to California, 1841*, ed. Francis P. Farquhar (1964).

ROCKWELL D. HUNT, *John Bidwell, Prince of California Pioneers* (1942).

CHARLES L. CAMP, *James Clyman, American Frontiersman* (1928, 1960).

IRENE PADEN, *In the Wake of the Prairie Schooner* (1943).

GEORGE R. STEWART, *Ordeal by Hunger* (1936, 1960).

CAUGHEY, *California Heritage*, 134–48.

chapter ten

American Take-over

I declare to the inhabitants of California that altho' I come in arms with a
powerful force, I do not come among them as enemy to California:
but on the contrary I come as their best friend; as henceforward
California will be a portion of the United States.

Commodore John D. Sloat,
July 7, 1846

The United States Looks toward California

1846
to
1848

A half century of contact with California preceded its annexation
to the United States. The flag followed trade, represented by otter
hunters, hide and tallow men, whalers, and beaver trappers. It
came only after several hundred Americans had moved into California as chance settlers, resident traders, or members of the first
covered wagon trains. Annexation was also preceded by several
preliminary moves on the part of United States officials which foreshadowed the eventual result.

Official interest is traceable to many of the same factors
which had attracted individuals. California's climate, fertile soil,
proven resources in furs, hides, and tallow, and the usefulness of her
ports for China ships and whalers were considerations which the

Customhouse and Flagpole at Monterey

William R. Hutton, 1848

155

government could not overlook. In addition the increasing body of Americans resident in California prompted official concern, and the idea of Manifest Destiny had obvious implications of particular interest to the men in charge of national policy. The inadequacy of Mexican control, furthermore, was significant because it foreshadowed some change in sovereignty. In view of the policy set forth in the Monroe Doctrine, leaders in Washington were concerned as to the outcome. British or French control of California, of which there seemed some possibility, would be viewed with alarm. The strategic value of San Francisco Bay was again something of peculiar significance to the government.

Andrew Jackson made the first overt attempt at acquisition when in 1835 he authorized his diplomatic agent in Mexico to offer half a million dollars for San Francisco Bay and the northern part of the province. His interest had been aroused by the representations of his minister to Mexico, the headstrong and unprincipled Anthony Butler, later branded "a national disgrace," and by Jackson himself as "a cantankerous, incompetent rascal." Early in his residence in Mexico Butler concluded that every Mexican official had his price; he advocated "bribery and corruption," or "presents if the term is more appropriate," as the open sesame to advantage in Mexico. His analysis may have been sound, though probably not when he estimated that $500,000 judiciously applied would secure any desired portions of the Mexican domain, but he erred grievously in making this unflattering opinion openly known in Mexico City. The Mexicans were naturally insulted, Butler's usefulness in Mexico was at an end, and the prospect of a successful purchase was shattered.

Although foiled in this effort, Jackson did not give up. Butler had enlarged his original interest in Texas to take in "the whole of that tract or territory known as New Mexico, and higher and lower California, an empire in itself, a paradise in climate, . . . rich in minerals and affording a water route to the Pacific through the Arkansas and Colorado rivers." Butler's rosy geographical fallacies were supplemented by the sober praise of San Francisco Bay by Lieutenant William A. Slacum, whom Jackson sent to Oregon and California in 1836 to obtain all information "interesting or useful to the United States." Although Slacum's observations were mostly of the Northwest, he was no more enthusiastic about the Willamette Valley than insistent that the United States must obtain Puget Sound and San Francisco Bay. Jackson was already moving in that direction.

Early in 1837, when Santa Anna came to Washington following his defeat at the hands of Sam Houston, Jackson proposed American mediation between Mexico and Texas on the basis of annexation of Texas with a boundary along the Rio Grande and the thirty-eighth parallel, on the erroneous assumption that this would include San Francisco Bay. Mexico would be indemnified with $3.5 million. He also urged the Texans to lay claim to California as a means of paralyzing the opposition of the North and East to annexation by giving a harbor on the Pacific. Yet neither through Butler, Santa Anna, nor Texas was Jackson able to acquire California.

During Van Buren's presidency (1837–41) there were no direct attempts to acquire California, but the question was kept open by several reports concerning the province. Alvarado's pronouncement for California independence in November, 1836, was viewed with alarm by the United States consul at the Hawaiian Islands. A Russian protectorate was rumored, he reported, in which case the United States' designs on California would be thwarted. Slacum's report was laid before Congress in December, 1837, where its Oregon proposals were taken up by Senator Linn of Missouri and elaborated in his famous bill and report. Both to the Senate and to the nation Linn pleaded the Oregon cause, but California had a measure of attention as the tail to the Oregon kite. Again in 1839, when Hall J. Kelley, archproponent of the Americanization of Oregon, laid a long memorial before Congress, he devoted half his space to California, particularly the northern part. He explained this attention to California not merely on the score of the negotiations between the United States and Mexico with regard to the province but more because he regarded its future addition to the United States as "most unquestionably a matter to be desired."

Later in Van Buren's administration the Graham affair stirred further official interest. The British consul and vice-consul at Tepic were primarily responsible for the release of the prisoners, and the United States is sometimes attributed a Machiavellian cleverness in delaying interference in order to build up a claim against Mexico which might eventually lead to the cession of California. Certainly successive American agents in Mexico, Powhatan Ellis, Waddy Thompson, and Duff Green, endeavored to make the most of the incident as a bargaining point. It led also to a petition from American merchants in California that the Navy station a ship permanently in California waters to protect them against arbitrary miscarriage of justice. The Secretary of the Navy responded by enlarging the Pacific squadron and instructing the commander to explore and chart the Gulf of California, to protect American whalers, and to guard the interests of Americans in California.

With the arrival of Waddy Thompson as Tyler's minister to Mexico in 1842, the proposal of ceding California to the United States was again brought forward. Although he had never seen the land of which he wrote, Thompson was a California enthusiast. In his first letter from Mexico he lauded the province as "the richest, the most beautiful, and the healthiest country in the world." He mentioned the commercial ascendancy that the United States would have through possession of the ports of San Francisco, San Diego, and Monterey, together with internal communications by way of the Arkansas River. He dwelt on the advantage to American whalers and praised California as potentially "the granary of the Pacific." He was highly hopeful that both California and Texas might be secured through cancellation of American claims on the impoverished Mexican treasury, but of the two he considered California incomparably the more valuable.

Secretary of State Daniel Webster showed interest in Thompson's plan and cautioned him about approaching the Mexican officials. It would be better, he wrote, to express interest only in the port of San Francisco and if possible to maneuver the Mexicans into offering the cession as a means of settling American claims. Webster also tried to arrange the cession of California by means of a three-party arrangement between the United States, Great Britain, and Mexico. By the terms of this Tripartite Agreement the United States would have contented itself with the Columbia as the northern boundary, received Texas and Upper California, and paid off American and English creditors and bondholders of Mexico. Although hopes were high and Webster was once on the point of sailing to England to conclude negotiations, the plan fell through. American expansionists balked at surrendering so much of Oregon, and the English did not warm to the plan. A more fundamental defect was that Mexican benefits would have been so indirect; she was to receive no cash but merely to have her indebtedness somewhat reduced. Finally, a circumstance beyond Webster's control, the famous Jones incident, made his scheme completely unworkable.

Commodore Thomas ap Catesby Jones was then in command of the American naval forces in the Pacific with general instructions which recognized the supposed British designs on California. When a dispatch delivered to him at Callao, Peru, gave him the impression that the United States and Mexico were at war, he concluded that it was his duty to hurry to California and take possession before Mexico could hand the province over to England for safe-keeping. Arriving at Monterey on October 19, 1842, Jones seized the town. Because Californians were unaware of any war and the defenses were in their usual state of disrepair, no fighting was necessary. The next day Jones decided that it was all a mistake, that there was no war. He apologized, restored Monterey undamaged to the proper authorities, and sailed south to San Pedro. There a carriage was provided to take him to Abel Stearns' house in Los Angeles, where Jones and his staff were wined and dined by Governor Micheltorena—and presented with a well-padded bill for the damages done. The Californians let the Monterey incident pass as a joke, though a rather humiliating one. Micheltorena had fumed, boasted of the measures he was about to take to expel the invader, and "advanced" from San Fernando to Los Angeles. In Mexico there was deeper indignation, fanned still higher by the bitter denunciation of Jones' action by anti-administration Americans. Thereupon, Thompson was forced to admit that it was "wholly out of the question to do anything as to California."

Jones' seizure of Monterey, though based on misinformation, illustrates the widespread belief that the British had designs upon California. Thompson had reported such designs. "I have information upon which I can rely," he wrote in one of his letters, "that an agent of this government is now in England negotiating for the sale, or what is precisely the same thing, the mortgage of Upper California for the loan of fifteen millions." Later he reported certain knowledge that the treaty had been made and that within 10 years the province would be English.

But Thompson did not originate the bogey of British designs. As early as 1839 the proposal to write off Mexican debts through the transfer of California had appeared in a published book written by a British official, Alexander Forbes, vice-consul at Tepic. His *History of California* was the first book in English devoted specifically to California. Although containing much historical material it was frankly intended as propaganda to bring about British colonization. Forbes outlined a detailed plan whereby British creditors could write off $50 million of Mexican bonds, take over California, and recover their investment through operations modeled after those of the Hudson's Bay Company or the British East India Company. Many American journalists jumped to the conclusion that Forbes' proposal was actually in operation, an opinion shared by Sir George Simpson of the Hudson's Bay Company, who visited San Francisco in 1841. After commenting on the natural advantages of the province, Simpson affirmed his belief that the Californians would "require very little encouragement" to declare their independence of Mexico and place themselves under the protection of Great Britain.

Actually, the British government was not at this time ready to take aggressive measures toward securing California, but in view of semiofficial statements such as the above, England's established reputation for imperial ambitions, and the Anglo-American rivalry in progress over Texas and Oregon, it was natural for American officials to conclude that England was moving to acquire California. However uninterested the home government was, British officials in California and Mexico and on naval vessels in the Pacific were determined to snatch the province out of the grasp of the United States and to turn it over, if possible, to Great Britain.

Warnings of British designs on California were reiterated. Duff Green in 1844 and Wilson Shannon in 1845 reported from Mexico that "the mortgage on the Californias" was about to be foreclosed. The amount now became $26 million. The American press took up the refrain. Santa Anna's opponents in Mexico added to the furor by disclosing that he had been negotiating with Britain for the alienation of Mexican territory, and the Americans seized upon this as more positive proof of British machinations.

Polk's Aggressive Program

Anglophobia took a further upward turn with the inauguration of James K. Polk as president. A native of Tennessee, nurtured in Jacksonian democracy, and elected on a platform stressing a firm stand against Britain in Oregon and Texas, Polk believed the worst about British designs upon California. In addition to the information that he found in the files of the Department of State, Polk's own agents furnished evidence of Britain's aggressive attitude. William S. Parrott, his confidential agent in Mexico, sounded the old alarm in a new guise. "Great Britain," he wrote, "has greatly increased her Naval Forces in the Pacific, the object of which as stated is to take possession of and hold Upper California, in case of war between the United States and Mexico."

Parrott reported still another British device for obtaining California.

A young Irish priest named Eugene McNamara had asked for a grant of land in the province. His aims, he said, were to serve Catholicism and his countrymen and "to put an obstacle in the way of further usurpations on the part of an irreligious and anti-Catholic nation." McNamara's plan of bringing 10,000 Irish colonists to a California grant of 3,000 square leagues was not immediately approved, but early in 1846 he was encouraged to go to the province to select suitable lands. In June he chose a location embracing most of the eastern half of the San Joaquin Valley. The provincial assembly at Los Angeles approved his request on July 6, and Governor Pío Pico made the grant at Santa Barbara a week or so later. Because of the raising of the American flag on July 7, Pico seems to have predated the grant as of July 4, thus making it illegal in that it was made prior to the action of the assembly. Furthermore, the grant considerably exceeded the legal maximum of 11 square leagues. McNamara made no effort to get the United States to confirm his title, but the scheme was potentially alarming to Americans in California and in Washington, and it was later adduced by Frémont and his friends in their rationalization of the Bear Flag revolt.

Of greater influence upon Polk's policy was a Larkin letter of July 10, 1845, reporting the rumor that British merchants were financing the impending Mexican reinforcement of California and that the appointment of British and French salaried consuls to California was particularly suspicious. Neither nation had sufficient commercial contact with the province to justify such an appointment, and the British appointee, James Alexander Forbes (not Alexander, author of the *History of California*), was undoubtedly a secret agent for his government and a servant of Larkin's "Colossus of the North," the Hudson's Bay Company.

Communications such as these confirmed Polk's distrust of Britain and determined several features of his presidential program. Fighting fire with fire, he commissioned Larkin as secret agent in California to "exert the greatest vigilance in discovering and defeating any attempts which may be made to acquire a control" over California. Larkin was to persuade the Californians to resist any attempts to transfer the province to Great Britain or France, and the United States, it was promised, would sustain them in such resistance. Likewise, the instructions to John Slidell, who was authorized to offer Mexico as much as $40 million for California, stressed the necessity of counteracting "the influence of foreign powers exerted against the United States in Mexico" and particularly the necessity of preventing the cession of California to any European power. In his first message to Congress Polk reasserted the Monroe Doctrine in clearer and more vigorous language. California was obviously in his thoughts when he said that "the people of this continent alone have the right to decide their own destiny. Should any portion of them, constituting an independent state, propose to unite themselves with our confederacy, this will be a question for them and for us to determine without any foreign interference." And it was equally so when he stated that "no future European colony or dominion, shall with our consent, be planted or established on any part of the North

American continent." Finally, the genuineness of his apprehension of Great Britain is revealed in a remark of his after the ultimate acquisition of California. "The fact that it has become a part of the Union and cannot be subject to a European power," he reflected at the close of the war, "constitutes ample indemnity for the past."

Nevertheless, it is misleading to suggest that Polk's interest in California was entirely a result of his anti-British bent. He was in step with other parts of Jacksonian philosophy, was a "Manifest Destinarian," and saw direct benefits to the United States through possession of the province. As early as September, 1845, Washington journalists were predicting the peaceful acquisition of California.

First, Polk attempted to purchase California. In Mexico, however, the cardinal political principle was still the same one reported by Duff Green in 1844, that it was regarded as "treason to sell any part of the public domain to the United States." That this was the situation Polk soon discovered. Having been given to understand that an emissary would be received, he sent Slidell with authorization to pay $40 million for California. Unfortunately, Slidell was preceded by a rumor that he had a million dollars with which to bribe the Mexican government. In a bid for popular favor President Herrera refused to receive Slidell, but that did not prevent the success of the Paredes revolution. The new government, perhaps encouraged by Britain and France, was even more opposed to treating with Slidell, who shortly abandoned all hopes of effecting a purchase.

Meanwhile, Polk had set in motion another procedure for acquiring California. He had commissioned Larkin as his secret agent and had ordered him to undertake, though discreetly, peaceful persuasion of the Californians to break away from Mexico and seek the protection of the United States. This was not the "Texas game," to be played by American settlers insinuating themselves into the province. Rather, as Larkin understood it, it was to be played by the Californians. To them he turned with discretion at least equal to Polk's. Abel Stearns at Los Angeles, Jacob Leese at Sonoma, and J. J. Warner in the extreme south were told about the scheme and threw in their support. Native Californians were also enlisted; Mariano G. Vallejo advocated annexation to the United States, and General Castro gave Larkin private endorsement of a written plan for liberating California from Mexico as soon as the number of foreign settlers increased sufficiently. Before relating how this second plan of Polk's failed, it is necessary to introduce another manifestation of United States interest in California, namely, the government explorer.

Slacum was the first official investigator. Then in 1841 Lieutenant Charles Wilkes arrived on the coast with the Pacific Exploring Expedition, which had been sent out in the interests of the American whaling industry. After extended observations in the Northwest, Wilkes sent a detachment overland to California and sailed south to join forces at San Francisco Bay. He developed no personal enthusiasm for the province, though after a thorough examination of San Francisco Bay he admitted that it was "one of the finest, if not the very best harbor in the world." An abbreviated account of Wilkes' expedition was published, but his full report was held confidential and then embalmed in a very limited edition.

Frémont's Adventures

Not so with the findings of John C. Frémont, a natural-born show-man and his own best publicity agent. His overland journeys abounded in electrifying experiences such as the winter crossing of the Sierra, which exerted a tremendous popular appeal. As the son-in-law of Senator Benton

John C. Frémont

From an early print

he was in line for special attention from the government, and his *Reports* benefited from his membership in that choice circle of writers who acquire by marriage a very attractive literary style. It is easy to understand how Frémont became the best-known westerner, how he was chosen by the Republican party as its first nominee for President, and how enthusiastic biographers came to do him excessive homage as "A Man Unafraid," "The Pathfinder," and "The West's Greatest Adventurer."

Of Frémont's five expeditions the second and third were most significant. The first, in 1842, reached no farther west than South Pass and the Rockies. On the second, in 1843 and 1844, he came west by Bent's Fort, South Pass, and the Oregon Trail to The Dalles, south along the eastern side of the Cascades and the Sierra Nevada, and across the Sierra by way of Carson Pass in the dead of winter. After recuperating for a month at Sutter's Fort and purchasing fresh horses and supplies, he moved up the San Joaquin Valley, crossed Tehachapi Pass, followed the Old Spanish Trail into southern Utah, and returned to the States by way of Sevier River, Utah Lake, the headwaters of the Grand and the Arkansas, and Bent's Fort.

This was a notable journey, even though most of it was over beaten trails except as Frémont turned aside to examine wonders of nature. And it was a personal achievement, even though Frémont relied heavily on his fur-trapping guides, Thomas Fitzpatrick, Kit Carson, and Joseph Walker. This journey illustrates the enigmatic nature of Frémont's career. Riddles persist despite the efforts of eminent historians from Bancroft and Royce to Nevins and Goodwin to solve them. Why, for example, did Frémont include a howitzer in the equipment of this supposedly purely scientific expedition? Did he really believe that the Buenaventura River existed? Was the wretched condition of his animals at the site of present-day Carson City sufficient explanation for his decision to cross the Sierra into California?

These and other questions may always baffle, but there exists no doubt that the principal importance of the journey was in fanning eastern interest in the West. From November, 1843, until the next July, while Frémont traveled from the Columbia to the Kansas, no word of his whereabouts reached the States. There were allusions to the "lost expedition," and national concern was felt for its safety comparable to contemporary anxiety over some unreported flier or polar expedition. The circumstance awakened interest; appearance of his volume clinched it. Thousands of copies were struck off by government and

Early California Home

private presses, and it became the principal popular source of information about the West.

In the spring of 1845 Frémont was on the trail again with a party of 62 men. His route was over the regular trail to Salt Lake and by the Humboldt Valley to Walker Lake. There, with winter fast approaching, he decided to take 15 men across to Sutter's Fort, while Walker led the main party across the Sierra by way of Walker Pass. A rendezvous was appointed at the "River of the Lake" just west of Walker Pass, but, failing to find the place, Frémont proceeded to Yerba Buena and Monterey and eventually was joined by his men in the Santa Clara Valley. Through Consul Larkin he obtained permission for his "scientific" party to spend the rest of the winter in California on condition that they remain back from the coast. The appearance of the entire party at Salinas convinced the provincial authorities that the American leader was acting in bad faith. A blustering correspondence passed back and forth, reaching a climax in Castro's order that Frémont depart at once. For three days Frémont remained in his fortified camp atop Hawk's Peak, then retired toward Oregon "slowly and growlingly."

In the Klamath Lake region he was overtaken by Lieutenant Archibald Gillespie, who, in the guise of a convalescent merchant, had hurried to California by way of Veracruz, Mazatlán, and Hawaii as a special messenger for President Polk. The dispatch that he delivered verbally to Larkin was the one described above. Its contents have long been known to historians. What message he delivered to Frémont has been the subject of much controversy. Presumably he related the substance of the dispatch to Larkin, though Frémont later expressed doubt and disbelief that Larkin had been commissioned as Polk's confidential agent. Gillespie delivered a packet of letters from Senator Benton, but their significance is minimized because of the Senator's slight connection with the Polk administration and because it was only an afterthought of the Department of State to send them by Gillespie. The special messenger was decided upon perhaps 10 days after the Larkin instructions were formulated. He was privately instructed by Polk and Secretary of the Navy Bancroft and again privately by the President. It is possible, therefore, as some writers suggest, that Gillespie brought Frémont a message that went considerably beyond the Larkin instructions. If, on the other hand, there were no secret instructions, the fact that Gillespie had traveled a dangerous 500 miles to overtake him was ample justification for Frémont's turning back to California. He was in no way hesitant that this was the thing to do, but there was another duty to discharge first, namely, to retaliate against the Klamaths for killing two or three of his men. Vengeance was swift and ample and apparently sweet.

By the latter part of May, Frémont was camped at Marysville Buttes on the Sacramento. His purposes were not transparent. To his wife and his father-in-law he wrote that he was on the point of returning to Missouri. The same intention was announced to Captain Montgomery of the U. S. S. *Portsmouth*, though qualified by the remark that emergencies might arise to detain him.

The emergency arose almost immediately; thus we cannot be sure of the genuineness of his intention. Opinions of his subsequent conduct vary. One suggestion is that he was fulfilling Polk's guarded orders to bring on hostilities in California which would perhaps lead to war with Mexico and certainly to the annexation of California. Yet his actions seem to indicate that his first endeavor was to avoid any hostilities which would jeopardize Polk's reiterated plan of acquiring California through the peaceful persuasion of the Californians.

Excited American settlers began to come to Frémont's camp. For some months they had been kept on edge by rumors of war. The Graham incident, the Hawk's Peak affair, and Castro's recommendation that the Mexican government buy out Captain Sutter, presumably as a preliminary to forbidding further American immigration, contributed to make these frontiersmen uneasy. It was also rumored that the Californians were inciting the Indians to attack the Americans, and Frémont's experience with the Klamaths was thought of as a case in point. The presence of his armed force served as a rallying point for these alarmed and disaffected settlers, yet Frémont at first would not join them against the California officials. He even dissuaded Carson and others of his men from resigning from the service to join with the settlers. Forty-five years later Frémont claimed that he "knew the hour had come" before he turned back from the Klamath region, but his actions at Marysville indicate that he was not yet ready to join in the violence and thereby ruin all chances of conciliating the native population and winning them over to the United States. He was not above suggesting lines of procedure to the settlers and thus had a measure of direct responsibility for what unfolded.

A band of settlers "who had nothing to lose" launched the revolt on June 10 by seizing a herd of horses belonging to Castro. The Californians supposed this to be an act of robbery rather than rebellion. Four days later a similar group descended upon Sonoma and surrounded the house of Mariano Vallejo. "Almost the whole party," according to one of its members, "was dressed in leather hunting-shirts, many of them very greasy; taking the whole party together, they were about as rough a looking set of men as one could well imagine." Vallejo's wife urged that he flee out the back door, but instead he opened the front door and asked the business of the intruders. He soon discovered that he was to consider himself a prisoner, and then, through his son-in-law, Jacob Leese, negotiations proceeded but in ludicrous fashion.

Ezekiel Merritt, Robert Semple, and William Knight entered as commissioners to arrange with Vallejo, Salvador Vallejo, and Victor Prudon the terms of surrender. After a long wait the Bear Flaggers sent John Grigsby to expedite the procedure, and after another long pause they sent in William B. Ide. The latter found the preceding emissaries befuddled by Vallejo's aguardiente. Ide declined Vallejo's "potent hospitality," and the negotiations were speedily finished. There was a written guaranty of protection for noncombatants. There was talk of paroling the prisoners but, instead, the Vallejos, Prudon, and Leese were sent to Frémont's camp and on to Sutter's Fort. The violence to Vallejo was an unfortunate mistake on the part of the Bear Flaggers, both in the way that it was mismanaged and because Vallejo had been a firm advocate of American acquisition.

The Bear Flaggers went on to construct their flag, a grizzly-bear passant and a lone star on a field of white, bordered at the bottom by a broad red stripe, and beneath the bear the caption "California Republic." William B. Ide proclaimed that the aim of the movement was to set up a "Republican Government" in place of the "Military Despotism" which had seized the mission property, oppressed the people, and made enormous exactions on imports. He promised that the new government would guarantee civil and religious liberty, would detect and punish crime, would encourage industry, virtue, and literature, and would leave unshackled "Commerce, Agriculture, and Mechanism." In peroration he summed up his political credo, saying "that a Government to be prosperous and happifying in its tendency must originate with its people . . . that its Citizens are its Guardians, its officers are its Servants, and its Glory their reward." In style and in ideology Ide's proclamation is at variance with the usual picture of the Bear Flaggers as uncouth ruffians.

Near San Rafael the Bear Flaggers fought their one battle, the practically bloodless "Battle of Olompali" in which one or two Californians were killed and a number of horses captured. Soon after, moved by the capture and execution (and some add mutilation) of two Americans on their way to the Fitch rancho on Russian River for a barrel of powder, Frémont announced his support. His 60 men joined, as did the other settlers of the vicinity. There was maneuvering back and forth in the north bay region and Castro cleverly extricated his small force from the Marin peninsula, but a few days later official news of the Mexican War arrived and the Bear Flag movement had no further necessity. The charge is made, in fact, that it never had any excuse, that it occasioned unnecessary violence, engendered ill will, ended all hopes of peaceful annexation, and neither saved the province from British seizure nor hastened American acquisition. It was, however, an interrupted movement that did not run its full course. Had the Mexican War postponed its intrusion, the Bear Flaggers might easily have extended their sway over northern California at least in a Texas-like preliminary to annexation to the United States.

The War with Mexico

The causes of the Mexican War pertain largely to Texas and to the question of title to all of Texas, not merely the strip between the Nueces and Rio Grande. Another factor was Polk's ambition to add California and other southwestern territory to the national domain. His efforts to purchase this area had failed. The method of peaceful persuasion upon the Californians through the confidential agency of Larkin was not given time enough to operate, nor was the Bear Flag Revolt, which Polk did not start but probably would have approved. The method of conquest remained.

The war was really fought and won south of the Rio Grande and in the Valley of Mexico, but Polk was careful to see that the coveted territories were occupied. The ap Jones drama was reenacted, this time by a less impetuous hero. Commodore John D. Sloat, commander of the Pacific fleet, had standing instructions that virtually duplicated Jones'. As soon as he was assured that war had broken out, he sailed to Monterey to forestall any possible intervention by Admiral Seymour of the British Navy. Although Sloat entered port on July 2, he delayed announcing the war or taking possession until the seventh. Just why he held off is not clear, though his instructions were to preserve if possible the goodwill of the inhabitants. It required a combination of Larkin's persuasion, the urging of his officers, the apprehension of British intervention, and the realization that the Bear Flaggers must be forestalled in acquiring control over the province to spur Sloat to action. On the ninth there were flag raisings at San Francisco and Sonoma and two days later at Sutter's Fort.

Sloat's proclamation may be criticized as a partisan document casting the entire blame for the war upon Mexico and exaggerating Taylor's initial success against General Arista. It is interesting, however, for the conciliatory tone which Sloat maintained and for the point-blank assertion that the United States would retain possession. He went on to promise the Californians full privileges of citizenship, freedom "to worship the creator in a way most congenial to each one's sense of duty," freedom from revolution, and the right to import from the United States free of duty and all foreign goods at one quarter of the duty Mexico imposed. He predicted that under the American flag the province was bound to "improve more rapidly than any other on the continent of America."

On July 15 Sloat resigned his command to Commodore Robert F. Stockton, and a more vigorous policy ensued. The Bear Flag men were enlisted as volunteers in the United States Army, with Frémont as major and Gillespie as captain. Stockton determined to extend the conquest into southern California. He also issued a bombastic and inflammatory proclamation full of threats against the California leaders and devoid of Sloat's assurances to the people of the province. On August 13 he entered Los Angeles and on the seventeenth proclaimed: "The Flag of the United States is now flying from every commanding position in the Territory, and California is entirely free from Mexican dominion." So far, so good; but again with unnecessary harshness he went on to decree martial law, to forbid the carrying of arms, and to establish a strict 10 o'clock curfew.

Revolt and Reconquest

In southern California, as in the north, the Californians offered no resistance to the forces of the United States, and the change was altogether peaceful. But Stockton erred in the tone of his proclamation. He also made the mistake of leaving Gillespie in command with an inadequate garrison, and Gillespie unwisely issued tactless regulations further restraining the Angeleños from certain harmless and accustomed enjoyments. On September 23 Gillespie was made aware of the extent of American unpopularity. Sérbulo Varela and other semioutlaws, filled "with patriotism and perhaps with wine," made a disturbing though innocuous attack on the American barracks, and, when Gillespie sought to arrest these disturbers, he found most of the populace against him.

The first major engagement was at Isaac Williams' Chino Rancho where B. D. Wilson and a score of Americans were forced to surrender to the Californians. Heartened by this victory, the Californians tightened their siege upon Gillespie's force, which had taken refuge on Fort Hill back of the plaza. Gillespie managed to get a messenger, Juan Flaco (Lean John) Brown, off to Stockton. After a narrow escape from the Angeleños, Brown rode madly to Monterey and on to San Francisco. He covered the 500 miles in five days, but Gillespie could not hold out even this long and surrendered. He was allowed to take his men to San Pedro on condition that they embark immediately.

Before this ship sailed, the relief party from San Francisco appeared, and Gillespie's men landed to assist in the recapture of Los Angeles. The ensuing Battle of the Old Woman's Gun, sometimes called the Battle of Domínguez Rancho, was a decisive California victory. On October 8 the Americans marched inland 15 miles to Domínguez Rancho. California horsemen hovered about, but the principal obstacles were heat, dust, and thirst. The next day José Carillo's men resisted further advance. They were indifferently armed with carbines and homemade willow lances but excellently mounted and had a four-pound swivel gun that they used with telling effect. A Mexican woman had secreted the gun at the time of Stockton's entrance into Los Angeles; now it was lashed to the front half of a wagon's running gear. Ignacio Aguilar fired it with a lighted cigarette, and reatas whipped it out of the Americans' grasp and back into position. The Americans wore themselves out in futile efforts to capture the gun; the Californians were "content to let the gun do the fighting," which it did so well that the invaders fell back to San Pedro. It was a victory for California horsemen, powder made at San Gabriel, and a salute-firing cannon from the plaza.

Two other forces were converging on the Angeleños. Frémont, with more than 300 men, was marching south from Monterey, and General Stephen W. Kearny was headed west from Fort Leavenworth. Kearny's march was part of Polk's general plan of occupying the Mexican areas whose cession was desired. New Mexico was the first objective; over this province Kearny gained control without serious difficulty. Leaving the greater part of his command as a garrison at Santa Fé, he set out with 300 dragoons by the Gila route for California. On the Rio Grande below Socorro he met Kit Carson on his way to Washington with dispatches from Stockton. When Carson, who had left the settlements prior to the Los Angeles outburst, showed him Stockton's official statement that American control was already established, Kearny decided to send most of his men back to Santa Fé, but he induced Carson to guide him to the coast.

The desert crossing involved frightful hardships. Then, before his men or animals had recovered their strength, Kearny found himself opposed by a large force of Californians under Andrés Pico. At San Pascual the Californians retreated before an American attack, but, as soon as the pursuers were strung out and disunited, Pico's men turned and attacked. Sixteen or eighteen Americans were killed and as many wounded, while the Californians had only a few minor wounds. The survivors were still at bay before the California

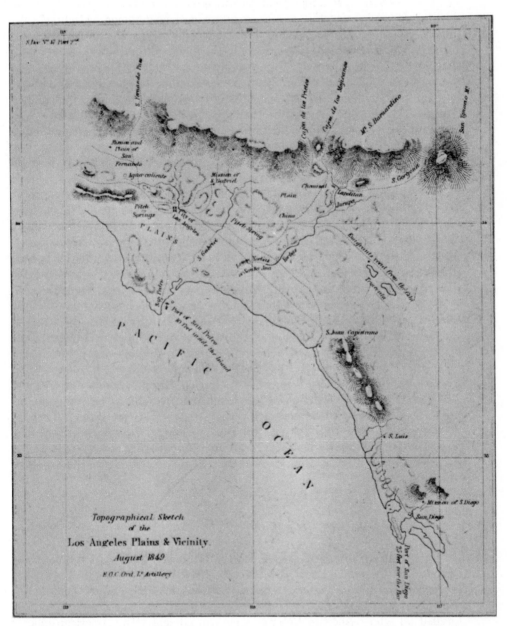

Los Angeles Plains and Vicinity

Topographical sketch, August, 1849

horsemen. Kit Carson and Lieutenant Edward F. Beale slipped through to San Diego, Stockton sent out 200 marines and soldiers, and with their help Kearny got in to San Diego on December 12.

To the War Department, Kearny reported San Pascual as an American victory. He had come off in possession of the battlefield, though with practically all the casualties. He could find, however, feeble excuse for bringing on the battle. Even had he won a decisive victory, the California revolt would have remained virtually as strong. He must answer for sending his men into battle on worn-out mules and half-broken horses, with their powder wet and with no weapons but clubbed guns and rusted swords, against skilled and well-mounted lancers. The conclusion must be that the Californians were underrated, yet Pico appears to have planned the battle and the tactics most vaguely and, when reinforcements arrived, he disappeared.

Weeks passed before Kearny and Stockton were ready to move on to Los Angeles. January 8 found them at the upper ford of the San Gabriel, with a California force under José María Flores commanding the opposite bank. The Californians were advantageously posted, but dissensions and bickerings within their ranks had dissipated most of the enthusiasm evidenced at Chino, Los Angeles, and San Pascual. Their powder also was poor and consequently their artillery fire, which otherwise would have been withering, did not hinder the Americans from crossing the river. At Los Angeles River the next day the performance was repeated, again with almost no casualties on either side.

Los Angeles surrendered to Kearny and Stockton on January 10; Flores turned his authority over to Andrés Pico and left for Sonora. Rather than surrender to Kearny and Stockton, Pico preferred to capitulate to Frémont, now as far south as San Fernando. Frémont's pardon of Jesús Pico, another leader in the revolt and a parole violator, doubtless had much to do with Andrés Pico's choice. Vindicating Pico's hopes, the Cahuenga Capitulation on January 13, 1847, ended the revolt without the least semblance of vindictiveness. No punishments were threatened or provided; conciliation was its pervading spirit.

Like the Bear Flag Revolt this southern California uprising may appear a fruitless and unnecessary outburst. But its causation is clear if not sufficient, and it at least demonstrated the gallantry, the dash, and the valor of the Californians.

The War in Baja California

After this spirited action in Alta California, American attention was directed to the peninsula. On March 29, 1847, Captain Montgomery of the *Portsmouth* raised the American flag at San José del Cabo and on April 13 did the same at La Paz. In each instance he exacted a pledge of neutrality and invited all who wished to become American citizens. The American officers were as emphatic as they had been in Alta California that the province would be retained permanently by the United States, yet Commodore Shubrick was more intent upon blockading the mainland ports than upon ensuring the complete submission of the peninsulares. In July Colonel Burton and 115 men of the New York volunteers arrived from Santa Barbara to garrison La Paz, and in November Shubrick left Lieutenant Heywood and 24 men to hold San José.

Several weeks earlier Captain Manuel Pineda had crossed the gulf from Guaymas to Mulege and begun preparations to oust the invaders. Waiting prudently until the American naval vessels had left, he launched attacks on the American barracks at La Paz on November 16 and on San José on the nineteenth. At La Paz the investment continued until the arrival of the *Cyane* on December 8, with the sharpest fighting occurring on November 17, 27, and 28. San José was temporarily relieved by two American whalers on November 21, and additional marines and sailors brought Heywood's force up to 46 men. In January Pineda renewed the attack. By February 10 he had possession of the town; two days later Heywood was in distress for lack of food and water, but on the fourteenth the *Cyane* came to the rescue and the siege was lifted. In March, reinforced from Alta California, Burton took the offensive and captured Pineda and several other opposition leaders.

Although the fighting in Baja California was many times bloodier than that in the northern province, the war was decided not in either California but by the victories of Taylor and Scott at Buena Vista and Chapultepec. The Treaty of Guadalupe Hidalgo, in February, 1848, disregarding the American victories in Baja California and the pronouncements of American officers there, restored that province to Mexico. In the American Southwest and in Alta California, however, the treaty confirmed the American hold and transmuted provisional control into permanent possession.

For Further Reading

ROBERT G. CLELAND, "Early Sentiment for the Annexation of California," *Southwestern Historical Quarterly*, three installments (1914–15).

BERNARD DE VOTO, *Year of Decision, 1846* (1942, 1961).

JOSIAH ROYCE, *California, from the Conquest in 1846 to the Second Vigilance Committee in San Francisco* (1886).

C. L. GOODWIN, *John Charles Frémont, An Explanation of His Career* (1930.)

ALLAN NEVINS, *Frémont, the West's Greatest Adventurer* (1928), slightly modified as *Frémont: Pathmarker of the West* (1939, 1961).

JOSEPH T. DOWNEY, *The Cruise of the Portsmouth* (1963).

WERNER MARTI, *Messenger of Destiny: The California Adventures of Archibald H. Gillespie* (1960).

EDWIN BRYANT, *What I Saw in California* (1848).

ROSS CALVIN, *Lieutenant Emory Reports* (1951), on Kearny's march.

GEORGE W. AMES, *A Doctor Comes to California, The Diary of John S. Griffin* (1943).

ARTHUR WOODWARD, *Lances at San Pascual* (1948).

CAUGHEY, *California Heritage*, 156–78.

chapter eleven

Gold

My messenger sent to the mines has returned with specimens of the gold; he dismounted in a sea of upturned faces. As he drew forth the yellow lumps from his pockets, and passed them around among the eager crowd, the doubts, which had lingered till now, fled. . . . The blacksmith dropped his hammer, the carpenter his plane, the mason his trowel, the farmer his sickle, the baker his loaf, and the tapster his bottle. All were off for the mines, some on horses, some on carts, and some on crutches, and one went in a litter.

Walter Colton, Alcalde of Monterey,
June 20, 1848

The Discovery

1848
to
1875

When the Spaniards came to California, they were the world's most famous treasure finders and producers of precious metals. With this reputation, one of the ironies of history is that they did not discover California's gold. Some of the forty-niners rationalized on the bases of the depravity of the natives and the Catholic religion of the Spaniards. The latter, according to this theory, would have used the California gold "to keep the world in darkness and to extend the dominions of popery," whereas the prevailingly Protestant Americans would put it to a better use. This argument was not entirely convincing, not even to the forty-niners; as one of them, after speculating on the point, went on to say of his fellows, "But still the majority,

The Mill at Coloma
William R. Hutton, 1849

172

[Sutter's Saw Mill]
Monday April 16 1849.
The first discovery of gold was in digging this mill race.

173

perhaps nine-tenths, are seeking it for wicked purposes," an observation heartily endorsed by many witnesses of the gold rush.

Without invoking the intervention of a divine and Protestant Providence, it is understandable that the Spaniards did not make the discovery. Those who came to the province were soldiers, settlers, and missionaries. In Mexico as in most of Spanish America, mining had been for silver more than for gold, and since the days when Columbus and his companions washed the gravels of Española, placer mining had been of slight importance. Also, the Spanish mineral discoveries were usually deposits which the Indians were already working, and the California Indians, of course, had not taken this preliminary step. Finally, and most significant, the Spaniards occupied only the coastal strip. Even when ranchos were extended farther inland, contact with the mother lode area was infrequent and superficial.

To be sure, California had yielded small amounts of gold prior to 1848, the most famous and most important find being that by Francisco López in San Feliciano Cañon in 1842. Several score prospectors followed López into the mountains back of Mission San Fernando and took out varying amounts of gold. From these placers came the first California gold presented to the United States mint, some 20 ounces forwarded by Alfred Robinson for Abel Stearns. These placers also influenced Deputy Manuel Castañares to report to the Mexican government in 1844 that mining promised to be one of the most profitable industries of the province. These southern deposits, however, did not live up to expectations; interest in them was local and short-lived, 'and it remained for James Wilson Marshall to make effective discovery of California's fabulous wealth in gold.

Jim Marshall

From a Britton & Rey broadside

On January 24, 1848, while constructing a sawmill at Coloma on the American River, Marshall chanced to notice flecks of yellow along the tailrace. The tailrace had cut across a bend in the river and was to all intents and purposes a rough sluice through a bar such as the Argonauts learned to look for. Marshall gathered samples of this "color," by the next day enough to make three ounces. On the fourth day, despite the incredulity of his companions, he rode off to Sutter's Fort to confer with his employer, the potentate of the Sacramento Valley. Behind locked doors the two men examined the contents of Marshall's pouch and applied every test that their ingenuity or the *American Encyclopaedia* could suggest. By all accounts Marshall, a peculiar and excitable young man, was quite worked up over the discovery, doubtless in large degree because some of the men at the mill had insinuated that he was crazy. Sutter records that his own sleep was disturbed that night by thoughts of the disruption of his ventures which a flurry of excitement about gold might cause. Yet many accounts read entirely too much drama and foreknowledge into the conference of Marshall and Sutter in the latter's office. The magnitude of the discovery was not yet discernible.

Sutter, still worried about keeping his laborers, went up to Coloma and persuaded the men there to promise to continue at their task for six weeks. Gold prospects in the vicinity, nevertheless, were sufficiently bright to suggest the advisability of acquiring title to the district. Accordingly, Sutter called together the Coloma Indians and dickered with them for a three-year lease of the 10 or 12 leagues of land surrounding the mill. The consideration was some shirts, hats, handkerchiefs, and flour, "and other articles of no great value." Next he dispatched Charles Bennett, one of the mill hands, to Monterey to get Colonel R. B. Mason to validate his title to the land.

Throughout these first weeks Sutter's course was inconsistent. He sought to minimize the importance of the discovery yet rushed to get title to the land. He bound Bennett to secrecy yet sent with him six ounces of gold. He made Marshall's men promise to work for six weeks yet allowed them to prospect on Sundays. He attempted to isolate Coloma from New Helvetia but sent teamsters back and forth to the mill. He was noncommunicative to his employees but as early as February 10 was writing to Vallejo at nearby Sonoma: "I have made a discovery of a gold mine, which, according to experiments we have made, is extraordinarily rich."

To keep such a secret was impossible; it escaped through numerous leaks. At Benicia on his way to Monterey Bennett could not resist trumping a rumor of coal near Mount Diablo by displaying his sample of a mineral "that will beat coal." At San Francisco and at Monterey he again showed the gold. At Coloma one of the Wimmer boys babbled of gold to a teamster, and his mother, to prove the boy not a liar, brought forth some of the metal. The teamster in turn, ordering a bottle of whisky at Smith and Brannan's store at Sutter's Fort, offered gold dust in payment. In February, Henry Bigler shared the secret with three of his Mormon friends who, as Bancroft put it, "united with them three others to help them keep it." So it went, and, before long, word of the discovery had permeated much of northern California.

Miner

From a contemporary lettersheet

Although the secret escaped, California was not immediately gripped with a furor for mining. The first newspaper mention of the discovery was a perfunctory notice tucked away on the second page of the San Francisco *Californian* of March 15. Three days later the *California Star* made an equally noncommittal statement and on March 25 reported that enough gold had been mined to make it "an article of traffic" at New Helvetia. In its next issue, on April 1, the *Star* ran a long installment of V. J. Fourgeaud's "The Prospects of California." He mentioned gold but bracketed the American River diggings with the old placero "a few miles from the Ciudad de los Angeles" and dwelt primarily on agricultural and commercial resources. On May 6 Editor E. C. Kemble, after a jaunt through the interior, made only this staccato report:

> Great country, fine climate; visit this great valley, we would advise all who have not yet done so. See it now. Full-flowing streams, mighty timber, large crops, luxuriant clover, fragrant flowers, gold and silver.

A few venturesome individuals stole off to Coloma, but not until the latter part of May did the gold fever really become virulent. Then it was Sam Brannan's quinine bottle full of the precious dust and his infectious shout of "Gold! Gold! Gold from the American River!" that started the rush. Alcalde Walter Colton described the excitement at Monterey on June 20. Everyone, except one old codger who insisted they were "some Yankee invention, got up to reconcile the people to the change of flag," admitted that the specimens of gold were genuine. Monterey was quickly depopulated; even the tapster left his bottle. An American woman who had opened a boardinghouse rushed off before her lodgers had a chance to pay their bills, and Colton was left to govern "a community of women," a gang of prisoners, and here and there a soldier. By July for lack of a servant he, Governor Mason, and Lieutenant Lanman of the *Warren* were their own cooks.

Other parts of California soon felt the effect of the gold excitement. San Jose was largely deserted; places as far south as Santa Barbara and Los Angeles contributed their quota of prospectors; rancheros and farmers hustled off to the diggings; Army pay of $7 a month did not suffice to keep men in the ranks; and ships which put in at San Francisco were quickly stripped of their crews and often of their officers as well. The immediate consequences were frequently grotesque. San Francisco and Monterey were on the way toward becoming ghost towns. Business, except in picks, pans, shovels, and mining outfits, was at a standstill, labor was not to be had, construction stopped, and real estate tumbled to give-away prices. A San Jose stablekeeper was urged by his brothers, already in the mines, to burn his barn if he could not otherwise dispose of it. On the other hand, mining equipment rose to fantastic prices and transportation to the mines was at a premium. Horses could still be had for about $15, but every small vessel on the bay was eagerly sought out, and Semple's ferry at Benicia did a tremendous business.

The Season of '48

Meanwhile, the field of mining operations spread rapidly from the initial point at Coloma. Henry Bigler and other employees at the mill discovered better diggings downstream, and friends of theirs dug the first gold at Mormon Bar. Upstream, Marshall discovered Live Oak Bar where Indians were soon set to work mining. On March 8 Isaac Humphrey, an experienced Georgia miner, began prospecting at Coloma and the next day had a rocker in operation. Later in the month John Bidwell visited Coloma, observed the alluvial deposits in which the gold was found, and was reminded of similar formations near his rancho at Chico. He soon had his Indian retainers at work at Bidwell Bar on the Feather River. P. B. Reading was inspired to put Indians to work far to the north at placers along Clear Creek and the Trinity. Soon other placers were being worked along Feather River. Here seven men from Monterey, assisted by 50 Indians, took out 273 pounds of gold in seven weeks. On the Yuba, principal tributary of the Feather, gold was still more abundant. The first five prospectors there made $75,000 in three months, and other miners are said to have averaged $60 to $100 a day.

Prospecting was extended also to the tributaries of the American River. John Sinclair was the pioneer at its forks, a Mormon group began work at Spanish Diggings on the middle tributary, an Irishman opened the Yankee Jim, and a party sent out by Charles M. Weber, after visiting the Stanislaus and the

Gold District of California

James Wyld, London, 1849

Mokelumne, mined the first gold at Weberville on the south branch of the American. One of the best strikes in this vicinity was at Dry Diggings, subsequently rechristened Hangtown and still later Placerville. Here the daily yield in the summer of 1848 was from three ounces to five pounds per man, and that summer, as Bancroft aptly observes, "the 300 Hangtown men were the happiest in the universe."

Such were the northern diggings. Except for Reading's placers far to the north it was a fairly compact district on the American and the Feather rivers and on their several tributaries, such as the Yuba, Bear, and Weber. The miners were principally Americans from the northern ranchos and towns, deserters from Mason's command, sailors from every vessel that anchored at San Francisco, and Indians native to the gold region.

Indians also were the pioneers in the southern diggings. Weber's company was partly responsible. Twenty-five Stanislaus Indians were taken to Weber Creek, given a short course in mining methods, and sent back to their native haunts with the promise of a ready market for any gold they might gather. The Indians brought in such quantities of coarse gold (one nugget is said to have weighed 80½ ounces) as to convince their white friends that they had found "the place where all the gold came from." The Weber group led a rush to the Stanislaus and was soon joined by others from the north, a large contingent of southern Californians, and many prospectors from Sonora. Phenomenal success greeted some of these gold seekers. At Knight's Ferry on the Stanislaus three men with no better equipment than pick and knife averaged $200 to $300 a day each. On the Tuolumne, Antonio Coronel took out 45 ounces the first day, another found a 12-ounce nugget, another secured 52 pounds in eight days, and a Sonoran known as Chino Tirador spent a short day cleaning out a pocket with a horn spoon and piled a tray with so much clean gold that he could hardly lift it. To be sure, not every miner fared that well but the average return seems to have been approximately an ounce a day.

Shallow mining was characteristic of 1848. Prospectors overran practically the entire area that was to be worked in the next decade but confined themselves to scratching the surface. With pan and rocker they washed the gravel convenient to the streams mentioned above. At dry diggings such as Auburn, Hangtown, and Sonora they creviced with pick, knife, and horn spoon and carried the pay dirt to water or else winnowed it by dry washing. Scarcity of silver coin resulted in a very low price for gold, $6 to $8 an ounce being common, while abundance of gold and shortage of supplies, particularly toward the end of the season, bred high prices for all commodities. Fantastic quotations could be cited: flour, $800 a barrel; whisky, $100 a gallon; hire of a rocker, $150 a day. Even the forty-niners were less prodigal.

Although the miners were beyond the effective reach of the arm of the law, the season of '48 was remarkably free from crime. The accounts all mention the safety with which equipment, supplies, and gold were left lying around unguarded. One reason was that the forty-eighters, drawn largely from California, continued as friends and neighbors. Another was that honest toil was yielding such high returns; still another, that the mining region was not yet crowded. That claim jumping very seldom occurred is one proof of this obvious proposition: the few thousand miners of '48 were spread over the same area occupied by several times that number in the following years. A measure of credit should go to Mason for his action invalidating the Mexican system of denouncing mining claims. Had a few individuals attempted to file on the best diggings, much friction would have developed. Already the miners were showing themselves capable of working out their own code of mining regulations and of punishing such crimes as were committed. Only two hangings are on record for 1848. That one victim was French and the other Spanish suggests that race prejudice was already in evidence.

The mining population for 1848 has been grossly overestimated by some writers. In May there were only a few hundred at work, by July 3,000 or 4,000, and Colton's estimate of 50,000 at the end of the season must be scaled down to 8,000 or 10,000. California contributed the majority but the contagion spread rapidly over the Pacific area. Oregon sent some 1,500 prospectors, and Hawaii and Mexico sent perhaps 2,500.

The Trek of the Forty-Niners

Gradually the excitement spread to eastern United States and Europe. By August and September, California letters telling of the gold discovery had been printed in various eastern papers. As had happened in California, however, the first reports were met with polite or raucous incredulity, and months passed before the nation began to believe. Finally attention was riveted by the arrival of official messengers from California. The Navy sent E. F. Beale by way of Hawaii, Peru, Panama, and Jamaica, and Governor Mason sent Lt. Lucien Loeser by way of Mazatlán, Veracruz, and New Orleans with his report and a tea caddy containing $3,000 worth of gold. In his message to Congress on December 5 Polk took official notice of the discovery, and his words became the signal for a stampede.

The news came opportunely in the midst of the period of postwar adjustment. The War with Mexico, to be sure, was not a great upheaval, but thousands of soldiers had been mustered out recently, many had not yet found peacetime employment, and others were dissatisfied with a humdrum existence and longed for new adventures. For them California gold mining had a compelling appeal, but the "yellow fever" did not confine itself to former soldiers. Farmers, shopkeepers, clerks, physicians, and politicians caught it too, not to mention "the briefless lawyer, the starving student, the quack, the idler, the harlot, the gambler, the hen-pecked husband, the disgraced."

California could be reached by three principal routes, Cape Horn, Panama, or overland. For New Englanders the sea route was the natural one, both from habit and for convenience. Ships were numerous, seafaring men even more so, and, thanks to the otter trade, the hide trade, and whaling, there were many men expert in the voyage to California. Astute shipowners withdrew their vessels from other commerce, some 71 from whaling, for example. They fitted these vessels to carry Argonauts to California and then, after the crews had deserted at San Francisco, wondered how to get their ships home. Other New Englanders formed joint-stock companies, bought vessels, provisioned them, selected ship officers, and sailed to California. Such a group was the Boston and California Mining Company whose members were exhorted by President Edward Everett of Harvard to go to California "with the Bible in one hand and your New England civilization in the other and make your mark on the people and country." In nine months 549 vessels arrived at San Francisco, many of course from Europe, South America, Mexico, and Hawaii but more than half from the Atlantic seaboard.

Although travelers by sea vied with Panama men and overlanders in stigmatizing their particular path as the worst, the Cape Horn route probably offered the easiest journey. It may, indeed, have been too easy, for many passengers were so softened by four to eight months of inaction as to be unequal to the hard labor in the diggings. It was something of a white-collar route, favored by gamblers, politicians, saloonkeepers, and prostitutes, as well as by Bible-bearing Yankees. Every forty-niner by sea visited San Francisco before proceeding to the mines, and many went no farther. The sea route also made a material contribution in bulky machinery, furniture, and foodstuffs which could not have come overland. Included in the cargoes was a choice assortment of patent mining machinery destined for un-Christian burial on the flats below San Francisco. By accident some shovels and picks were included along with pianos, printing presses, and other practical appliances.

Potentially the Panama route was the quickest way to California. The Pacific Mail Steamship Company was just beginning regular service from New York to Chagres and from Panama to San Francisco. From the tentative schedule it appeared that the journey might be accomplished in 30 days, but the forty-niners found Panama a snare and a delusion. To get across the isthmus one had to depend on the caprice and satisfy the avarice of native boatmen and mule drivers, and on the Pacific side ships were woefully lacking. On its initial Pacific Mail voyage the *California* picked up 365 passengers, some of whom paid as much as $1,000 for steerage accommodations. Other vessels were pressed into service but an impatient horde was left stranded. Some set out in tiny sailboats; others are said to have resorted to dugout canoes for the 5,000-mile journey; the majority had to wait.

While they waited, insects, tropical storms and heat, poor food, and bad drinking water harassed them. Yellow fever brought death. Yet some of the more enterprising Americans, notably Collis P. Huntington, recognizing the opportunity that the situation afforded, prospered through catering to the wants of these thwarted emigrants. With the Panama route may be lumped several variations attempted by smaller numbers. But whether one crossed Nicaragua, Tehuantepec, or central Mexico, the problem of finding passage up the Pacific still remained. Congestion was less than at Panama but delay undiminished.

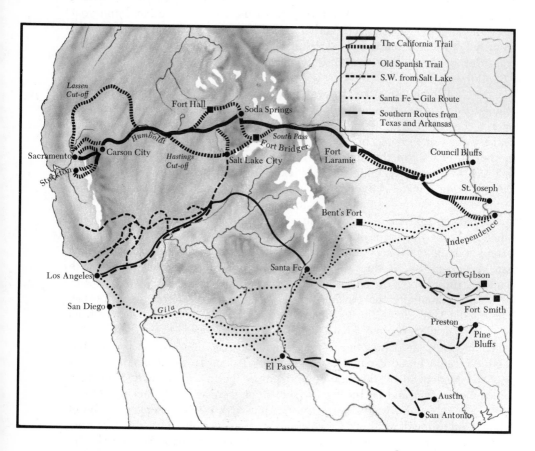

The California Trail
Old Spanish Trail
S.W. from Salt Lake
Santa Fe — Gila Route
Southern Routes from Texas and Arkansas

Overland to the Diggings

Almost 40,000 forty-niners followed these water and land-and-water routes. For most residents of the Mississippi Valley, however, the overland trails were nearer at hand and less forbidding. Editors in Texas, Arkansas, and Missouri vied in praising the routes from Corpus Christi through Mexico, across Texas to El Paso, from Fort Smith to El Paso, or down the Santa Fé Trail and on by the Gila or the Old Spanish Trail. These southern trails had the advantage of passing through a number of settled points in Mexico, on the Rio Grande, and in southern California where it would be possible to rest and reprovision. They were not subject to closure by winter snows; in fact, winter was probably the ideal season for crossing the southern desert into California. Opened by Spanish explorers and restless beaver trappers, these southern trails had been broadened and improved by the caravans of Santa Fé traders and by American military forces during the recent war. They attracted some 10,000 or 15,000 forty-niners, most of whom got through safely, however much they may have grumbled at delays and difficulties.

From Missouri north the consensus of opinion recommended the Platte–South Pass–Humboldt itinerary, which had been broken by the fur men, favored by the pioneer settlers, used in part by the Oregon missionaries and settlers and by the Mormons in their hegira to Salt Lake, and advertised by Frémont. Some 25,000 or 35,000 persons swarmed over this most direct route and made it known as the California Trail.

Although the major overland trails had been well worked out before 1849, few competent guides were available at the starting points along the Missouri, and reliable information was not available in print. Guidebooks were shortly produced to point the way and advise as to methods, yet it is a curious commentary that the best one was produced by a St. Louis newspaper writer, Joseph E. Ware, who had never been west of Missouri. Most of the forty-niners, lacking even such a guide, had to learn by experience the procedure of crossing the plains, the desert, and the mountains. According to a typical gold seeker, "There were few, if any, who possessed a definite knowledge of the road and, as a consequence, there was great suffering."

In outward appearance the migration of 1849 duplicated those of earlier years. The same prairie schooners and the same sorts of teams were used and the proportion of families to single men was only slightly less than in the earlier migration of agriculturists. In 1849, for that matter, many of the gold seekers carried the fundamental farming equipment with them. By reason of its very magnitude, however, this movement was basically different. In an earlier period the chief dangers had been from Indian attacks or from losing the way. Gold seekers on their way to California found the Indians harmless except for depredations on livestock along the Humboldt, and, as for getting lost, the only ones to go astray did so voluntarily.

Shortcuts, to be sure, lured the emigrants repeatedly, usually with unfortunate results. One such experience was on the shortcut or detour southwest from Salt Lake. Late season emigrants were advised to take that roundabout route rather than risk being snowed in as had happened to the Donner party. When Jefferson Hunt agreed to go as guide, enough forty-niners to make a 107-wagon train accepted the proposition. En route another Mormon overtook them and enticed most of them to turn off on another shortcut more directly westward. They soon ran into very rough country, broke up into many small groups, some shifting to packing and others struggling on with their wagons. A few returned to Salt Lake; others went back to Hunt's trail and straggled on into Los Angeles.

Others wandered into a below–sea-level desert basin which they named Death Valley. A dozen or more lost their lives not far from this spot. One small group, the Bennett–Arcane party, pitched camp in the valley and waited while two young teamsters pushed on to San Fernando, obtained a mule and two horses and a small quantity of food, and went back into the desert to bring out the imperiled men, women, and children. Lewis Manly's *Death Valley in '49*, a gold-rush classic, is a reminiscent account by one of the heroes in this rescue.

Lassen's Cut-off, from the Humboldt across Black Rock Desert to a northern pass, Pit River, and the upper Sacramento, lured ten or a dozen wagon trains. The most voluminous of all gold-rush diarists, J. Goldsborough Bruff, wintered and almost starved in the mountains on this route. Although some improvements were achieved by similar experiments, Sublette's Cut-off, for instance, the usual result was that voiced by Alonzo Delano concerning the Lassen Cut-off:

> Instead of avoiding the desert, instead of the promised water, grass, and a better road, we were in fact upon a more dreary and wider waste, without either grass or water, and with a harder road before us. . . . We had been inveigled there by false reports and misrepresentations.

Diaries and journals make much of the great concourse of people on the trail, of how each night's camp was made within sight of other campfires, of how the migration resembled a large city on the move. Delano gives this picture of the great trek:

> For miles, to the extent of vision, an animated mass of beings broke upon our view. Long trains of wagons with their white covers were moving slowly along, a multitude of horsemen were prancing on the road, companies of men were traveling on foot, and although the scene was not a gorgeous one, yet the display of banners from many wagons, and the multitude of armed men, looked as if a mighty army was on its march.

Exhaustion of the grass supply and ravages of cholera, the two most serious problems facing the forty-niners, were products of the crowded trail. At many camping sites where former caravans had found luxuriant pasturage the grass was cropped clean by the cattle of the earliest forty-niners and later parties found none. Then there were certain mendacious individuals who fired the grass as a deliberate hindrance to those behind, apparently hoping thereby

Death Valley

David Packwood

to reduce competition in the diggings. Nightly detours or side trips of two or three or four miles became the rule for the hindmost parties. From the Missouri to the Rockies the ravages of cholera were frightful. Men were struck suddenly. Some died after two or three hours of violent chills and fever; others lingered between life and death for days or weeks. Medical attention was seldom to be had, and relatives were rarely on hand to care for the afflicted. Supposed friends occasionally abandoned their companions, but in other instances utter strangers went out of their way to minister to those in distress.

Fortunately the cholera did not cross the Continental Divide; mountain fever took its place as the principal ailment and then it too was left behind. But the road became worse. The Platte Crossing, the alkaline lakes, Sublette's Cut-off with its 35 miles without water, the Green River Crossing—these earlier crises paled before the Humboldt. In its valley the forty-niners, excepting those

185

who had circled south of Great Salt Lake, had their first real taste of desert travel. It was hot and dusty. The landscape was cheerless and devoid of vegetation except for a little grass and a few small willows at the immediate margin of the river. As the grass along the south bank was exhausted, many of the later travelers had to cross the stream nightly to gather grass for their cattle, and these discomforts and annoyances made the Humboldt the butt of their grumbling, as numerous diaries attest. Argonaut John Steele opined that this was "the neighborhood of the rich man's hell"; versifying his salute, Horace Belknap started off in this vein,

> Meanest and muddiest, filthiest stream
> most cordially I hate you;

and the average Argonaut would have been ready to endorse Horace Greeley's observation, "Here famine sits enthroned, and waves his sceptre over a dominion expressly made for him."

The Humboldt Valley had its shortcomings, yet as an attenuated oasis stretching most of the way across the Nevada desert it made possible the use of this overland route. Unfortunately, the river terminated in the "Sink," beyond which lay 40 miles of unrelieved desert before one reached the Carson River or the Truckee. Because men and animals were weakened and worn out by the rigors of the long trail, the desert crossing was the more difficult. Milus Gay, one of the more restrained diarists, described it in these terms:

> Continuing across the Desert got across to Carsonville on Carson River about 4 p.m. 12 or 15 miles of the latter part of the Journey being sandy was very hard on our cattle the distance across is perhaps about 40 miles— Such destruction of property as I saw across the Desert I have never seen I should think I passed the carcases of 1200 head of cattle and horses and a great many waggons—Harneses—cooking utensils—tools water casks &c. &c. at a moderate estimate the amount I would think the property cost in the U.S. $50,000. We also see many men on the point of starvation beging for bread. We stopped an hour in this wagon and tented ville. bought 2 lb Beef for which we paid $1—and eat it all for supper. went up some 3 or 4 miles and encamped Grass scarce ☞ (N. B. Water 8 miles from C[arson] R[iver] sold for $1 gallon.)

After tarrying briefly to recruit their cattle on the luxuriant grasses at the eastern base of the Sierra, the emigrants hurried on. Several routes were available but there was not much choice. The route by the Truckee and Donner Pass was in some respects the easiest but in ill-repute because of the Donner tragedy. The Truckee could be followed to Henness Pass and the Yuba, or one could ascend the Carson to either Johnson's Pass or Carson Pass and Placerville on the American, or one could go up the Walker to Sonora Pass and the Stanislaus. By any route the rocky fords and steep ascent made it hard pulling for man and beast. Some wagons and much baggage were taken no farther. Adding to the difficulty, winter set in earlier than usual but, thanks to the energetic measures of relief directed by Major Rucker of the United States Army, duplication of the Donner tragedy was averted.

The migration of 1850 was a repetition differing only in detail. The number was as great, the cholera was worse, ferry service was now available at a dozen rivers along the way, and the regular trail along the Humboldt was under water as the result of most unusual rains. The desert took its accustomed toll, and again California relief agencies, this time managed by William Waldo of Sacramento, saved thousands from impending disaster in the Sierra.

In the Diggings

These overlanders plunged immediately into mining. They imitated the old-timers' use of pick and shovel, pan and cradle. Even when the more efficient long tom and sluice were introduced, they found that gold mining was backbreaking business. One moved as much dirt as a ditch digger, frequently standing in icy water and under a broiling sun. There was excitement, of course, and any day might bring a rich prize, but the excitement was a temptation to overwork and to neglect such prosaic tasks as cooking. The miner's home was an uncomfortable tent or shanty and his clothing was nondescript and often inadequate protection against the elements.

Miners at Work with Long Toms

From a contemporary lettersheet

The rewards, furthermore, were not only uncertain but on the average unsatisfactory. The "pound diggings" of 1848 were succeeded by the "ounce diggings" of 1849 and 1850, and thereafter came a further decline. The statistics are incomplete and conflicting, but it has been calculated that the mean return after 1850 was about $2 a day per man. Apart from the few who struck it tremendously rich, the wisest forty-niners were those who turned to saloonkeeping or merchandising or hauling or farming or dishwashing, where the compensation was not only surer but higher.

Frank Marryat offers this eyewitness description of an active camp:

A turn of the road presented a scene of mining life, as perfect in its details as it was novel in its features. Immediately beneath us the swift river glided tranquilly, though foaming still from the great battle which a few yards higher up, it had fought with a mass of black obstructing rocks. On the banks was a village of canvas that the winter rains had bleached to perfection, and round it the miners were at work at every point. Many were waist deep in the water, toiling in bands to construct a race and dam to turn the river's course; others were entrenched in holes, like grave diggers, working down to the "bedrock." Some were on the brink of the stream washing out "prospects" from tin pans or wooden "batteaus"; and others worked in company with the long tom, by means of water sluices artfully conveyed from the river. Many were coyote-ing in subterranean holes, from which from time to time their heads popped out, like those of squirrels to take a look at the world; and a few with drills, dissatisfied with nature's work, were preparing to remove large rocks with gunpowder. All was life, merriment, vigour and determination, as this part of the earth was being turned inside out to see what it was made of. . . .

Small patches of garden surrounded the village which bore so palpably the stamp of cheerfulness and happy industry, that I was disappointed on learning that its name was "Murderers' Bar."

A glance at the miners' amusements reveals that the favorites were drinking, gambling, and dancing, with certain men delegated for the ladies' parts. Dissipation and roistering, however, were less prevalent than is sometimes represented. Horse racing, cockfights, and practical jokes were frequent. Evenings were devoted to conversation and song, some of the ballads being only less distinctive than those in the cowboy's repertory. Sundays were largely given over to frolic (and washing and baking), but many of the miners set an example of rectitude with debating societies or even religious services. The theater also came to the mines. There was a regular circuit from Rabbit Creek to Mariposa, played by such celebrities as Lotta Crabtree, Lola Montez, Katherine Sinclair, and Edwin Booth.

The effects of the gold rush were not confined to gold mining. As on most mining frontiers, many who came to prospect never washed a pan of gravel, and others experimented only briefly in the diggings before turning to farming, merchandising, transportation, and other familiar work. Some were

Sunday Morning at the Mines

Charles Nahl
E. B. Crocker Art Gallery, Sacramento

not physically equal to the hard life in the mines; some became disgusted with their luck and threw up the work. Enough miners were deserting the diggings to afford William Harlan a profitable business buying their implements for a song and reselling them to greenhorns at California prices. Some of these disappointed ones returned to the States, but vast numbers remained in the West, the majority in California and particularly at San Francisco. The urban forty-niner developed as great a significance as his red-shirted brother of the placers.

When gold was discovered, San Francisco was a village boasting two hotels, two wharves nearly completed, and 812 persons. Early in the summer of 1848 the population shrank almost to zero; everyone had gone to the mines, and the town was dead. It revived rapidly under the impetus of hundreds of thousands of dollars in gold pouring in from the diggings. The miners wanted supplies, and San Franciscans assumed the twin responsibilities of providing supplies and an outlet for the miners' gold. Although business flourished during the last months of 1848, the next year saw the real boom with 40,000 Argonauts avalanching upon the town.

No amount of stretching and crowding would make facilities planned for the accommodation of 800 commodious for the sudden throng. Hotels and lodging houses put 10 or 20 men in a room and charged exorbitant prices. Rents skyrocketed to $40,000 a year for the El Dorado gambling saloon tent and $3,000 a month for a small store. Other prices jumped correspondingly. A meal

Placerville

Lithograph by Quirot & Co.

cost $3 or more, drinks 25¢ and 50¢, and coppers and small coins were virtually unknown. Wages went up in proportion. Unskilled labor commanded $10 to $12 a day.

Excitement surcharged the entire atmosphere. Everyone was in a hurry. Loans were for a month rather than a year. An abnormal fraction of the population was in the streets or the gambling saloons, adding to the bustle. Gambling itself was rapid-fire, for the tables were crowded and others were anxious to make their bets. The regal splendor of the fifties was not yet attained, but plate-glass mirrors, prism chandeliers, ornate bars, and appropriate paintings had already arrived.

Whereas San Francisco had at least a municipal existence prior to the gold rush, several other communities owed their origin to it. Such were Grass Valley, Auburn, Placerville, Columbia, and Sonora, which flourished mightily and then with the eclipse of mining went into as sudden a decline. Sacramento and Stockton also came suddenly into existence on the flood of gold but demonstrated commercial, industrial, and political reasons for continued existence after the passing of the mining era.

The rise of San Francisco and these satellite cities was only one consequence of the gold rush. Others included the drastic alteration of the price structure in California and to a lesser extent in the world at large. Commerce, agriculture, lumbering, and countless other pursuits were greatly stimulated in northern California and up and down the Pacific coast. New arguments and incentives were created for transportation development. California's population was multiplied many times over. Additional foreign strains intensified its cosmopolitan character, while the predominance of Argonauts from the States greatly accelerated the change from Mexican to American society. The worldwide interest in California, so suddenly created, reduced the intellectual as well as the physical isolation of the province. Most important, perhaps, were the psychological consequences, the unrestrained and masculine society of gold-rush California, the willingness to believe that the fabulous could be realized, and a fortification of the historical heritage as a unifying factor for all Californians. Gold, without question, exerted a powerful influence on the state's history.

For Further Reading

JOHN W. CAUGHEY, *Gold Is the Cornerstone* (1948).

H. H. BANCROFT, *California Inter Pocula* (1888).

E. L. EGENHOFF, *The Elephant as They Saw It* (1949).

RODMAN W. PAUL, *The California Gold Discovery* (1965).

California Historical Society, *California Gold Discovery* (1947).

JOSEPH E. WARE, *The Emigrants' Guide to California* (1849; reprinted 1932).

E. GOULD BUFFUM, *Six Months in the Gold Mines* (1850; reprinted 1958).

BAYARD TAYLOR, *Eldorado* (1850).

OSCAR LEWIS, *Sea Routes to the Gold Fields* (1949).

ALONZO DELANO, *Life on the Plains and among the Diggings* (1854).

G. W. READ and RUTH GAINES, *Gold Rush: The Journals, Drawings, and Other Papers of J. Goldsborough Bruff* (1944).

W. L. MANLY, *Death Valley in '49* (1894).

RODMAN W. PAUL, *California Gold* (1947, 1965).

LOUISE AMELIA KNAPP SMITH CLAPPE, *The Shirley Letters* (1854; reprinted 1922, 1933, 1949).

C. H. SHINN, *Mining Camps* (1885).

C. L. CANFIELD, *The Diary of a Forty-niner* (1906), fictional.

CAUGHEY, *California Heritage*, 188–245.

chapter twelve

Mushrooming Economy

When I awoke in the morning, and looked from my windows over the city of San Francisco, with its store-houses, towers, and steeples; its court-houses, theatres, and hospitals; its daily journals; its well-filled learned professions; its fortresses and light-houses; its wharves and harbor, with their thousand-ton clipper ships, more in number than London or Liverpool sheltered that day, itself one of the capitals of the American Republic, and the sole emporium of a new world, the awakened Pacific; when I looked across the bay to the eastward, and beheld a beautiful town on the fertile, wooded shores of the Contra Costa, and steamers, large and small, the ferryboats to the Contra Costa, and capacious freighters and passenger-carriers to all parts of the great bay and its tributaries, with lines of their smoke in the horizon,—when I saw all these things, and reflected on what I once was and saw here, and what now surrounded me, I could scarcely keep my hold on reality at all, or the genuineness of anything, and seemed to myself like one who had moved in "worlds not realized."

Richard Henry Dana,
"Twenty-Four Years After,"
at the time of his 1859 visit to California

1848
to
1875

Most of the Argonauts had no intention of becoming Californians. They came to make their pile and then to return to civilization in the States, Europe, Sonora, or from wherever they had come. Many held to this purpose. The earliest instance was in July, 1848, when a party of twoscore Mormons, including several of Marshall's associates at Coloma, turned their backs on the gold area and set out over the Sierra and across the desert to join their brethren at Great Salt Lake. The overland forty-niners met a few other parties headed east. When the onset of winter closed down most of the diggings, the departures by ship and by southern trails mounted. In the fifties the number leaving was much greater; the Panama route was the favorite and passage from San Francisco was frequently at a premium. The magnitude of this backwash of the gold rush is borne out by the

San Francisco Waterfront

The Bancroft Library

records of the transportation companies and by the large number of forty-niner diaries that have come to light in the East. Its significance lay first of all in the attitude of many of the gold seekers toward California, and secondly in the wide dissemination of information about the state.

Nevertheless, numerous as were the miners who came and went, a larger number came and stayed. By the end of 1849 population exceeded 100,000; in 1852 the state counted 224,435, and in 1860 the official census showed 380,015. This sudden increase in a province that for generations had lain practically dormant was at once symptomatic of and conducive to far-reaching change. The state shortly acquired among other things a new political setup, a new social structure, and a new economy.

Mining Techniques

Fundamental to this economy was gold mining itself. For a while almost every Californian was a gold miner, and as late as 1863 mining employed more of the state's workers than any other pursuit. Production also held up well. The peak was attained in the early fifties, followed by a gradual tapering off. In the first decade and a half, however, the average annual output was $50 million. After 1865 gold production displayed remarkable stability at approximately one third of this amount annually. Although in recent years other minerals, particularly petroleum, have far overshadowed gold, to the end of the century gold was the unchallenged leader in the state's mining industry.

In the first hectic years placer mining predominated. Techniques

Ground Sluicing

From a contemporary lettersheet

improved rapidly. The pan and cradle were superseded by the long tom and it in turn by the sluice, which became the essential apparatus in all gold washing. A standard form developed, each section of open trough 12 feet long, 1½ or 2 feet in depth, and 16 or 18 inches wide (though sometimes wider). Sections or boxes of this pattern were fitted together to make a sluice 200, 300, or even 1,000 feet long, with a drop of from 8 to 20 inches per section. Riffle bars or cleats were wedged in transversely, or diagonally, to catch the heavy gold, and mercury was thrown in to amalgamate with the smaller particles of floating gold. A 2-inch stream of water coursed down the sluice. Every 6 to 10 days the run was stopped in order to remove the riffle bars and clean up the accumulated gold.

In the more elementary form of sluice mining, the gold-bearing clay, sand, or gravel was shoveled into the upper sections of the sluice from adjacent bars or riverbank deposits. Often it was brought more laboriously from a greater distance, from a deposit from which the topsoil had first to be stripped off or from a streambed exposed by damming and diverting the water. The hydraulic method, feasible only in hill country, was the easiest way to deliver gold-bearing dirt to the sluice. With a nozzled canvas hose or iron pipe delivering 50 or more feet of water pressure half a dozen men could wash more dirt than a couple of hundred wielding pick and shovel. The method was so cheap that it could be employed profitably on dirt yielding as little as one cent to the cubic foot, which would have been considerably beneath the attention of the non-hydraulic miners. Popularity of the hydraulic method is revealed by statistics of 1854 which indicate 4,493 miles of ditches delivering water for mining operations.

Almost from the beginning, the placer miners were eager to work back to the source of the gold. An early and pseudoscientific theory was that a volcanic eruption had splattered gold over the area of the diggings. Most of the miners, however, believed that it had washed down from veins or from a single vein and that sooner or later this mother lode would be brought to light. The vein theory was ridiculed by Dr. Philip T. Tyson, the first geologist of reputation to report on the gold region, but before the end of 1849 quartz or lode mining had been started on Frémont's Mariposa grant, and many reckoned this hard-rock branch of mining most likely to endure.

The first step in quartz mining was that of quarrying. At Mariposa and the other early mines the deposits were surface or shallow; later, auriferous quartz was pursued a mile or more beneath the surface. The next step was to powder the quartz. Various devices were employed, ranging from the Mexican arrastra, in which mules pulled a heavy stone drag, and the Chilean mill, in which heavy wheels rotated around a pivot, to batteries of square and rotary stamps. The latter, run by steam or water power, operated on the pile-driver principle with a straight fall or a twirling motion. The final step was to mix the powdered ore with water and mercury, and then by gravity process to separate the amalgamated metal. Although the early quartz mills were so inefficient as to bring the method into disrepute, improvements were soon made. By 1863 one third and by the end of the decade more than half of the gold mined was from quartz.

Much of the mercury required in California gold mining was produced within the state. The New Almaden mine near San Jose had been opened in the Mexican period and named after the famous quicksilver mine in southwestern Spain. Under the impetus of increased demand and price the working of this mine was boosted until production reached 220,000 pounds a month. Both the mining and the reduction of the ore were fairly simple processes. The ore occurred in large and irregular masses rather than in veins. For reduction it was placed in a furnace. When heated the mercury was driven off in gaseous form and recovered by passing through a series of condensing chambers opening into each other alternately at top and bottom. In the period here under discussion California's other mineral resources were almost entirely neglected.

Trade and Freighting

Of the three quarters of a billion dollars' worth of gold, a conservative estimate of what was produced in California up to 1865, an indeterminate fraction was carried out of the state by the miners returning eastward. A much larger quantity changed hands at least once in California. The effects of this tremendous increase in purchasing power and of the accompanying spurt in the number of customers and consumers challenge the imagination. Stores sprang up throughout the diggings to cater to the miners' wants. At the outset many stores stocked only the basic commodities, salt pork and beef, flour, and whisky. As quickly as circumstances permitted, however, the list was extended. The storekeepers, it was generally agreed, were surer to profit than the diggers of gold. Perhaps on that account there was a tendency to look down upon them as a class. Although John Bidwell, Charles M. Weber, Alonzo Delano, and certain other storekeepers were highly respected, the majority were not held in such high esteem; in fact, the Yankee merchant was reckoned not much above the professional gambler, another familiar figure in the diggings.

Closely associated with the storekeepers were the freighters who replenished their stocks. By wagon or pack train over abominable roads and the roughest of trails they moved a varied cargo from Sacramento and Stockton to the most remote mining camps. They took the first consignments of gold away from the diggings and by easy transition became the pioneers in mail, express, and banking services. Although superseded by railroads, buses, and trucks, the freighters were less transitory than those who made their living by hunting game for the miners or by driving up cattle and sheep to be butchered at the diggings.

San Francisco and Sacramento soon boasted wholesale and retail merchants who became the commercial czars of California. The fortunes of the "Big Four" of Central Pacific fame were laid on foundations of this sort of commerce, and the well-known stories of Collis P. Huntington's warehouse, his dealings with ship captains, and his corner on shovels amply illustrate the complexities, the uncertainties, and the ethics of this first big business in California. At first there was no such thing as ordering goods from the East; merchants merely dealt in whatever commodities New England, New York, or foreign shippers had seen fit

Freighter on the Placerville–Carson Route

Vischer's Miscellaneous Views, 1861

to send to San Francisco. The result was an unpredictable schedule of prices. Of some goods there was an oversupply, hence the San Francisco sidewalks paved with tierces of tobacco, sacks of flour, and in another instance with cook stoves. Again, a dearth of some other commodity resulted in a price that seemed exorbitant even to Californians. A frequent comment was that the spread between wholesale and retail prices was out of all proportion.

Besides the round-the-Horn shipments the movement of goods to gold-rush California involved many other avenues. Wagon trains on the overland trails brought household goods, tools, and implements that in the aggregate were important. These trains and more formal drives brought horses, cattle, and sheep. Ships from Puget Sound and the Columbia delivered lumber, while the agricultural settlements in the Willamette Valley sent eggs, garden produce, and grain. Dried beef—charqui, or jerky—came from Chile, and diversified cargoes were sent from Hawaii and the Orient. In 1849 California was producing few of the things required by her new population. It is said, for example, that San Francisco's soiled linen was sometimes sent to Hawaii or China for laundering. Soon, however, local producers and enterprisers came to the rescue. Existing branches of agriculture and industry were stimulated, and new branches were started to supply the gold seekers. In many instances it was found that a much broader market existed or could be developed.

Agriculture

Cattle raising was the branch of agriculture that could most readily be expanded to meet the new opportunity. Cattle which had found no market at $5 and $6 a head brought as much as $500 at the mining camps. The price did not long remain at this fantastic figure, but in the fifties beeves often brought from $50 to $100 a head. With its Mexican ranchos California was well grounded in the cattle business. Additional herds were driven in from Texas and the Midwest, several hundred head in 1850 and as many as 40,000 a year in the middle fifties. It was a "long drive" antedating the more famous one from Texas to the northern plains, and as beef cattle the California breed was somewhat improved. Southern California rancheros suddenly became prosperous, though the easily acquired wealth was in most instances as rapidly dissipated. In the San Joaquin Valley, Henry Miller began to build up the more enduring Miller and Lux ranches and fortune. From less than 300,000 head of cattle in the state in 1848 there was an increase to 3 million head in 1860. In the great drought of 1863–64 cattle died by the tens of thousands. The distress of the cattlemen was aggravated by the extremely high interest rates that then obtained. In 1870 the official inventory showed only 630,000 head of cattle in the state.

At the missions sheep had been almost as numerous as cattle, but after secularization they fell into disfavor, and in 1849 there were less than 20,000 in the state. With the miners providing a market for mutton, the industry revived. There were drives from Chihuahua, from New Mexico by way of the Old Spanish Trail, and from the American Midwest by way of the Salt Lake–Los Angeles route, with Kit Carson, Wilson Flint, and the Bixbys as some of the better-known participants. The peak years seem to have been 1853 and 1856, when 135,000 head and 200,000 head, respectively, were brought in. By 1860 the state had 1 million sheep, yielding, however, only 2 million pounds of wool. Importation of blooded stock brought an improvement, and by 1870 the number of animals had increased to 2.75 million and the wool clip to 11 million pounds.

A Bonanza in Wheat

Another mission activity which revived and expanded in the golden era was cultivation of the small grains. The rancheros of the postsecularization period, being less abundantly supplied with laborers than the friars had been, allowed grain cultivation to lapse. Sutter was sowing large fields of wheat in the Sacramento Valley on the eve of the gold discovery, but he also found the labor supply inadequate. The farming of the fifties was more directly an outgrowth of Sutter's agriculture than of the earlier cultivation at the southern California missions. The local market created by the hungry gold diggers led to a "back-to-the-farm" movement. The lower San Joaquin and Sacramento valleys and northern California provided the lands first brought under cultivation, though subsequently the San Joaquin Valley became the center of California's

Threshing Barley, Simi Valley, 1880

Los Angeles County Museum of Natural History

wheat belt. California soil and climate proved most congenial for wheat production. The yield per acre surpassed the midwestern average, and the dry summers prolonged the harvest season and made the wheat very dry and hard. It was unimpaired by shipment to distant markets, and flour milled from it was preferred in tropical markets. Another advantage was that ships which had been sailing from San Francisco in ballast could now take cargoes of wheat. In the late sixties the business boomed, with the acreage trebling within half a dozen years. In 1850 wheat production was estimated at 17,000 bushels. It rose to 5.9 million bushels in 1860, to 16 million in 1870, and to 40 million in 1890.

The characteristics of this farming were large holdings, mining of the soil with no rotation of crops, a high degree of mechanization, emphasis on export around the Horn to Liverpool, and speculative returns because of the uncontrolled variables in the cost of seed, sacks, and shipping and in price on the Liverpool market.

California's wheat frontier parallels the better publicized prairie-farming frontier in the belt from Texas to Saskatchewan. It had a character of its own in more absentee ownership and in several other features. In a procession of new machinery from the Stockton gangplow to giant steam-powered combines it ran a jump or two ahead of the midcontinent wheat belt. Rail rates meant little to the Californians and elevator middlemen were not in the picture. The California wheat moved in the sack from farm to flatcar or barge to the hold of the ocean transports.

The best-known entrepreneurs were Dr. Hugh J. Glenn, who had the equivalent of an old California rancho, some 55,000 acres, in production along the Sacramento, and Isaac Friedlander, who, besides being a major grower, was the leading ship charterer, seed and sack dealer, and handler of selling at Liverpool. Many farmers were convinced that their hard work was piling up profits primarily for Friedlander the Grain King.

In 1873–74, through the State Grange which then had 104 locals, the disgruntled farmers tried to band together in a loose-knit cooperative pledged to ship and sell through a broker of their own. They also pledged to buy their sacks through this agent, and, the prospects appearing good for higher prices later in the season, they agreed to hold off selling in order to take advantage of that rise. Everything went wrong. More ships were chartered than the cooperating farmers were ready to fill, and Friedlander picked them up at reduced rates. The sack monopolists cut prices and spoiled that investment. The market did not rise and the returns were disappointing. The cooperative dissolved and Friedlander resumed his dominant position. As Rodman Paul has recited, the eulogist at Friedlander's funeral in 1878 was not far wrong when he said, "He gathered the grain crops of California in the hollow of his hand."

Wheat growing continued to expand, reaching its peak in the early nineties. It required many teams of horses or mules at planting time and harvest time. The labor demands also were seasonal and held down by the mechanization. This was a spectacular branch of agriculture, and the number of ships filled in a year rose as high as 500.

Wine Making

California's suitability for a wide variety of other crops was thoroughly proven in the fifties and sixties. In 1854, for example, B. D. Wilson wrote to his brother in Mississippi that Los Angeles County produced "every species of grain and fruits in the greatest abundance." To prove his point he listed the different fruits growing on a farm he had just purchased: grapes, oranges, pears, apricots, peaches, apples, almonds, English walnuts, cherries, figs, olives, quinces, and plums, all growing so luxuriantly that he did not know which grew best.

In his *Resources of California* a few years later John S. Hittell catalogued the state's subordinate agricultural products: oats, maize, hay, potatoes, kitchen vegetables in great variety, berries of all sorts, and fruits of the several kinds listed above. The potatoes he described as half again as large as those in the States, and he vouched for a 10-pound carrot, a 26-pound turnip, a 53-pound cabbage, a 118-pound beet, and a 260-pound squash. At the time of his writing in 1863 half the state's 2,500 orange trees were in the grove of William Wolfskill at Los Angeles. Much of this horticulture was carried over from the mission period, but Johnny Appleseeds were not lacking, bringing in additional stock and new varieties from the East. In California, fruit trees were more precocious, practically every vegetable was in season twice as long as in the East, and San Francisco had a year-round supply of strawberries from the Santa Clara

Valley. In the fifties and sixties, however, all these foodstuffs, though grown commercially, were limited to the California market. Consequently, they did not rival the big four in the state's agriculture: beef cattle, sheep, wheat, and barley.

Through its associated industry of wine making, grape culture offered better possibilities. As a heritage from the Franciscans, California possessed a number of plantings of "mission grapes," hardy vines and good bearers, though not extraordinary in quality. This was the stock on which the earliest commercial vintners depended, notably Luis Vignes of Los Angeles. By 1842 he was doing a thriving business in supplying northern California and the coastal trade with wine and brandy. After the gold rush created an enlarged market, others entered the business. It was profitable because vines could be brought into production more rapidly than fruit trees. There was good demand for table grapes, and the derivatives, wine and brandy, had the great advantages of being compact and relatively imperishable. The assessment records indicate 1 million bearing vines by 1855, 8 million by 1860, and nearly 28 million by 1870. In 1870 production approached 2 million gallons of wine. One fourth of the total, mostly in sweet wines, was from Los Angeles County; a sixth, mostly in dry wines, came from Sonoma County.

Meanwhile, sanguine hopes arose that the ideal industry for California would be silk raising. In 1864 the legislature offered a bounty of $250 for every planting of 500 two-year-old mulberry trees and $300 for every 100,000 salable cocoons. Under this impetus some 10 million trees were set out by 1869. The leading enthusiast was Louis Prévost. He organized the California Silk Center Association, which bought some 8,500 acres in the Jurupa district (later to be called Riverside) and went in for sericulture on a grand scale. Predictions were freely made that silk would become the state's most valuable product. Silkworm eggs sold for a time at $10 an ounce, and a few men profited greatly. When Prévost died and the legislature, somewhat alarmed over the drain on the state treasury, withdrew the bounty offer, agriculturists turned unanimously from this glamorous fad.

Cotton also was in style for a brief season. In Civil War days William Workman and others made a few plantings. In 1876 Matthew Keller planted 60 acres in a field just north of what is now the University of Southern California campus. He got a good crop but found no satisfactory market, the experience of other cotton planters. The ambitiousness of their plans, however, was reflected in the formation of the California Cotton Growers and Manufacturers Association, which had 10,000 acres at Bakersfield and a colony of Negro cotton pickers imported from the South. These Negroes, however, preferred other work, and, since white labor was expensive and marketing difficult, California cotton growing was postponed for another half century.

Notwithstanding these failures California agriculture was shifting from the pastoral economy of the ranchos to a stress on cultivation of the soil. The droughts of the early sixties dealt a body blow to the cattle industry and the positive success with grain and grapes confirmed the shift. By 1872 the trend had advanced to the point where there was overpowering sentiment in favor of the "no-fence law," an act which placed the responsibility for the restraint of livestock upon their owners rather than upon the planters, who formerly had to fence other people's stock out of their fruit groves, vineyards, and grain fields. Characteristic of the shift from stock ranching was the experience of B. D. Wilson. In the fifties he had run thousands of head of cattle and sheep, but in 1873 he considered a herd of 100 cattle overlarge. The new agriculture included cattle and sheep but centered on grain and grapes and other fruits.

Expanding Industry

Hand in hand with the development in mining, commerce, and agriculture, manufacturing began to flourish in the northern towns. The discovery of gold, it will be recalled, had come about as a by-product of lumber manufacture sponsored by Sutter. The gold rush, though it wrought havoc with Sutter's affairs, returned the compliment to lumbering by creating a great demand for sawmill products. The placer miners required quantities of planks for their sluices, flumes, and wing dams. A special 12-foot plank, 2 inches thick, 14 inches at one end and 18 at the other, was turned out for sluice bottoms so that the sections could be fitted together without nails. Quartz miners also required timbers and planks for bracings in their shafts and tunnels. For building purposes also, lumber was the favored material, at least after San Francisco passed the canvas and paper stage. Railroad construction provided another important market for lumber, and, since barbed wire had not yet appeared on the scene, fencing called for many rails and planks as well as posts.

Mendocino and Humboldt counties boasted the largest mills and produced the most lumber, 35 and 30 million feet, respectively, in 1860. Most of

Logging Team in the Redwoods

C. C. Pierce Collection

it was redwood, sawed from logs averaging 4½ feet in diameter. Schooners from 150 to 300 tons transported the lumber to San Francisco. Santa Cruz County was next with 10 million feet a year, all redwood, much of it shipped to southern California. Santa Cruz lumber was distinguished also by the fact that much of it was split rather than sawed. For a skilled workman, redwood splits straight and smooth; consequently this technique was efficient for getting out fence posts, rails, rough planks, joists, beams, and shingles. More than one Argonaut found that he could make his pile more quickly and surely by splitting shingles in the Santa Cruz Mountains than by wielding pick and shovel in the diggings. Other sawmills, many of which were portable, operated in the Sierra forests, turning out lumber for the miners.

For flour the forty-niners provided an excellent market, but not until three or four years later was the raw material available in adequate quantities. The first two mills in the state, in fact, were largely engaged in remilling spoiled imported flour, but as wheat raising boomed, flour milling followed suit. The flinty character of the California wheat made the local flour excellent for shipment, even through the tropics, and, when the Crimean War and the Civil War handicapped older areas of flour production, the California industry was greatly stimulated. In the late sixties California flour was exported not only to the mining camps throughout the Rocky Mountain West but also to Japan and China, to the British Isles, and to continental Europe. By the end of the decade the state had over 200 mills, several capable of milling 1,000 barrels a day.

Of even wider distribution throughout the state was the business of wagon and carriage making. As a Spanish and Mexican province California had gotten along without such establishments, but with the coming of the Americans the wheeled-vehicle complex was introduced. The first wagon shops were crude because the state lacked hardwoods and foundries. Soon, however, wagon and carriage making was as universal as the automobile repair shop is today. The most famous names connected with the business were those of John Studebaker of Placerville, of subsequent fame as an Indiana manufacturer of wagons and automobiles; George P. Kimball of Oakland, who built a quarter-million-dollar factory in 1868; and Phineas Banning of Wilmington, whose specialty was coaches of the Concord type.

The abundant supply of cowhides, coupled with the great demand for heavy boots in the mines, harness and pack saddles in the freighting business, thoroughbraces on the Concord stages, and belting in all sorts of machine operations, suggested the erection of tanneries and leather-working establishments. The first large tanneries were on the San Lorenzo River in Santa Cruz County. San Francisco soon took first place and tanneries appeared at Sacramento, Benicia, and several other northern towns. The output was mostly heavy leather goods until Civil War days when an additional impetus was given the manufacture of shoes. In spite of the relatively high wage scale in California this industry flourished until the advent of hard times in the nineties.

Quartz mining in California, silver mining in Nevada, and excavation and tunneling for railroad construction created a heavy demand for explosives. When the Civil War made the continued importation of powder both dangerous and expensive, its manufacture was begun. The California Powder Works put up a $150,000 plant on the San Lorenzo River. The Pacific Powder Works in Marin County was even larger. In 1868 these two mills manufactured 1 million kegs of blasting powder. Contra Costa County boasted half a dozen smaller plants.

Textile mills were introduced at about the same time and under similar provocation. Those designed for cotton, such as the one William H. Rector built at Oakland in 1864, did not succeed chiefly because cotton raising did not flourish as expected. Manufacture of grain sacks out of jute from the Orient was temporarily more profitable, but the largest and most thriving mills were those turning out woolens. Of these the best known was the Mission Woolen Mills of San Francisco. Other plants were located at Marysville, Santa Rosa, and Sacramento.

Among industries of incidental importance in the fifties and sixties sugar refining and cigar making should be mentioned. The former industry used raw cane sugar from the islands of the Pacific and from China, though a number of unsuccessful efforts were made to promote sugarcane cultivation in southern California. In the early American period William T. Coleman and Claus Spreckels were the leading refiners. San Francisco was also the cigar-making center, with predominantly Chinese labor.

Of broader importance was ironworking. California did not furnish the raw material but brought it in at low cost as ballast on wheat ships. The state and the adjacent West, through the several industries mentioned above and especially through mining and railroad building, furnished a large market

Locomotive Calistoga Issuing from the
Vulcan Iron Works, San Francisco

Vischer's Miscellaneous Views, 1863

for cables, pipe, wire, pulleys, and machinery of various sorts. The Union, the Neptune, and the Vulcan Iron Works of San Francisco were the earliest large plants. Besides smaller products they turned out locomotives and iron riverboats.

Banking

Prior to 1848 California had had only rudimentary banking as carried on by the government account keepers, the prefects of the missions, the hide and tallow traders, who extended credits, and the Army and Navy quartermasters in the period of the conquest. As gold came into production, facilities for storing and transmitting it were called for, and as commerce and industry sprang up, some means of handling financial transactions was required. Merchants and saloonkeepers provided the first banking service, that of safekeeping the miners' sacks of gold. Then by easy transition were added the buying and selling of gold, the arranging for its transmission to the East, and the making of loans. The earliest banking was simply a side line to other businesses; soon, however, it became a business in itself. A number of Californians entered it, and eastern firms such as Adams and Company, Palmer, Cook and Company, and Page, Bacon and Company opened branches in the state.

The first banking was largely in the hands of inexperienced men and was entirely unregulated by the state. Remoteness from the financial centers of the world made the matter of remittance and exchange difficult and expensive. Nor were the unsettled conditions in California conducive to the most conservative banking practices. In consequence, the early record is full of irregularities. For half a decade most banks prospered; interest rates were from 2 to 5 per cent a month, and the miners did not object to a substantial charge on drafts on eastern banks. In 1855, however, a panic gripped San Francisco, which several banks could not weather. Most spectacular was the closing of Page, Bacon and Company. News of the failure of its St. Louis branch precipitated a run on the San Francisco house. For a week the bank met every demand but on February 23 was forced to close its doors. Other banks were affected, notably Adams and Company, whose crash was rendered all the more disquieting by reason of the eleventh-hour transfer of its remaining assets to Palmer, Cook and Company. Not until the sixties did California banking fully recover from the shock of 1855. Then its recovery was greatly assisted by the upsurge of local industry and agriculture and by the outpourings of the Nevada silver mines.

These early banks helped much less than might have been expected in the provision of a circulating medium of exchange. Out-of-state exchange was managed fairly well, though it was so expensive that California exporters often resorted to conversion of their receipts into commodities for shipment to San Francisco. Locally, the banks were not privileged to issue bank notes, and Californians had such an addiction to gold that it is probable such paper money would not have circulated anyhow. Throughout '48 and '49 most payments were in gold dust, weighed or guessed at, a pinch passing for a dollar. Then slugs of approximately three ounces passed for $50. Even after a government mint was established in San Francisco in 1854 much Mexican silver remained in use. In the sixties, when the rest of the nation was doing business chiefly in greenbacks, California scorned them and stuck to hard money, the favorite being the double eagle, the $20 gold piece.

The Comstock

California's financial history in this period was profoundly affected by the opening of the silver mines of Washoe, now called Nevada. For the better part of a decade after Marshall's discovery in 1848, mining had been confined to the California diggings, but in the late fifties prospectors began to turn up mineral wealth all over the mountainous West. There were strikes in Colorado and eastern Oregon, in Idaho and along the Fraser, in Arizona and Nevada, and eventually in Alaska and the Klondike. In many of these rushes Californians predominated, and for the majority of the new fields San Francisco was the logical supplier. Most intimate were the relations with Washoe and its Comstock Lode. California contributed most of the miners, supplied food, machinery, whisky, and even water, and in turn felt a Nevada influence upon its literature, commerce, and transportation, and particularly upon its banking and finance.

To Nevada history belongs the detailed story of the discovery of the Comstock, the working of the mines, the experiments conducted in milling the ore, the problems of mine drainage, cooling, and ventilation, and life in Virginia City. The discovery in 1859 followed several years of desultory gold panning. The eastward rush across the Sierra in the late fall of that year sorely overtaxed the accommodations of Virginia City and the other mining camps in the vicinity of Mt. Davidson, but nothing could daunt these men in the staking out of claims, the organization of companies, and the floating of stock. In the first season some 37 companies were organized with a stock issue exceeding $30 million, and in 1861 an additional 49 companies incorporated, all clustered on the slopes of Mt. Davidson, though some had no footage on the Comstock Lode.

Silver mining, the erstwhile gold seekers soon discovered, was a business entirely different from the operations of gold placers. It had a closer affinity to quartz mining but required even more elaborate machinery and heavier capital investment. Financing by sale of shares was thus the most obvious procedure, and San Francisco was the most convenient money mart. Mining stocks have a reputation for speculative character and sudden fluctuation. Under the most favorable circumstances those for the Comstock would have surged up and down because the vein unpredictably widened or pinched out, the miners worked in bonanza and then in borrasca, and there were floods, cave-ins, and fires to reduce still further the regularity of output. Other factors made the Washoe shares plummet wildly. Neither Washoe nor California had seen fit to provide any restrictions on stock issuance or exchange or any regulation on banking. The door was open for the most unscrupulous rigging of the market.

When mining first began on the Comstock, San Francisco bankers and investors had their fingers burned. They bought shares indiscriminately and then found to their chagrin that many of the properties were nowhere near the real lode. Other mines, however, were pouring out ore assaying from $50 to $2,000 a ton, such solid encouragement that investors could not be scared away permanently. For several years the strategically located mines all paid well. The ore was rich and located near the surface, mechanical difficulties encountered were surmounted successfully, and those who could raise the money did not hesitate to put millions into a mine's excavation, timbering, hoists, and pumps, hundreds of thousands into a mill, or tens of thousands into a Virginia City saloon. Capital investment on the Comstock mounted rapidly, much of it from mining profits plowed back into the enterprise but another large fraction derived from California.

Until about 1864 all went well. Then several of the mines ran into borrasca and at the end of the year only the Gould and Curry, with a $9 million gross, was producing satisfactorily. Seasoned operators, engineers, and geologists believed that still richer ores were to be had for the digging. Whether they actually knew of these may be a different question. In the meantime most mines had to levy stock assessments in order to proceed, and the mill owners had to borrow money to tide them over until quantity production was resumed. For their loans they turned almost without exception to William C. Ralston's Bank of California.

Launched in the summer of 1864 with a paid-up capital of $2 million, this bank promptly established branches in Nevada. Its Nevada manager, William Sharon, adopted a liberal lending policy. He established an interest rate of 2 per cent a month in place of the prevailing 3 to 5 per cent, and he seldom refused a prospective borrower. When he had lent $2 million on mills and mines and Ralston came over to reason with him about such plunging, Sharon was able to persuade his employer that the risk was good, that sooner or later the mines would strike another bonanza and the bank would recover its money and more. Without a bonanza the bank would be ruined, because the mills and mining machinery to which it held mortgages or title were of value only where they were. No mean plunger himself, Ralston gave the order to proceed. Shortly the bank was involved to the extent of $3.5 million and had foreclosed on most of the mills. Through 1865 and into the next year the outlook continued very dark. Sharon and Ralston, however, hit on a device to keep their heads above water. With D. O. Mills and one or two other bank officers they organized the Union Mill and Mining Company to operate the mills which the bank possessed, and through the bank they exerted pressure on the mines to deliver their richest ore to these mills. To the distress of the private mill owners, the scheme worked. It also appealed to Sharon and Ralston because, when a bonanza was struck, the profits would go to this small group rather than be dissipated among all the stockholders of the bank.

While matters stood thus, the Ralston–Sharon forces were threatened from another quarter. Adolph Sutro, a young mill owner who was subsequently to be mayor of San Francisco and a generous benefactor of that city, was proposing a plan which would divert most of the business from the bank's mills. His proposal was for a tunnel tapping the lode at the 2,000-foot level which would ventilate the mines, carry off the excess water by gravity flow, and save correspondingly on ore-hoisting expense. Though sound from an engineering viewpoint, Sutro's tunnel would have made the bank's mills and hoisting machinery obsolete. The bank, therefore, refused to cooperate; it opposed Sutro on every turn and delayed for more than a decade the completion of the tunnel.

Throughout the late sixties and into the next decade Sharon as the bank's manager was unquestionably King of the Comstock. He controlled the railroad built up from Carson City, his lumber company had a virtual monopoly on supplying the mines and mills with timber and fuel, and in other departments of business the bank's power was equally felt. All these years the mines were in borrasca more often than in rich ore. Although the bank's monopolies continued to show a profit, a few straws in the wind intimated that Sharon's hold might be broken. A disastrous fire in the Yellow Jacket enabled Sutro to rouse the miners to support his tunnel. Two members of the bank ring, John P. Jones and Alvinza Hayward, went off very profitably on their own. Finding new ore bodies in the Crown Point, they quietly bought up its stock and, by organizing the Nevada Mill and Mining Company, excluded the bank from any direct share in the Crown Point bonanza. Another syndicate comprising two mining men, John W. Mackay and James Fair, and two San Francisco saloonkeepers, James C. Flood and William S. O'Brien, acquired control of four mines: the Bullion, the Kentuck, the Hale and Norcross, and the Savage. On the Hale and Norcross they struck a small bonanza, the profits from which were promptly reinvested in exploration digging and in buying up the stock of the Virginia and the California, two mines which had yielded little though located between the rich Ophir and the Best and Belcher.

With $212,000 raised by assessment on the Virginia and California stock, Fair began a search for pay ore. There were discouragements which enabled the partners to buy up still more of the outstanding shares, but in March, 1873, Fair came to a rich vein 54 feet wide. Having gained control of practically all the Virginia and California stock, the partners neglected no opportunities to publicize their good fortune. Dan De Quille, the most reputable mining reporter in Nevada, was invited to appraise the ore in sight. He published a figure of $116,748,000, while the director of the mint estimated the value at $300 million and practical miners were ready to multiply the figure by five.

With this bonanza pouring out an unprecedented treasure, with Jones' Crown Point continuing to do well, with the bank's mines and mills taking a new lease on life, and with English money at last available for the Sutro Tunnel, Virginia City prospered as never before. Speculative investment in Comstock shares also touched a new high with San Francisco the scene of the most hectic trading. Because of the great advance of the most interesting stocks, trading was now principally upon margins and thus subjected to a new hazard. A rumor that the bonanza was exhausted produced a panic in which, within a single week, the market value of Consolidated Virginia and California dropped $24 million. The bonanza kings professed to be undisturbed. Their profits, they said, were in ore and not in stocks; when the price went low enough they bought a few more shares. Among the players of the market, however, the distress was great. As increasing bullion output disproved the rumor of exhaustion, the market recovered with another wave of margin purchases, only to crash again in the summer of 1875. This time the book loss was over $60 million, and this time the Bank of California was carried down in the crash.

Sharon, Mills, and some others of the bank ring were able to salvage their personal fortunes, but Ralston was not. Ousted as cashier, he walked to North Beach for his customary swim and, by accident or design, drowned. An audit of his books showed unsecured liabilities in excess of $4.5 million. The temptation is to condemn Ralston as a predatory economic royalist. He had taken the lead, however, in many enterprises of great civic importance. The Palace Hotel, his estate at Belmont, and the Bank of California had been his principal monuments, but steamship lines, the Spring Valley Water Company, the Lone Mountain Cemetery, the University of California, and so many other projects had benefited from his promotion as to suggest to a biographer the title "The Man Who Built San Francisco."

On the ruins of Ralston's bank the bonanza kings erected the Nevada Bank of San Francisco and assembled a Comstock monopoly more complete than its predecessor's. In another few years, however, the bonanza was exhausted, and Virginia City soon dwindled to ghostlike proportions. Fortunes based on the Comstock, such as those of Mackay, Fair, Flood, O'Brien, Sharon, Mills, Jones, Sutro, and Hearst, were prominent in subsequent chapters of the nation's and particularly of California's history. To San Franciscans, however, the Comstock is above all memorable for the two decades of great excitement and the glorious opportunity for speculative investment that it afforded. In popular fancy it dwarfed such enterprises as wheat ranching, flour milling, carriage making, or lumbering.

For Further Reading

R. G. CLELAND and OSGOOD HARDY, *March of Empire* (1929).

GERALD D. NASH, *State Government and Economic Development; A History of Administrative Policies in California* (1964).

OTIS E. YOUNG, JR., *How They Dug the Gold* (1967).

VINCENT P. CAROSSO, *The California Wine Industry, 1830–1895* (1951).

PAUL W. GATES, *California Ranchos and Farms, 1846–1862* (1967).

JOHN W. CAUGHEY, "Don Benito Wilson," *HLQ*, 2 (1939), 285–300.

WALTON BEAN, "James Warren and the Beginnings of Agricultural Institutions in California," *PHR*, 13 (1944), 361–75.

RODMAN W. PAUL, "The Great California Grain War," *PHR*, 27 (1958), 331–49.

ROBERT L. KELLEY, *Gold Versus Grain* (1959).

R. G. CLELAND and FRANK B. PUTNAM, *Isaias W. Hellman and the Farmers and Merchants Bank* (1965).

JULIAN DANA, *The Man Who Built San Francisco* (1936).

WILLIAM WRIGHT (DAN DE QUILLE), *The Big Bonanza* (1876).

GRANT H. SMITH, *The History of the Comstock Lode* (1943).

CAUGHEY, *California Heritage*, 268–79.

chapter thirteen

Political Experiment

What we have here to do is to understand what forces worked for and against
order in this community of irresponsible strangers.

Josiah Royce,
California

Military Government Protested

1846
to
1865

When he raised the American flag at Monterey in 1846, Commodore
Sloat proclaimed that California was to be a permanent possession
of the United States, its inhabitants to enjoy the rights and privileges
of citizenship and the advantages of stable government. Stockton was
even more explicit in promising that territorial government would
be provided.

For the time being, however, in accordance with the precedents set in other newly acquired American territories, military
government was put into operation. Although this action had further
justification after the southern California revolt necessitated recon-
quest by force, even in this district the military governors tempered

Thomas Starr King

California State Library

211

martial rule by encouraging the alcaldes and other local officials of the Mexican regime to continue functioning. From the native Californians, despite the childish wrangling of Stockton, Kearny, and Frémont over precedence and authority, there appears to have been no objection to the type of government that prevailed.

In contrast, the Americans in California protested bitterly against government by the military, asserting that the Constitution accompanied the flag and demanding immediate provision of civil government. Curiously enough, the one feature of civil government that did exist, alcalde rule, struck them as particularly un-American and was the target of their sharpest shafts. Alcaldes were orthodox Spanish-American local officials, unhampered by the Anglo-Saxon fetish of separation of powers. Anglo-Americans looked aghast at the wide range of their authority, which, it must be admitted, was occasionally misused. A writer in the *California Star* complained that alcaldes exercised "authority far greater than any officer in our republic—the president not excepted. . . . The grand autocrat of the Russians . . . is the only man in Christendom I know of who equals him."

Whether the constitutional guaranties of civil government entered California with Sloat's proclamation, the Cahuenga Capitulation, or the Treaty of Guadalupe Hidalgo is a question on which the jurists have engaged in inconclusive hairsplitting. Certainly the Californians did not delay their criticisms of the military regime until after the signing of the treaty. Exactly one month after Cahuenga the *California Star* urged the formation of a constitutional convention, and a year later, on January 22, 1848, "Pacific" complained in the same paper that California, "since the United States flag was hoisted over it, has been in a sad state of disorganization . . . , we have had no government at all during the period, unless the inefficient mongrel military rule exercised over us be termed such." Other journals called on the military governors to take the necessary steps or advised the people to assume the initiative.

With the end of the war and the definitive cession of California to the United States the arguments against military government gained added weight. Washington recognized that civil government was in order for California but saw also a number of complicating circumstances. For one thing, the Mexican Cession possessed populations that eastern Americans distrusted. Congress granted Oregon territorial government in the spring of 1848, but an amendment to broaden the act to provide the same governmental machinery for California and New Mexico was voted down on the ground that "native-born" Oregon should not be unequally yoked with territories "peopled by Mexicans and half-Indian Californians." A worse drawback involved the question of slavery extension. President Taylor advocated procrastination because he feared the flare-up that would inevitably attend Congressional attempts to provide civil government. Delay lasted two and a half years after the Treaty of Guadalupe Hidalgo. To the Californians this seemed unconscionable; as a matter of fact it was not extraordinary, for Oregon had waited two years for territorial government and New Mexico was to wait 60 years for statehood.

In California the impatience with military government was mounting. Colonel Mason, in announcing on August 7, 1848, the formal cession to the United States, attempted to mollify the Californians by predicting that Congress would provide civil government within a few months. He also issued a code of *Laws for the Better Government of California* (published by S. Brannan, San Francisco, 1848), but the rarity of this volume and its infrequent contemporary mention indicate that the reform was not entirely effective. Throughout the summer and fall of 1848 Californians were so preoccupied with the search for gold that they gave little thought to things political, but, with the onset of the winter rains and interruption of mining, many gold seekers had time either at their camps or in the settlements to reflect upon the injustice of Washington's delay. On February 12, 1849, some 400 or 500 assembled San Franciscans resolved that a better-defined government was absolutely necessary. They proceeded to organize a town government along American lines, but Mason's successor, General (and Governor) Persifer F. Smith, refused his support.

The inrushing forty-niners shortly thereafter changed the whole outlook of the province. Although politics was not their major interest, they were not in a mood to accept complacently the disenfranchisement symbolized by military government. Whatever the jurists might say, they were absolutely certain that they had brought their constitutional prerogatives with them across the plains, across Panama, or around the Horn. They quickly fell in line with the proposals for direct action such as that mentioned at San Francisco and with the plan for a constituent assembly. Mass meetings at San Jose, Sacramento, Santa Cruz, and Monterey endorsed this plan and set the date for its convening on the first Monday in August.

Organizing a State

Facing this situation upon his assumption of the governorship in April, General Bennett Riley concluded that it would be more proper for a convention to gather at his invitation. Accordingly, as soon as he learned that Congress had adjourned without acting for California, he issued a call for a convention to meet at Monterey on September 1. San Franciscans particularly resented his "interference," but in the end they concluded that more might be gained by cooperating than by resisting. The elections were held and early in September the delegates gathered.

Riley's proclamation had designated ten districts: San Diego, Santa Barbara, and San Luis Obispo to send two delegates each; Los Angeles, Sonoma, Sacramento, and San Joaquin, four each; and Monterey, San Jose, and San Francisco, five each. An optional clause, however, authorized any district that considered itself entitled to a larger representation to elect additional delegates. The southern districts sent only the 10 delegates specified, but the northern districts increased Riley's allotment by 11, which enlarged the membership of the convention to 48.

Monterey in 1849

Joseph Revere, A Tour of Duty

The convention proceeded to frame a state rather than a territorial government. Because of the gold rush California had received such a great influx of population that it could skip the territorial stage. Forty-niners, however, did not dominate the convention. Not more than a dozen of the 48 members had come in the rush. The others were "old-timers": a few native Californians, such as Vallejo, Carrillo, and De la Guerra; some Americans of long residence, such as Stearns and Larkin; others like Semple, who had come with the overland immigrants in the forties; and Mexican War veterans, of whom Halleck is representative. These old-timers who were to be California's Founding Fathers were not old in years; only four had passed 50, thirty were not yet 40, and nine were still in their twenties.

The most debated question before the convention was where to locate the eastern boundary. The large-state faction urged the Rockies; the small-state faction, the Sierra. Six or eight compromise lines were proposed, and the convention repeatedly switched its approval from one to another. From the debates it was evident that the territory west of the Sierra and that fronting on the Colorado was what really mattered. Beyond that, the prime consideration was to get a line that Congress would approve promptly. Exclusion of the Mormon district around Salt Lake seemed advisable because the Mormons were not represented in the convention and preferred to remain apart. Another argument of the small-state advocates was that the national government should be left responsible for protecting and relieving emigrant parties in the intermountain desert basin. The present line was the eventual compromise.

The work of the convention was much simplified because of the availability of other state constitutions. Chief reliance was on that of Iowa, the most recent constitution in the West, and on New York's newly revised frame of government, but the influence of six or eight others can be detected.

Several circumstances tended to impair the reputation of this first California constitution. It was suspect because it had been drawn up in the wild and boisterous West and by a body irregularly convened. The disgracefully low standards of political conduct in California in the following decade also reflected unfavorably upon the constitution's standing. Furthermore, within 30 years the state discarded it in favor of a new one. On the other hand, it is worth noting that the work of the Monterey convention was approved almost without dissent when submitted to popular vote. Congress criticized the procedure followed but made no complaint about the constitution. Moreover, political scientists agree that this first constitution was a superior document. It was a simple statement of fundamental principles and procedures, not cluttered with a multitude of technical provisions really legislative in character.

A most striking tribute to the excellence of this constitution of '49 is that it was a principal inspiration and model for the Argentinian constitution of 1853. Comparison of the two documents reveals their similarities. We have also the testimony of Juan Bautista Alberdi, father of the constitution of 1853. Acknowledging his indebtedness, Alberdi had this to say of the California document:

> Without universities, without academies or law colleges, the newly-organized people of California have drawn up a constitution full of foresight, of common sense and of opportunity.

California statehood was not approved by Congress until almost a year later. The constitution, some Congressmen charged, had been "concocted" by President Taylor through Governor Riley. Others objected that the Californians were a miscellaneous grab bag of adventurers who could not be trusted to operate a state government; furthermore, they were ill-mannered upstarts who had not waited for an enabling act as the signal to draw up a frame of government. Such a dangerous show of disregard for Congress should be rebuked as an example to the rest of the West. The real reasons for the delay, however, were eastern rather than western. They concerned the overlapping claims of Texas, New Mexico, Deseret, and California in the Mexican Cession; they had to do with party jealousies and with factional disputes between the President and Congress; above all, they were inherent in the disagreement between the North and the slave-holding South. Only through the exercise of Henry Clay's suave peacemaking could these several issues be compromised. In the end the national government approved what the West had done and on September 9, 1850, California took her place in the family of states.

State Government in Operation

This admission to statehood is widely heralded and celebrated. It is not so well known that the impatient Californians had not waited for formal admission to start operating their state government. After approval of the constitution at the election in November, 1849, the first legislature assembled in December, and on the twentieth of that month Peter H. Burnett was sworn in as the first civil governor of the state. The wheels of government creaked not so much because they were new as because money raising was practically impossible so long as ultimate recognition of the state government was uncertain. In this intermediate stage, of course, California had no representation in Congress. Consequently, admission to the Union meant much to the state. It dispelled the specter of military government, regularized the state government which was already operating, seated California's Senators and Congressmen at Washington, and set a seal of approval upon a state constitution which was a lasting monument to the good sense and wise decision of the Californians of '49.

Whereas the constitution of 1849 demonstrated the political capacity of the Californians, their day-to-day citizenship was more nearly of the caliber predicted by the Congressional pessimists who had hesitated to entrust state government to these gold-mad westerners. Inexperience was one obstacle to good government. A contributing factor was inattention induced by the absorbing and highly profitable nature of private enterprise. In the conduct of state government the result of this crass neglect was a record of the grossest abuses. The legislature of 1849, as has been intimated, faced a peculiar handicap in that the delay of admission left all its acts in a position of dubious legality. This first legislature enacted a code of laws and chose the first United States Senators, but it is better known as the "Legislature of a Thousand Drinks," in remembrance of Senator Thomas J. Green's constant advocacy of adjournment for liquid refreshment. The legislature of 1851, it pleased a San Francisco journalist to observe, was "an infamous, ignorant, drunken, rowdy, perjured and traitorous body of men."

In the Mexican period the capital had been shifted from Monterey to San Diego, Santa Barbara, or Los Angeles at the caprice of the governor. As the American period began, one of the major issues was where to bring the capital to rest. The military governors had stationed themselves at Monterey. There likewise the constitutional convention assembled, but the sudden importance of the mining area seemed to dictate removal to some point nearer the center of population. Local aspirations influenced the decision. For the first legislative session San Jose was designated. Then arose the question whether to continue at San Jose, return to Monterey, go to New York of the Pacific, a budding metropolis on Carquinez Straits, or cross the straits to a site tendered by Mariano Guadalupe Vallejo. By offering 156 acres of land and a contribution of $370,000 to the building fund, Vallejo prevailed.

In 1852, however, when the legislature convened at Vallejo, it found none of the conveniences which the general had promised. The decision was shortly to take ship for Sacramento, and, the merchants of that town having thoughtfully chartered a riverboat for the purpose, the legislature moved, lock, stock, and gavel. The next year it tried Benicia but in 1854 returned permanently to Sacramento. As long as gold mining dominated the economy this site had the recommendation of convenience, but with the shift of population to southern California the argument lost weight. Certainly the removal from Monterey meant the abandonment of a distinctive geographical environment, rich in historical associations, for one with climatic handicaps reminiscent of the midwestern states.

Gwin Versus Broderick

Throughout the fifties California was emphatically Democratic. Only once did the governorship fall to the opposition, and the United States Senate seats, regarded as much higher political prizes, were reserved exclusively for Democrats. Within the party, however, a most bitter rivalry developed. Leadership was in the hands of two most astute politicians, each of whom had come to California with a determination to dominate the politics of this new commonwealth. The bitterness of their spirited contest, fortunately, has seldom been surpassed in the subsequent political experience of the state.

First on the scene was William M. Gwin of Tennessee and Mississippi, well-educated and magnetic, a veteran of Jacksonian politics and a protégé of the Polk regime. His leadership was particularly acceptable to the southerners in California, and his faction of the party was often spoken of as the Chivalry or Chiv Democrats. Gwin assumed leadership at the constitutional convention at Monterey and immediately impressed himself upon the Californians as a most capable and experienced political leader. He encountered little opposition in his candidacy for the first full-term seat in the United States Senate, Frémont being chosen for the other place.

David C. Broderick, who was to enter the lists against Gwin, had brief experience in Tammany-Hall politicking in New York City. Within a few months after his arrival in San Francisco he had made himself well enough known to be elected to the first legislature and there had the honor of defeating a bill to forbid entrance of free Negroes. In the next legislature he unsuccessfully opposed a stringent fugitive slave law. In 1851 and 1856 he was an open critic of the illegal actions of the San Francisco vigilance committees. A likable young Irish-American, he became the leader of the anti-Chivalry faction of the California Democrats.

Although the federal patronage was beyond his grasp, Broderick quickly built up a personal following through the state patronage, the municipal machines at San Francisco and Sacramento, and control of the party conventions. By 1854 his control of the legislature had reached the point where he thought it safe to call for the choice of a successor to Gwin in the Senate, though normally the vote would not have been taken until the following year. This proposal was narrowly defeated, but only after most bitter and abusive debate. The breach widened, and in 1856 the Know Nothings, who in California were more antiforeign than anti-Catholic, were able to take advantage of it to elect J. Neely Johnson governor.

In 1857, when the Senatorial question was finally brought to a vote, Broderick was able to dictate the terms. He got himself elected to succeed John B. Weller, whose term was to expire that year. The other place went to Gwin, but only after he had agreed to place the federal patronage in Broderick's hands. Gwin gave evidence of a sincere intention of going through with his part of this hard bargain, but President Buchanan would have nothing to do with Broderick, who had vigorously opposed the President's policy regarding Kansas. His colleagues in the Senate likewise failed to warm to him, with the result that Broderick returned to California in 1859 very much embittered and, because of his noncontrol of the patronage, with fewer supporters in the state than when he had left.

Broderick plunged immediately into strenuous campaigning, featuring angry tirades against Gwin and his associates. There were responses in kind, including a rebuke volunteered by Justice David S. Terry of the state supreme court, who had been a testy member of the Law and Order faction at the time of the Second San Francisco Vigilance Committee. Broderick made a scathing reply which prompted a friend of Terry's to challenge Broderick to a duel.

Resort to "the field of honor" was so common in this era that the framers of the constitution in 1849 felt impelled to decree in Article 11, Section 2, that any citizen participating in a duel would be excluded from voting or holding office. Dueling continued with at least a couple of hundred encounters in the 1850's. Broderick had participated in one in 1852. He scorned the challenge by Terry's friend, who happened to be a noncitizen, but immediately after the election, when Terry's second delivered the formal demand for "satisfaction," Broderick promptly accepted.

Friends interposed with a writ on the morning of September 12, 1859, but early the next morning the two men met at close range at a spot near Lake Merced, just across the line into San Mateo County. Broderick was an expert marksman, but Terry had practiced with the pistols that were used and knew their hair-trigger set. When the signal was given, Broderick's pistol fired prematurely, with the ball striking the ground a short distance in front of him. Terry's carefully aimed shot went true to its mark.

Public opinion turned against Terry and reacted against Gwin. As a martyr Broderick gained stature. The formalized shoot-out at Lake Merced discredited dueling more effectively than had the constitutional provision. The immediate political consequence was a deeper split in Democratic ranks, and in 1860 the state's votes in the electoral college went to the Republican candidate, Abraham Lincoln.

Movements for State Division and for a Pacific Republic

Throughout the fifties a strong undercurrent of feeling ran in favor of a division of the state. The southern delegates had raised the question at the constitutional convention in 1849 because they thought territorial government more suited to the needs of their section, and as state government went into operation, the worst expectations of the southerners were realized. The southern counties were given less than their due share of representation in the legislature, legislation was selfishly or thoughtlessly directed for the exclusive benefit of the mining counties, and taxation rested most heavily upon the nonmining cow counties. In 1852 Governor McDougal admitted that the six cow counties with a population of 6,000 paid $42,000 in property taxes and $4,000 in poll taxes, while the north with 120,000 population paid only $21,000 and $3,500, respectively. Los Angeles newspapers protested in similar vein and fumed over the inadequate representation of the south. Even the San Francisco *Daily Alta*

Celebration of Washington's Birthday, San Francisco, 1852

Lithograph by Pollard and Britton

protested that the majority of representatives from the mining counties acted as though "no bond of connection or sympathy existed between their interests and those of the commercial cities and other sources of wealth of our infant state."

Skeptical about producing any change of heart among the established politicians, southern Californians began to advocate state division. In 1851 a Convention to Divide the State of California was called to meet at Los Angeles. The men who summoned this convention asserted that state government had proved a "splendid failure" and that Los Angeles in particular was tasting the bitter fruits in political neglect, paralyzed commerce, insupportable taxation, and the complete lack of protection against Indian depredations. Separation, "friendly and peaceful but still complete," they asserted to be an imperative necessity. Other efforts followed, and in 1859 Andrés Pico secured legislative approval for the incorporation of the counties from San Luis Obispo south as the Territory of Colorado. A two-thirds vote of approval in the counties affected was assured, but, before Congressional approval could be gained, the Civil War broke out and blocked the step completely.

Discriminations against southern California continued far into the twentieth century. Superficially there was annoyance in such terms as non-American, backward, rustic, disloyal, and cow counties, and in San Francisco's appropriation of the expression "the City." Taxation for many decades bore more heavily on the south, and appropriations for highway construction, education, and many other functions favored the north. Southern Californians furthermore were consistently underrepresented at Sacramento and in Washington. Although the census of 1920 revealed that the population majority had passed to the south, reapportionment of the Assembly and House seats did not take effect until 1933, and not until 1967, by intervention of the Supreme Court, was the principle of one man, one vote applied to the state Senate.

Of the remaining political issues of the fifties the one of broadest potentialities was doubtless the recurrent suggestion of a Pacific Republic. Back in the Mexican period there had been a tendency toward independence, which the Revolution of 1836 put largely into effect. Certain early Americans in the province, Lansford W. Hastings in particular, also dreamed of a western independence. The Bear Flag movement, had it been allowed to run its full course, might have led to such a result. For a decade and a half thereafter the scheme was proposed as often as California had a real or fancied grievance. When military government was prolonged and statehood denied, the idea came to the fore. Again, during the days of the Second Vigilance Committee, when there seemed to be a possibility of federal interference, a "strong undercurrent of secession" animated the vigilantes. They made no public announcement to that effect because such a statement would have justified the interposition of national arms, but later several of the leaders admitted that it had been so. Whenever the Californians felt that they deserved better mail service, more protection against the Indians, a transcontinental railroad, or additional ports of entry, their dissatisfaction with Washington was apt to inspire visions of a Pacific Republic.

Lincoln's election raised the question in earnest. Although a free state, California had been consistently Democratic and in 1858 had endorsed Buchanan's Kansas policy. The state was isolated. Its population was drawn mostly from the North, but a substantial minority was of southern extraction. Should any Californian be called upon to fight against the "land of his nativity"? Governor Weller advised escape from the dilemma of choosing between the North and South by founding on the shores of the Pacific "a mighty republic, which may in the end prove the greatest of all." Other officials agreed, particularly Congressman John C. Burch, who became the leading advocate.

California's gold and her population, comprised of "the most enterprizing and energetic of the country," were counted on to secure the new nation favorable reception into the family of nations. Advantages were also foreseen in the rivalry of North and South for California's trade. On the other hand, western population was small, Oregon and Utah could not be counted on for financial support, the bulk of trade had been with northern states, and the national government had been spending millions for California's benefit. Consequently, sober second thought discouraged westward secession.

The Civil War

The choice of supporting North or South remained. The legislature passed loyal resolutions, while the governor repudiated Lincoln's policy. "I do not believe," he said, "that an aggressive war should be waged on any section of the Confederacy, nor do I believe that this Union can be preserved by a coercive policy." Loyalty demonstrations answered pro-South appeals and men rallied to both sides. The plain truth was that California was a border state, fairly evenly divided between Union and secession sentiment.

Although a divided Democratic vote in 1860 had allowed the Republicans to carry the state for Lincoln, they had polled only three votes out of every eight; loyalty was not absolutely proved, and the state election of 1861 was looked upon as a significant test. The "Secesh" faction redoubled its efforts; Union sympathizers organized the Home Guard and made a systematic effort to swing the state to Leland Stanford, the Republican candidate. Helped by the firing on Fort Sumter, the death of Douglas, and especially the oratory of a Unitarian divine, Thomas Starr King, the Republican and Union ticket carried.

Far from being silenced, the "Secesh" faction continued its protests in press and pulpit, poem and harangue. Sometimes the criticism was direct, with the Union Army assailed as "a whining running army, that has disgraced our flag, lowered our cause and dishonored Republican chivalry," or with Lincoln called an "unprincipled demagogue," an "illiterate backwoodsman," and a "narrow-minded bigot." At other times there was more subtle reference to "Mr. Lincoln" and "President Davis." The Visalia *Equal Rights Expositor* "prayed" on Thanksgiving Day, 1862:

> O Lord we thank thee for letting the rebels wallop us at the battle of Pittsburg Landing—for letting them smite us hip and thigh, even unto the destruction of 9,600 of our good loyal soldiers, and 463 of our officers; and for giving speed to their legs through the awful swamps of Chicahominy; and, O Lord, most especially do we thank thee for the licking they gave us at Bull Run the second, and assisting our flight from that fatal field; and, O Lord, never while we live will we forget Antietam, where we had 200,000 and they only 70,000—if they, O Lord, had a happened to a had as many men as we, we'd a been a done gone in—and that friendly creek between us, the mountains that kept our men from running. . . .

General George Wright responded to the most vicious of these attacks by excluding half a dozen papers from the mails. When this and other forms of persuasion failed to moderate the editors of the *Expositor*, some 30 soldiers without consulting their officers broke into the newspaper office, broke the press, and pitched type, paper, and ink into the street. The Rev. William Scott, a clergyman in San Francisco, had the temerity to insist before presbytery that Jefferson Davis was no more a traitor than George Washington had been. Berated by the press and threatened by a mob, Scott was forced to resign his pulpit and leave the state, although he later returned to his pastorate.

Southern sympathizers in California made one effort to strike for the Confederacy. Under the pretext of a commercial venture to Manzanillo, they loaded a quantity of ammunition and arms on the schooner *Chapman*, intending to intercept a Pacific Mail steamer, convert it into a privateer, and ravage Union shipping in the Pacific. Federal authorities got wind of the plot, seized the *Chapman* before she passed the Golden Gate, and interned the men involved.

Since Confederate sentiment was so strong, the government hesitated to draw many loyal volunteers out of California. Of some 16,000 who were enlisted, a few did garrison duty along western trails but the majority remained in the state. The "California Hundred" and the "California Battalion" were attached to the Second Massachusetts Cavalry and participated in more than 50 engagements. The next nearest approach to active service was when the California Column under General Carleton marched through Yuma and Tucson to the Rio Grande to repel the Confederate invasion of New Mexico. The invaders had already fallen back, and the principal consequence of the march was that a number of deserters started a mining rush to Bill Williams Fork. Gold shipments rather than fighting men were California's greatest contribution to the northern cause.

Although California was not in the heat of the conflict, several of her citizens gained great fame for their war work. There was, for example, Leland Stanford, the war governor. A more popular figure was Colonel E. D. Baker, a great orator and one of the most prominent members of the California bar. Shortly before the war he had gone to Oregon where he was promptly elected to the United States Senate. His speeches did much to strengthen the Republican cause in California and to bring about the election of Stanford, and in the Senate he was one of Lincoln's most valued supporters. Upon the outbreak of hostilities he resigned his place in the Senate to serve brilliantly in the northern army and to die at Ball's Bluff. The Reverend Myron C. Briggs of the Methodists was another favorite patriotic orator, only less famous than his Unitarian colleague, Thomas Starr King. King had been a very popular lecturer on nature topics. He spoke for Lincoln in 1860 and for Stanford in 1861, but his greater fame rests upon his eloquent solicitation for the Sanitary Commission, the Civil War precursor of the Red Cross. Largely through his efforts California contributed $1,233,831.31, more than one fourth of the entire amount received by the Commission. For humanitarian as well as patriotic reasons, therefore, Thomas Starr King is considered second only to Junípero Serra among California's heroes.

For a decade after the end of the war Californians were more alive to national issues and the problems of Reconstruction than to local politics. No arresting questions arose comparable to the contest between Gwin and Broderick or to the crucial election of 1861. The Civil War had laid to rest several of the issues of the fifties, such as the questions of state division and of a western secession. Others, such as the location of the capital, had died a natural death or had gone into protracted hibernation. The problem of governmental inefficiency and corruption held over but was not considered particularly pressing. Attack upon it was delayed until the late seventies when it was caught up in a wave of more general unrest and discontent.

For Further Reading

THEODORE GRIVAS, *Military Governments in California* (1963).

WALTER COLTON, *Three Years in California* (1850).

LAWRENCE CLARK POWELL, *Philosopher Pickett* (1942).

CARDINAL L. GOODWIN, *The Establishment of State Government in California* (1914).

WILLIAM H. ELLISON, *A Self-Governing Dominion: California, 1849–1860* (1950).

JOSEPH ELLISON, *California and the Nation, 1850–1869* (1927, 1969).

JOSEPH A. B. SCHERER, *Thirty-first Star* (1942).

JAMES O'MEARA, *Broderick and Gwin* (1881).

A. RUSSELL BUCHANAN, *David S. Terry of California, Dueling Judge* (1956).

MILTON H. SHUTES, *Lincoln and California* (1943).

AURORA HUNT, *The Army of the Pacific* (1951).

FRED B. ROGERS, *Soldiers of the Overland* (1938).

CAUGHEY, *California Heritage*, 257–64.

chapter fourteen

Vigilantes and Filibusters

Their majesties the mob, with that beautiful consistency which usually
distinguishes those august individuals, insisted upon shooting poor Harry—for,
said they, and the reasoning is remarkably conclusive and clear, "a man so
hardened as to raise his hand against his own life, will never hesitate to
murder another!"

Louise Amelia Knapp Smith Clappe,
Dame Shirley Letters

Law and Justice in the Diggings

**1848
to
1860**

The bold, impetuous, swashbuckling temper of the Californians of
the golden era is apparent in their approach to the problems of economic development and state politics. It is observable also in their
attack upon the problems of law.

In the diggings a peculiar situation existed. Gold seekers
poured in so rapidly that regular agencies of government could not
keep pace. The season of 1848 caught California in transition from
Mexican to American administration, with a military governor stationed at Monterey but nothing more than makeshift alcalde governments at the scattered towns. Because these conditions persisted
through the next year, the men in the mining camps were left pretty
much to their own resources both as to law making and law enforcement.

The Hanging of James Stuart

From a contemporary print

225

Taking matters into their own hands, the miners devised a system of claim law beautiful in its logic and simplicity. Some indebtedness is traced to the lead miners of Iowa and more to Spanish colonial and European precedents which the California miners freely adapted. Although specifics varied from camp to camp, the essentials were that each miner was entitled to one claim of reasonable size and that the only way to perpetuate title was to work the claim. Absentee and speculative owners thus had no place in the miners' society, nor was anyone allowed to enclose natural resources or to place them out of the reach of labor, which was recognized as the prime agency in wealth production.

Each camp or gulch or section of a river had its own way of applying these principles. Local practices were not identical as to what the size of claim was to be, how it was to be marked, what frequency of working was required, how disputes were to be resolved, and what power should reside in the camp alcalde, recorder, arbitrator, or chairman. Disputes not otherwise resolved would come before a general meeting of the camp.

As mining advanced from the washing of surface gravels to stream diversion for working the bed of a river, to hydraulic washing, and following a vein of quartz far beneath the surface, the codes had to be elaborated. There were also attempts at standardization at the county level, with Nevada County's quartz laws providing a much used example, and at the state level. What is sometimes called "the California common law on mining" spread to Nevada and many other western territories and states and gained national recognition and acceptance in the western half of the nation.

In 1848 and 1849 the setup was far less elaborate. "The beginning," as E. Douglas Branch observes, "was a signboard on a California gravel bar: CLAIME NOTISE,—Jim Brown of Missoury takes this ground; jumpers will be shot."

Claim law was an everyday necessity in the diggings. Throughout 1848 there was very little occasion for anything more, but later intermittent need for criminal law arose, and the extralegal democracy of the forty-niners was extended to meet these emergencies.

Dry Diggings near Coloma provided the first memorable instance. In January, 1849, five men were caught red-handed in an attempt to rob a Mexican gambler. Courts, jails, and authorities being far away, the alternatives seemed to be to turn them loose or to set up a local substitute for court machinery. The miners chose the latter alternative. A jury of 12 was formed and its verdict of 39 lashes duly executed. Then new charges were made against three of the culprits for crimes committed during the preceding fall on the Stanislaus. Hanging was the popular verdict. E. Gould Buffum entered a vigorous protest but the mob was not to be dissuaded. Three corpses soon dangled from a convenient oak, and Dry Diggings was ready for its new name, Hangtown.

As occasion arose, other mining communities followed the Hangtown example until, as Bancroft put it, the quiet oaks were "tasselled with the carcasses of the wicked." Again, procedure varied from camp to camp but, in general, suspected thieves or murderers were brought before a miners' meeting, testimony was heard, a jury returned the verdict or in smaller camps the decision was reached by an open vote of all assembled, and the group promptly executed the sentence. Since imprisonment was out of the question, hanging, banishment from the camp, ear cropping, and whipping were the customary penalties. A typical account of miners' justice is recorded in Gay's diary:

> I was called up last night 11 or 12 o'clock to assist in taking and trying a man for stealing money—George Gillin late of Ioway—Took him up to Dry Town—went into the "Southern House" I was appointed Judge—selected 12 men for Jury tried him—found him guilty—sentenced him to 39 lashes on the bare back—blind folded. Tryal occupyed the night—Jury rendered their verdict about sun up—took him out—tied him up and applyed the lash —required him to leave by 3 p.m.

Some writers insist that the miners' justice was no justice at all, with the innocent suffering as often as the guilty and with only the most haphazard correlation between crime and punishment. Bret Harte, for example, tells the apocryphal tale of the jury that was told its verdict had better be right because the defendant had already been hanged. Yet until very recently the consensus of opinion has been that the miners administered justice admirably in civil cases and remarkably well in criminal cases. That result has been attributed to the Anglo-Saxon genius for spontaneous self-government, a genius balanced at the time only by the gross corruption in the municipal government of San Francisco.

The miners' justice savored of lynch law, not only in retrospect but also to many contemporary observers, to Buffum at Dry Diggings in January, 1849, and to residents of Hangtown who saw that as an opprobrious name and transmuted it to Placerville. David P. Barstow, a witness of the execution of Juanita at Downieville in 1851, characterized the participants as "the hungriest, craziest, wildest mob" he had ever seen and insisted that "the hanging of the woman was murder." "Since that time," he continued, "I have had no sympathy with or confidence in mobs; I prefer the law for redress of grievances."

In the first couple of years, although the diggings were within 40 to 200 miles of a seat of government and perhaps of regular justice, no machinery existed for bringing mining-camp suspects to trial there. There were no marshals to conduct the accused and the witnesses to that distant bar and no funds to meet the costs. To the gold miners it did not look practicable to send their suspects, some of whom were caught red-handed, to a remote and uncertain jurisprudence.

Unavailability of regular justice, even in 1849, was not as verifiable in the mines as for the overland parties en route to California. Months out on the trail these travelers were beyond the reach of any regular court and in a jurisdictional vacuum as well. When confronted by an act of violence, their alternatives were to improvise a court or to let the assault, robbery, or murder go unpunished.

On the Sweetwater, on June 20, 1849, a man named Williams shot and killed a teamster who had repeatedly threatened his life. Williams went to several wagon-train camps and offered to stand trial but none would act. On July 3 a man named Brown killed one of his messmates. The volunteer posse sent in pursuit did not catch Brown but brought back Williams, and at Green River Ferry the next day an open-air court was convened. Partly because the participants were deeply involved in a "spirited" celebration of the Fourth of July, the trial did not get beyond vigorous debate on a challenge of jurisdiction, after which it broke up. Williams took the cue and left, by inference cleared of the murder charge.

Later in the summer on the southern trail near the Gila two young men from Arkansas quarreled and fought. They were pulled apart, but one boy pulled out a knife and made one fatal lunge. The men of the train immediately picked a judge and jury and the entire company confirmed the verdict. The next morning 12 rifles were handed out, six loaded with blanks and six with powder and ball. Over the grave they posted a brief statement of what they had done.

As to these trail incidents and to a number of the earliest in the mines it can be maintained that at the time there was no law, and the only valid comparison must be with the anarchy that would have prevailed except for the functioning of an extralegal court.

This justification of lynch law decreased in validity as regular courts and sheriffs appeared on the scene. Often, however, there was a preference for direct action even after the orthodox machinery was available. Many of the forty-niners enjoyed the excitement of taking the law into their own hands. On other occasions local chauvinism entered in, as in 1857 when the prospectors at Grass Valley preferred to try their own culprits rather than turn them over to the county authorities at the rival town of Marysville. Politics also figured, as in the case of the hanging of Hamilton McCauley at Napa in 1851. He had been convicted in regular court for the murder of the municipal judge, but fellow Chivalry Democrats brought persuasion to bear upon Governor McDougal and procured a reprieve to be delivered by the sheriff from the rival town, Benicia. The Napans got wind of the sheriff's coming and delayed him on the road just long enough for the prisoner to be properly hanged, thus serving the ends both of party politics and of town pride.

The San Francisco Committees

Related and yet distinct from these rustic manifestations were the famous popular tribunals of San Francisco. As early as 1849 the ineffectiveness of police, prosecutors, and courts led to the appearance of the Hounds, or Regulators. Ostensibly a volunteer police organization, this group of young men was actually a gang preying chiefly upon the weak and the inoffensive. Few Americans suffered but the various groups of foreigners were victimized in turn. Not until the Hounds perpetrated a particularly atrocious raid upon Little Chile were the San Franciscans sufficiently aroused. Led by Sam Brannan, the citizens took a day off, gathered at the Plaza, contributed money for the rehabilitation of the Chileños, and ordered the arrest of the leading Regulators. Banishment and other penalties were decreed for several of these "Sydney Ducks," others fled before the wrath of the citizens, and the gang was broken up.

Ordeal by fire resulted in another civic improvement. In 18 months San Francisco was devastated by six fires that did at least $12 million damage. Rebuilding on a grander but no less combustible scale had followed each fire. Volunteer fire companies were organized but their service was more social and political than protective. The fire houses became clubs and later powerful political organizations. A fire alarm started a race to the conflagration. The hook-and-ladder companies had a glorious time ripping off the side of the building to give the hose companies a chance to stop the fire's spread. The engine companies, meanwhile, were pumping water from one engine to another and eventually to the fire. They jerked the hand rails up and down at frantic speed, far less anxious to extinguish the flames than to "wash" the next crew, that is, to produce an overflow by pumping water in faster than it could be pumped out.

Early in 1851, after a brutal assault and robbery of merchant C. J. Jansen, two Sydney Ducks were arrested as suspects, one of them identified by the victim and taken to be the notorious criminal James Stuart, known as English Jim. Angry citizens led by Sam Brannan seized these two men and were about to string them up, but another merchant, William Coleman, protested that first they should have a trial. A people's court was hastily set up. The principal suspect insisted that he was Thomas Berdue, not English Jim. This doubt, compounded by some question about Jansen's ability to recognize his assailant, led to a divided jury, whereupon the two suspects were given back to the sheriff. Berdue, or Stuart, was tried in regular court, found guilty, and sentenced to 14 years in prison. He thereupon was forwarded to Marysville to stand trial for murder in the mines.

A continuing crime wave, together with the belief that arsonists had set some of San Francisco's fires, revived the vigilante group. Another Sydney Duck, John Jenkins, was caught in the act of stealing a small safe. The vigilantes assembled at once, tried him that very night, and immediately took him to the plaza and hanged him. When some of their number were identified at the inquest, the committee published its membership roll. It went on to arrest other suspects, hold trials, and assess penalties.

Among the suspects brought in to vigilante headquarters, the committee was surprised to find another man alleged to be English Jim. When confronted with this charge, he at first denied it, then confessed and went on to recite a long list of crimes he had committed. Convinced after a time that he was the man they should have been trying two months earlier, they came to a verdict of guilty and in broad daylight marched him to the end of the Market Street Pier, a site in full public view though easy to protect against any attempted rescue, and proceeded with the hanging. Meanwhile, two vigilantes were hurrying to Marysville, arriving after Berdue's conviction for a James Stuart murder but before sentence was pronounced and carried out. The committee tried 90 suspects, hanged two others, whipped one, banished 28, and handed 15 over to the regular authorities.

The provocation had been great, with crime rampant, the regular courts weak and not to be relied on, and the citizens of San Francisco most inattentive to civic responsibilities. The summary actions of the Vigilance Committee are said to have been more of a lesson to the criminal element than were 50 regular hangings.

That estimate, however, must be drastically revised downward because the cure was only temporary. Robbery and arson declined for a time, but within a few years new abuses developed. Municipal offices fell into the hands of unprincipled persons. Scandals occurred in connection with public-works contracts, local government expenses shot up, and elections were brazenly manipulated. The courts also were notoriously corrupt. They tolerated and connived at the sharp practices of criminal lawyers to such an extent that it was practically impossible to get a conviction for murder no matter how clear the evidence. The Chivalry Democrats reaped political profit from this sad state of affairs, but it was the apathy of businessmen and of the people generally that made its existence possible.

When the panic of 1855 redirected attention to governmental problems, the editor of the *Bulletin,* the dynamic James King of William, launched a vigorous campaign for better government. Conceiving of himself as "a moral gadfly" and "the conscience of San Francisco," he was in vituperation and invective another John Randolph of Roanoke. In fearlessly outspoken fashion he systematically exposed the iniquities of Palmer, Cook and Company, one of the leading financial concerns of the city, and went on to analyze the workings of the courts, the practices of leading lawyers, and the operations of the sheriff's office. He mentioned men by name, specified their misdeeds, and called upon the citizens to demand legal steps toward reform. Among others he antagonized James P. Casey, a county supervisor. Because King had broadcast that he was a former inmate of Sing Sing and had refused to give any space in the *Bulletin* to a denial or rebuttal, Casey challenged the editor to a duel, and, when the latter declined, threatened to shoot him on sight. At least a score of like threats had been made by others pilloried in the *Bulletin,* and King apparently took this one no more seriously. But fired up by his cronies, Casey intercepted King as he left his office and shot him down.

King had not been in all respects admirable. One of the most reputable attorneys then practicing in the San Francisco bar insists that he was a notorious broken-down money dealer, that his paper was small and scurrilous, and that its leading columns were devoted to daily abuse without much regard to facts. This attorney further asserts that King refused to publish evidence disproving his charge against Casey, that he declined the latter's challenge to a duel, that he provoked a street fight, and that he was warned to draw and defend himself and had his cocked pistol half drawn when Casey fired. Had the latter withheld his fire one second longer, according to this informant, the fracas would have been called a fair fight rather than an assassination. As it was, Casey lifted the somewhat unworthy James King of William to martyrdom.

Public indignation ran high and Casey was put in the county jail for safekeeping. He had abundant confidence in the courts, and well he might, for Charles E. Cora had just escaped conviction for the murder of a United States marshal. For like reason, many San Franciscans had no confidence that the courts would administer justice to Casey. A mob swarmed around the jail, but the mayor, police, and militia succeeded in quieting it. Mass meetings followed, but the matter might have been dropped except for an advertisement in the morning papers calling a meeting of the Vigilance Committee.

Fundamentally the Committee faced the same problem as in 1851, but, whereas then the legal government had been marked principally by inefficiency and weakness, it was now characterized by corruption and abuse of authority. City and county officials, the forces of the police and the sheriff, the powerful political machine, the leading newspapers, a majority of the bar, and a substantial number of sober citizens stood for "Law and Order," then as now an appealing phrase, and opposed illegal action by the vigilantes. Furthermore, since the corrupt officials might be able to get state or national troops to suppress an insurrection, the Second Vigilance Committee had to move cautiously. The leadership of such men as William T. Coleman and Clancy Dempster proved of inestimable value.

Solemnity, secrecy, and deliberateness marked the Committee's work. Advisable because of the psychological effect upon the entire populace as well as upon the vigilantes, this policy was necessary because of the strong opposition forces. The Committee could not afford to take an overt step until its membership had risen to several thousand trustworthy men, its military equipment and discipline had been brought to a satisfactory stage, and a definite plan of action had matured. To many the delay seemed interminable, but actually only three days was required for the preparations.

On Sunday, May 18, 3,000 armed men surrounded the jail, a cannon was brought to bear upon the door, and a mounted horseman rapped on the window and handed the jailer a note demanding Casey's surrender. Thereupon two carriages drove up, and Casey was brought out and carried off to the vigilante headquarters. On a second trip Cora was taken. The trials of these men were not hedged about by legal technicalities but otherwise they were fair. Just before sentence was passed, word came that James King of William had died but the outcome of the trial was already certain. Both men were condemned to die. On Thursday, at the first stroke of the bell signaling the start of King's funeral procession, the platforms under the two murderers were dropped.

Casey and Cora were, of course, only the symbols of what the vigilantes were striking at. The Committee worked on down through its black list, banishing from the city men it identified as thugs, robbers, murderers, and other criminals and turning certain offenders over to the regular courts, which, significantly enough, promptly sentenced them, though previously convictions had been rare. Besides these obvious criminals the Committee banished a dozen hitherto respected characters, such as Judge Edward McGowan, who had no police records but were regarded as undesirable citizens.

Governor J. Neely Johnson vacillated, as he did on every vital ques-

Escorting Judge Terry to Fort Gunnybags

From a Noisy Carrier lettersheet

tion, but his sympathies were chiefly with the Law and Order faction. William Tecumseh Sherman served as military commander against the vigilantes and later slandered them in the forgetfulness of his *Memoirs*. Judge David S. Terry left the bench in Sacramento to rush to the assistance of the so-called Chivalry. Other men, less famous but more substantial, cast their lot with the opponents of the vigilantes. Their stand was that, even if conditions in San Francisco were as bad as represented, the proper remedy was to bring the pressure of public opinion to bear on the officials then in office or to wait less than two years until the next regular election provided an opportunity for legal reform. In theory and in practice there is much to be said for the Law and Order distrust of extra-legal procedures.

The Second Vigilance Committee, however, avoided the worst pitfalls in its path and rapidly gained strength. The vigorous but dignified punishment of Casey and Cora lent confidence; revelations of the iniquities of the political machine helped, as did blunders by the opposition. Terry ended whatever chances the Law and Order party may have had when he plunged a knife into one of the vigilantes, thereby exemplifying the illegal tendencies of the Law and Order faction. He was taken prisoner and indicted before the Committee on a number of counts including four other attacks upon citizens. The Committee was convinced that Terry deserved punishment, but it was a ticklish problem to attempt to impose a sentence upon a Supreme Court Justice. After 25 days' deliberation—his victim in the meantime having recovered—it was decided to acquit. Although Terry was not punished, the incident discredited the opposition to the Committee. State interference had shown its impotence before Fort Gunnybags, the vigilante headquarters, and the federal authorities, especially General Wool in command of the military department of California, had declined to provide men or arms to suppress the Committee. Its work done, the Committee displayed its strength in a mammoth parade of 6,000 armed men, held a public reception at Fort Gunnybags, and adjourned sine die.

The Seal of the Committee of Vigilance

Vigilante action, especially as symbolized by San Francisco's Second Committee, has come down in popular tradition as a noble example of community action. The majority of eastern editors at the time, while granting that the provocation was great, refused to admit that tribunals operating outside the

Fort Gunnybags

From a Noisy Carrier lettersheet

law were justified and branded them as "pregnant with lamentable and dis-astrous consequences." The New York *Courier and Enquirer,* however, said, "Our admiration is commanded no more by the promptness and decision of their action than by the dignity and decorum which seems to have accompanied it"; the New Orleans *Delta* affirmed that "the people of San Francisco acted well"; and the Boston *Journal* and the New York Sunday *Times* endorsed the summary proceedings and the peremptory justice "which the venality of the courts had made necessary." With the exception of the *Herald,* most San Francisco papers, in step with the thinking of the business community, endorsed the work of this committee.

Historians improved on these phrases. Bancroft hailed the 1856 committee as "the greatest popular tribunal the world has ever witnessed." Theodore H. Hittell, in more labored prose, saluted it as "one of the purest and best intentioned bodies of men ever assembled in San Francisco" and its work as "the most remarkable municipal reform ever known in this country." In the volume on the forty-niners which he wrote for Yale's *Chronicles of America* series Stewart Edward White said that "the effect was the same as though four hundred had been executed." Robert Glass Cleland in 1922 concluded a gen-erally favorable treatment with the slightly guarded comment that "few today will deny that San Francisco profited from this over-riding of law to save law."

In 1964 in his book on the 1851 committee George Stewart quotes with approval Richard Henry Dana's judgment with more special reference to the Committee of 1856 in which Dana says that San Francisco was

> rescued and handed back to soberness, morality and good government, by that peculiar invention of Anglo-Saxon Republican American, the solemn, awe-inspiring Vigilance Committee of the most grave and responsible citizens, the last resort of the thinking and the good, taken to only when vice, fraud, and ruffianism have intrenched themselves behind the forms of law, suffrage, and ballot, and there is no hope but in organized force, whose action must be instant and thorough, or its state will be worse than before.

A hundred and more years later, historians arrived at a judgment considerably more critical. In 1950 in his *A Self-Governing Dominion* William H. Ellison charged that the Committee of 1856 failed in its administration of jus-tice, disregarded the safeguards for the rights of individuals, was a menace to organized society, and "shockingly demonstrated the ease with which lawless-ness in the form of mob or extralegal action" may arise.

In *Their Majesties the Mob*, a book described as a brief for due process, another historian in 1960 concluded that, "whatever the temptation to escape the technicalities of legal justice by substituting direct action, the wiser course is to handle all such cases through the regular courts."

Walton Bean, in 1968, in his *California, An Interpretive History,* wound up his account of the California committees with this evaluation:

> As for vigilante jurisprudence, its record of violations of due process was appalling. The leaders of the vigilance committees would have served

California far better if they had confined their activities to legal methods and to genuine reforms. It is doubtful that they accomplished anything whatever of real value, and they left a vicious, dangerous, and persistent tradition of contempt for the normal processes of government.

Rustic Vigilance

Although in San Francisco the immediate sequel to vigilante action was less commission of crime and more prompt and vigorous functioning of regular justice, throughout the rest of the state, not to mention other parts of the West, the much more prominent result was a stimulation of vigilante action in imitation of that in the metropolis. Vigilante action became so common that it was the accepted order of the day. In some instances it was kept at the high plane of dignity and dispassion attributed to the Committee of 1856, but in other instances it sank to the lowest level of mob vengeance and lynch law. The excuse given, as in San Francisco, was that the regular courts were totally ineffective or that the cleansing of San Francisco had shunted habitual criminals to the provinces or that horse stealing and cattle stealing must be stopped.

William Graham
Rural Scene

Again, judgments differ as to the adequacy of these excuses. Undeniably the arm of the law was of much more rudimentary development in most parts of the back country than in urban San Francisco.

In 1851 there was reason to believe that a statewide criminal ring existed. The burning of Stockton on May 6, just two days after the great San Francisco fire, was an incendiary attempt at jail delivery. Sacramento, Marysville, Nevada City, and other communities seemed to be caught in the same toils. Accordingly, there were proposals for a statewide organization under the sponsorship of the San Francisco Committee. Some correspondence was exchanged both in 1851 and in 1856, chiefly warnings as to the whereabouts and past records of known criminals. The Sacramento Committee used the constitution of its Bay City counterpart. This spirit of cooperation strengthened the position of local committees and helped forestall any effective state interference in San Francisco in 1856, but the metropolitan leaders wisely refused to assume any responsibility for possible excesses by local bodies beyond the limits of their control.

Their fears proved well founded, for in the smaller communities the vigilante movement ran the entire gamut from fair and temperate trial to the most degenerate and revolting forms of mob violence. A few random illustrations will suffice. At Weaverville in the early fall of 1852 a certain Michael Grant was charged with murdering a Missourian named Holt. Arrested by the sheriff, he was taken in hand by the miners, who appointed judge and jury and attorneys for prosecution and defense. Fairly tried and convicted, Grant was allowed a 10-day stay of execution and the ministrations of a clergyman, after which he was solemnly hanged. At Visalia in 1858 vigilantes brought pressure to bear upon a certain William C. Deputy in an attempt to force him to restore properties fraudulently taken from his nephew. The pressure was in the form of marching the old man out to a tree, adjusting a rope around his neck, and swinging him. After three or four trips skyward he agreed to the demands of the vigilantes and was returned to the jail. In the morning a lawyer and a notary called and took the necessary depositions, after which the sheriff turned his prisoner loose. Sonora had one of the most active committees. In the summer of 1851 it disposed of a case almost every day, usually by laying on 50, 75, or even 150 lashes but sometimes by branding horse thieves with the appropriate initials.

In Los Angeles lynch law frequently supplanted regular justice. In rationalization it is asserted that Los Angeles was one of those proverbially tough cow towns, with cowboys, teamsters from the Salt Lake freighting line, desperadoes expelled by the San Francisco vigilantes, Latin bad men like Joaquín Murieta and Juan Flores, and Indians crazed with the poisonous liquor dispensed in "Nigger Alley." The press lashed out against the mounting crime wave—44 homicides in 15 months and not a conviction was the figure in 1851; by 1854, though doubtless with appropriate exaggeration, the rate was quoted at a murder a day. (Licensed automobile drivers today do not quite treble that figure.) The courts proving inadequate, lynch law was invoked.

Although responsible persons usually condemned the resort to lynch law, a vigilance committee was called into being on July 13, 1851, by formal action of the mayor and city council of Los Angeles. Among its more famous actions were the hanging of two alleged Mexican murderers in August, 1852, and, a few months later, the hanging of three others charged with the murder of Major General J. H. Bean. Five years later proof came to light that one of these young men had been innocent.

In January, 1855, Mayor Stephen C. Foster resigned his high office to take active part in lynching a certain Dave Brown. The good work done, he was promptly reelected mayor. This particular lynching, besides being personally directed by the mayor, was outstanding because a full report of it was printed in the *Southern Californian* some hours before the actual hanging. This anachronism occurred because the enterprising editor of this sheet wanted to feature the story in his issue for the 10 o'clock San Francisco steamer. At three, when the hanging actually occurred, the vigilantes had, so to speak, a full printed script for their performance, complete even to a last-minute confession by the murderer. The chief divergence from the printed program was that Brown objected to being hanged by "a lot of Greasers," and in deference to his wishes the Spanish-American volunteers stepped aside and let an all-American crew haul on the rope.

Thus was justice served at Los Angeles. The ranger company, in other words the vigilantes, in 1854 and 1855 brought about 22 executions "in accordance with the law or without the law, whichever was most convenient." Two years later some 200 men turned out to avenge the slaying of Sheriff James R. Barton by the Flores gang. Not counting those killed in the process of apprehension, 11 members of this gang were hanged at the jail. As late as 1863 a single month witnessed seven lynchings.

These popular tribunals of town and country have only a fraction of the fame enjoyed by the two great committees of San Francisco. In nicety of organization and in dramatics they were far inferior. Few of them would be held up as high examples of good citizenship triumphing over difficulties occasioned by corrupt and venal officials. They were, nevertheless, close kin to the vigilance of San Francisco and belong in every general picture of extralegal justice in California. In fact, they perhaps should have the principal attention, for in number of hangings these rural tribunals exceeded San Francisco's two committees by at least twenty to one. In the year 1855 alone there were 19 vigilante hangings for murder, 24 for theft, and four for minor crimes, a total of 47, not one of which took place in San Francisco.

Southward the Course of Empire

Californians of the fifties expressed their lofty disdain for the due process of criminal law through the vigilance movement. Their corresponding disregard for international law was revealed in numerous filibustering expeditions. California was merely the starting point for these expeditions directed toward Sonora, Baja California, Hawaii, or Central America. The main operations lay outside the state and none of these forays succeeded, yet the work of these filibusters sheds considerable light on the state of mind of many Californians of the day.

The United States, it should be recalled, had just taken long strides westward with the annexation of Texas in 1845, the Oregon treaty in 1846, and the Mexican Cession of 1848. Manifest Destiny, as Americans were repeatedly told, had ordained all this. Many Americans and particularly many Californians of the fifties were reluctant to believe that this much expansion was all that had been ordained. These surely were not the final limits of the nation but merely marked a pause before the advance should be resumed. Many filibusters of the fifties considered themselves logical successors of Pike, Austin, Houston, Jed Smith, Bidwell, Frémont, and their comrades, who by venturing across into foreign soil had prepared the way for American acquisition.

Furthermore, several other provinces seemed to be as eligible for American picking in the fifties as Texas and California had been in the preceding decade. Baja California and Sonora were remote from and neglected by Mexico's central government. Sonora lay open to Apache inroads, from which no force short of that of the United States promised relief. Hawaii's native government was decrepit, her commercial ties were with the United States, and her foreign colony was largely American. Even Central America, by virtue of the faltering of its national governments and because of the popularity of the Panama and Nicaragua routes to California, came within the scope of American interest. California's proximity and its volatile and adventurous population made it the inevitable rallying point for the filibusters and, as in most other matters, San Francisco led.

California's first filibuster was Joseph C. Morehead. He seems to have had invitations of a sort to bring a force into Sonora and Baja California to assist in Indian control and doubtless in a revolution. Recruits were not lacking, and inasmuch as he was Quartermaster-General of California it was easy for him to outfit his followers. Drawing on the funds and supplies left over from the Yuma campaign of 1850, he purchased what was necessary, including the bark *Josephine.* In the spring of 1851 his men left for the lands which they expected to seize for the United States. Some 200 arrived at La Paz in June. They engaged merely in trade and soon dispersed. Meanwhile, a larger party was moving through Los Angeles toward the Gila River and the Sonora frontier. It likewise broke up. Morehead in person was to lead a third detachment to Mazatlán. At San Diego most of his men deserted and he narrowly escaped arrest. Warned of his approach, the Mazatlán authorities were ready for him, but to their surprise they found no arms, ammunition, or other warlike manifestations on board the *Josephine.* Morehead's filibusters proved entirely innocuous.

In the *Game Cock* in 1851 Sam Brannan took out a band of armed men intent on liberating Hawaii, only to find that no such ministration was wanted. To the Mexican government the Morehead expeditions suggested the advisability of strengthening Indian defenses on the Sonora frontier. Various expedients were considered, but the decision was to recruit colonists from the French of California. Of the foreigners contributed by the gold rush the French were second only to the Chinese in clannishness and picturesqueness. English and Irish were soon assimilated, Germans were temporarily conspicuous because of their fondness for large watches and heavy watch chains, Sydney Ducks created a special problem for the vigilantes, and Chileños were numerous enough to give their name to a section of San Francisco. The French outranked all these in numbers. Individual migration was supplemented by several companies devoted to exporting Frenchmen to the land of gold. Most famous of these was La Société de l'Ingot d'Or, which by 1853 was credited with sending 3,046 Frenchmen to California. In the mines these immigrants encountered miscellaneous persecution, plus the discriminatory foreign miners' tax. Many of them, therefore, turned back to San Francisco where some of their number became prominent as merchants and importers, hotel and restaurant keepers, gamblers and bankers. Others turned to more menial employment as barbers, bootblacks, waiters, scullions, woodcutters, or hunters. It was from this latter class that the recruits for Mexican ventures were chiefly drawn.

Such were the 88 Frenchmen who sailed with Charles Pindray for Guaymas in November, 1851. Augmented by later arrivals to about 150 men, Pindray's party moved inland to an assigned tract near one of Kino's old missions, Cocóspera. There they set about developing an agricultural colony as an outpost against the Apaches and, they hoped, as a base for mining operations. The colony did not flourish. The Apaches ran off their stock and the Mexican authorities did not furnish the promised support. Pindray went to Ures to protest and on the return journey was shot, by himself, another Frenchman, a Mexican, or a tool of the Mexican government—just which is not clear. His colony soon dissolved. Near Tucson in the Santa Cruz Valley a smaller group under Lepine de Sigondis and T. P. Sainte-Marie was equally unsuccessful.

Despite these discouragements the California French rallied almost immediately to send new expeditions to Sonora. A new leader took charge, Count Gaston de Raousset-Boulbon, an imperious, reckless, and magnetic scion of France's decayed nobility. At the invitation of certain Mexican officials and with some indications of support from the imperial agents of Louis Napoleon, Raousset led expeditions from San Francisco to the promised land of Sonora in 1852 and again in 1854. On the first occasion his following was ostensibly a mining organization known as La Compañía Restauradora de la Mina de la Arizona. From Guaymas it moved on to the frontier, though not without considerable friction with the local authorities of Sonora. This eventually led to outright hostilities, culminating in a brilliant exploit for Raousset, the capture of Hermosillo and its 1,000 defenders by his 240 followers. As the hero of Hermosillo, Raousset was in a fair way to make himself the "Sultan of Sonora," an intention once attributed to him. On the other hand, the Sonorans had no enthusiasm for the victors. With Raousset laid up with dysentery, his lieutenants ordered a retreat to Guaymas to await expected reinforcements from San Francisco. En route they were opposed by General Blanco and 1,200 troops, to whom in discouragement they capitulated.

Back in San Francisco the next spring, Raousset began recruiting a force of 1,000 men. Enlistment proceeded satisfactorily, but the promised financial support for the expedition did not materialize and the principal result was to stimulate the Sonora authorities to strengthen their defenses. Hopes revived when Raousset was invited to Mexico City to confer with President Santa Anna about bringing 500 Frenchmen to defend the Sonora frontier. These two worthies failed to agree, and the Count returned to San Francisco still further discredited. Shortly thereafter, a confederate of his at Mazatlán exposed proposals for a grandiose west coast revolution to be supported by 5,000 California Frenchmen.

Meanwhile, the "grey-eyed man of destiny," the famous William Walker, was openly recruiting filibusters in California. After his offer of "assistance" to Sonora had been rebuffed, Walker sailed from San Francisco with 45 men in the brig *Caroline*. At La Paz he seized the Governor of Baja California and issued a bombastic proclamation as President of the Republic of Baja California. The hostility of the countryside led him to retreat to Enseñada just below San Diego, but in his proclamations he became more pompous and annexed Sonora to his republic. His project ended ignominiously in May, 1854, when he scurried back into the United States after a farcical attempt to march around the head of the gulf to conquer Sonora. His filibustering had embarrassed the negotiation of the Gadsden Treaty and contributed to the exclusion of Baja California from that purchase.

The incident also led to renewed Mexican overtures to Raousset to establish a French outpost on the Sonora frontier. The Mexican and French consuls at San Francisco were taken to court on charges of violating the United States law against filibustering. Although there were other obstacles, in the spring of 1854 Raousset was able to dispatch 400 men. He followed most uncomfortably and hazardously on an overloaded schooner. Arriving at Guaymas, he and his men were viewed with suspicion by the local officials. Misunderstandings led to conflict, culminating in the Battle of Guaymas on July 13, 1954, in which the French were completely defeated. Raousset's execution 30 days later was the coup de grace to French filibustering from California.

The following year Walker embarked with some 58 Californians for Nicaragua. After much adventure and some good fortune he became the master of this Central American republic, only to incur the wrath of the Vanderbilt transportation interests. Walker lost prestige as rapidly as he had gained it, and after a series of disappointments and humiliations he faced a firing squad at Truxillo, Honduras, in 1860.

Less deserved and consequently more tragic was the fate of the Stockton lawyer and California state senator, Henry A. Crabb. Interested in Sonora because of his wife's property holdings there, Crabb took some 50 colonists to the province in 1856. By a local revolutionist, Ignacio Pesquiera, he was urged to recruit a still larger force of Californians to assist in the revolution and to prepare the way for annexation to the United States. Crabb raised 100 men, most of whom he marched by the Los Angeles–Yuma route to Sonora. At the frontier the filibusters encountered unexpected opposition offered by the very man who had urged their coming. Pesquiera had gained his end without the necessity of armed revolt and now was utterly opposed to the entrance of filibusters. Crabb pushed on as far as Caborca where, partly by superior force and partly by treachery, he was induced to surrender. The next morning the 59 prisoners were taken out in batches and butchered.

That this senseless savagery was protested in only perfunctory fashion by the United States government contributed to the impression that Crabb's fate was fully deserved. On the contrary, it appears that his expedition was more colonizing than filibustering in character, his followers high in reputability, his coming to Sonora by semiofficial invitation, and the opposition to him motivated by a desire on Pesquiera's part to cover up his own misdeeds.

Others might talk about further southwestward expansion of the United States but Crabb was the last of the California filibusters. The actual expeditions, from Morehead to Crabb, are less significant than the restless, adventurous, and imperialistic attitude of the Californians, which made them ready to enlist in such enterprises, ready to condone actions which violated the statutes of the United States, and as jurymen unwilling to convict leaders like Walker who were brought to trial for violation of the antifilibustering law. To a degree the West was a law unto itself and did not yet realize that Manifest Destiny had run its complete course.

For Further Reading

HUBERT HOWE BANCROFT, *Popular Tribunals* (1887).

CHARLES H. SHINN, *Mining Camps* (1885).

JOSIAH ROYCE, *California, from the Conquest in 1846 to the Second Vigilance Committee in San Francisco; A Study in Character* (1886).

MARY FLOYD WILLIAMS, *History of the San Francisco Committee of Viligance of 1851* (1919).

GEORGE R. STEWART, JR., *Committee of Vigilance, Revolution in San Francisco, 1851* (1964).

JAMES O'MEARA, *The Vigilance Committee of 1856* (1887).

A. RUSSELL BUCHANAN, *David S. Terry of California* (1956).

JOHN W. CAUGHEY, *Their Majesties the Mob* (1960).

WALTER VAN TILBURG CLARK, *The Ox Bow Incident* (1942).

RUFUS K. WYLLYS, *The French in Sonora* (1932).

RUFUS K. WYLLYS, "The Republic of Lower California, 1853–1854," PHR, 2 (1933), 194–213.

RUFUS K. WYLLYS, "Henry A. Crabb, A Tragedy of the Sonora Frontier," PHR, 9 (1940), 183–94.

ANDREW F. ROLLE, "California Filibustering and the Hawaiian Kingdom," PHR, 19 (1950), 251–64.

CAUGHEY, *California Heritage*, 197–99, 233–37, 283–86.

chapter fifteen

Challenge to Land Ownership

The injury done to the country by the delay in the settlement of the land-titles is, to a considerable extent, irreparable. That delay caused us to lose, or has prevented our gaining, a population of a million citizens, of the most valuable class.

John S. Hittell,
Resources of California

The Problem and the Policy

1848
to
1875

The foregoing narrative of vigilance and filibustering illustrates the unsettled condition of California in the early American period. This unrest is further illustrated and in part explained by the awkward, faltering, and unjust procedure whereby the United States government dealt with the land titles carried over from the Mexican period.

Sloat's proclamations, not to mention other official statements in the course of the conquest, had assured the Californians that their property ownership would not be disturbed. The Treaty of Guadalupe Hidalgo also clearly obligated the United States to confirm titles to lands held, and the military governors gave repeated

Diseño Accompanying Application for Grant of Rancho Parage de la Laguna de Temecula

The Bancroft Library

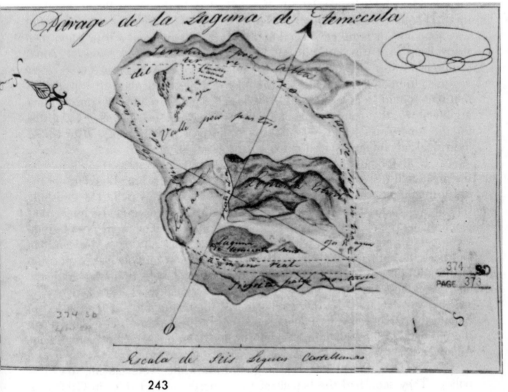

assurance that the national government would act in good faith. Instead, the United States followed a policy which placed an unreasonable burden of proof upon the grant holders, involved them all in court action, kept most of their cases in litigation for a decade and a half and some for much longer, piled up legal expenses which cost most of the grant holders the bulk of their property, and throughout this period deprived California of any security or certainty in land titles.

On the surface the issue would seem to have been very simple. By all the evidence available it appears that it would have been no superhuman task to distinguish between valid and invalid grants. Documents in the provincial archives, supplemented by sworn testimony that could have been taken from former officials, would have enabled any competent investigator familiar with the land system which had functioned in the province to determine which titles would have continued valid had the Mexican regime continued. These grants, probably nine tenths of all claimed, should have been duly surveyed and their titles confirmed. The task might reasonably have been completed within two or three years at the most.

Numerous hindrances arose. The earlier experience of Americans had not prepared them to understand the propriety of such large grants as were customary in California. For cattle raising as it had been conducted in the province and as it was later to be conducted on the Great Plains, holdings up to 11 square leagues (that is, up to 50,000 acres) were not excessive. Land was abundant; it required several acres to graze a cow, and a man could own many head of cattle and still not be rich. Few Americans, however, could comprehend this situation. Furthermore, most of the Mexican grants were vague as to boundaries or seemed irregular in other particulars. It was argued that they should be reduced to the American norm before confirmation. Another argument was that confirmation of all these titles would leave none of California for the Americans, whereas Manifest Destiny was usually expected to confer individual advantage as well as national aggrandizement.

Before any decision was reached, the entire issue was complicated by the great gold rush. In the eyes of eastern Americans the broad holdings of the Mexican grantees now appeared fabulously and inexcusably rich. The inrushing tide of Americans increased the pressure upon California's land supply, thus jeopardizing the older titles, while at the same time these newcomers as a group were more strongly afflicted with race prejudice against all things Mexican than had been the earlier arrivals from the States. The most forcible mass expression of this attitude was in the Sacramento squatter riots, a bold attempt to eradicate all preconquest titles without so much as the formality of legal action. The scheme was defeated "by the good sense of the community," but squatterism remained a potent force, its influences constantly directed toward breaking down the old and the large holdings and throwing them open to the "conquering" Americans.

The authorities at Washington, meanwhile, were moving toward a policy. They soon had the benefit of two reports on land titles in California, one by Captain H. W. Halleck and the other by William Carey Jones. Halleck intimated that there were imperfections in most of the Mexican titles which would give the United States an entering wedge for breaking them. Jones, after a careful examination of the California archives and consultation with Mexican and American officials in the province, reported that most of the titles were valid and that the few which were fraudulent could easily be detected. An official survey, he said, would be a sufficient preliminary to confirmation of most of the grants. The chief flaw in Jones' report was that it provided a more sensible basis for action than was desired by the majority at Washington or in California.

Jones' proposals were echoed in the Senate by Benton and Frémont. Benton stoutly opposed the creation of a special tribunal to pass on land titles. Such a step, he insisted, would be a violation of the recent treaty. He wanted confirmation made very simple, with the district court's findings final for values not exceeding $5,000. Frémont proposed a commission from which the claimant only could take an appeal. Senator Gwin countered with a substitute bill eliminating the restrictions on appeal by the United States. He argued plausibly that there was precedent in the Louisiana claims and that the courts could be counted on to decide justly, but neither he nor anyone else answered Benton's protest that the prolonging of litigation would spell confiscation rather than confirmation. Reading between the lines of the debates, it is clear that the Senators were more in sympathy with the squatters than with the grantees, that they suspected many of the grants to be fraudulent and most of them excessive in size, that they were alarmed by rumors concerning the McNamara colony, and that they pictured every California rancho as a prospective gold mine. Gwin's bill was enacted by the Senate with but a few negative votes on February 6, 1851, and by the House without debate on March 3.

The Course of Litigation

In accordance with this act a board of three commissioners was installed at San Francisco in January, 1852. Every claimant of land was required to appear before it within two years to present proof of title. The commission is probably the least denunciated feature of American land policy in California. It is admitted that the several commissioners were honest and conscientious men, though totally unfamiliar with local usage and with the Spanish and Mexican land system. They went as far as legal-minded persons might have been expected to go in simplifying the hearings and the taking of testimony from the non–legal-minded Californians. Even so, it was no easy matter for many of the Mexican grant holders to marshal the necessary proof for presentation. Their expenses were much increased because the commission, except for a short session at Los Angeles in the fall of 1852, held all its meetings at San Francisco. The commission acted fairly expeditiously on the 813 claims presented; by the date of its final adjournment on March 1, 1856, it had confirmed 521, rejected 273, and discontinued 19. The worst feature was one prescribed by the law, that claimants were considered guilty until they had proved their innocence. Their claims were reckoned faulty or fraudulent until positive proof to the contrary was brought forward.

The decisions of the commission, as already stated, were subject to appeal by either party for retrial in the district court. Some 132 claimants availed themselves of this privilege, and, through the introduction of new testimony to strengthen their cases, some 98 won reversal of judgment. The government attorneys were much more persistent in appealing. Their infinitesimal ratio of success, five out of 417 cases, is proof positive of excess of zeal. Following a consistent "make-work" policy, these lawyers laid great emphasis on petty technicalities and refused to content themselves with test cases. This needless persecution of the grant holders was applauded by the squatters. It was also a great boon to the legal gentry retained by the claimants. This group fattened on the additional fees, most of which could be raised only by sacrificing land or cattle or by mortgaging at ruinous interest rates. In many cases the cost of fighting an appeal was out of all proportion to the risk involved. Some 90-odd cases were carried on further appeal to the United States Supreme Court. Here again the majority of decisions favored the claimants. They, however, were put to heavy expense, the most vexatious being that of paying for transcripts of the records of the lower courts, even though the government had lodged the appeals. The Supreme Court heard no new testimony, but certain cases in which fraud was suspected were remanded to the lower courts for retrial. Even without retrial the process was long drawn out and costly.

The long-suffering claimants soon found that the end was not yet. Confirmation of title did not lead automatically to the issuance of a patent. In the first few instances a deputy of the Surveyor-General made a survey of the grant, which he forwarded to Washington where the commissioner of the land office, if he found everything in order, issued the final patent. By a law of 1859, however, this procedure was changed. It was required that the survey be submitted to the district court, whose decision as before was subject to appeal to the Supreme Court. Thus the unfortunate claimants were subjected to another long round of ruinous litigation with its full complement of delay, expense, and uncertainty. It meant that every claim might have to be defended six times against the United States: before the board of land commissioners, in the district court, and in the Supreme Court; then before the Surveyor-General and the land office, again in the district court, and again in the Supreme Court. It is appalling that such an unjust course was followed, but it certainly is not surprising that the government's unrelenting opposition kept most of the titles unsettled for a full 15 years.

Many of the claimants, needless to say, found that the confirmation and patent of their titles gave only an empty victory. For some it was a matter of their property having been eaten up by the heavy expenses of the protracted litigation. For others the real difficulty was that squatters refused to get off, even though the land case had been decided in favor of the grant holder. The squatter spirit is in evidence in a proposal of Gwin's in 1852 to allow squatters to "home-

Hay Field

Edward Weston

stead" 80 acres on Mexican grants, the grantees to be allowed a like number of acres from the public land. A state law four years later required grant holders to pay for improvements which squatters might have made or to sell at the appraised value of the land. This law was declared unconstitutional in 1857.

Barbecues to celebrate the defeat of Pico's Moquelumne claim in 1876 and of Berreyesa's Milpitas claim in 1877 may be considered proper manifestations of squatter feeling, though not the six-month imprisonment of Domingo Peralta by militant squatters in the East Bay area or the defiance of the sheriff who had come to evict them by 1,000 armed squatters near Santa Clara in 1861. Other examples might be cited of obstruction of justice and defiance of the authorities by squatters who had been worsted in the regular courts. Even where such tactics did not succeed they added to the expenses and the difficulties of the grant holders.

It is not easy in a few words to indicate the methods followed by commission and courts, the principles developed, and the points of law established. Obviously, the prime requisite was to prove that the grant had actually been made by an authorized agent of the Spanish or Mexican government. In support of such a grant the archival record was the preferred evidence. If archival evidence no longer existed the testimony of witnesses was considered,

247

but the court insisted that such testimony be full and conclusive. In the absence of archival evidence the Cambuston claim for 11 leagues in Butte County was confirmed by the commission and the district court largely because the United States did not contest the point. The Supreme Court, however, remanded the case, and upon retrial the district court decided that the original grant was not proved.

One point on which the courts were insistent was that no grant would be considered legal if dated after July 7, 1846, the date of Sloat's taking possession at Monterey. Although Governor Pico and the diputación had been still at large and still functioning, it became a fiction agreed upon that the Mexican regime had ended then. Incentive was thus offered for claimants of later grants to see that they were antedated, and this was the fraud most frequently alleged. The government attorneys, on the other hand, cited the statement of Mexico's treaty commissioner that no grants had been made after May 13 and urged invalidation of all grants made subsequent to the outbreak of the "war of conquest." The courts ruled, however, that July 7 was the magic date. The Palmer claim to Point Lobos, for example, was rejected upon proof that Governor Pico had not been at Los Angeles on the date when the grant was claimed to have been signed.

To many claimants it was equally vital to have determined the date of perfection of title to the grant. Under a Spanish grant of 1820 Luís Peralta claimed the San Antonio, comprising the sites of present-day Berkeley, Oakland, and Alameda. In 1842 he had divided this rancho among his four sons, a step confirmed also by his will nine years later. The courts upheld the titles thus created, excluding the sisters' claim, which would have been valid had the title of 1820 been considered perfect. Another example was provided by the descendants of Manuel Nieto. Occupation dated back to a grant from Governor Fages in 1784. Fifty years later Figueroa approved a division between two sons and the widows of two others. One of the widows, Josefa Cota de Nieto, sold her portion. Confirmation having been made by the United States courts on the basis of the grants of 1834, the California state courts decided that Josefa's sale was valid. Had the title derived from the grant of 1784, the sale would have been held illegal, and her children, as heirs of Don Manuel, would have been placed in possession.

Practically all the Mexican grants were conditioned upon occupancy and improvement within a year from the date of the grant. The district court was at first inclined to insist upon literal fulfillment of such conditions. But in the first case decided by the Supreme Court a rejection on these grounds was overruled, and thereafter reasonable excuses were accepted for the failure to meet the conditions. The line was usually drawn to bar claims to lands completely neglected or abandoned until the rise in value in the American period led to occupancy—for example, Noé's claim to an island in the Sacramento. Confirmation of Frémont's Mariposa claim represented perhaps the ultimate stretching of excuses for nonfulfillment of conditions; grantee Juan Bautista Alvarado had never set foot on the land and there was no attempt to improve it until after

California in 1858

J. H. Colton & Co.

the Mexican period had ended. In the same case it was judicially determined, although the Spanish-Mexican grants had not covered mineral rights, that mineral title accompanied land ownership.

The government attorneys attempted to invoke the Mexican statute prohibiting any grant within 10 leagues of the coast, but the courts wisely declined to give sudden effectiveness to a law which had been so frequently honored in the breach. The limitation to 11 leagues in grants to any individual was scrupulously upheld. William E. P. Hartnell, for example, presented adequate proofs for a 5-league grant to the Todos Santos at Santa Barbara and to 11 leagues at the Cosumnes. The latter was arbitrarily reduced to 6 leagues so that his total would not exceed 11. Other grants were for so many leagues, poco más ó menas, which came to be interpreted to mean plus, not more than one additional league.

Floating grants were a problem in themselves. These were grants usually within a specified area but with undefined boundaries. Needless to say, many such claims overlapped. In the second case that came before it the land commission adopted the procedure of permitting rival claimants to appear and contest the confirmation of conflicting claims. The method apparently was necessary, but the government attorneys abused it by encouraging opposition to claims that otherwise would have been incontrovertible. Where a floating grant, such as the Cajón at San Diego, was not impinged upon by others, no particular difficulty arose. But where there was conflict, decision was more difficult, particularly if priority in grant, occupancy, and confirmation was distributed rather than concentrated. Generally the earliest perfect title held, though with the proviso that in making out his boundaries the grantee must start with the land he had actually occupied. In a number of instances confirmed and patented grants left no room for other claims confirmed slightly later. For the Butano near Santa Cruz, for example, the surveyor could find only half a league of unpatented land left; worthless mountain land was thrown in to complete the amount allotted.

Sutter's claim to 11 leagues in the Sacramento Valley was confirmed as valid even though the original document had been burned in 1851. Location of the grant, however, proved a most difficult problem, which was not in the least simplified by Sutter's sales of parcels of land all up and down the valley. These land parcels are said to have been scattered over 100 leagues. On the basis of an error in the statement of the latitude of the southern boundary, the Sacramento squatters sought a ruling that their city and Sutter's Fort were not included in the New Helvetia grant, but the courts ruled otherwise. The first survey approved a 2-league tract embracing the fort and Sacramento City and a 9-league tract on the Feather including the site of Marysville. The district court preferred a gerrymandered survey which attempted to weave in all the lands the General had sold, but the Supreme Court returned to the first and simpler survey. Sutter claimed an additional 22 leagues under supplementary grant from Micheltorena in 1845, but the Supreme Court ruled adversely. Nor would it countenance the "general title" grants, claimed on certificates from

Sutter, which had been issued on the basis of a permit from Micheltorena dated December 22, 1844. The court ruled that the document from Micheltorena was nothing more than a bid for support against the Castro–Pico revolutionists, and that it was irregular and illegal. Bidwell's was the only "general title" claim upheld. The charge was made that he was favored because of his prominence, but in theory confirmation was on the basis of an earlier permission to occupy.

A particular cause of resentment was the tendency of the courts to decide land cases on what appeared to the laymen to be trivial technicalities. Thus one judge was ready to rule that P. B. Reading's grant was invalid on the ground that Mexico would have revoked it because of his participation in the Bear Flag movement. Vallejo's claim to the Soscol was rejected, though the documentary evidence was admittedly excellent. The grant had been made by Micheltorena in partial satisfaction of bills for supplying the provincial garrisons. Rejection was on the fantastic ground that the Mexican governor had been empowered to give away land but not to sell it. Another unpopular decision was that against Serrano for the Temescal near San Diego. Serrano had occupied the land in question ever since 1819. Such long and uncontested occupancy based on some sort of initial permit would probably have sufficed to establish title, but the document which Serrano submitted in support of his claim was a temporary permit of 1819. The court ruled that it ruined his claim to permanent title, though without the document title would presumably have been confirmed. The logic of such a decision was baffling.

Another apparent injustice was in the New Almaden case. In 1845, with the sanction of the Mexican authorities, Andrés Castillero had denounced the quicksilver mine a few miles south of San Jose. The surrounding land had previously been granted in two ranchos. In the American courts the New Almaden mining claim and the New Almaden land claim were purposely confuted by the government attorneys with these rancho claims. The Castillero land claim had not a leg to stand on. The mineral claim, having passed into the hands of a British company, was upheld by the land commission and the district court after prolonged hearings whose record ran to 3,584 printed pages, but the Supreme Court by a four-to-three decision reversed the verdict. The mining company strove mightily to get the survey modified to include the mine in the rancho it had acquired. Here again the result was failure. For the mine the company received only nominal compensation to the amount of $1,750,000, whereas the new syndicate which acquired it extracted $12 million worth of mercury within 15 years. The British mining company sought redress through the "Alabama" claims commission at Geneva in 1873 but without success. The impression is inescapable that this particular claimant was the victim of sharp practice on the part of the United States government.

Of outright fraudulent claims the most famous was José Limantour's. In February, 1853, this intrepid Gaul astounded the residents of San Francisco by laying claim to a 4-league grant including the better part of their fair city. The decade-old grant had never been announced, yet the documents and the testimony of witnesses seemed to be in order and the land commission approved the claim early in 1856. San Francisco was immediately in turmoil, and excited lot holders rushed to pay tribute to the Frenchman's gall by paying handsomely for quitclaims. William Carey Jones denounced the claim as fraudulent. Henry W. Halleck insisted that the grant would be invalidated because it included practically all the pueblo lands. John S. Hittell, on the other hand, gave his opinion that the claim was valid and that the squatters' only recourse was to deal with Limantour. Two years later in Judge Hoffman's court, the fraud was laid bare. Documents, it was proved, had been antedated, signatures had been forged, witnesses had committed perjury, and finally the seals on the Limantour grants were demonstrated to be counterfeit. Limantour not only abandoned his claim but prudently fled the country.

Several other fraudulent claims were exposed though none so grandiose as this one. A smaller number escaped detection until after the titles had been patented. The policy of the courts then was not to permit the reopening of the case by the government, certainly a tempering of justice with practical wisdom. A patent, however, did not protect against third parties. In 1870, for example, a litigant named Majors was awarded one third of the Rancho Refugio near Santa Cruz, though it had previously been patented to a certain Bolcof. Majors proved that the original grant had been to the Castro sisters, one of whom he had married, but that in the earlier trials the document had been presented with Bolcof's name fraudulently substituted for theirs.

Mission and Pueblo Lands

A special set of claims concerned the mission lands. In their original status under Spain and Mexico the missions had been granted no lands. The system was merely that the government refrained from granting to anyone else such lands as were needed by the neophytes. After secularization parts of the mission tracts had been granted to individuals, both Indian and white, and these grants were handled by the land commission exactly as any other Mexican grants to individuals. In a special category, however, fell some 17 claims based on sales by Governor Pico in 1845 and 1846. Differing from the regular colonization grants to which conditions of residence and improvements were normally attached, these sales were regarded as emergency measures partially necessitated by the crisis in provincial affairs. The validity of these titles was at least doubtful: sales had been private rather than at auction; a communication from Mexico City, dated November, 1845, had ordered suspension of such sales; and a subsequent order giving Pico and Castro "ample powers" for the defense of the province had not arrived until after most of these sales had been consummated. Eight of these titles were confirmed. The rest, including those of greatest intrinsic value, at San Francisco, San Gabriel, and Santa Barbara, were finally blocked by a Supreme Court ruling. Through its archbishop the Catholic Church entered a claim for a league of land at each mission, but, since no semblance of a grant could be produced, these titles were refused. The courts did confirm title to the actual mission sites, the cemeteries and gardens attached thereto, the Santa Inés College tract, and La Laguna at San Luis Obispo.

The Act of 1851 gave due recognition to the Spanish-Mexican practice whereby a town was entitled to 4 leagues of land. San Jose and Los Angeles as pueblos and Branciforte as a villa were obviously eligible; the pueblos subjoined to the presidios at San Diego, Santa Barbara, Monterey, and San Francisco could present a strong case for inclusion; and a number of Indian villages located at secularized missions were also qualified. Branciforte and several villages of the third class, including Las Flores, San Dieguito, San Pasqual, San Juan de Argüello, and San Juan de Castro, presented no claims. The post-Mexican towns of Sonora and Sacramento presented claims which were promptly thrown out, and the commission and courts were left with eight or ten claims of respectable antiquity. Several of these had complicating factors. Los Angeles asked for a tract 4 leagues square instead of 4 square leagues. Process of adjudication began, but before it was carried to a decision the city relinquished its claim to the larger area to get clear title to 4 square leagues. At San Jose the tract claimed was interspersed with parts of ranchos and other private grants, a condition that prevailed elsewhere as well. Litigation delayed confirmation of most of these titles until the sixties and the issuance of patents until the seventies or eighties.

The great contest, meanwhile, involved San Francisco. Government attorneys in fighting the claim charged that San Francisco had never been a pueblo. They insisted that Kearny had had no authority to relinquish the United States' claim to beach and water lots or even to ordinary town lots. They pointed out irregularities in the sale of lots by the town council and by a justice of the peace. Further complications included such matters as the sheriff's sale at nominal prices of many lots to satisfy Stephen Smith's claims against the city, and a variety of delineations of the town limits. Uncertainty was at its height in the late fifties when Limantour's claim was still pending, when parts of the city were being claimed as parts of other similar grants, and when a claim under Pico's sale of the mission lands had not yet been invalidated. San Franciscans could not be sure whether their title to lots should derive from the pueblo, from Limantour or some other "ranchero," from the purchase of the mission lands, or directly from the United States. Under such circumstances the difficulty of conveying title to town lots can well be imagined.

Various attempts to cut the Gordian knot were made. In 1851 the state legislature ceded water lots to the city. In 1855, by the Van Ness Ordinance, the city legalized lot holdings as of 1851. The legislature approved in 1858, and in a test case two years later the State Supreme Court upheld the pueblo title. Congress made the ordinance effective against any possible federal title, and in 1867 the pueblo title was finally confirmed. The matter of survey remained, and not until 1884 were attendant difficulties sufficiently ironed out so that the patent could be issued.

In Bancroft's opinion the United States' system of dealing with the California land claims "was thoroughly bad in almost every respect" and "merits only condemnation." Josiah Royce stigmatized it as "legalized meanness." John

S. Hittell's verdict was that it was outright "persecution." That the grant holders were unjustly treated is a patent fact. The damage, however, was by no means confined to them. All Californians suffered, the squatters included. For throughout the long period of this litigation, lasting until after the Civil War, no land title in the state was secure. It was impossible for a settler, whether businessman or agriculturist, to get certain title to any real property. All enterprise was thus subjected to an extra hazard. Since real estate was a doubtful collateral, interest rates were kept abnormally high, successful forty-niners hesitated to send for their families, and many of the most substantial men who had come in the gold rush reluctantly left the state. In 1863 Hittell estimated that California's population was a million persons less than it would have been had the question of land titles been settled promptly, fairly, and generously. The figure may be too large, but, excepting the land lawyers, it does appear that every class in California would have been much better off.

Mineral Rights

A companion evil, one for which the Californians were largely responsible, was the delay in providing for private ownership of mines. In the first years of gold washing, it was simpler that the entire mother lode country should be reckoned public domain and the individual ownership of a mining claim be purely usufructuary. By the middle fifties the drawbacks came to outweigh the advantages. Because of the impossibility of acquiring permanent title, miners were discouraged from installing expensive and efficient equipment. Like the ranch owners with clouded titles, they found it impossible to borrow money at reasonable rates. Consequently, they had no incentive to build adequate or respectable houses, and they wasted inordinate time and energy in moving about from one digging to another. But the roving habit was strong, and, since the system seemed to embody freedom, it was praised, though perhaps inaccurately, as a safeguard against monopoly. It did render the miners largely untaxable, which, despite the hardship on the tax-ridden cow counties, undoubtedly was a boon to the miners. As an unsettling factor, however, the practice was subject to most of the criticism leveled against the delay in providing sound titles to the state's urban and agricultural lands.

For Further Reading

W. W. Robinson, *Land in California* (1948).

Robert H. Becker, *Diseños of California Ranchos* (1964).

Ogden Hoffman, *Report of Land Cases Determined in the United States District Court of the Northern District of California* (1862).

JOHN W. DWINELLE, *Colonial History of San Francisco* (1863).

JOSIAH ROYCE, "The Squatter Riot of '50 in Sacramento," *Overland*, n.s. 6 (1885), 225–46.

HENRY GEORGE, *Our Land Policy, National and State* (1874).

PAUL W. GATES, "The Adjudication of Spanish-Mexican Land Claims in California," *HLQ*, 21 (1958), 213–26.

PAUL W. GATES, "California's Embattled Settlers," *CHSQ*, 41 (1962), 99–130.

PAUL W. GATES, "Pre–Henry George Land Warfare in California," *CHSQ*, 46 (1967), 121–48.

GREGORY YALE, *Legal Titles to Mining Claims and Water Rights in California* (1867).

IDWAL JONES, *Vermillion* (1967), a novel.

CAUGHEY, *California Heritage*, 299–301.

chapter sixteen

A White Man's Country

The California valley cannot grace her annals with a single Indian war bordering on respectability. It can boast, however, a hundred or two of as brutal butcherings, on the part of our honest miners and brave pioneers, as any area of equal extent in our republic.

Hubert Howe Bancroft,
History of California

"Wars" and Massacres

1848 to 1875

The first Indian policy in California was introduced in 1769 by the Spaniards. Its underlying principles were that the Indian should be preserved, civilized and improved, and used as the basic element in the permanent population. In coastal and southern California, mission, presidio, and pueblo had carried this process well along toward realization, at least to the degree that most of the labor at mission, town, and rancho was performed by "domesticated" Indians. The earliest arrivals from the United States accepted this attitude and soon came to regard the California native as a useful and acceptable element in the local population. Sutter, Bidwell, and others even extended the practice into the Sacramento Valley, and the mining

Mojave Mother and Children, 1908

A. L. Kroeber, Lowie Museum

season of 1848 witnessed something of the sort in the gold area, where the two races worked side by side and for the most part without friction in the extraction of the precious metal.

After the secularization of the missions, however, the Indian policy derived from Spain lost its vital features. The Indians already civilized or "domesticated" might continue so, though many reverted to their ancestral customs; no effective agency was at work for the training of additional Indians. Besides that decline grave abuses developed in the treatment of many former mission Indians. Walter Colton tells of the problems created by the ex-neophytes at Monterey. The year-by-year records of Los Angeles for the late forties and fifties abound with mention of the Indians reduced to starvation, beggary, and petty crime, of their hopeless addiction to drink, of Indians rounded up like cattle for the work season, and of the Monday slave mart at which their services for the week were auctioned off to cover the fines for their inevitable drunkenness. This shameful practice was matched by callous indifference to the killing of an Indian. The prevailing attitude seemed to be that such an act was by no means a crime.

In retrospect this misuse of derelict humanity may seem the darkest phase of local Indian history, but most southern Californians of the day were more alarmed by the depredations by Indians from the mountainous and desert interior. Such thievery had occurred during the Spanish and Mexican periods. Now renegades from the missions and a growing taste for horse meat and beef aggravated the practice, and at the same time the greatly improved market for ranch products magnified the value of the losses. To the local military and to the federal and state authorities southern rancheros clamored loudly for protection and for punitive expeditions against these marauders.

With the gold rush the great central valley, the Sierra foothills, and northern California were suddenly overrun by headstrong Argonauts engulfing whole tribes and dispossessing others of their hunting and food-gathering lands. These gold seekers had had no opportunity to absorb the Spanish philosophy of race relationships. Most of them had been nurtured on the contrary Anglo-American principle that the Indian should be made to give way before the advancing tide of white settlement, a principle alternately practiced through wars of extermination and treaties for Indian removal. On the overland routes to California, difficulties with the Pawnees and the Humboldt Valley Diggers inflamed hatred of Indians, and many miners transferred this hate to the California natives. The whites are charged with the first violence, though the mere entrance of miners into certain districts roused the Indians to resistance. Thereafter retaliation flowed in both directions, often without any discrimination between the original sinners and the innocent. For the operations that followed, the name "wars" is sometimes employed. It is a sordid and disgraceful chapter, never stressed in local histories.

The first of the so-called wars occurred in the spring of 1848. Outrages attributed to former members of the New York Volunteers led to retaliation by the natives of the Coloma district, whereupon the miners organized parties for Indian hunting. McKay's party is credited with killing 30 at one ranchería and capturing seven men and 40 women, while Greenwood's party at another village killed 20 and captured others, of whom six were sentenced to run before a firing squad. Only one escaped. For the rest of the year hostilities were avoided but in 1849 they broke out again, particularly on the Yuba and in the Kings River region, where the natives perpetrated a number of atrocities such as flaying intruders alive. The Yumas also inflicted insults and damages upon immigrants passing through their territory. In the Clear Lake country two settlers met a well-deserved death at the hands of the Indians. They were promptly avenged by a force under Captain Nathaniel Lyon which killed 175 Indians.

Indian depredations continued, often provoked by inconsiderate whites, and had cumulative effect in a series of campaigns in 1850. Regulars and militia after several pitched battles brought the Yubas to terms in May. Yet opportunities for friction were numerous and the peace did not last. When hostilities spread up and down the valley, the governor authorized Sheriff Rogers of El Dorado County to lead 200 volunteers into action. This time most of the Indians managed to elude Rogers. Those who put up a fight gave good account of themselves with their arrows. All the damage the posse could do was limited to the destruction of huts, acorn stores, and the like, and its exploits were reckoned far from brilliant. Campaigns in the San Joaquin foothills had similar results.

From Los Angeles, meanwhile, a company was raised to punish the Yumas for killing 11 Americans who had operated a Colorado River ferry. The campaign won little popular support, the general opinion being that the ferrymen were murderers and robbers who had deserved such a fate. By conscripting from emigrant trains, Joseph C. Morehead got together 125 men. He found the Indians quiet but prodded them into a fight in which a score of Indians were killed. The principal achievement of this campaign was an expense account of $76,588.

In 1851 the Yumas and the Luiseños gave southern California a more serious scare. The Luiseño chief claimed that 3,000 warriors would take the field. But regulars and volunteers were gathered at Los Angeles and San Diego, and the obstreperous Luiseño chief was seized by the Cahuillas and handed over for execution. Major H. P. Heintzelman made war on the Yumas and at length captured and executed their chief, and southern California returned to normal.

The most famous campaign of 1851 was that of the Mariposa Battalion under James D. Savage. After strenuous efforts the people of several hostile and semihostile rancherías were rounded up, but by a clever ruse Chief Tenieya and 350 Yosemites and Chowchillas gave their captors the slip, making a second campaign necessary. To recapture the chief the whites resorted to trickery. Exciting though the campaign was, the Mariposa Battalion's greatest achievement was the effective discovery of Yosemite Valley. Walker's fur men had looked down on the valley 17 years earlier, but not until these Indian hunters of 1851 came along was the majestic beauty hailed and appreciated. Yosemite soon became one of the show places of the state.

The northern fringe of the state was the next scene of conflict. Oregon was then in the throes of a bloodier war than any this state has witnessed. The Klamaths showed a disposition to follow the example of their northern neighbors but were held fairly well in check by army posts established at Humboldt, Reading Valley, and Scott Valley. Then in 1852 the Shastas went on the warpath, and the contagion spread to the Pit River Indians and the Modocs. The latter were held responsible for a midnight onslaught on an immigrant train on its way to California. Nearby miners organized to strike back. Negotiations were opened. Both sides suspected treachery, but the whites struck first, slaughtering some 40 Modocs in what is known as Ben Wright's Massacre.

The melancholy narrative continues: Oregon's Rogue River War kept on disturbing the northern California tribes. The Shastas were on a rampage in 1853, and other tribes committed depredations. Regulars and volunteers retaliated upon the lower Klamaths in 1854 and 1855, forcing them to accept reservation life. The fighting in Siskiyou County was drawn out longer. Even the mission Indians of southern California provided a war scare in 1857 but were placated by the appointment of agents, supposedly to provide for them. To hostilities in the San Joaquin Valley, General Kibbe responded in 1858–59 by campaigning in the Coast Ranges along its western edge, where he killed more than 100 natives and rounded up several times that many for the reservations.

Similarly, on Mad River and Eel River in the north, cattle stealing was the excuse for campaigns in which more than 200 Indians were massacred. The grand jury entered a courageous protest against these atrocities, but the prevailing sentiment is clearly indicated by the fact that Francis Bret Harte was practically run out of Humboldt County for sharply criticizing the massacre in his paper, the Union *Northern Californian*. The Hoopas held out obstinately for five years and were rewarded with an excellent reservation in the lower Trinity Valley.

Owens Valley supplied the next massacre. As advancing settlements cut down on their forage grounds, the natives were forced into cattle stealing. To abate this nuisance the settlers took the field in 1862 and again in 1865. In January of the latter year more than 40 Indians were massacred at one rancheria. The next month 100 or more were driven into the brackish waters of Owens Lake, where the whites "saw to it that they perished." This was the last major engagement in southern California though there was occasional sniping back and forth. In 1866, for example, the owner of Rancho San Pascual, at present-day Pasadena, was killed by Indian arrows. In 1867 the scene shifted to Pit River, where there occurred the usual sequence of depredations by the Indians, answered by a punitive campaign directed by General Crook.

The Modoc War

Nearby the stage was already being set for the dramatic climax of California Indian fighting, the Modoc War. In 1864 the Modocs had been forced to agree to move to a reservation in Oregon. They reckoned their lot doubly unsatisfactory because they were thrown in with a larger number of Klamaths who made their life miserable. After a short taste of reservation life Captain Jack (Chief Kientepoos) led his people back to their old haunts on Lost River. In 1869 he was persuaded to give the reservation another chance, but in the spring the 200 Modocs decamped once more in favor of their home land. Again overtures were made to persuade them to return to the reservation, but, the Indians proving adamant, the army was called to round up Captain Jack's band.

Warned of the advancing column, the Modocs took refuge in the impenetrable lava beds near Tule Lake. Captain Jack had only 50 fighting men equipped with muzzle-loading rifles and a few revolvers and encumbered with at least 150 women and children. Arrayed against them were 400 well-armed soldiers, 225 of them regulars, supported by a battery of howitzers. Colonel Frank Wheaton came to the natural conclusion that the quickest way to end the war was by an immediate attack in force. The attack was made on January 17, 1873. The Americans advanced bravely enough. They saw no Modocs, but from howitzers and rifles they poured a heavy fire into the lava beds. The Modocs answered with careful shots from their places of concealment, killing nine and wounding 30 before the Americans fell back. Wheaton sent for four more howitzers and 410 more men. Other attempts to dislodge the Modocs were no more successful; in fact, by means of captured rifles and ammunition the Indians were probably stronger than at the outset.

In such circumstances the Americans turned to a renewal of negotiations. Late in March, Captain Jack was persuaded to come out to a peace conference. He soon found that the only terms his antagonists would consider were those of absolute submission, this in spite of the fact that the Modocs had by no means been vanquished. His moderate proposals, such as a mutual surrender of thieves and murderers, were brushed aside as naive, as perhaps they were. The American commander, General E. R. S. Canby, would not concede the Modocs a reservation anywhere except among the overbearing Oregon Klamaths. Captain Jack seems to have had no illusions of success but agreed to consult with his tribesmen. They opposed his plan of working for peace and, by taunting him as a "fish-hearted woman," won him over to a plot to kill the American leaders at the next peace conference. The commissioners were warned by a Modoc woman, Winema or Tobey, but they proceeded with the conference on April 11. At Captain Jack's signal the Modocs whipped out revolvers and knives and even rifles. Canby and the missionary, Reverend Eleazer Thomas, were killed and Indian agent A. B. Mecham was wounded.

The Modoc leaders got off to the lava beds. More soldiers were brought up and battle was joined again. Another attempt to storm the Modoc position was as disastrous as had been the assault in January. But with supplies running low, the Indians had given up hope of attaining any favorable terms from their opponents. Split into smaller groups, they fled from their haven in the lava beds. One band was captured and its leader, Hooker Jim, offered to help take his former chief. At length, accompanied by three forlorn followers, Captain Jack came out and surrendered. With the loss of five men, two of whom were killed while trying to open an unexploded howitzer shell, Captain Jack had held off a far superior force for over three months. The Americans, meanwhile, had lost eight officers, 39 privates, 16 volunteers, two Indian scouts, and 18 civilians, besides numerous wounded. The expenses of the war were a round half million, whereas the Modocs would have been satisfied with a 2,000-acre reservation, worth at the most $20,000, or even with the worthless lava bed area. Besides having the best of the fighting, Captain Jack seems to have advanced the more reasonable arguments and proposals in the conferences held. His captors, however, were not swayed by any sentimental admiration. They tried him for his violation of the code of the whites, and in company with Black Jim and Boston Charley he was hanged at Fort Klamath.

Introducing the Reservation System

Throughout these years of warfare the United States government had employed its customary peaceful devices to solve the Indian problem in California. The first agents, Sutter, Vallejo, and J. D. Hunter, were named as adjuncts of the military by Kearny in 1847. Two years later they were followed by Subagent Adam Johnston, whose responsibility was to the newly created Department of the Interior. That same year California Indian affairs were given cursory examination by an emissary extraordinary of the Department of State, the cavalier Thomas Butler King. Far more important was the arrival in January, 1851, of three commissioner agents, Redick McKee, G. W. Barbour, and O. M.

Pomo Baskets

Wozencraft. These men found that the militia had just been called out for an Indian campaign in Mariposa County and that the legislature had just set up a "war chest" of $500,000.

The three commissioners plunged immediately into negotiations with the Central Valley and Sierra foothill tribes. Their basic theory was that the tribes whose lands had been taken over by the miners should be assigned tracts on the floor of the valley and suitably indemnified with beef, blankets, and other supplies. The theory was that to feed the Indians for a year would be cheaper than to fight them for a week. Eighteen treaties were negotiated, calling for the settling of some 139 tribes or villages on reservations adding up to about one fourteenth of the total area of the state. The program was endorsed by Edward F. Beale, newly appointed superintendent of the California Indians, but the Senate promptly rejected all 18 treaties. The Senate may have been aghast that the three commissioners with $50,000 appropriated for their expenses had laid out more than $700,000; it certainly was moved by the vehement protest lodged by California's representatives that the treaties deeded to the red men some of the best land in the state.

The summary rejection of the treaties encouraged further encroachment upon Indian lands and necessitated new expedients by the Indian superintendent. This officer, the spirited young lieutenant who had made the perilous trip to San Diego to get relief for Kearny after the battle of San Pascual, was equal to the occasion. He arrived on the scene in mid-September, 1852. Six weeks later he submitted a detailed proposal for a new program calling for a system of military posts "for the convenience and protection of the Indians." At each post there would be a resident agent vested with disciplinary authority and responsibility for instruction of the natives. The reservations thus created would have exactly defined limits. The Indians would be required to stay on the reservation and be taught civilized pursuits, such as farming and the simpler trades which would enable them to be self-supporting. This plan sounds very much like a revival of the Spanish mission, shorn only of its religious aspects. It sounds very little like the old-style "reservation" system through which the United States had been shunting the Indians out of the way of the juggernaut of white settlement.

On the basis of the blueprint drafted by Beale and his southern California subagent, B. D. Wilson, the new-style reservation system was inaugurated in California. From there, with slight modifications, it was taken to Oregon, Kansas, Nebraska, and New Mexico and became the kingpin of the United States' Indian policy. It became so much the standard that few persons would guess that its first use was as recent as the 1850's or that its place of origin was Beale's California.

Although Beale and Wilson are to be credited with devising and introducing the policy which the nation adopted, immediate results in California were far from brilliant. In the fall of 1853 they launched the first reservation at Tejon. The neighboring Indians were not easily persuaded to come in and experiment with the new life, but the superintendent's boundless energy and optimism, together with the loyal support of Wilson and other assistants, overcame the initial reluctance. The next June, Beale could report 2,500 Indians on this reservation and a first harvest of 42,000 bushels of wheat and 10,000 bushels of barley. Already, however, Beale was in disfavor at Washington, where political opponents had been after his scalp. They found a talking point in the irregularity of his financial accounts, and, although subsequent investigation absolved him of all blame, this attack led to his dismissal.

The next superintendent, Thomas J. Henley, expressed himself as fully in sympathy with Beale's program. He established four more reservations: at Fresno, at Nome Lackee near Tehama in the northwestern extremity of the Sacramento Valley, at Klamath River, and at Cape Mendocino. He even found a way of circumventing the legal limitation of the reservations to five by setting up "farms" that were reservations in disguise. Unfortunately, however, the increase in reservations seems to have appealed to Henley primarily because of the multiplication of the lucrative positions at his disposal. Most of his appointees were not of the high caliber of Beale's, and they were soon joined by their chief in cheating the government and the Indians. An official investigation in 1858 by J. Ross Browne disclosed the grossest mismanagement; for example, Indian supplies had been issued to laborers at a private sawmill, and other supplies had been bought at inflated prices through a store in which Henley had an interest. Consequently, there was a new superintendent in 1859, a sharp reduction in the appropriation, discharge of many persons who had in theory been working for the Indians, and abandonment of most of the farms and reservations.

Other vicissitudes followed. Tejon was abandoned in 1863. At the end of the decade only three stations were left, Hoopa and Round Valley in the north and Tule farm in the San Joaquin Valley. In 1870 these were transferred from army to Methodist supervision, a change that seemed to be for the better. The relocation of Tule farm in 1873, however, was to a new site which could support only about one fourth of the agency population. In 1870 there was a half-hearted attempt to provide a reservation for the mission Indians of the south. The Pala and San Pascual valleys were set aside for their occupancy, but white settlers of the vicinity took the announcement as an invitation to rush in and occupy this land. A resolute agent might have prevailed against these squatters, and a tribe like the Klamath probably would not have given in without a fight. These mission Indians, however, had repeatedly been imposed upon. They seemed aware of the futility of resistance. Their resignation in the face of injustice was at length rewarded with sturdy championing of their cause by Helen Hunt Jackson, Charles F. Lummis, and others, but not until much later was their lot ameliorated.

Decline in Number

Although early census figures on the number of "wild" Indians in California are not helpful, it is clear that in the third quarter of the nineteenth century the number of wild and of domesticated Indians was alarmingly and shamefully reduced. Wars and massacres contributed as did the expansion of white settlements and industries, which diminished the food resources of the natives. The reservation system or its abuses bore heavily on many tribes. Also, the government played fast and loose with the natives, keeping only those promises that suited its convenience. And finally disease, respiratory and venereal, took a heavy toll. By 1875 not more than one fourth as many natives remained as had occupied the state a quarter of a century earlier.

The crushing of the natives in numbers and in spirit is sometimes given the credit for the state's freedom from Indian "troubles" in the years thereafter, yet this happy result seems due primarily to the still more rapid increase of the white population. Reduced to so insignificant a minority, the Indians had no choice but to accept the white man's regulations.

For the present generation the natural tendency is to take the side of the Indian. For a long span of years—in fact, the mind of man now runneth not to the contrary—we have been in perfect safety from Indian attack or depredation. Anthropological studies have played up the aboriginal virtues and attainments. The Indian was the underdog, and the land, we freely admit, was originally his. In the early American period, however, even this justice was denied the California native. The Treaty of Guadalupe Hidalgo, it was held, had transferred full title to the land from Mexico to the United States government and therefore no further formalities or compensations were necessary for extinguishment of Indian title. This legalistic argument is a clue to the attitude then current. Rather than idealized as at present, the redskin was feared, hated, and despised. That state of mind explains but does not excuse the heartless liquidation of the California Indians.

Discriminations against Other Races

Race prejudice showed itself against other groups. Vicente Pérez Rosales, a distinguished Chileño, on one occasion rescued some of his countrymen from discriminatory abuse by giving the impression that they were Frenchmen. The French themselves ran into difficulty in the diggings, though the principal incident, the so-called French Revolution, passed off without a pitched battle. Australians in San Francisco were particular targets of the vigilantes in 1851. It was, however, against Indians, Negroes, Mexicans, and Chinese that white or Yankee superiority was most glaringly asserted.

By the fall of 1849, when the constitutional convention assembled, the miners had made clear that they wanted no competition from slave gangs. Relatively few southerners had brought slaves, which meant that the threat was remote. A related contingency pressed the issue of making California a free state; only thus was there prospect that the Congress would approve statehood. The convention went further and tried to ward off any suggestion of future division which might have produced a slave territory or state in southern California. Many who were against slavery were as adamant against admitting free Negroes. This proposition was debated at length before being set aside.

The antislavery provision in the constitution lacked teeth against the holding of slaves brought earlier into the state and was weakened further by a state fugitive slave law enacted in 1852. Masters asserting intention of taking slaves back to a slave state had some color of protection. The most famous case on this issue reached the California supreme court in 1858. Justices Peter H. Burnett, who had been the first elected governor, and David S. Terry conceded that the master was not legally entitled to possess Archy Lee as a slave, but, since this was the first case and would be a hardship to the owner, they were "not disposed to rigidly enforce the rule." They returned the slave to his owner.

The owner promptly started for Mississippi. In San Francisco he was intercepted by a new court action which hinged on the fugitive slave issue, and by court order Archy Lee was set free. Perhaps as a carry-over of the condescension toward Negroes, this case comes down in history not as *Lee* vs. *Stovall* but as *ex parte Archy*.

Meanwhile, the first legislature had barred testimony by a Negro against a white in criminal litigation, and the second legislature had extended the ban to civil cases. Prominent Negroes such as William Yates, Mifflin Gibbs, and Jonas H. Townsend petitioned the legislature to rescind these actions and won support from such notables as Edward D. Baker, David Broderick, and J. Neely Johnson. In 1863, stimulated by the war for the Union, the legislature authorized Negro and Indian testimony, though not testimony by Chinese.

Discriminations against Negroes continued. In 1870 a Negro couple in San Francisco objected to the practice of school segregation. They tried to enroll their child in the school nearest their residence and were refused admission. They went to court for an order to the principal of the school to admit their child, but were rebuffed in the decision in *Ward* vs. *Flood* in which the court fully accepted the rationale of separate but equal.

Discriminations against Mexicans are much better known, in part because there were so many more Mexicans. Yankee newcomers conceded themselves a superiority, demonstrated, so they said, by the victory in the War with Mexico. Old-line Californians as well as gold seekers from Mexico were forced out of the better diggings. This discrimination was legalized in the Foreign Miners Tax of 1850, aimed more against Mexicans than anyone else. The prejudice was made more explicit in the Anti-Greaser Act of 1855, ameliorated only slightly the next year by deleting the word "greaser" though retaining the impact. Vigilantism, as indicated, was also carried out prejudicially against Mexicans and other "foreigners."

These pressures caused resentment, again especially by the Mexicans, who found a way to express it in banditry. The legendary hero here was Joaquín Murieta, in Martin Noble Burns' phrase, the Robin Hood of Eldorado, who took it upon himself to avenge the slights and cruel slings to his countrymen. His deeds of brigandage were rivaled by those of Juan Flores in the fifties and Tiburcio Vásquez in the sixties and seventies.

Murieta so terrorized the southern mines and the San Joaquin that the legislature commissioned a posse headed by former Texas ranger Harry S.

Joaquín Murieta

Charles Nahl, The Bancroft Library

Love to run him down. Love and his men returned with a head that they represented as Joaquín's and collected the reward, plus a $5,000 bonus added by the legislature. Murieta lived on in legend, claimed by Chile as well as Mexico, painted in heroic pose by Charles Nahl, and acclaimed in a best seller, *The Life and Adventures of Joaquín Murieta* (1854), by John Rollin Ridge, perhaps the more sympathetic because he was a Cherokee.

Many of the Mexican forty-niners went back to Mexico and some Mexican Californians also repatriated. In northern California the old-timers almost immediately became a minority; in southern California they were not outnumbered for another twenty years. Their relative share of California wealth fell off as they were shunted out of the diggings, lost their titles by the Land Act or the cost of litigation, and had difficulty competing with the more aggres-

Young Aristocrats

Arnold Genthe

sive newcomers. Yet many of this group accommodated to the new regime and assimilated into the new society.

The first Chinese to come to California were given a place of honor at San Francisco's celebration of admission to statehood. In the diggings, however, the hardy miners acted on the assumption that Providence as well as the Mexican War had made California a white man's country. They had no intention of letting Chinese stake out claims and compete on equal footing. Chinese swarmed to the area. By 1852 there were 25,000 in the state, making them the largest minority, and most of them were in the mines. For the state, one person in ten was Chinese; in some of the mining counties, three out of ten.

In 1852 Senator George B. Tingley introduced a measure to authorize contract labor on a ten-year basis, supervised by the state. The assembly approved, but the senate, alert to what this would mean in the mines, defeated the bill. When Governor John Bigler urged a law to check the tide of Asiatic immigration, Rev. William Speer, a former missionary, spoke up in praise of the Chinese, but others bore down on them as morally depraved transients and a menace to the state's tranquillity. The legislature responded with a renewal of the foreign miners' tax with full expectation that its principal application would be to the Chinese. There were evasions and peculations by some of the collectors, but from that date, 1852, through the sixties nearly a quarter of the state's receipts would be from this tax.

In 1854 the state government added another thrust. In *People* vs. *Hall* the state supreme court extended the constitutional ban on testimony against a white by an Indian to exclude the Chinese as well. The reasoning was that "Indian" was a generic term intended to cover all nonwhites, to which the justices added what was then the quaint notion that Indians and Chinese were of the same "Mongolian" branch of mankind.

The Chinese endured these and other discriminations. In the sixties the building of the Pacific Railroad improved the market for labor and, though thousands were imported, little friction resulted. Chinese also proved themselves in agricultural labor. They began the process of establishing a welcome as launderers, houseboys, cooks, and vegetable growers and peddlers. Yet in these first decades there was a foretaste of greater discriminations to come.

For Further Reading

SHERBOURNE F. COOK, *The Conflict Between the California Indian and White Civilization*, part III: *The American Invasion, 1848–1870* (1943).

WILLIAM H. ELLISON, "The Federal Indian Policy in California, 1846–1860," *MVHR*, 9 (1922), 37–67.

EDWARD E. DALE, *The Indians of the Southwest* (1949).

THEODORA KROEBER, *Ishi in Two Worlds* (1961).

LAFAYETTE H. BUNNELL, *The Discovery of the Yosemite and the Indian War of 1851* (1880).

JOHN W. CAUGHEY, *The Indians of Southern California in 1852* (1952).

STEPHEN BONSAL, *Edward Fitzgerald Beale, A Pioneer in the Path of Empire* (1912).

J. ROSS BROWNE, *The Indians of California* (1864).

KEITH A. MURRAY, *The Modocs and Their War* (1959).

MAX HEYMAN, *Prudent Soldier*, (1960), a biography of E. R. S. Canby.

RUDOLPH M. LAPP, "Negro Rights Activities in Gold Rush California," *CHSQ*, 45 (1966), 3–20.

WILLIAM E. FRANKLIN, "The Archy Case," *PHR*, 32 (1963), 137–54.

ELMER SANDMEYER, *The Anti-Chinese Movement in California* (1939).

PING CHIU, *Chinese Labor in California, 1850–1880* (1963).

GUNTHER BARTH, *Bitter Strength: A History of the Chinese in the United States, 1850–1870*, (1964).

CAUGHEY, *California Heritage*, 20–24, 248–57, 262–64.

chapter seventeen

Cultural Awakening

Between 1848, when James W. Marshall discovered gold at Coloma, and 1869, when San Francisco celebrated the building of a railroad that ended its isolation, a people lived through a condensed version of the world's economic and cultural growth. To this phenomenon the writers of El Dorado owe their distinction and western literature its absorbing interest.

Franklin Walker,
San Francisco's Literary Frontier

Church and School

1848
to
1875

From the sordid accounts of land cheats and the tragedy of Indian slaughter it is a pleasure to turn to a more creditable manifestation of gold-rush influence, the stimulation of a cultural awakening. This awakening found expression in the establishment of schools and churches, a flourishing theater, a lush growth of journalism, and a sudden outpouring of creative and entertaining writing.

Long before the coming of the Americans the Spaniards had made California a Christian land. To them, of course, Christian meant Roman Catholic. By contrast, the American pioneers and most of the gold seekers came from an environment where Protestantism

Ballard's Little Red Schoolhouse
in use continuously since 1883.

King Merrill

prevailed. Their impact on the province included holding Protestant services and organizing Methodist, Baptist, and other churches. Several denominations sent missionaries to California, the American armed forces brought chaplains, and the forty-niners included a goodly number of clergymen. One observer, doubtless exaggerating, put the preachers at one in ten. San Francisco as in all else took the lead. In November, 1848, a conclave of its citizens invited Rev. Timothy Dwight Hunt to be city chaplain on a nondenominational basis. Thirteen months later there were 12 bona fide ministers established in their work, and by the mid-fifties San Francisco could boast 32 churches, ranging from African Methodist to Welsh Presbyterian.

The pioneer period is better represented by William Taylor's street preaching in San Francisco or by the circuit rider in the diggings who persuaded a saloonkeeper to clear a space before the bar for a Sunday morning discourse. Except in the suddenness with which organized churches took shape California's experience was that of the West in general. Many of her pioneers had no interest in churches. Others out of homesickness or conviction wanted the solace of religion. They tried to achieve as close a reproduction as possible of their accustomed church.

How well they succeeded is another matter. Sarah Royce, perhaps with excess of charity, remarks on the "fixed attention," the "intense earnestness," and the "reverence, devotion, and glow of intelligence" characterizing the congregation she observed in San Francisco. Visiting that city in 1859, Richard Henry Dana, author of *Two Years Before the Mast*, met a Harvard man, a regular churchgoer in New England, who could not even direct him to Bishop Kip's church. Once he found it, Dana observed that the congregation was "precisely like one you would meet in New York, Philadelphia, or Boston." In mundane terms this was exactly what those who brought Protestant Christianity to the Pacific coast wanted to accomplish.

Although it was said of San Francisco at the time that being a religious man was considered "not exactly a crime but only a misfortune," men of outstanding talent labored in its churches. Among them Episcopalian Bishop W. Ingraham Kip, Catholic Archbishop Joseph S. Alemany, Presbyterian William A. Scott, and Unitarians Thomas Starr King and Horatio Stebbins were leading and influential citizens.

In one respect the results were far inferior to the Spanish achievement. Notwithstanding some lapses, as at San Luis Rey, the massive architecture of the missions was well suited to the land. The church buildings of the early American period were of all shapes and styles or of no style at all. They disfigured the scene more often than adorned it, though they did symbolize the cosmopolitan character of gold-rush California. To all concerned, what went on within them was all that mattered.

The story of formal education in California begins with the Franciscan missions. For pupils other than Indians Bancroft lists 55 schools of the Spanish and Mexican periods. Except for W. E. P. Hartnell's Colegio de San José all were elementary and most functioned only briefly. It is understandable that, when it could be afforded, boys were sent away to Honolulu, Valparaiso, or even to Paris for their elementary schooling. In 1847 several American-type schools were opened, the first at Santa Clara. On April 3, 1848, San Francisco pioneered with a public school taught by Thomas Douglas, formerly of the Young Chief's School in Honolulu. By the end of May, when four of the five trustees and all but eight of the pupils had been carried away by the gold fever, schoolmaster Douglas closed his classroom and took himself off to the mines.

The upsurge of population, wealth, and, more gradually, of stability contributed by the gold rush gave momentum to the demand for schools. Organized religion lent its support. Several of the missionary pastors engaged in teaching as well as in preaching. Schools were opened under other private auspices. This development was all very well, but in the American culture pattern being transfixed upon the state a cardinal feature was recognition of the public responsibility to provide for instruction. The state constitution obligated the legislature to provide for a school, operating at least three months every year, in each district in the state. The legislature in 1851 passed an implementing act, later improved and broadened.

The first state superintendent of schools, John C. Marvin, was elected in 1851. He worked diligently for a state commitment to a system of public schools which would be free, secular, compulsory, state financed, and relevant for Californians by including geology and mineralogy and stressing Spanish and French rather than Latin and Greek. The legislature moved gradually in the direction Marvin recommended, and within two years public schools were opened in 47 counties. In 1853 the Democrats paid a political debt by giving the nomination and the job to a venerable state senator. In 1862 the state by good fortune found a dedicated, energetic, and persuasive apostle of education in the person of a young San Francisco teacher, John C. Swett.

John C. Swett

The Bancroft Library

Twice reelected, Swett had a total of five years in which to make his imprint on the state school system. His achievements included a rewriting of the school law in 1866 and completion of the transition to a free public school system. He has been hailed as the Horace Mann of California and the father of this state's public school system. Swept out of office in the Democratic landslide of 1867, Swett went back to the ranks of teacher and principal of the Denman Girls School at Fifth and Market in San Francisco. He continued as a principal in San Francisco until 1890 when, upon challenging Blind Boss Buckley's exercise of the patronage in school appointments, he was forced to resign.

California's first kindergarten opened in San Francisco in 1863, and its most famous one, the Silver Street kindergarten in Tar Flat, a slum as tough as the Barbary Coast, was opened by Kate Douglas Wiggins, later a very successful children's writer. Meanwhile, a number of academies and seminaries, approximately of high school level, had been started, and in 1856 San Francisco pioneered with the first public high school.

The University of Santa Clara traces its origins back to the College of Santa Clara and to classes conducted in 1851. The University of the Pacific, through a college, traces back to 1851, and the University of California, through the private College of California which it later absorbed, goes back to 1855.

In 1868, encouraged by the federal subsidy offered through the Morrill Land Grant Act, the legislature chartered the University of California as a state institution. It enrolled its first students at Oakland in 1869 and the next year took the radical step of admitting women students. In 1872 it gained distinction through the appointment of Daniel Coit Gilman as president and the following year shifted to its campus designate at Berkeley. From the start the university had some excellent men on its faculty, including John and Joseph LeConte, professors of physics and geology, and Ezra S. Carr, professor of agriculture and horticulture. It was not, however, a university in today's sense, associating several collegiate programs or offering advanced work. In 1874 a controversy came to a head over whether the stress should be on agriculture and mechanic arts with instruction in carpentry, blacksmithing, and other practical fields or on a more comprehensive and liberal program of instruction. The general education advocates prevailed, but before the year was out President Gilman decided that he would find a more congenial climate of opinion in the East and resigned to go to Johns Hopkins where he developed the first genuine graduate school in the United States.

The Theater

The theater was a culture form that could respond buoyantly to the stimulation of gold. Although there had been amateur performances such as those by the men of Stevenson's regiment, bored by garrison duty at Monterey, the first professional to take a turn apparently was Stephen Massett from England. In June, 1849, he put on a one-man show at San Francisco. In a rich baritone he sang several of his own compositions; in falsetto he mimicked an operatic diva. Next came a series of monologues in Yankee dialect, climaxed by a seven-voice rendition of a New England town meeting.

Massett was followed by a minstrel show at the Bella Union, its run cut short when one of the "bones" was killed. Later in 1849, in a large tent at Clay and Kearny, Joseph Rowe presided over a circus featuring nine acrobats and equestrians and a posing horse.

At Sacramento the Eagle Theater company opened with "The Bandit Chief; or, The Forest Spectre." Plays such as "The Wife," "Dead Shot," "Othello," "Batchelor Buttons," "William Tell," "Rent Day," and "Charles II" were also in the repertoire. In January, 1850, this company brought legitimate theater to San Francisco. Although the manager of the troupe lost the first week's receipts at monte, the popular response encouraged other impresarios to provide similar entertainment. Rowe built a platform across one end of his tent and substituted actors for acrobats. As an annex to the Parker House saloon and gambling hall Tom Maguire opened a theater which he called the Jenny Lind. When this theater burned he built a second Jenny Lind; when it burned, a third, which the city fathers bought for a city hall. With $50,000 raised by popular subscription Dr. David Robinson built the Adelphi. He was responsible also for the American Theater and had a share in Bryant Minstrels, later converted into San Francisco Hall and still later into Maguire's Opera House.

The ebullience of the audience often made playing the San Francisco stage an exciting experience. Making the circuit of the mining camps was even more of a test. Traveling by stagecoach or on horseback, putting up at primitive hotels, living on rough fare, and performing in makeshift theaters, the troupers had to rise above circumstances. A play, often sharply curtailed, was the feature of each performance. To it the artists added solos, dances, readings, impersonations, and skits, so that the evening's entertainment combined legitimate theater and vaudeville.

Although their critical faculties may have been dulled by long absence from the theater, the mining camp playgoers were exacting. As in San Francisco, when lines were cut, forgotten, or muffed, they stamped and hooted. On the other hand, if a performance caught their fancy, they showered the stage with coins, nuggets, and bags of gold dust.

The theater faced competition from cockfights, bull-and-bear fights, and other bizarre amusements. The saloon and the gambling hall were more potent counterattractions. Borrowing from the theater, the larger of these establishments added musicians, dancers, variety acts, and minstrel acts. That the theater did compete successfully was in part due to the headline talent that came to the Gold Coast. Representing the minstrels were Ed Christy, end man Eph Horn, soft-shoe dancer Dan Bryant, and banjo virtuoso Thomas F. Briggs. Singers Elisa Biscaccianti and Kate Hayes joined the trek. So did a host of noble actors, including the Booths, the Chapmans, Edwin Forrest, Catherine Sinclair, and such personalities as Lola Montez, Adah Isaacs Menken, and Mathilda Heron.

Above all others the paragon of the gold-rush theater was Lotta Crabtree. Her debut was at a tiny log theater in Rabbit Creek. In long-tailed green coat, knee breeches, and tall hat, she bounced onstage and danced a vigorous Irish jig and reel. After encores she reappeared in a white dress with round neck and puffed sleeves and sang a plaintive ballad. The hardened miners went wild, showering the stage with coins, nuggets, and a 50-dollar slug. Black-eyed, red-haired Lotta, all of eight years old but looking no more than six, was their darling.

Tutored by her ambitious mother, Mart Taylor, and other willing helpers, Lotta made a rapid tour of the camps. She learned new songs and steps. A Negro minstrel taught her to do a soft-shoe breakdown. Lola Montez introduced her to Spanish dancing and Jake Wallace taught her how to make a banjo ring. From others she picked up buck and wing and new bits of pantomime. Thus equipped she could put on a whole show in the style of Stephen Massett. By the mid-fifties, however, talent was so abundant that the real problem was to get a chance to perform. Lotta's mother was a persistent agent. With barrel-top numbers at auctions, variety billings in the mines and at San Francisco, bits in the regular plays, and specialties between acts, Lotta had a busy childhood. In one little vibrant bundle of energy she represented the things the Californians of this generation most prized: humor and pathos, high skill and lower buffoonery, mastery of the traditional forms and indulgence in pyrotechnics.

The theatrical pageantry that Lotta represents rested on the gold rush. Without the rewards so manifestly present none of the name talent would have come all the way to California. Probably, had it not been for the confidence lent by the gold, the provincial audiences would not have been so free about molding actors and vehicles to suit the California taste.

Less spectacularly the gold rush encouraged the pictorial arts. In illustrated books, in canvases hung on widely scattered walls, and in illustrated letterheads issued by California stationers, this record is partly preserved. Delano's drawings, Charles Nahl's group scenes, J. W. Audubon's travel sketches, J. Goldsborough Bruff's sketches, the paintings of W. S. Jewett and Thomas Hill, and Edward Vischer's lithograph prints are examples of this work. Realism is in conflict with romanticism and usually realism prevails.

Journalism

California writing began long before the golden era. The classics include Palou's *Life of Serra,* Font's *Complete Diary,* Shaler's *Description,* Pattie's *Personal Narrative,* Robinson's *Life in California,* Bryant's *What I Saw in California,* and Frémont's *Report.* Most of these books are distinguished for content more than for style, yet they are usually pronounced readable, and one of their company, Dana's *Two Years Before the Mast,* besides being widely circulated, is frequently used in academic courses as a model of style in English composition.

Palou's and Font's writings were works of Christian duty, but these writers, like the others, were inspired by a conviction that the exciting California experiences of which they had direct knowledge were eminently worth recording and would be read with interest in Mexico and Spain or in the States. The same is true of the trail journals, ocean logs, and miners' diaries of '49. Like their predecessors, these chroniclers were writing for the effete East rather than for local consumption. The first book printed in the province, Figueroa's 16-page code of laws (1834), though intended for local use, was hardly literature; nor was the arithmetic book *Tablas por los niños que empiezen a contar* printed two years later. The same charge may be safely leveled at Mason and Brannan's *Laws for the Better Government of California* printed in 1848.

The outset of the American period was marked by an improved demand for reading matter, a demand that was met after a fashion by the shin-plaster journals started by Semple and Colton at Monterey and by Brannan and Kemble at San Francisco. With the gold rush this demand greatly increased. It was evidenced by the long queues at the San Francisco post office, the special fees readily collectible for delivery of letters at the mines, the popular excitement whenever a steamer entered the Golden Gate, and the high prices current for eastern newspapers which were part of the incidental baggage of the Argonauts. Fifteen hundred copies of Greeley's *Tribune*, brought by a fellow passenger of Bayard Taylor, sold within two hours for a dollar apiece.

The first repercussion of the gold excitement in the summer of 1848, drawing away editors and compositors as well as subscribers and advertisers, was the suspension of publication of the pioneer weeklies, the *Californian* and the *California Star*. The secondary effect was the creation of a much larger field for journalism. Reviving their moribund sheets, the editors decided on January 4, 1849, to pool their resources in a new venture, the subsequently famous *Alta California*. In May the *Placer Times* blossomed at Sacramento, followed shortly by a motley assortment of papers scattered through the bay region and the mining towns. Included for a short time in the fall of 1850 was the *Illustrated Times*, which lived up to its name by featuring woodcuts. Also of short duration was the allegedly humorous *Hombre* of 1851, a pioneer in its field. Reflecting California's cosmopolitan character, the press quickly became multilingual. In 1850 there appeared the first French paper, in 1852 a German organ, two years later the first Spanish journals, and shortly after one in Chinese. Eventually there were publications in practically all languages including the Scandinavian.

Quantitatively, California journalism scaled heights that, without the gold rush, would not have been attained for decades. For many years the state could boast a per capita circulation exceeding even that of New York. As to quality, praise must be more niggardly. The presses, type, and paper available were uniformly inferior, composition and presswork were indifferent, and proofreading was an undeveloped art. Most of the sheets were blatantly partisan and reflected the malodorous state of local politics. News coverage was haphazard, editors depended largely on their shears, and much that was printed seemed to have no other justification than that it filled space. The most hopeful sign was a tendency to escape some of the current inhibitions of eastern journalists.

San Francisco, naturally enough, had the lion's share of these early newspapers, yet some of the most influential journals were not of the city. Two examples stand out, the Sacramento *Union* and the Virginia City *Territorial Enterprise*. In the fifties the Sacramento *Union* was of moderate significance. It had the advantage, however, of being near the seat of state government and the greater advantage of honest, patriotic, and high-minded management. Its proprietors, James Anthony, Paul Morrill, and H. W. Larkin, aimed to be fearless champions of the common people and to the best of their ability they adhered to that policy. The most momentous example was doubtless in the early sixties when the paper was one of the staunchest supporters of the Union cause and was credited with greater effectiveness than an army corps. Most dramatic was the refusal of the three partners to move their paper to San Francisco even though it was clear that in no other fashion could it be maintained as a dominant journal. They elected to stand by their guns, with the result that the *Union* declined in importance and in 1875 was purchased and absorbed by its rival, the *Record*.

The *Union's* proprietors wielded a remarkable influence and employed and subsidized a notable staff of writers, among whom Henry Clay Watson and Samuel Seabough were the most notable examples and Mark Twain, the most famous. It was a "travel grant" from the *Union* that made possible Twain's jaunt to the Sandwich Islands, which in turn led to his career as a platform lecturer, his world tour, and the travel book *Innocents Abroad*.

The *Territorial Enterprise* issued from Washoe, later labeled Nevada, but the society which it vocalized was part and parcel of the California culture area, and it is no violence to the facts to include it in a discussion of the state's early journalism. In addition, the *Enterprise* had special ties with California. Joseph T. Goodman, its editor and guiding genius, was a graduate of California's *Golden Era*, as was Rollin M. Daggett, whose principal fame is as cofounder of that magazine. Mark Twain heads the list of those who reached California publishers by way of the Nevada paper which he immortalized so satisfactorily in *Roughing It*. The journal flourished in the lush environment of sagebrush and alkali, nurtured on the white gold of the fabulous Comstock. The Washoe community was, if possible, more masculine and more unrestrained than had been the camps of the forty-niners. Journalism in this unreal setting was free to follow any path of hyperbole or to perpetrate any outlandish hoax and under no obligation to print a story just because it was news. With what gusto the "sagebrush school" embraced this opportunity is to be seen in the books of Mark Twain and Dan De Quille (William Wright) or, better still, in the broken files of the *Territorial Enterprise*.

From *Golden Era* to *Overland Monthly*

Most early California newspapers contained a few literary pieces, which were received with enough favor to suggest in 1852 the issuance of a weekly paper largely devoted to such materials. This journal, the *Golden Era*, included ordinary news but its distinction lies in its emphasis on literature. Its popularity was both immediate and sustained; it flourished for almost half a century and was read more widely than any of its competitors. This very popularity made the journal suspect. Superior and condescending critics have often remarked that the *Era* catered to low tastes, specifically to those of California's rustics and miners. The accusation may be true; attired in miner's boots and flannel shirt, coeditor Daggett did tour the diggings soliciting subscriptions. The editors furthermore chose to emphasize California themes. To start the paper off, Daggett had written up an episode experienced on the overland trail from the States, and his partner, J. Macdonough Foard, had drawn similarly on his recollections of Cape Horn. To the end the *Era* dealt mainly with matters within the comprehension or even the experience of a majority of Californians. Only in dramatic criticism did it take on airs; for years it constituted itself the mentor of the San Francisco stage.

For all its popularity the *Era* did not draw the best writing. Contributors, having acquired a reputation through its columns, were quick to desert to more pretentious journals. Thus surprisingly little of the prose and poetry that appeared in the *Era* was judged worthy of inclusion in the collected works of Mark Twain, Bret Harte, and the rest. With one or two exceptions, however, the entire galaxy of early California writers found their initial opportunity in the *Era*. Alonzo Delano's pen name, Old Block, was a frequent signature during the fifties, as were also Caxton (William A. Rhodes) and Yellow Bird (John R. Ridge). In the sixties the new editor, Colonel Joe Lawrence, was even more indefatigable in casting the net for local writers. Mark Twain, fresh from his triumphs with the *Territorial Enterprise*, contributed enough sketches to make a small volume. Bret Harte entered "by the backdoor" as compositor and before long contributed "M'liss," archtype of the California short story. Ina Coolbrith, Joaquin Miller, Charles Warren Stoddard, and Charles Henry Webb, better known to his readers as Inigo, are representative of others who got their start with the miners' favorite. So notable a roster is ample justification, if any is needed, for the *Era*'s policy of being popular and unpretentious.

Competitors were numerous but for the most part short-lived. One of these was the *Pioneer*, launched as a monthly in January, 1854, and kept afloat only two years. Its editor, Ferdinand C. Ewer, is better known for his fervent espousal of one ism after another. He was in turn a Unitarian, an Episcopalian, an atheist, a Trinitarian, a spiritualist, and finally an Episcopalian again. His excursion into mysticism, entitled "The Eventful Nights of August 20th and 21st," was the toast of the spiritualists—until he announced that it was a hoax. The *Pioneer* was of too short duration to exemplify his theological mutations and was, furthermore, only slightly philosophical.

In the first issue, probably to emphasize the contrast to the *Golden Era*, Ewer announced that the new magazine would be devoted to literature, politics, science, belles-lettres, poetry, and "the more flowery paths of Literature." The contributions of California writers, he predicted, would make the magazine a credit to "the noble State in which it had its origin." The promise was in fair degree realized. Descriptive pieces and semihistorical reminiscences outbulked fiction, and space was devoted in each number to a commentary on the contemporary scene—music and the stage, books and magazines, recent law decisions, and "Gossip with Readers and Correspondents." The poetry was often notable. Edward Pollock contributed some of his best, including "Evening" and "The Chandos Picture." Among the lesser luminaries were Charles Havens, J. P. Anthony, Frank Soulé, and John Swett.

Nevertheless, the fame of the *Pioneer* really rests on certain prose contributions. Early issues contained a serial, "California in 1851," now known as the *Shirley Letters* and hailed as one of the most accurate, penetrating, and charming descriptions of life in the diggings. Another outstanding contributor was Stephen Massett. His column, signed James Pipes of Pipesville, contained many a sparkling gem. Ewer's greatest triumph was to entice George Derby to contribute. Beginning in June, 1854, nine successive issues contained humorous sketches representative of the best achievements of his alter ego, John Phoenix, the more remarkable because they were composed in the somnolent desuetude of San Diego. Eastern journals hailed the *Pioneer* as "a capital periodical . . . freighted with good things," and, said the Boston *Post,* "we prize it like a nugget of gold for its many excellencies." These journals paid the *Pioneer* the more obvious compliment of copying its material wholesale, especially the John Phoenix sketches. In spite of such wide and favorable notice and notwithstanding its fine roster of writers, the *Pioneer* could not continue beyond its second year.

Next in the field was Hutchings' *California Magazine,* begun in 1856. Two years later the number of woodcuts was increased, though without corresponding improvement in quality, and for the remaining three years of its existence the word "illustrated" was added to the title. Although it contained nothing so uproarious as the Phoenix sketches, the new magazine was on the whole in a lighter vein. The most quoted example was Editor James H. Hutchings' "The Miner's Ten Commandments." Hutchings' favorite theme is illustrated by his "In the Heart of the Sierra," an impassioned tribute to the beauty and grandeur of the Yosemite Valley. He is often regarded as the first of the California nature enthusiasts, a company shortly joined by Charles Warren Stoddard, Thomas Starr King, Clarence King, John Muir, and a host of others.

The *Hesperian,* begun in 1858, gained distinction by falling into the hands of Mrs. F. H. Day. She improved the quality of illustrations, introduced a juvenile department, and gave the magazine something of a homey tone, yet managed to retain a measure of masculine interest. "The contents," it is asserted, "vary from sublime thoughts upon Milton to the best method of making muffins and embroidering flannel skirts." In 1863 the *Hesperian* got a new editor and a new name, *Pacific Monthly,* but did not long survive. Minor ventures included the *San Francisco Pictorial Magazine,* the *Sunday Mercury,* the *Golden Gate,* and, from Tuolumne, the *California Mountaineer.*

The *Californian,* established in 1864, ran for only three years, but its quality was so high and its contributors so distinguished as to make it of more than passing interest. Editor Charles Henry Webb had left the *Era* with the avowed intention of producing a more "high-toned" magazine. Assisted by such literati as Stoddard, Coolbrith, and Twain, he succeeded in this laudable purpose only to find the market totally inadequate.

One other magazine of importance graced the field of early western publishing, and in it California's first literary tradition reached its culmination. The reference, of course, is to the *Overland Monthly,* launched in July, 1868, and terminating its first series in 1875. Revived in 1883, the *Overland* survived

Bret Harte

California State Library

various vicissitudes but did not duplicate the achievements of the initial series. Origin of the magazine is credited to the publisher, Anton Roman, and to him goes a further plaudit for vesting absolute editorial control in Francis Bret Harte. It was Bret Harte's editorial genius, and often his pen, that gave the *Overland* its high repute. This fact is illustrated by the steady decline of the magazine after he relinquished the editorship and also by the rueful remark of Roman's successor, John H. Carmany, that in pocketing the loss on the *Overland* he had "spent thirty thousand dollars to make Bret Harte famous."

As the vehicle in which the best of his stories and poems appeared, the *Overland* was an important chapter in Bret Harte's personal development yet no more so than in the literary evolution of the West. In its heyday this journal drew the writings of practically every promising local author and by its high standards challenged them to improve. Significant also was the stress it laid on the potentialities of the West. Its subtitle proclaimed that the *Overland* was "devoted to the development of the country." This pledge was redeemed in a number of ways. Besides a quota of enthusiastic descriptive pieces the early numbers contained items such as "High Noon of the Empire," "The Tropical Fruits of California," "Art Beginnings on the Pacific Slope," and "Farming Facts for California Immigrants," all of which were frankly promotional.

Even more noteworthy was the determined effort to give the *Overland* an unmistakably western flavor. The *Atlantic Monthly* is often cited as its model and inspiration; the *Overland*, however, was not a mere imitation of the

Boston monthly but rather its Pacific counterpart, differing from it as West from East. A glance at the contents of the first volume reveals a few contributions, such as the Reverend E. C. Bissell's "Egotizing" or T. H. Rearden's "Favoring Female Conventualism," which were environmentally detached. A much larger number would have seemed outlandish in the *Atlantic*. They are by no means confined to California but range broadly over the American West and the Pacific area, illustrating the expansive outlook of the *Overland* and of Californians. Random examples are: "Portland-on-Wallamett," "The Apache Race," "A Ride on the Texas Frontier," "The French in Mexico," "Carthagena," "Lima," "Hawaiian Civilization," "Japanese Holy Places," and "In Nankin." Yet to catalog the subjects tells only half the story. Much of this writing had about it a vibrancy, a freshness, a western aroma, difficult to analyze but unmistakably recognizable. It was this quality which won the *Overland* so warm a reception on the Atlantic coast as well as on the Pacific.

Books along with magazines made their appearance. Included were such compendia as *The Annals of San Francisco*, by Soulé, Gihon, and Nisbet (1855); *The Resources of California*, by John S. Hittell (1863); *The Natural Wealth of California*, by Titus Fey Cronise (1868); and two anthologies of western poetry. Two thrillers were far more widely read: John R. Ridge's *The Life and Adventures of Joaquín Murieta* and Royal B. Stratton's *Captivity of the Oatman Girls*. Treatises on philosophy and political economy are conspicuously absent, and history has no better representatives than Frost and Dwinelle. Thus, nonfiction was at the level of simple reporting and narration rather than of contemplative inquiry.

The Galaxy of Writers

By posterity, if not by their contemporaries, many of the writers of this early period have been judged worthy of no more than passing attention. The majority of the poets, in particular, may be dismissed with the remark that their outpourings were indifferent in quality and contributed little to American letters. Quantity was not lacking. The wares of these poets may be sampled in the files of the early magazines and newspapers and in anthologies such as *Poetry of the Pacific*, assembled in 1865 by May Wentworth, and *Outcroppings*, sponsored the following year by Bret Harte. The modern reader is apt to close these volumes with little reluctance. As to early acclaim, Bret Harte and Joaquin Miller were the leaders, together with Ina Coolbrith, Charles W. Stoddard, and Edward Pollock.

In the field of prose the percentage of distinction was somewhat higher. In the fifties, for example, there was the miners' particular favorite, Alonzo Delano, who wrote under the name of Old Block, contributing to many papers and journals and illustrating many of his pieces with appropriate caricatures. It was inevitable that Delano's fame should decline with the passing of the forty-niner generation, for much of his writing was dated and presupposed familiarity with the diggings. Furthermore, Delano's readers in the fifties were under the spell of his personal magnetism: his nose, California's largest, and his integrity, demonstrated so forcefuly in the panic of 1855 when he undertook to pay off the obligations of his bankrupt employer. Posterity, less acutely aware of these admirable qualities, has a lesser appreciation for his *Pen Knife Sketches* (1853) and the play *Live Woman in the Mines* (1857). Today readers are much more apt to turn to his narrative of 1849, *Life on the Plains and Among the Diggings*.

Of greater fame and doubtless of greater stature was George H. Derby of the Topographical Engineers. He came to California in 1849 with an excellent military record and left half a dozen years later with the reputation of being the nation's favorite humorist. This rocketing to popularity was in part because of his penchant for practical jokes, a vice to which Californians of the fifties were particularly addicted. An unconscionable number of pranks are attributed to him, many of them no doubt erroneously. Tastes having changed, most of these jokes seem to be mere encrustations on the portly lieutenant's real

Phoenixiana

John P. Squibob

Yours respectively
John P. Squibob

NOTE.—This autograph may be relied on as authentic, as it was written by one of Mr. Squibob's most intimate friends.

humor, but in the fifties they were an effective stepping-stone to fame. More important were the sketches he published in the *Alta California* under the name Squibob and then in the *Pioneer* under the name John Phoenix. Immediately the vogue, these hilarious sketches were reproduced in journals far and near. In 1856 a hastily assembled collection was brought out as a book, *Phoenixiana*, which soon ran through 35 editions. Some of his choicest bits can be appreciated today only by antiquarians immersed in the nicer details of late gold-rush California, yet even the most modern reader will find that the wit has not lost all its savor.

Derby's place in American letters is something on which the pretenders to authority cannot agree. The tendency to call him a crude and ill-mannered buffoon seems to be waning, and some critics, veering to the other extreme, rank him as a polished and skillful workman and the founder of a new school of American humor. He was one of the first to demonstrate that one could evoke laughter without resorting to illiteracy and bad grammar. His salty burlesques were also diametrically opposed to the artificial romanticism whose stronghold was then New England. With all his horseplay Derby was still an exponent of realism, and much of his popularity was due to the conviction of his readers that his finger was on the fundamental verities.

Whatever the effect on national letters through the wide circulation of his *Phoenixiana* and through his subsequent contributions to the *Knickerbocker*, it is obvious that Derby's influence upon western writing would be more marked. Punsters like "Inigo" Webb, pranksters such as the members of the sagebrush school, and, above all, Mark Twain profited greatly from the exploits and the tradition of this earlier artist in fun making.

Mark Twain and Bret Harte need no introduction. Their place in California letters is only exceeded by their indebtedness to it. It was in the West that Mark Twain found himself and there that he had his first practice in writing and as a platform lecturer. Western themes were his first stock in trade, and western readers were his first, his most loyal, and his most consistent supporters. The Derbyesque realism which he attained was a quality which Californians were best prepared to commend. Bret Harte's debt to California was even greater. Not only were California journals his first medium of publication, but in gold-rush California he found the setting for all that was meritorious in his writing. He had, to be sure, a mastery of expression which tempts forth such adjectives as felicitous, choice, sparkling, exquisite, but for all its excellence this style availed him little except when he was exploiting the unique background of California in its golden era. His later eastern writings are flavorless, and when he tried to revive the western theme it was as though his perception of detail had been dulled.

Joaquin Miller also became a world celebrity through strictly western writing. He is accused of playing up the outward manifestations of the West in a bid for attention, as when he paraded in London society attired in miner's boots and red flannel shirt. The genuineness of his westernism, nonetheless, is beyond dispute. He wrote with the fervor of sincerity. He did not desert California and it was constantly recurrent as the theme of his poetry. Discerning critics today point out that he made slips in grammar, that his poorer poems detract from his best, and that his paean to the West is not distinctive. Nevertheless, he still stands above the other California poets of his day.

Mark Twain

California State Library

To single out Delano, Derby, Twain, Harte, and Miller may obscure the picture of the broader ranks of California writers. That these were numerous is an elementary fact; that they produced an astonishing quantity of creditable literature is also admitted. An explanation must include comment on the caliber of the individuals brought to California in 1849, allowance for the early material prosperity, recognition of the stimulation afforded by the majesty of Nature in the West, and allusion to the isolation which dictated western publishing instead of the mere purchase of eastern goods. These early Californians also had a high estimate of their own importance. They were the pioneers who had reached continent's end; they were erecting overnight a magnificent state; their gold was a decisive factor in preserving the Union. California writers, steeped in this feeling, were sure they had something important to write about.

This confidence is of more fundamental significance than some of the more noticed characteristics—the fascination, for example, with California's novelty that elicited poems to "The Sequoias," "The Golden Gate," and "An Abalone Shell." The penchant for pen names is another superficiality in which the psychoanalyst might detect a hidden meaning. Besides being nearly universal, these pen names in a number of instances, among them Mark Twain and Joaquin Miller, succeeded in vanquishing the original names. Broad humor as a prominent feature of this writing has a more obvious significance, for the relish for laughter was a key trait among Californians of this generation. Impatience with artificial restraints, as when Bret Harte balked at censorship of "The Luck of Roaring Camp," is also important. It again illustrates the impulse toward realism witnessed a little later by the coolness toward Bret Harte when it seemed that he had lost his grasp on the West as it actually was.

The Californians had abundant assurance in the significance of their land, themselves, and their era. History, they were confident, was being made. For literature, therefore, what better function than to depict them and their achievements as they really were. The earnestness thus imparted to a generation of writers did not become sterile through deadly seriousness. Instead, it contributed a sense of high purpose, which proved an effective stimulant to noteworthy attainment. California writing was launched on a high plane, and an invigorating influence was imparted to the nation's literature.

For Further Reading

PAULINE JACOBSEN, *City of the Golden 'Fifties* (1941).

T. A. BARRY and B. A. PATTEN, *Men and Memories of San Francisco* (1873).

ROBERT E. COWAN, *Forgotten Characters of Old San Francisco* (1938).

DAVID F. FERRIS, *Judge Marvin and the Founding of the California Public School System* (1962).

WILLIAM G. CARR, *John Swett, The Biography of an Educational Pioneer* (1933).

CONSTANCE ROURKE, *Troupers of the Gold Coast* (1928).

G. R. MACMINN, *The Theater of the Golden Era* (1941).

JOHN BRUCE, *Gaudy Century: The Story of San Francisco's First Hundred Years of Robust Journalism* (1948).

WILLIAM B. RICE, *The Los Angeles Star, 1851–1864* (1947).

FRANKLIN WALKER, *San Francisco's Literary Frontier* (1939).

RODMAN W. PAUL, "In Search of Dame Shirley," *PHR*, 33 (1964), 127–46.

GEORGE R. STEWART, JR., *John Phoenix, Esq.* (1937).

IVAN BENSON, *Mark Twain's Western Years* (1938).

DAVID M. GOODMAN, *A Western Panorama, 1849–1876, The Travels, Writings, and Influence of J. Ross Browne* (1966).

THURMAN WILKINS, *Clarence King* (1958).

ROBERT LOUIS STEVENSON, *From Scotland to Silverado*, James D. Hart, ed., (1966).

CAUGHEY, *California Heritage*, 257–62, 268–83.

chapter eighteen

Stages and Steamers

As a motion-picture man once told me: We don't *want* to present the stage-coach as it was. We must show it as the people *think* it was. Or else they won't believe us.

William and George Hugh Banning,
Six Horses

Initial Steps

1848
to
1868

In the drowsy calm of the pastoral period California had made no transportation demands which could not be met by a saddled horse, an ox-drawn carreta, or the irregular sailings of the trading vessels. The Argonauts were not so easily content. Their restlessness led them to clamor for more convenient and more modern means of getting about, while their affluence enabled them to pay whatever was charged. The result was a revolution in communications within the state and a speedy provision of land and sea connections with other parts of the world, particularly the eastern states.

Local improvement began humbly in hit-or-miss fashion and by private initiative. For example, the first to give thought to the problem of mail delivery seems to have been a certain Alexander

The Overland Mail

*Theodore R. Davis. Harper's Weekly, February 8, 1868.
From collections of Library of Congress*

Todd, who came down from the diggings to the San Francisco post office, commissioned by a hundred-odd prospectors to carry up their letters. His rate was an ounce a letter, and his business acumen is further attested by his purchase of a skiff for $300 and his charge of $16 a head for the privilege of pulling an oar the hundred miles to Sacramento. Then came Bill Ballou, cutting the rate for letter delivery to a quarter-ounce and carrying a thimble as a measuring cup. With more competitors the rate was slashed to a dollar and eventually to two bits.

These private mail carriers extended their operations throughout the diggings, supplementing the skeleton service which the national postal authorities, with only 34 post offices in the state by June, 1851, were able to provide. By easy transition, letter carrying merged with gold delivery, and the two were often conducted in conjunction with pack-mule freighting. Banking was a more impressive outgrowth, and the national firms that opened California branches, such as Adams and Company in 1849 and Wells, Fargo and Company in 1852, reaped their largest income through commissions on remittances of gold. For many years, however, these larger concerns were supplemented throughout the interior by one-man express companies and middle-sized outfits carrying on where Alexander Todd and Bill Ballou had left off. Collectors of the franks of these lesser companies are able to list literally hundreds of outfits.

To provide for passenger conveyance was another golden opportunity. The first artery opened was the so-called river line to Sacramento. Sutter's launch had been an irregular forerunner, but Marshall's gold dictated more adequate appointments. At first all sorts of smaller craft were pressed into service. Ocean-going brigs and schooners could be worked up to Sacramento and many were utilized thus. Competent pilots in the summer of 1849 charged $200 to $500 a trip, which seemed worth it to those who undertook the voyage on their own. George F. Kent's journal, for example, has an exasperated entry about the grounding of the 123-ton *Rudolph* in the mud off what he called "Mosquito Creek," between Benicia and New York of the Pacific. The *Rudolph* stuck fast twice more before reaching Sacramento, but, reconciled by this time to the uncertainties of California navigation, Kent was able to attain a more philosophic resignation.

Although the bay had boasted a tiny side-wheeler, brought from Sitka in 1847 and promptly wrecked, steam navigation really began in August and September of 1849 when several flat-bottomed side-wheelers and steam scows were put into commission. The *Washington*, launched at Benicia, seems to have been the first; it was followed by the *Edward Everett, Jr.,* assembled from parts brought out from New England, the *Sacramento*, and several others of clouded name and uncertain prowess. To judge from the record of wrecks, breakdowns, and short service, these pioneer vessels were poor makeshifts.

In October these experimental craft were eclipsed by the *Mint*, small and careening but fast, the 400-ton *McKim*, a propeller steamer, and the still larger *Senator*. Traffic was heavy and rates were high; in her first year of operation the *Senator* is said to have netted her owners $60,000 a month. By the end

Sacramento from the River

The Bancroft Library

of 1850 there were 50 steamers, large and small, operating on the bay and the inland waterways. A notable addition to the fleet was the palatial *New World*, built in 1848 for excursion duty on the Hudson, boarded up and spirited away from the sheriff's attachment, so the story goes, and sailed around the Horn to far-off California. She was able to cut the *Senator*'s time on the San Francisco–Sacramento run from 10 hours to six.

Competitive rate wars, lowering the Sacramento fare from $25 or $30 to $1, led to the organization in 1854 of the California Steam Navigation Company, capitalized at $2,500,000. Stabilizing fares at $10 for cabin, $7 for deck passage, and $6 and $8 a ton for freight, the monopoly made comfortable profits. Would-be competition was forced out or bought out, and public protests against what were regarded as overcharges proved unavailing. Only the coming of the railroads caused the powerful company to unbend, and then, as far as the public was concerned, it amounted merely to the substitution of a new monopoly for the old. Besides dominating inland navigation the Steam Navigation Company acquired control of several coastal routes: to Humboldt Bay, to San Diego and way points, to the Columbia River, and finally, in 1867, to Alaska.

In the early years disasters were all too common. California waters had not been thoroughly charted, many of the vessels in use were outworn hulks, masters and crews were frequently lacking in skill and discretion, and steamboat inspection was lax. In 1852 local inspectors still had to refer their reports to the

New Orleans district office, and the passion for racing led to numerous boiler explosions. In the first half-dozen years the riverboats had a score of accidents with fatalities running as high as 50 persons. Still the Californians delighted in the luxury of steamboat rides, and the more steam was carried the better they liked it.

California Staging

Back in the autumn of 1849, when the first paddle wheels churned the river waters to Sacramento and Stockton, the modernization of California land transport had begun. The pioneer seems to have been John Whistman, who, with an old French omnibus and a mixed team of mustangs and mules, offered an adventurous ride from San Francisco to San Jose. Passengers came forward at 2 ounces each and were elated at the nine-hour schedule. Winter rains curtailed the service to the 8 miles between San Jose and Alviso, where steamers picked up passengers for San Francisco. The following spring a competing line was introduced by Ackley and Maurison, furnished, so it was advertised, "with the best stages and horses the country can produce." In the summer Whistman sold out to two experienced stage operators, Warren F. Hall and Jared B. Crandall, who reduced the fare to $16, extended their line to Monterey, and a year later won a four-year contract to carry the mail to San Jose. In their lyric advertising Hall and Crandall divided the emphasis between the safety of their stages, the beauty of the Santa Clara Valley, and the skill of their drivers. California offered "no more charming drive," Hall and Crandall insisted, than on the line to San Jose, and they promised that passengers would find "pleasure united with business" as they were "whirled through the oak openings and across the level plains under the skillful driving of Professor Dillon or Crandall." Professor Crandall's most famous drive through the oak openings was in the fall of 1850 when, with Governor Burnett on the box beside him, he raced toward the state capital to beat the rival stage and carry the news of California's admission to statehood.

Meanwhile, at Sacramento in the fall of '49, young James Birch had appeared with an old ranch wagon and four fractious mustangs, offering a 30-mile ride to Mormon Island at a fare of 2 ounces. The enthusiastic response to this initial service to the diggings attracted other men to the business, many of them, like Birch, experienced stage operators from New England or the Ohio Valley. Lines multiplied and service was extended to the major camps in the northern diggings, even as far as Shasta, 180 miles distant. By the fall of 1851 the San Francisco papers were ready to admit that Sacramento rather than the metropolis on the bay had become the hub of the stage lines. The *Alta's* Sacramento correspondent in November, 1851, listed the daily stages: six to Marysville, two to Coloma, and one each to Nevada City, Placerville, Auburn, Stockton, and Drytown-Jackson. Passengers, he added, were plentiful, the daily haul on the Sacramento–Marysville run averaging 70 each way and most of the other stages drawing a full complement. Fares had been reduced from the original dollar a mile, but they were still high enough to make the business very remunerative.

More striking than the spreading network of lines was the phenomenal improvement in equipment both in horse flesh and rolling stock. The high prices current in California's flush times go far toward explaining this improvement, but in addition there was a healthy rivalry between the several proprietors, and these veterans of eastern staging took an intense pride in outfitting their lines with the very best. American horses soon replaced the native cow ponies. A few superior carriage horses had been brought out by the overland forty-niners; more were ordered from Ohio, Kentucky, Pennsylvania, and Virginia, and from $2,000 to $4,000 a span was not an unheard-of price for matched leaders, swing, or wheelers.

As to vehicles the trend was toward the Concord type, manufactured by Abbott, Downing and Company of Concord, New Hampshire. The first such vehicle appeared at San Francisco on June 25, 1850, creating a sensation and inducing nostalgia on the part of the editor of the *Alta*. Additional Concord coaches were freighted round the Horn or caravaned overland until, by the mid-fifties, the California lines boasted newer and better equipment than was in use anywhere else.

The Concord was a work of art. Of its excellence the present automobile generation, viewing only battered and patched museum specimens of this vehicle, is naturally skeptical. In design the essentials were a conventional running gear with a pair of *C*-shaped springs anchored to each axle, and stretching from these the thorough braces (manifold straps of stoutest leather), on which was cradled the egg-shaped body. Most significant was the thorough-brace suspension, which allowed the body to sway fore and aft. However much passengers might be inconvenienced by the constant pitching, the device was an effective shock absorber for the teams, and to spare the horses was the ruling purpose.

Abbott and Downing exploited this model to perfection. They chose materials most carefully—iron from Norway, well-seasoned ash and oak, and poplar for the body paneling. After some four decades of experience, workmanship had attained a high standard. The coaches combined strength with lightness, and dependability when put to the most exacting use with beauty of line and ornamentation.

Nine or ten passengers could be squeezed into the standard stage with another dozen on top. Boots at front and back carried mail and baggage. The vehicle weighed only about 2,500 pounds, considerably less than our "light automobiles" today, and delivered in California cost from $1,200 to $1,500. Although drawn at breakneck speeds—10, 12, or even 15 miles an hour over roads of unconscionable roughness—these stages ran for years with almost no necessity for repairs. Over heavy grades or heavy roads the lighter and lower "mud wagons" were favored. The mud wagon seated about a dozen passengers in a more conventional wagon box, with or without an awning, but slung on thorough braces as in the standard coach.

The stage driver or "whip," as he preferred to be called, was one of the heroic figures of the old West. His wizardry in piloting a stage on a night run, his skill in careening down a mountain road, his prodigies in profanity, and later his exploits in foiling Indian attacks or attempted holdups surrounded him with the aura of a superman. And indeed, to manipulate whip and brake, to play upon the six reins so that each horse was individually controlled, and to be ready to act instantly in whatever emergency might arise called for a virtuoso.

The schedules maintained, 60 miles in 6 hours, and the record runs, 160 miles at 13 miles an hour, inadequately convey the attainments of the California stage lines. By the mid-fifties service was unsurpassed except perhaps by England's Royal Mail. And Englishmen who contrasted California's rough trails with England's macadamized post roads were astounded at such speed.

In 1854, the year of the consolidation of the riverboats, five sixths of the state's stage lines were amalgamated in the California Stage Company. Two New England whips headed the company, James Birch, the pioneer, and Frank Stevens, who until 1851 had operated a Sacramento tavern offering "Rest for the Weary and Storage for Trunks." Neither had passed 25 years of age and most of their partners were also in the exuberant vigor of youth. The new company, capitalized at $1 million, advertised regular service on lines totaling 1,500 miles and "the most extensive and complete Line of stages in THE WORLD." Two years later, with 3,000 miles of stage lines in regular operation, not to mention the large fleet of steamboats plying the inland waters, the state could boast excellent facilities for handling intrastate passengers, mail, and express.

Panama Steamers

A companion need was to break down California's isolation from the rest of the world. Under Spain and Mexico the greatest deterrent to development had been the remoteness of the province, and the authorities had never been able to overcome the obstacles symbolized by the Yuma Massacre, the inadequacy of San Blas, and the hazards of sailing up the coast. With the removal of the seat of government from Mexico City to Washington, the problem was altered without being perceptibly simplified. The overland routes from Missouri were as difficult as the Anza trail from Sonora, and, in spite of improvement in ships, the round-the-Horn sailings or the broken voyage by Panama presented hardships comparable to those in sailing up the coast from Mexico.

At the very outset of the new regime, gold intensified the need for better contacts with California. The golden harvest must be channeled to the States and a California suddenly populous must be integrated with the rest of the nation. In the prevailing atmosphere of sectional distrust both these arguments had particular weight.

The most obvious answer to the problem seemed to be the development of the Panama route. Even before news of gold Congress had undertaken to subsidize steamship lines by way of the isthmus to California and Oregon. The legislation was premised not upon consideration for Pacific coast settlements but upon the supposition that commercial steamships could easily be transformed into auxiliary cruisers for the navy. Under terms of the first legislation in 1845 and 1847 the Post Office Department did not succeed in finding a contractor, even though the cooperation of naval officers was promised. Later in 1847, however, the Navy Department was authorized to act. It contracted with the United States Mail Steamship Company for semimonthly voyages from New York and New Orleans to Chagres and with the Pacific Mail Steamship Company for monthly voyages from Panama to Oregon. The annual subsidies were to be $290,000 and $199,000, respectively.

Service commenced just in time to catch the first flood of California-bound Argonauts. The rush of passengers brought others into the business, notably the mogul of Hudson River ferries and steamboats, "Commodore" Cornelius Vanderbilt, and the Atlantic and Gulf operator, Charles W. Morgan. Using the Nicaragua transit, they offered sharp competition from 1851 to 1856. In the ensuing three years the Pacific Mail paid Vanderbilt $40,000 and then $56,000 a month to stay out of the business. In 1859 he won the mail contract. A sharp rate war was followed in 1860 by an agreement that Vanderbilt should have the Atlantic run and the Pacific Mail, the Pacific run, and in 1865 the Pacific Mail purchased the Atlantic fleet.

For several seasons, despite the impressment of many smaller craft and a number of additions to the Panama fleet, accommodations were greatly overtaxed. The *California*, for example, though built for a maximum of 250, carried 365 on her maiden voyage, and a decade later the Vanderbilt line was accused of shipping 1,100 on a vessel licensed to carry 750. Vanderbilt's steamers also had the reputation of being dirty and badly manned. Worse than the discomfort was the hazard to life. In the first half-dozen years of steamship operation to California no less than a score of disasters occurred, several with appalling loss of life. The Pacific Mail had one loss, the $300,000 *Tennessee,* which went down off San Francisco in 1853; the Vanderbilt line lost five; independent coastal and round-the-Horn shipping suffered the rest. In 1857 occurred the crowning disaster when, some 400 miles below Cape Hatteras, the palatial *Central America* spread her seams and foundered, carrying to a watery grave more than $2 million in gold and 400 men.

Notwithstanding the risks these wrecks symbolized, the Panama route came to be the favored path between California and the States. Completion of the Panama railroad reduced the transit schedule from three or four days to four hours. The larger steamers put into service also reduced the running time, especially on the Pacific, and by 1866 the schedule had been pared from 33 or 34 days to 21. The fare fluctuated wildly, but in the later years it was usually less than half the original rate of $450 for first class and $225 for steerage. Government officials, politicians, businessmen, and men of means were almost unanimous in their choice of the Panama route. It was the choice also of the miners who, having struck it rich, wanted to return home. Much California mail was carried by way of Panama even after the opening of the overland stage line and was delivered quite as expeditiously. Express was also carried, and the shipments of California gold, which in Civil War days assumed such significance, were all by way of Panama. Perhaps the best indication of the importance of the steamship line is that the surplus of westbound over eastbound passengers accounted for a fifth of California's population increase in the fifties and for a half in the next decade.

The Pacific Railroad Surveys

The Panama steamers, however, especially in their early operations, did not seem the ultimate solution of California's transportation problem. They were too slow, too crowded, too roundabout. Also, it was felt that California, as a contiguous part of the United States, ought to have a direct connection rather than be treated as an overseas possession, distant two ocean voyages and an isthmian transit through the territory of a foreign nation. Californians, aware of their importance and of the shortcomings of the Panama service, loudly demanded an overland connection, arguing that it was the manifest duty of the federal government thus to provide for their convenience. In the East a number of men prominent in politics and journalism joined them and urged the authorities to forge a transcontinental link. The arguments they advanced were less those of constitutional obligation to the Californians and more those of national defense, national solidarity, and American opportunity on the Pacific.

The type of overland communication uppermost in the thoughts of most of these men was, strange to say, the railroad. It was only a score of years earlier that the first trains had begun operations near Baltimore. In those few years, however, the steam horse had proved a precocious upstart. By 1850 the section of the nation east of the Mississippi and north of the Ohio was crisscrossed by a maze of rail lines. The total mileage, some 9,818, was impressive, but practically all was accounted for by short lines of local inception and construction, built to handle a traffic already existent. To throw a line across 2,000 miles of unoccupied plains and mountains to the Pacific coast was beyond the resources of any magnates then in the business, and with the small prospect for traffic it was not a proposition attractive to private enterprise. The advocates of a Pacific railroad seem not to have grasped the fundamental distinction just as they underestimated the difficulties of actual construction. Besides, to any such practical objections there was the ready answer that the federal government should see to the construction of the transcontinental.

That a road was not immediately authorized was largely because of sectional squabbling over location of its eastern terminus. True, the Panama steamship companies lobbied against such bills, many easterners were unconvinced that the federal government should embark on so grandiose an internal improvement, and the exact technique of federal aid was not immediately agreed upon. Nevertheless, had there been unanimity as to route it seems probable that construction would have been begun in the early fifties. At any rate, the federal government's first step toward establishing an overland connection with California was to appropriate $150,000 in 1853 for the survey of the several feasible Pacific railroad routes.

The surveys, thereupon conducted by the army, resulted in the accumulation of a vast quantity of topographical, ethnological, botanical, geological, zoological, and climatic information, impressively stored up in the ponderous tomes of the *Reports*. The surveys thus are of considerable geographic and academic interest, though, beyond the assertion that there were a half-dozen possible railroad routes to the Pacific, their practical utility was slight. Sectional bickerings prevented Congressional action until 1862, at which time the politics of war determined the choice of route, and before actual construction took place a more thorough plotting proved necessary.

The Overland Stage

In the meantime Californians renewed their clamor for overland communications and at the end of the decade were rewarded with stage line, pony express, and telegraph. Although the telegraph was something of permanent utility, overland mail and pony express functioned only briefly. The latter did shorten the interval for communications between California and the States, though, as we have seen, improvements on the Panama line soon reduced its schedule to approximately the equivalent of the transcontinental stage. Toward the movement of passengers the pony express contributed nothing and the overland merely a negligible amount. On the score of practical utility, then, they deserve only a fraction of the attention which their spectacularity has won them in so many works of popular nature and sober history. Their true significance is that they gave practical demonstration of the possibility of through service on the overland routes, that by their very shortcomings they helped to evoke the railroad, and that by the boldness of their design they drew attention to the problem of western communications. Incidentally, it is worth noting that the pony express was started precisely as an advertising medium.

For the stage line there were antecedents in certain mail contracts, such as one in 1850 to a "camping-out" company which freighted the mail from Independence to Santa Fé and another in 1851 for a line from Independence to Salt Lake City. Birch's flourishing California Stage Company was much better supplied with the wherewithal to provide rapid through service.

Californians were giving much thought to the matter, but, like their eastern brethren, they fell into the error of wasting most of their energy in bickering about the choice of route. Persuaded that Johnson's Pass was the best Sierra crossing, the state appropriated funds for road building, and in 1857 the intrepid Crandall inaugurated stage service across the Sierra from Placerville to Washoe. Meanwhile, some 75,000 California voters had memorialized Congress to construct a military wagon road to California by way of Salt Lake. This colossal petition, the largest thus far laid on the Congressional doorstep, led to one appropriation of $200,000 for roadwork along the southern route and another of $300,000 for the Salt Lake line, but with the western terminus fixed far to the north of Johnson's Pass. Thus was the confusion in California worse confounded.

Hot on the heels of this road appropriation came another measure most heartening to the advocates of the overland. The Postmaster-General was authorized to contract for six years at $600,000 a year for semiweekly service on a 25-day schedule from the Mississippi to San Francisco. Ostensibly, the contractor would designate the route, but it was a foregone conclusion that Postmaster-General Aaron Brown of Tennessee would dictate the circuitous southern route. It was also freely predicted, despite the bid of an eastern coalition of seven men headed by John Butterfield, that the award would go to California's James Birch, hailed by the New York press as "a gentleman of large capital and much experience, and more competent, perhaps, than any other single man in the United States to execute this great mail contract."

Birch and Brown seemed to think so too, for, as an apparent preliminary to the larger contract, the Postmaster-General awarded the Californian a $150,000 contract for monthly mail stages from San Antonio to San Diego. This line "from nowhere to nowhere," partly by relays and partly by camping out, and partly horse-drawn and partly mule-drawn (hence its nickname, "the Jackass"), defies explanation except as a subsidiary of the larger overland. It went into operation late in 1857, giving Birch the honor of operating the first transcontinental stage line. By Presidential intervention, however, the greater opportunity was deflected from him into the hands of Butterfield and his associates. Birch had little time to ponder on the strange ways of statesmen, for that very fall, when still in his twenties, he perished at sea in the wreck of the *Central America*.

To the fore now came the new ruler of the stages, John Butterfield. The task confronting him called for all the experience he had gained in midwestern freighting and staging and for all the executive ability he possessed. In 12 months, according to the terms of his contract, he must man, stock, and equip some 2,800 miles of stage line. For efficiency of administration he divided the line at El Paso into an eastern and a western section, each section consisting of four divisions 300 to 400 miles in length. West of El Paso the line was manned by Californians and stocked with California equipment.

With hard work the preparations were completed on the appointed day, September 17, 1858, and stages set out simultaneously from Tipton, Missouri, the railhead west of St. Louis, and from San Francisco. Each completed the run with more than a day to spare, the eastbound coach to be greeted by a congratulatory telegram from President Buchanan and the westbound to encounter exuberant enthusiasm at San Francisco. As the *Bulletin* described the event:

> At a quarter after four o'clock the coach turned from Market into Montgomery Street. The driver blew his horn and cracked his whip; at which

the horses, four in number, almost seemed to partake of his enthusiasm, and dashed ahead at a clattering pace, and the dust flew from the glowing wheels. At the same time a shout was raised, that ran with the rapidity of an electric flash along Montgomery Street, which throughout its length was crowded by an excited populace. As the coach dashed along through the crowds, the hats of the spectators were whirled in the air and the hurrah was repeated from a thousand throats, responsive to which, the driver, the lion of the occasion, doffed his weather-beaten old slouch, and in uncovered dignity, like the victor of an old Olympic race, guided his foaming steeds toward the Post Office.

Diverse and contradictory are the descriptions of travel on Butterfield's Overland Mail. With no stopovers except to change horses, with no pretense at facilities for sleeping, and with not much preparation for meals en route, traveling the overland was hard work. For one passenger it induced insanity, and another pair got on each other's nerves enough to provoke a duel. Others, inured to western hardships, pronounced the ride a thrill and a pleasure. But with an eye to the mail rather than to the passengers, the overland ran on, occasionally disturbed by floods or by Indian attacks on the stations and a few times requiring more than the allotted 25 days, though usually getting through with two or three days to spare.

Northern California never really warmed to the Butterfield line, principally because of the conviction that a faster schedule was easily possible on the central route. Crandall's stages were demonstrating the feasibility of the Sierra crossing. In 1858 Postmaster-General Brown loosened the federal purse strings slightly to contract with John M. Hockaday for weekly mail from Independence to Salt Lake City and with George Chorpenning for carriage on to Placerville. Commencing a few weeks prior to Butterfield's line, the central combination brought the mail through regularly, winter as well as summer, and often in less than the 38 days which the schedule allowed; the administration, however, was careful not to build this line up into a dangerous rival of the favored southern line. In December, 1858, the government's preference was brought into the open in connection with the President's annual message to Congress. Advance copies were promised to the Tehuantepec steamer, the Butterfield line, and the Hockaday line, but to the latter's dismay no copy was forthcoming for the Central Overland. Thus handicapped, the race went not to the swift but to the favorite. The week's head start enabled the Butterfield messenger to win, but Hockaday and Chorpenning's elapsed time of 17 days and 12 hours was quicker by more than two days. Northern Californians, none too cordial toward Buchanan's southerners to start with, were all the more convinced of the superiority of the central route.

Postmaster-General Brown, though limiting the Central Overland to a niggardly $320,000 subvention, was ready to lay out funds for still other lines to California. He let a contract for a monthly stage along the thirty-fifth parallel from Kansas City to Stockton, another for a stage from Neosho, Missouri, to Albuquerque, and a third for steamers from New Orleans to Tehuantepec and on to San Francisco. The San Antonio–San Diego, also established in 1858, was enlarged to a semimonthly line. Brown's death early in the following spring brought in an economy-minded successor, who saved a million dollars a year by eliminating several of these lines and curtailing all the others with the conspicuous exception of the Butterfield.

Deprived of their mail contracts, Hockaday and Chorpenning found themselves in trouble. Hockaday was overshadowed and then bought out by the reigning entrepreneurs of Plains freighting, Russell, Majors, and Waddell. Their stages, known as the Leavenworth and Pike's Peak Express, and then as the Central Overland California and Pike's Peak Express (COC and PPE), did a good business to the Colorado mines and Salt Lake City, even though the cancellation of Chorpenning's contract left no through service to California.

The Pony Express and the Close of an Era

When a new menace appeared in the form of competitors on the Colorado run, William Russell decided to gamble. He announced to Senator Gwin that the COC and PPE would establish a pony express on a 10-day schedule. His partners were skeptical but considered their firm pledged to the venture, and on April 3, 1860, this most dramatic of transcontinental mails went into action.

> Away across the endless dead level of prairie a black speck appears in the sky.... In a second or two it becomes a horse and rider, rising and falling, rising and falling—sweeping toward us nearer and nearer, and the flutter of hoofs comes faintly to the ear—another instant and a whoop and hurrah... a wave of the rider's hand, but no reply, and a man and horse burst past our excited faces, and go sweeping away like a belated fragment of storm.

Mark Twain's magic pen has captured the contemporary and the permanent spell of this miracle of horseflesh and horsemanship. Practical details fade into insignificance, such as the half-ounce letters in oilskin pouches, the boy jockeys, unarmed and depending on their ponies' speed to escape the ambushes of designing savages, the 75 relays, the $5 postage, and the disappointingly small volume of westbound letters. As an advertisement of the central route the Pony Express might or might not have been successful. Popular fancy was captivated, but, before Congress attacked the problem of revamping the California mails, Lincoln had been elected, South Carolina had seceded, her sister states, Texas included, had followed, Fort Sumter had been fired upon, and the Civil War was under way. The Butterfield route was abandoned and its stock hustled northward to the Salt Lake line. Although the ponies ran a little longer, gladdening California with news little more than a week old, even that service was outmoded on October 26, 1861, by the completion of the Pacific telegraph. In actuality, the ponies' contribution was to expedite communications in the 19 months immediately preceding the telegraph and, more important, to become the symbol of all the gallant efforts of the prerailroad era to provide the transcontinental link.

The day of the Concord was not over. Concentrating now on the central route, Congress on March 2, 1861, authorized a million-dollar subsidy for a daily stage. Arrangements were complicated by the necessity of compensating Butterfield for transferring northward and by the financial difficulties of the COC and PPE because of the heavy drain of the Pony Express. Efficiency also demanded a route which would include on the main line both Denver, the metropolis of Colorado mining, and Salt Lake City, the Mormon metropolis. By July these problems were on the road toward solutions. The first run was accomplished in 17 days, and despite Indian hostility, the severe winter of 1861–62, and floods in the following spring, the stages kept rolling.

Financially, however, Russell, Majors, and Waddell were at the end of their resources and in March, 1862, had to surrender to a new magnate, the expansive Ben Holladay. By those who did not like him, Holladay was accused of having all the vices of the unprincipled, domineering, coarse, and ruthless tycoons who were then riding the crest of big business' sudden rise. He was not in the traditions of staging as, for example, was Birch. He knew little of its niceties as a craft, took no pride in the superlative qualities of Concords or of matched wheelers, and was a demanding taskmaster rather than an inspiring leader for his employees. On the other hand he had an astounding ability to get things done, had adequate finances at his command, and was adept in the financial deception, shady and otherwise, practiced by so many of his contemporaries. In the four years of his control western staging attained its largest scale. Holladay had some 3,300 miles of regular lines in operation and enjoyed a reputation, attested by Mark Twain, of getting the mail through. In 1866, on the eve of eclipse by the transcontinental railroad, Holladay gave further proof of his financial genius by selling out at a good price to Wells, Fargo and Company.

Most published accounts of prerailroad communication concentrate on the most dramatic ventures, such as Butterfield's Overland Mail, Russell's Pony Express, the army's experiment in the fifties with a camel caravan, or John A. "Snowshoe" Thompson's ski trips across the Sierra with as much as 100 pounds of mail on his back. Some of the phases usually neglected seem to be of comparable or of even greater significance, particularly the development of communications within the state by steamboat and stage, California's contribution to overland staging, the role of Crandall, Hockaday, and Chorpenning as pioneers on the central route, the culmination of the overland system under Holladay, and finally the continued dependence of Californians on the Panama sailings of the Pacific Mail Steamship Company. Pony and stage sometimes outraced steamer and often monopolized public attention, but it took a doughtier foe to wrest away the bulk of the business in passengers, express, and even mail. Steamer patronage was well maintained, the peak being reached in 1868. The

Los Angeles and San Pedro Train at Wilmington, 1870

next year the joining of the rails at Promontory terminated a colorful and significant epoch and reduced both steamers and stages to roles subordinate to that of the new hero, the puffing locomotive.

For Further Reading

ERNEST A. WILTSEE, *The Pioneer Miner and the Pack Mule Express* (1931).
JERRY MacMULLEN, *Paddlewheel Days in California* (1944).
JACK McNAIRN and JERRY MacMULLEN, *Ships of the Redwood Coast* (1945).
WILLIAM and GEORGE HUGH BANNING, *Six Horses* (1930).
OSCAR WINTHER, *Express and Stagecoach Days in California* (1936).
JOHN H. KEMBLE, *The Panama Route, 1848–1869* (1943).
A. H. CLARKE, *The Clipper Ship Era, 1843–1869* (1910).
RAYMOND RYDELL, *Cape Horn to the Pacific* (1952).
LEWIS B. LESLEY, *Uncle Sam's Camels* (1929).
HARLAN D. FOWLER, *Camels to California* (1950).
W. TURRENTINE JACKSON, *Wagon Roads West* (1952).
WALTER B. LANG, *The First Overland Mail* (1940; 1945).
LYLE H. WRIGHT and JOSEPHINE M. BYNUM, *The Butterfield Overland Mail* (1942).

WILLIAM B. TALLACK, *The California Overland Express, the Longest Stage Ride in the World* (1935).

HORACE GREELEY, *An Overland Journey* (1860).

GLENN D. BRADLEY, *The Story of the Pony Express* (1913).

RAYMOND W. and MARY LUND SETTLE, *Saddles and Spurs, the Saga of the Pony Express* (1955).

ROBERT LUTHER THOMPSON, *Wiring a Continent* (1947).

CAUGHEY, *California Heritage*, 265–68, 286–92.

chapter nineteen

Rails over the Sierra

Let the great line be adorned with this crowning honor, the colossal statue of the great Columbus, whose design it accomplishes, hewn from the granite mass of a peak of the Rocky Mountains, overlooking the road, the mountain itself the pedestal, and the statue a part of the mountain, pointing with outstretched arm to the western horizon, and saying to the flying passenger, "There is the east! There is India!"

Senator Thomas Hart Benton

From Asa Whitney to Theodore Judah

1845 to 1869

In California the first quarter-century of the American period was filled with epochal changes and remarkable achievements. They are encountered in law and politics, in agriculture and industry, in literature, and in transportation. Most grandiose of all the projects attempted was one which was major in the nation as well as California, the building of the Pacific railroad.

First proposed with any seriousness in 1845, a transcontinental railroad was for a number of years regarded as a most visionary scheme. Gradually its advocates gained a more sympathetic hearing. The gold rush added incentive, the surveys of 1853 to 1855 pronounced several routes feasible, overland stages and pony express

Through to the Pacific

Lithograph by Currier & Ives, 1870

305

popularized the idea, and the sectional crisis emphasized the necessity of binding the Far West to the nation. Notwithstanding the formidable and complex difficulties encountered, Asa Whitney's dream of 1845 was realized in 1869, just 24 years later. The story obviously belongs to the nation and to the East, yet much of the drama was enacted in California, and this railroad's influence on the state has been pervasive and powerful.

Prior to the gold rush it was perfectly natural that the planners of a Pacific railroad should look toward Oregon rather than toward California. In the fifties, when sights were shifted, hopes were pinned not merely on California but on the entire Pacific area which the railroad would unlock: Oregon and British Columbia, the Russian empire on the North Pacific, the islands of the South Seas, the Japan whose door Perry was even then opening, ancient China, and Columbus' India. The railroad, significantly, was always called the Pacific railroad.

Throughout the fifties the prospect for such a railroad was dimmed not only by calculations of probable cost and engineering difficulties but also by sectional jealousies which prevented agreement on any single route. Those interested in the existing transportation system by stage and steamer exerted their influence against active federal support. Also, though many individuals warmed to the notion that a railroad should be constructed, only a very few had any concrete ideas on how to engineer or finance it, how much it would cost, how long it would take, how much private capital could be raised for the enterprise, or how much business the completed road might expect.

The first to rescue the Pacific railroad from the limbo of hazy generalities and to discuss it in terms that would impress engineers and bankers was a young construction engineer named Theodore D. Judah. Before 1854 he assisted in rebuilding the section of the Erie Canal between Jordan and Seneca and helped build the bridge at Vergennes, Vermont, and various New England and New York railroads, including the Niagara Gorge Railroad. At the ripe age of 28 he was brought to California to build the Sacramento Valley Railroad to Folsom, 22 miles distant, and then perhaps to Shasta or even to Oregon. To Folsom the rails were laid expeditiously, at a cost only slightly in excess of Judah's original estimate. Since it cut a day from the time required for freighting to the mines, the road became immediately profitable. Stage lines also transferred their depot to Folsom. This railroad was California's earliest. On a hand-car over its first 400 feet of track, Judah enjoyed the first railroad ride in the state. Logically, other sections of track might have been added, but at this point Judah became disturbed by the company's heavy interest charges. He severed his connections with it and track laying stopped.

Judah's miscellaneous employments in the next few years were overshadowed by his preoccupation with the idea of a Pacific railroad. When commissioned to chart a wagon route across the Sierra, he made his report primarily an argument for the railroad. With a one-horse wagon equipped with barometer, compass, and odometer, he made no less than 22 reconnaissances of Sierra passes and approaches, finally selecting the Dutch Flat route, which the Central Pacific

Theodore D. Judah

The Bancroft Library

eventually used. Selection of this route was one of Judah's major contributions to the ultimate railroad.

Meanwhile, he was still more active in advocating the idea. "Crazy Judah," people called him, because of his incessant harping on this theme. He calls to mind that earlier enthusiast for the Americanization of Oregon, the eccentric Hall J. Kelley. There was this difference, however: Although Judah talked indefatigably about his obsession, his enthusiasm was backed by a seemingly inexhaustible store of facts and figures about the actual problems of construction. Although he may have been infatuated with the idea, he was singularly well-informed, thoroughly practical, and unquestionably an expert.

Besides riding his hobby in California, where he gradually built up a following of more or less enthusiastic converts, Judah made several bids for support at Washington. He was there in 1856 and again in 1857, urging his favorite project upon Congressmen, Senators, and others influential in the government. The nature of his proposal is well summed up in a pamphlet that he had printed at Washington on the occasion of his second visit. It is entitled *A Practical Plan for Building the Pacific Railroad* and it was just that. Judah began with a devastating criticism of the government surveys of 1853 to 1855, which the irrepressible John Phoenix was even then lampooning in the California press. Judah argued that most of the botanical and zoological information which the military surveys had amassed was irrelevant and that prospective builders needed to know more about actual grades and alignments, about the requirements for tunnels, fills, and bridges, and about the availability of fuel, timber, and building stone. He urged Congress to appropriate $200,000 for such an "actual and reliable survey," which he represented as necessary if private capital was to be induced to take up the project. Seeing a model in the way that squatter sovereignty had taken the question of slavery extension out of the halls of Congress, he proposed that the choice of route be left to the capitalists and thereby removed from politics. Sound though most of these arguments were, they were unavailing, and Congress in 1857 adopted none of the legislation proposed.

Two years later Judah had partial success in another quarter. The California legislature was persuaded to call a Pacific Railroad Convention, which met at San Francisco on September 20, 1859, with 100 delegates in attendance and John Bidwell presiding. Although the convention was an oratorical rather than a legislative body, it achieved a unified statement of western recommendations regarding the transcontinental railroad. As its most active member, Judah was the natural choice to convey the convention's proposals to Congress. He sailed on October 20 in company with California's new Congressman, John C. Burch, who quickly became a convert to Judah's idea. Other California and Oregon representatives gave support, as did Congressman John A. Logan of Illinois, who procured a room in the Capitol for Judah's more effective lobbying. There Judah set up a Pacific Railroad Museum filled with maps, surveys, reports, and other materials calculated to sell the idea of the railroad. Notwithstanding the persuasiveness of his exhibit and his speeches, the time was not yet ripe for federal action. When Judah sailed for the Pacific coast, he had not yet realized his hopes.

Organizing the Central Pacific

Back in California, Judah was off at once to the high Sierra to spend the entire summer in search of the best route. By the time winter snows drove him down to the habited lowlands his fieldwork had removed from his mind any uncertainties about the feasibility of a trans-Sierra railroad. Encouraged by his close friend, the Dutch Flat druggist, Dr. Daniel W. Strong, he drew up articles of association for a company to build such a railroad. Its name was to be the Central Pacific Railroad of California.

Before such a company could be incorporated, state law required that its stock be subscribed to the amount of $1,000 for each mile of trackage proposed, which in this instance meant $115,000. Judah, Strong, and a few Dutch Flat associates were good for $46,500. It was with optimism, therefore, that Judah left for San Francisco to raise the remainder. For a time prospects seemed rosy, but in the end the metropolitan financiers proved too coldly calculating and the Central Pacific had to go begging to Sacramento. From the Wall Street of the West to the humble merchants of Sacramento was quite a comedown; it was the latter, however, whom Judah was finally able to wheedle into giving the necessary support.

The process of extracting this support was not without drama. After many conferences and conversations and after a first meeting had failed, a second meeting was called in a small room over the hardware store owned by Mark Hopkins and Collis P. Huntington. Those in attendance included Judah and

Strong; James Bailey, jeweler; Cornelius Cole, lawyer; B. F. Leete, surveyor; the Robinson brothers; Lucius A. Booth; Leland Stanford, wholesale grocer; Charles Crocker, dry-goods merchant; and the hosts of the evening. Stanford was shortly to be the Republican candidate for governor and Cole later went to the United States Senate. At the time of the meeting, however, none of those present had a reputation more than local, none had previous experience in large-scale construction or financial enterprises, and their combined resources would not have paid for even as much of a railroad as the Sacramento Valley line to Folsom. This certainly was not the most promising personnel for the heroic venture of spanning the Sierra.

Judah's persuasive powers were equal to the emergency. He mentioned the plan for a transcontinental railroad in which the Central Pacific was to be a unit, but he had the good judgment to build his plea on arguments which small-town merchants would be better able to comprehend. Eventually would come the railroad, but for the present all that was necessary was to charter the company and run the survey over the mountains to the state line. With this accomplished, the company would be in excellent position to get federal, state, and local government subsidies. More to the point, it would control the lucrative traffic to and from Washoe. Even with a wagon road, Judah subtly pointed out to these Sacramento merchants, the Washoe market would be theirs. Thus persuaded, these tradesmen entered upon the speculation that was to bring four of their number fame and wealth beyond their wildest expectations.

It was conservatively that they ventured. At the meeting at which that minimum subscription for incorporation was reached, Huntington took no stock. Only after further appeal from Judah did he agree to lend a hand. He then promised to get six men to pay for the projected instrumental survey across the mountains, a valuable contribution to be sure but one for which the six struck a hard bargain. Judah put at the disposal of the company practically without compensation his fund of knowledge about railroad building, the Dutch Flat route, and lobbying at Washington. Dr. Strong's early support was soon forgotten, but the six merchants, Stanford, Huntington, Bailey, Hopkins, Booth, and Crocker, who took only 800 of the original 85,000 shares, were rewarded with the positions, respectively, of president, vice-president, secretary, treasurer, and directors of the company. There is a poetic injustice that control should have passed from the hands of Chief Engineer Judah to these men, but, putting sentiment aside, the enlistment of these men into the enterprise was unquestionably one of Judah's major contributions to the Pacific railroad.

Work on the survey began at once. Judah was greatly heartened to have at least a portion of the load lifted from his shoulders. The vast majority of Sacramentans, however, were most skeptical that the Central Pacific Company would surmount the Sierra by rail. Even with the $1,000-a-mile requirement railroad planning was a favorite California pastime, usually with abortive result. Judah's project, more fantastic than the average, seemed most unlikely to succeed, for, as the survey progressed and demonstrated that a trans-Sierra railroad was an engineering possibility, the obstacles to be overcome were brought more

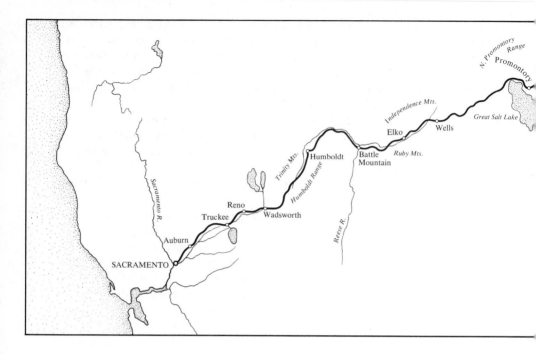

clearly to view. Never before had a railroad attempted to scale so formidable a barrier, an abrupt rise of 7,000 feet in 20 miles, with rugged mountainsides, deep canyons, dangerous slide areas, hard granite almost everywhere a cut or tunnel was indicated, and winter snowfalls of as much as 30 feet. Judah never minimized these difficulties, but in his reports he achieved an optimistic tone by harping on the magnitude of the Nevada traffic and the resources, such as timber, that the road would open up.

Next on Judah's program was another jaunt to Washington. Again he sailed in company with a Congressman-elect, Aaron Sargent, and again he was able to instill much of his enthusiasm into the representative. Sargent not only agreed to sponsor the Pacific railroad bill but at the first opportunity spoke energetically for it, got a subcommittee appointed to take the measure in charge, and saw to it that Judah was named clerk of this subcommittee. Judah was already secretary of the corresponding Senate committee and soon acquired similar opportunity with the House's main committee on railroads, thus becoming a triply effective lobbyist. Even without his influence a Pacific railroad bill might have been enacted in 1862, because the secession of the southern states had removed opposition to a north-central route and because the Civil War set a special premium on California's gold and Nevada's silver. The bill, however, bears the unmistakable stamp of Judah's hand, particularly in the provision that the western unit, from Sacramento to the state line, should be built by the

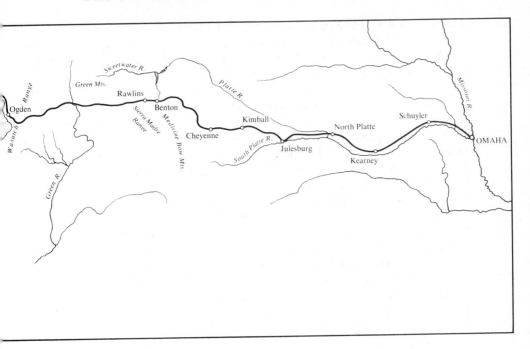

Route of the Pacific Railroad

Central Pacific Company of California. Other provisions of the act were that the road should extend from the Missouri River to Sacramento and that, in addition to the 400-foot right-of-way, the companies should receive from the public domain the odd-numbered sections within 10 miles of the line, that is, 10 for each mile of track. Most important of all, the federal government agreed to advance, on 30-year 6 per cent bonds for each mile of track laid, $16,000 to the mountains, $48,000 in the Rockies and the Sierras, and $32,000 on the intermountain section.

Returning to the coast, the master lobbyist found himself the hero of the hour, honored on all sides except in his own company. Among the Central Pacific moguls the bone of contention was the perhaps inevitable one between builder and speculators. Judah envisioned the road as a link in the Pacific railroad, a permanent asset for future generations and something that should be built accordingly. The partners seemed to have designs merely on the Nevada business and the government subsidy, especially the latter. Track laying they regarded as a necessary evil, prerequisite though it was to collection of the subsidy. Survey beyond the mountains could also be postponed, and any other device that would cut expenses or expedite collection of the subsidy was sure to meet with their favor. The rift widened. Judah insisted that as chief engineer, indeed as the only competent engineer, he should have the final decision on construction matters. The partners responded by excluding him from any voice in company affairs. They called on him to pay up the 10 per cent deposit on his stock, though his initial services to the company had been accepted as an in lieu payment. The last straw was his refusal to certify to the federal authorities that the line entered the mountains some 20 miles sooner than was actually the case. By enlisting the support of the state geologist, Professor J. D. Whitney, the partners "moved the Sierra into the middle of the valley" and profited thereby to the tune of some $640,000, but Judah would not be a party to the deception.

The parting of the ways was now at hand. In October, 1863, Judah sailed for New York. He had accepted $100,000 for his interest in the Central Pacific and had taken options to buy out Stanford, Huntington, Hopkins, and Crocker at $100,000 each. His plan apparently was to persuade eastern capitalists, perhaps the Vanderbilt interests, to buy out his shortsighted and unprincipled antagonists. But the gods overruled. Contracting yellow fever at Panama, Judah was brought ashore at New York a very sick man, and on November 2, four months short of his thirty-eighth birthday, he died. Thus for good or ill the Central Pacific Railroad was left in the hands of the Californians who were soon to be ticketed the Big Four. They exhibited a perfect willingness to allow Judah to pass into oblivion. For a decade he had been the most active promoter of the Pacific railroad. The Dutch Flat route, the Central Pacific Company, and the Pacific Railroad Act were monuments to his competence as engineer, promoter, and lobbyist. His former partners did not so much as name a whistle stop in his honor, nor did they share any of the profits of the enterprise with his widow.

The Big Four at Work

The four men whose sway over the company was now complete are among the most famous in California's history. Making due allowance for sporadic essays and for Oscar Lewis' successful venture in group biography, these men still await full and exacting biographical treatment. They and their relatives frowned on early proposals, and recent scholars have not been attracted to the task, in realization, no doubt, that many essential materials would not be available and that to do the subject justice would call for the collaboration of a Horatio Alger, an Ida Tarbell, and a Sinclair Lewis.

The four had much in common. Each had a vigorous youth in the East before coming to California in the gold rush. Each turned quickly from gold mining to the more profitable and less speculative avenues of trade, demonstrating full capacity to look out for his own interests. Hopkins was tall and spare, the other three tall and robust; all were conspicuous by their abundance of energy and their capacity for sustained effort. Huntington and Crocker, in particular, had given early indication of indomitable will. Crocker later indulged in periods of lethargy and Stanford was chided by Huntington for laziness, but, through the sixties at least, the four were unremitting drivers of themselves as well as of those who worked for them. Convinced by experience that the pursuit of wealth was man's highest calling, in common with their contemporaries in the mushrooming of American big business, the group which Matthew Josephson has labeled the "Robber Barons," they had few scruples about the methods to be employed in the accumulation of wealth and power. In fairness, however, they should be measured not against an absolute standard but in the light of the thought patterns of their own generation.

Like-minded though these four individuals were, each was fitted for a special function, as a result of which a division of work soon developed. Stanford became the titular head, the public-relations chief in California, and the spokesman of the company in seeking subventions from the state and the counties. Huntington stepped into Judah's place as contact man with the national government and became the purchasing agent and the chief money raiser in the East. Hopkins' role as office man was the least conspicuous, but as the balance wheel he restrained his rasher partners from steps that would have jeopardized the company. Crocker superintended construction, a task to which he was ideally suited and which later enabled him to discomfit Stanford and Huntington with the complacent assertion that, whatever the others had accomplished, he had built the road.

One of Judah's criticisms of his partners had been over the way in which construction contracts were handled. The first, to grade 32 miles of road-bed, was let at an inflated figure to the Charles Crocker Company, whose owners were the Big Four. With the chief critic silenced by death this technique continued. Its effect is obvious. To the disadvantage of the numerous smaller stockholders in the railroad company the executives voted themselves construction contracts that soon made them multimillionaires. Small wonder that the Charles Crocker Company was anathema to the unsuspecting purchasers of the Central Pacific stock and that the railroad acquired the sobriquet "the Dutch Flat swindle." The device was essentially the one made notorious by the Union Pacific and its dummy, the Crédit Mobilier.

Forty miles of track had to be laid before the federal subsidy was collectable. With materials at inflated prices because of the Civil War, with round-the-Horn shipping commanding emergency rates, and with the war and Nevada silver competing in the California labor mart, the Big Four found it very difficult to complete this first unit. Their own resources were inadequate, for they were still men of very moderate means, and investors were not expressing confidence by rushing forward to purchase stock. Early in 1863 Crocker was so discouraged by the outlook as to be willing to "take a clean shirt, and get out." It was Stanford who pulled a rabbit from the hat. The state government and several interested counties were induced to buy $1.5 million worth of stock and to assume the interest payment on bonds to a like amount. Without this timely assistance the Central Pacific would have had difficulty building far enough to collect the initial federal subsidy.

On July 2, 1864, the company recorded another financial triumph when President Lincoln approved an amendment to the Pacific Railroad Act doubling the land grant, permitting advance payment of certain subsidies, and extending the time limit. Most important, the government agreed to reduce the security for its loans from a first to a second mortgage. Lobbyist Huntington had good reason to congratulate himself.

Brightening financial skies gave new zest for road building. Construction had gone forward haltingly, and two years after work had started there were only 31 miles in operation. The next six months witnessed better progress. By midsummer of 1865 trains were running 56 miles to Illinoistown, soon to be renamed in compliment to Vice-President Schuyler Colfax. Business was good too and, at 10 cents a mile for passengers and 15 cents a ton-mile for freight, operating revenue exceeded $1,000 a day. Central Pacific had surpassed the Union Pacific, which by the end of 1865 had only 40 miles of track jutting westward over the open prairie from Omaha. At the rate of construction thus far attained and with no allowance for the greater difficulties ahead, it would have required 40 years to join the rails.

Assurance of adequate financial support was one factor speeding up construction. Another factor that seemed equally fundamental was the solution of the Central Pacific's labor problem. At first Crocker had relied upon California whites: Irish, Americans, Germans, and those of other nationalities. The wage scale had to be high and, worse yet, a majority of the recruits seemed to look upon railroad work as merely a convenient dodge for getting a free ride toward the Nevada mines. In spite of all that could be done the labor turnover was excessive. In desperation the Big Four considered heroic cures. One proposal was to bring up several thousand Mexicans, a solution of the labor problem to which southwestern railroads later turned for maintenance work and southern California agriculturists for crop harvesting. But Mexicans did not build the Central Pacific, nor did the 5,000 captured Confederate soldiers whom the federal government was requested to provide. The solution was found nearer at hand.

Crocker had the inspiration to try the Chinese. In the mines and in the northern towns the little yellow man was already a familiar figure. Because of his small stature, most of Crocker's associates were skeptical that the Oriental would be equal to the heavy work required, but the initial experiment with 50 Celestials proved that Oriental stamina was a more than adequate substitute for Occidental brawn. Thereafter, the Chinese contingent was steadily increased. California supplied 2,000 in April, 1865; by the end of the season the number had increased to 6,000 and by 1869 a peak of 15,000 was reached. The Chinese never threatened to strike as had the Irish-Americans. They were tireless; pick, shovel, and wheelbarrow were no mystery to them, and they soon became adept with drill, blasting powder, and the other fairly simple equipment with which the line across the Sierra was to be carved out.

At San Francisco labor leaders frowned on the importation of shiploads of coolies. In the sixties violence was threatened but not actually visited upon the hapless immigrants. At the railhead, however, the expected opposition did not materialize. The construction crew was being enlarged so rapidly that most of the whites could be promoted to superior work as teamsters, powdermen, or gang foremen, and there was little objection to the Chinese taking over the backbreaking tasks.

Secrettown Trestle, Sierra Nevada, 1867

Just beyond Colfax the railroad confronted a practically vertical granite cliff 1,000 feet high. Cape Horn was its name, and rounding Cape Horn became the problem of the year. Lowered by ropes from above, Chinese chiselers chipped out a narrow ledge, which after herculean effort was widened to accommodate the tracks. A most spectacular achievement, it gave passengers the tingling sensation of being suspended in midair.

Cape Horn, for all its difficulty, was child's play compared with the difficulty of holing through the quarter-mile Summit Tunnel. The hard granite of the upper ridges defied the hand drills and black powder on which the tunnelers had relied. Crocker put crews of Chinese to work at both portals and sank a shaft in the center so that they could peck away on four cutting surfaces. Drills and chisels dulled after a few blows, however, and the powder charges fizzled out of the drill holes. Progress was counted by inches and not until September, 1867, was the tunnel finished. In an endeavor to speed up the work Crocker began to use a new explosive, the dangerous and unpredictable nitroglycerin. He could not be persuaded, however, to experiment with the newly invented steam drill. Although his partners fumed and stormed and Stanford sent one up to the railhead, Crocker stuck by his hand drills. A year or two later these were completely outmoded.

315

The Race with the Union Pacific

With a new construction engineer in charge, the Union Pacific was rapidly advancing its tracks across Nebraska. Grenville Dodge was a driver comparable to Crocker, and his Irish paddies were worthy rivals of "Crocker's Pets." In the race for track mileage, the collateral for the government subsidy, the Central Pacific could not wait for Summit Tunnel to be holed through. Locomotives, flatcars, and rails were hauled on huge sledges across the divide, and grading and track laying were pushed down toward the Nevada line. These measures added $2 million to expenses, but because of the prospect of the subsidy beyond the mountains it was counted good economy. The competitive urge for haste also dictated work right through the winter in spite of heavy snows and subzero temperatures, which cut efficiency to a fraction.

Clearing, grading, and track laying went forward at a snail's pace during the winter months, but the higher portion of the completed line could not be kept open. Even five locomotives could not push a snowplow through the 30-foot drifts above Cisco. In the interest of subsequent operations as well as of current construction, something had to be done. Snowsheds were the answer and some 37 miles of them were built at a cost of another $2 million.

By June, 1868, the road was finally completed to the state line. Ahead lay the plums for which the Big Four had been straining, the open floor of the intermountain basin, across which tracks could be laid for half the amount of the subsidy, and the traffic of the Mormons at Salt Lake. Authorized in 1866 to build beyond the state line, the Central Pacific girded itself for a final sprint. All was not smooth sailing. Prices of steel rails, locomotives, cars, and powder had not dropped as expected at the end of the Civil War. Freight rates round the Horn were still high and ships not always easy to charter. As the road pushed into Nevada the cost of ties and timber, fuel and hay, once nominal, rocketed upward. And with every mile of track built, the railhead became that much more difficult and expensive of access. This latter difficulty came to bear even more heavily upon the Union Pacific as its single-track line stretched farther and farther westward.

Answering the demands for speed, both Dodge and Crocker whipped their construction crews into highly expert machines. Using the factory method of division of labor, they perfected their techniques so that the rails went down at the rate of three, four, and five miles a day. In a final inspired burst of superefficiency Crocker's Chinese laid 10 miles in a single day.

As the two lines approached each other, the nation suddenly realized that they might not meet. Why should they? As the law stood, each road might continue on across the continent with uninterrupted enjoyment of land grants and subsidies. An alarmed Congress intervened at the eleventh hour to designate Promontory, Utah, as the place where the rails should meet.

The completion of construction afforded an irresistible temptation for dramatics. The stage was set early in May. By Saturday, the eighth, Stanford had arrived by special train, ready for his histrionic role, but Vice-President Durant of the Union Pacific was delayed by washouts and by a strike occasioned by lack of money with which to pay off his workmen, and the celebration had to be postponed until Monday.

The people of Sacramento, with Judge Nathaniel Bennett of Sacramento as the orator of the day, went ahead with their celebration on May 8. Judge Bennett congratulated his fellow Californians that they were "composed of the right materials, derived from the proper origins.... In the veins of our people," he declared, "flows the commingled blood of the four greatest nationalities of modern days. The impetuous daring and dash of the French, the philosophical and sturdy spirit of the German, the unflinching solidity of the English, and the light-hearted impetuosity of the Irish, have all contributed each its appropriate share." With never a thought to the contribution of the Chinese, Judge Bennett moved along to his peroration. "A people deducing its origins from such races, and condensing their best traits into its national life, is capable of any achievement."

On the afternoon of May 10 Durant's special finally arrived at Promontory. With suitable flow of oratory, and to the tune of music from the Twenty-First Infantry Band, the stage properties were brought forward; a laurel tie; the last rail; spikes of Comstock silver, of Arizona gold, iron, and silver, of Idaho and Montana gold and silver, and of California gold; and a silver sledgehammer from California. At last the final gold spike was ready to be driven home, with Stanford to have the honor of giving the coup de grâce. His blow missed.

Held Up!

N. H. Trotter. Department of Civil History, Smithsonian Institution

Durant's courtesy was equal to the occasion. He also scored a miss and left the driving for Dodge and the Central Pacific's construction engineer. Over the last rail two locomotives touched cowcatchers. Their engineers had the first drinks of champagne and then the celebration became general.

The fashion often is to belittle this first Pacific railroad. Construction methods had been wasteful, and excessive haste had encouraged faulty construction. Much of the track was almost immediately in need of replacement and considerable portions were subsequently realigned. Both sections of the line had been built with a view to collecting the subsidies rather than to profiting through operations, witness the promptness with which the Union Pacific directors severed their connection with the company.

One feature not to be belittled is the federal subsidy totaling more than $60 million in government bonds and 20 million acres of land. The bonds were almost enough to cover the actual construction costs, which means that private investors had to put up only a very small fraction of the outlay and that private enterprisers—on the western half, the Big Four—emerged with the railroad, the land, and the handsome profits through the construction contracts. By business standards the railroad in the 1860's was premature. How many years it would have been before traffic would have justified the investment cannot be calculated because the railroad itself helped generate such patronage. The road was built for reasons of state and public opinion, for the Union, progress, and the development of the country. It was by all odds the largest federal subsidy thus far and would not be exceeded until the twentieth century.

In the High Sierra

William Graham

Although speculation may have overshadowed construction, the Pacific railroad remains one of the epochal developments in western history. Perhaps even more significantly than the discovery of gold, it marked the end of an old era and the opening of a new. For exactly a century, since the coming of Portolá and Serra in 1769, isolation had imposed a powerful restraint upon California's development. Now the barrier was broken through. Subsequent improvements were to batter it down still further, and what California was to lose in provincialism was to be more than compensated for in stimulus to new and greater attainments. The Pacific railroad heralded transformation of California and the West.

For Further Reading

GRANT FOREMAN, *A Pathfinder in the Southwest* (1941), reproducing Whipple's Pacific Railroad Survey on the thirty-fifth parallel.

CARL I. WHEAT, "A Sketch of the Life of Theodore D. Judah," *CSHQ*, 4 (1925), 219–71.

OSCAR LEWIS, *The Big Four* (1938).

GEORGE T. CLARK, *Leland Stanford* (1931).

HARRY J. CARMAN and CHARLES H. MUELLER, "The Contract and Finance Company and the Central Pacific Railroad," *MVHR*, 14 (1927), 326–41.

WESLEY S. GRISWOLD, *A Work of Giants: Building the First Transcontinental Railway* (1963).

ROBERT WEST HOWARD, *The Giant Iron Trail: The Story of the First Transcontinental Railroad* (1963).

JOHN D. GALLOWAY, *The First Transcontinental Railroad* (1950).

JACOB R. PERKINS, *Trails, Rails, and War; the Life of General* [Grenville] *Dodge* (1929).

ROBERT WILLIAM FOGEL, *The Union Pacific Railroad, a Case in Premature Enterprise* (1960).

SAMUEL BOWLES, *Our New West* (1869), a passenger's account.

ROBERT LOUIS STEVENSON, *Across the Plains* (1892).

chapter twenty

Social Unrest

The worst railroads on the Pacific Coast are those operated by the
Southern Pacific Company. The worst railroad operated by the Southern
Pacific Company is the Central Pacific. It owes the government more
millions of dollars than Leland Stanford has vanities; it will pay fewer cents
than Collis P. Huntington has virtues. It has always been managed by
rapacity tempered by incompetence. Let Leland Stanford remove his dull
face from the United States Senate and exert some of his boasted
"executive ability" disentangling the complexities in which his frankly
brainless subordinates have involved the movement of trains.

Ambrose Bierce,
San Francisco *Examiner*,
July 22, 1888

A Monopoly of California Rails

**1870
to
1880**

California's initial enthusiasm for the Pacific railroad soon gave way
to annoyance, distrust, and dislike. The change was an echo of the
national conviction that the railroads were responsible for most of
the country's economic ills, including the panic of 1873. California
not only shared this opinion but also saw much local evidence that
the railroad was to blame for the most pressing afflictions of the body
politic, economic, and social. For all its promise of vitalizing the
West, the railroad yielded a first crop of bitter fruit. Local shopkeepers found their business thrown into confusion by the stocks of
new goods brought in by the iron horse; western publishers encountered unprecedented competition in the deluge of printed matter
flowing in from the East; and Sacramento, though it had taken the

The Tables Turned

UCLA Library

THE TABLES TURNED

YOU SABE HIM ! KEALNEY MUST GO !

lead in building the Central Pacific, shortly found itself declining to a way station on the line to San Francisco. The railroad became a monster, or more con-
cretely, the Octopus. It was the target for criticisms by all those whom the hard
times of the seventies made discontented and bitter.

The railroad thus pilloried, though dominated by the same Big Four,
was not just the transcontinental line so boldly, wastefully, and profitably constructed in the sixties. It had become much larger, much more complex, much
more powerful; in the figure of speech of the period, the Octopus had thrown
out additional tentacles.

Because of the meager documentation available concerning the early
operation of the Big Four, it is not possible to speak with absolute precision
about the evolution of their plans. There is no question, however, that their
original purpose did not go beyond the building of the transcontinental link,
and that, having skimmed the cream of cash subsidies and land bounties, they
regarded railroad operation as an unpromising business. Their eastern counterparts, the Union Pacific executives, being philosophers of the same stamp, left
that company promptly when the subsidies ended. But there was no one on
whom the Big Four could unload; they had no choice but to hold on to the
Central Pacific.

However reluctant they may have been to continue in railroading,
the Big Four quickly saw that their further success hinged upon establishing a
monopoly of California rails, particularly with regard to San Francisco Bay.
To this end they moved rapidly. The Western Pacific Railroad Company, the
Big Four under another alias, was chartered to build from Sacramento to San
Jose, and a branch from Niles to Oakland gave virtual monopoly of the Oakland
waterfront. To control another approach they absorbed the California Pacific
which had a Sacramento–Vallejo franchise. Its tracks were carried to Benicia,
a ferry crossed to Port Costa, and rails continued to Oakland, completing the
stranglehold on the East Bay.

Through grants from the state legislature the Big Four next sought
control of San Francisco's waterfront, but because of violent protests from the
press this grant was reduced to a mere 60 acres. The newspapers also foiled an
attempt to get Congress to donate Goat Island, which under its more limpid
name Yerba Buena is now the stepping-stone for the Bay Bridge. Undaunted,
the Big Four purchased the San Francisco and San Jose, acquired two lesser
lines circling the southern arm of the bay, and effectively bottled up peninsular
traffic.

In addition to the encirclement of San Francisco Bay, the railroad
magnates took steps toward dominating the rest of California. As early as 1865
they had chartered the Southern Pacific, ostensibly as a competitor, to build
down the coast to San Diego. They also gobbled up an assortment of lines in
the San Joaquin Valley, constructed occasional links, and extended through
service to Goshen in Tulare County. By 1871 their plans for the south came
more clearly into the open. To the chagrin of the people of the southern coastal
counties it was announced that the Southern Pacific would shift to the valley

route. Public interest would have been much better served by a coast line, but along the latter were some 350 privately owned ranchos, whereas the inland route passed through government land from which the railroad's magnificient bounty could be carved. Also, the inland route was in easier striking distance of Needles and Yuma, gateways to the state which the Big Four wanted to control. Equally illuminating to the people of the state was the disclosure that the Southern Pacific was but another name for the Central Pacific. When its construction work was placed in the hands of Crocker's Contract and Finance Company, little doubt remained on that score.

Nor was public opinion reassured by the Southern Pacific's practice of holding up cities and towns for special subsidies on the threat of leaving them off the main line. This form of legalized blackmail was by no means confined to California and the Southern Pacific, but it was nonetheless galling. Los Angeles, for example, though the largest municipality in southern California, was threatened with a "run-around" if it did not hand over the Los Angeles and San Pedro Railroad, deed a sixty-acre depot site, and pay a bonus of $600,000. Spurning San Bernardino, the Southern Pacific built its own division point at Colton, three miles away.

Besides absorbing as many as possible of the local railroads, the Big Four took into account the menace of competing transcontinental lines. Many such lines had been projected, and several had advanced to the stage of more or less active construction. There was, for example, the Oregon Shortline, a northwestward extension of the Union Pacific to Portland. If it were completed, the Union Pacific would be in position to route California shipments over its own lines to Portland and from there by steamer to California, to the great discomfiture of the Central Pacific. To counterbalance such a potentiality and also for the land grants that could be obtained, the Big Four bought the California and Oregon Railroad and began to build north from Sacramento, following closely the route outlined in the Williamson–Abbott survey of the fifties. In 1887 the tracks were joined at Ashland, staving off the competition not only of the Oregon Shortline but also of Henry Villard's Northern Pacific.

Meanwhile, the southern gateways to California were more seriously menaced, particularly by Thomas A. Scott's Texas and Pacific. Backed by the resources of the Pennsylvania Railroad, of which he was president, and extracting full benefit from the bestowal of passes, Scott was able to get Congress in 1871 to charter the Texas and Pacific to build from Texarkana and Marshall, Texas, along the thirty-second parallel to San Diego. Land-grant subsidies promised were calculated at $68 million. Huntington was no less active as a lobbyist. First he persuaded Congress to grant a comparable subsidy to the Southern Pacific to build from San Francisco to Yuma. Then he endeavored to get Congress to cancel the Texas Pacific franchise west of Yuma, where for many miles its tracks would have to parallel those of the Southern Pacific. From this beginning the contest between Scott and Huntington expanded into a battle royal. Huntington emerged with the spoils of victory, partly because he was able to enlist support from the territorial governments of Arizona and

Collis P. Huntington, about 1886

C. C. Pierce Collection

"Out of three drops of rain which fall in the San Joaquin Valley,
two are owned by Collis P. Huntington."

popular folksaying

New Mexico and partly because the Southern Pacific set a more rapid pace in actual construction. For a time Yuma seemed to be the probable meeting place, then Tucson, then El Paso. With Scott's successor, Jay Gould, Huntington finally agreed on a junction at El Paso, with a traffic agreement, and with a transfer of the Texas Pacific land grant to the California company. Advantageous though this arrangement was, the Southern Pacific was ambitious for a line of its own to New Orleans; it built on eastward, local lines were bought up, and by the end of 1882 the goal was reached.

Although the Texas and Pacific was the first great rival in the south, the Atlantic and Pacific also cast a covetous eye westward along the thirty-fifth parallel toward the California entrance at Needles. Having crossed Tehachapi Pass on the way south toward Los Angeles, the Southern Pacific could comparatively easily build eastward from Mojave to Needles, a development designed, paradoxically enough, not to open that door but to close it against a competitive railroad. By the early eighties, therefore, the Big Four had made the monopoly of California rails almost complete. San Francisco Bay had been encircled. The coast line was not built, but spurs from Gilroy to Soledad and to Tres Pinos blocked the approach of any rival. The Central Valley was pre-empted, and Tehachapi Pass and San Gorgonio Pass were grasped. Transcontinental rivals from the north or by way of Needles or Yuma seemed to be adequately guarded against. In 1884 nomenclature was simplified when this entire system was effectively coordinated in a new Southern Pacific Company, incorporated under the laws of Kentucky. To Californians, however, it was still the Octopus.

Rising Resentment against the Railroad

The paramount position of the railroad in the seventies is not easily understood by the present generation. Big business today is multiple; in modern California it is represented by banks, oil companies, utilities, airplane and space industries, various manufacturers, chain stores, large department stores, metropolitan newspapers, and so forth. In the late nineteenth century all other enterprises were so overshadowed by the railroad as to be reduced to the stature of small business. The railroad was the biggest landowner and the biggest employer of labor, its owners were the richest men in the state, its influence on government was supreme, and by arbitrary manipulation of freight rates it could make or break almost any merchant, industrialist, or agriculturist in the state.

Had this unusual power been used with generous and studious moderation, the monopoly could have had a high place in popular esteem, for its contribution to California development far surpassed that of any other man-made factor. But since its power was not exercised with such utopian beneficence, and no doubt in part because of its very magnitude, the railroad supplanted Joaquín Murieta as public enemy number one and was blamed for everything that went wrong.

It was a period, furthermore, when many things seemed to be going wrong. California state government, never a glorious achievement of probity and efficiency, sank in the seventies to the nadir of disreputableness. San Francisco officials had reverted to the roguery of the early fifties, while at Sacramento the manifestations of corruption were equally prominent. No branch of government seemed to be exempt—not the courts, the tax assessors, or the executive officers; yet it was the legislature that seemed to be guilty of the most flagrant abuses. The scandalous laxity was in conformity with the mores of the day as represented by New York's Tweed Ring, Jay Gould's Black Friday, the Crédit Mobilier, the Star Route scandals, the Indian Frauds, and the Whisky Ring. It also arose from frontier examples, vigilante precedents, speculative enterprise, the prominence of the nouveaux riches, and, Californians would have added, the machinations of the railroad.

At the time that the agencies of government were being perverted for the advantage of a few and to the disadvantage of the majority, Californians were becoming conscious of other economic abuses. One had to do with land monopoly, long to continue a burning issue. Many a writer since Henry George has railed against the vast feudal estates of hundreds of thousands of acres held off the market and out of production for a speculative profit. Prospective farmers in the 1870's, as in the twentieth century, found that much of the best land was withheld from them, and it was the railroad's millions of acres that stood out most prominently. Water for irrigation was controlled to an even greater extent by the monopolists, thereby contributing to the building up of still larger holdings.

"Flood's Wedding Cake," the Menlo Park residence of
James A. Flood, 1877

Added to these factors were numerous instances when the railroads played fast and loose with prospective purchasers, raising the price after the settler had put in expensive improvements or proceeding with summary evictions. The dramatic climax for disputes of this sort was in the Mussel Slough tragedy in Tulare County in 1880, where an attempted eviction led to the killing of seven men. The railroad had the law on its side, and five settlers were sentenced to jail; but public opinion persisted that the railroad was in the wrong.

Overshadowing these complaints against the railroad was the more obvious one that its rate structure was unjust and antisocial. The railroad magnates replied that their rates were within or below the legal limit set in 1861 of 10 cents a passenger-mile and 15 cents a ton-mile and that railroad earnings were not excessive. The counterblast was that the Big Four had become very rich. Some of the practices criticized, for example, that of terminal rates to meet ship competition, have been upheld by the Interstate Commerce Commission and the courts. Others, such as the granting of rebates to favored shippers, have been outlawed. The fundamental contention of the critics, that transportation rates should be subject to government regulation, is taken for granted today. In the California wonderland of the seventies that contention was inverted; state government was regulated by the railroad.

With these conditions, it is natural that a popular hue and cry should have arisen for curbing the railroad. With their characteristic faculty for obscuring the issue, the reform leaders gave first attention to another only slightly related problem, the Chinese.

326

The Anti-Chinese Movement

In gold-rush days, when the first Celestials had appeared in California, they were given a cordial reception. Chinese had positions of honor at San Francisco's celebration of admission to statehood and again a few weeks later at the memorial services occasioned by Zachary Taylor's death. Never thereafter were they completely without friends in California, though some of their advocates distinguished sharply between houseboys, cooks, launderers, vegetable peddlers, and Chinatown merchants on the one hand and coolie laborers on the other.

In the diggings, however, there was less of the race tolerance that often prevailed among the white-collar whites in cosmopolitan San Francisco. The hardy miners were convinced that Providence as well as the treaty negotiators at Guadalupe Hidalgo had intended that California's mineral resources in particular were to be reserved for "Americans." Accordingly, they exerted pressure to get laws enacted, such as the Foreign Miners' License Law of 1850, which would discourage mining by non-Americans, and they took many forceful measures outside the law to make foreign miners uncomfortable. Objection was not raised to Englishmen, Germans, Scandinavians, or Irish but with varying intensity was raised against Frenchmen, Spanish Americans, Indians, Negroes, and especially the Chinese.

Conspicuously different in color, language, dress, and customs, the Chinese were looked upon as a race apart. Because of their clannishness and the great dissimilarity of their culture, they appeared destined to continue as such, while at the same time the easy accessibility of the teeming homeland held promise that their number would mount rapidly. The matter of numbers was certainly a fundamental cause for concern. By 1852 there were some 25,000 Chinese in California, making them the largest minority group. For the state at large one person out of ten was a Chinese, and in some of the mining counties the ratio was three out of ten. In the light of American conviction then prevailing regarding the superior privileges of the white race, it is not surprising that hostility arose toward the Orientals.

It began with local discriminatory measures, followed by the state tax on foreign miners. The first move on a statewide basis to be directed expressly against the Chinese was the proposal of Senator George B. Tingley in 1852 that the state authorize and agree to supervise the contracting of Chinese labor on a 10-year basis. While admitting that California needed laborers as industrious and as orderly as the Chinese, the press remonstrated vigorously against Tingley's proposal. Speaking for the opposition, Senator Philip A. Roach asserted the doctrine that white labor should not be subjected to unfair competition with Orientals, who were content with an abnormally low standard of living. A modification of Tingley's bill had passed the Assembly, but public opinion welled up so vigorously that rejection by the Senate was by a vote of 18 to 2.

On the heels of this action, Governor John Bigler addressed to the legislature a message urging the necessity of measures to check the tide of

Asiatic immigration and to prevent the exportation of gold to China. Unquestionably this was a political maneuver in Bigler's campaign for reelection. Whether it represented his studied conviction is questionable, but his reputation as an unprincipled and opportunist politician makes his use of this issue all the better index to the prejudice of the California voters.

Bigler's message did not lead to an exclusion act, but it did bring out into the open certain criticisms of the Chinese as transients, as morally depraved, and as a menace to the state's tranquillity. It stirred up a former missionary, the Reverend William Speer, to lecture on behalf of the Chinese, but on the other hand it encouraged a wave of anti-Chinese demonstrations and pogroms, especially in the mining counties. Presumably as a consequence, immigration slackened, and in 1853 the Chinese population had decreased by three or four thousand.

In April, 1855, hard times again having called attention to the straits of white labor, a law was enacted to impose a head tax of 50 dollars on immigrants not eligible for citizenship. Although this basis of classification later provided the most effective curb upon Asiatic immigration, the State Supreme Court ruled the act unconstitutional. Chinese continued to enter the state. Popular with capitalists, employers, and well-to-do householders, their entrenchment in certain occupations came to be relatively secure. Labor, however, had a constant tendency to regard them as unwelcome competitors, and, whenever the demand for labor fell off, this intolerance was apt to manifest itself vociferously or even violently.

In the sixties the Civil War, Nevada silver, and the building of the Central Pacific improved the market for labor and, to that degree, lessened the disposition to molest the Chinese. Because of the firm demand for white as well as yellow labor, Crocker's importation of thousands of coolies to man his construction crews did not lead to immediate trouble. But with the completion of the road and the laying off of entire gangs, labor's position became much less favorable, and, running true to form, labor leaders heaped most of the blame on the hapless Chinese.

The following biennium witnessed a new wave of repressive measures, most of them outside the law. There was mob violence at such widely separated places as Chico and San Diego, with houses and laundries burned, stores looted, and an occasional Chinese killed. The bloodiest pogrom was at Los Angeles, where resistance to a police raid on the Chinese quarter ignited the fuse. "The scum and dregs" of the city to the number of 1,000—incidentally, a sizable hoodlum element for a town of only 6,000 persons—descended furiously on Chinatown, tore it to pieces, and killed at least 22 Chinese. Local editors deplored the violence and the notoriety, for this was the first time that Los Angeles had made the nation's headlines, but no serious attempt was made to bring the mob leaders to justice.

Simple economic causation, as represented by hard times and unemployment, is not a sufficient explanation of this outburst of race hatred. Hate for the Chinese had been built up over the years by charges that they were unsanitary, a disease menace, and addicted to strange vices; that most of their women were prostitutes, that their tong organization was un-American and subversive; that they spoke an outlandish jargon, subsisted on peculiar food, and worshiped pagan gods. As the first skirmishers for an army of 400 million Celestials, they were seen as a towering Yellow Peril. Such was the California hysteria of 1871.

The hysteria was increased, furthermore, by a feeling of frustration as a result of the failure of all previous attempts to regulate immigration. By 1871 the state and its subdivisions had enacted a whole series of regulatory measures, which had succeeded merely in harassing the Chinese without deterring them from coming or staying. In the state courts or the federal courts the more far-reaching of these measures had been declared void, as contraventions of the commerce clause in the national Constitution. In the immediate postwar years three further barriers to state action were erected: first, the Fourteenth Amendment, with its "due process" and "equal protection of the laws" clauses; second the Burlingame Treaty of 1868, with its express guaranty of free migration; and third, the Civil Rights Act of 1870, with its prohibition of discrimination in the courts against any person and of immigration taxes upon any particular group of foreigners. These several actions were decided upon with some knowledge of California problems, but by easterners who naturally did not have such acute awareness of the problem as did west coast residents.

As interpreted by the courts, this trilogy of amendment, treaty, and act seemed to close the door to state regulation. Justice Stephen J. Field of the United States Circuit Court, for example, passing on the state's attempt to require shipmasters and owners to give bond that persons brought into the state would not be likely to become public charges or prostitutes, ruled that the act, for all its ingeniousness, was in conflict with the Fourteenth Amendment, the Burlingame Treaty, and the Civil Rights Act. A similar fate was in store for the Lodging House Law, imposing penalties for the renting of lodgings with less than 500 cubic feet of air space for each occupant, and for the reenacted Queue Ordinance, requiring that every prisoner committed to the county jail have his hair cut to within an inch of his scalp. By this time the legislature was convinced that the only hope lay in national action. Consequently, it financed a lobby at Washington that arranged the appointment of a Joint Congressional Committee of Investigation, which came to San Francisco in October, 1876.

The Kearneyites

In California, meanwhile, the forces opposed to the Chinese, the railroad, the land monopoly, and the corrupt state government achieved a temporary fusion. Earlier organizations such as the Workingmen's Alliance, the Anti-Chinese Association, the Industrial Reformers, the People's Protective Alliance, and the Supreme Order of Caucasians had paved the way, while the Granger movement then sweeping the agrarian Midwest supplied inspiration and example. Newton Booth had won the governorship in 1871 on a platform stressing Chinese exclusion and railroad regulation, but it was not until six years later, when the full effects of the panic of 1873 were belatedly making themselves felt in California, that an effective organization was achieved.

In July, 1877, the discontented laborites of San Francisco displayed a tendency to get out of hand. Their demonstrations against the local Chinese and against the Pacific Mail Steamship Company, the principal carrier of Chinese immigrants, were so alarming that the conservative element made haste to organize a committee of safety. William T. Coleman, of vigilante fame, was placed in charge with a war chest of $100,000 and rifles and ammunition for 1,760 men. He armed more than 1,000 men, most of them with pick handles, and undertook to patrol the city. There were several clashes, some damage to property, and the loss of a few lives, but on the whole the rioting was less bloody than in the similar and practically simultaneous labor riots at Philadelphia.

By the fall of the year the San Francisco labor leaders had developed a policy of political rather than direct action. Their program may be viewed in the platform of the Workingmen's party, organized on October 5. Included were demands for the eight-hour day, direct election of United States Senators, compulsory education, a better monetary system, abolition of contract labor on public works, abolition of the pardoning power of the executive, abolition of fee payments to public officials, state regulation of banks and industry including railroads, and a more equitable taxation system. Prosaic as most of these planks, except perhaps the last, would sound today, the platform was regarded in the seventies as alarmingly radical.

Still more alarming was the way in which the leaders of the Workingmen's party appealed for support and maintained their following. Their method was to gather crowds at the sandlots across from the city hall and, by inflammatory speeches, rouse the passions of their hearers. Most popular among the speakers, and thereby head of the Workingmen's party, was a young Irishman, Denis Kearney. In his youth a seaman and more recently a San Francisco drayman, Kearney had a close intellectual kinship with his audiences. A born orator and a practical one, he delighted the sand-lotters with fiery denunciations of the capitalists and the monopolists and their hirelings, the corrupt politicians. His speeches bristled with such catch phrases as "The Chinese must go" and "Every workingman should get a musket." For the capitalists he recommended "a little judicious hanging," and if San Francisco did not accede to his demands he threatened it with "the fate of Moscow."

Such rabid incendiarism terrified the conservative element, especially when a mob of 2,000 was harangued in the very shadow of Crocker's mansion on exclusive Nob Hill. A few days later Kearney and five of his associates were arrested and sentenced to a fortnight in jail. Emerging from prison as a martyr, Kearney blithely resumed his habits of inflammatory oratory. Nor was he quieted by a state law making it a felony to incite a riot or to advise and encourage criminal violence. He was lionized at a mammoth labor parade on Thanksgiving Day, 1877, and he dominated the first state convention of the Workingmen's party, which assembled at San Francisco the following January. In the literature of the day and in most historical writing, Kearney is depicted as a hotheaded anarchist who played upon the coarsest impulses of the rabble, yet in fairness it should be remembered that for all his vocal advocacy of terrorist measures

Election Day in the Mines

Frank Leslie's Illustrated Newspaper, *December 9, 1876*

he precipitated no riot and produced no violence; his incendiary talk was but a means of promoting political action.

In local elections in the bay region Kearney's Workingmen's party demonstrated such strength that it appeared altogether possible that the party could dominate the state constitutional convention, for which an election had been called for June 19. The campaign was well contested. Democrats and Republicans, alarmed by the patent strength of the Kearneyites, sank their differences in most parts of the state and named nonpartisan candidates. Even so, the Workingmen's party might have seated a majority had it not been that dissension arose among its leaders, some of whom resented Kearney's extreme radicalism and others his personal ambitions. The final count indicated the election of 51 Workingmen, 78 nonpartisans, 11 Republicans, 10 Democrats, and two Independents. The Workingmen thus had a potent minority, especially since a number of delegates not of the party were committed to Granger ideals.

The New Constitution

The convention which assembled at Sacramento in September, 1878, is often compared with its predecessor at Monterey 28 years earlier. With 152 delegates, contrasted to 48, it was obviously much more unwieldy. Its deliberations, or at least its debates, were likewise much longer, and the finished product which it presented to the state was a much more cumbersome, detailed, and complicated document. As to political sagacity it would be rash indeed to argue that the men of '78 were an improvement over the smaller group of '49. It was true, however, that the first constitution-makers had worked under a double disadvantage. In the first place, they had to draft a frame of government for a commonwealth whose future, however golden in prospect, was still inscrutable. In the second place, they had to keep a weather eye on national policies; while they were under some obligation to produce a constitution satisfactory to the Californians, it was imperative that the document be acceptable to the national authorities. The framers of the second constitution were not inhibited by fears of a federal veto; they were free to tackle the state's own problems. Also they had the benefit of three decades of experience under the old constitution. California's problems had become well-defined actualities, and proposed solutions had been amply and repeatedly aired in electoral campaigns. Most noteworthy was the new consciousness of the social responsibilities of government. The convention in '49 had hardly considered social problems. It disposed of the whole matter of taxation, for example, in two sentences reputedly derived from Texas' first constitution. In a generation the pressing issues had come to be almost entirely social: the tax base; the regulation of banks, railroads, and big business; the land monopoly; and the Chinese.

Toward the solution of these problems the convention accomplished astonishingly little. It continued in session for almost half a year. Its 30 standing committees brought in wordy and conflicting reports. With its membership so evenly divided between liberals and conservatives, between Kearneyites and anti-Kearneyites, it was inevitable that the final product should be a "bundle of compromises."

The most prominent innovations included the following: To equalize tax valuations in the several counties and to assess intercounty railroad property a State Board of Equalization was created. To regulate a variety of railroad matters an elected Railroad Commission was provided. Another section increased the accountability of bank directors and stockholders, while still another specified the eight-hour day on public works. After bitter debate, a four-section anti-Chinese article was adopted which authorized the legislature to enact all measures necessary to protect the state from aliens who might prove "dangerous or detrimental," prohibited employment of Chinese by corporations, prohibited such employment on public works, and, in an omnibus section, outlawed Asiatic coolieism as slavery and authorized measures to prevent further immigration and to deal with those already in the state. More stringent restrictions were argued down as certain to be declared in conflict with the national Constitution. Indeed, warnings were voiced that the sections adopted would not be upheld in the federal courts.

With the completion of the convention's labors, the arena of debate was transferred to the state at large. One hundred and twenty delegates approved the constitution but, when it was referred to the electorate, bitter opposition developed. The opposition of the railroad, the banks, and the Sacramento Board of Trade, an antecedent of the Chamber of Commerce, is readily understandable, if for no other reason than the radicalism of the Kearneyites. The Workingmen were equally dissatisfied, because the constitution did not go far enough in extending a protecting arm over labor. Party spokesmen attacked the constitution as vehemently as they had the capitalists, in consequence of which the parts of the state where the Workingmen's party was strongest voted against adoption. But the rural vote, swayed by Granger optimism concerning the Railroad Commission and the Board of Equalization, carried the constitution by a margin of less than 11,000 out of 145,000.

The outcome substantiated the fears of the liberal opposition. There were a few incidental improvements. The legislature was brought under more suitable restraint by a ban on special legislation and on appropriations of state funds to corporations or institutions not directly under state control. The governor's pardoning power was curbed, and the judiciary was remodeled for greater efficiency and expedition. But federal judges promptly invalidated the anti-Chinese sections and the legislation enacted to implement them. The Board of Equalization and the Railroad Commission fell far short of the expectation of the farmers; the latter came to be spoken of popularly as a state-financed publicity bureau for the railroad. To illustrate the abortive nature of the reforms a cartoonist in 1881 depicted a distraught farmer in the coils of a huge snake labeled "The New Constitution." James Bryce in his *American Commonwealth* cited the new California constitution as a "horrible example" of western democracy at work.

Chinese Exclusion

Frustrated though the California reformers had been, the dawn of the new decade brought one rift in the clouds. Effective restriction of Chinese immigration was soon a reality. California's efforts through local ordinance, state law, and constitutional provision had failed because they ran counter to the commerce clause, the Fourteenth Amendment, the Burlingame Treaty, and the Civil Rights Act. Repeated pleas for national action met opposition in the East, because most eastern Americans knew the Chinese only through the more favorable channels of missionary work or lucrative trade. Finally, the barrage of western protests, including a long memorial from the constitutional convention, broke down this eastern apathy. In 1878 Congress enacted the Fifteen Passengers Bill, which, as its name suggests, imposed a quantitative restriction on Chinese immigration. President Hayes vetoed the measure as a violation of the Burlingame Treaty, but in response to popular demand he sent a commission to China to negotiate a new treaty. The Chinese government agreed readily to permit the United States to "regulate, limit, or suspend" the entrance or residence of Chinese laborers, provided, however, that the action should be reasonable rather than absolute. Under the terms of this treaty in December, 1881, Congress voted a 20-year exclusion bill, which President Arthur vetoed as unreasonable. A few months later he approved a 10-year exclusion bill.

Partial success seemed to fan the flames of anti-Chinese feeling in California. The drive was renewed to make the Celestials in the state uncomfortable and thus perhaps to force them out. At San Francisco, for example, there was a regulation concerning laundries which, by discriminatory enforcement, drove some 200 Chinese out of that business. There were also threats to move Chinatown to South San Francisco. On some of these local matters the courts came to the rescue of the persecuted yellow men. The Scott Act of 1888 forbidding reentry of Chinese laborers and the Geary Act of 1892 prohibiting Chinese immigration for another 10 years were protested vigorously by China, but not until 1894 was she placated by the gesture of treaty revision. At long last, by treaty in 1901 and by legislation in 1902 and 1904, exclusion was put on a permanent basis and was made to apply to the insular as well as mainland possessions of the United States.

The other problems of the "discontented seventies" also proved too formidable for immediate and local settlement. The Octopus went on untrammeled, if not even abetted, by the Railroad Commission. The land monopoly had its wings only slightly clipped by the regulatory measures of the new constitution. Farmers discovered that the expected boon of lower taxes, lower rail rates, and lower interest rates had slipped from their grasp; nor was there immediate abatement of the nuisance of hydraulic mining. Most of these problems, the state and the nation were learning, were so large in scope that they could be met only by national regulation. In the eighties and the nineties California followed the nationwide tendency to look to the central government for regulation of big business; and local attention, diverted by the upward trend in economic conditions, was concentrated on the expansion of agriculture, the introduction of new crops and new farming methods, the stimulation of population growth, and the fascinating pastime of speculation in real estate.

Ineffectual and barren of result though it may appear to have been, the political ferment of the seventies is not without historical significance. In the hard times of that decade the common people of California, the urban laborers and the rural small farmers, saw themselves about to be crushed between the upper millstone of big business and the nether millstone of coolie labor. That they struck out somewhat blindly and with passion is not surprising; nor is it surprising that they accepted the leadership of a self-tutored, emotional, and flighty young Irishman. The meagerness of immediate results was not entirely because of the local personnel. By the accident of our federal system, Chinese exclusion, though a matter of purely local importance, was the exclusive prerogative of the national authorities. Control of the Octopus, on the other hand, though constitutionally within the jurisdiction of state government, proved to be so herculean a task as to require national attack. In the last analysis, therefore, these Lochinvars of the West were merely expressing in higher dramatics the common national experience.

For Further Reading

Doris M. Wright, "The Making of Cosmopolitan California," *CHSQ*, 19 (1940), 323–43; 20 (1941), 65–79.

Paul S. Taylor, "Foundations of California Rural Society," *CHSQ*, 24 (1945), 139–61.

Stuart Daggett, *Chapters on the History of the Southern Pacific* (1922).

Wallace Smith, *Prodigal Sons, The Adventures of Christopher Evans and John Sontag* (1951).

C. B. Glasscock, *Bandits and the Southern Pacific* (1929).

Elmer C. Sandmeyer, *The Anti-Chinese Movement in California* (1939).

Paul M. De Falla, "Lantern in the Western Sky" [Los Angeles Chinese Massacre], *SCQ*, 52 (1960), 57–88, 161–85.

William R. Locklear, "The Celestials and the Angels," *SCQ*, 52 (1960), 239–56.

Carl B. Swisher, *Motivation and Political Technique in the California Constitutional Convention, 1878–1879* (1930).

Leonard Pitt, *California Controversies* (1968), 262–64, 324–29.

chapter twenty-one

Health Seekers
and Speculators

No such growth had ever before been seen in any part of the world,
and would have been impossible anywhere except under the climate of
Southern California, which has for years infatuated a certain proportion of
its visitors, and will continue to infatuate them to the end of time.

T. S. Van Dyke,
Millionaires of a Day

The Cow Counties in Transition

1850
to
1900

Throughout the first decades of California's American period, growth
and development were largely confined to the northern part of the
state. That was where the population increase had centered, where
most of the city building, practically all the mining, the most rapid
increase in grain production, the lion's share of industrialization, most
of the banking and merchandizing, the main transportation improvements, the major innovations in politics and government, and the
principal cultural advances had occurred. The southern counties,
meanwhile, were undergoing a much more gradual transformation.
Since the chief business of history is to record and analyze change
in its myriad aspects, it is natural that for these years attention has

Wolfskill's Orange Grove

Thompson and West, History of Los Angeles County

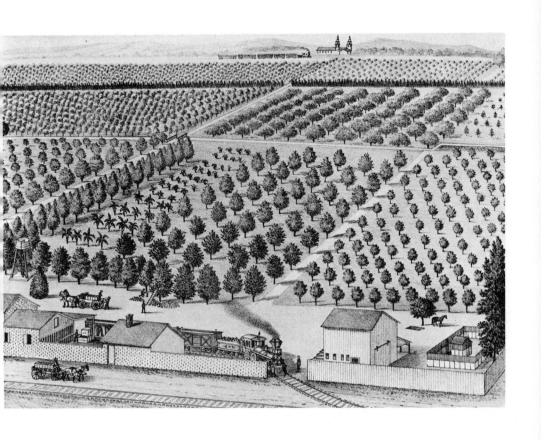

been heavily weighted toward the north rather than toward the relatively "unhistorical" south. In succeeding years, however, the south registered a phenomenal growth and became the cynosure of attention.

This late-century development rested on a real though unspectacular transition in the fifties, sixties, and seventies. While central and northern California mushroomed to half a million inhabitants, the counties south of the Tehachapi had a more modest but substantial increase from some 6,000 citizens in 1850 to about 26,000 in 1860, 39,000 in 1870, and an estimated 60,000 in 1875. Most of the newcomers were from the United States. In numbers they overwhelmed the natives of Spanish and Mexican extraction. The culture of these newcomers was more aggressive and, borne on the tide of mounting numbers, overwhelmed most of the habits of the old regime.

Nevertheless, the adaptation was mutual. Certain older elements persisted or gave way only gradually to the new. Through the fifties adobe continued to be the standard building material, though bricks and boards began to enter competition. By the seventies new construction was almost entirely in the form of frame buildings. To the towns and irrigated fields of the early-American years water was brought, as in the past, by zanja. The cattle business, which boomed and then declined with the droughts of the sixties, carried over the essential methods, many instruments, and an extensive vocabulary from the pastoral era of the Mexican period. The sheep industry, boomed by the Civil War and curtailed by the droughts of the seventies, had a smaller but important Spanish content. The tillage branch of agriculture, especially where it involved vineyards or irrigation, continued patterns that had prevailed at the missions. Into these patterns, however, many American and foreign elements were incorporated. By the seventies, for example, agriculture was turning from Indian labor to Chinese. Furthermore, the broad crop-list tolerance of the environment gave farming an exotic touch and helped it toward a distinction of its own.

In transportation a more pronounced revolution came about. Saddle horses, carretas, and the hide ships had been the carriers in the Mexican period. Of these only the horses persisted and their relative importance went down as other facilities came into use. The transit of American pioneers and gold seekers through the region brought wagons, which soon supplanted the creaking carretas. A more purposeful introduction of freighting equipment followed. At an early date Alexander and Banning were freighting, virtually on a public-carrier basis, between Los Angeles and San Pedro. Wagons did the hauling to the ranchos, army posts, and Indian reservations. In the fifties wagon freighters operated between Los Angeles and Salt Lake City. In the seventies they gave the Cerro Gordo mines of Inyo County their line of shipment and supply.

The stage was a more dashing symbol of the new era. In its idealized form, a Concord coach drawn by six matched and blooded horses, or in its lesser manifestations with mud wagon and a pick-up team, it seemed to be progress on wheels. Here also the earliest line was between Los Angeles and San Pedro. Other lines, some on intermittent schedules, were added before 1858 when the Butterfield line swept through from Tejon Pass to Yuma on its transcontinental way.

The Vintage in California

Harper's Weekly, *August 5, 1878*

The rise of coastal shipping came about even more rapidly and meant considerably more to the region. Sailing ships and then steamers began where the hide ships left off. They quickly established themselves as the fundamental link for passengers and for freight between southern California and the affluence of San Francisco and the mines. Except as the lurching stage entered the picture, coastal shipping continued for a quarter century to be southern California's basic connection with the outer world. The region's economy was oriented coastward, and steamer day was the climax of the week.

Stage and freighting mogul Phineas Banning brought southern California its first railroad. In 1863 he persuaded the legislature to authorize a bond issue by the city and county of Los Angeles for construction of a line connecting the pueblo and its port at San Pedro. The $150,000 bond issue was finally put to a vote in 1868, and late the next year this first railroad in the south began to operate. The next road, incorporated as the Los Angeles and Independence, was projected by a group of local citizens to link Los Angeles with the Cerro Gordo mines near the Nevada border. Taken over by Senator John P. Jones, the company went forward with elaborate plans for building over Cajon Pass and out onto the Mojave desert, but the only rails laid were between Los Angeles and Santa Monica. Late in 1875 Los Angeles thus acquired a second railroad to the sea.

From the fifties on, local editors and politicians had been clamoring for a transcontinental railroad to, or at least through, southern California. When at last the Southern Pacific came down the San Joaquin Valley pointing toward the gateway at Yuma or Needles, a civic crisis arose about how to persuade the Big Four to come through Los Angeles instead of veering off from Tehachapi Pass to Antelope Valley. The price set by the railroad was a depot site, the Los Angeles and San Pedro Railroad, and a donation in the amount of 5 per cent of the assessed valuation of the county, or $602,000. Benjamin F. Peel and former governor John G. Downey headed a vociferous opposition, but Harvey K. S. O'Melveny argued persuasively that the pueblo had to have the railroad. The city council and the board of supervisors agreed to put the issue on the ballot. A torchlight procession and more oratory persuaded the voters, and the agreement was approved by vote of 1,896 to 650. In 1876 when the Tehachapi was surmounted and the San Fernando tunnel holed through, Los Angeles could celebrate that the iron horse had really arrived.

The rise of newspapers, schools, and churches symbolized and assisted the transition from Mexican to American. Meanwhile, along with the north, the southern area had profited by the general untangling of the fetters that had restrained the state as a whole. With the outmoding of vigilante justice, the cessation of filibustering, the elimination of any menace of Indian attack, the fading of Civil War issues, the final adjudication of land titles, the achievement of Chinese exclusion, and the resolvement, at least temporarily, of the reform demands of the Grangers and Workingmen, southern California was ready to face a new day.

The Health Rush

At a very early date, as far back as Cabrillo, in fact, there was recognition of advantages in southern California's climate. At quite an early date the climate was seen as a health asset. One of the Mexican governors moved to the south for his health. The gold rush brought a liberal sprinkling of persons more intent on regaining health than on getting rich. Other health seekers came from time to time, a few by overland stage, more by ship or by covered wagon. As early as the forties, travel by prairie schooner was recommended as a sort of fresh-air cure. In some instances it did cure; in others it proved too heroic a remedy.

For a while, southern California was too remote and too rough a frontier to have much appeal as a health resort. By the seventies, however, it was less beset by wild Indians, bandits, and desperadoes; it was outfitted with some improvements in transportation and accommodations; and it had developed a number of new pursuits in which invalids or their relatives might find opportunity or employment. At the same time the medical profession was entering a phase in which change of climate was a favorite prescription. This combination of circumstances touched off a rush of health seekers which proved to be a chief dynamic for southern California development in the seventies, eighties, and nineties.

Tuberculosis of the lungs, then called consumption, was the malady that did most to promote the health rush. Asthmatics and rheumatics were numerous also, and, indeed, there was hardly an illness known to man from which some sufferer did not seek relief, on doctor's orders or on his own initiative, by moving to this region. At the outset the invalids usually went to the established towns, Los Angeles, San Diego, Santa Barbara, or San Bernardino. They found fewer conveniences than they would have liked and relatively few qualified physicians. In many instances, however, there was a quick recovery and as often a tendency to attribute it to the mild and equable temperature and the abundance of sunshine. To spread these tidings became a duty and a pleasure. The good news encouraged other afflicted ones to migrate to this health-giving land, crowding its housing to a still greater extent.

There were, of course, two obvious ways in which the housing shortage could be remedied: by building more hotels and houses in the old towns or by starting new towns in which such facilities might be made available. Both remedies were resorted to. The old towns were enlarged, particularly Los Angeles, and a dozen or more new towns took shape, including Pasadena, Riverside, Sierra Madre, Altadena, Santa Monica, Palm Springs, Ojai, and Nordhoff, many of them primarily health resorts.

In the course of this expansion a realization grew that, although there were underlying similarities, southern California had not one climate spread over its entire area but many. This gave basis for intercity rivalries in bidding for health seekers. Los Angeles and San Diego, for example, each claimed more equable temperatures and more sunny days. The fact of diversity led also to an assessment of local advantages in a great many places in southern California and to something approaching a medical climatology. Not all the claims made were valid, but some had general medical endorsement at the time, for example, that the seaside towns were advantageous for asthmatics and that the drier interior and foothill locations were to be preferred by consumptives.

The area also abounded in thermal and mineral springs. To capitalize and encourage internal and external use of these waters was the next step. Some developed into spas comparable to the famous watering places of Europe, the California Carlsbad, for example. A feature of this phase of health seeking in southern California was that use did not wait for analysis. Years later, when a state chemist was commissioned to run tests, it was revealed that some of the

Orange County Bean Field

Edward Weston

waters so freely drunk were harmful rather than beneficial. On the other hand, testimonials to the success of the water cure were not lacking.

The migration of thousands and then tens of thousands of invalids to southern California was accompanied by a migration of doctors, some of them health seekers themselves. Through their coming and through the experience gained in local practice with this bonanza of patients, a medical advance took place. It was evidenced in part by the opening of rest homes, convalescent homes, hotel-hospitals, and eventually sanitaria and hospitals specializing in tuberculosis and other maladies. Through much of the period, however, it was a matter of putting up in an ordinary hotel room, finding a room or house in town, or taking a small place in the country, and depending primarily on the health-giving environment for improvement.

Along with the medical advance there was a great deal of quackery and a high susceptibility to cults and fads. There were vegetarians and fruitarians, apostles of fresh air and those who stressed indirect ventilation, advocates of complete relaxation and others who were for hard work. One tubercular attributed his cure to clearing the brush and shouldering the stones from the field where he was setting out his vineyard.

Even with the rapid population growth southern California had a limited amount of so-called light work in which convalescents could engage. They flooded the white-collar fields. A sizable number, the majority townspeople rather than farmers in the East, turned to agriculture. In the fifties, when cattle raising was in the ascendant, they certainly could not have qualified as vaqueros. By the seventies, however, the region's agriculture had evolved to include many branches in which the physical demands were much lighter. Vines could be set out and brought to production without backbreaking labor.

342

Oranges and other fruit trees could be grown with only intermittent attention. There was instances of women successfully embarking on this work. But perhaps the ideal agricultural opportunity that offered itself to the invalids was bee keeping.

A few hives of Italian bees were brought to San Diego in 1857. In the seventies bee keeping spread rapidly, especially to the unoccupied interior of the southern counties. It was an agricultural frontier exceptional in several respects. It moved eastward, and advanced with minimal alteration of the landscape. In addition, its frontiersmen were mostly of urban backgrounds and recruited from the poor in health. By 1884 these apiarists achieved a production of 9 million pounds of honey and then went on to push California to first place among the states in honey production.

Important as they were in agriculture, the health seekers were perhaps even more significant in calling attention to southern California. Before their time, and after, the slogan "California for Wealth" drew people to the Golden State. Recognition of the region's potential as a place of retirement and as a vacation land remained in the future. Pilgrimages to Hollywood in hopes of getting into the movies also lay ahead. These and other practical talking points for boosting the region would prove effective. But they were worldly and even sordid as compared to the news of the healing climate. In time, promoters, realtors, and professional Californians would sound the region's praises; none, however, with so high a sense of calling as was felt by those who could hold out the promise of health.

The response was the first big rush to southern California, the health rush. Gaining momentum in the seventies, it was abetted by railroads and real-estate speculation in the eighties. It continued in the nineties, and still goes on, though much less spectacularly, because at the turn of the century medicine found a new prescription for consumption and substituted institutional care instead of a better climate.

The census reports score the growth of southern California population to 76,000 in 1880, 221,000 in 1890, and 325,000 in 1900 but do not specify why these people came. After making exhaustive study of this great rush, John E. Baur concluded conservatively that at least a quarter of those present in 1900 had come as health seekers or with a relative who was a health seeker.

Advertising Railroad Lands

Rail connection with San Francisco and with the East by way of Sacramento was achieved in 1876. It gave southern Californians an added sense of inclusion in the nation, then celebrating the centennial of its declared independence. With banquet, oratory, editorials, and parade the Angeleños hailed the coming of the railroad as the advent of a new era. To their chagrin they discovered that the immediate consequences of the entrance of the Southern Pacific, even with its additional lines to Needles and through Yuma to El Paso and New Orleans, were much less gratifying than had been expected. The major reason was probably that local economic productivity had not yet reached the point where it could take full advantage of the new facilities for rapid transit. Local citizens, however, were less aware of this condition than of another deterrent to use of the railroad, the rate schedule, which was not only high but also discriminatory in favor of San Francisco. Nevertheless, the coming of the Southern Pacific was worth much. The sharpest contrast between the first and second quarter-centuries of American southern California was that the former was prerailroad and the latter a railroad era.

Although in the first decade after its entrance into the southern part of the state the Southern Pacific was not carrying a great many passengers or a great deal of freight, it was operating through another channel to advance the development of the region. For its construction activities the company had been rewarded with millions of acres of land; the company agent in 1882 set the figure at 10,445,227 acres, most of it in the southern half of the state. The railroad moguls quickly saw that sales, especially to new farmers who would live on the land, would be doubly advantageous, for in addition to the purchase price the Southern Pacific would profit by the operating revenue which the new settlers would create.

Animated thus, the railroad embarked upon real-estate promotion. It set up a land office at Sacramento which professed to have a better listing of available land than any of the government offices. Jerome Madden had charge of this office and of the publicity that issued from it. He arranged for special pictorial editions of various newspapers such as the San Francisco *Spirit of the Times*. He ran advertisements in local newspapers and in eastern newspapers and periodicals. He prepared illustrated pamphlets such as the *Southern Pacific Sketch Book*, of which 10,000 copies were printed in 1887, and these were distributed by ticket agents throughout the country. He was the author of another pamphlet, *The Lands of the Southern Pacific*, directed more especially at prospective settlers. Numerous editions beginning in 1877 were distributed through these same channels. He also enlisted or appropriated the aid of several authors of established reputation and integrated their volumes of travel and description into the campaign to sell the railroad land.

The stamp of railroad subsidy is unmistakable in Charles Nordhoff's *California for Health, Pleasure and Residence: A Book for Travellers and Settlers* (1873) and *A Guide to California the Golden State* (1883), and also in Ben C. Truman's *Homes and Happiness in the Golden State of California* (1883), I. N. Hoag's *California the Cornucopia of the World* (1884), and Madden's own *California: Its Attractions for the Invalid, Tourist, Capitalist, and Homeseeker* (1890). Equally effective, though apparently independent in origin, were such glowing descriptions as *Between the Gates*, by Benjamin F. Taylor (1878); *Old Mexico and Her Lost Provinces*, by W. H. Bishop (1883); *California of the South*, by Lindley and Widney (1888); and *Eine Blume aus dem goldenen Lande oder Los Angeles*, by Ludwig L. Salvator (1878). Since many of these books ran through several printings, the number of readers reached was considerable.

The Modern Ship of the Plains

R. F. Zogbaum, Library of Congress

Another avenue for inexpensive advertising of the railroad lands was through cooperation with certain independent agencies for immigrant promotion such as the California Immigrant Union and the Pacific Coast Land Bureau. These organizations maintained representatives in the East and in Europe. Their publications, such as the Union's *All About California and the Inducements to Settle There* (1870) and the Bureau's *The California Guide Book*, made a particular point of stressing the advisability of buying railroad land in California. In addition, the railroad had its own agents, including I. N. Hoag, who conducted the California Immigration Commission at Chicago, E. Hawley at New York, a Mr. Schriever and a Mr. Meyer at New Orleans, and W. G. Kingsbury at London and on the continent.

California-bound emigrants were afforded several accommodations by the railroad. One was the emigrant car, in which, at no extra charge, sleeping and cooking facilities could be improvised. In Texas the railroad maintained emigrant houses where travelers might put up for a week without charge while seeking work or earning money to enable them to go on to California. The railroad ran an informal employment service; its agents would telegraph ahead to arrange for passengers to meet prospective employers, and for a fee the European agents would locate young men as "farm pupils." Interpreters offered assistance to foreign-speaking immigrants. Fares to the West were made attractively low, and attached to the "landseeker's ticket" was a nontransferable voucher which could be applied at the full cost of the ticket on a purchase of railroad land. The land, furthermore, could be paid for on the installment plan.

Notwithstanding its patent efforts to develop the country, the Southern Pacific was the target of much criticism and abuse. Its refusal of service or connections to towns which would not meet its demands for bonus and right-of-way, its arbitrary selection of certain sections to colonize and develop, while

Los Angeles and Outlying Towns, 1888

Los Angeles Lithograph Company

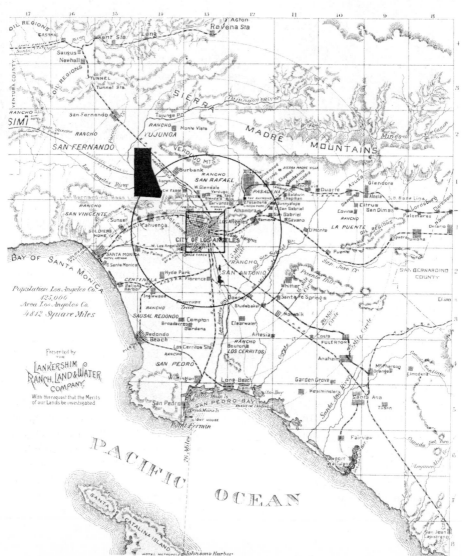

others were held off the market, and its high rates for freight and local fares were the principal causes for dissatisfaction. In the late seventies, as related above, political reform and the creation of a state commission were counted on to regulate the great monopoly. By the mid-eighties hopes were pinned on the appearance of a competing railroad.

The Coming of the Santa Fe

Tom Scott's Texas and Pacific had promised to be the competitor but, thwarted by Huntington's implacable opposition, had fallen by the wayside. Through Kansas a much less pretentious road was inching southwestward. This was the Atchison, Topeka and Santa Fe, chartered by Cyrus K. Holliday in 1859. Construction was not started until 1868, but within four years the rails stretched across Kansas to Dodge City where an entirely unexpected business was encountered, the hauling of Texas cattle to market. This operating revenue was a godsend to the Santa Fe, which, with a land grant of only 3 million acres, had not appeared strong enough to build all the way to Santa Fe, much less to the Pacific. It did dispose of much of its Kansas land to good advantage, utilizing most of the promotional devices which the Southern Pacific was employing in California and also running excursion trains in June when the prairie farms were looking their best.

From its limited scope as a cattle carrier through Kansas the Santa Fe was lifted by William B. Strong, who became general manager in 1877 and president in 1881. The franchise of the Atlantic and Pacific was purchased; tracks reached El Paso in 1881 and Guaymas, on the Gulf of California, in 1882, and another line of greater ultimate significance crossed Arizona toward Needles. Theoretically, the Southern Pacific had closed this gateway by building its Mojave–Needles line, but, since the Santa Fe had reached Guaymas and could threaten competition by steamship to the California ports, Strong could demand concessions.

First came a lease of the line to Mojave. Then by rapid strides the Santa Fe expanded its California facilities. Crossing Cajon Pass, it reached San Bernardino in 1885. It purchased the California Southern and gained an outlet at San Diego. It acquired rights to run over Southern Pacific tracks from Mojave to San Francisco and from Colton to Los Angeles. Finally, in 1887, by building from San Bernardino to Azusa and buying the Los Angeles and San Gabriel, it got its own line into Los Angeles. Thus, some 18 years after the completion of the first transcontinental railroad, the Big Four's monopoly was finally challenged.

To the resulting competition is due a large share of the credit for California's, especially southern California's, subsequent development. More spectacular was the immediate influence in producing the boom of 1887. Other conditions of course were favorable, what with new vistas opening in agriculture, the Southern Pacific's advertising campaign in full swing, and the country in general enjoying greater prosperity. But competitive rail rates touched off the charge. Competition might have been minimized had the Southern Pacific been willing to concede 50 per cent of the southern California business and 27 per cent of the northern. Refused this prorate, the Santa Fe started a rate war that saw passenger fares from Kansas City to Los Angeles brought down to five dollars and for a time even to one dollar, and freight rates reduced, though not in proportion. The natural result was a stimulation of shipments and settlement and, for the first time, a large stream of tourists to southern California. Trains on both roads had to run in sections to accommodate all who wanted to come.

The Boom Begins

The influx of so many visitors, their enthusiasm about southern California as a place in which to live, to farm, and to do business, and the concurrent arrival of new residents led to a sudden awareness of glorious prospects. Astute real-estate promoters, many of them experienced boomers from the Midwest, capitalized on this spirit of optimism. Few of the devices employed were of local invention, but southern California proved a most congenial clime into which to transplant them. Flourishing vigorously, they attained such proportions as to seem unquestionably Californian.

The first step was for an enterprising promoter to acquire title to some tract of land on which his town or suburb could be plotted. It seemed to matter little what sort of land was chosen. The site of Ballona was swamp land; Chicago Park nestled in the rocky wash of the San Gabriel; Carlton perched precariously on a steep hillside east of Anaheim; Border City and Manchester were stranded on the far slope of the Sierra Madre, their only real asset a noble view of the Mojave Desert. Elsewhere the subdivider ruthlessly hacked his way through orange groves.

The devastation thus wrought is often compared to the blight of the *Icerya purchasi*, or cottony cushion scale, which was introduced from Australia almost exactly at the time the boom began. Seemingly immune to all chemical sprays, the scale wrought great havoc. The Wolfskill grove was one of the first devastated, and the entire citrus industry seemed threatened with ruin. To the rescue the Department of Agriculture summoned the Australian ladybug, which quickly exterminated the *Icerya*. No comparable antidote was discovered to stay the hand of the subdivider.

Having plotted his tract, at least on paper, the real-estate promoter embarked upon his sales campaign. Choice of name was important. The Gladstone promoters, for example, circulated the report that the British prime minister was coming to erect a winter home. Lithographers and printers were called upon to produce brochures and pamphlets effulgent with roseate predictions. Slogans such as "Buy Land in Los Angeles and Wear Diamonds" were blazoned across newspaper pages and flaunted on handbills. Another standard device was to start the construction of some conspicuous building, usually a rambling frame hotel or sanatorium. When the boom was over, these monstrosities and the white

A Boom Hotel

The Henry E. Huntington Library and Art Gallery

corner stakes were the only surviving landmarks for several of the towns so boldly conceived.

As contributory causes of the boom these untenanted buildings pale before some of the other antics of the boomers. Sales depended less on the printed word and on buildings in construction than on ballyhoo of a more direct sort. At barbecues and free lunches, with brass bands, processions, and free excursions, through the build-up of individual sales talks and the spellbinding of the auctioneer, they expatiated on the abundant prosperity that southern California was just about to grasp. They specialized in overstatement, quoted one another's exaggerations, admitted that they exaggerated, but insisted that the truth would not fall far short. Through such techniques prices were puffed up and excitement swelled.

The magnitude of the boom is indicated by several sorts of testimony. Real-estate transfers brought to record in the country in 1887 totaled $98,084,162, and, since many sales were on time contracts and since many of the contracts were reconveyed at a substantial advance, it is a conservative estimate that the year's sales surpassed $200 million. There are statistics likewise for the amount of subdividing that went on. Thus from January, 1887, to July, 1889, the records indicate some 60 new towns plotted, with a total acreage of 79,350 acres. Or we may turn to the reminiscences of old-timers who before the boom had known everyone in town and suddenly found Los Angeles filled with strange faces. This was literally true. The census-taker in 1880 had found only 11,183 Angeleños; in the summer of 1887 he would have found six or seven times as many.

Climax and Denouement

It was a boom replete with ridiculous features, many of which were recognized at the time. Editors in northern California held these excited southerners up to no end of ridicule even before the real-estate market broke, and as early as 1890 T. S. Van Dyke lampooned them deliciously in his volume *Millionaires of a Day*. On the other hand, it is worth noting that outside the locality there was much trading in southern California futures. Simon Homberg, for example, the promoter of Border City and Manchester, marketed his lots solely in northern California, Oregon, and the East, and extracted from the gullible a cool $50,000.

Nevertheless, the boomers directed most of their fanfare toward swelling the local excitement. A measure of their success is that the record for real-estate transfers in a single day rose to $664,000, to $730,000, and finally to $930,000. Those who had sold made every effort to buy in again. Men stood in line for hours to get choice lots in new subdivisions and refused as much as $500 for a place in the queue. The querulous few who questioned the soundness of the inflated values were silenced by pronouncements such as that of Philip D. Armour of the great packing company:

> Boom—will it break soon? There is no boom to break! This is merely the preliminary to a boom which will so outclass the present activities that its sound will be as thunder to the cracking of a hickory nut!

This was in July. For a time it appeared that Armour was right. Early in 1888, however, purchasers began to be more wary, prices were reduced and still no takers appeared, and suddenly the whole top-heavy price structure came tumbling down. Expectations were rudely shattered. A host of purchasers on contract had no alternative but to forfeit the down payments they had made. Others who had stretched their credit to buy real estate were cleaned out. Among them were a number of long-time residents who had resisted the early excitement only to succumb in the end and plunge their all on the eve of the collapse. Departing trains now had the heavier business. Several of the communities for which the most roseate predictions had been made became deserted villages. Carlton, Nadeau, and Santiago were left without a single inhabitant; Chicago Park and Sunset had one resident each, the watchmen at the hotels with which the sucker list had been baited.

The setback was serious enough. A number of business houses were forced to the wall, local banks were hard put, and population and volume of business declined sharply. On the other hand, the catastrophe was not absolute. Even after the departure of thousands, 50,395 persons were present in Los Angeles at the time of the census of 1890, and twice that many were in the county. The banks were all able to weather the crisis, and the largest losses were in anticipated profits. As Van Dyke has one of his characters put it: "I had half a million dollars wiped out in the crash, and what's worse, $500 of it was cash."

Indeed, the collapse of speculative real-estate prices had its beneficial effects, for it terminated the complete infatuation of southern California with this artificial source of profits and redirected attention to the neglected opportunities for production of wealth through agriculture and industry.

The postboom years witnessed a back-to-the-farm movement. Groves that had been blighted by *Icerya* or subdividers were restored to productivity, and thousands of acres of new lands were put to the plow and set out in vines or citrus. Not only did production mount, but with freight rates stabilized at a more reasonable level, the actual income for southern California was increased even further. In terms of percentages the nineties appear to have been a slack decade, yet the population increment for Los Angeles County was slightly larger than for the eighties (68,844 as against 68,073), and for Los Angeles City it was considerably larger (51,084 as against 39,212). The other southern counties made a more gradual recovery, but they likewise were soon participating in the general uptrend. It would be too much to say that the lesson had been learned with absolute perfection, yet never again was there so cavalier a disregard for the more fundamental elements of southern California economy.

For Further Reading

JOHN E. BAUR, *Health Seekers of Southern California* (1959).

J. J. WARNER, Benjamin Hayes, and J. P. Widney, *An Historical Sketch of Los Angeles County* (1876).

REMI A. NADEAU, *City-makers, The Men Who Transformed Los Angeles from Village to Metropolis* (1948).

GLENN C. QUIETT, *They Built the West* (1934).

NEILL C. WILSON and FRANK J. TAYLOR, *Southern Pacific, The Roaring Story of a Fighting Railroad* (1952).

L. L. WATERS, *Steel Trails to Santa Fe* (1950).

JAMES MARSHALL, *Santa Fe, The Railroad That Built an Empire* (1949).

CHARLES NORDHOFF, *California for Health, Pleasure, and Residence* (1873).

WALTER LINDLEY and J. P. WIDNEY, *California of the South* (1888).

T. S. VAN DYKE, *Millionaires of a Day* (1890).

GLENN S. DUMKE, *The Boom of the Eighties in Southern California* (1944).

CAUGHEY, *California Heritage*, 304–13, 319–23.

chapter twenty-two

Broadening the Base

The water [from Owens Valley] was released into the San Fernando reservoir
in November 1913, in the presence of some forty thousand spectators,
as the climax of a two-day civic celebration. The one really noteworthy
speech of the occasion was Mulholland's laconic remark as the foaming
water roared down the spillway: "There it is; take it."

Robert Glass Cleland

Selling California Oranges

**1870
to
1914**

California's economy had its first period of ebullient growth in the
gold-rush epoch when development centered on gold and grain, lumber and beef, and was accompanied by a succession of transportation
improvements culminating in the transcontinental railroad. A second
period followed the First World War. Its more conspicuous characteristics were large-scale production of petroleum, the moving-picture
industry, an augmented stream of tourists, and a number of grandiose
engineering achievements. The attendant improvements in communication included the Panama Canal, the automobile, and the network
of highways, airlines, and radio. Between these two peaks intervened
a middle period, overlapping the last years of the nineteenth century

Spillway, Shasta Dam

Bureau of Reclamation

and the first of the twentieth. Relatively quiet, this period was by no means devoid of advancements, and, although the economic elements introduced between 1875 and 1914 were less spectacular than gold and the movies, several were of a very solid nature and long-term value.

One such element was the establishment of citrus raising as an industry. After secularization, the mission citrus trees were neglected. In the fifties orange, lime, and lemon plantings were regenerated by seeds and seedlings from Hawaii and Central America, but the results were only mildly encouraging. By 1860 the state had only 4,000 bearing orange trees and 600 bearing lemon trees. Practically all were in southern California, and by all odds the largest concentration was in William Wolfskill's Los Angeles grove. A decade later the bearing citrus trees numbered 45,000, including some extensive plantings as far north as Porterville and Oroville. The volume of production, however, was still small. In 1868 Los Angeles sent only 2,200 boxes of oranges to San Francisco, and there they had to compete with fruit from Hawaii and Sicily.

In the seventies and eighties orange growing forged to the front. Two innovations share the credit. The first of these was the discovery of the agricultural possibilities of the uplands, such as those at Riverside, which opened new vistas. The Riverside tract had been poor grazing land; according to the current phrase, even the coyotes carried canteens. Louis Prévost's Silk Center had failed there, but, when the colony led by J. W. North watered the land with a $50,000 canal and set out orange trees, several natural advantages came to light. The higher land proved less subject to frost than the lowlands, and there was no danger of tree roots reaching the water table and drowning.

A more dramatic innovation was the introduction of the Washington navel orange. The Department of Agriculture at Washington, having received from a Presbyterian missionary at Bahia, in Brazil, a dozen budded trees of a seedless variety, sent two of the dozen to Mr. and Mrs. L. C. Tibbetts of Riverside. In the new environment these trees lived up to their Brazilian reputation, producing large, seedless oranges of excellent color and fine flavor. Budwood from these pioneer trees was transferred to thousands of specimens of the older stock. So great was the demand that the Tibbetts had to enclose the trees with an extra-high barbed-wire fence to discourage thievery. One of the parent trees still flourishes at Riverside, and the myriad progeny of these trees, filling grove after grove, has been fundamental to the success of the California citrus industry.

In 1884 these oranges took practically every prize at the New Orleans exposition. Two years later shipments amounted to 2,250 carloads, and orange growing was southern California's most popular enterprise. In 1888 a blight on the grapevines led the Anaheim colonists to abandon viticulture in favor of oranges and English walnuts. In other localities vineyards gave way to tree planting. For the most part, however, the orange groves sprang up on lands hitherto unimproved, largely the highlands that had not been considered eligible for irrigation. Not all the skills of orange culture were acquired immediately, but the orange growers succeeded in getting good crops of good fruit.

Marketing was a harder nut to crack. By the close of the century there were not quite a million and a half potential orange consumers in California. If the industry was to flourish on a scale commensurate with the groves already set out, a much larger market outside the state had to be built up. The coming of the railroad and the invention of the refrigerator car opened the door for distant marketing. At the most, these were enabling acts and not the full explanation of the industry's rise.

Early experience with shipments to the eastern states was discouraging. Freight charges, though moderated in the course of the rate war, were high. Delivery was not as rapid as it should have been for a somewhat perishable product. And worst of all, the growers were at the mercy of eastern commission houses and middlemen to whom the California fruit was merely an incidental matter. They did little to push its sale, and the remittances they sent were often disappointingly small. There was need for more effective management of the distribution of orange shipments, for expediting delivery, and stimulating demand. Eastern middlemen were not responsible for the fact that the orange was regarded as a luxury goods, as an ornament for the Thanksgiving Day table or the Christmas stocking, yet it was clear that they could not be counted on to elevate it from an exotic curiosity to a staple.

Orange Grove and Snow-covered Mountain

Title Insurance and Trust Company, Los Angeles

As the solution of these two problems of inefficient distribution and inadequate demand, the orange growers resorted to a cooperative association, the California Fruit Growers' Exchange. This association brought about some improvements in production, for example, in pest control and frost prevention and in the substitution of clipper picking for hand pulling. It also standardized packing on a much higher level of efficiency and attractiveness. Early shipments had been too nearly orchard-run. The Exchange installed machinery for cleaning and grading the fruit and introduced techniques of wrapping, labeling, and packing. Grocers could order California oranges with more precision as to size and quality than was true of most of the goods they handled in this prepackaged era.

All these improvements influenced marketing, but the real work of the Exchange was to tackle the latter problem directly. The essential method was a simple one. Agents, stationed at the larger population centers in the East, kept close tab on the ratio of supply and demand in each locality. It was then a simple matter to reroute cars from an overstocked center to another that was running low. Thus the price structure was protected against breaks through the glutting of a particular market, and at the same time prospective purchasers seldom had to be turned away because a local supply had been exhausted.

The Exchange also set about systematically to whet the national appetite for California oranges. The devices it employed were many. Special fruit trains were festooned with banners and became, in effect, moving billboards. The common billboard was also pressed into service, and newspaper advertisements throughout the land sang the praises of the California orange. "Oranges for Health—California for Wealth." A test campaign in Iowa in 1905 led to marked increase in sales and encouraged the Exchange to blanket the nation with the same sort of propaganda. The word "Sunkist" was entered in the national vocabulary. To stimulate consumption and to prevent the substitution of non-California and ipso facto inferior fruit, a silver orange spoon was offered for a dozen Sunkist wrappers and a dozen pennies. The Exchange followed up this offer with other gadgets, notably the electric juice extractor, which by all that is reasonable would seem to have been a far more effective consumption stimulator than its antecedent.

At the head of the Exchange during its formative years was Francis Q. Storey, to whom is due much of the credit for the phenomenal rise of the association and the industry. In recent years the association has modernized its sales campaign. It has not neglected the golden opportunity afforded by the discovery of the vitamins and by the dictum of the pediatricians that every infant and youngster should have his daily ration of orange juice. Here was a greater godsend than a smudgeless orchard heater, another marketable by-product, or a new formula for profitable disposal of culls. The Exchange embraced the opportunity with appropriate zest, though at the same time it took whatever steps were necessary to consolidate its advantages. For example, when the sawmills which had been furnishing the boxes suddenly doubled their price, the Exchange bought itself a sawmill and a stand of timber and demonstrated its readiness to make its own boxes. In other directions the association expanded, yet fundamentally it adhered to its original principles.

One of the largest concerns in the state and a leading contributor to the material prosperity of southern California, the Exchange became a phenomenon of more than local interest. It ranks with the world's most successful cooperatives and has often elicited that sincerest flattery, imitation. In California walnut growers and avocado growers took the same course. In New Zealand and Australia the citrus industry followed the blueprint. In these instances success was considerable, but not always are the results so happy. The method seems to have its best application in an association that can control the major fraction of production of some commodity for which the national market can be expanded. Some products, such as cotton, wheat, corn, hogs, and eggs, are raised by so many farmers that a cooperative to handle marketing would be extremely unwieldy. For other items, such as dates, domestic production is so small in comparison to imports that a cooperative association has uphill sledding. The California Fruit Growers' Exchange, in 1952 rechristened the Sunkist Fruit Growers' Exchange, remains a model cooperative and one that probably will not soon be surpassed.

George Chaffey, Irrigator

There is more to the record of agricultural expansion during this middle period. These were the years of peak production of wheat and barley, a holdover from the older economy. They witnessed also an expansion of grape and prune production, of dairying, and of wine making that would be interesting to explore, though less arresting than the record of orange growing and marketing. In the realm of agriculture, however, the second great advance was in irrigation. This was nothing new, for irrigation was an old California trait, one of the first that the Spaniards implanted in the province. It had declined with secularization but did not disappear, even though it had no part in the cattle raising of the pastoral days and little significance on the wheat and barley ranches of the early American period. Then, as California agriculture was broadened and particularly as the railroad era brought settlers into the San Joaquin Valley, irrigation increased. Some of the valley projects were cooperative ventures, laid out without much benefit of engineering and built by hand or by ordinary farm tools. Elsewhere in the valley the railroad controlled irrigation development, or some large company, such as Miller and Lux, took up the water rights and monopolized irrigation. Disputes over water rights were responsible for much of the resentment against the railroad in the valley. Yet here, as south of the Tehachapi, irrigation was required for all but a few crops.

By the eighties and nineties California irrigation was experiencing both expansion and refinement. Many individuals contributed, but the new developments are well typified and summarized in the work of an engineer from Canada, George Chaffey. When he arrived in southern California in 1880, the transforming power of irrigation was most strikingly apparent at Riverside, where the poorest grazing land of Rancho Jurupa had been made a show place of citrus culture. Brief residence at Riverside convinced Chaffey of the practicability of further development through irrigation. Late in 1881 he persuaded his brother to join with him in acquiring a tract of land, bringing water to it, and selling it as small farms and home sites.

On Thanksgiving Day of that year the brothers contracted for 1,000 acres of García's Rancho Cucamonga with an accompanying water right in the adjacent mountains. Subsequently they added another 1,500 acres. After a famous Indian chief of Michigan and Ontario the colony was named Etiwanda. Construction of concrete pipe lines to deliver water to the upper corner of each 10-acre tract began at once, and before the end of 1882 some 1,400 acres had been sold. The features of particular significance were: use of concrete pipes which insured against water loss, generation of electric power in conjunction with the delivery of the water, adequacy of private capital for financing the development, and, most important, addition of perpetual water rights to ownership of each acre of land by means of a mutual water company. The problem of water law had been one of the thorniest faced by western jurisprudence. Chaffey's device of a mutual water company owning the water supply and the distributing system and in turn owned by the landholders in the district, one share for each acre of land, proved a simple, sensible, and practical solution of a problem that had seemed insoluble.

From Etiwanda the Chaffeys went on to a larger project on the gently sloping plain at the mouth of San Antonio Canyon. The site for this colony, to be named Ontario, was acquired from Rancho Cucamonga, the Kincaid ranch, the holdings of Henry Hancock, and by purchase of railroad and government lands. To the skeptical it seemed that San Antonio Canyon could not furnish enough water to supply so large a tract, especially since the town of Pomona was able to make good its claim to half the surface flow in the canyon. Chaffey, however, acting upon the Spanish adage that "the rivers of California run bottom upward," drove a tunnel into the canyon bed. Penetrating some 2,850 feet, he struck a strong subterranean flow, which was conducted through a cement-lined ditch to a junction with the diverted surface flow. As an ocular demonstration of the abundance of water he built a fountain near the Southern Pacific depot, which was turned on to spout water high in the air whenever a train came through.

Ontario and Pomona engaged in more or less good-natured rivalry throughout these early years. Ontarians delighted in the anecdote, good enough to be apocryphal, that a circus owner had refused to take his circus to Pomona because there was not enough water there to give his elephant a drink. Chaffey was responsible for a comparable quip on Ontario. Asked by the Baptists for a church site, he replied that he had it on good Pomona Baptist authority that there was not sufficient water in Ontario to meet the requirements of Baptist ritual. This byplay, however, should not obscure the fact that both communities flourished. Ontario had a special honor conferred on it when it was chosen in

1903 as the model irrigation colony and was played up as such at the St. Louis World's Fair in 1904. The tribute was not only to the efficient use of water in crop production but also to the high achievement in town planning, educational provisions, home beautification, and social benefits, much of which Chaffey had planned.

In 1886, largely because of his success at Ontario, Chaffey was invited to undertake an even larger project in Australia. Mildura and Renmark were the results, both capably engineered but unprofitable because of political jealousies, inadequate transportation, and insufficient markets. When Chaffey returned to California in 1898, penniless and expecting to find himself discredited, he found on the contrary that Ontario very much wanted his services. Prolonged drought had reduced the water supply alarmingly. Put under contract of $500 a month to develop additional water, Chaffey resorted to portable pumps and artesian wells with tunneled outlets, thereby saving the colony from disaster. By bringing in artesian wells on an adjacent tract he was able also to recoup his personal fortune.

At this point Chaffey was drawn into a scheme to bring Colorado River water to the Colorado Desert, a proposal advanced intermittently since as early as 1853. The river had water in abundance. Aridity, it was widely believed, was a guaranty of fertility, but the general belief had been that a white population could not endure the heat of the Colorado Desert. Chaffey's Australian experience convinced him to the contrary and, when C. R. Rockwood's California Development Company approached him as the leading irrigation engineer of the Southwest and invited him to cut the Gordian knot of its difficulties, he responded with alacrity. A six-week reconnaissance of the region led to discovery of a canal route that could be developed for an estimated $100,000, a mere pittance compared to the vast acreage that could thus be brought under cultivation. Chaffey hastily contracted to do the work and then discovered that the company did not have either the promised option on the diversion point at Hanlon Heading or the represented right-of-way through Mexico, that it was bankrupt and in jeopardy of losing its charter, and that it was obligated to accept some $350,000 worth of land scrip at par, which was about 10 times the market value. His friends advised a break with this jumbled company, but he was determined to do the job. Within 12 months water was being delivered to Imperial Valley, its name another reminder of Chaffey's Canadian and Australian background. In modified form his mutual water company device was also employed. By 1905 valley population had mounted to 14,000, and 120,000 acres were under cultivation. That same year, because of further difficulties with the California Development Company, Chaffey sold out his interests in the valley for $100,000 and retired as engineer of the water company.

The immediate sequel was a blunder by his successors. Troubled by silt at Hanlon Heading, these engineers opened a new and dangerous intake, and at the next high water the river broke through and began to pour all its water into the valley. Salton Sink changed into the Salton Sea, the railroad was forced to move its tracks, and Imperial Valley was threatened with complete inunda-

Lettuce and Dates, Imperial Valley

William Graham

tion. The California Development Company's resources were entirely inadequate for damming a river 2,500 feet wide and 30 feet deep. In June, 1905, it transferred its assets and the responsibility of stopping the flood to E. H. Harriman's Southern Pacific. The railroad engineers made two abortive attempts later in the summer and early in 1906 constructed a quarter-million-dollar dam, later washed out by the first summer flood. Appeals to President Theodore Roosevelt were fruitless because the break was below the line in Mexico; therefore, in the winter of 1906–07 the railroad tried again. A heroic 52-day drive, involving 6,000 carloads of rock and gravel and 1,200 piles and costing $1.6 million, finally closed the break and saved Imperial Valley. Yet the precarious position of the valley a few hundred feet below the level of the river denied the valley residents complete ease of mind until 30 years later when Boulder Dam brought the river under final control.

Meanwhile, Chaffey had developed artesian water for another flourishing colony at Whittier and had laid plans for extending irrigation in Owens Valley in conjunction with hydroelectric development and an electric railway to Los Angeles. In this last project he was foiled by Los Angeles' own water and power designs, and his principal monuments remain Etiwanda, Whittier, Ontario, Imperial Valley, and, less ponderable but equally significant, the methods which he devised for California's material and social advancement.

Taming the Sacramento

California had another river, wetter than the Colorado, which posed perennial flood hazard. In its lower course the Sacramento ran through a wide alluvial plain of deep, rich soil. The river greeted the forty-niners with floods that drove them to the roofs. The hydraulic miners aggravated the problem by sending down huge quantities of debris that buried good farmland and raised the bed of the river many feet.

As early as 1868 farmers along the west bank of the Feather built a 17-mile levee to protect their lands. Their neighbors to the east objected that the effect would be merely to shunt floodwaters onto their lands. The levee had that effect but it did not hold against recurrent floods. Piecemeal attempts to restrain the river by privately built levees were supplemented by a state program under the Drainage Act of 1880, which, however, was declared unconstitutional in 1881. Valley residents showed much more enthusiasm for a ban on hydraulic mining and were rewarded in 1884 with an injunction.

In 1893 the Caminetti Act opened a new era. It authorized a revival of hydraulic mining provided debris was controlled. More important, it set up a state agency, the California Debris Commission, in essence an authority for flood control. Under the commission's auspices Marsden Manson and C. E. Grunsky brought in an engineering report based on providing bypasses or standby auxiliary riverbeds. The mechanics proposed was to make the Sacramento and its tributaries run full for maximum scour but to use the bypasses to carry off quickly any excess floodwaters.

Levee construction proceeded but without shutting off the bypasses and with some leveeing of these auxiliary channels. The state and the federal government invested in dredging, jettying, and removing snags to give better depth and tidal scour at the mouth of the Sacramento. Much of the responsibility was still left to private leveeing, and every few years a flood demonstrated the inadequacy of these efforts.

A climax came with the mammoth flood of 1907. Up to that time it had been calculated that the Sacramento might rise from its normal flow of 6,000 to as much as 300,000 second-feet. In 1907 the engineers were astonished to learn through strategically placed gauges that the flood rate was 600,000 second-feet, in other words, equal to a hundred Sacramento Rivers at normal flow.

The California Debris Commission now was convinced that, instead of concentrating on penning in the great mass of debris along the lower Yuba, it must tackle the problem of the entire flood plain. A report was assembled. Late in 1911 Governor Hiram Johnson called a special session of the legislature, which approved the Sacramento Flood Control Plan, calling for joint efforts by the state, the federal government, and private enterprise. Work began immediately, although it was not until 1917 that Congress provided funds for flood control on the Mississippi and the Sacramento. In 1928 the federal government accepted broader responsibility for flood control.

After 1911 California efforts were accelerated. In 1910 protected productive acreage in the Sacramento Valley comprised 300,000 acres. By 1913 it had risen to 400,000 and by 1918 to 700,000 acres. Levees averaged 15 feet in height, though some were higher, and as much as 30 feet wide at the top. The farming behind these levees was phenomenally productive, much of it high-value crops, fruits, vegetables, and rice. In 1911 only 160 acres were in rice; by

1915 the valley produced 720,000 sacks worth $1.5 million and in 1916, 2.5 million sacks worth $5 million. As Robert Kelley observes, "The sea of flood-waters was replaced by a sea of waving grain."

Irrigation, often by siphoning water over the levee, was easy. Transportation to market, by short haul to river landings and by barge to San Francisco or to ship, was convenient and cheap. The intensified farming that developed broke up some extremely large landholdings and increased the number of farms. Cooperative action, state and federal aid, and decision making by government agency were fundamental to success in reclaiming the lower Sacramento and Delta area, as had been true also in Imperial Valley. The Sacramento and Delta area went on in subsequent decades to become a major fruit and bread basket in California's thriving agriculture.

Borax and Petroleum

Broadening agriculture was the keynote of the state's economic advance in this period, but substantial expansion also occurred in industry. Meat packing, the canning and preserving of fruits and vegetables, and cement manufacture were prominent on the list, together with some holdovers from the earlier economy, such as flour milling, lumbering, and foundry work. Two new industries will serve as illustrations, borax and petroleum.

Although known to the ancients—Roman arenas were sometimes cleansed with it after gladiatorial combats—borax was not discovered in the New World until 1856. The first deposits were disappointingly small, but by 1880 Nevada prospectors were agog with hopes of finding a dry lake with a thick crust of the valuable chemical. In that year Aaron and Rosie Winters, marginal ranchers at Ash Meadows to the east of Death Valley, heard about the excitement in Nevada and picked up information as to the appearance and the simple flame test for the mineral. Applying the test on the salt marsh near Furnace Creek in Death Valley, they were rewarded with a green flame, indicative of the genuineness of the deposit. For $20,000 Winters sold out to William T. Coleman, former leader of the Second Vigilance Committee and the Pick-handle Brigade, and F. M. (Borax) Smith of Nevada. These two men organized the Harmony Borax Company, later changed to the Pacific Coast Borax Company, in popular terminology, the Twenty Mule Team Company.

The difficulties confronted in the production of borax were severe and unusual. The deposit was located in a spot as forbidding as its name and generally believed to be uninhabitable for half the year. At best, work could proceed from October through May. The borax had to be extracted on the spot by boiling and crystallizing, and Death Valley had precious little fuel for such purposes. Greasewood, desert pine, and cedar were used; also loads of "desert hay," or sagebrush. A road had to be opened to the rails at Mojave, 165 miles distant. Most of the road was the tortuous, unimproved type customary in the mountain and desert West, but for an eight-mile stretch across the salt-encrusted floor of the valley it was an improved road—improved by sledge hammer. The salt crust here was a tangle of peaks, ridges, and irregularities entirely impassable except in the six-foot swath beaten down by sledge hammer.

For this hauling great wagons were built at Mojave, with 5-foot and 7-foot wheels, 10-ton capacity, and fixed axles, so that turning was always by skidding. Two such wagons and a water-tank trailer made a train, pulled by two wheel horses and 18 mules and conducted on a 20-day schedule over the round trip by a driver and a swamper. The driver presided over whip and "jerk line," the single rein that stretched to the lead team. The swamper manned the brake on the second wagon, helped with the hitching and unhitching, the feeding, and the watering, and usually acted as cook. At this distance it all sounds very picturesque, but to the swampers and mule skinners of the eighties it was hard and monotonous work, and not enhanced by the imminence of disaster if wagons broke down or teams gave out, or if water tanks or supply stations were looted.

In the late eighties this spectacular phase of the borax industry was terminated by the discovery of colemanite, a lime and borax compound, first in the Calico Mountains near Daggett and shortly thereafter in the Funeral Mountains near Ryan. Railroad tracks penetrated to these mines, refining operations were transferred to San Francisco, and the 20-mule team rolled into the limbo of tradition, leaving its reflection on the company's trademark and reechoing a half century later in a radio serial.

The petroleum industry may be introduced by a paraphrase of the preceding comments on borax. Although known to the California ancients, who used it both medicinally and to caulk their cooking baskets, and used by the Spaniards in roofing, petroleum was of no significance until the American period. In the fifties there were a few attempts to distill lamp oil from the seepages in Pico Canyon, La Brea, and Carpintería. It remained, however, for the Drake well in Pennsylvania in 1859 to show the way in well drilling. Under the stimulus of this example and encouraged by the numerous surface indications in California, wildcatting became a popular pastime in the sixties. Colonel R. S. Baker sank some $65,000 on a tract not far from the present intersection of Wilshire and Hoover in Los Angeles. Colonel Phineas T. Banning, B. D. Wilson, and others formed the Los Angeles Pioneer Oil Company and sank holes 75, 100, and even 200 feet deep at Wilmington, but their reward was more often water than oil. In Humboldt County a new town was optimistically named Petrolia. Santa Rosa, Santa Clara County, and the ocean front between Santa Barbara and Ventura had their wells, but the best early results were attained at Sulphur Mountain, back of Ventura, and by tunneling rather than by well drilling.

In the sixties, of course, the big oil industry in California was whaling. Shore stations operated at Monterey, Palos Verdes, and all along the coast from San Diego to Trinidad. In addition, large fleets were dispatched from San Francisco each summer to Arctic waters. The magnitude of this industry is indicated by some of the losses sustained. In 1871 an entire fleet of 33 vessels, carrying oil, bone, and ivory valued at $1.6 million, was lost in the ice field. In

1876, 12 vessels with cargo worth $2.5 million were lost, and in 1890 six vessels out of a fleet of 52 were lost. In view of the dimensions of this industry, both in shore stations and in the Arctic fleets from San Francisco, additional meaning attaches to the bold prediction of geologist Benjamin Silliman in 1865 that California would be found to have more oil in its soil than in all the whales in the Pacific Ocean. He ventured to suggest that this oil would eventually "lubricate the wheels of commerce and set a trade at work excelling in variety any that has thus far been known on this coast," a brash prediction, concerning which said the San Francisco *Bulletin* on January 8, 1866, "We admit to being a little skeptical."

Almost a decade later J. DeBarth Shorb, a southern Californian who had dabbled in oil, concluded a 10-page review of the southern fields with this pronouncement:

> As a question of financial importance to the state at large, the petroleum interests of this State can never amount to anything. To obtain oil at all a large sum has to be expended; and when obtained nothing can be done with it that will give profit to the manufacturer.

His correspondent, the state geologist, incorporated this opinion in his article on California for the *Encyclopaedia Britannica*. Indeed, such pessimism seemed to be justified. The wells thus far, if not dug by pick and shovel, were drilled by spring pole. Transportation was in barrels on wagon, freight car, or ship. Tank cars and tankers were yet to come, and the first pipeline, a two-inch pipe from the Pico Canyon wells to the Newhall refinery, was not built until the next decade. Still farther off was the four-inch line from Pico Canyon to the sea at Ventura, completed in 1885. Nor was an adequate market immediately at hand. Kerosene had to compete with whale oil as well as candles, and, because the California oil had an asphaltum rather than a paraffin base, the derivation of lubricants was difficult. Consequently, the growth of the industry had to await the introduction of new uses and a broadening of demand as well as an increase in production.

The eighties saw new wells brought in and the opening of major fields in the Puente Hills, at Whittier, and at Summerland. Production reached a peak of 690,000 barrels in 1888. At Los Angeles what was known as the Los Angeles–Salt Lake field was opened in 1893, this being the time and place of E. L. Doheny's entrance into the oil business. Although Doheny was to become Los Angeles' best-known oil man, his start was unpretentious enough. With pick and shovel and a hand windlass he and his partner, C. A. Canfield, brought in a shallow well in the West Second Street district. The more important fields dating from the nineties were north of the Tehachapi at Coalinga, McKittrick, Midway-Sunset, and Kern River. In the main they were responsible for the production increase to 4 million barrels in 1900.

Small companies had predominated in the earlier oil production, but now larger companies began their domination of the field. The Harbison and

Doheny Discovery Well, Los Angeles

C. C. Pierce Collection

Stewart Company became the Union Oil Company, the local Pacific Coast Oil Company was acquired by the Standard of New Jersey, and the Puente Oil Company enlarged into the California Petroleum Company, later to become a subsidiary of the Texas Company. Partly through these connections with the oil industry elsewhere California came to share in the technological advances in methods of locating fields, drilling, and refining. The relationship was by no means one-sided, for many engineering improvements originated in California and were copied wherever oil was produced.

Even more noteworthy were the new uses discovered for California oil. An early use was to mix the nonvolatile residue with sand to make asphalt blocks for street paving, foreshadowing large-scale use in highway construction. A far more important step is credited to E. L. Doheny. In the declining years of the century he persuaded the Santa Fe Railroad to experiment with crude oil as fuel for its locomotives. The experiment was a complete success, providing a cheaper, hotter, cleaner, and more convenient fuel, and oil-burning locomotives soon became standard equipment throughout the Southwest, to the great relief of the passengers and the fireman's shovel. Success with oil-burning locomotives led to many other opportunities for fuel oil. In southern California, at

365

least, it was the first source of industrial power made available in adequate quantity and at reasonable cost.

From 1900 to 1914 oil output mounted steadily and rapidly from 4 million to 104 million barrels, and not so much through new fields as by drilling more and deeper wells in the old fields. Oil consumption likewise was principally according to the developed pattern, the demand being for fuel oil, oil to be used in paving, illuminating oil, and lubricants. A new consumer, the internal-combustion engine, destined to be the most voracious of all, was beginning to make its appearance. In these early years, however, the automobile was a luxury and not altogether reliable, the airplane was a curiosity, and the tractor, an experiment. Horse and mule power were not yet bested on street, road, or furrow, though the handwriting was on the wall with a promise for oil producers of a much greater demand to come.

In the long run the oil industry out of local production and imports would be blamed for the most irritating components of California smog. From the 1880's through the 1930's there were complaints that the oil fields were unsightly, the tank farms a blot on the landscape, and every refinery detectable downwind for miles. These, however, were limited impacts on the environment and a tolerable price for the convenience offered by the new fuel.

No glance at the formative years of California's oil industry would be complete without some mention of speculation. Even today the increased expertness of oil geologists has not taken the gamble out of well drilling, and the stabilized market has not eliminated the hope of sudden wealth through a share in a new gusher. In this period chance was a more potent factor and investing in oil stocks a more reckless gesture. From the angle of promotion and stock trading, however, the California branch of the industry was part and parcel of the national phenomenon and little worse or better than other parts of the whole.

Here it is more to the point to notice the local effects of the industry: the development for the state of a new money crop worth annually an increasing number of millions of dollars; the growth of the industry with its steadily mounting payroll and capital investment in wells, refineries, tank farms, and pipelines; and the provision for the first time of adequate power for the machinery of transportation and industry.

The Railroad Age

As to transportation the turn-of-the-century generation was predominantly the railroad age. By 1880 trackage in the state amounted to 2,195 miles. In the next decade, through the Santa Fe and Southern Pacific construction already described, it mounted to 4,356 miles. Thereafter the rate of increase tapered off and popular fancy was less captivated by the achievements of railroad builders; for another quarter century, however, activity continued. In 1901 the Southern Pacific completed its Coast Line between San Francisco and Los

Angeles. Four years later Senator William A. Clark brought southern California into closer connection with the Rocky Mountain states with his San Pedro, Los Angeles and Salt Lake Railroad, which in 1921 became a part of the Union Pacific system. In 1910 the Western Pacific entered northern California by way of Feather River Canyon. These lines, together with a number of lesser projects, brought the total trackage at the outbreak of the First World War to approximately 8,000 miles, at which figure it has remained almost constant ever since. This generation not only built California's railroads but used them to the practical exclusion of other avenues of transportation, such as waterways, highways, and air lanes. This generation also took pleasure in the railroad, especially after the conversion to oil-burning locomotives. In many a scene the passing train was an attractive accent, its whistle a welcome sound, and its pulsating machinery a delight. As compared to the dusty wagon roads of earlier day and to the wide bands of pavement that the truck and automobile would require, the railroad was gentle. Its rails lay innocently on the roadbed, and native vegetation persisted along the right of way when virtually eliminated elsewhere. Furthermore, transportation by rail, channeled travelers across the deserts and through the Sierra without giving them much chance to harm these delicate balances of land and biota.

Municipal Problems

Amplification of economic pursuits had as its corollary an increase in California population, in round numbers from 700,000 in 1875 to 3 million in 1914, which in turn created certain municipal problems. San Diego faced several such problems, especially after the crash of the real-estate boom in 1887. It came to have several prominent residents of wealth, energy, and vision, such as Edward W. Scripps, but the city's regeneration was largely the work of John D. Spreckels. Spreckels kept the Santa Fe's San Diego branch operating. He took over Coronado and built it up as a tourist attraction. Organizing the Southern California Mountain Water Company, he assured the city an adequate water supply. Several business blocks, the public library at Coronado, the city traction system, and the railroad to Yuma were among his contributions, and the Panama–California Exposition of 1915 was made possible chiefly through his generosity. Other cities which had no such godfather wrestled in these years with comparable problems and worked out acceptable solutions.

At the turn of the century through the practical genius of Henry E. Huntington the Los Angeles metropolitan area acquired a most excellent system of interurban and street railways, the Pacific Electric. It grew by absorption of older electric lines and by new construction, some of which was mainly for opening new real-estate subdivisions Huntington wanted to promote. Despite these ulterior purposes, the network of lines interlocked in such a way as to make the whole area readily accessible. At the peak some 600 cars were in operation on more than a thousand miles of track reaching out as far as Riverside, Santa Monica, San Fernando, and Balboa. Schedules were fast and frequent and fares averaged less than three fourths of a cent a mile.

Besides the routine work of hauling passengers and freight throughout its empire, the Pacific Electric was a great recreational asset. It ran chartered excursions for Sunday School picnics and the like and featured day-long tours to the beaches, to Mission San Gabriel and the ostrich farm, to Long Beach, Balboa, and Santa Ana, and to the orange empire east of the city. Together with the inclined railway and trolley line up Mt. Lowe and the excursion steamer to Catalina, these tours for years channeled the tourist view of southern California and the inspection by most residents as well. Unfortunately for the popular repute of the Pacific Electric its lines and equipment were continued without perceptible modification into the thirties, by which time the local transportation load was vastly greater, not to mention the snarls of automobile traffic. Eventually this system gave way to buses, which have never remotely approached the satisfaction given an earlier generation by the big red cars.

In the nineties the attraction of tourists and the promotion of trade were taken in hand by a Chamber of Commerce reorganized as an aftermath of the bursting of the boom, and its functioning has been a prominent feature ever since. In the nineties the city waged war with the Southern Pacific over the issue of a free harbor; between 1905 and 1913 it achieved its first "final" solution of the problem of water supply.

A dry winter in 1904 put the city fathers into a receptive mood to listen to a proposition to bring in more water. An engineer and former mayor, Fred Eaton, alert to the problem, had located a large supply of water in Owens Valley and an ancient riverbed that would greatly simplify the problem of

Receiving the Water from Owens Valley, November 5, 1913

Los Angeles Department of Water and Power

diverting this water to the parched city some 250 miles distant. Having acquired the necessary options, Eaton broached the matter to City Engineer William Mulholland, who endorsed it wholeheartedly to the city water board. That body acted at once. It acquired the site, approved Mulholland's plan for a $25 million aqueduct, and broke the news by asking the voters of the city to authorize the necessary bond issue. As an engineering venture the aqueduct was a most creditable performance. Mulholland completed it within his estimate both as to time and money, and Los Angeles benefited not only by the 400 second-feet of water delivered but also by the provision of electric power at a very moderate cost.

In other respects the results of the aqueduct were less happy. Owens Valley residents, who had success in their grasp in the reclamation of the valley, found their prospects dashed by the diversion of the water. Plenty of water for valley and city could have been impounded by a dam upstream from the cultivated area. Instead, the engineers proposed to follow the quicker and cheaper expedient of taking the water right out of the river. They were aided and abetted by the Secretary of the Interior, who stopped homesteading in the valley by declaring it forest land, and by President Roosevelt, who promptly endorsed a bill to give Los Angeles right of way for its aqueduct through Inyo, Kern, and Los Angeles counties. It was all done on the presumption that it would accomplish "the greatest good for the greatest number," yet the conviction has mounted that the planners of the aqueduct, besides devastating the valley, bilked the citizens of Los Angeles in order to reap swollen profits on San Fernando real estate irrigated with the first flow of water. When disgruntled ranchers resorted to dynamiting and other violent action, the city had excuse to proceed still more ruthlessly in forcing the settlers out of the valley. Vehement critics, including Walter Chalfant, Morrow Mayo, and Will Rogers, tilted a lance for the settlers and stirred the city's conscience to consider belated compensation, but this did not allay the desolation of the valley, or salve all the wounds, or undo the baleful publicity that redounded to the city because of the "rape of Owens Valley."

For Further Reading

JOSEPHINE KINGSBURY JACOBS, *Sunkist Advertising* (UCLA dissertation, 1966).

WALLACE SMITH, *Garden in the Sun* (1939), the San Joaquin Valley.

MERLIN STONEHOUSE, *John Wesley North and the Reform Frontier* (1965).

J. A. ALEXANDER, *The Life of George Chaffey* (1928).

ROBERT L. KELLEY, "Taming the Sacramento," *PHR*, 34 (1965), 21–49.

ROBERT M. FOGELSON, *The Fragmented Metropolis, Los Angeles, 1850–1930* (1967).

GERALD T. WHITE, *Formative Years in the Far West, A History of Standard Oil Company of California* (1962).

MARY AUSTIN, *The Land of Little Rain* (1903).

REMI A. NADEAU, *The Water Seekers* (1950).

CAUGHEY, *California Heritage*, 324–29, 334–37.

chapter twenty-three

Strong Individualists

It is a habit of mine, when troubled in thought, to go for a long walk.
One late afternoon I found myself at the top of Russian Hill. Around me ran
the full circle of what I would be giving up if I were to leave San Francisco,
a city I had grown to love and where I had made so many fine friendships.
I began to see clearly that teaching would never bring me the happiness
I wanted. It was here I belonged, in this new country which had
broadened my horizons, opened my eyes to a new conception of life, and
shown me a way to satisfy my desire for beauty. Having absorbed something
of the American spirit of independence, I made my decision according to
my own lights. I took the first step on my career as a portrait
photographer. I started in search of a studio.

Arnold Genthe

A Robust Victorianism

1875 to 1914 For California in the 30 or 40 years prior to World War I the key to the social and intellectual characteristics was the fading of frontier conditions. Improvements in communication broke down the barriers of isolation. Cumulative increase in population did away with much of the roughness that had characterized gold-rush days. In the closing decades of the century California came closer to the national average in ratio of the sexes in the population, proportions of age groups, occupations, and habits of thought. Distinguishing qualities existed, but, to a far greater extent than before, descriptions of the life of the nation became applicable to California.

John Muir

Culver Pictures

On landing in San Francisco, John Muir asked the first man he met how
to get out of town. "But where do you want to go?" "Anywhere that is wild."

In retrospect, the outstanding intellectual experience of that generation was exposure to the theory of evolution which Darwin had advanced in 1859. Although the protest of religion, especially Protestant theology, is often assumed to be the entire story, the impact actually was much broader. The postulate of evolution turned philosophers from transcendentalism to pragmatism. It fostered the concept of law as an organic growth changing with society rather than as a set of fundamental and immutable principles. It gave teachers an impetus to make education "functional," that is, articulated with social needs and ends. It stimulated the churches to socialize Christianity, as may be observed in such phenomena as medical missionaries, Christian Endeavor, Jane Addams' Hull House at Chicago, or Donaldina Cameron near San Francisco's Chinatown. Although Californians participated in this change of outlook, geographical remoteness from the centers of culture at Boston and New York and chronological proximity to frontier days seemed to ordain for them an inconspicuous place in American arts and letters. Nevertheless, in several fields of creative endeavor these Californians achieved and deserved wide renown.

Socially speaking, the state was divided into rural California and San Francisco. Life in small towns and in the country was the lot of a majority at the start of this generation and of a substantial minority at its close, yet nowhere has it been adequately described. Whenever nonfictionists have considered this countryside, they have been engrossed with the technological advances in railroad building, irrigation, new crops, and real-estate promotion, or they have centered on political issues to the neglect of sociological description. Novelists, when they depict these people, as Frank Norris did in *The Octopus*, center on the problems of law, government, and economics. Rural California before the First World War saw an agricultural expansion equaling that in the Plains region, yet no Willa Cather has risen to write an *O Pioneers*, much less an Ole Rölvaag to produce an epic *Giants in the Earth*.

The explanation is multiple. The rise of California farming had the characteristics of the growth of a great industry and seemed about as promising material for an absorbing human drama as the concurrent rise of the Standard Oil Company. Ownership tended toward capitalistic concentration. Labor ranks were manned largely by Orientals, first by Chinese coolies and later by Japanese. Expansion was achieved more by invoking machines and factory techniques or by scientific discoveries and inventions than by the sweat of pioneer homesteaders. The openness of the climate, the productiveness of the land, and the usually favorable market for California crops minimized the distress and uncertainty that made the saga of the Prairie farmers so throbbing a narrative. It all simmers down, perhaps, to the fact that life in rural California, for all the expansion and the innovations, was no longer pioneering.

Furthermore, the hinterland was eclipsed by the metropolis. San Francisco had great advantages. The fortunes of the railroad builders and the kings of the Comstock, added to the tribute paid by California gold, agriculture, and the commerce of the Pacific slope, made it a center of opulence. Picturesqueness of setting and of history were additional assets. Cosmopolitan population put San Francisco in a class with New Orleans for distinctiveness. Unchallenged as yet by any other American port on the Pacific, it had the further advantage of being on the most favored route for travelers to and from the Orient or round the world. Thus, it was a mecca for globe-trotters, numbering among its more distinguished visitors former President Grant, Henry Ward Beecher, Adelina Patti, King Kalakaua, Rudyard Kipling, and Oscar Wilde. Still others who contributed to the tone of society were the officers of the United States Navy assigned to the San Francisco station and those of other navies who found frequent occasion to visit the bay.

The prevailing testimony of these visitors is that San Francisco was a fascinating place. Physically, its charm sprang from the conjunction of bay and mountains and the cool, gray briskness that is the standard weather.

To this noble setting buildings contributed little. Most business blocks were nondescript and unsubstantial. Residences were unpretentious except for the ornate palaces of the plutocrats on Nob Hill, and these monstrosities, high-lighted by Charlie Crocker's 30-foot spite fence and the brass fence that gave a man full-time employment as a polisher, were admired only as conspicuous proofs of great wealth. The old Palace Hotel was a showplace because of its very immensity. Cliff House overlooking Seal Rocks was also on the itinerary of every visitor, and the underground passages in Chinatown had a reputation rivaling that of the sewers of Paris, but the two man-made features most often complimented were the generous width of Market Street and the cable cars. In these the architects of the city had triumphed.

In more intimate details San Francisco made a better impression. The excellence of her restaurants was a tradition zealously upheld. Marchand's and the Poodle Dog offered a dollar dinner unsurpassed; Louis' spread a four-course dinner that stirred Will Irwin to rhapsodies, and the price was 15 cents with wine or 20 cents with coffee. The French colony dating from the days of gold supplied the leading restaurateurs. Home cooking by Chinese houseboys also attained a high standard of excellence. The best foreign schools of cooking made contributions to the California cuisine, where they were interlarded with American dishes and recipes.

Further advantages were in the profusion of fresh vegetables which the gardens of the bay region provided so abundantly, in the many varieties of sea foods conveniently available, in the game readily obtained throughout this period, and in the fruits, as luscious as they were inexpensive and abundant. Here was the wherewithal for epicurean feasts. San Franciscans, it must be admitted, did their part nobly by supplying the restaurants an exacting but large and appreciative patronage. According to the reminiscences of the period, gourmets and bon vivants constituted a large fraction of the population of the city. Good food and drink thus received the most appropriate compliment.

Preliminary to dining, San Franciscans were in the habit of strolling along the Cocktail Route. The cocktail, it was claimed, was a San Francisco invention; certainly it had a strong hold on these sturdy sons of the pioneers. From the Reception Saloon at Kearney and Sutter the route led to Haquette's Palace of Art, which was practically a museum, to the Cardinal, to the Occidental Bar, to the Bank Exchange, famous equally for its marble floors, fine paintings, and Pisco Punch, to another score or so of first-class saloons, and finally to Dunne Brothers at Eddy and Market. Offering the most prodigal of free lunches, including such dishes as terrapin in a sauce of cream, butter, and sherry, and Virginia baked ham cooked in champagne, the Cocktail Route based its principal appeal on its provision for masculine conviviality. The habitués embraced, so it is claimed, every San Franciscan who mattered, and many sampled the food, drinks, and conversation at practically every station along the Route.

Since 1849 the theater had been one of the more prominent embellishments of San Francisco. In the Champagne Days, Evelyn Wells' apt designation of the generation, San Franciscans could choose between Walter Morosco's Grand Opera House, which, under "the largest chandelier in America," specialized first in melodrama and then in opera; the Tivoli, with light and grand opera and each seat equipped with a tray on which beer was served between acts; the Bella Union; the Alcazar, with its excellent stock company; the California; the Stockwell; the Columbia, sometimes with vaudeville, sometimes with concerts, sometimes with standard plays; the Baldwin Theater, touted as the finest outside of New York; a Chinese theater in Chinatown; the Wigwam; and perhaps most distinctive, the Orpheum, where, for half a century after its founding in 1887, vaudeville reigned as a high art. A list of the artists who performed in these always packed theaters would be a roll call of the generation's celebrities: Melba, Homer, Caruso, Alice Nielsen, Nat Goodwin, Lillian Russell, Julia Marlowe, Otis Skinner, De Wolf Hopper, Sarah Bernhardt, Weber and Fields. To enumerate the theaters, the players, and the plays gives but faint recognition to one of the most vital elements in old San Francisco.

Worth mentioning also were the city's clubs. Of these the most individualized was the Bohemian Club. Organized in 1871 by a group of newspaper men, of whom Henry George was one, this club was at first rigorously limited to writers, actors, musicians, painters, sculptors, and the like. Gradually the bars were lowered to admit prominent citizens who made no pretensions as creative artists. Membership advanced to 750 and the club treasurer ceased worrying about bills and deficits; nevertheless, the emphasis on things artistic persisted. The best exemplification was in the annual High Jinks, an elaborate and ambitious two-week toast to Nature, staged in a magnificent natural amphitheater in the redwoods, some 50 miles north of the city. The High Jinks represented amateur theatricals raised to the ultimate. It also displayed the penchant of the people of San Francisco for convivial communing with one another and for giving generous attention to the amenities of life.

The pictures usually offered of San Francisco society before the Fire contain few reminders that some business was transacted in between visits to the Cocktail Route, the restaurants, the theaters, and the clubs. When the earthquake and fire wiped out so many of the material elements of these Champagne

Days, the effect was to give free rein to the imagination in reminiscences about "the city that was." After allowing all the bubbles to rise, there is left a heady drink that suggests a gay, volatile, open-handed society in which Victorianism was well ventilated by gusts of robust westernism.

The Arts

In the practice of the arts Californians of this period seem to have been practically sterile in such fields as architecture and sculpture and to have achieved moderately in such others as painting and writing. After a beginning of some promise in the religious art of the missions, painting broke off to start again with the coming of crude limners in the late Mexican period, though the best "California art" of the era was in the form of portraits and landscapes to illustrate the accounts of foreign visitors to the province. The Mexican War brought other artists who recorded their impressions with pencil or brush and the gold rush brought still more. Charles Nahl, with his numerous genre pictures of California life, was the most famous of these, but there were many others: R. J. Holt, Thomas F. Ayres, W. S. Jewett, S. W. Shaw, S. S. Osgood, Thomas S. Officer, F. A. Butman, Thomas Hill, and Albert Bierstadt. Jewett not only brought the California landscape into its own but was commissioned to do a portrait of John A. Sutter for the State Capitol at a fee of $5,000. Ayres is noteworthy as the artist–discoverer of Yosemite Valley. A large pastel of his, when redrawn on stone by Nahl, became a most popular lithograph print. Tom Hill and Bierstadt worked the Yosemite vein even more assiduously.

The California nature theme, particularly Yosemite, came to be such a standard motif as to occasion complaint from one critic in 1875 against these "hackneyed landscapes," which he said were repainted year after year with only "a new rock and a cow or two introduced to give an air of originality." The theme and several of the artists continued, though the most prolific and popular painter at the end of the century, William Keith, turned from the grand view to more poetic studies in lighting effects and to intimate glimpses of the university campus at Berkeley. The missions were another favorite subject. Edward Vischer's etchings, which survive now only in the form of lithograph prints, formed the first complete series; Keith painted them all in 1880, and his example was followed by artist after artist.

Douglas Tilden, best known for the Donohue Fountain in San Francisco, the gigantic lever-punch operated by five muscular mechanics, is reckoned the leading sculptor. Southern California had its painters, including Gutzon Borglum, William L. Judson, Elmer Wachtel, and William Wendt. Wendt devoted himself especially to realistic portrayal of the brilliantly lighted southland. Other artists could be mentioned, but more significant was the organization of the San Francisco Art Association in 1871 with Virgil Williams as its leading spirit, Judson's Arroyo Guild at Pasadena in the nineties, and the California Art Club at Los Angeles with Wendt as its most active member. These organizations encouraged painting by widening the circle of appreciation of art and enlarging the clientele for the purchase of canvases. Throughout the generation there was much talk about California as a future center of art. It was a goal, however, very much for the future, and apart from a bolder use of color California painting was dominated by the precepts laid down at Düsseldorf, Barbizon, and Paris.

The Californians of this period had the further good fortune to sit for a great photographer, Arnold Genthe. He came to California as a tutor, experimented in picture taking as an avocation, and went on to make it his career. His specialty was portrait photography and, thanks in part to his practice in unobtrusive camera work in Chinatown, he succeeded remarkably well in achieving naturalness. On the morning of the earthquake, all of his possessions having been ruined, he went to a Montgomery Street shop to ask for a camera. The proprietor told him, "Take anything you want; it's all going to burn anyhow." From the small camera that he selected came the best pictures of this disaster.

Poets and Novelists

In writing, a more promising tradition had been shaped by the gold-rush generation, a tradition so closely interwoven with the conditions of that earlier day that their successors were unable to uphold it. No humorist attained the dimensions of Derby; no California stories could compete with Mark Twain's "Jumping Frog" or Bret Harte's "Outcasts of Poker Flat," and, except for Gelett Burgess' "Purple Cow," no bit of doggerel had the vogue of Bret Harte's "Heathen Chinee." Nor was there any literary journal so distinctively and meritoriously western as the old *Overland Monthly*.

Poets were in good number but their verse, with very few exceptions, was not of superior quality. Joaquin Miller and Ina Coolbrith continued to write, and Miss Coolbrith was belatedly chosen poet laureate of the state. The most famous poem of the generation was Edwin Markham's mawkish "The Man with the Hoe."

Quantity of output in novels, meanwhile, exceeded even that in verse. In the front rank marched an oddly assorted quartet: Gertrude Atherton, Helen Hunt Jackson, Frank Norris, and Jack London. After them trooped a legion of lesser writers who occasionally produced an important book, such as Charles Tenney Jackson's *The Day of Souls*, a poignant drama of San Francisco before the Fire.

Gertrude Atherton set her stories against backgrounds as diverse as Periclean Athens, modern Austria, colonial Jamaica, and pastoral California, and suffused them with the flavor of reality. Her many novels gained a following in England and on the Continent as well as in the United States. Locally, she is of most interest when interpreting early California in *Rezanov*, in *The Splendid Idle Forties*, or in her *Intimate History*. In these works her imaginative reconstruction of bygone scenes was assisted by traditive materials from her people, her husband's people, and their friends in old San Francisco.

Helen Hunt Jackson came late to California. She had served a long apprenticeship in New England and the East writing children's stories, romantic verse, and sentimental novels. In 1872 a transcontinental trip to view Yosemite introduced her to California. Nine years later, when she first came to southern California, she was a much-changed person. Marriage to William S. Jackson of Colorado Springs had given her a broader outlook and a more mature attitude. She had also become vitally interested in the problem of Indian rights, and that very year she was bringing together her philippics against the United States Indian policies under the title *A Century of Dishonor*. This treatise led to her appointment with Abbot Kinney, founder of the California replica of Venice, to make a report on the conditions and needs of the Mission Indians, published later at Washington in 1883. Mrs. Jackson, however, felt that thus far she had not sufficiently stirred the nation's conscience. She turned, therefore, to the medium of the novel and strove through *Ramona* (1884) to obtain effective reforms. Although *Ramona* did not achieve all that its author had hoped, it swept the nation. After many years it is still read, besides being dramatized year after year at Hemet in the Ramona country and periodically on the screen. Strictly speaking, Helen Hunt Jackson was not a Californian but it was here she found her noblest theme.

Frank Norris was an author wholly Californian. His first published works were romantic. By some, this romanticism is regarded merely as a passing phase from which he soon turned to naturalism; others see it as his device to build up a popular following for the more solid works to come. With *McTeague* in 1899, though he retained certain romantic devices, Norris became the first thoroughgoing disciple in America of the naturalism which Zola had popularized in France. Written with power and with insight into Mac's brutal sadism that would do credit to a trained psychologist, *McTeague* is a study in character disintegration induced by economic pressure.

After another exercise on the debasement of an individual through the play of inexorable circumstances, Norris, in the unfinished work "Vandover and the Brute," turned from the psychological to the sociological. His final works, *The Octopus* (1901) and *The Pit* (1903), hinge again on economic determinism, but this time it was a whole farming population caught in the arms of a man-made machine. Both works have an epic sweep that is in keeping with the broad valley in which *The Octopus* is set. Rich in action and peopled with a large cast of characters whose metamorphosis by the wheat is magnificently portrayed, *The Octopus* would have gone far just as a novel. But in it Norris deserted the amoral attitude of naturalism to pass judgment and to cry out for social reforms. Whatever this may have done to the book as literature, it gave it additional significance historically by linking it directly with the reform movement which culminated in the election of 1910 and the legislature of 1911.

Many readers of Jack London see him merely as a master storyteller, vivid in his landscapes, authentic in his settings, apt in characterization, and attaining high velocity of action. *The Call of the Wild* (1903), *The Sea Wolf* (1904), and most of his later popular writings were of this stamp, but, as *The*

Jack London
Arnold Genthe

PERDRIX, MÂLE ET FEMELE, DE LA CALIFORNIE.

First Published Portrait of the California Quail
Voyage de la Pérouse, 1797

"There are still some places in the west where the quail cry 'cuidado'."

Mary Austin

Iron Heel (1908) and *The Revolution* (1910) clearly show, London was a Marxian Socialist and revolutionist. Elsewhere in his publications are other preachments on the struggle of the classes. More restraint and polish would have put him in Norris' "respectable" bracket but probably at the expense of the spontaneity and forthrightness of style which won him so many readers. Even more than Norris, London represents the bitter reaction against capitalism on the part of a small but vocal minority in his generation. *Martin Eden* (1909), one of two excursions into autobiography, offers an unusual perspective of Jack's unorthodox student days.

With the exception of Jack London at his best, writings more enduring came from a little woman who made herself the voice for the desert that creeps across the Tehachapi into the southern end of the San Joaquin Valley and crowds more relentlessly on the Owens Valley. Mary Hunter came with her parents to bleak years of homesteading in the parched fields near Bakersfield and the Grapevine, then with her husband, Stafford Austin, moved to Lone Pine, east of the Sierra. Developing an intimacy with the land, the Indians, and the Mexican and Basque sheepherders, she wrote eight books and many shorter pieces about this marginal part of California. These works vary in effectiveness. *The Flock* (1906) is a classic on the men who followed the sheep. *Basket Woman* (1904) and shorter writings on the Indians have a jewel-like quality. *Land of Little Rain* (1903) is sensitive nature writing illumined by a sense of oneness with the people of this stark land.

Reminiscence Glorifies the Past

Not far removed from the novelists were those who committed their reminiscences to print. The principal works of this nature, by Horace Bell, William Heath Davis, and Harris Newmark, are improperly weighted with two for the south and one for the north, though by including Frémont's memoirs and more recently published reminiscences by Cornelius Cole, Frank A. Leach, Sarah Bixby Smith, J. A. Graves, Amelia R. Neville, Boyle Workman, and William T. Ellis, the balance is readjusted. Bell's *Reminiscences of a Ranger,* published in 1881, has claim to fame as an early Los Angeles imprint. Bell's primary consideration, and to a degree this is true of Davis also, seems to have been not to let his story lose anything in the telling. He mixed legend and rumor with sober fact and made no pretense of following a chronological outline. With his memory jogged by a searching of the old newspaper files, Newmark was far more literal and much more cyclopedic. In common with Bell and Davis, and for that matter with practically all those who indulge in reminiscences, he pushed the horizon back as far as possible.

Davis was largely concerned with the processes leading up to American acquisition of California. Bell's chief interest was in Los Angeles during the fifties and the period of the Civil War. Newmark, though continuing toward 1913, gave three fourths of his space to the fifties, sixties, and seventies.

Cole in 1908 was content to carry his memoirs up to about 1875, and Mrs. Neville saved but one chapter for the gay nineties. Even Leach, who as Director of the United States Mint at San Francisco in 1906 had an exciting and important role in the weeks following the earthquake and fire, could not resist dallying for half his volume with the fabulous fifties and sixties. So it went for most of those who reminisced, including the scores of personages who were waited upon, notebook in hand, by Bancroft's secretaries. The result is that the American conquest, the gold rush, and the Civil War period are better covered in reminiscences than is the subsequent epoch. On the other hand the publication of the first of these memoirs in the eighties indicates that Californians were ready to take an active interest in the history of their state.

In southern California reminiscence was carried a step further by the dynamic Charles F. Lummis. Lummis had walked out from Cincinnati, with a stopover in New Mexico's Indian country. He engaged in some orthodox journalism as city editor of the Los Angeles *Times* but soon gave himself over completely to his enthusiasms, the Indians, the Spanish pioneers, and the wonders of the Southwest. Practically all he did can be related to one or more of these causes. The monthly that he created, *Land of Sunshine,* later renamed *Out West,* boosted California and the Southwest with eulogies of the climate and resources and with descriptions of expanding agriculture and industry.

Out West was also the organ for the Sequoia League, a Lummis society dedicated to the rehabilitation of the first Americans, and for the Landmarks Society, whose name is self-explanatory. It was Lummis' habit in his journal to run translations of basic documents relating to the Spanish pioneers, for example, Benavides' *Memorial on New Mexico.* Still another monument to him is the Southwest Museum, an endowed institution which has done more than any other one factor to put Los Angeles on the anthropological map.

Constitutionally a rebel against the dictates of convention, Lummis preferred the company of kindred spirits. His house, which was of his own devising and making, was a constant resort for ambitious artists and writers, a bohemian salon offering hospitality in the old California tradition. Lummis also incorporated his ideas in books. *The Spanish Pioneers and the California Missions* proclaimed his admiration for Spanish achievement and argued its significance to the people of the United States. His *Land of Poco Tiempo* is a New Mexican travel book by one most simpático. His *Little Flowers of Our Lost Romance* is a delightful excursion into the epoch of the Spanish borderlands.

The Great Bancroft and Lesser Historians

Meanwhile, California's past was attracting the attention of several local historians. As such it is hardly fair to include Josiah Royce, because by this time he was a Harvard professor; he wrote his *California* by request rather than in response to an irresistible inner urge, and the suggestion had arisen because Houghton Mifflin Company was embracing all the states in the American Commonwealths Series. But the multivolume histories of Bancroft, Hittell, and Eldredge issued unmistakably from the California environment and the times. They are still the best of the large and comprehensive histories of the state.

Hubert Howe Bancroft was a historian the like of whom has very seldom if ever been produced. He was first of all a San Francisco book dealer and publisher. Having one day in 1859 ranged on a shelf some 50 or 75 works on California that happened to be in his stock, he fell into the habit of adding other volumes to this collection. The habit grew, and from sporadic forays in other book shops in San Francisco he soon went on to systematic purchases in the East. Personally and through agents he searched through catalogs and stocks in London and Paris, in Spain and Italy, and throughout the Continent, meanwhile broadening his interest to take in the entire Pacific slope of North America. On the cogent theory that completeness of the collection was most to be desired and that even the most insignificant item might have real value when placed in such company, he made it his policy to buy every book or pamphlet that had any material whatsoever on the history of this area. Under this impetus his collection mounted rapidly. At first the 50 volumes had seemed a creditable showing. Within three years the total reached 1,000 titles, shortly thereafter 5,000, and by 1868, 10,000.

Hubert Howe Bancroft

Bradley & Rulofson
The Bancroft Library

At this point Bancroft recites that he was ready to rest on his oars. Then came an announcement of an auction sale of some 7,000 volumes of Mexicana, the library of José María Andrade, former intimate of Maximilian and now a refugee from the republicans. The catalog opened to Bancroft a new vista for rounding out his collection. It had not occurred to him that Mexico, with a history of publishing reaching back a full century earlier than Massachusetts, had untold riches for the collector of Pacific coast materials. Equally patent was the fact that a collection such as the Andrade would not come on the market again in Bancroft's day, if ever. There was not time to check the catalog against his own holdings; nor could he attend the auction at Leipzig. All he could do was authorize his London agent to spend $5,000 on his behalf. The result was an addition of 3,000 volumes, printed and manuscript. Very few were duplicates of Bancroft's earlier purchases, and these were more than offset by works of the greatest importance.

Other auctions and special sales found Bancroft a discriminating but liberal bidder, notably the dispersals of the E. G. Squier collection of Central American materials, of the Caleb Cushing library, and of the collection of José Fernando Ramírez, another Maximilian exile. At this latter auction in 1880 prices of Mexicana had advanced so sharply that Bancroft's bill for a much smaller lot than he had taken of the Andrade collection amounted to almost $30,000. In terms of that valuation he calculated his whole library as worth a million dollars.

The total number of titles eventually ran to some 60,000. Besides books and pamphlets, two other classes of materials were collected. One was newspapers, of which Bancroft acquired runs totaling almost 500 years, the approximate equivalent of 5,000 volumes. The other was manuscripts. Some of the highest prices he paid were for transcripts from the official archives of church and state or for original documents. In the seventies he encouraged many old-timers to record their experiences and recollections, and these statements, together with many documents, family and otherwise, which were turned over to him, constituted a most valuable branch of his collection.

Had Bancroft been content with collecting, his name would still be first in the roster of contributors to California historiography. The Bancroft Library, while in his possession and later as the property of the University of California, became the focal point, foundation, and inspiration for most of the subsequent exploration of this field. Although he began as a collector, Bancroft soon conceived a much more gargantuan task, that of sifting, correlating, and evaluating all the material he had collected and of writing from it a complete history of the Pacific slope. Needless to say, no human being could have done all this alone. Bancroft made no pretense of doing so. He employed numerous assistants, some of whom, such as Henry Oak, Thomas Savage, and Frances Fuller Victor, became historians in their own right.

By trial and error a technique developed. At first Bancroft set men to work making literal extracts from the sources. These proving too cumbersome and less satisfactory than the originals in their context, he turned to an elaborate index, which also proved too complex. The next resort was a simple subject index on three by five slips, which were organized on a topical basis and then subdivided locationally and chronologically. This master index to his library was years in the making and cost an estimated $35,000, yet Bancroft considered that a bargain price for a key that would unlock the knowledge stored up in his vast collection. It was an Aladdin's lamp, as he worded it, enabling a man to "seat himself at a bare table and say to a boy, Bring me all that is known about the conquest of Darien, the mines of Nevada, . . . [or] the town of Querétaro . . . and straightway, as at the call of a magician, such knowledge is spread before him, with the volumes opened at the page."

With the aid of the index, Bancroft and his staff went through the subject matter of Pacific slope history item by item, viewing the evidence, weighing it, comparing, and interpreting. The facts as they saw them were written up in the text proper, while divergent or variant testimony fell into the footnotes in company with verbatim quotations from many supporting witnesses. Thus the work proceeded, with the mark of the index in evidence in such matters as the general organization, in which chronological arrangement was made subordinate to the geographical divisions. The end result was 39 fat volumes, uneven in quality, but cyclopedic in detail and crammed with citations of every conceivable authority. Particularly on its center, which is California, a more comprehensive amassing of information would be difficult to imagine. Eighty and more years after the first publication, Walter Hebberd of Santa Barbara is paying Bancroft the compliment of issuing a facsimile reprint of his seven-volume *History of California.*

The historical profession, perhaps in outstripped jealousy, for many years looked down on Bancroft, ridiculing his cooperative technique, scoffing at his "factory" methods, and denying him the recognition of authorship. The latter criticism has a measure of justification, for Bancroft wrote far less than half of the actual text, yet the criticism might come with better grace if research assistants and secretaries were unknown in the profession.

The defects in the Bancroft *Histories,* however, are traceable to human frailties, to occasional intemperateness of expression, and to the non-existence of any considerable number of preceding monographic studies to chart the way for his general account rather than to flaws in the system itself. In history proper the method has not been reapplied except perhaps in the Federal Writers' Project, the Historical Records Survey, and some of the works on the military services in World War II, but the employment of a staff under sentence of anonymity by the editors of *Time* and of *Fortune* and by the Walt Disney Productions are modern recrudescences of Bancroft's literary workshop.

Concurrently with the great Bancroft, Theodore H. Hittell was turning aside from his law practice to undertake a history of California. Hittell worked alone; he utilized just such materials as did Bancroft, though of necessity on a selective rather than on an all-inclusive basis; he was accorded many facilities at the Bancroft Library; his legal background made him particularly well qualified to deal with certain phases of California history, and he was gifted in literary style. Consequently, his four-volume work, published in 1885 and 1897, is a notable milestone in local historical publication, reckoned second only to Bancroft's.

Whereas other historians were overshadowed by these two, their activity in the pursuit of local historical studies is symptomatic of the outlook of the generation. Mention should be made of George Davidson, Nestor of California geographers and author of half a dozen important works on California's Age of Discovery. At the Santa Barbara Mission, Father Zephyrin Engelhardt devoted himself to a study of the missions of Baja and Alta California. Like Bancroft a devotee of compendiousness rather than discrimination, Engelhardt suffused with his own religious ardor the record of Jesuit and Franciscan labors in the Californias.

The third of the larger state histories was a by-product of the Panama–Pacific Exposition of 1915. Sailing under the name of its editor, Zoeth Skinner Eldredge, the first three and a half volumes were actually written by Clinton A. Snowden and the fifth volume is made up of articles by selected specialists. Eldredge, however, deserves recognition for the general planning of the work and also for a two-volume study of the beginnings of San Francisco, published three years earlier.

Henry George and Ambrose Bierce

In the field of political economy California was producing an even greater luminary, Henry George. George has been called, rightly, America's most original economist; in the vigor of his thinking he need share the laurels only with Thorstein Veblen. The young George showed few signs of oncoming greatness. Leaving school at 14, he sailed before the mast from Philadelphia to Australia, came on to Salem, Oregon, where he worked in a print shop, and at length to San Francisco, where he moved from one print shop or newspaper to another, his chief reward being the experience gained.

A Jeffersonian and a Democrat, George found in California as well as in his own experiences much food for thought on the injustices of the economic order, for California in the sixties, though endowed with abundant resources that should have made it a land of almost limitless opportunities, was rapidly falling into the hands of land monopolists. The swollen fortunes of the railroad builders, the tremendous land grants with which the United States subsidized them, the scandals current in connection with swamplands and fraudulent grants, the speculative profits at Oakland when it was made the terminus of the transcontinental railroad, the opulence of the Comstock fortunes —such was the atmosphere of San Francisco in the formative years of George's thinking. Here certainly was basis for placing the blame on land monopoly and for seeking to eliminate private enjoyment of unearned increment.

True enough, the same general conditions were noticeable elsewhere. On a visit to New York, George was struck by the juxtaposition of a most

Henry George

The Bancroft Library

flourishing, profitable commerce and of slums in which thousands lived in direst poverty. Throughout American history the thread of land speculation had been present, from the Ohio Valley before the Revolution to the Oakland water-front after the railroad and from the Yazoo frauds to the California swamplands.

The economic philosophy that George worked out owed little to academic economists, for whom, by the way, he had the utmost contempt. He was a free-lance thinker, a seeker after origins, thinking, as Tom Paine had recommended, "as if he were the first man who ever thought." His cardinal principles were the inequity and iniquity of land monopoly, the viciousness of unearned increment, the conception of the landlord as a parasite, the assertion of the right of every human being to himself and to the use of his rightful share of the free gifts of nature, and the advocacy of a tax on land—that is, on rent, which he identified with unearned increment—as the panacea for the ills of society. An interesting corollary was that capital and labor were linked, that interest and wages would rise and fall together, and that what was good for one would be beneficial to the other.

Nowadays George is charged with oversimplification, both in his analysis and in the remedy proposed. Not all unearned increment, to cite one example, is to be classified as rent. Nor is reason alone an adequate agent for the achievement of social reform. He was an arch-idealist, a quixotic "knight-errant from out of the newest West." In spite of the correctness of these suggestions and notwithstanding that the single tax has not been adopted, Henry George has been the most influential American economist. A pioneer in analyzing exploitative capital, he attempted to bring the science of economics out of its ivory tower and make it face the problems of the common man. In this his success, of course, was only relative, yet he more than any other humanized and democratized the science of economics.

Measuring in terms of total circulation, no other California writer compares with George. Heading the list is his magnum opus, *Progress and Poverty*, which was rejected by all the eastern publishers. George's printer friends in San Francisco had more confidence in him; they helped him set up the type, make the plates, and run off an edition of 500 copies. With the chief expense of publication thus covered, D. Appleton and Company agreed to take over the book, but the firm's lack of confidence in it is apparent in their refusal to take out an English copyright. Certain San Francisco reviewers derided the book, but the American press was warmer, and British critics on such journals as the *Times* and the *Edinburgh Review* hailed it with the greatest enthusiasm. George also made a triumphant tour de force of England and Scotland on the lecture platform. Thereafter he continued to be doubly successful as lecturer and writer but not as the Socialist candidate for mayor of New York. Of *Progress and Poverty* a conservative estimate is that two million copies were printed in the 25 years subsequent to 1879, while in the same period there circulated at least three million copies of his other writings, notably *Protection and Free Trade*. More years have elapsed and still George is read wholesale. Although his books would not have died, their vigor is additionally sustained by his ardent disciples, who still spread the gospel according to George.

Ambrose Bierce

The Bancroft Library

George, the mild-mannered, the self-effacing, was not the only prodigy supplied to letters by San Francisco journalism. The hallmark of genius was equally unmistakable in caustic, perverse Ambrose Bierce. His road to writing was also an indirect one. After a boyhood of poverty and deprivation in Ohio and Indiana, he enlisted in the northern army, saw active service in the Civil War, during which he was brevetted major, and came in 1866 to San Francisco, where he was soon at work as a watchman at the Mint. The San Francisco press at this time was filled with boisterous comments on the passing scene from such writers as Mark Twain and Dan De Quille. Bierce was moved to try his pen at this sort of writing, first as a sideline and then instead of his work as watchman. He became "Town Crier" for the *News Letter* and, beginning in 1868, doubled as editor as well as columnist.

For the next three decades, with only an occasional interlude, Bierce regaled San Franciscans with a regular column in which he impaled whatever or whoever incurred his displeasure. First it was as "Town Crier" for the *News Letter*, then as "Prattle" for the *Wasp*, and then as "Prattle" for Hearst's *Examiner*. Much that he wrote was drivel but, Homer having nodded, a columnist can be excused. By their hidebound conservatism and by their negative character the ideals Bierce stood for do not stir the imagination. The people, in his estimation, "were a great beast," and democracy he decried as a prelude to anarchy. For the *Argonaut* he turned loose his siege guns on Denis Kearney and the Sand-Lotters, and he had equal contempt for social reformers like Henry George who used an intellectual approach. His early writing, too, was monotonously devoted to bludgeoning invective suffused with venom, and many of his most acerbic attacks were upon innocent young authors whose only offense was in publishing an imperfect book or one which violated a Biercian canon.

By the eighties, when he carried his "Prattle" to Hearst's paper, Bierce was still the implacable critic, but he had acquired a more appropriate adversary in the Southern Pacific and had exchanged his sledgehammer for a rapier. These should have been his pleasantest years, if the word may be applied to one whose business was insult and abuse. Certainly they were his most productive, for in addition to his regular column he wrote much else. It was then that he wrote and published most of his Civil War stories, which, together with his horror stories, are the basis for much of his reputation as a writer. It was also under Hearst that Bierce achieved his greatest journalistic triumph. When the Southern Pacific in the nineties brought up the Funding Bill, which would have postponed for 99 years its reckoning with the federal treasury, the young publisher sent the old misanthrope, admittedly his ace writer, to do battle for the people against the great corporation. Victory was his, and Bierce could exult that the pen was mightier than the pocketbook.

Subsequent years added little to Bierce's literary stature. He continued for a time in California and then transferred his residence to the East. Finally in 1913, old and ill and embittered, he crossed over into Mexico, making a dramatic departure from history but a glamorous entrance into the realm of fantastic legend. Most astounding rumors filtered back about his mythical deeds, none of which, however, has been corroborated under scrutiny. This mysterious denouement, along with Bierce's virtuosity as a gadfly, has deprived him of full consideration as a literary figure. The man has eclipsed the writer. His war stories, to be sure, have been praised as among the best short stories of all time, precision-built and forceful. His horror stories, though less famous than Poe's, attain comparable effects without the necessity of invoking the supernatural or the abnormal.

Bierce's greatest genius was not in the short story or even in the retort discourteous. Rather it was in phrasing pithy, catchy statements of truths eternal. In verse, in doggerel, in simple phrases and sentences, or in the form of short fables, he turned out these aphorisms by the hundreds. For the production of inevitable sayings such as these Bierce had the necessary attributes. He was, as all who knew him would admit, sufficiently cynical, competent to see beneath the surface to the essential realities, and blessed with a superiority complex that encouraged him to pass judgment. In addition, he had developed an exquisite style, perfect in structure and unerring in word choice.

Such a genius, one might say, must be independent of time and place. Bierce might just as well have written proverbs for Confucius or King Solomon as for San Francisco's champagne generation, yet it is easy to see that Bierce was encouraged by his environment. California writers of the gold-rush era had established a tradition of outspokenness bordering on impertinence, and Bierce's position on Hearst's yellowing journal provided the ideal sounding board plus the necessary incentive for the grinding out of these immortal pungencies that best establish his genius. By no means a normal specimen of his generation, he was, nonetheless, a product of it.

John Muir and the Sierra Club

The late nineteenth century Californian of most enduring influence may well have been John Muir. A native of Scotland whose early years were spent in rural Wisconsin and at the University of Wisconsin, Muir arrived in San Francisco in 1868. His immediate impulse was to escape the city. Asking the first man he met how to get to "anywhere that is wild," he was directed to the Oakland ferry. From its terminal he walked southward 60 miles to Gilroy, turned eastward, and ascended Pacheco Pass. From its summit he beheld the Sierra Nevada in its luminous majesty, in his phrase, "the Range of Light."

Walking on across the San Joaquin Valley, Muir entered the foothills and Yosemite Valley and began to make acquaintance with the surrounding wilderness. In 1869, for the express purpose of seeing more of the high country, he signed on to take a flock of 2,000 sheep to the high pastures for summer grazing. He herded as he had hiked, notebook in hand, botanizing by the way, learning about many other aspects of nature, and reading the geological record.

El Capitan, Yosemite Valley

Ansel Adams

Granite Pavement, Yosemite

Philip Hyde

That winter he took a subsistence job at James M. Hutchings' station in Yosemite Valley, with time off for occasional explorations. The summer of 1870 permitted more ambitious jaunts and climbs. The summer was enlivened also by visiting tourists, among them an English noblewoman who made him the ill-concealed hero, Kenmuir, in the novel *Zanita* (short for manzanita). By invitation Muir also joined a Sierra trek by a group of University of California students with their geology professor, Joseph LeConte, in tow.

For another half dozen years Muir spent most of his time in these wilds, going often on solitary rambles and sometimes with a companion or two or a small group. He became the most knowledgeable person on the Tuolumne-to-Sequoia wilderness and the high Sierra and their most articulate champion. Presidents Roosevelt and Taft sought his guidance three decades later.

Muir early came to the conclusion that the Yosemite Valley and the "yosemites," as he called them, of the Tuolumne and the Kern were not products of cataclysmic convulsions, as the state geologist insisted, but of glacial grinding and polishing. Muir argued his theory persuasively to many visitors, including Professor LeConte. Bolstered by his subsequent discovery of living glaciers in the Sierra, Muir gained wide acceptance for his theory, which in 1934–35 was verified by seismic explorations which revealed that, underneath a thick layer of alluvial deposits, Yosemite is a U-shaped glacial valley.

In his early years Muir wrote and published voluminously in eastern and western magazines and in the New York and California newspapers. His forte was nature writing, benefiting from sharp observation and scientific understanding, together with bits of personal narrative, but gathering its principal appeal from his passionate enthusiasm. In 1894 his first book, *The Mountains of California*, appeared, followed in 1901 by *Our National Parks*. Later, some 40 years after the events, the essays describing his learning experience when he followed the sheep into the mountains were assembled as a book, *My First Summer in the Sierra* (1911). His *Yosemite* was published in 1912. These four were soon outnumbered by posthumous collections and selections from his writings.

In 1892 Muir was a leader in founding the Sierra Club and the natural selection as its first president. An alpine club with stress on camping and climbing, the new organization had a companion dedication to the protection of the Yosemite and Sierra wilderness area. Almost immediately the club was confronted by a bill to authorize mining, lumbering, and grazing concessions in the near vicinity of Yosemite Valley. The membership was prestigious. It elicited a resolution from the legislature and support from eastern conservationists and defeated this bill in committee. The club also prevailed in having

Tuolumne Meadows

Philip Hyde

the state reconvey Yosemite Valley to the federal government for administration as a National Park.

These contests were but shadowboxing compared to the battle for Hetch Hetchy. Shortly after 1900 San Francisco saw a need for additional water supply. The Mokelumne was one source investigated, but preference went to Hetch Hetchy, a smaller and less accessible yosemite on the Tuolumne within the bounds of Yosemite National Park. The first several applications for use of this site were rejected in the courts, but in 1905 Gifford Pinchot announced that the Roosevelt administration would support the application. Pinchot saw this action as consistent with conservation by maximizing the benefits from natural resources.

When Muir and others tried to muster the forces of the Sierra Club to block this raid on the wilderness preserve, they found that some of the staunchest members sided with utilitarian conservation. By a substantial majority, however, the "nature lovers" won support for a vigorous campaign against a dam at Hetch Hetchy, which would create a reservoir that would fluctuate 240 feet each season and thereby change a beautiful valley into an eyesore.

The battle went on for years. During Taft's presidency the nature lovers staved off final approval. But Woodrow Wilson's Secretary of the Interior, Franklin K. Lane, had been city attorney of San Francisco. To him it seemed proper for the greater good of the greater number that San Francisco should have this water. By that ploy the Sierra Club lost this nine-year battle. Muir died the next year. In 1916 Congress voted the National Park Act, which was intended to close the door to any repetitions of Hetch Hetchy.

Colleges and Universities

Another tangible expression of the cultural interests of these times was the development of institutions of higher learning. The state's population growth, coupled with the national tendency to put more emphasis on going to college, set the stage for such expansion. The transcontinental railroads made it convenient for young people to go east for their schooling and many did. Notwithstanding these "exports," California far exceeded the rate of the nation in expanding and improving her colleges and universities.

Carried over from the gold-rush epoch, there were a number of colleges and universities, so-called, among them the state university, the College of the Pacific, several Catholic schools, a state normal school established at San Francisco in 1862, and another at San Jose dating from 1871. In the ensuing years, a dozen or more institutions were added, the majority under denominational auspices. With a donated site in the southwestern part of Los Angeles, the University of Southern California was founded in 1879 by the Methodists. Three years later Los Angeles qualified for a branch of the San Jose state normal school, the cell from which the University of California at Los Angeles would eventually develop. In Oakland, Mills Seminary, which had been functioning for a number of years, was reinstituted as Mills College in 1885. A charter was obtained in 1887 for the Occidental Presbyterian University of Los Angeles, later simplified to Occidental College, and a few months later the Congregationalists chartered Pomona College. In September, 1888, these institutions enrolled their first students. At the Quaker colony of Whittier there was talk of a college almost from the beginning. It materialized in 1901. In 1891 the Church of the Brethren launched Lordsburg College, later named LaVerne, and in 1909 the University of Redlands opened classes in the First Baptist Church.

Most of the schools founded in this period had the primary aim of providing a general education in the liberal arts tradition and of supplementing this program with teacher training. One exception was Amos G. Throop's school at Pasadena, which went through a succession of name changes from Throop University, to Throop Polytechnic Institute, to Throop College of Technology, to California Polytechnic Institute, to California Institute of Technology, meanwhile evolving into an institution with primary stress on engineering and the physical sciences.

In all these institutions the achievement of true collegiate status came only gradually. For example, the University of Southern California in 1891 had 192 students enrolled in the preparatory department and only 25 in the collegiate department. Furthermore, each college started on the most meager of financing, a few acres of ground, perhaps a hotel building in which classes could meet, some town lots that could be leased or bought, and seldom more than a few thousand dollars in pledges and cash.

This being the setting, the announcement of the Leland Stanfords late in 1885 that, as a memorial to their son, they would bestow the bulk of their fortune upon a university was electrifying news. The initial conveyance was of properties appraised at six million dollars, with another million and a quarter for buildings. The Stanfords promised additional gifts and bequests, to bring the total to about $30 million. At the time, Columbia's productive capital was $4,680,590, Harvard's was $4,511,862, and Johns Hopkins' was $3 million. Thus the prospect was that Stanford would start as the richest of all universities.

Even this largess did not dispel skepticism that a first-rate university could be achieved. Since the peak enrollment at the University of California was only 332, experts wondered whether there would be any students at Stanford. The difficulties in getting good men to come to Berkeley, or to stay there, made others doubt that a competent faculty could be assembled at the new university. There was some awareness, too, that the strength of a university is in large degree a matter of spirit and tradition and not to be acquired overnight. The founders, however, had an inspiring model in mind—Cornell University, a happy combination of the applied sciences of engineering and agriculture and the humanistic studies. They were even more fortunate in the selection of the first president, David Starr Jordan, an ichthyologist of the first water, a man of vision and initiative, forceful and compelling in expression both in writing and in speaking, at heart a poet, and an inspiring leader.

With its wealth, its dynamic head, and its fresh purpose, Stanford

University was likened to a giant meteor flashing across the western firmament. Lack of students was never a problem; the 1891 registration was a surprising 490, and three years later 1,100 were enrolled and growth continued. Notwithstanding its incomparable riches, Stanford did not immediately outshine all other American universities; the law of momentum, to which universities are particularly subject, would have precluded any such result. Furthermore, with the hard times following the Panic of 1893, it looked as though the university's wealth would evaporate. Mrs. Stanford came to the rescue, drawing on the estate left by her husband to round out the now meager income from the properties previously assigned to the university. In the intellectual life of the West, Stanford University quickly became an active factor. Life and study in the environment that it offered could be ennobling as well as quickening to the mind. President Jordan and members of the faculty took leading roles in public affairs. And the existence of Stanford University prompted those controlling the destinies of other California schools to improve their institutions.

The prime example of this response was in the revitalizing of the University of California during the presidency of Benjamin Ide Wheeler, 1899–1919. Aware that personal interferences by members of the board of regents had been a handicap to the institution, he conditioned his acceptance of the presidency on the board's adoption of a set of rules that he held to be "absolutely essential to the existence of anything like a proper university spirit, indeed, of a university." These were that the president should be the sole organ of communication between faculty and regents, that the president should have sole initiative in appointments, removals, and matters of salary, and that, however divided in discussions during meetings, the board as a unit should support the president. The balancing factor did not have to be stated—that should the board lose confidence in the president, it could have his resignation.

As the real leader of the university, Wheeler built soundly. The school of commerce and the summer session were early additions. Through an open contest the university had previously gained a comprehensive building plan, the work of M. Bernard of Paris. Although never to be realized in its entirety, this plan and the rapid increases in enrollment inspired active building. California Hall, Boalt Hall, the Hearst Mining Building, the Agriculture Building, the Doe Memorial Library, and Wheeler Hall all rose during Wheeler's presidency. Mausoleum-like in white stone, they seemed somewhat alien to the land, especially in contrast to the warmth of tile and terracotta in the Stanford quadrangle.

In addition to his talent for rallying support for the university, Wheeler offered it his personal philosophy. The phrase in which he summed it up was "the abundant life." He wanted the students while they were at the university not to be superficial and not to narrow themselves to a single specialization but to live abundantly. He wanted them also to prepare for, and to get into the proper frame of mind for, a lifetime characterized by this same breadth and depth. In his day the University of California faculty made advances in research and taught a great many practical and useful subjects. To Wheeler the things of greater importance were the kind of experience the students could be led to have and the outlook and inspiration that they could carry away. Therein he was in step with Jordan and the more thoughtful heads of other California schools of his day.

In another generation the fields of honor in a university would be the recondite and deadly sciences and the practical professions, such as medicine and engineering. Of the California faculty in Wheeler's day it is revealing that the brightest luminaries included, and perhaps were, a professor of English and a professor of history. Charles Mills Gayley had a long and fruitful career in research and writing. His popular lectures to the public and to undergraduates were his chief glory. He developed a course on great books long before their Chicago discovery, and it soon filled the largest hall and became a campus institution. Its only rival in popularity was H. Morse Stephens' survey of the history of the Western world. Both men mingled freely with the students; Stephens, as a bachelor living at the Faculty Club on the campus, had an advantage here. He was seldom mistaken for a profound scholar, but he had a great hold on the students which persisted with the alumni. When he died, the legislature adjourned out of respect to his memory; the Student Union building was named in his honor. Gayley and Stephens arrived independently at the pattern which they gave their careers. Both were exemplars of the abundant life that Wheeler stressed.

For Further Reading

EVELYN WELLS, *Champagne Days of San Francisco* (1939).

AMELIA R. NEVILLE, *The Fantastic City* (1932).

EDGAR M. KAHN, *Cable Car Days in San Francisco* (1940).

FRANKLIN WALKER, *San Francisco's Literary Frontier* (1939).

FRANKLIN WALKER, *A Literary History of Southern California* (1950).

HAROLD KIRKER, *California's Architectural Frontier* (1960).

IRVING STONE, *Jack London, Sailor on Horseback* (1938).

ANNE ROLLER ISSLER, *Stevenson at Silverado* (1939).

PAUL FATOUT, *Ambrose Bierce, The Devil's Lexicographer* (1951).

JOHN W. CAUGHEY, *Hubert Howe Bancroft* (1946).

CHARLES ALBRO BARKER, *Henry George* (1955).

LINNIE M. WOLFE, *John of the Mountains* (1938), John Muir.

HOLWAY R. JONES, *John Muir and the Sierra Club: The Battle for Yosemite* (1966).

W. A. SWANBERG, *Citizen Hearst* (1961).

R. L. DUFFUS, *The Innocents at Cedro* (1944).

CAUGHEY, *California Heritage*, 299–319, 330–43.

chapter twenty-four

Political Housecleaning

The richest thing in San Francisco was not shattered by the earthquake.
Neither did it shrivel in the fire. Nor did its market value diminish.
It is way above par. The spirit of the people of San Francisco today is
the grandest and most practically valuable asset which the
metropolis ever has possessed. . . .

It was agreed by the San Francisco Real Estate Board that the calamity should
be spoken of as "the great fire" and not as "the great earthquake."

San Francisco *Chronicle*,
April 21, 23, 1906

**1880
to
1918**

State politics in 1880 was at one of those peaks of exaltation with
all problems seemingly solved. The new constitution, elaborated
by the convention in 1879, contained, if not the summation of all
human knowledge, at least a working compromise on the issues
that had been central in the unrest of the seventies. Kearneyites and
Grangers found satisfaction in the provisions for a state railroad
commission and a board for tax equalization and in the prospect
of Chinese exclusion. Conservatives were relieved that the whole
program of the malcontents had not been carried into effect. With the
air cleared, interest in state government flagged.

Other factors prompted the disregard of state politics.
For one thing, California found itself on an economic upturn. The
pinch of hard times, which had contributed to urban and rural dis-

San Francisco Earthquake and Fire

Arnold Genthe

content in the preceding decade, was largely forgotten in the more prosperous eighties. For another, national issues absorbed much attention, what with Garfield's assassination; Arthur's Civil Service reforms; the "rum, Romanism and rebellion" campaign, in which Cleveland squeezed in ahead of Blaine, the "plumed knight"; much talk about tariffs, silver purchase, interstate commerce regulation, and trustbaiting; and international incidents concerning Venezuela, Samoa, and Hawaii.

State elections, meanwhile, seemed a subordinate branch of politics. Democrats and Republicans were alternately in office, but the margin of victory was usually slight and the distinction of party objectives not much greater. Few individuals were of sufficient importance for their names to intrude upon a general history. Washington Bartlett, who was inaugurated governor in 1887 with popularity unsurpassed, died in office just a few months later. His successor built up an unenviable reputation as the "Great Pardoner." The election of 1890 was supposed to hinge on the question of state division but, although the southern California candidate was elected, no steps were taken toward division. Four years later James H. Budd won the governorship by emphasizing that he was young, a graduate of the state university, and traveled by buckboard rather than by railroad.

Combating the Southern Pacific

Gradually local issues recaptured attention. As early as 1880 the settlers at Mussel Slough near modern Hanford in Tulare County were disillusioned concerning the effectiveness of the new constitution as a check upon the Southern Pacific. They had occupied and improved the land under what they thought were bona fide offers. On various pretexts the railroad delayed conveying title and finally quoted a price far in excess of that originally contemplated. The settlers demurred and began to organize for more effective protest. When the railroad attempted to get evictions in favor of two hired purchasers, Walter J. Crow and M. J. Hart, a clash ensued. In a few moments of gunplay Hart and five of the settlers were killed outright or given mortal wounds. Crow slipped away and hid in a wheatfield, but when he tried to climb the fence and get away he was picked off by an unidentified settler. Under indictment for resisting a United States officer, seven of the settlers were taken to San Francisco for trial. Five of them were convicted and sentenced to eight months in the San Jose jail. In the climate of opinion that prevailed they rather than the railroad emerged as heroic. Several crusading novels, including Josiah Royce's *The Feud of Oakfield Creek* and Frank Norris' *The Octopus*, seized on the Mussel Slough incident as a dramatization of the burning resentment against the railroad's heartless domination.

To what extent the railroad was guilty of the many malpractices charged is difficult to say. Denunciation of big business was then the national pastime, and, since it was by all odds the biggest of California's corporations, the railroad stood out as the natural target. On the other hand there was hardly an office, from the seats in the United States Senate down through the governorship and the courts to the most inconsiderable town office, in which the right man could not do the railroad a service. Suspecting the worst, critics charged freely and proved occasionally that California was governed by the Southern Pacific machine. The railroad became the stalking-horse of the demagogue and attack on it the touchstone of California politics.

Three times in the eighties and nineties the railroad's willingness to influence government was exposed with unmistakable candor: in the publication of the Colton Letters, in Los Angeles' fight for a free harbor, and in the defeat of the Funding Bill.

In the seventies David D. Colton had annexed himself to the Southern Pacific to the extent that its moguls were often referred to as the Big Four and a Half. As the phrase suggests, Colton never quite attained a parity with Stanford, Huntington, Crocker, and Hopkins, but he did enjoy Huntington's confidence, and the latter wrote to him freely and candidly about his experiences as a lobbyist in Washington. The partners went so far as to define the conditions under which Colton might join the inner circle, but at the time of his death in 1878 they were busily engaged in squeezing him out. His widow at first accepted a modest settlement, but, when she saw that identical securities in the Hopkins estate were valued at a much higher figure, she charged that she had been defrauded and brought suit to recover. Mrs. Colton's lawyers got little satisfaction for their client, but they contributed much to the entertainment of the railroad baiters and to the enlightenment of historians by reading into the record letter after letter in which Huntington had described with utter frankness his methods as a lobbyist. Some 600 of these letters were spread upon the court record ostensibly to demonstrate that Colton had been a key man in railroad councils. To the public, however, they were a devastating indictment of the railroad's chicanery.

The Free Harbor Fight

The free harbor fight is a longer story. Since Spanish days the inadequacy of the natural harbor at San Pedro had been recognized as a serious barrier to the development of Los Angeles. In the Mexican period hide traders did their largest business with the cattlemen of the district and imposed no price differential because of the atrocious harbor, but as an American city Los Angeles obviously could not go far without better port facilities. For many years Phineas Banning was the leading advocate and almost the only advocate of action. To him are credited most of the federal appropriations from 1869 to 1892. Aggregating more than $500,000, they were expended upon deepening, widening, and improving the entrance to Wilmington Estuary so that vessels of 18-foot draft could be accommodated.

As larger ships came into service on the Pacific, more heroic steps seemed to be indicated, and as early as 1881 there was a concerted demand for a large breakwater which would provide a deep-water harbor. The Chamber of Commerce endorsed the idea and several newspapers also took up cudgels in its behalf. Whenever an influential person visited southern California, the Chamber of Commerce would take him in tow and seek to impress upon him the merits of the harbor project. Senator William P. Frye of Maine, chairman of the Senate's Committee on Commerce, was such a visitor in 1889. To the discomfiture of the local boosters the Senator was not favorably impressed. He made embarrassing remarks such as: "Where are all the ships?" "You propose to ask the Government to create a harbor for you, almost out of whole cloth!" and "It will cost four or five millions to build you say. Well, is your whole country worth that much?" As crowning insult he suggested a removal of Los Angeles to San Diego's excellent harbor. After this contretemps the harbor advocates were greatly heartened by an appropriation of $5,000 the next year to finance an investigation of possible sites for Los Angeles' deep-water harbor.

Three sites came under active consideration. One was Santa Monica, which a Comstock mine superintendent and Nevada Senator John P. Jones had fostered as the seaport for what he thought would prove another Comstock Lode in southwestern Nevada. The ore output was not up to his expectations, and Jones was glad to sell the railroad line from Los Angeles to Santa Monica and the wharf jutting out into the ocean to the Southern Pacific. Redondo, a few miles to the south, was a parallel case. The monotony of its open beach was broken by a wharf constructed by John C. Ainsworth of Portland, and threading inland to Los Angeles was a narrow-gauge railroad. The other possibility, of course, was San Pedro. There nature had not been much more generous than at Santa Monica or Redondo, but the deep water, which a breakwater would make calm, was at least adjacent to the already improved Wilmington Estuary, and San Pedro was reached not only by the Southern Pacific but also by the Terminal Railroad, which would assure access for all competing lines. The commission reported in favor of San Pedro and estimated the cost of the proposed breakwater at $4 million.

Thus far the problem of the harbor advocates had seemed to be merely that of extracting an appropriation from Congress, and in view of the pork-barrel character of the biennial Rivers and Harbors Bill this did not promise to be a hopeless task. In 1892, however, Collis P. Huntington jolted Los Angeles from its complacency by announcing to a Senate committee that, since piles could not be driven into the rocky bottom at San Pedro, the Southern Pacific was abandoning that port in favor of Santa Monica. Army engineers were again dispatched to examine the sites and again reported in favor of San Pedro, but the Southern Pacific continued work on its million-dollar wharf at Santa Monica. The real explanation obviously was not any difference in ocean bottoms but that, owning all the ocean frontage below the Palisades at Santa Monica, the Southern Pacific had a sure monopoly there.

From this beginning the harbor fight widened and deepened. Huntington advised the Chamber of Commerce to abandon its "hopeless" advocacy of San Pedro, urged the Chamber to join forces with him to get an appropriation for Santa Monica, and reminded that he had "some little influence at Washington —as much as some other people, perhaps." He revealed that 83 members of the Chamber had signed an endorsement of Santa Monica, whereupon a poll of the members was ordered, the result being 328 to 131 in favor of San Pedro.

Organizing the Free Harbor League, Angeleños sent a barrage of letters to old neighbors and friends who were now representing eastern states and districts in the national Congress. With its population so largely and recently recruited from the East, Los Angeles was in better position to exert such pressure than almost any other city in the nation. The Santa Fe Railroad was also a potent advocate of San Pedro. Its $500 million investment, it represented to Congress, would be jeopardized if public funds were appropriated for the improvement of Huntington's private harbor at Santa Monica. Los Angeles newspapers, notably the *Times,* were actively engaged. Several eastern journals were equally outspoken; the New York *World,* for example, pointedly inquired whether this was "a government for the people, or a government by Mr. Huntington, for Mr. Huntington."

The Congress of 1896 being economy-minded, a $390,000 request for inner harbor improvements at San Pedro were judged all that it was politic to ask. When the Rivers and Harbors Bill came out of committee, however, it surprisingly contained a $2.9 million item for a deep-water breakwater at Santa Monica. In view of Huntington's well-nurtured prowess as a lobbyist this development was perhaps not so surprising after all, but it threw consternation into the San Pedro camp. The brunt of the battle was borne by Senator Stephen M. White, whose statue in consequence has long embellished the Los Angeles Civic Center. Before the Senate he berated government by special interest, debating the issue vigorously with Senator Frye, who had cast so many aspersions on Los Angeles' seagoing aspirations. The $2.9 million was voted, but still another commission was delegated to decide whether it should be spent at Santa Monica or San Pedro. The decision again favored San Pedro, and thus, with irony that was not lost on the Angeleños, the money Huntington had extracted from a parsimonious Congress became available for the harbor he opposed.

This was the real turning point in the fight, but Huntington had not exhausted his stock of obstructionist tactics. He persuaded the Secretary of War, Russell A. Algers, who was soon to acquire notoriety in connection with "embalmed beef," to delay the start on one pretext and then another: alleged sunken rocks at the harbor entrance, no money to call for bids, and so on ad infinitum. A Senate resolution failed to produce results, and not until President McKinley prodded him did he act. In the House in 1898 there was one more protest against the expenditure of public funds for a harbor when the Southern Pacific stood ready to build one free of charge at Santa Monica, but this suggestion was excoriated by Representative Harry A. Cooper of Wisconsin, and San Pedro was saved again. Finally in 1899 the President touched a button that was supposed to dump the first load of rock for the breakwater. The transcontinental hookup was faulty and the rock had to be dumped by hand, but the work at last had started. San Pedro had prevailed over Santa Monica and, more important, Los Angeles' deep-water harbor was to be its own rather than enmeshed by the Southern Pacific.

In comparison with later expenditures on harbor improvements this initial appropriation was small. By the 1960's the federal government had contributed an estimated $50 million for breakwaters and dredging. Through its Harbor Commission the city of Los Angeles had invested by that time some $126 million, and the city of Long Beach, blessed with large royalties on tidelands oil, had exceeded that amount in improvements to its harbor, protected by the same breakwaters. That is not to minimize the importance of federal aid. The beginnings and the manner of the start in developing a harbor at this location were fundamental. Establishment of a free harbor rather than one approachable only by a single railroad was an indispensable basis for the growth that has ensued.

To the railroad the Funding Bill considerably overshadowed the harbor fight. It proposed that the 30-year 6 per cent bonds which had secured the government's original subsidy be replaced both for principal and interest by 99-year bonds at one half of one per cent. This, of course, would have been almost tantamount to cancellation, yet except for three or four impediments Huntington would probably have succeeded in putting the scheme over.

One obstacle was the determined opposition of Adolph Sutro, Mayor of San Francisco. Sutro had become incensed because the street railway company of San Francisco, a Southern Pacific subsidiary, would not concede a five-cent fare to the gardens which he proposed to give to the city. More specifically against the Funding Bill, young William Randolph Hearst arrayed the power of his press. To Washington he sent acerbic Ambrose Bierce to train his brilliant and caustic pen upon Huntington and his Funding Bill. With Bierce was an expert cartoonist, Homer Davenport, who turned out a daily representation of Huntington in the act of despoiling the nation. Bierce is credited with defeating the Funding Bill, yet assists should be scored for the Colton Letters and the Los Angeles free harbor fight. Against such a background the Funding Bill had too rough a course to run.

At the close of the century Californians in common with other Americans had their attention diverted from local problems by Bryan's Cross of Gold speech, the blowing up of the *Maine*, Dewey at Manila Bay, Hobson at Santiago, and Roosevelt's Rough Riders at San Juan Hill. Not until 1901 did the Southern Pacific become news again. By that time Huntington, last of the Big Four, had passed on to his reward, and the Southern Pacific properties were gathered up by Edward H. Harriman and merged with the Union Pacific system, which he had just resuscitated. This concentration of more than 15,000 miles of track under one management paralleled the rise of other gigantic trusts, the United States Steel Corporation and the Northern Securities Company, against which Theodore Roosevelt's spectacular trust-busting campaign was launched. Repercussions reached California but, meanwhile, San Francisco's municipal problems held the center of the stage.

San Francisco Prosecutes Graft

As of the late eighties San Francisco public job holding was firmly controlled by a saloonkeeper, Blind Boss Buckley. He operated with a certain courtliness. Story has it that when a schoolteacher applicant was advised that a prerequisite was to take five gold pieces to the boss at this saloon, he picked them up and purred, "I can't imagine why a young lady like you is bringing me this present." He also was remorseless, as in the cashiering of the venerated John Swett as school principal in 1890. Buckley lost out, not to reform, but to another boss.

In 1901, after bitter turmoil between organized labor and the Employers' Association, Eugene E. Schmitz was elected Mayor of San Francisco as the standard-bearer of a newly organized Union Labor party. Schmitz' qualifications for office were not impressive, his previous occupation being that of theater musician, but he was reelected in 1903 and again in 1905. The admitted power behind the throne was a member of the San Francisco bar, Abe Ruef, and the Union Labor label, though still good for many votes, was something of a misnomer. Prior to the election of 1905 it was a recognized fact that the Schmitz government, or rather the Ruef machine, was in unseemly intimacy with established vice and guilty of corrupt practices. The would-be reformers, however, conducted so ineffective a campaign in 1905 that Ruef not only reelected his mayor but also carried into office for the first time his full slate of supervisors.

Throughout this half decade San Francisco had been growing even more rapidly than California as a whole. The rate of increase was approximately 10 per cent a year. Such growth naturally meant that public utilities would expand and that in the course of this expansion they would have to make franchise and other arrangements with the city government. Ruef's machine exacted tribute from saloons, gambling houses, houses of prostitution, French restaurants, prize fights, and the like, but its more ambitious levies were upon telephone, gas, water, and streetcar companies. Ruef's hand in demanding a payoff was oftentimes strengthened by an aroused public opinion as to what sort of expansion would be best. Thus, in the case of the United Railroads Company, its proposal of an overhead trolley system was violently opposed by Rudolph Spreckels, James D. Phelan, and other leaders in wealth and civic pride, who insisted that for beauty and for fire protection their city should have the underground conduit system along with Washington and New York.

Then came San Francisco's greatest ordeal. Early on the morning of April 18, 1906, there was slippage on the San Andreas fault, and the city and other communities north and south along the fault were struck by a severe earthquake. Fire broke out and, with water mains broken and pressure practically nonexistent throughout the city, the flames swept through four square miles including most of the business district. Some 400 persons were killed and 28,000 buildings destroyed. Thousands of refugees were evacuated; other thousands camped in Golden Gate Park.

Predictions were hazarded that the city would not be rebuilt and certainly that Market Street would not flourish again, but, almost before the ruins ceased smouldering, the work of rebuilding began. Two men took the lead: General Hugh S. Johnson, better known to a later generation for his place beside the blue eagle at the head of the National Industrial Recovery Administration, who headed the relief work of the United States Army; and E. H. Harriman of the Southern Pacific, who put every resource of the railroad at the disposal of the emergency workers. Aided by $300 million in fire-insurance payments, San Franciscans built their city anew, finding in the adversity a determination and a sense of civic pride which even they had not known to exist.

The earthquake and fire reversed the population trend in San Francisco, but the rebuilding that was necessitated presented even greater opportunities for the Ruef machine. Alleging that the earthquake had closed the cable slots, the United Railroads began substituting trolley lines on Market Street. Notwithstanding a wave of protest the city fathers granted the company on May 21 a blanket franchise to install trolley lines throughout its system. This affront to the popular will, together with a sharp lapse in police efficiency and lavish expenditures on the part of Mayor Schmitz and the $100-a-month supervisors, led to a mass meeting at which the Ruef machine was denounced and then to an announcement by District Attorney William H. Langdon that charges of graft and malfeasance in office would be laid before the Grand Jury. Langdon revealed that Francis J. Heney, who had made a reputation by exposing timber frauds in Oregon, had been taken in as a special deputy to direct the graft prosecution, that William J. Burns had been retained as investigator, and that Rudolph Spreckels had agreed to underwrite the necessary expenses.

The battle royal that followed had all the elements of drama. The machine struck the first blow by having acting-Mayor Gallagher remove Langdon as District Attorney and name Ruef in his place. Langdon, however, refused to vacate the office and Heney would not be dismissed as deputy. At the impaneling of the Grand Jury the presiding judge recognized the right of Langdon and Heney to proceed, and in another court they got an injunction against Ruef's attempt to take over the office of District Attorney.

The Grand Jury was not long in bringing in five indictments each against Ruef and Schmitz for practicing extortion against the French restaurants. Trial should have proceeded at once, but Ruef's lawyers, availing themselves of every possible stratagem, were able to delay it some three months. Meanwhile, the prosecution found proof that Ruef's henchmen, the supervisors, had taken bribes from several public-service corporations. Seventeen of the 18 supervisors signed detailed affidavits to this effect and repeated their stories before the Grand Jury, explaining how some $200,000 in bribe money had come to them: $9,000 from the prize-fight trust, $13,350 from the Pacific Gas and Electric Company, $62,000 from the Home Telephone Company, $85,000 from the United Railroads, and the balance from the Pacific States Telephone Company and the Parkside Transit Company. Thereupon, the Grand Jury returned 65 more indictments against Ruef and a lesser number against various persons for giving these bribes. On the extortion charge Ruef pleaded guilty, and Schmitz was convicted on the jury's first ballot.

Langdon and Heney next sought convictions of the bribe-givers. They were not surprised that these men brought to court an even larger battery of legal talent than had represented Ruef and Schmitz or that these lawyers again raised all possible objections to the Grand Jury that had returned the indictments. These attacks were fought down successfully in court, but not so the out-of-court campaign waged against the prosecution. Small newspapers in San Francisco and elsewhere in the state were subsidized to attack the prosecution. The San Francisco *Chronicle* came out with all manner of criticism, Hearst's *Examiner* systematically pilloried Langdon and Heney, Burns, Spreckels, and Phelan, and the Los Angeles *Times* savagely attacked Heney and his associates. Social distinctions were thrust upon the defendants—Patrick Calhoun of the United Railroads Company, for example, was inducted into the Olympic Club—and discrimination both social and economic was made operative against the prosecution.

Although the prosecution secured a conviction against Louis Glass of the Pacific Gas and Electric Company in the first bribe-giving case brought to trial, the tide turned rapidly. Tirey Ford, chief counsel for the United Railroads, was tried three times on three separate counts. The first jury divided; the other two returned verdicts of not guilty. That was about as close as the prosecution came to getting another conviction for bribe-giving. At several elections the people of San Francisco recorded a vote of confidence in the prosecution. Langdon was reelected district attorney in 1907, Judge Frank H. Dunne was reelected to his office in 1909, and Judge William P. Lawlor in 1912, but the main objective of Prosecutor Heney, that of procuring punishment for the men of wealth who had done the bribing, could not be attained. Spreckel's expectation that the trail would lead to William F. Herrin, attorney for the Southern Pacific and boss of its political machine, also was not fulfilled. On appeal, even the conviction of Louis Glass was reversed.

For a time it appeared that Ruef would also go scot free. The higher state courts, in decisions that must be reckoned very bad law, reversed the findings of the Grand Jury and the trial court and released both Schmitz and Ruef. The latter was immediately brought to trial on one of the bribery charges, and, when the jury divided, the process was repeated on another bribery charge. Midway in this trial Prosecutor Heney was shot down in open court by a juror whom he had challenged. In jail, this assailant was silenced by what may have been murder or suicide. With Heney unable to continue, Hiram Johnson and Matt Sullivan stepped into the breach and won a conviction. Ruef was sentenced to fourteen years in San Quentin.

Meanwhile, the prosecution was proceeding as best it could with the trial of Patrick Calhoun, President of the United Railroads. Calhoun's legal staff was even larger and more brilliant than that which Ruef had employed. To secure a jury, 2,370 veniremen had to be called and 922 examined, a process that took three full months. The trial itself consumed five months and eight days, after which the jury failed to agree. The prosecution began a second trial, but, before half a jury was impaneled, the election of 1909 intervened. Langdon declined to run again and it was Heney against Charles M. Fickert for district attorney. Fickert's election was perhaps not a valid index to San Francisco's attitude toward the graft prosecution and defense, but it was so interpreted, and thereafter no serious effort was made to secure convictions of any of the defendants. Over the protests of Judge Lawler the second Calhoun trial was terminated and the remaining indictments were dismissed.

In some respects the most striking features of the four-year program of graft prosecution had been the kidnapping of Fremont Older, outspoken partisan of the prosecution and editor of the *Bulletin*, the bombing of the house of Supervisor Gallagher, a key witness, and the courtroom shooting of Prosecutor Heney. This violence, whether or not directly instigated by the graft defendants, hampered the prosecution, even though it also enhanced it somewhat in popularity. With regard to the legal procedures themselves, a more prominent feature was the hamstringing of the prosecution by the refusal of many witnesses to testify, the departure of witness after witness from the state, the secreting or removal of much documentary evidence, for example, the cash book of the United Railroads, the subornation of witnesses, and the fixing of juries.

Yet all this pales into insignificance in comparison with the propagandist methods whereby public opinion in San Francisco was converted to sympathy for the defendants. In less than five years the determination to call to an accounting all those who had prostituted the city's government had softened into an attitude that it would be "best for business" to forget all about it. Any animosity left was directed against the prosecutors; they were held up to scorn as the vicious monsters. The tactics in the courtroom, in the press, in politics, in business, and in society whereby this was accomplished have been suggested. No better illustration could be asked than Fremont Older's sudden compassion for Abe Ruef and his agitation for a pardon after the latter had languished in San Quentin for twelve months.

Historians also, though admitting that more penitentiary sentences would have been in order, have usually been content to gloss the conclusion over with such innocuous platitudes as the assertion that "the political atmosphere of the city was cleansed" or that there was "a renaissance of idealism." The plain fact seems to be that the political atmosphere of San Francisco remained foggy, and so important a step as the cleaning up of the Barbary Coast was left for a later administration.

The Good Government Movement

Partly out of the San Francisco example and partly by independent origin, a movement for reform in municipal government cropped up in other parts of the state. In Los Angeles the spearhead was Dr. John R. Haynes. Some years earlier he had turned from medicine to real estate with substantial profit.

He also had become an ardent enthusiast for direct legislation. Almost single-handedly he saw to it that Los Angeles' new city charter, adopted in 1902, incorporated provision for the initiative, referendum, and recall. The first use of the recall seemed proper enough, to remove a councilman who had voted to award the city's legal advertising to the Los Angeles *Times* even though there was another bid $15,000 lower. Nevertheless, there were staid citizens who looked upon the experiment in thoroughgoing democracy as revolutionary and dangerous.

Direct legislation was merely one facet of the push for better government in Los Angeles, and many others in addition to Haynes took part in the work. Some of the interest in reform was traceable to the shortcomings of local officials, some to the disclosures in the muckraking literature then so popular, but much of it was in direct protest against the undisguised political control of southern California by Walter Parker of the Southern Pacific machine. A Good Government League was organized to work for a cleanup. In 1906 a slate of reform candidates was entered in the city election. On 17 of 23 positions the reformers were successful, though they did not beat the machine candidate for mayor, A. C. Harper. A year later, the *Herald* began an exposé of vice protected through purchased shares in nebulous oil and sugar companies. These engraved documents led to the mayor, set the stage for a recall election, and prompted Mayor Harper to withdraw from the race.

Other cities indulged in lesser reforms. Sacramento voted itself a new charter and employed the initiative to grant a franchise to the Western Pacific Railroad. Santa Barbara and Palo Alto adopted new charters, San Francisco adopted the recall in 1907, and in several other municipalities the trilogy of initiative, referendum, and recall was made available.

With so much reform in the air locally and Theodore Roosevelt chanting the same refrain nationally, it was natural that similar proposals should be made concerning the state government. Provocation was not lacking. James H. Budd had given the state a notably economical administration from 1895 to 1899, and George C. Pardee proved his integrity and his independence of machine politics and of the great corporations during his term of office from 1903 to 1907. On the whole, however, its state government was something in which California could not take pride. The legislature progressively and inexcusably padded its payroll. Legislative elections of United States Senators were handled on a frankly partisan basis with every indication of venality. Machine control of nominating conventions was particularly galling, notably at Santa Cruz in 1906, when the Republicans summarily shelved Pardee in favor of a more compliant tool. At this convention the most powerful boss was none other than Abe Ruef. Additional cause for dissatisfaction was provided aplenty by the legislature of 1907, which set a new record for wastefulness, unscrupulousness, and subservience to the machine. That gave the immediate impetus to the reform movement which culminated in 1910, but of course the legislature of 1907, the Santa Cruz convention of 1906, and the Senatorial deadlock of 1899 were only surface symptoms. Underneath ran a deeper current of resentment that the state was in the grasp of the machine set up by the Southern Pacific.

For many years certain Californians had been working for electoral reforms. Stuffing of the ballot box, sometimes through use of ingenious devices such as the false-bottomed box in which a quantity of ballots could be stowed, was frequently charged. Other irregularities included false counting, repeat voting, marching in hired voters, and intimidating honest voters. The voter supplied his own ballot or the party did. The party ballots were distinguishable by size and color, which meant that a watcher could readily see how anyone voted. Party ballots on occasion were counterfeited to benefit a particular candidate. Party nominations meanwhile were manipulated through the conventions and handpicked rather than representative.

As early as 1874 the legislature authorized parties to apply in elections to their conventions the safeguards operative in general elections. Because it was merely optional, this measure had little effect. Furthermore, the safeguards referred to were feeble protections. Other legislation followed, including introduction of the Australian ballot, provided by the state and marked in private and therefore secret. In 1900 a constitutional amendment offered a direct primary for choosing convention delegates. But not until the constitutional amendment in 1908 and supplementary legislation in 1909 did it become mandatory that party nominees be chosen by popular vote.

Other reform efforts were made in the nineties and in the following decade. Public ownership of railroads and utilities was one solution suggested, and at Fresno early in 1906 a Public Ownership Party was launched. It proved no more successful than the Iroquois Clubs organized in the Democratic party and designed to coerce that party into more progressive action. Another group of Democrats organized the Independence League and boomed Langdon for governor in 1906 but without success.

The Lincoln–Roosevelt League

The next year the Lincoln–Roosevelt League took shape. Plans were first discussed at Los Angeles by a small group assembled by Chester H. Rowell of the Fresno *Republican* and Edward A. Dickson of the Los Angeles *Express*. Formal organization, with Frank R. Devlin as president, was achieved at Oakland in August, 1907. The platform, in brief, called for "the emancipation of the Republican party in California from domination by . . . the Southern Pacific Railroad Company and allied interests, . . . the selection of delegates to the next Republican national convention pledged to . . . Roosevelt's policies, . . . the election of a free, honest, and capable legislature, . . . the pledging of all delegates to conventions against the iniquitous practice of 'trading,' " direct election of United States Senators, and direct primaries for the nomination of candidates for all state and local offices.

To rouse support for this program the League depended primarily on volunteer and personal work. Half a dozen newspapers, influential but not the largest in the state, supported the League from its inception. Besides Rowell's and Dickson's papers these included the Oakland *Tribune,* the Sacramento *Bee,* and Older's San Francisco *Bulletin.* Many smaller papers joined in and an official organ, the *California Weekly,* was launched. Even a few Democratic papers, such as the Los Angeles *Herald,* were cordial. Reform advocates organized clubs in almost every part of the state, and speakers headed by Chester Rowell carried the campaign from one end of the state to the other.

As a first major objective the League's executive committee focused on the election of 1908 and determined to win enough seats in the legislature to enact direct primary law. In the meantime, a few trial balloons were sent up in the shape of candidates in municipal elections, and as early as September of 1907 the first of these came in a winner, Clinton L. White, who was elected Mayor of Sacramento. The League gained valuable publicity at the special session of the legislature called in November of 1907, and the work of organizing and agitating went steadily forward.

In May of the following year the League sought to win control of the state convention to elect delegates to the Republican national convention. Since only a minority of the members of this convention were to be elected and the rest named by county conventions, the League was at a considerable disadvantage and did well to gain approximately 44 per cent of the seats in the convention. This percentage was not enough to enable it to name the state chairman or to control the state central committee or its executive committee, but at least the League members were encouraged to continue their war against special privilege.

Seeing the handwriting on the wall, the old political bosses had allowed the legislature of 1907 to propose to the people at the election in November, 1908, a constitutional amendment authorizing enactment of a direct primary law. Heartily advocated by the Lincoln–Roosevelt forces, this amendment carried by a large majority. The new legislature also was sufficiently Lincoln–Roosevelt that a comprehensive measure on the subject was enacted early in 1909. Since the direct primary had been regarded as the means for gaining all other reforms, there was some talk of disbanding the League. The vast majority, however, believed that the League faced an equally important task in the election of 1910.

For that campaign Hiram W. Johnson was prevailed upon to be the Lincoln–Roosevelt candidate for governor. He had built up a most successful legal practice and had greatly enhanced his personal popularity by volunteering to assist in the San Francisco graft prosecution after the shooting of Heney. He put on a whirlwind campaign for the Republican nomination, traveling some 20,000 miles by automobile, and this at a time when such travel was far more arduous than today. Everywhere he went Johnson reiterated his promise to "kick the Southern Pacific Railroad out of the Republican Party and out of the state government." He won the nomination handily and carried with him the League candidates for almost every nomination.

Although the Democrats had elected only one governor in the preceding 20 years, they managed to make the campaign of 1910 an interesting

Hiram Johnson Campaigning

The Bancroft Library

one. The liberal faction controlled the Democratic convention and against Johnson put up Theodore A. Bell, who had been the party's national chairman two years earlier. Bell and the Democrats could insist with a measure of accuracy that they were even more progressive than Johnson and the Lincoln–Roosevelt Republicans. History, as represented in previous platforms, corroborated Bell's claim, and current intentions, as represented by the platforms of 1910, were also not unfavorable to the Democrats. There were in fact some 14 major points on which the two parties made equally radical demands. These included initiative, referendum, and recall, regulation of public utilities, a nonpartisan judiciary, the Australian ballot, conservation of natural resources, segregation of first offenders in a reformatory, direct election of United States Senators, Asiatic exclusion, simplification and tightening of the administration of justice in criminal cases, government support for a Panama steamship line, government appropriations for roads, rivers, and harbors, votes for women, an income tax, and elimination of corrupt control, a euphemism for Southern Pacific machine control, of politics. With the voters it was not so much a question as to which group was sincere but as to which group would best be able to carry out the platform promises. By a margin of 177,191 to 154,835 the task was entrusted to Hiram Johnson and his Lincoln–Roosevelt cohorts.

Reforms Accomplished

To expedite the enactment of the many reform measures contemplated, the triumphant Republicans assembled immediately after the election at Santa Barbara and then adjourned to San Francisco, where a dozen committees were appointed to draft bills and constitutional amendments. Some legislators disapproved of this procedure, though a number of Democrats joined in. It served, at any rate, to give the legislature of 1911 a running start, and it went far toward enabling that body to enact, in the words of Theodore Roosevelt, "the most comprehensive program of constructive legislation ever passed at a single session of an American legislature." Even the opposition gave grudging recognition. The San Francisco *Call* continued to refer to the "Legislature of a Thousand Freaks," but the San Francisco *Chronicle* conceded that it was the most industrious legislature in the state's history and that most of the laws enacted were excellent.

Johnson deserves much of the credit. His inaugural address was a clarion call to progressives in both parties to fulfill the promises they had made. He injected a controversial note by urging that the state ballot be shortened and responsibility concentrated by instituting the appointive cabinet system for most of the state offices, and his advocacy of making the recall applicable to the governor and to all judges was also regarded as ultraradical. Under his dynamic leadership, however, the legislators set aside party jealousies. Insofar as they were constitutionally empowered, they enacted laws to carry into effect the Lincoln–Roosevelt program. To cover other points they initiated 23 constitutional amendments, on which the people voted on October 11. A short session gave effect to the amendments thus adopted.

Some of these measures, such as the workmen's compensation act and the law for the regulation of weights and measures, aimed at social betterment. Most were designed, however, to insure the voters effective control of the government and thereby make impossible machine-controlled corruption such as had prevailed. The creation of a new railroad commission was in some respects the most direct blow against the old regime, yet it was only one element in a much more comprehensive attack. The Southern Pacific, incidentally, made public announcement of its retirement from the political arena.

The Lincoln–Roosevelt or Johnsonian progressives continued in the ascendant for some years. In Johnson and his handpicked successor, William D. Stephens, they held the governorship for a dozen years, and throughout most of this period they had effective control in the legislature. Nevertheless, they were unable to maintain the pace set in 1911. Some legislation of importance was enacted at the next session, but thereafter the Johnson and Stephens administrations were relatively unproductive.

The main reason for this slowing down was that the Lincoln–Roosevelts had run out of ideas. By 1914 they had achieved practically complete success in translating their platform into law. Some of them envisioned other vital steps that might be taken—some, for example, were hard at work for public ownership of utilities—but the group was not agreed on a program for further action. Nor was public opinion prepared for it. Even with the most dynamic and purposeful leadership a few years would properly have gone to consolidating the gains already made.

On top of this factor there were great distractions. In 1912 the patron saint of the League, Theodore Roosevelt, broke with the Republicans and rallied his forces as the Progressive party. Most of the California progressives went along with him. In recognition of the strength of progressivism in California, Johnson was nominated as Roosevelt's running mate on the Bull Moose ticket. Because they still had control of the Republican party organization in California, the Johnson forces were able to keep Taft off the California ballot. As a write-in candidate he ran far behind. Roosevelt and Johnson carried 11 of the state's electoral votes and Wilson picked up the other two.

Four years later, when in theory, at least, the Republican party was reunited, Johnson won the senatorship by almost 300,000 votes, but the presidential nominee, Charles Evans Hughes, ran far behind and by 3,773 votes lost the state and the presidency to Wilson. Though an eminent figure, Hughes was a man of a good deal of reserve, coldness, and conservatism. He had shown no sympathy with labor and no appreciation of the achievements of the California progressives. Furthermore, when he made a campaign visit to California in August, he allowed himself to be taken completely in tow by William H. Crocker and Francis V. Keesling, Old Guard Republicans. On the train from Oregon he slighted Chester Rowell; in San Francisco he ignored Mayor James Rolph; and in Long Beach, though under the same hotel roof with Governor Johnson, he did not see to it that a meeting was arranged.

The Long Beach affront no doubt was unintentional, but Hughes' complete neglect of the Johnson wing of the party was so consistent that it inevitably gave the impression of being calculated. After the votes had been counted, the Old Guard Republicans threw the entire blame on Johnson, charging that out of vindictiveness he had not given Hughes' candidacy genuine support. Johnson angrily retorted that the Old Guard had so misused Hughes and his California visit that the injury could not be undone. Most of the contemporary and later discussion of this election concerns what might have been. The fact most clearly established is that the Old Guard alone could not carry California. Even with the advantage of the Republican label and of Johnson on the same ticket, Hughes needed to give more convincing demonstration of agreement with Lincoln–Roosevelt Johnsonian progressivism.

The 1916 campaign had another aftermath that illustrates a weakness among the California progressives. As a political move to appeal to the southern California voters, William D. Stephens had been persuaded to run for lieutenant governor rather than for reelection to Congress. The understanding was that if elected to the Senate, Johnson would resign the governorship to Stephens. Johnson, however, made no move to do so in November or December. In January, when the legislature assembled, he continued as governor. When some of Stephens' friends protested and intimated court action, it merely threw Johnson into choleric fury. He delayed his resignation until March when a special session of Congress was called and no alternative was left. This was one among a number of occasions when deep rifts developed within the Lincoln–Roosevelt group. Many, perhaps most, of these men were strong-minded individuals. Common cause had held them together for a while, but this was not an amalgam that would endure the fire of Johnsonian rage and vindictiveness.

For Johnson the Lincoln–Roosevelt League was a springboard to the United States Senate. On the whole, however, the leaders in the League did not move on to public office. Roused to political action by the manifest abuses in California government, they organized, campaigned, and captured the Republican party, and through it the state government. With systematic determination in the legislature of 1911, they enacted their program. Incidental additions were made in the years that followed, and by momentum the group retained control of the state government throughout the decade, gradually relinquishing leadership to regular Republicans who were less or not at all progressive. Lack of a program for continuing reform, the distractions of national politics and the First World War, and a series of personal quarrels within their ranks weakened the movement, but not before it had given the state a decade of remarkably high-minded and uncorrupted government.

Lincoln–Rooseveltianism was a reform movement that captured the popular fancy with unprecedented rapidity. Here were reformers who translated their theories into practice with unusual thoroughness and efficiency. They were most astute politicians. Californians rightly took great pride in this demonstration of political acumen and statesmanship, and the nation gave it an attention not completely distracted by the fiasco of Rooseveltian progressivism or by the First World War. It stands as a high-water mark in California's record of political achievement.

For Further Reading

W. H. HUTCHINSON, *Oil, Land, and Politics, the California Career of Thomas Robert Bard* (1965).

ALEXANDER CALLOW, JR., "San Francisco's Blind Boss," *PHR*, 25 (1956), 261–80.

EDITH DOBIE, *Political Career of Stephen M. White* (1927).

CHARLES D. WILLARD, *The Free Harbor Contest at Los Angeles* (1899).

WILLIAM BRONSON, *The Earth Shook, the Sky Burned* (1959).

MONICA SUTHERLAND, *The Damndest Finest Ruins* (1959).

WALTON BEAN, *Boss Ruef's San Francisco* (1952).

The Autobiography of Lincoln Steffens (1931).

GEORGE E. MOWRY, *The California Progressives* (1951).

SPENCER C. OLIN, *California's Prodigal Sons: Hiram Johnson and the Progressives* (1968).

JACKSON K. PUTNAM, "The Persistence of Progressivism in the 1920's," *PHR*, 35 (1966), 395–411.

CAUGHEY, *California Heritage*, 378–81, 394–97.

chapter twenty-five

Race Prejudice
and Labor Conflict

California was given by God to a white people, and with God's
strength we want to keep it as He gave it to us.

William P. Canbu, Grand President,
Native Sons of the Golden West,
April, 1920

The Anti-Japanese Movement

**1890
to
1930**

In the period spanning the turn of the century California experienced
a gratifying development along almost every line. Improved transportation, expanded agriculture, and increased activity in commerce
and industry yielded a substantial economic growth. The traditional
bulwarks of society—the home, the church, and the school—registered
noteworthy gains during the period. On the political front, too, it
was an epoch of truly remarkable achievement. In the light of all
these advances it is surprising and regrettable that these years are
equally characterized by bitter class conflict. Some of it was racist;
the greater part was in the area of labor relations and had as its crux
the question "Should labor be permitted to organize?"

Sun Rise and Mikado Restaurant Ads

Los Angeles County Museum of History

Sunrise...
Restaurant

I. INOSE, Propr.

209 East First Street
Near Los Angeles Street

Free Pudding For Dinner

Free Stewed Fruit for Supper

Nice Lunches Put Up to Order

Chicken Dinner Every Sunday 15c.

21 Meals Ticket $2.00

BEST 10 CENT MEAL HOUSE IN THE CITY.

...MIKADO...

..Restaurant...

HIDEO MUTA, Propr.

301 Commercial Street, Los Angeles.

Meals 10 cents with Wine and Ice Cream,
... Pie or Pudding Every Day ...

Turkey or Chicken Dinner with Wine and Ice Cream,
...or Pie Every Sunday. ..

One feature of this social conflict was a rising clamor for Japanese exclusion. Until the nineties very few Japanese had come to California. In that decade immigration was at the nominal rate of about 1,000 a year, but in 1900 entrants numbered 12,626, while the 1910 census showed a total of 41,356 in the state and the 1920 census, a total of 71,952. Representing only 2 per cent of the total population, this racial minority may seem too trivial to have caused much concern, yet Californians worked themselves up to a high pitch of excitement; a state historian in 1922, disturbed by the influx of Japanese and other foreigners, feared that California's most difficult task would be to remain American. California still harbored a remembrance of the long and bitter contest for Chinese exclusion, and many of the arguments employed against the Celestials seemed equally applicable against the Nipponese. Distinguishable by pigment, stature, conformity, language, and customs, they were regarded as not likely to prove completely assimilable. Furthermore, having congregated in certain localities, the Japanese were much more conspicuous than their actual numbers would have predicated.

As early as 1886, when there were only 400 in the state, the slogan "The Japs Must Go" was first voiced. In 1900 San Francisco was the scene of a mass meeting for a similar purpose. Five years later trade-union men there organized the Asiatic Exclusion League, and the *Chronicle* ran a series of articles advocating exclusion. Then, in 1906, the San Francisco school board precipitated an international incident by announcing that Japanese students, numbering about 90, would have to go to the Chinese school. After President Roosevelt intervened, this order was rescinded but only temporarily. With the doctrine of "separate but equal" the law of the land, the federal government could do nothing for California-born Japanese, but on behalf of those who were foreign-born the United States Attorney General brought suit against the school board. Mayor Schmitz went to Washington for a conference and a compromise was worked out.

The federal authorities, meanwhile, undertook to limit the immigration of Japanese laborers. Early in 1907 Congress legislated against the admission of Japanese from Canada, Mexico, or the United States' Pacific islands. Shortly thereafter Elihu Root and Ambassador Takahira drafted the Gentlemen's Agreement whereby Japan promised to grant passports to nonlaborers only, or to laborers who were going to join a parent, wife, or child, resume a domicile in the United States, or take possession of a previously acquired farm. So far as California was concerned this was a palliative rather than a solution. The smuggling of Japanese across the Mexican border continued, and the agreement itself contained loopholes for further immigration. Most colorful of these was the permission for Japanese to come to the United States to join their spouses. Under this authorization picture brides by the thousands entered California. Sociologically there was much to be said for the coming of these women, for otherwise the Japanese in the state would have been virtually under sentence of involuntary bachelorhood. On the other hand Californians denounced it as a subterfuge, were shocked at the high birth rate among the Japanese, and protested that the picture bride was usually another field laborer.

Japanese Packing Oranges

Los Angeles County Museum of History

Much of the talk about the menace of Japanese laborers was merely window dressing. Throughout the nineties and the following decade, when they were functioning primarily as agricultural laborers, the Japanese were accepted with a minimum of distrust. They did work that white workers did not want to do and were not generally regarded as competitors. Even the San Francisco school incident was very much magnified by the supersensitiveness of Japan and did not signify a unanimous stand against the Japanese.

Shortly thereafter the crusade against the Japanese mounted in intensity. By organizing and demanding higher pay, they incurred the displeasure of their employers. At the same time they showed an increasing tendency to move from farm labor to farming. In the rice districts of Glenn, Colusa, and Butte counties, in the Delta area, in vineyards and orchards around Fresno and Tulare, in Los Angeles and Orange County vegetable and berry gardens, and in Imperial Valley, Japanese growers such as George Shima in the Delta, who earned fame as the "Potato King," became more numerous. By 1920 the farmland owned or leased was set at 535,000 acres, much of it the most productive land in the state. This advance into the entrepreneural class put the Japanese into competition with established producers, and, though in the agitation that followed appeal was made to the old shibboleths against coolie labor, the drive came to be more against the Japanese capitalists.

The first major salvo of the campaign was the Alien Land Law, the Webb Act of 1913. The burden of this measure was that aliens ineligible for citizenship could not acquire farmland or lease parcels of agricultural land for more than three years. Ostensibly it applied to all Orientals and to other aliens who could not or would not seek United States citizenship; practically its appli-

417

cation was to the Japanese alone. The national authorities, as repeatedly before, became alarmed that the measure would jeopardize cordial relations with Japan. President Wilson sent telegrams to Governor Johnson and, while the bill was still before the legislature, dispatched Secretary of State Bryan to Sacramento to lobby for its defeat or modification. Despite this pressure, the legislature passed the bill and the governor promptly signed it.

Had the act been enforced rigorously, Japanese agriculturists would soon have been squeezed out. It developed, however, that there were many ways to escape its full rigors, through indirect leasing, incorporation, or vesting ownership in California Japanese who had already acquired citizenship. By the end of the decade the Japanese, still constituting only 2 per cent of the population, controlled more than 11 per cent of the state's agricultural land. California thereupon resolved to try again. The legislature in 1919 had before it a more stringent land law, which failed to pass only because Secretary of State Lansing certified that to offend Japan would endanger the peace negotiations at Paris. Deference to the makers of the Versailles Treaty was only a temporary staying of California action. The following year the State Board of Control published an elaborate and highly partisan report entitled *California and the Oriental,* which the governor prefaced with a fervid justification of the California attitude. Later in 1920 an initiative measure, approved by a majority vote in every county, tightened the restrictions. In 1952, after an interval of forty years, the State Supreme Court belatedly ruled the Webb Act unconstitutional.

Regulation of immigration, of course, was a prerogative of the central government. Californians were not reticent about proposing national legislation, and beginning in 1911 various measures designed to achieve exclusion were introduced in Congress. None succeeded until 1924 when Congress had under consideration a general curb on immigration. Californians, in what must be regarded as an excess of zeal, had written into this bill a provision forbidding the entrance of immigrants not eligible for citizenship. Translated into practical terms this meant no Japanese. Secretary of State Hughes urged the more diplomatic procedure of applying the same quota arrangement being set up for European nations, which would have worked out to admit only 246 Japanese a year. This counsel of tact, however, was set aside. Ambassador Hanihara protested that the measure would have "grave consequences." Congress took umbrage at this "veiled threat" and passed the bill promptly, and President Coolidge, though regretting the anti-Japanese clause, approved the bill as a whole. Needless to say, the Japanese entrants after 1924 were few and were considerably exceeded by the number departing. The California Japanese, however, 71,952 in number in 1920, increased to 97,456 in 1930, and declined to 93,717 in 1940. They continued to be prominent in the agricultural areas mentioned above, in flower growing, operation of vegetable markets, as residential gardeners, and in the fishing industry, especially at San Pedro.

The California campaign for Japanese exclusion, although generating more international friction than had the earlier move against the Chinese, was not accompanied by so much violence. It produced quicker action than had the anti-Chinese drive, mainly because the United States was concerned about Japanese immigration to Hawaii and the Philippines. Most Californians in 1940 were probably content that Japanese immigration had ceased. The more reflective, however, could not take pride in the methods whereby that end was achieved, nor did they subscribe to the alarmist arguments of the Anglo-American nativists of the teens and twenties. As for assimilation, the nativists certainly had been in error. True enough, Japanese blood was not disappearing in the general stream, but the more important process of cultural assimilation was taking place rapidly. By 1940 almost two-thirds of the Japanese were second generation Californians and therefore citizens, Americans in fact as well as in technicality.

Other Labor Recruits

With Japanese immigration forbidden and with most Japanese in California preferring to work for themselves, the state's agriculturists stood in need of a new supply of cheap labor. In the Filipinos they found such a supply providentially available, for raising the American flag over the islands had made the inhabitants nationals if not citizens. In 1923 some 2,426 Filipinos were brought in, and for the rest of the decade the number mounted until the total stood at about 35,000. At first the Filipinos were regarded as very good and docile workers. Within a few years, however, the pendulum of employer opinion swung against them. The accumulated criticism of earlier Orientals was applied against them, a few knifing affrays were magnified, and their association with white dance-hall girls was adjudged a scandal. Violence was inflicted on them, notably at Watsonville in 1930 and in the Salinas lettuce fields four years later. There was also a proposal for their exclusion, which in 1935 was achieved indirectly through a "free transportation" measure specifying that no Filipino who accepted free passage home could return to continental United States. Pursuant to this law thousands were deported.

The attitude toward the Mexicans went through a similar pattern of change. Until the late teens Mexicans were of little significance in farm labor except in Imperial Valley, but as the older sources of labor supply were cut off or proved inadequate, an increasing dependence was placed upon Mexicans. The year 1920 is referred to as a Mexican harvest, and throughout the twenties Mexicans were the most numerous element in California fieldwork. In the late twenties, however, Congress had under consideration bills to put Mexicans on the quota basis.

With the depression urban communities began to object more strenuously to maintaining aliens on relief through the winter so that they could work on the farms for low wages during the harvest season. Inspired by the Hoover administration's program in the early thirties to reduce unemployment by deporting aliens, Los Angeles County set in motion repatriation of Mexicans. In theory the operation was benevolent and it drew some cooperation from the

Mexican government. There were objections, however, that it was damaging to trade in Los Angeles' eastside barrio and that it was counterproductive in terms of goodwill in Latin America, which caused the Chamber of Commerce to withdraw its endorsement. After tens of thousands had been sent to Nogales and Juárez, these deportations ceased.

The next group given a twirl on the vicious circle of recruitment, low wages, hard working conditions, and talk of ejection and exclusion were the Dust Bowl refugees from the Midwest. These Okies and Arkies were not Orientals, but the cycle of changing attitude toward them was almost precisely the one previously enacted with the Chinese, the Japanse, the Sihks, and the Filipinos.

While other states from British Columbia and Idaho to Arizona and Sonora felt the urge for Oriental exclusion, the experience was not nationwide, or anywhere so pronounced as in California. Other local issues corresponded more closely to those of the nation, notably the one that was long the key social problem, the relationship of capital and labor.

Labor Versus Capital

Beginning with a printers' union in 1850, San Francisco added many labor organizations in the years that followed. These trade unions did much to stabilize wages and control working conditions, and they also brought to pass several items of labor legislation, including a mechanics' lien law and an eight-hour day in government work. In the troubled seventies labor's aims were unfortunately diverted to the crusade against the Chinese, but in the following decades, initially under the leadership of Frank B. Roney, attention was turned to more fundamental problems. Roney centered his efforts on the waterfront, notorious for shanghaiing and other abuses.

After a waterfront strike which failed in 1886 and a brewery strike and one by the metal workers, leadership in San Francisco unionizing passed to the Coast Seamen's Union, organized in 1885 and after 1887 with Andrew Furuseth as its mainspring. In the early nineties this union contested vigorously with an Employers' Association for control of crew hiring at San Francisco and all the other ports from San Diego to Vancouver in British Columbia. The union's chances were good until crimped by the Panic of 1893 and demolished by a bomb explosion at a nonunion boardinghouse. Who set the bomb was never discovered, but public opinion jumped to a conclusion and the Seamen's Union was years in reestablishing its strength.

When the Spanish-American War and the gold rush to the Klondike provided a new basis for prosperity, labor made another effort to strengthen its position. Again the employers were equally alert. The waterfront and seagoing workers joined in the City Front Federation, which soon was countered by the Employers Council. On July 30, 1901, the Federation called a waterfront strike, and a large number of sympathetic strikes soon followed. The employers with a war chest of $250,000 fought back. Altogether there were some 30 assaults reported and five men were killed. After three months the strike ended in a stalemate. The net effect, however, was advantageous to labor because of the continuing strength of the unions. San Francisco became a closed-shop city, the first in the nation. At the polls, too, the Union Labor party prevailed and held control of the city government for a decade.

Meanwhile, the scene of sharpest controversy had shifted to Los Angeles. The contest began in 1890 with a walkout of typographers on four newspapers which had threatened a 20 per cent wage cut. Three of the papers settled quickly, but the *Times,* commanded by the militant Harrison Gray Otis, would have nothing more to do with union printers. Nonunion men were imported, with the natural consequence of altercations both verbal and physical. Other unions expressed sympathy, and Otis expanded his diatribes to include not only union printers but everything that smacked of unionism. The unions attempted a boycott of the *Times* and of merchants advertising in it. Their campaign was more ingenious than effective, but against a less resourceful fighter than Otis and in a city more stable than Los Angeles it might have succeeded. Los Angeles was growing so rapidly that new subscribers and purchasers were constantly entering to take the place of those participating in the boycott, and the farming folk who comprised a good fraction of the increase were little disposed toward regimentation in the cause of unionism.

Taking advantage of the railroad strikes of 1893–94, which interfered seriously with the marketing of southern California fruit crops, Otis berated the unions for their "robber rule" and "organized despotism." He did not hesitate to vilify merchants who stopped advertising in his paper, and with others of like sentiment he organized an aggressive employers' union, the Merchants and Manufacturers Association, which soon had 6,000 dues-paying members.

The M & M had other pretexts for existence but its primary function was to combat unionism. In this battle it obviously had extraordinary powers of coercion, particularly upon businessmen who, forgetful of their class obligations, showed a disposition to truckle to labor. Bank loans could be withheld, settlement of accounts could be delayed, orders could be diverted to other firms, and a blacklist could be employed. The structural resemblance to labor's boycott is striking, but the effectiveness was considerably greater. The M & M, in fact, was one of the biggest guns in Otis' artillery.

Otis' pugnacious attitude was instrumental in making the Los Angeles controversy a national issue between capital and labor. There were other factors, of course, such as the wage differential as compared to San Francisco, which made Bay City employers and labor leaders desirous of seeing Los Angeles unionized, but it was largely because of the truculence of the *Times* that Los Angeles became the battle front for the nation's forces for closed shop and open shop.

A number of strikes took place with a full complement of violence and always with the *Times* a willing participant against the strikers. Then, in the summer of 1910 matters came to a climax with a strike of the Structural

Iron Workers, in which the local union was aided by a contingent from San Francisco. Strikers and strikebreakers slugged and blackjacked each other, and, when the city council passed an antipicketing ordinance and the Superior Court granted injunctions against the strikers, the police entered the fray. Hundreds of pickets were arrested and sentenced to a $50 fine or 50 days in jail. When jury trials were demanded, however, most of the strikers were acquitted, which encouraged the unions to believe that public opinion after all was on their side. The atmosphere, meanwhile, continued tense. Otis mounted a small cannon on his automobile, and the *Times* surpassed itself in derogation of the unions. Fomenting the excitement still further, the police reported discovery of unexploded bombs planted at the Hall of Records and the Alexandria Hotel.

In this atmosphere of hate and recrimination surcharged with hysteria Los Angeles was aroused just after one o'clock on the morning of October 1 by a series of explosions, their roar audible for 10 miles. The scene of disaster, it was soon discovered, was the Times Building. The explosions immediately turned the building into an inferno in which 20 men were killed and 17 injured.

From an auxiliary plant a few blocks away the survivors got out a morning edition in which the blame for the disaster was placed squarely upon unionist bombs. Police and grand-jury investigations, as well as special reports by investigators for the mayor and the city council, supported the opinion that the building had been dynamited. Labor retorted that the basement showed no effect of dynamite's downward action, that broken windows were conspicuously absent, that escaping gas had overcome several persons in the building during the day, and that because of his "criminal negligence" in maintaining a "gas-polluted fire-trap" Otis should be tried for manslaughter. People in Los Angeles and over the country knew not what to think, whether the cause had been dynamite or gas, and the majority answered the riddle according to their previous predilections for the *Times* and the open shop or for unionism and the closed shop.

Almost seven months later the *Times* blazoned forth with headlines announcing that the dynamiters had been caught and were en route to Los Angeles in custody of William J. Burns private detectives. Still more sensational was the identity of the men seized: Ortie McManigal and J. B. McNamara, apprehended in Detroit, and J. J. McNamara of Indianapolis. McManigal and J. B. McNamara were well-known union men, while J. J. McNamara was secretary of the Structural Iron Workers' Union. The *Times* did not play up the method of the seizure of the first two in Detroit, their conveyance to Chicago, and irregular extradition from Illinois, or the irregularities surrounding the extradition of J. J. McNamara from Indiana. Union sympathizers over the nation, however, well remembered the kidnapping of three other labor leaders in 1907 and their arraignment for a dynamite murder in Idaho. Prosecuted by William E. Borah and defended by Clarence Darrow, these men had been acquitted after a sensational trial. The secret arrest of the McNamaras had all the earmarks of another "capitalist conspiracy" and was denounced as such by Samuel Gompers of the American Federation of Labor, Eugene V. Debs of the Socialist party, and numerous other national figures.

The ensuing trial was much more than a personal and local issue. The American Federation of Labor retained Darrow to conduct the defense, and by appropriation and private donation union labor and its adherents supplied him with a quarter of a million dollars. The prosecution, similarly, had ample financial support from such organizations as the National Manufacturers' Association as well as from local interested parties. In addition, the trial had a political hookup. Job Harriman, attorney for the local labor council and an associate in the McNamaras' defense, was running for mayor of Los Angeles on the Socialist ticket. His candidacy was inextricably bound up with the insistence that the McNamaras were victims of an iniquitous conspiracy. Furthermore, victory in Los Angeles would be of inestimable value as a stimulant for the rising trend toward socialism then sweeping the country.

In October, 1911, the trial of J. B. McNamara at last got under way. Neither side seemed anxious to hasten its course. Darrow, according to the statement subsequently recorded in his autobiography, was convinced before the trial had started that his clients could not be saved. Delay, however, would enhance the Socialist–Labor chances in the election, while the prospect of Darrow's cross-examination of Otis and others was by no means reassuring to the prosecution. Consequently, though there was nothing on the surface to indicate it, settlement out of court seemed the best solution for both sides. Through the mediation of Lincoln Steffens a bargain was struck, and on December 1, to the stupefaction of all who were not in on the secret, the McNamara brothers appeared in court and changed their pleas to guilty. Two days later they were sentenced, J. B. to life imprisonment and J. J. to fifteen years.

Just why the defense took this course is not entirely clear. For socialism and for organized labor it was a most bitter blow. Instead of being swept into office as he confidently expected, Job Harriman was hopelessly snowed under in the Los Angeles election. Socialist candidates elsewhere were adversely affected, and the Socialist party never regained the strength or promise that it enjoyed prior to the McNamara confession. For the next 20 or 25 years the same can almost be said of the American Federation of Labor. For socialism and for the union, conviction without confession would have been a more satisfactory outcome, for then many would have believed that the brothers were really innocent. Darrow doubtless realized all this, but he may have believed it the only way to save his clients from the gallows. The McNamaras may have thought so too, for some most sinister rumors were being circulated, as of a Burns dictaphone installed in Darrow's office, and to this day it has not been revealed how conclusive was the proof amassed by the prosecution.

The McNamara case still has many mysterious angles. It is impossible, for example, to reconcile the statements in the McNamara confession with the description of the planting of the bomb as elaborated in the *Times* or with the version given to the *Saturday Evening Post* 20 years later. The participants in the deal that led up to the confession, though voluble on some points, have been close-mouthed about the most essential features and to a considerable extent have carried the secret with them to their graves.

The evidence is clear, at any rate, that the bargain turned out to be more one-sided than had been expected. The prosecution made no recommendation of leniency; the judge, who had been a party to the bargain and whom Steffens had advised to speak to the defendants "as one criminal to another," instead denounced them bitterly and sentenced J. J. to 15 years instead of the expected 10. Los Angeles capitalists, furthermore, did not take the steps of which Steffens had been so confident toward establishing a peaceful understanding with labor. With the wind taken out of the sails of the labor movement the employers pushed their advantage and were able to keep Los Angeles for some years longer the stronghold of the open shop.

The IWW and Mooney

Even before the McNamara case monopolized the headlines, the Industrial Workers of the World (IWW) had invaded California. Ridiculed as the "wobblies" and attributed the slogan "I Won't Work," the IWW was well fitted to implant ideas of labor organization in fields thus far neglected by the trade unions. Organizers, drifting south from the lumber camps in the Northwest, found willing listeners in California mine and lumber crews and in the agricultural labor gangs. Most of the workers involved were relatively unskilled, which placed them outside the preferred province of the American Federation of Labor and made a union's effectiveness uncertain, but the wobblies were not daunted.

In 1910 their local at Fresno reacted to interference with IWW meetings and launched a fight for free speech. The technique was simple. The wobblies got themselves arrested singly and in groups until the jail could hold no more. Wobbly endurance and willingness to absorb punishment were pitted against the capacity of the law enforcement agencies and the patience of the community. Capacity and patience were exhausted first. Antiwobbly demonstrators burned the IWW headquarters, and the police, exasperated by the wobbly ritual of singing in jail, tried to silence it with a fire hose. After months of strife, Fresno made partial concessions.

Two years later the IWW mobilized for a similar campaign against San Diego. There were very few wobblies in the vicinity and only a few thousand in the entire state, but, summoned by grapevine and moving in by boxcar, they rapidly converged on the city to reenact the Fresno routine of getting arrested and going to jail. The San Diego police inflicted rough treatment; one of the jailed wobblies was kicked to death. With police encouragement a vigilante group rounded up several hundred wobblies, ran them through a gauntlet, and drove them away. Governor Johnson then sent an investigator to the scene, and after a time the state lent its support to the principle of free speech. These free speech fights demonstrated the fanatical devotion of the wobblies to their cause. This fanaticism in turn gave them influence, especially among unskilled labor, out of all proportion to their numbers.

A case in point was the Wheatland riot in August, 1913. On the

Durst hop ranch near Wheatland some 2,800 workers were camped in unspeakable filth and discomfort. They had been recruited by advertisements for twice as many pickers as were needed, were paid wages that fluctuated between 78 cents and a dollar a day, were gouged by a company store, and were detained in the camp by a 10 per cent holdback on their wages. At that, conditions were not unlike those that had prevailed for years in California farm labor camps. In this camp an IWW local was formed by some 30 men. On August 3 they called a meeting to demand better living conditions. As the meeting closed, a sheriff's posse, accompanied by the district attorney, arrived on the scene and attempted to arrest Blackie Ford, the IWW leader and spokesman. A shot in the air, fired "to sober the mob," started a riot in which the sheriff, the district attorney, and two workers were killed and many others injured. Most of the workers fled the camp. The National Guard was ordered out and patrolled Wheatland for a week, while the Burns operatives combed the state for wobblies. How many were arrested no one has been able to compute because many were jailed without proper booking or were held privately by the Burns detectives. Herman Suhr, an associate of Ford's who had left the camp before the riot, was seized in Arizona, popped into a boxcar, and without formality of extradition shipped back to California. Eight months later Ford and Suhr were convicted on charges of murder and sentenced to life imprisonment. Though less famous, they are more genuine martyrs to labor's cause than the McNamara brothers could have been.

The Wheatland tragedy called attention to the plight of California's agricultural laborers. The state government was stimulated to begin regulation of labor camps. A Commission on Immigration and Housing was created with Simon J. Lubin as chairman, and working and living conditions were somewhat improved. Another episode drawing greater public attention to the problems of the unskilled and seasonally unemployed workers was the march of Kelley's Army on Sacramento. Modeled on Coxey's Army, Kelley's 1,500 men encamped at Sacramento to demand "charitable assistance." They were greeted instead by a pick-handle brigade which drove them across the river, burned their blankets, and denied them access to the city.

The First World War, meanwhile, was exerting new influences on labor–capital relations. In all quarters the tendency was to identify strikes with breach of patriotism. In Los Angeles, however, the war years witnessed a strengthening of unions, perhaps because business leaders had a more immediate interest in reaping profits than in keeping labor in check. In the north the war years were chosen as the time for a new campaign for the open shop, this time in the guise of a preparedness measure. This, in brief, was the psychological setting for San Francisco's Preparedness Day bombing on July 22, 1916, with its toll of 10 lives.

Union activists Tom Mooney and Warren K. Billings were arrested and put on trial. The key testimony against them was by an Oregon rancher who volunteered that he saw a party including the two defendants drive up to the curb at Steuart and Market and deposit on the sidewalk a battered suitcase

Tom Mooney in San Quentin

which contained the bomb. The defense offered testimony that Mooney and Billings were elsewhere, but the jury returned a verdict of guilty and the judge sentenced Mooney to death.

Labor partisans immediately charged that Mooney had been railroaded, and at the same time more neutral analysis cast doubt on the verdict. A deluge of protest came in, including a strong suggestion from President Wilson. Governor Stephens responded by commuting the sentence to life imprisonment.

Investigative work on Mooney's behalf brought to light a picture of Mooney on a rooftop some distance from the scene of the bombing with a clock registering a time that made it almost impossible for him to have planted the bomb. Police on traffic duty did not believe that any car had been permitted to make the described trip. Later it developed that the key witness had not arrived in San Francisco until after the explosion. His was perjured testimony, the only doubt being whether it was prearranged.

Motions by counsel for reversal and for a new trial were refused. Even after the jury and the trial judge publicly retracted their decisions and two of the three prosecuting attorneys recommended pardon, such action did not occur. For 22 years Mooney stayed in jail and his case continued to be American labor's leading cause célèbre.

Finally in January, 1939, when Culbert L. Olson took office as governor, Mooney was granted an unconditional pardon. Billings presumably was no more guilty than Mooney, but as a second offender he was not eligible for pardon. Nine months later by commutation of sentence he also was released.

The evidence has long since convinced historians that Mooney had not been proved guilty as charged. That conclusion was made all the more explicit a half century after the event in Richard H. Frost's meticulously researched *The Mooney Case* (1968).

As to Mooney, the hard-hearted have insisted that he was worth more to the labor cause in San Quentin than out. Be that as it may, his detention there long after it was clear that he had been convicted on perjured testimony was certainly not advantageous to the anti-union cause; the gentlemen of this persuasion might better have exerted their influence for his release.

Criminal Syndicalism and the Decline of the Unions

Immediately after the First World War the American people entered a period of particular hysteria. The tensions of the war were partly responsible. Resort to dynamiting as a means of persuasion toward unionism was another factor, as was the IWW's practice of sabotage, and by easy extension all Socialists were assumed to be anarchists and nihilists. With the Russian Revolution of 1917 engineered by men presumed to be of the same stripe, social conflict in America acquired an international overtone which suggested that world upheaval was the menace to be feared. The infamous Palmer raids and the unseating of the Socialist members of the New York legislature are two well-known consequences. California fell in with the hysteria with her accustomed vigor and, as might have been predicted in terms of prior episodes of social conflict, aimed retaliation primarily against unionism.

As modus operandi, the state legislature in 1919 enacted a criminal syndicalism law similar to the one with which Idaho had led the way two years earlier. The act defined criminal syndicalism in dragnet fashion as "any doctrine or precept advocating, teaching or aiding and abetting the commission of crime, sabotage . . . , or unlawful acts of force or violence or unlawful methods of terrorism as a means of accomplishing a change in industrial ownership or control, or effecting any political change." In terms of the act, guilt attached equally to doing the deed, advocating it, or belonging to an organization that advocated it. Penalty was set at imprisonment for one to 14 years. The California act bore general resemblance to those legislated by some 21 states, mostly western, and by Alaska and Hawaii. Elsewhere the acts soon became dead letters, but in California there was rigorous enforcement. In the first five years 531 persons were arrested, 264 were brought to trial, and 164 were convicted.

The most widely noted criminal syndicalism prosecution was of a respected philanthropist, Anita Whitney. In 1919, when the Socialist party local of which she was a member broke off and joined the Communist Labor party, she went as a delegate to a state convention in Oakland. At the convention, open to reporters and the public, she took a strong stand against revolutionary unionism and in favor of working for reform through the ballot. The state convention, however, voted a preference for the other method. It also gave pro forma approval to the national convention's program, which in passing included endorsement of the IWW. Three weeks later Miss Whitney was arrested for violation of the criminal syndicalism law.

In the protracted trial the bulk of the evidence adduced concerned alleged atrocities committed by the IWW. On the basis of her attendance at the state convention of the Communist Labor party, which approved the national convention's program and thereby endorsed the IWW, she was convicted of the felony of association with a group which advocated, taught, or aided and abetted criminal syndicalism. Appeals kept this case in court until 1927 when the United States Supreme Court by a split decision upheld the conviction. Foiled on that front, Counsel John Francis Neylan urged Governor C. C. Young to issue a pardon. Impressed by this appeal and by the dissenting opinion of Justice Brandeis and convinced that Miss Whitney, "lifelong friend of the unfortunate," was "not in any true sense a criminal," the governor decided that "to condemn her to a felon's cell" was "absolutely unthinkable." Instead, he issued a pardon.

Practicing idealists from the upper strata could be caught in the coils of the criminal syndicalism act. Members of various unions as well as of left-wing political groups also were jeopardized. Its most frequent targets, however, were the IWW members. They constituted the bulk of the persons arrested, tried, and convicted. In the free-speech fights, on charges of sabotage, and on other charges, the wobblies had seen a great deal of the courts prior to the enactment of this particular law and on the whole had little confidence in them. They seldom carried their disdain so far as the 53 "Silent Defendants," indicted earlier in 1919 for mass trial at Sacramento, who declined to attempt any defense. Many a wobbly, however, pleaded his own case, and, even when there was counsel, the main batteries of legal talent were always with the prosecution. In these trials it became almost impossible to present defense witnesses, whereas the prosecution again and again relied on Elbert Coutts, W. E. Townsend, and John Dymond, professional witnesses. Furthermore, in the temper of the times mere membership in the IWW or association with it was regarded as felonious. Ease of obtaining convictions undoubtedly explains the frequency with which this particular charge was brought.

In 1923, when the IWW called a waterfront strike at San Pedro, the immediate response was to invoke the criminal syndicalism law against the strike leaders. Attempts to suppress the strike by direct action followed. There were wholesale arrests; one haul was variously estimated at 700 to 1,200 men taken off to stockades in Griffith Park. When Upton Sinclair came to a strike meeting and started to read the Constitution of the United States, he and his companions were arrested and jailed. Within a month the strike was called off. The Sinclair episode led directly to the founding of the southern California branch of the American Civil Liberties Union, an affiliate that would rival the national office in number of actions taken to court.

Resentment against the IWW continued, in fact, mounted. In March, 1924, the Ku Klux Klan demonstrated against it. Other incidents followed, including a sacking of the IWW headquarters, a vigilante assault on a benefit party in which a number of children were beaten and tortured, and a tarring and feathering of several of the leaders. After 1924 the IWW ceased to be a power at San Pedro, though its influence lived on in other waterfront and maritime unions. Its hold on farm and forest laborers also declined rapidly, partly because of pressures from without and partly because of dissensions within.

At about the same time public opinion took a turn against the criminal syndicalism statute. J. W. S. Butler, president of the State Bar Association, David Starr Jordan, Max Radin of the University of California Law School, and other responsible citizens urged its repeal. It was not removed from the statute books, but after 1924 actions under it ceased for the time being. It was not revived until the late sixties, and then survived only on appeal. The major reason may well have been that the IWW was no longer the threat it once had seemed to be.

Throughout the twenties the general tenor of labor–capital relations was one of greatly diminished strength for unionism. Following the defeat of a waterfront strike in 1919 and a building-trades strike in 1921, San Francisco was more open shop than closed. In Los Angeles unionism declined at about the same rate and some of the accompanying features eclipsed the plain fact. The meretricious label "American plan" supplanted the term "open shop," the menace of Red Russia was taken very seriously, property rights were exalted as the citadel of patriotism, and organizations such as the Better America Federation made anti-liberalism and anti-unionism the prime virtues. The decade ended with unionism and liberalism at low ebb.

For Further Reading

Roger Daniels, *The Politics of Prejudice: The Anti-Japanese Movement in California* (1962).

Thomas A. Bailey, *Theodore Roosevelt and the Japanese-American Crisis* (1932).

Carey McWilliams, *Prejudice: Japanese Americans, Symbol of Racial Intolerance* (1945).

Paul S. Taylor, *Mexican Labor in the United States* (1929).

Carey McWilliams, *North from Mexico* (1939).

Hyman Weintraub, *Andrew Furuseth, Emancipator of the Seamen* (1959).

Louis Adamic, *Dynamite* (1929).

Wallace Stegner, *The Preacher and the Slave* (1950).

Robert H. Frost, *The Mooney Case* (1968).

Eldredge F. Dowell, *Criminal Syndicalism Legislation in the United States* (1939).

Caughey, *California Heritage*, 385–94, 397–403.

chapter twenty-six

The Boom of the Twenties

You know, I think we put too much emphasis and importance and advertising on our so-called High standard of living. I think that "High" is the only word in that phrase that is really correct. We sure are a-living High.

Will Rogers

1914 to 1930 Since the gold discovery gave its fillip, California has enjoyed practically uninterrupted growth. There have been intervals of hard times, such as in the nineties, but every successive census has shown a population increase and the other indexes have moved constantly upward. More dramatically, the steady climb has been punctuated by spurts of very rapid growth. One such was touched off by gold; another came with the boom of the eighties; still another arrived in the aftermath of the First World War and was most pronounced in the twenties.

In 1914 the state's population was less than three million. By 1930 it was five and two-thirds million, by 1940 just short of seven million. The statistics on bank clearings, postal receipts, freight shipments, property assessments and tax receipts, building permits, crop harvests, and industrial production advanced even more. This rapid

Traffic Congestion, Downtown Los Angeles, 1925

Title Insurance and Trust Company, Los Angeles

growth, furthermore, involved a wholesale transformation. By 1940 the majority of Californians lived in dwellings constructed within the quarter century, did business in buildings equally recent, and moved about on a network of paved streets and highways that had not existed in 1914. For a few commodities like gold, wheat, and beef, the aggregate totals for pre-1914 production were not matched in the span between 1914 and 1940. For other old standbys, including oranges, walnuts, wines, and deciduous fruits, the output of this quarter century surpassed that of all the preceding years. For another long list, including cotton, moving pictures, head lettuce, airplanes, and raisins, the years this side of 1914 were the only ones of importance. These new products suggest that the economic development of this more recent period was not a mere automatic outgrowth of the processes initiated by the historic heroes from Serra and Anza to Stanford and Huntington. The new era gave promise of earning eventual recognition as the most significant thus far in the pageant of local history.

The Automobile Age

The new day is perhaps best characterized as the automobile age. The preceding years had belonged to the railroad; now the motorcar was in the ascendant. In car manufacture California lagged far behind Michigan and its neighboring states and consequently did not generate any great corporation of its own comparable to the Central Pacific–Southern Pacific Railroad. Through local emphasis on designing and building racing cars it did contribute to the evolution of the automobile. In the matter of using the new machines, furthermore, Californians yielded to none. Here the contributions are even more notable, including the center line that bisects highways the world over and the automatic traffic signal that also has become universal in distribution.

As the most avid of car users, Californians geared their culture to the machine in a degree unexceeded. Los Angeles citizens, to cite one example, became more dependent on their private automobiles to get to work and play than did the inhabitants of any other city, and the University of California at Los Angeles earned the doubtful distinction that a larger fraction of its faculty and students drove daily to and from its campus than was the case with any other reputable university. In 1936 California exceeded even New York in the number of fatalities charged to the automobile. Pleasanter clues may be mentioned. Radio came to the state virtually as an automobile accessory, with the first large stations controlled by the Packard and Cadillac distributors, and an automobile club organ, *Westways*, ranked as the best California monthly.

This enthusiastic reception came in spite of the fact that acquisition and operation of automobiles were not entirely easy. California car registrations were surprisingly large in view of the price differential of $150 to $300 maintained against western purchasers under the guise of rail freight charges from Detroit. Even after assembling plants were put in operation at Oakland, Long Beach, and Los Angeles this charge was maintained. California's urban parking facilities were by no means ideal; her streets were originally laid out for horse and buggy traffic. The San Francisco Bay barrier to vehicular circulation was conquered only in part by ferries and bridges, and after a quarter century of construction the state's network of paved highways was still less extensive than those of several more compact states, such as New York, Illinois, Pennsylvania, and Ohio.

Offsetting these disadvantages were numerous favorable conditions, in particular the benign climate, which imposes no closed season for automobile use. Large-scale production of petroleum made for a reasonable gasoline price. A most conservative height limit for office buildings and the preference for individual houses rather than apartments promoted in Los Angeles a tendency to spread out. In this city and elsewhere throughout the state, population grew more rapidly than existing systems of public transportation could be expanded to meet the demand, and dependence on private automobiles seemed a simpler solution. The automobile, at any rate, became an integral element, if not the dominant note, in the California scene.

Many of the consequences seem to have been inevitable or were a part of the national experience. Every American soon took it for granted that a large fraction of any city's police force would be assigned to traffic duty, that state troopers, officers, or rangers would patrol the highways by motorcycle, that state and local governments would spend more for highway construction and maintenance than for any other function except public education and perhaps relief, and that there would be a garage with every house and a filling station at every other corner. California lived up to this standard, if not beyond it, and, when a historian or sociologist arises to assess the role of the automobile in American civilization, this state should provide many of the more striking illustrations.

Passing notice should be accorded several industries subsidiary to the automobile, such as the manufacture of Portland cement. This product, of course, has a variety of uses. It goes into sidewalks and foundations, by the carload into steel-skeletoned business blocks and factories, and by the trainload into such structures as Boulder Dam. Nevertheless, it was the demand for paving material that maintained California cement manufacturers a comfortable second to Pennsylvania's through the thirties with annual production at times mounting as high as 13 million barrels.

Advertising California

Advertising of the booster sort, often branded as ballyhoo, was another prominent characteristic of the period. Earlier enthusiasts, newspaper editors, railroad land agents, and chambers of commerce had established a tradition of proclaiming California's advantages. Such organizations as Californians, Inc., and the All-Year Club expanded this art and obtained city, county, and state funds allotted to finance such promotion efforts. Whereas the stress was once upon getting agriculturists to move to California, the emphasis now shifted to persuading industries to locate new plants on the west coast, opening new markets for California products in the East or abroad, bringing conventions to California cities, and promoting tourist travel into the state. The time-honored devices of illustrated brochures, special editions of newspapers, and dissemination of booster literature continued; and in the moving pictures those who would make California appear at her most glamorous found an invaluable ally.

Two other advertising media proved effective. One was annual celebrations, such as Santa Barbara's summer fiesta, the Salinas rodeo, and the San Bernardino Orange Show. Most famous and most successful were Pasadena's Tournament of Roses and the Rose Bowl game, the latter flattered by imitation all across the continent. Special celebrations, though less numerous, were even more pretentious. In beautiful Balboa Park, San Diego staged the Panama–California Exposition in 1915, and San Francisco celebrated the completion of the canal with an even larger display, the Panama–Pacific Exposition. In 1932 Los Angeles hosted the Olympic Games, and, in 1939 and in 1940 on an island created for the purpose in the bay just north of Yerba Buena, San Francisco signaled the completion of her great bridges with the Golden Gate International Exposition. How many visitors were brought to the state by these special attractions would be difficult to measure, for the standard inducements such as Yosemite and the big trees, Death Valley, Catalina, San Francisco, and Hollywood drew large numbers even in exposition years.

In the longer view the fairs and the parades were only surface waves on a much deeper current. They were for the most part merely excuses to visit California, and probably second in frequency of effectiveness to something much more prosaic, the excuse of visiting friends or relatives. With California's population drawn so largely from outside its borders, the number of persons who could avail themselves of this excuse was legion. For some, doubtless, it was the real reason for a trip to California; for a larger number, however, the impulse was more profound. The majority set out not merely to see Treasure Island or Uncle Henry but for a look at Hollywood and Yosemite, for a taste of the California sunshine, a glimpse of orange trees in blossom and in fruit, and for a sample of the life abundant for which California had become a synonym. Thus did advertising bear fruit, or, if you please, the truth came into its own. For a quarter century, at any rate, one of the steadiest and most profitable California crops was the tourist crop. As in the preceding generation, those who visited were very apt to want to stay, and tourists thus were important not only for the money they spent and for the business they created but also for their contribution to the increasing permanent population.

These elements were among the more conspicuous characteristics. It may be objected that they are unsubstantial, that the state was not assured of prospering just because hordes of persons came flocking in, because the whole population was seized with a frenzy for gadding about in motorcars, because advertising budgets reached new highs, or because the state's recreational opportunities gained wider recognition. As a matter of fact, these elements form a sounder economic base than might be assumed. Although Californians could hardly make a living by washing one another's cars, with so large a population hundreds of thousands could be engaged in the service occupations as grocers and haberdashers, as druggists and bankers, as salesmen and clerks, as lawyers, teachers, physicians, dentists, and barbers. Thanks to the funds of the tourists and to a considerable income from investments outside the state, California could afford a larger budget for "non-productive" service and distribution than the average commonwealth. Enterprises unquestionably "productive" more than kept pace.

First Place in Agriculture

Among these the advance of agriculture is noteworthy. In 1909, a representative year toward the close of the second American generation, the total value of California field crops was calculated at $95,757,000 and of fruit crops at $48,718,000. By 1937 the total figure had advanced to $648,200,000, which put California first among the 48 states. This phenomenal advance was achieved through far-reaching alteration of the crop list and by innovations of method in several of the older branches of agriculture. Certain crops, such as the grains, shared in this advance hardly at all. Others, like potatoes, sugar beets, and alfalfa, advanced as much as 150 per cent in the three decades, but without keeping pace with the industry as a whole. Most of the increase is accounted for by expansion of orange raising and wine production and by several crops insignificant prior to 1914.

The California orange since the seventies had been the winter-ripening navel, but early in the new century growers began to set out Valencias. The new variety possessed several points of superiority, not least of which was that it ripened in the summer when the nation's appetite for cool drinks was at its best. The two varieties made available a year-round supply of California oranges, which fell in line admirably with the marketing program of the Fruit Growers' Exchange. By the early twenties the Valencia had caught up with the navel and thereafter continued to gain steadily until in 1936 the acreages were 143,000 and 88,000, respectively. In 1909 the value of the orange crop was put at $12 million. In the thirties, despite adverse prices, there were several $100 million years, and acreage and total production still increased.

Most of the expansion of orange plantings was predicated on uninterrupted prosperity. When the depression of the thirties slashed prices 60 per cent or more, the growers faced serious difficulty. A satisfactory remedy was not easy to find. Production costs, including irrigation, fertilizing, spraying, and orchard heating, were more or less fixed, and production itself was not subject to annual control by such devices as plowing under every fourth row. The Exchange continued its efforts to expand the market, but the main reliance was upon the prorate, a device to regulate the quantity of fruit offered for sale. By this method, which entailed destroying quantities of good fruit, the industry bolstered its price structure, though according to the growers' definition, prices were still too low. It is a narrow and artificial view, however, to judge an industry solely in terms of the money value of its product. The more significant criterion for the orange business is its phenomenal increase in acreage, production, and consumption, not only in the prosperous twenties but also in the hard times of the thirties.

On a smaller scale the walnut growers enacted the same drama. From very modest beginnings in the prewar era they expanded their plantings so that the annual crop approached 100 million pounds. This, they found, was somewhat more than could be marketed, and through their Exchange they, too, attempted to set up a prorate to peg the price above the cost of production. In size the walnut industry compared with the orange industry approximately as does a walnut with an orange. The walnut, however, was not to be despised; 100 million pounds of walnuts was a considerable quantity in the twenties and thirties, surpassing in value the total crop production of New Hampshire, Vermont, Rhode Island, Delaware, Nevada, or Wyoming.

Viticulture ranked as the second branch of California agriculture. Building on the Spanish foundation and benefiting from the new varieties imported by Agoston Haraszthy in the fifties and from the experience gained by the pioneer vineyardists in succeeding decades, the industry became one of California's most distinctive and at the same time most successful. In 1918 the Eighteenth Amendment threatened the vineyardists with ruin, for up to that time by far the largest fraction of California grapes had gone into wine. Long before repeal the wine market was reentered through the sale of "grape concentrate" and "wine bricks" from which wine of a sort could be concocted in the home.

Meanwhile, the vineyardists set out to sell their produce in two other guises, as table grapes and as raisins. The former had long been esteemed in the local markets; now refrigeration and rapid transit made it possible to whisk them across the continent to eastern markets. Raisins, on the other hand, had been so indifferent in quality that they were practically unmarketable. Dried grapes was their unappetizing name. A modern triumph of the industry was the introduction of better methods of manufacture and the stimulation of sales under the Sun Maid label and organization. Science was enlisted to assist other branches of viticulture, particularly for the improvement of wine-making processes, and the gains were less spectacular chiefly because the start was not from zero as it was with raisins. By the late thirties wine grapes, table grapes, and raisins brought California vineyardists an annual income of approximately $50 million. In 1937 the state produced almost two and a half million tons, or 90 per cent of the nation's total.

The list of crops in which California by that time led the nation is by no means ended. In fruits for canning and drying she was easily first. The peach crop exceeded the total for the next 10 states on the list, and domination in apricot production was still more pronounced. The pear crop was a trifle larger than the Oregon–Washington total and almost as large as the total for the other 45 states. The prune, once regarded as being as plebeian as the dried apple, was another California specialty. Production mounted steadily throughout the thirties, as well as the twenties, until the annual output reached half a billion pounds. At the same time, improved techniques in drying made the prune a much more delectable morsel and removed much of the stigma that used to be attached to it.

Although they doubtless will never rise to first place in national production, California apples reached the $10 million class in the twenties. The potentialities appeared greater for certain subtropical fruits. Figs had been raised for many years. The date palm was introduced by the Spanish missionaries as a decorative tree, but commercial plantings were of little significance until this century. The avocado, a still more recent importation from Mexico, gained popularity rapidly. Miscellaneous groves of olives, almonds, cherries, and the like aggregated still another $10 million annually. The grand total was a diversified yet specialized fruit industry comprising almost half of the state's crop production.

In field crops, likewise, phenomenal expansion characterized the period. Truck gardening, which had flourished earlier for the supply of the local market, led in the expansion. The state's increased population and the trend toward a larger per capita consumption of vegetables would have permitted a trebling of production. That the increase was much greater was because a nationwide market was opened by the twin devices of canning and refrigeration. Canneries operated before 1914 but with disturbing uncertainty as to the quality of output. Only more recently were processes perfected to insure standardized and palatable products. Refrigerated cars to make possible Atlantic seaboard delivery of Salinas Valley lettuce, Imperial Valley cantaloupes, or Tagus Ranch pears were a new facility. On this multiple basis California advanced to first place in production of tomatoes, lettuce, asparagus, artichokes, cantaloupes, carrots, cauliflower, celery, peas, and garlic. Truck farmers were capitalizing on California's long season which makes possible several harvests, the early season which gives her first call on the eastern markets, and the boon of irrigation which accounts for much of the uniformity in size and the attractive appearance of California vegetables.

In the Sacramento Valley, Japanese introduced the cultivation of rice. The acreage was smaller than in Louisiana, Texas, or Arkansas, but the yield per acre was the highest in the United States and placed California third in production. In 1937 the harvest exceeded 10 million bushels. The reclaimed swamp land on which the rice plantations were located soon ranked with the most valuable farm land in the state.

Another lusty upstart was cotton. Early experiments had been made in the sixties and seventies but with disappointing result. In 1910 a fresh attempt was made with a new variety, the Acala. Results were more encouraging, and, when World War I boomed the market, plantings were greatly increased in Imperial Valley, Riverside County, and the southern part of the San Joaquin Valley. Largely because the plantings throughout were restricted to the single variety, thereby avoiding mongrelization through cross-pollinizing, the yield per acre was more than twice the national average and because of longer staple the price was better too. Cotton became a $40 million crop, which put California ahead of Oklahoma, Missouri, Tennessee, Virginia, and Florida and within challenging distance of such cotton-kingdom strongholds as the Carolinas, Georgia, Alabama, and Louisiana.

The remaining third of California agriculture centered on livestock and poultry. Dairying headed this division, consuming the larger share of the state's $50 million alfalfa crop, and producing enough milk and cream, butter and cheese, ice cream and condensed milk to meet the major requirements of the state's population. As a dairy producer California by 1940 was surpassed only by some eight states clustered around Wisconsin. Meat production was second to dairying on California stock farms. Although the state lagged far behind Texas in cattle and Iowa in hogs, and although East Los Angeles and South San Francisco did not rank with South Chicago or Kansas City in meat packing, California had more cattle than any state in the old South or west of Kansas. In wool production its rank was third. Poultry raising was much emphasized, with many turkey ranches in the semiarid south and with myriad chicken ranches all over the state. Petaluma and San Fernando were the egg centers par excellence, but the standardized and streamlined versions of the old-fashioned hen-roost were encountered almost everywhere. In 1929 the egg count was 159 million dozen.

In butter and eggs, meat and potatoes, cabbage, onions, and numerous incidental crops, modern California had, so to speak, lifted herself by her own bootstraps. Increased local demand required a threefold increase in production. These lines were important but not the essence of the state's agriculture, for which the distinctive note was provided rather by production for the national and to some extent the world market. This production spread over a long list of commodities from exotic dates and avocados to things as common as carrots, yet in each instance California climatic and soil conditions afforded either a monopoly of opportunity or at least a very great advantage over the less fortunately situated portions of the United States. Availing themselves of these opportunities and contributing no little ingenuity, California agriculturists forged into first place.

A prevailing characteristic of this agricultural development was its industrial technique and method. Profiting by the findings of agricultural research, tooling for assembly-line operations, and incorporating on the scale of big business, the typical farms became factories in the fields. A correlative fact was the presence of an exploitative attitude toward farm labor. From Indians to tramps, to Chinese, to Japanese, to Filipinos, to Hindus, to Mexicans, the farm labor force had been in a position of inferiority. This inherited pattern and the nationwide practice in the twenties go far to explain the prevalent attitude.

Black Gold and Other Minerals

In mineral production California rose to third, with Texas and Pennsylvania in the van. Annual value of output ran beyond $440 million, most of it accounted for by the yearly outflow of more than 200 million barrels of oil. Even without petroleum California would have been an important mining state. The annual gold output exceeded a million ounces and the price had been boosted to $35.02 an ounce. Other metals were of less significance, but the list of nonmetallic minerals was long and imposing, some 50 different minerals being produced in San Bernardino County alone. The cement industry, with a yearly production in excess of 10 million barrels has already been mentioned. Sand and crushed rock were used in proportion, and clay products, from rough tile and brick to glazed tile and tableware, were an embellishment and a continuation of one of the old mission industries.

The petroleum industry after 1914 was furnishing fuel for locomotives, heating furnaces, and orchard heaters. It was finding favor in paving operations and gaining an even larger market in gasoline for automobile consumption. There was technological progress also, especially in the latter portion of the period, including improved methods of drilling and refining, the construction of pipelines, tank cars and tankers, and the solidification of financial control in the hands of a few large companies.

From 1914 to 1920 production ranged between 89 million and 105 million barrels, with no new fields of importance being opened. Whatever excitement was missing in these years was more than made up for in the ensuing decade when one fabulous strike followed another. First came the Huntington Beach field in 1920 and the next year Santa Fe Springs and Signal Hill. By 1923 these three fields, all in the Los Angeles area, were producing, respectively, 113,000, 332,000, and 244,000 barrels a day, carrying the state's total for the year to 264 million barrels. In such an outpouring the existing facilities for storage and refining were completely engulfed. The oil companies escaped inundation by putting their tankers on a rapid shuttle service through the Panama Canal to refineries on the Atlantic seaboard. There were in 1924 some 1,704 transits by tankers, the best business the canal had enjoyed up to that time, and good business for the oil companies too, since this was a cheaper method of delivering oil than to ship it from the midcontinent fields.

Canal shipments of oil soon fell off about a third, partly because of the availability of Mexican and South American oil and the opening of the tremendously productive midcontinent field in Texas and Oklahoma. California production, however, declined only slightly. In the late twenties it maintained an average of 241 million barrels, in the early thirties was off to 184 million, but then mounted again to more than 200 million barrels. The same major fields were still heavy producers, in some instances from deeper sands, and in 1928 Kettleman Hills near Coalinga came in as another bonanza.

New wells, however, were a less striking feature than were some of the other changes in the industry. One development was the expansion of storage facilities with huge tank farms at Richmond, Bakersfield, Coalinga, El Segundo, and Long Beach so that almost two years' production could be held in storage. Refineries also expanded, turning out three and a third billion gallons of gasoline annually and other products in proportion. Significant also was the expansion of the local market. The state's automobiles, airplanes, trucks, buses, and tractors consumed annually a quantity of gasoline exceeded only in New York, and the demand for fuel oil grew correspondingly, thanks to diesel motors and engines, the augmented number of orchard heaters, and the expansion of California industry. Only an eighth of the electricity consumed was generated in steam plants such as the huge installation of the Southern California Edison Company at Long Beach, but the cost of this oil-generated current was the yardstick for determining the price of hydroelectric power from Boulder Dam.

After 1920 the production and consumption of natural gas also increased tremendously. For domestic uses, including home heating, it became the favored fuel and had industrial significance as well. Over a 16-year period the increase in billions of cubic feet consumed was from 66 to 320, while other large quantities were converted into casinghead gasoline or reintroduced into the oil sands to rejuvenate faltering wells.

Industry

In the twenties and thirties one set of industries catered primarily or exclusively to California consumers. This group included certain lines of manufacturing that are of necessity conducted near the point of consumption, for example, baking, printing, the operation of foundries and machine shops, the manufacture of concrete products, and the operation of planing mills. These were generously represented in the state, and in the latter two, because of the demands of irrigation and flood-control projects and because of the great activity in the building trades, California rose to first rank. The presence by 1940 of almost seven million persons and the remoteness from eastern industrial centers led to a considerable development of industry.

California plants supplied outlying areas as well. This was true, for example, in the manufacture of drilling and refining equipment for the petroleum industry, in the production of mining machinery, in the making of furniture, and in the manufacture of automobile tires and tubes.

In the last analysis, however, manufactures only incidentally for the local market made California an industrial center surpassed by only seven states in the Middle Atlantic and Great Lakes area. These more ambitious branches included oil refining, the canning and preserving of fruits, vegetables, and fish, wine making, the manufacture of clothing, especially for women, and, by no means least, motion-picture production. In few of these lines was output large prior to 1914.

Some years prior to that date the movies were transferred from

Edison's laboratory to a set of unpretentious studios in Brooklyn. There the earlier masterpieces such as *The Great Train Robbery* were filmed, and until 1910 no films were even shown in Hollywood, the city fathers looking askance at recreational establishments of dubious morality. In 1910, however, the Horsley brothers, tiring of the handicap of Brooklyn's gloomy skies, transferred their business to a Hollywood barn. Other companies followed suit, and Hollywood soon came to be the industry's recognized capital. Early arrivals included the Bison Company and Biograph, David Wark Griffith, Mack Sennett, Owen Moore and Mary Pickford, Jesse L. Lasky, Cecil B. DeMille, William Farnum, and Charlie Chaplin. For some years the industry coasted along on its curiosity value, which was in showing pictures that moved. Modern critics are most disdainful of early filmdom, charging that from the beginning it "was almost exclusively in the hands of the lowest type of business men, the lowest type of actors, and the lowest type of writers; to wit, honky-tonk impresarios, hams and hacks."

By 1915 the movies could demand at least quantitative respect; Mary Pickford was on salary at $1,000 a week and Griffith's *The Birth of a Nation,* having cost a million dollars to produce and destined to gross 15 times that sum, was by any definition colossal. With this epic the movie magnates entered into direct competition with the olive bottlers for a lien on the adjectives of magnitude. The film makers used these adjectives indiscriminately, though justifiably in such instances as *The Four Horsemen of the Apocalypse, Ben Hur, The Big Parade,* and *Snow White and the Seven Dwarfs.*

The passing years brought, naturally enough, a number of changes and some improvements. A wave of scandals in the early twenties—the Arbuckle incident, Wallace Reid's death, and the Taylor murder—led the magnates to cast their problems in the lap of Will H. Hays, who left Harding's cabinet to become czar of the movies' public relations. Introduction of sound and color brought further alteration. By running up the cost of shooting they set a penalty on interminable retakes and a premium on workmanlike performances. The talkies, furthermore, made demands on the players almost comparable to those of the stage. They led, in fact, to a great influx of experienced actors and thus contributed to the artistic refinement of the movies. Doubtless the number of true artists who have found expression in moving pictures is larger, but the critics are agreed on two in particular, Chaplin and Walt Disney. Although readily distinguishable they had this much in common: they both recognized that a picture is not merely a transplanted stage play, that its strongest point is action and its most powerful expression is through pantomime.

In proceeds the moving-picture industry plotted itself a most astounding graph. Particularly spectacular was the up-curve for exhibitions. The beginnings had been very humble; Los Angeles' first projection parlor was operated in connection with a peep show and was arranged accordingly. Through holes in a partition seven patrons could peek into the darkened room at the screen. By 1910, however, the number of theaters equipped to show movies had grown enormously and throughout the next two decades the trend continued.

Even at nominal admission charges—a nickel was for some years the standard price—the revenue to the producers became fabulous. Money poured in so rapidly that the movie people literally did not know what to do with it. The players offered to take a share, and salaries of the stars were boosted to five, ten, or twenty thousand dollars a week. Writers, directors, producers, and technicians shared in the bonanza. There were expenses, of course, for film, costumes, sets, transportation, and so forth, but the principal loot was still in the hands of the magnates. Some of it went into publicity, many of the fabulous salaries of the stars being chargeable thus. Other millions were plowed back into new productions or into equipment. Lesser sums went into what might be called research, though most of the improvements in film, cameras, sound-recording machines, color processes, and the like were made by the supply houses rather than by the producing companies. After all these deductions a tidy sum remained, and this along with much of the income of the players, directors, and writers was poured out lavishly in conspicuous expenditure.

Hollywood's nouveaux riches had been held up to greater ridicule than perhaps any suddenly wealthy group since the dawn of history. In large degree the lampooning was based on fact, for the atrocities committed at their behest by architects, interior decorators, automobile salesmen, caterers, and entertainers have been wonderful and fearful to behold. The social impact upon the community through premieres and previews, night life and progressive marriage, also became a source of much concern to the guardians of southern California taste and morals. Gossip-mongering reporters broadcast these details to the world at large, with nothing lost in the telling but often with special impingement upon the Los Angeles area.

The moving-picture industry released in southern California a very considerable purchasing power, esteemed alike by builders, tradesmen, salesmen, domestics, and members of the professions. Quantitative statement is not easy because not even the stars spent all their income locally, and, since the industry put its financial center in New York, some of the profits were diverted from the state. Nevertheless, the residuum was large. In 1935, salaries and wages totaled $98 million and cost of production stood at $165 million. How far income exceeds cost was not revealed, but even these figures establish the industry as a California asset comparable to the orange.

The movies in addition had a publicity value almost impossible to exaggerate. What suburb the world over had been so widely heralded as Hollywood? The films acted as a lodestone drawing countless tourists to the state, tourists who are said to have spent $200 million in southern California in 1938. Hollywood's contribution to certain allied industries must be mentioned too. The studios created a style center for women's apparel rivaled only by Paris, and California clothing manufacturers capitalized on this advantage. In radio the congregation of talent near the movie lots led the nation's broadcasting systems to establish studios in Hollywood secondary only to New York's Radio Center.

Public Improvements

In this era of prosperity the engineers were working on a variety of projects and planning others still more ambitious. One important project had to do with highways. In the 1850's stage lines had spread to the far corners of the state over unimproved roads. With the coming of the railroads, wagon roads fell back into strictly local use from which the automobile elevated them only gradually. However, new ideas took hold: roads should not merely be graded and graveled but paved, and they should extend from one end of the state to the other. In 1909 the legislature ordered a survey for a state highway system, and in 1911 it set up a Highway Commission to supervise such a program. In 1910 bonds were voted in the amount of $18 million, followed by $15 million in 1915 and $40 million in 1918 to finance paved roads approximating the course of present highways 99 and 101 and with connections with every county seat.

In 1923 the legislature followed the Oregon inspiration and voted a two-cent-per-gallon gasoline tax, together with higher fees for trucks, the income to be allocated to highway improvements. This device had the virtues of pay-as-you-go financing and also was a neat approximation of payment in proportion to use. From that time on, the gas tax has been the main reliance for highway and later freeway construction, assisted at intervals by federal aid, much of it derived from a superimposed federal gas tax. One testimony to the inherent logic of the gas tax is that the representatives of the people have seen fit step by step to advance the tax to bring the state and federal levy up to as much as 11 or 12 cents per gallon. There have been pressures to divert part of this tax to other worthy purposes, such as school support, but for the most part that temptation has been resisted. In 1969, for instance, one cent was added temporarily to the current total of 11 cents per gallon, but it was for repair of flood damages and principally to streets and highways. A few years earlier there was a similar temporary hike to cover repairs of the Redwood Highway.

As was true elsewhere, the first so-called highways were not much more than surfaced wagon roads, not engineered specifically as a runway for motor-driven vehicles. By the twenties, however, rapid progress had been made. One main artery followed the approximate route of El Camino Real, through the Santa Clara, Salinas, and Santa Maria valleys from San Francisco to Santa Barbara, and then by the inland route to San Fernando and Los Angeles, and on by the coast to San Diego. The other main artery reached south from Oregon, took advantage of the open expanse of the great Central Valley, and crossed Tejon Pass to Los Angeles. Laterals attached most of the centers of population with these main arteries, and highways reached eastward to the Colorado crossings at Yuma and Needles and to the trans-Sierra gateway at Reno. Extension of the Redwood Highway northward along the coast came more slowly, but by mid-decade it was surfaced and open all the way to Oregon.

Discarded Remnant of the Plank Road, Colorado Desert

California Department of Public Works, Division of Highways

Since many of the property lines in California antedated the quadrangular surveys typical of the United States as a whole, roads and highways were less rigidly held to the straight lines and square corners of the section lines. The terrain set up many difficult problems. One, on the coast route, was to negotiate the transfers from valley to valley, as at Cuesta grade near San Luis Obispo. Another was to cope with the constantly shifting sands near Yuma. Several miles of movable plank road were the initial solution to this problem. Still another difficulty was how to surmount the mountain barrier between Bakersfield and Los Angeles. The twisting switch-backing old ridge route was a devious answer to that problem, achieved in the pattern of the period with as little earth moving as possible and with no compunction about the number or sharpness of the turns. It was an adventurous ride, blamed for much carsickness and calling for prodigious exercise of the steering wheel.

The arms of San Francisco Bay, such a boon to water transportation, were an equivalent obstacle to automobile traffic. An obvious response was to add automobile ferries to those already serving railroad passengers and commuters. In the twenties this service was available from San Francisco to Sausalito, Oakland, and Berkeley, from Richmond to San Rafael, and across Carquinez Straits at Vallejo and Benicia. Bridges, it was suggested, would speed up this traffic. Several were built—at Antioch, Crockett, Dumbarton, and San Mateo. They helped but in each instance they merely cut off the end of an arm of the bay. A bolder remedy in the form of bridges direct from San Francisco to Oakland and to Marin County advanced to the planning stage, but in the twenties neither got beyond paper.

The problems of water and power were recognized as even more vital. In earlier days the water resources most conveniently available for irrigation and for municipal supply had been developed. In the time of George Chaffey several more dramatic steps had been taken, most rewardingly in the diversion of Colorado River water into Imperial Valley and most flamboyantly in the siphoning of the Owens River to Los Angeles. In many instances hydroelectric energy had been generated as a sort of by-product of the water supplying. In the teens and twenties still other power plants were installed along Sierra streams. Just prior to the completion of the big dams at Boulder, Shasta, and Friant the aggregate of this hydroelectric output was almost a fifth of the national total.

Through the twenties the Owens Valley Aqueduct was much in the news. In 1923, following a succession of dry years, Los Angeles began to buy up additional farms in the valley and to transfer their water to the aqueduct. The remaining residents of the valley, especially the townspeople, were incensed at this blighting of their homeland. The Owens Valley champions protested vocally and editorially, then by placing a token charge of dynamite alongside the aqueduct, then by seizing a spillway in the Alabama Hills and turning the flow of water out upon the desert, and finally by more damaging sabotage of wells, pumps, and aqueduct sections. The city put detectives to work but never brought any of the dynamiters to trial. The protesters took it the more amiss because much of their water was not piped to Angeleños' homes but was used instead to irrigate the San Fernando Valley. A syndicate dominated by the Otis–Chandler interests had bought 47,000 acres in this valley in 1910. The aqueduct water increased its value as much as a hundredfold.

More serious violence seemed likely, but on August 4, 1927, Owens Valley had a great setback. The principal bank of the county closed its doors. Its president, N. N. Watterson, and cashier, M. G. Watterson, who had symbolized the cause of the settlers against the city, had misapplied the bank's funds to the tune of some $2 million. The settlers, many of them bankrupt through this speculation, had no alternative but to give in.

The following March 12, a 180-foot dam that Mulholland had built in San Francisquito Canyon near the southern end of his aqueduct suddenly gave way, sending a monstrous wall of water cascading down the narrow valley of the Santa Clara. When it struck Santa Paula, 50 miles away, the crest was still 25 feet high. The toll of lives was between 400 and 450, almost as many as in San Francisco's great fire. The property damage was millions of dollars. An appraisal committee assessed the property losses and the city promptly met these claims. With the dynamite blasts along the aqueduct still in mind, there was an impulse to blame the disaster on sabotage, but inspection revealed that the dam was built on and anchored to a weak and faulted rock formation. Capable geological advice would have prevented this catastrophe.

San Francisco was also at work on its water problem. Initially it had depended on local wells. By 1901, however, when it was apparent that a supplement was needed, Mayor James D. Phelan filed an application for water from the Tuolumne River just north of Yosemite. Nature lovers protested and nothing was accomplished until 1913 when Congress authorized the diversion and confirmed San Francisco's title to water rights in the amount of 420,000 acre-feet a year. Legal, financial, and physical difficulties, together with the opposition of Pacific Gas and Electric and the Spring Valley Water Company, delayed the work. Finally, in 1931, after an expenditure of $121 million, the Hetch Hetchy Dam, the transmission lines, and the 186-mile aqueduct were realities, and San Francisco had all the water it would need in the foreseeable future.

The Speculative Urge

For the United States as a whole the postwar twenties was a sort of binge, with prohibition, bootleggers, and speakeasies, a runaway stock market, an increasing degree of corporate concentration as exemplified in chain stores, and a resurgence of hyperpatriotism and nativism as expressed in isolationism, the Ku Klux Klan, and the Scopes and Sacco–Vanzetti trials. California shared in these aberrations and with some distinctiveness.

Through mergers and consolidations, locally-owned and directed banks gave place to the branches of a few mammoth organizations, chief of which was Gianinni's Bank of Italy. By removing much of the personal equation from their lending and collecting, these banks improved soundness and security, at the same time concentrating power to an alarming degree. They also had a hand in broadening interest in investment, some of it highly speculative. A host of persons who had never previously paid attention to stock quotations bought shares in Transamerica and other such issues and hung on the rise and fall of the market.

The speculative urge was more purely evident in the uncritical support given to real-estate schemes, such as were promoted at Atascadero, and in the rage especially in Los Angeles for oil stocks. The particular darling of the Los Angeles public was C. C. Julian, an ornate showman and a master of breezy, folksy, spellbinding appeal. In the chatty monologue of his newspaper ads he invited the folks to take shares in the bonanza of Santa Fe Springs' gushing wells. Julian Petroleum stock sold rapidly and paid handsome divi-

Oil Wells, Speedway, and Beverly Hills in 1921

C. C. Pierce Collection

dends. From 1922 to 1925 his ventures spiraled upward, but at that point the major interests protested his stock issues, pressured the newspapers to refuse his advertising, and persuaded the refineries to stop handling his oil. In the crisis that ensued Julian lost control of his company.

His successors, S. C. Lewis and Jacob Berman, had to borrow money extravagantly to keep the company afloat. A favorite speculation was in lending money at exorbitant interest and bonuses to Julian Petroleum. It was participated in by a bankers' pool from the most respected element in the community, a Jewish pool made up of affluent merchants and bankers, and the Tia Juana pool, composed of gamblers and race-track habitués. As security for these loans, Lewis and Berman resorted to counterfeiting stock, eventually in the amount of 3,000,015 shares. On May 7, 1927, this bubble burst and $150 million in supposed worth vanished from the grasp of 40,000 eager investors. Julian perhaps had set the stage for such a disaster but there is no evidence that he was culpable for what others did to Julian "Pete."

This spectacular failure was followed by the receivership of the Richfield Oil Company in 1931, with revelation of unconscionable extravagances by its officials and an operating loss of $56 million. Embezzlement, fraud, and poor judgment brought many other companies to bankruptcy, including the Guarantee Building and Loan Association and the American Mortgage Company. Indeed, in bankruptcies for fraud Los Angeles led the nation at the end of the twenties.

Slightly translated, the speculative urge of southern Californians in the twenties was expressed also in attention to new cults of philosophy and religion. The region abounded in health faddists, naturopaths and other exponents of medical unorthodoxy, apostles of new thought variously defined, and indigenous sects. The latter may be illustrated by a funerary establishment designed to banish all that is somber and depressing.

The dramatic evangelism of Aimee Semple McPherson was even more innate to the twenties. Sister Aimee began to preach the Four Square Gospel in Los Angeles in 1922. Within a very short time she had a devoted following of thousands, who built the huge Angelus Temple with an auditorium to seat 5,000. In 1926 Aimee disappeared. Last seen on the beach near Ocean Park, she was presumed to have drowned. Eight days later she reappeared at Agua Prieta, Sonora, returned to a triumphal reception at Los Angeles, and gave out a story that she had been kidnapped. When reporters exposed this story as a hoax, she was arrested on the charge of falsifying and thereby interfering with the orderly processes of the law. The charge was later dropped. Her followers continued loyal to the time of her death in 1945, never, however, exceeding in numbers or vigor the peak attained in the twenties. Because of her penchant for showmanship the Los Angeles press and the more sophisticated element in the community dealt lampooningly with Aimee. Thereby they obscured the substantial amount of real good that she did in helping the sick and needy, cheering the unhappy, providing social opportunity for the lonely, and uplifting her followers.

Politics as Usual

Prosperity tends to promote complacency. The American people exhibited this attitude toward their national government during the twenties, and Californians did the same both with regard to business and to state and local government. In William D. Stephens, Friend W. Richardson, and C. C. Young a succession of Republican governors spanned the decade. Legislatures met with calendrical regularity but enacted few measures of much moment. In fact they sedulously avoided one issue that many of their constituents regarded as imperative, that of reapportionment.

The unequal growth of the state, with the center of gravity shifting more and more southward, lent increasing unreality to the representational system. In the normal course of events each decennial census should have been followed by a revision of electoral districts for the House of Representatives and for the state legislature, provided, of course, that there had been a sufficient population shift or increase. The federal constitution strongly implies this by providing that representation be apportioned among the several states according to population, and the state constitution is even more mandatory in its requirement.

Such an apportionment had been made by Congress in 1911, with California assigned 11 representatives, and the legislature had supplemented it with an appropriate local measure. When the census of 1920 established the increase in California population at 44.1 per cent, the natural expectation was that the state would be allotted three or four additional Congressmen and that in local reapportionment Los Angeles and southern California would be the chief gainers. Successive congresses, however, neglected to act, and their remissness gave the legislature excuse not to reapportion its own districts.

For five years this condition prevailed. In the state, meanwhile, several alignments were discernible: Republicans versus Democrats, the north versus the south, San Francisco versus Los Angeles, and the rural districts versus the urban centers. Some had little to do with reapportionment. The Republican party, for example, was so preponderant that no conceivable redistricting could do it much harm or good. The north–south rivalry, though frequently a rallying cry in the controversy to follow, seems to have been invoked primarily out of deference to tradition. Certainly in its more extreme form, the threat of state division, it was able to gather only the most limited support. The rivalry of the two cities had more reality, and the issue between city and country was sharply drawn.

In 1926, the legislature having indicated clearly that it would not act, two contradictory initiative amendments were laid before the electorate. One, ineptly named the Los Angeles plan, called for reapportionment according to population for both houses of the legislature, delegated power to act to a commission of ex officio members if the legislature failed to act, and also made available judicial remedy. The other plan was advanced by various farm groups, the Farm Bureau Federation, the State Grange, the Farmer's Union, and the Agricultural Legislative Committee, and also by the San Francisco Chamber of Commerce. Labeled the Federal plan, it apportioned seats in the lower house according to population and in the upper house according to the counties at the rate of not more than one to a county and not more than three counties to a district. Most of the arguments advanced for this plan do not stand up under examination. The analogy to the national practice was erroneous and misleading. Distribution would not have been on anything like an equal-area basis, nor did the plan assure a well-balanced legislature in which neither the cities nor the farm areas would predominate. More realistic and more effective was the unvoiced argument that by its rotten-borough system the plan would perpetuate the countryside in its control of the senate, while rural assemblymen would often hold the balance of power between the Los Angeles and San Francisco representatives.

The voters in their wisdom chose the Federal rather than the Los Angeles plan, only the latter county expressing a preference for representation on a straight population basis, and the legislature in 1927 marked out the districts. Opponents of the plan staged a forlorn protest by invoking the referendum against this act in 1928 but interest was apathetic. Half a million persons who participated in the presidential vote did not bother to cast their votes on the referendum and, though San Francisco joined Los Angeles on this vote, the referendum lost.

This action, however, laid reapportionment to rest only temporarily. In 1929 Congress at last decreed reapportionment of representation in its own lower house to be computed on the basis of the forthcoming census of 1930. So rapid had been the state's increase that this enlarged California's representation from 11 to 20. By reason of this law, together with the initiative amendment of 1926, the legislature in 1931 had the double duty of relocating assembly and congressional districts.

The reapportionment contest began before the legislature convened, with drives for the speakership by Edgar C. Levey of San Francisco and Walter J. Little of Santa Monica. Both professed to favor reapportionment on the basis of population, but it was generally understood that Little's program would be more in accord with the census figures and therefore more favorable to Los Angeles and southern California. Levey won the speakership, 41 to 39. The committee he appointed drafted bills assigning 10 Congressmen to each section and dividing the assembly seats almost evenly between north and south. A senate committee countered with a proposal to allot the Congressmen 9 and 11 and the assemblymen 38 and 42, north and south. After a bitter fight in which all manner of pressure was exerted to influence the votes of assemblymen, the San Joaquin Valley delegation cast the balance in favor of the senate's bill, the McKinley–Little program.

Los Angeles and the south reckoned it a great victory for justice and for themselves. It marked, so they felt, the attainment of political maturity and would put an end, so they hoped, to the political domination which San Francisco and the north had been able to prolong for some years after the center of population had shifted southward. In practice it became clear that San Francisco's voice in state government was still large, and clearer still that the Federal system gave rural California relatively the greatest representation in the legislature. Hearst and others agitated against the Federal system and proposed various remedies, from the mild device of making the rotten boroughs slightly less rotten by permitting the lumping of five counties in a senatorial district to the more drastic step of adopting the unicameral legislature. With the urban centers leaning toward Democratic liberalism and the farm provinces a stronghold of Republican conservatism, the question acquired a partisan flavor hitherto lacking. None of the schemes for revision, however, came anywhere near acceptance.

Reapportionment was followed shortly by a revision of the taxation system which amounted, in effect, to reassessment. The change was a complicated one but necessary, it was pleaded, to keep the schools functioning in the districts hardest hit by the depression. Several steps were involved. One was to make state funds available to local public schools up to and including junior colleges in proportion to daily attendance. To get the necessary funds into the state treasury, the property of public-service corporations was to be transferred from local assessment rolls and placed under state taxation, and two new taxes were to be instituted, a one per cent sales tax and an income tax.

Largely on the argument of saving the schools, the program was voted in in 1933. Two important details, however, did not work out according to the blueprint. The transfer of a large part of the school burden afforded only slight and temporary relief to local taxpayers, because removal of the corporations from the assessment rolls narrowed the tax base while other branches of local government immediately raised their demands. Local property owners, accordingly, paid practically as much as before. The other slip was that the sales tax, which everyone recognized would bear more heavily on the poor, was not balanced by an income tax. Governor James M. Rolph found excuse to veto the latter measure. A fair interpretation, it may be said, was that those who paid the sales tax had the privilege of saving the schools, while taxable incomes went unscathed and the corporations had their tax burdens lightened.

For Further Reading

Westways (December, 1950), celebrating the 50th anniversary of the Automobile Club of Southern California.

JOHN C. BURNHAM, "The Gasoline Tax and the Automobile Revolution," *MVHR*, 48 (1961), 435–59.

EARL S. POMEROY, *In Search of the Golden West: The Tourist in Western America* (1957).

FRANK J. TAYLOR and EARL M. WELTY, *Black Bonanza* (1950), a history of Union Oil.

FRANK LATTA, *Black Gold in the Joaquin* (1949).

JULIAN DANA, *A. P. Giannini, Giant in the Land* (1947).

MARQUIS JAMES and BESSIE ROWLAND JAMES, *Biography of a Bank: The Story of Bank of America* (1954).

GILES T. BROWN, *Ships That Sail No More* (1966).

LEWIS JACOBS, *Rise of the American Film* (1939).

NANCY BARR MAVITY, *Sister Aimee* (1931).

VINCENT OSTROM, *Water and Politics: A Study of Water Policies and Administration in the Development of Los Angeles* (1953).

CAREY McWILLIAMS, *Southern California Country* (1947).

MORROW MAYO, *Los Angeles* (1933).

CHARLES F. OUTLAND, *Man-Made Disaster: The Story of St. Francis Dam* (1963).

THOMAS S. BARCLAY, "Reapportionment in California," *PHR*, 5 (1936), 93–129.

CAUGHEY, *California Heritage*, 373–77.

chapter twenty-seven

The Great Depression

The cars of the migrant people crawled out of the side roads onto the great cross-country highway, and they took the migrant way to the West. In the daylight they scuttled like bugs to the westward; and as the dark caught them, they clustered like bugs near to shelter and to water. And because they were lonely and perplexed, because they had all come from a place of sadness and worry and defeat, they huddled together; they talked together; they shared their lives, their food, and the things they hoped for in the new country. Thus it might be that one family camped near a spring, and another camped for the spring and for company, and a third because two families had pioneered the place and found it good. And when the sun went down, perhaps twenty families and twenty cars were there.

In the evening a strange thing happened: the twenty families became one family, the children were the children of all. The loss of home became one loss, and the golden time in the West was one dream.

John Steinbeck,
The Grapes of Wrath

**1929
to
1940**

Viewed with hindsight, imperfections show up in the American prosperity of the twenties, some of which were suspected at the time. The boom in business was highly selective; automobiles and radios sold as never before, but such key industries as soft coal mining, textiles, and agriculture were not prospering. Labor-saving machinery gave production a tremendous boost; no means, however, had been devised to give a similar lift to consumer purchasing power. Installment buying was the closest approach, but at most it was a palliative, a method of putting a mortgage on future orders. The unevenness of prosperity showed in the 312 per cent increase in speculative gains from 1923 to 1928, while wages crept up only 12 per cent. In the midst of the prosperity, too, there was an alarming amount of poverty; unemployment, to cite one example, went up from 1.5 million in 1926 to 1.8 million in 1929.

Emigrant Family from the Dust Bowl

Dorothea Lange, Farm Security Administration

The speculative superstructure toppled first. To many Americans it seemed a matter of comparative indifference that the paper profits of the market players were swept away. Soon, however, the paralysis spread through the whole economy. Wages, salaries, and dividends were slashed; national income dropped from $81 billion in 1929 to $41 billion in 1932; stores and fac-tories closed, Hoovervilles and apple-selling came into being; and the roster of unemployed mounted to 10 million in 1931 and to 14 or 15 million the next year.

Earlier drops in the business cycle, such as the panics of 1857, 1873, and 1893, had had only a delayed reaction in California. By 1929 the state was closely enmeshed with the nation. Furthermore, much that it had to offer in the national market was particularly sensitive to recession. Its fruits were only partially regarded as staples. Its moving pictures were somewhat less than absolute necessities. Its vacation opportunities would go begging in a period of austerity. This time California felt the impact as abruptly as any part of the country except perhaps Wall Street itself. Before the depression was over, some of its consequences would be brought home in aggravated form. For example, California became a special asylum for the unemployed. They were attracted by the mildness of the climate, which made it seem a better place in which to endure privation, and they were lured by the state's traditional aura as a land of promise and opportunity.

In the state as in the nation the very volume of distress among the impoverished and the unemployed called aloud for action. The Hoover admin-istration sought to cope with the depression by pronouncements of confidence in America. Later, through the Reconstruction Finance Corporation, it gave aid to major industries. Its philosophy, however, was that relief to individuals should come from private sources or local governments, and only with reluctance did it move on at length to federal contributions for such purposes. The California state government was equally hesitant. The first major decision in coping with the depression was in the election of James (Sunny Jim) Rolph as governor in November, 1930.

In his long tenure as mayor of San Francisco the major qualifications Rolph had evinced were as official greeter, hand shaker, and parade reviewer. Unfortunately in his term at Sacramento there was not much to be sunny about. It was not in the cards that he would mobilize the state government to meet the emergency. With the accession of Franklin Delano Roosevelt as President in 1933 the national government launched the New Deal as an effort to achieve relief, recovery, and reform. Many phases of the New Deal had impact on California. Its state government, however, declined to get in step and con-tinued, insofar as possible, to practice the philosophy of Coolidge and Hoover Republicanism.

The Coming of the Oakies

In at least one part of the nation the depression struck harder than in California. On the southern plains falling prices, foreclosures, and unemploy-

The Road West

Dorothea Lange, Farm Security Administration

ment coincided with a shift toward larger farms and more mechanization. Some people had to leave because of foreclosures; others spoke of themselves as tractored off. In addition there came a series of dry years which turned the whole region into a Dust Bowl.

Such was California's reputation that when refugees had to leave they almost automatically went West. This flight was by families in their run-down jalopies, a migration vividly depicted in Dorothea Lange's *American Exodus* and in the first part of Steinbeck's *Grapes of Wrath*.

Displaced farmers and their families came pouring in from many states, particularly those in the tier from Texas to the Dakotas. Oklahoma had the best nickname and lent it to the whole migration. Being farmers, these newcomers looked for work in the fields of California. They came in sufficient numbers to glut the market for migratory farm labor and at a time when the growers were least able to pay a living wage. The Oakies brought more women and children than had characterized earlier harvests. Consequently, even at a time when people were suffering almost everywhere, the distress of these new arrivals was extraordinarily heartrending. The Oakies, with the Dust Bowl and the rigors of Highway 66 behind them and the organized, implacable, and police-supported growers confronting them, stand as the most touching symbols of the Depression.

The Restiveness of Labor

A predictable feature of the depression period was the restiveness of labor. With prices cascading, employers sought to protect their interests by slashing wages, and workers often felt this tendency was carried too far. The feature of greatest novelty was the attempt to organize farm labor and to stage a series of great agricultural strikes.

Prior to 1929 there had been some gestures toward organizing agricultural workers in the state, by the American Federation of Labor (AF of L) among the cannery workers, by racial associations among the Japanese and the Mexicans, and by the IWW in its peculiar and impractical program among the casual laborers. None of these efforts had appreciable effect on the status of farm labor.

Early in 1930 two spontaneous strikes occurred in Imperial Valley protesting lowered wages in the fields and the packing sheds. After the strikes failed, the heads of the Trade Union Unity League (TUUL) called a conference of worker delegates from the entire valley. This move provoked arrest of some 100 workers, trial of a number of the leaders for violation of the criminal syndicalism statute, and conviction of eight of them.

Capitalizing on the resentment that this repression produced, the Communist party began a drive to organize the farm workers. The strategy was to take advantage of every labor dispute and every strike that developed spontaneously and to try to build these pieces into a cohesive statewide movement. This foreign label, Communist, added to the rise of unionism where it had never existed before, roused bitter resistance. At Vacaville late in 1932 a masked mob answered a fruit workers strike by seizing six of the leaders, flogging them, shearing their heads, and annointing them with red enamel. Strikes followed among the pea pickers at Decoto, the cherry pickers at Mountain View and Sunnyvale, the peach gatherers at Merced and elsewhere, the grape workers at Lodi and Fresno, in the pear harvest in the Santa Clara Valley, and in the general fruit gathering on the Tagus Ranch.

Although not always initiated by Communist organizers, these strikes were incorporated into the program of the Cannery and Agricultural Workers' Industrial Union (CAWIU). It went on in the fall of 1933 to organize a cotton pickers strike that boycotted the fields throughout the San Joaquin Valley, maintained a headquarters camp of some 5,000 persons near Corcoran, and withheld 18,000 workers from the fields. This was followed by an Imperial Valley strike in the winter of 1933–34 and another wave of walkouts in the northern fruit districts in 1934.

Opposition to these strikes took the form of bitter denunciation in the press, vigilante violence aimed primarily at the leadership, and use of local police, sheriffs' deputies, and state police to break up strike meetings and disperse their camps. As in the routing of the TUUL, the criminal syndicalism law was invoked against the CAWIU. After its second state convention in 1934, all its leaders who had not previously been taken care of were brought to trial and convicted under this act. In this fashion the union was broken, despite its record of winning 21 strikes out of 24 and advancing the prevailing wage from 15 to 25 cents an hour.

Paralleling this effort to unionize farm labor was an effort to rebuild unionism in San Francisco. From 1921 to 1933 the city's unions were at minimum strength and the port was on what amounted to an open-shop basis. During these years, notwithstanding its natural advantages, San Francisco by no means kept pace with other Pacific coast ports. Its share of tonnage decreased from 36 to 21 per cent and other indexes went down in proportion. The open shop was not to blame but did not prevent this decline.

In the company-controlled hiring, grave abuses developed and were aggravated by the depression. When Section 7A of the National Recovery Act outlined a procedure whereby labor could choose its bargaining agency, the waterfront workers with little delay chose the International Longshoremen's Association (ILA). In May, 1934, this organization felt strong enough to make a series of demands for a minimum wage of a dollar an hour, a six-hour day and a 30-hour week to spread the work among a number of men, union control of the hiring halls, and various lesser concessions.

The operators rejected all these demands and countered with the charge that the ILA was Communist and radical. President Roosevelt, Senator Robert Wagner, and members of the national and regional boards tried to bring about a settlement but failed, and on May 9 the strike began, tying up all the ports on the coast. Almost immediately it erupted into violence at San Francisco. A climax came on July 5 when strikebreakers under police escort tried to move cargo. The strikers resisted, overturned trucks and burned them, dumped goods into the streets, and answered tear gas and pistol fire with cobblestones and brickbats. Two of the strikers were killed and more than a hundred seriously injured. A funeral procession 10,000 strong marched up Market Street and created a profound impression on the entire community. Governor Merriam deployed the National Guard, and as a protest against the partisanship of the forces of government the labor leaders decided to invoke a general strike, that is, a strike designed to paralyze the community and force surrender.

This strike took place from July 16 to 19. Except for a few authorized necessities nothing was sold or delivered. The more conservative union leaders were not willing to see it through to a conclusion. In effect they sabotaged the strike. The "sympathetic strikers" including even the teamsters went back to work. By the end of July the longshoremen were back on the job also. By arbitration award in October control of the hiring hall was assigned to the union. With Joseph P. Ryan having to yield to Harry Bridges in the ILA, and with the organization of the Maritime Federation of the Pacific, the strike marked a long step in the direction of industrial unionism, a trend represented on the national scene by John L. Lewis and the CIO defection from the AF of L.

There was, however, a division of opinion. Bridges and the longshoremen went with the CIO; Harry Lundeberg and the sailors' union stayed with the AF of L. Out of this schizophrenia of labor arose a bewildering array of petty strikes and work stoppages—561 between October, 1934, and November, 1936—crippling to operators and shippers, a nuisance to the public, and extremely damaging to the goodwill that union labor might otherwise have deserved. At the time these jurisdictional disputes were more damaging to labor's reputation than the recurrent charge that the unions were Communist dominated.

Despite the drawbacks the maritime unions continued in strength throughout the thirties. Unionism in general likewise made great strides, first under the temporary benediction of the Blue Eagle of the National Industrial Relations Administration (NIRA), and later under the National Labor Relations Board. By 1940 San Francisco and the Bay region had more union members than ever before, including even newsboys and bootblacks. Although Los Angeles still purported to be open shop, it had a nucleus of solid unionization in the harbor district; the more concentrated industries, such as airplane building, automobile assembly, tire manufacture, and oil production and refining, were thoroughly organized; the motion-picture industry was practically solid; and organizers had made some progress in other lines, such as the building trades and truck driving. Between 1933 and 1940 union membership advanced from 33,000 to 200,000.

Pea Pickers Waiting for the Weigh-in

Dorothea Lange, Farm Security Administration

As to rural labor, however, after the liquidation of the CAWIU in 1934 there was no revival of effective unionism. On the contrary, the larger agriculturists formed a union of employers, the Associated Farmers, and, whenever labor troubles occurred, they supplanted or subordinated the regular peace officers, armed enough men with guns, pick handles, and tear gas, and resorted to enough violence to crush the strike. Farm fascism or, in other parlance, vigilantism seemed an effective check on the movement to unionize farm labor. The most hopeful sign was at the close of the decade when Carey McWilliams' *Factories in the Fields* and John Steinbeck's *The Grapes of Wrath* called attention to the plight of the migratory workers in clarion voice and stirred the public conscience.

Technocracy and Utopia

In the prosperous twenties Californians had shown a remarkable waywardness in philosophy and religion. In the depression decade the state spawned equally fantastic schemes for economic legerdemain. Since the state had contributed Henry George and the Single Tax and had harbored communitarian ventures at Kaweah, Delhi, Llano, and elsewhere, perhaps this susceptibility should not surprise. The degree with which visionary and unscientific programs took hold was, nevertheless, amazing.

The first of any consequence was Technocracy. Technocracy had honorable origin at Columbia University as a study of energy as the foundation of civilization. Howard Scott brought it to California as a crusade encrusted with an impressive pseudoscientific vocabulary. He quickly recruited a large number of adherents, who, as a group, made up in enthusiasm for whatever they lacked in understanding. The most notable of the new disciples was Manchester Boddy, owner and editor of the Los Angeles *Daily News*. He used its columns to spread the new gospel and did so with such effectiveness that Technocracy swept the state. Twenty years later a few clubs devoted to economic salvation through the proper use of modern science were still meeting.

In July, 1933, a competitor arose in the Utopian Society. An "educational" society, with initiation ceremonies, secret rituals, and pageantry borrowed from the old morality plays, it claimed to be the answer to the ills of society. From modest beginnings with initiation cycles performed in private homes, it gained adherents so rapidly that the largest auditoriums in Los Angeles were filled. At the peak a half million Utopians was the estimate, practically all of them in southern California. The doctrine of Utopia was, in essence, that private ownership and the profit system were to blame for all evil. With modern machines and proper management, three hours' work a day by those between 25 and 45 years of age would produce all that was needed by the entire population. Education until 25 and pensions after 45 was the motto. The truth probably was that the social and inspirational qualities of the meetings had more to do with the popularity of the society than did its teachings. After about two years the movement faded away almost as rapidly as it had risen. It was part of the ferment out of which arose Epic.

The Epic Crusade

The Epic movement obviously was nurtured on the distress of the depression. It also was encouraged by the New Deal, by Roosevelt's remarks about the forgotten man, and by the nationwide fervor that was engendered when the NIRA was introduced to the country. Some months before the primary a group of liberal Democrats and Socialists persuaded Upton Sinclair to register as a Democrat and seek that party's nomination for governor. A lifelong Socialist, a writer rather than a speaker, an idealist rather than a practical politician, Sinclair was in some respects as unpromising a candidate as could have been found. On the other hand he had boldness of imagination, determination, an incorruptible character, and unexpected powers of dynamic leadership.

Upton Sinclair in 1934

The Henry E. Huntington Library and Art Gallery

Already the author of some 48 books, plays, and pamphlets, Sinclair adopted the novel expedient of building his campaign around a book. Formulating the program he wanted to carry into effect, Sinclair envisioned the obstacles that would confront him, the way they would be overcome, and the eventual triumph of his plan. All this he wrote up in a booklet entitled *I, Governor of California, and How I Ended Poverty: A True Story of the Future.* The campaign was then simply an endeavor to make this book come true.

Sinclair's plan had 12 points, chief of which were the proposals for state land colonies where the unemployed might farm under the guidance of experts, similar operation of idle factories, and a state distribution system for the exchange of these various products—all to be financed by state-issued scrip. His plan proposed repeal of the sales tax, enactment of a steeply graduated income tax, and increases in inheritance and public utility corporation taxes. It contained a proposal for tax exemption on homes occupied by the owners and on ranches cultivated by the owners, provided the assessed value did not exceed $3,000. There was a Georgian proposal for a 10 per cent tax on unimproved building lots and on agricultural land not under cultivation. Finally there was provision for $50-a-month pensions to the aged needy, the physically incapacitated, and widows with dependent children.

How the plan would have worked can be answered only on the basis of theory. It had elements that were most attractive to the unemployed, the poor, and the left wing. Those same elements antagonized and alarmed the propertied classes. The campaign was waged, therefore, with reforming fervor and hope arrayed against distrust and resistance to change. The Epics had only a minimal financial support, not enough to buy much radio time or to make available the other channels of campaigning usually employed. Sinclair's supporters had to depend instead upon volunteer workers, rallies, and clubs, upon their candidate's pamphlets, which, after all, were better than his radio performances, and upon the mistakes of the opposition.

Although handicapped with the colorless Frank Merriam as a candidate, the opposition had a wealth of political experience and an unlimited war chest. Practically all the newspapers were against Sinclair. The radio beat out heated warnings against giving him office, billboards carried the same message, and the voters were deluged with handbills, pamphlets, and letters urging them to "save the state" with Merriam. Sinclair was maligned as "an Anarchist, a free-lover, an agent of Moscow, a Communist, an anti-Christ." Just before the election the motion-picture industry released what purported to be newsreels introducing the tramps who would allegedly descend upon California if Epic were adopted. In actuality they were bit players from Central Casting. A Literary Digest poll, perhaps in honest error, found 62 per cent of the voters for Merriam, though in the election he got only 49 per cent.

On top of all this, Sinclair was opposed by many Socialists and Democrats. Norman Thomas and other Socialists complained that he had deserted true socialism. Conservative Democrats announced for Merriam, and many liberal Democrats threw their votes to Raymond Haight, the Progressive candidate. George Creel, a leading Democrat, denounced Sinclair, and President Roosevelt withheld his support. In the end it was virtually Sinclair and the Epics against the world.

In retrospect it is difficult to recapture the feeling of bitter partisanship that suffused the state. Part of it was due, no doubt, to the threat to entrenched privilege which Sinclair's plan obviously contained. Others were sure that his real intentions were to go far beyond the announced plan and that the latter was merely an entering wedge for a program of socialization which would exceed anything Russia had seen. Many conservatives were also habituated to the thought that the Soviets were behind every movement in America bearing the reform label. The combination of fear and hate, of concern for the preservation of property rights and national institutions, and of political experience and financial resources was more than the Epics could overcome. The Epics won Sinclair the nomination and elected a number of assemblymen, state senators, and Congressmen, but they fell short in the final vote for governor. It was 1,138,620 for Merriam, 879,557 for Sinclair, and 302,519 for Haight. The state was saved from however much of his platform Sinclair might have tried to carry into effect and had instead a continuation of the cautiousness and the laissez faire with which Merriam had been facing the depression crisis.

The Townsend Plan

In its timing Epic encroached on its precursors, Technocracy and Utopianism. In like fashion it had to compete with a counterattraction, the Townsend Plan. The inspiration for this panacea came to a retired physician of Long Beach, Dr. Francis E. Townsend, about the time Epic was taking shape. He proposed to cure the depression by the simple device of giving $200 a month to every person over 60, with the proviso that each installment be spent within the month, the funds to be raised by a 2 per cent transactions tax. Notwithstanding the obvious fallacies involved, the package of old-age pensions and limited inflation had instantaneous appeal. Townsend clubs sprang up as if by chain reaction, contributions from hopeful oldsters poured in to the "national headquarters," and the publications that Townsend set up sold in great quantity.

Although not launched until a few months before the 1934 election, the Townsend Plan was a factor in its outcome. Sinclair denounced the plan as economic heresy. Merriam endorsed it and there can be no doubt that it helped elect him. At the 1935 legislature, too, an early order of business was to consider a memorial to Congress in favor of enactment of the Townsend Plan. Republican votes put it over, and the Townsendites in appreciation began to boom Merriam for President. That the Republicans, who had been so righteous about saving the state from Sinclair's experiments, should plump for the folly of Townsendism is only explainable as politics, or as confidence that the federal government would not be stampeded.

The Townsend idea had a lively persistence. It moved out into the national arena and got support from candidates in many states. As a matter of fact, its original intention was that the federal government should be the agency to give it effect. At the state level it also continued to exert pressure. Exactly how much influence can be attributed to it is hard to measure, but certainly it is credited with accelerating the increase in California old-age pensions and the adoption of the national social security program.

In California derivative programs threw other scares into the camp of economic stability. In 1938 a certain Robert Noble conjured up a plan for rewarding everyone over 50 with $25 every Tuesday in state warrants redeemable at the end of the year, provided that a weekly stamp tax of 2 per cent was affixed. Since its moneymaking apparatus was self-contained, the economic fallacy should have been apparent even to the most unwary, but such was not the reception. Taken in hand by an astute promoter, Willis Allen, the scheme came close to adoption. By advancing the amount and the day, Allen achieved an alliterative title, Thirty Dollars Every Thursday. In the course of the campaign the nonsensical nickname Ham and Eggs was added, and for a while this seemed to help in the promotion. With relative ease Allen got 700,000 signatures, far more than were needed to qualify his proposed constitutional amendment for the November ballot. He took a leaf out of Townsend's method in appealing to the old folks for contributions for the drive to get them something for nothing and at the same time stimulate recovery from the depression. Backed by these contributions and by the advertising revenue of the pension paper that he published, Allen staged a vigorous campaign. It made use of the radio but depended largely on mass meetings and volunteer solicitation of votes. Certain candidates for office, among them Culbert Olson and Sheridan Downey, Democratic aspirants for governor and United States Senate, made a bid for the pensioner vote by endorsing Ham and Eggs, but the sober element in the state was solid against it. There was something of a countercampaign, but the general attitude was that a proposal so fantastic really had no chance of adoption. It was a shock, therefore, when the count showed more than a million votes cast in its favor and that a shift of a few hundred thousand more would have enacted it.

A greater shock came in Allen's announcement that the Retirement Life Payments proposal would immediately be requalified for the ballot, this time with a million signatures. The petition went into circulation, the radio and the newssheet were kept going, and the campaign of soliciting dollars from the aged was intensified. The Chamber of Commerce and its business cohorts had no choice but to continue and step up their opposition. The million signatures were achieved, and publicly delivered to Governor Olson on May 18, 1939, and he was put on the spot to call a special election. The Ham and Eggers hoped for an August date, but Olson set November 7, and by that time the fervor had waned to the extent that the proposition got only 993,000 out of 2,975,000 votes. That was not the end of pension schemes but it was the last of Ham and Eggs.

Except for the scene-stealing Epic campaign, Californians throughout the thirties were more absorbed in national issues than in those of the state and were more attentive to national politics. The recovery and reform efforts of the New Deal, the reciprocal trade agreements, labor relations as provided for in Section 7A, agricultural benefits, devaluation of the dollar, the threat to pack the Supreme Court, and the third-term issue—questions such as these got attention almost to the exclusion of matters concerned merely with the state. California voting behavior was equivocal and contained a paradox easier to describe than to explain. At each opportunity the state went for Roosevelt, and as regularly it returned its old hero, Hiram Johnson, to the Senate. It elected a fair number of New Dealers to Congress but not until 1938 did it choose a Democratic governor or legislature. Throughout most of the decade, in fact, the state government was so out of sympathy with the New Deal program that it held cooperation to a minimum. For example, not until the very end of the Public Works program were the regents of the University of California willing to accept federal money for much-needed university buildings.

In national politics bitterness intensified as it became apparent that Roosevelt would seek a third and a fourth election. As for California politics, however, the reactionary and radical factions of 1934 moved toward each other and by 1938 were merely conservative and liberal. Another four years of depression made almost everyone accept the procedure of government relief as a matter of course.

In 1938 the Democrats offered a more conventional candidate for governor, the politically experienced Culbert L. Olson, and elected him without much difficulty. A former Epic, Olson was committed to modest reforms, which incorporated a few of the Sinclair planks, for example, relief through production for use. He entered office handicapped by ill health; his friends in the assembly were a majority, but proved disunited and inept; and the unrepresentative senate was still dominated by the conservatives. It was Olson who pardoned Mooney and took a few other steps that might be called liberal. He appointed Democrats to office and among his selections some were egregiously bad. At the time, however, Hitler and Mussolini were plunging toward war. The war came in the ninth month of his governorship, and thereafter the thoughts of Californians ran far more to national and world problems than to what might be done at Sacramento.

In retrospect, the most notable fact about the Olson administration was a facing up at last to the problems of the migratory laborers in California agriculture. By the thirties the pattern was well established that a great part of the state's agriculture, including practically all the larger operations, depended seasonally on a large force of casual laborers. Employers wanted the labor force amply large and unorganized and wage ceilings set and held to throughout the season and throughout the state. Local associations in effect set these ceilings, and after 1920 there was statewide coordination through the Agriculture Committee of the State Chamber of Commerce. Following the strikes and attempts at unionizing in the early thirties, still another agency was created, the Associated Farmers, its prime function being to break strikes and to keep the casual labor force fluid and unorganized.

Until the thirties the laborers had been tramp or foreign and thus had an inferiority handicap. In the thirties the general depression and the local

Company Housing

Dorothea Lange, Oakland Museum

distress in the Dust Bowl sent some 300,000 old-line Americans, the so-called Oakies, to California, most of them intending to do farm work.

The problems faced admittedly were complicated and difficult. How to assure a living wage and yet keep costs within bounds, how to provide adequate housing and yet keep this labor mobile, how to have labor available at the right season and not swamp the relief rolls in the intervening months—these were some of the difficulties innate to the setup. Some of them still plague California.

Under Olson the state government, in cooperation with federal agencies, moved toward ameliorating the conditions. One action was to enforce minimum sanitary requirements at the labor camps and to set up government camps where at least a part of this working force could be accommodated. Another action was to try to regulate the calls for labor in particular harvests so that they would not exceed the actual needs. Still another was to try to restrict the police to police activity rather than have them act as auxiliaries to strikebreaking. A contributory factor of great importance in this approach to the farm labor problem was the detailed investigation carried out by the LaFollette Committee. Before major corrective legislation could be achieved at the state or national level, however, the labor requirements of defense preparations and then of the war effort siphoned off the labor surplus and decidedly altered the problems. The working out of durable and mutually satisfactory farm labor relations consequently was deferred to a later day. Meanwhile, the Oakies and the Arkies, who for a time were regarded as such a problem group, were quickly assimilated into California's already heterogeneous population.

The Boulder Canyon Project

In a planned economy, which California has never had, a depression would be the time for public works. One such enterprise of major proportions was ready for action early in the thirties, the project of damming the Colorado.

In 1921 Phil Swing went to Congress as representative of the seven southern and southeastern counties of the state. His foremost purpose was to win federal support for a flood control program that would make impossible a repetition of the 1905–07 disaster to Imperial Valley. Prior to that time the Southern California Edison Company had under consideration a hydroelectric power installation on the Colorado in Boulder Canyon and the Reclamation Service had proposed dams far upstream to impound floodwaters. In 1920 Arthur Powell Davis of the Reclamation Service had proposed coalescing these two functions in a great dam in Boulder Canyon, which would control the flow of the river and yield a tremendous amount of electric power. Swing had knowledge of this proposal and, en route to Washington, made a detour to Boulder Canyon and inspected the site.

As a lawyer who had represented an irrigation district, Swing saw the advisability of federal involvement in control of the Colorado and in resolution of the claims of the seven basin states and of Mexico. The upper states pushed ahead with a compact reserving to themselves half the flow of the river. In collaboration with Senator Hiram Johnson, Swing introduced a bill to authorize federal construction of a multipurpose dam in Boulder Canyon. By regulating the flow of the river, this dam would safeguard against flooding, and as a high dam it would produce electric power. Over a 50-year period the sale of power was to return to the federal government its investment plus interest.

In the 67th Congress this bill died in committee. In the 68th Congress, Democrats bottled it up as a favor to Senator Carl Hayden of Arizona. In the 69th Congress, Republicans defeated it as requested by private power interests. In 1928, following the Teapot Dome scandal, the private power lobbyists were at a low ebb of influence and passage was possible. It took a few more years before an appropriation was made—$10 million on July 3, 1930. On March 11, 1931, a contract in the amount of $48,890,990 was signed for the construction of the dam and powerhouse.

In September, on the occasion of the driving of the first spike of the access railroad, Secretary of the Interior Ray Lyman Wilbur seized the opportunity to christen the dam-to-be in honor of the then President, Herbert Hoover. Hoover had presided over the drafting of the compact in 1922. From start to finish he had preferred a low dam merely for flood control. Those alert to the steps by which enabling action had been achieved were outraged at this stealing of the dam. Johnson was not one to take such an affront philosophically but, as Beverley Moeller reports, Swing did, merely remarking that "many a child has been named for a man who admittedly was not its father."

Swing had one more task to perform in Washington, the funding of the All-American Canal, which would disentangle the delivery system from international complexity, bring the water in at a higher level, and make lands on the east side of Imperial Valley irrigable. In 1933, when he set out on this mission, there was no need to ask Congress for the money. As one means of combating the Depression, Congress had authorized $3.3 billion for public-works projects. Secretary of the Interior Harold L. Ickes and the Public Works Administration held these purse strings, but the President was the man to see.

Los Angeles Chamber of Commerce

Parker Dam on the Colorado

After carefully laying the groundwork and gathering a delegation representing most of the basin states, Swing successfully took his appeal to Franklin D. Roosevelt. The irrigation customers in prospect were a good risk to repay the $78 million involved.

In addition to their obligations to the federal government for electric power to be picked up at the dam, the southern California contractors planned and prepared to finance $56 million worth of transmission lines. Los Angeles and 44 neighboring communities joined in the Metropolitan Water District and prepared to invest $200 million building Parker Dam, the Metropolitan Aqueduct, its branches, pumping plants, storage reservoirs, and treating plants, through which Colorado River water would be delivered at the rate of a billion gallons a day.

Because the great dam, 1,282 feet in length, 727 feet high, 661 feet thick at the base and 45 feet at the top, was a bigger job and risk than any one company was prepared to handle, the contract was taken by a combine known as the Six Companies. Under the driving direction of Frank Crowe, the task, including preliminary diversion of the river, the building of a railway spur to the site, and the creation of Boulder City to house the workmen, was completed by March, 1936. The dam freed Imperial Valley of flood danger. It created a lake that would store 32 million acre-feet of water, and its generators would produce power at the rate of more than one million kilowatts.

While the dam was rising, work began on the delivery adjuncts, the transmission lines, the All-American Canal, and the Metropolitan Aqueduct, which in sum cost several times as much as the dam itself. By 1941 all three were in operation. They, too, were products of the depression decade.

The Central Valley Project

In this decade California finally decided to come to grips with the water problem of the Sacramento–San Joaquin Valley. The basic idea was to divert surplus water from the northern half of the valley to the southern, thereby minimizing flood danger in the north and alleviating aridity in the south. Supplementary aims were to develop hydroelectric power, improve navigability of the Sacramento, prevent saline intrusion in the Delta area, and furnish water to several towns and cities along the straits.

As early as 1874, B. S. Alexander had proposed such a project. In 1919 Robert Bradford Marshall adopted it and began to popularize it as the Marshall Plan. Some of his details were unduly simplified; he made drawings of canals, wide enough for sailboats, leading down both sides of the great valley. In 1921 the legislature appropriated $200,000 for a scientific study of the plan, but voted down a Water and Power Bill which would have supported the project. In 1922, 1924, and 1926 William Kent, John R. Haynes, James D. Phelan, and Rudolph Spreckels saw to it that the proposal was on the ballot as an initiative measure. Each time the Pacific Gas and Electric Company vigorously opposed it and the measure did not pass.

In 1933, however, the legislature, conservative though it was, passed the Central Valley Project Act, authorizing a bond issue of $170 million to cover construction costs. The private utility companies forced a referendum in which the measure was upheld by 459,712 to 426,109. Instead of trying to find takers for the bond issue, the state government pinned its hopes on getting the federal government to adopt the project and succeeded in 1935 to the extent of a $12 million initial appropriation. Two years later Congress officially declared it a federal reclamation project. The engineering plans, meanwhile, were carried forward, and by the end of the decade work was launched on the two major dams, Shasta and Friant. The role of Shasta Dam is to impound some 4.5 million acre-feet of water on the upper Sacramento, regulate the flow, and generate electric power, some of which is budgeted to pump to the canal that carries water a hundred miles up the San Joaquin Valley. Friant Dam, near Fresno, impounds the San Joaquin River, and the 160-mile Friant–Kern Canal diverts this water southward to the driest part of the Central Valley.

Most of the work on these key units was to fall in the following decade, and other amplifications of the project were reserved for the more distant future. Decision was deferred also on many knotty problems of admin-

Furrows for Sugar-beet Planting, near King City

Dorothea Lange, Farm Security Administration

istration and control. Should the Reclamation Bureau, the Army Engineers, or the state exercise control? Should publicly owned distributors have preference in sales of power? Should the Reclamation Bureau's customary 160-acre limitation on water sales be enforced? These and other fundamental questions were left to be answered later. Because the project lay entirely within the state, some of the patterns in other river developments were not entirely applicable. Since if fully developed, its potentialities so far exceeded others, such as the Tennessee Valley Authority, the ultimate arrangement would be a matter of very great moment. With the advocates of effective public control on the one hand and private interests, as represented by the Pacific Gas and Electric and the great landowners on the other, an epic tug of war was in the making. The depression-ridden thirties left these matters unresolved but did posterity the inestimable service of crystallizing the plans and launching this most ambitious project.

In the never-ending task of modernizing the state highway system and in a public building program involving schools, libraries, courthouses, and government office buildings, much of it federally financed, California advanced during the thirties. It was a period during which private enterprise was less venturesome. With the Federal Housing Authority as angel, however, a fair amount of residential construction did take place. The railroads also began to reequip with diesels and streamliners. In agriculture, cotton raising and dairying expanded rapidly as did the commercial fishing based at California ports. Several branches of industry gained, notably cement making, but the most striking innovation was the rise of airplane building.

Until the mid-thirties California's best-known contribution to aviation was that Lindbergh's *Spirit of St. Louis* had been assembled and conditioned at San Diego. Shortly thereafter the plants of Douglas, Lockheed, and North American at Santa Monica, El Segundo, Inglewood, and Burbank gave the state high rank in airplane manufacture. The availability of electric power was a factor as was the reservoir of skilled labor. The climate of southern California was congenial to the sprawling plants and afforded open weather for test flights the year round. By the end of the decade this industry accounted for more than 10 per cent of industrial employment in the state.

In a way, the inescapably dominant note of the thirties was the reality of the depression, its body blows to the economy and its disjointing of society. A feature of almost comparable significance was the tendency to look to the federal government to provide a remedy. It was a time when the graphs and the indexes were down. Nevertheless, in addition to construction on the Colorado and planning in the Central Valley, California made substantial progress during this troubled decade. The annual totals in many lines of production advanced, including cotton, fruits, milk, canned goods, oil refining, moving pictures, airplanes, and paved highways. Though not so spectacularly as in better times, the state continued its population climb, moving from 5,677,251 in 1930 to 6,907,387 in 1940, thereby acquiring a larger increment than any other state. All told, there was solid achievement despite adversity.

For Further Reading

DOROTHEA LANGE and PAUL S. TAYLOR, *American Exodus* (1939; 1969).

JOHN STEINBECK, *In Dubious Battle* (1936).

JOHN STEINBECK, *The Grapes of Wrath* (1939).

CAREY MCWILLIAMS, *Factories in the Fields* (1939).

CLARKE A. CHAMBERS, *California Farm Organizations* (1952).

PAUL ELIEL, *The Waterfront and General Strikes, San Francisco* (1934).

MIKE QUIN, *The Big Strike* (1949).

LUTHER WHITEMAN and SAMUEL LEWIS, *Glory Roads: The Psychological State of California* (1936).

UPTON SINCLAIR, *I, Governor of California, and How I Ended Poverty* (1933).

UPTON SINCLAIR, *I, Candidate for Governor, and How I Got Licked* (1934).

ABRAHAM HOLTZMAN, *The Townsend Movement, A Political Study* (1963).

WINSTON MOORE and MARIAN MOORE, *Out of the Frying Pan* (1939), Ham and Eggs.

ROBERT E. BURKE, *Olson's New Deal for California* (1953).

BEVERLEY R. MOELLER, Phil Swing and the Boulder Canyon Project (UCLA dissertation, 1969).

ROBERT DE ROOS, *The Thirsty Land, The Story of the Central Valley Project* (1948).

CAUGHEY, *California Heritage*, 414–28.

chapter twenty-eight

A Distinctive Culture

Physically attached to the West rather than belonging to the West, culturally isolated from the rest of America during decades when it grew ''like a gourd in the night,'' California has always struggled, however uncomprehendingly, for independent expression.

Carey McWilliams,
Southern California Country

The Environment Rediscovered

**1914
to
1945**

The men of the gold-rush era, though engaged in work that was often peculiar, did their utmost to reproduce the pattern of living they had known back home. Likewise, the people of the next generation, though operating an economy that was distinctive, felt a compunction to conform to the national standard in things cultural. California women, to the best of their ability, dressed exactly like their sisters in the East, and male attire ran to the conventional somber colors, hard collars and cuffs, high shoes, and no laying aside of vests or hats. In architecture the fearsome ornateness and eclecticism of the period had full force locally as well as in the East.

Upon the next generation, bounded roughly by the two world wars, national urges in things social continued to have great effect. The people of the state were Americans first and Californians

Robinson Jeffers

Sonya Noskourak, The Huntington Library and Art Gallery

second. They went hand in hand with the rest of the country in discarding chewing tobacco and taking up the cigarette, in accepting women at the polls and in employment, in filling the home with gadgets and machines, in going along with the trend toward chain stores and packaged goods, in moving about with increased ease, and in recognizing that many of the problems of the time were beyond solution by local authority or by private initiative. In some respects the Californians of these years went beyond the national average; for example, in gearing themselves to the automobile, in shifting to suburban residence, and in adapting their dress and dwellings to the climate. In these and in other perhaps more significant particulars they moved toward a cultural pattern distinctively Californian.

Not least among the factors promoting this movement was what might be called a rediscovery of the environment. The wonders of the Yosemite, it is true, had been extolled for a generation, and the High Sierra had its devotees. The health rush had involved appraisal of the state's many subclimates, and the state's agriculture, by trial and science, had achieved an adjustment to the environmental facts. Yet overall appreciation of what Nature offered waited until the twentieth century when highways and the automobile made the remote parts of the state accessible.

With literally thousands and tens of thousands turning out where only dozens had gone before, problems arose of how to accommodate such crowds and at the same time preserve the beauties and wonders of Nature against such an onslaught. One answer, now commonplace, was through the National Parks Service and the taking charge of parks, monuments, forests, beaches, and historic sites by federal or state custodians.

As long ago as 1864 Yosemite Valley was designated a state park. In 1890, alerted by the intrusions of cattlemen and sheepherders, the federal government set aside about a thousand square miles adjoining this valley as Yosemite National Park. At the same time, stirred by the Kaweah communitarians and their project for lumbering in the vicinity of the big trees, Congress also created Sequoia and General Grant National Parks, embracing about 250 square miles. In most cases the military was put in charge, which usually meant control without specialized personnel. This was one reason for the friction with the civilians whom the state had placed in charge at Yosemite Valley. In 1906 Yosemite was unified through reconveyance of title to the federal government, but not until 1916 with the creation of the National Parks Service was the care put on a really satisfactory basis. At Sequoia civilian control began in 1914. The modern program has this degree of recency.

More recently further additions were made to the areas protected by park control. In 1926 about 350 square miles in the Mt. Whitney–Kern River district were added to Sequoia. In 1933 Death Valley and its environs, almost 3,000 square miles of exposed geology and unbelievable color effects, became a national monument. In 1940 the Kings Canyon area immediately north of Sequoia, some 700 square miles in extent, was made a national park. Mt. Lassen, the Lava Beds, the Pinnacles, the Devil's Post Pile, and Muir Woods are other national parks or monuments.

The state too has taken jurisdiction over a number of sites, some of them historic, such as the Mother Lode town of Columbia and the Marshall monument at Coloma. But most of them were at favored and threatened beach frontages or at the most spectacular of the redwood groves from Del Norte County south as far as the Big Sur. A few of these sites, such as Santa Cruz Big Trees, were subject to earlier pilgrimage by rail, but practically all came to be of major interest only in the automobile era. Thus the state park system like the national assumed its real proportions and importance in the period after the First World War.

In 1915 San Francisco celebrated the completion of the Panama Canal with the Panama–Pacific Exposition on the flats to leeward of the Golden Gate. Notable for its encouragement of arts and letters, for its exhibits and lighting effects, this fair was of less enduring influence than the concurrent Panama–California Exposition at San Diego. The directors of the San Diego fair dramatized the regional culture of the Southwest, presenting a review of the patterns of living from prehistoric times to the twentieth century, with stress on the blossoming of the desert and the semiarid land whenever irrigation was applied, and displayed an architecture skillfully attuned to the land and climate.

Some of the buildings were permanent structures for Balboa Park, but the architectural influence was even more pervasive. Asked to accent Pan American relationships, Bertram Goodhue drew on the elements of the Spanish Renaissance and the Spanish colonial. Working primarily in bright tones of tile and stucco, with towers, domes, and arcades, he achieved variety, sparkle, and brilliance. Enthusiastically received by visitors to the fair, this theme infected the architectural trends of the time especially in southern California.

In the realm of residential design Richard Neutra, Frank Lloyd Wright, and others began to use the functional approach and took into account the opportunities of the locale. Once it was conceded that a California house did not have to look like a Spanish castle, a Cape Cod cottage, or a midwestern farmhouse, it was possible to open it so that the patio or garden became an integral part of the living area and to make other innovations to fit the surroundings. A great deal of construction was as conservative as ever, but the leaven of seizing upon the local advantages was increasingly present. The Los Angeles Union Station, Cliff May's Sunset Building at Menlo Park, and Carmel as it was in the 1930's are examples of this adaption of architecture to its environment.

In dress also this generation of Californians came to be less formal and less confined. The escape from corsets, collars, and excess layers of cloth was, to be sure, not confined to California, but the benign climate, the prevalence of vacationers, and the boldness of the state's own clothing designers made this unconventionality more tempting.

In addition to the day-to-day enjoyment of the outdoors and the daily adjustments to it, Californians devised a number of ways to capitalize on it. One was through the staging of special events such as the Los Angeles performance of the Olympic Games in 1932, another fair at San Diego in 1935, and the Golden Gate International Exposition at Treasure Island in 1938. Other activities were annual performances such as the Salinas Rodeo, the Santa Barbara

Fiesta, and the Pasadena Tournament of Roses and Rose Bowl game. Still another salute to the climate was in carrying the theater and the concert outdoors. Here again something of the sort is done at Tanglewood, by the Potomac, at the Red Rocks Theater in Colorado, and in Santa Fe. The beginning may have been the High Jinks of the Bohemian Club of San Francisco. Then came outdoor theater and pageantry in Marin County and in the Greek Theater in Berkeley. John McGroarty's Mission Play ran for many years at San Gabriel, and Ramona had even longer popularity at Hemet. Hollywood's Pilgrimage Play was another hardy perennial.

At the turn of the century the Point Loma Colony had an amphitheater in which Greek plays and classical music were performed. Open-air concerts at the Ford Bowl in Balboa Park were a feature of the 1915 exposition. At Ojai some years later an annual music festival was initiated. Most ambitious of all were the Symphonies Under the Stars in Hollywood Bowl, begun in 1921 and continued in spite of the competition of radio and television and the handicaps of traffic congestion and airplane interference.

Besides these al fresco concerts, Los Angeles had opportunity to hear its Philharmonic Orchestra established in 1919 through the philanthropy of W. A. Clark, Jr. The San Francisco Symphony Orchestra was much older and since 1911 had been in part municipally supported. San Francisco also supported its own opera company and in 1932 outfitted it with a home in the Civic Center, the first municipal opera house in the United States. No less significant as an institution in this epoch, and reaching a much larger audience, was the Standard Hour, a weekly radio program in which the San Francisco and Los Angeles orchestras were the most frequent performers.

Creative Artists

Since the time of the first railroad and Comstock fortunes, the number of privately owned masterpieces of art in California constantly mounted. Hung side by side these would make something less than a Louvre but a very creditable, instructive, and inspiring display. Although many of these canvases remained in sterile seclusion, there was most encouraging progress in making them available to the public. Old museums, such as the M. H. De Young in Golden Gate Park, were enlarged and enriched, and new galleries of even greater size and distinction were opened. These include the Palace of the Legion of Honor in San Francisco, the Los Angeles Museum of History, Science and Art, the Fine Arts Gallery in San Diego's Balboa Park, the Louis Terah Haggin Memorial Galleries at Stockton, and the Henry E. Huntington Art Gallery at San Marino.

Several of these galleries served as focal points for contemporary art work. The Carmel and Laguna Beach art colonies attracted large contingents of painters, poets, composers, and kindred spirits. Many another creative artist rose above outward circumstances and served his muse though dwelling in an orthodox bungalow hard by a bustling boulevard or in the lee of a movie lot.

The Watts Towers, Simon Rodía's Gift to His Neighborhood

Nick King

Of the notable artists of the period two men working in different media illustrate a tendency that was growing. Edward Borein of Santa Barbara used his exceptional talent in print-making to revitalize on copper the life of the western range. Edward Weston, using camera and tripod rather than easel or drafting board, found beauty lurking not only at California's showplaces but also in the most casual scenes. Borein saw artistic values in the state's past; Weston had sharper discernment of the artistic implications of this land and climate and a readiness to use new approaches in capitalizing upon them.

The patronage of music brought many performers to California. Other artists were attracted by the no longer silent films and still others by the climatic advantages of life in California. A few, such as Lawrence Tibbett and Luisa Tetrazzini, are listed as California contributions to music, but to what extent the state can lay claim to Amelita Galli-Curci or to the recent German exiles, Arnold Schoenberg and Otto Klemperer, is a debatable point. The important thing is that there was mustered in the state a generous allotment of the world's most talented musicians.

The Fishing Fleet, Monterey

Edward Weston

A Galaxy of Writers

California in the twenties and thirties was enriched through writers of eminence imported by the moving-picture studios. Theodore Dreiser stayed only briefly; F. Scott Fitzgerald and Eugene Manlove Rhodes, a little longer; and others, from a few weeks to the rest of their lives, including Irvin S. Cobb, Will Rogers, James M. Cain, John O'Hara, Nathanael West, and Aldous Huxley.

Every one of these writers made contributions in scenario or treatment or other working papers preliminary to the shooting of a picture. That, however, is not a recognized or readily accessible branch of literature. As California writers, therefore, these artists are judged by their moonlighting: Huxley for his *After Many a Summer Dies the Swan* (1939), West for *The Day of the Locust* (1939), and Fitzgerald for *The Last Tycoon* (1941).

In 1969 Huxley's *Brave New World* (1932) was target for savage attack by a clique of far rightists in Tustin bent on keeping the book off high school reading lists. *After Many a Summer* is memorable for its deflating of Los Angeles, William Randolph Hearst, and Forest Lawn, a formidable trinity. *The Last Tycoon,* unfinished at the time of Fitzgerald's death, gave promise of being the most revealing vignette of Hollywood, a role devastatingly essayed by Budd Schulberg in *What Makes Sammy Run?* (1941).

The attitude of the eastern establishment toward writers in the plush exile of Hollywood is well illustrated in Edmund Wilson's greeting to *The Day of the Locust* (from *The Boys in the Backroom,* 1941, pp. 68–69).

> Nathanael West, the brilliant author of *Miss Lonelyhearts,* went to Hollywood several years ago, and his silence had been causing his readers alarm lest he might have faded out on the Coast as so many of his fellows have done. But Mr. West, as this new book happily proves, is still alive beyond the mountains, and can still tell what he feels and sees—has still, in short, remained an artist. His new novel, *The Day of the Locust,* deals with the nondescript characters on the edges of the Hollywood studios....

> Mr. West has caught the emptiness of Hollywood; and he is, as far as I know, the first writer to make this emptiness horrible.

The state had more than its share of writers of westerns, including the inordinately productive Frederick Faust. It abounded in mystery writers. Raymond Chandler, as Philip Durham has pointed out in *Down These Mean Streets* (1963), used the medium of the detective story to support a vivid documentary on the southern California scene.

Edwin Corle in *Mojave* (1934), *Fig Tree John* (1938), *Three Ways to Mecca* (1947), and several other books proved himself an adept storyteller, primarily interested in the southern California interior, with which he dealt in a few works of nonfiction, notably *Desert Country* (1941).

John Steinbeck
The Bancroft Library

Another writer versatile in fiction and nonfiction was George Stewart, who also kept his hand in as a professor of English. His *Names on the Land* (1944), *Committee of Vigilance* (1964), and *Ordeal by Hunger* (1936, 1960) are representative of the scholar at work. *Ordeal by Hunger* is the most reliable account of the Donner tragedy. *Storm* (1941), his best-known title, is based on field work, interviews, and consulting the authorities as scholars are supposed to do. The packaging, however, is as a dramatized biography of a weather front moving in from the Pacific and depositing its sudden burst of precipitation on the Bay area, the inner valley and foothills, and the Sierra. *Fire* (1947) by the same formula is the life history of a forest fire and its impact on man.

William Saroyan, a more freewheeling writer, was at his most fluent in the 1930's and 1940's. He wrote innumerable stories and descriptions, favoring particularly the Armenians in and around Fresno and the personnel of the seedier parts of San Francisco. A set of short stories, *The Daring Young Man on the Flying Trapeze* (1934), and two plays for the screen, *The Time of Your Life* (1939) and *The Human Comedy* (1943), are representative.

At about the same time John Steinbeck began to publish intimate stories about the paisanos of Monterey County—*The Pastures of Heaven* (1932), *To a God Unknown* (1933), and *Tortilla Flat* (1935). With *In Dubious Battle* (1936) and *Of Mice and Men* (1937) he spoke forcefully for the downtrodden laborers in California agriculture. Then in 1939 he capped this arch with a novel of epic proportions on the hegira of the Dust Bowl refugees and their grievous mistreatment and suffering as migratory farm laborers in California. This book, *The Grapes of Wrath*, dwarfs the earlier novels of protest, such as Helen Hunt Jackson's *Ramona* and Frank Norris' *The Octopus*, and transposed readily into a trenchant film. Steinbeck, it has been suggested, had learned from the films and in his writing was "going part of the way to meet the producers."

Steinbeck continued writing and in the forties moved to New England. In some of his later works he returned to California themes, though less felicitously. The award to him of the Nobel prize was principally for the sequence that culminated in *The Grapes of Wrath*.

Alongside these writers of prose range a multitude of poets among whom Robinson Jeffers stands out in solitary greatness. In 1925 Jeffers attracted immediate attention with the publication of *Roan Stallion*. More than a dozen volumes set against the background of the Carmel region and the rugged Big

Bixby Creek Bridge on the Big Sur Coast

Department of Public Works, Division of Highways

Sur country followed. He acknowledged a large debt to "the magnificent un-spoiled scenery" of the Monterey peninsula, "the introverted and storm-twisted beauty of Point Lobos," the bold headlands jutting out into fog and ocean, and "the savage beauty of canyon and sea-cliff." The surging ocean, the gulls and hawks, the tortured cypress and redwoods—these and a thousand other elements of the "Jeffers country" are interlinked with his themes.

Universals are his chosen subjects and a steady seriousness dominates his writing. To him only Nature is significant and worthy of being eternal. He relentlessly rages against man's inhumanity, shortsightedness, and lack of respect for truth. In poem after poem he warns of the inevitable destruction of the human race if man continues the senselessness and horror of war, his onslaughts on the planet, and the population explosion—"the torrents of new-born babies, the bursting schools."

In one of his short poems, "Diagrams," he describes two curves in "the air that man's fate breathes": the rise and fall of the Christian culture-complex that now "drifts to decline" and the curve of the future that began at Kittyhawk. He predicts that when the two curves cross "you will see monsters."

Jeffers has not been the people's poet. He has had harsh criticism for his obsession with tragedy and violence. Random House, which had published his earlier books, brought out *The Double Axe* in 1948 with a foreword dis-sociating itself from some of the political expressions in the poems. The state-ment ended: "Time alone is the court of last resort in the case of ideas on trial."

The time may not be far in the future when considered opinion will reverse its verdict on Jeffers and acclaim him for the warnings and angry denunciations that at first were uncomfortable and therefore repugnant. In this gentle man the people may realize that they had a poet passionately concerned for man's plight.

Schools and Libraries

In facilities for the spread, care, and increase of knowledge California registered a substantial advance in the interval between the two world wars. For the dissemination of knowledge the dependence was chiefly on institutions established much earlier but substantially modified. In large degree the reliance was on the public school system. At the elementary and secondary levels these schools were organized in districts and were locally controlled, subject, how-ever, to certain standards enforced by the state board of education. The certi-fication of teachers, for example, was set up as a state function, part of the requirement being graduation from college to qualify for elementary teaching and a year of advanced work to qualify for high school teaching. The state specified minimum salaries and, to eliminate the extreme differences in tax burden, adopted the practice of making sizable remittances to each district proportionate to the average daily attendance.

As the richest state in the West, California could afford to appropriate generously for the school program. As of 1940 the per capita expenditure was exceeded only in New York. The problem, however, was made difficult by the extremely rapid increase in school population, which more than doubled between 1914 and 1940. School districts had to race to catch up with the needs for buildings, equipment, and staff.

California schools showed a moderate willingness to experiment. Architecturally, and most markedly at the college level, they followed closely the stereotyped imitations of midwestern business blocks and medieval castles. On occasion, however, a school board authorized a functional structure designed to take full advantage of the sunlight and the fresh air that are California's priceless heritage. By 1940 this type of school architecture was on the increase. As for teaching methods a restrained experimentalism was in vogue. One trend was toward the project method in the grades in place of formal drill. An early example of change was in the introduction of laboratory science in the high schools. A subsequent example was the fusion course.

Other innovations that developed were in the degree to which bus transportation made possible the consolidation of small schools, toning up of standards in high schools through the state university's system of entrance requirements and accrediting, generous provision for vocational and adult education, and the popularity of the junior college. The junior college had a shadowy beginning in 1907 when high schools were authorized to offer postgraduate work. A decade later junior colleges were made an integral part of the state school system. By 1939, with 49 institutions of this rank, 42 of them public, California was far and away the leading utilizer of this mechanism. By 1951 the number had grown to 75, with total enrollment at 302,130, more than in all the rest of the nation.

The higher echelon of the state's educational system included seven or eight state normal schools, a larger number of privately controlled colleges and universities, and the state university. In the course of these years the normal schools broadened their programs and became state colleges though still putting much emphasis on teacher training. The private schools, headed in enrollment by the University of Southern California and Stanford, in most instances rested on foundations laid in the preceding generation. The state university was in the midst of a rapid expansion, in 1919 annexing the Los Angeles State Normal School as a seventh campus and throughout the twenties and thirties gaining in enrollment at an unprecedented rate. By 1940 its student body was larger than any other university's anywhere. More significant, its Berkeley faculty, according to the findings of a Carnegie Institution survey, was surpassed in "distinction" only by the faculty of Harvard and that only slightly.

In library building California had done well also. No library in the state in 1940 was on a par with the British Museum, the Bibliotèque Nationale, the Library of Congress, the Harvard Library, or a dozen others in the older parts of the nation and world. By their essentially accumulative nature, libraries are the product of time, and in California time had been short. The oldest of its major collections was the State Library, in its early years a victim of mismanagement but later vastly improved. The most notable general collection was that of the University of California, which in 70 years had carried its accessions well

Berkeley Campus, University of California

Ansel Adams, Fiat Lux, University of California Press

beyond the million mark. Less venerable and less extensive holdings included those of the Los Angeles Public, Stanford University, the University of Southern California, Claremont Colleges, and the University of California at Los Angeles. Special mention should be made of the device of branch libraries and inter-library loans whereby the state, county, and city libraries conspired to make books readily available at a multitude of stations. Without such machinery the Los Angeles Public would not have achieved the largest circulation among American libraries.

By a liberal outlay of funds, a tireless zest in pursuit of materials, or a combination of the two, several world-famous special collections had been assembled. The Bancroft Library of Pacific States materials has been described. Stanford University boasted the Hoover Library of War, Revolution, and Peace, unsurpassed on certain phases of the First World War, the Russian Revolution, and the relief efforts. At San Marino the Henry E. Huntington Library and Art Gallery was opened to visitors and researchers. Its rich store of English paint-ings, English history and literature, and Californiana represented lavish expen-diture of the Huntington millions. As for California materials, the Huntington had become a good second to the Bancroft. In this field, too, research was greatly assisted by the special collections of the California Historical Society and the Southwest Museum, the Cowan collection at the University of California at Los Angeles, the assemblage started by Lummis at the Los Angeles Public, the Mason collection at Pomona, and the Layne collection at the University of Southern California. Other collections, such as the Clark in Los Angeles and the Sutro in San Francisco, had special resources in other fields.

In sum, these aids and materials for research in the humanities make a respectable total, yet it would have been quite out of step with modern times if they had been as impressive or represented a tithe of the investment in facili-ties for research in the sciences. Needless to say, they did not. In research laboratories maintained by many of the industries, such as the oil and the air-plane companies, and in laboratories at the major universities, special provisions were made for a great variety of scientific research. Some of it was intended to be immediately practical. On the whole, this was the case in the industrial research centers. The university's researchers in agricultural science were also, in effect, on call to try to solve any problem that might arise in crop production. Hopes of allaying suffering and improving health underlay the researches in medicine.

The practical utility of the study carried on, however, was not always expected to be direct. Into this category of basic research some of the largest investments went, particularly into the "unapplied" branches of astronomy, chemistry, and physics. Private, state, and federal funds were drawn upon in varying proportion and fashion to underwrite these research preparations. The astronomical record will serve as an example.

In 1874 an eccentric millionaire, James Lick, donated $700,000 to the University of California with which to build an observatory. His first thought was to put it at Fourth and Market in San Francisco, then he veered to the idea of a mountaintop and settled on Mt. Hamilton, south of San Jose, partly because it overlooked the site of a flour mill of his. Thus was initiated the scientifically advantageous device of perching a telescope in the clear atmosphere of the mountains. With a 35-inch refracting telescope, for many years the second most powerful in existence, the Lick Observatory was a focal point for astronomical research.

Thaddeus S. C. Lowe, Lewis Spence, and other promoters and popular scientists were inspired by the Lick Observatory and longed for something like it, only larger, in southern California. Their notion was taken up at the turn of the century by a trained astronomer, George Ellery Hale, who raised support for a scientific search for an ideal observatory site. The specifications included such factors as latitude 30 to 35 north, moderate but not excessive altitude, equable temperature, stability of weather, a minimum of clouds and overcast, no undue turbulence of air currents, and accessibility to an inhabited center where machine shops, supplies, and accommodations for visitors could be had. Mt. Wilson met the specifications. Hale then went to work on acquaintances of means, many of whom had retired to Pasadena's millionaires' row. By 1917 he had a 100-inch telescope ready to operate, for the next 20 years the world's largest, together with the other appurtenances for effective study and research.

As the work at Mt. Wilson progressed, Hale raised his sights to a still more ambitious project. In 1928 he persuaded the Rockefeller Foundation to commission a still larger telescope and to budget $6 million for the purpose. The sea of lights that had developed on the plains below Mt. Wilson ruled it out as the location. While the 200-inch refractor was being ground, southern California was combed for the most eligible site, the choice falling on Mt. Palomar in San Diego County. The partly ground glass arrived in Pasadena in 1936; another 12 years of painstaking work were necessary before the telescope was completed and installed, ready to reach out to the very boundaries of the universe.

Meanwhile, other arsenals for scientific research were being prepared. At Pasadena, as a sort of adjunct to his observatory, Hale envisioned a scientific institute. He convinced a number of wealthy Pasadenans to finance the idea. In 1917 Robert A. Millikan joined forces with Hale. He was as adept as Hale in enlisting benefactors of great wealth and he had a remarkable gift for selecting areas of research in which the prospect for significant findings was at a maximum. Within a very few years the California Institute of Technology won recognition as one of the most effective agencies of its kind in the country. The assembled staff and faculty deserved much of the credit, enabled, however, by the material equipment supplied by Hale, Millikan, and the donors.

In quantity and caliber of research facilities the institute was surpassed by the university at Berkeley. There a noteworthy improvement also took place in the period before 1940. It was interdisciplinary, embracing practically all the branches of science, but its most arresting feature was the Radiation Laboratory at work on the then mystical experiment in atomic fission.

Perhaps the most surprising thing was that a state as new as California, only recently graduated from frontier status, should be almost without peer in its marshalling of forces for exploration of the frontiers of scientific knowledge.

Historical Scholarship

So far as appreciation of scholarship was concerned, the scientists of this epoch collected the major plaudits. Astronomers such as Hale and Edwin Hubble certainly deserved them. Berkeley had an active coterie of anthropologists of great reputation. Its department of physics and its school of chemistry had equal distinction, and the college of agriculture, though somewhat narrowed to California's peculiar problems, ranked with the best. These examples could be extended. Scholarly attainment, however, was not confined to the sciences. It occurred also in the humanities, for which the field of history may be taken as an example.

The new and improved libraries became veritable arsenals for the researcher in history. Monographs published under the auspices of the Hoover Library by 1940 were into their second dozen, which indicates but inadequately the extent to which this collection had been used. Although at the Huntington the casual observer saw first of all the crowds pressing in to view the book exhibits, paintings, and gardens, behind the scenes an ever-growing group of "readers" was hard at work on problems in English literature and history, and California history. Certain new techniques, notably interlibrary loan service and the perfection of the photofilm method of copying books and manuscripts, opened unexpected doors to California historians. Among the results made possible were California books on such outlandish subjects as the modern French Empire in Africa and the Orient, the Spanish Floridas, and the dissolution of the Carolingian fisc.

California history, meanwhile, was brought under scrutiny by a number of very competent amateurs, that is, historians in the business for the fun of it rather than because of any economic urge. Many of the best results in this quarter century were achieved by historians of this group. Their works are cited by the score in this book's reading lists and bibliography, but too much emphasis cannot be laid on the great service to local historiography rendered by these men in the pursuit of their avocation. At the head of the lists in their respective divisions stand the bibliographies of Wagner and Cowan, Hanna's chronological commentary, Wagner's analyses of cartography and explorations, the biographies by Harding, Lyman, Watson, and Dana, and the miscellaneous writings of a host of others, among them Camp, Wheat, Chalfant, Robinson, Glasscock, and McWilliams. In this connection it is significant that the California Historical Society, the Historical Society of Southern California, and numerous local societies actively meeting, collecting, and publishing were maintained by energetic groups of nonprofessional enthusiasts.

The normal expectation in this era of specialization was that historical research should be primarily the work of professionals. In Bancroft's day California history was not written thus and, as recently as 1907 when the Native Sons of the Golden West proposed to endow a chair of California history, the president of the University of California demurred, in chagrin we hope, because there was no scholar at the university or elsewhere competent to fill such a chair. To the credit of the university it must be admitted that, assisted by the Native Sons, it set out at once to remedy that defect. Nevertheless, at this writing, more than 60 years later, no such chair has been set up.

In 1906 the university acquired the Bancroft Library, consisting of some 60,000 volumes of books, manuscripts, and newspapers. Then in 1910 H. Morse Stephens, head of the history department, persuaded the Native Sons to advance funds sufficient for two annual traveling fellowships. The following year Herbert E. Bolton was brought to the department expressly for the purpose of directing and leading the utilization of the resources of the Bancroft Library in graduate work and research. These elements, the Bancroft materials, the fellowships, Morse Stephens and Bolton, explain much of the renown earned by the Berkeley history department.

Recognition was also due the department for its all-round strength. A few years earlier the department had been said to consist of a sham giant surrounded by real pygmies, but the addition of Americanists Priestley, McCormac, and Chapman and of a group of specalists in the European field headed by Morris, Paetow, Palm, and Kerner gave the university a distinguished staff unequaled within a radius of half the breadth of the continent. Later this brilliance was further enhanced by the provision of two endowed chairs to which were called James Westfall Thompson, the celebrated medievalist, and Frederic L. Paxson, outstanding authority on the American frontier and the recent history of the United States.

There were, however, two particular concepts fundamental to the flourishing of the Berkeley graduate work in history. One was the realization that the archives of Spain and Mexico contained a marvelous wealth of materials for the history of California and of every other part of the New World in which Spain had once been interested. Bancroft had had only a slight awareness of the existence of these materials; Stephens gained a notion of the extent of the Spanish archives when he made a preliminary survey in 1910; Bolton was already conversant with Mexico's archival riches, for he had examined them with care and had prepared a guide to their resources for United States history. For the other fundamental, Bolton was primarily responsible. It was a simple idea, yet revolutionary, namely, that American history is best studied not within state or national confines but on a continental or, better still, on a hemispheric basis. Thoughtful analysis of California's history would seem to point inevitably to this deduction, but, if Bancroft grasped it, the only evidence is that he decided to broaden his project to take in the entire Pacific slope, and other historians had been content to stay within the United States, or even within a portion of it.

Catalyzed by this vision of broader horizons, nurtured on the riches that Bancroft had stored up, vitalized by the magnificent documentation preserved in the Spanish and Mexican archives, stimulated and assisted by the Native Sons Fellowships, and inspired by the leadership of Stephens and Bolton, the Berkeley graduate group in American history made itself one of the most dynamic, prolific, and significant in the country. Its doctors of philosophy predominated in the field of Hispanic American history; they became major workers in the field of the Spanish borderlands, prominent in the field of the American westward movement and the American West, including Hawaii, and the leading exponents of the study of the history of the Americas, the Western Hemisphere in its entirety. Concerning this group the term "California school" gained currency and more legitimately than if it were applied to any set of the state's poets, novelists, painters, or sculptors.

Many of these historians engaged in studies that relate distantly or not at all to California. Others turned their attention to local problems with such commendable result that of the references, other than first-hand accounts, tabulated in the accompanying bibliography more than a third are credited to this California school. Outstanding among these are Bolton's works on Kino, Anza, Crespi, and Paloú, Charles E. Chapman's *Catalogue,* his volume on the founding, the Chapman-Cleland *History,* Owen Coy's work on the gold-rush era, Cardinal Goodwin's studies of the establishment of state government and of Frémont, and Joseph Ellison's account of early federal relations. Thus the list begins: it goes on to include published items running the whole gamut of the state's history, not to mention scores of manuscript theses deposited in the university library. These works naturally are as variegated as the men who produced them, yet practically all exemplify these characteristics: they are based to a very large degree on sources and on fresh sources, and they treat California as an element in continental and world relationships rather than as a state poised in a vacuum.

For Further Reading

EDWARD WESTON, *California and the West* (1940).

ANSEL ADAMS, *The Sierra Nevada* (1938).

FRANCOIS E. MATTHES, *The Incomparable Valley: A Geologic Interpretation of the Yosemite* (1950).

FRANCIS P. FARQUHAR, *History of the Sierra Nevada* (1965).

RODERICK B. PEATTIE, *The Pacific Coast Ranges* (1946).

ANNE B. FISHER, *The Salinas, Upside-down River* (1941).

JOHN FONTENROSE, *John Steinbeck, An Introduction and Interpretation* (1964).

LAWRENCE CLARK POWELL, *An Introduction to Robinson Jeffers* (1932; 1940).

DAVID BROWER, *Not Man Apart; Lines from Robinson Jeffers; Photographs of the Big Sur Coast* (1965).

GEORGE STERLING, *Continent's End: An Anthology of Contemporary Poets* (1925).

JOSEPH HENRY JACKSON, *Continent"s End: A Collection of California Writing* (1944).

DAVID O. WOODBURY, *The Glass Giant of Palomar* (1946).

JOHN W. CAUGHEY, "Herbert Eugene Bolton," *American West,* 1 (1964), 36–39, 79.

CAUGHEY, *California Heritage,* 348–94, 403–29.

chapter twenty-nine

Wartime Upsurge

The Second World War removed the last traces of California's isolation; it increased her manufacturing output, measured in dollars, more than three times over; it established her as the center of American aviation, military and civilian; and, because a Japanese submarine popped out of the ocean one day and took a random shot at a pier near Santa Barbara it made her the only State in the Union to lose even a few slivers of wood by enemy action. . . .

The hold of venerable traditions loosened. Even in San Francisco people didn't look back to the Gold Rush or to the "Earthquake and Fire" as earnestly as they used to; they looked forward; after all, they did have those bridges. In Los Angeles the annual Iowa picnic would never again be the event of the year.

R. L. Duffus,
Queen Calafia's Island (1965)

1939 to 1945

In 1939, though the decade just closing had been one of travail, California could look back on an epoch of lusty growth. In the comparatively short span of 90 years as an American state she had come from nowhere to be fifth among the states in population, fifth in taxable income, at the top in agricultural production, and perhaps over the top in attention claimed. No other state had matched this increase; sober opinion doubted that even California could maintain the pace.

In September, 1939, however, Hitler sent his Panzers into Poland, and overnight Europe was caught up in a war that soon had world dimensions. For a time the United States remained neutral, though this was a war about which it was impossible to remain dispassionate and from which it was most difficult to remain detached.

Building a Bomber, Long Beach

Palmer, Office of War Information

The fact of world war, even though the United States was not a belligerent, radically changed the outlook for California. Then, on December 7, 1941, by attack without warning on Pearl Harbor, Japan snatched away America's neutrality and plunged the nation into the vortex of the European as well as the Pacific war. This development was a stimulant to the economy such as the state had never experienced. It involved a degree of planned and coordinated effort that had not been present before, and it provided a special patriotic incentive that was entirely new. Thus mobilized, California achieved material gains that surpassed even the greatest of her earlier attainments.

Plant and Potential

When the war started, California's economy was set up and adjusted to the needs and opportunities of peacetime. Annual income as of 1939–40 was approximately $5 billion. Primary production in fisheries, forests, mines, farms, and factories accounted for about half of the total. Fisheries yielded some $20 million; forests $87 million; mines about $400 million, the greater part in petroleum; agriculture $625 million; construction $417 million; and manufacturing, on goods with a market value of $2,798 million, was credited with addition of $1,135 million through processing. The other half of the annual income came from values added through distribution and services, a broad category including everything from wholesale and retail trade to utilities and transportation, hotels, laundries, theaters, personal service, and the professions. Part of this income was derived from investments outside the state and from expenditures by tourists and other visitors within the state.

A peculiarity of the economy was that, whereas the nation as a whole had an almost equal number engaged in primary production industries and in the distribution and service trades, in California the division was more nearly on a one-third, two-thirds basis. Clerks, salesmen, businessmen, service-station operators, teachers, money lenders, lawyers, and the like outnumbered mill hands, farmers, construction workers, and miners two to one. For the waging of old-fashioned war this personnel factor would not have been a good omen.

Several lines of production also seemed unwarlike. An early move was to shut down the $50 million a year gold-mining industry in an effort to shift its skilled labor to producing more critical minerals. In the nineteenth century the fruits and nuts that constituted about 30 per cent of the agricultural output and the vegetables that ran to another 18 per cent would not have been counted sinews of war. Of the 381,000 persons engaged in manufacturing it appeared that the 71,700 engaged in food and beverage production, the 31,000 moving-picture makers, the 22,400 apparel workers, and the 13,200 furniture makers, to cite just a few examples, were hardly in position directly to win the war. Iron and steel workers in 1939 numbered only 26,900 and aircraft and ship builders, only 22,600. The war, of course, was waged in a more modern fashion, utilizing a new assortment of skills and materiel. Even so, to meet the requirements of the war many Californians would have to shift to entirely different work.

The other side of the picture was that by 1939 California had in production a number of the requisites for up-to-date warfare. Since this war would not be fought on hardtack and embalmed beef, the state's agriculture did not have to be completely revamped. In gasoline and fuel oil the petroleum industry was producing two prime essentials. In machine shops, automobile assembly plants, tire factories, electrical equipment plants, and precision instrument shops the state had nuclei for military production. Furthermore, it was off to a good start in airplane building and possessed certain natural advantages for shipbuilding.

In the face of Japanese aggression against China and the rise of militarism in Europe, the United States began to step up its preparedness for war. Before Pearl Harbor there were several dividends for California. The most spectacular was in the awarding of contracts for training and combat planes and for ships, mostly Liberty and Victory type freighters and transports. With federal funds made available to cover part of the cost of airplane factory expansion and to cover almost the entire outlay for shipbuilding facilities, a rapid buildup of plants occurred. Employment rolls in these industries mushroomed by 1941 to some five and a half times what they had been in 1939, and production advanced from $106 million to $708 million—all before the United States became a belligerent.

Capitalizing on the mildness of the climate and the open spaces available, the federal authorities also turned to California for troop training sites. Held over from earlier wars and alarms were a number of installations, including Mare Island Navy Yard, lesser facilities for the Navy at San Francisco and San Diego, Army headquarters for the Ninth Corps Area at the Presidio in San Francisco, subordinate centers at Fort Ord and Fort MacArthur, and air bases at March Field and Hamilton Field. The Navy was at work on an airfield at Alameda and had plans for Treasure Island when the exposition closed. As the prewar draft put more and more men into uniform, California began to bristle with an array of mammoth training stations.

The defense contracts and the involuntary visitors in uniform hardly balanced the specter of disruption of the economy. Pessimists wondered what would happen to the state's more frivolous enterprises, such as the production of fruits, wine, off-season vegetables, moving pictures, and sports apparel, if the nation had to buckle down to an all-out war effort, which in turn would exercise first claim on transportation facilities. When the emergency actually came, the dislocation was as serious as had been forecast but not in the exact pattern predicted.

A more realistic expectation would have been that in a mechanized, aerial, and global war California's size, position, wealth, agriculture, oil, minerals, manufacturing, and science fitted her for a most active part.

War Industries

In the 27 months following Hitler's invasion of Poland the United States moved closer and closer to war, insofar as possible solidifying its position with the Latin American nations. A perimeter was marked off in hopes of sealing the western hemisphere against aggression. American forces undertook patrols and convoying half way across the Atlantic. Firing on submarines was authorized and generous credits were arranged for Britain and her allies. In the destroyers-for-bases deal the United States strained neutrality still further. There was attention to the menace of Japanese aggression, but throughout this period the primary concern of the American government was the danger represented by totalitarianism in Europe. With Pearl Harbor the tempo changed but not the emphasis. Confronted with the problem of waging war on two fronts, American strategists determined to be content with holding tactics in the Pacific until the Germans were coped with. Meanwhile, the problem was to build up military strength. It was a setting in which the munitions maker was a heroic figure.

Toward aircraft production in California a good beginning had been made. This program was now stepped up to an all-out effort. The national government put up $150 million for plant expansion, to which was added $79 million in private capital. Vast, sprawling plants soon took shape at Burbank, Santa Monica, El Segundo, Inglewood, Long Beach, and San Diego, camouflaged in imitation of residential subdivisions. A rumor circulated that the Ocean Park pier, which drew a bead on the Douglas plant, was to be re-aligned to set up the UCLA campus as a decoy. To Douglas, Lockheed, North American, Vultee, Hughes, and a host of subsidiary parts suppliers, the contracts poured in. By June, 1945, they totalled $2,136,119,000 in San Diego County and $7,093,837,000 in Los Angeles County.

From considerably fewer than 20,000 employees on the job in 1939 these plants built up their working force to a peak of 243,000 in August, 1943. A fraction of these workers came to the job sufficiently skilled. A larger number had to be trained as riveters, welders, machinists, and the like. The saving factor was that a division of labor approximating the assembly line was possible and narrowly specialized skills sufficed.

The shipbuilding story is strikingly similar. From a mere 4,000 men on the job in 1939 there was an upsurge to a peak of 282,000 in August, 1943. Contracts for wartime shipbuilding amounted to $5,155,516,000. The greater part, some $3,053,119,000, went to yards at Richmond, Sausalito, South San Francisco, and elsewhere in the Bay region. Los Angeles trailed with $1,709,974,000 in contracts. The plants were financed almost entirely by the federal government, which posted $409 million to go with $29 million in private capital. Several companies engaged in the work, but the one enterpriser who emerged as a public figure was Henry J. Kaiser. His fame derived in part from his other interests, which included cement, aluminum, and steel, a tank factory at Willow

Los Angeles Harbor, After the War

Los Angeles Chamber of Commerce

Run, and plans for automobile manufacture, but for a time he was thought of primarily as Kaiser the shipbuilder. His approach to the problem was not unlike that applied in the great construction projects at Boulder, Friant, or Shasta. Here were plans and blueprints to be transformed into reality. The methods of organization and procedure and some of the key personnel that had been used in such projects could be readily applied to the new assignment.

Although by 1939 California had some 675 plants producing and fabricating iron and steel, the majority were relatively small, supplied only a small fraction of the western market, and were at the fabricating level. A regional deficiency long recognized was the slight development of basic production of iron and steel. As of 1939 the available capacity was no more than a million tons of ingots a year. Wartime concern about decentralizing industry, lessening the load on the railroads, and insuring a supply of material to the western warplants led to a sudden expansion of plants. At Geneva, Utah, the federal government built a $200 million steel mill rated at 1,280,000 tons capacity. Through government loans it assisted in the enlargement of the United States Steel, Bethlehem Steel, and independent mills at San Francisco and Los Angeles. Also, with a loan from the Reconstruction Finance Corporation, Kaiser built at Fontana an integrated blast furnace and rolling mill of 700,000 tons capacity. Some 50 miles east of Los Angeles, dependent on coal from Utah 500 miles away, on iron ore from Eagle Mountain 150 miles away, and on rail freight for the delivery of its products, it was expected to be at a disadvantage in competition with tidewater-located mills. Nevertheless, the mill prospered sufficiently to justify a postwar enlargement of its capacity. Percentagewise, the California steel industry seemed an almost infinitesimal part of the national total. By 1945, after all this expansion, the state accounted for only 1.5 per cent of the nation's pig iron. The wartime increase, however, was a tonic to the West and a harbinger of a better rounded and possibly unmonopolized setup of basic industry.

After those in aircraft, ships, and steel, the next most conspicuous industrial change of the war years was in the oil industry. With the particular assignment of fueling the war in the Pacific, the California oil companies stepped up their production of crude oil, added to their refineries, and increased the output of gasoline and fuel oil by more than 50 per cent between 1939 and 1945. New cracking equipment enabled them to distill a considerably higher proportion of high test aviation gasoline. Alongside the refineries arose another series of plants dedicated to the transmutation of crude oil into rubber. To begin with, the process was fantastically expensive and noisome in odor, but, as Japanese conquests in Malaya and the Dutch East Indies cut off access to natural rubber, it was a war necessity. The end result was a synthetic with certain marked superiorities over natural rubber and therefore of continuing importance beyond the war years. Eventually, too, the cost of production was brought down.

Many other industries were boosted by the war effort. In some instances it was a matter of an older factory being converted, for example, from the making of furniture to plywood boats or from radios to sonar equipment. In more instances entirely new factories were improvised to produce airplane parts, shell casings, landing field lights, electronic equipment, and other such war supplies. The largest expansion in this miscellaneous industrial activity was in machinery, electrical equipment, rubber goods, sheet metal, and light metal products. Other lines, such as chemicals and clay and sand products, advanced more gradually. Even with certain industries, such as automobile manufacture, artificially restrained, the overall picture was one of tremendous growth. Factory output rose from $2,798,180,000 in 1939 to a resounding $10,141,496,000 in 1944.

Theoretically, there might have been advantages in a dispersal of this manufacturing as widely as possible over the state. In practice there were reasons of convenience which tended to cluster most of it in the localities where industrial beginnings had already been made—the Los Angeles area, the San Francisco Bay region including the East Bay, and the San Diego area. Los Angeles had the largest population increase during the war years, better than 300,000, but more startling gains included San Diego's spurt from 203,000 to 362,000; Richmond's from 23,000 to 93,000; and Alameda's from 36,000 to 90,000.

Agriculture at War

At the outset of the war certain lines in California agriculture such as flower growing were candidates for curtailment. By plan or otherwise there was a reduction in the acreage planted to strawberries and sugarbeets. Of the 50 crops on the Department of Agriculture's list, all the others held their own or showed an increase. The handicaps of competition for labor supply and transport to market were offset by the nationwide prosperity, the enlarged number of consumers in California, and government purchases for servicemen in training in the state and for provisioning the armed forces in the Pacific theater.

In actual distribution through the branches of agriculture the increase was without great distinction as to crop. From 1940 to 1944, for example, the income from dairying advanced from $91 million to $192 million, that from beef cattle, hogs, and lambs rose from $88 million to $175 million, that from poultry went up from $45 million to $119 million, with the total for livestock and livestock products going from $232 million to $500 million.

Cotton, meanwhile, advanced from $25 million to $51 million, other field crops from $74 million to $161 million, and vegetables from $123 million to $284 million. In this general category, as in livestock raising, farm income more than doubled during the war.

Fruits and nuts showed an even more striking growth. Citrus went from $91 million to $262 million, grapes from $35 million to $184 million, the deciduous fruit crop from $57 million to $217 million, and nuts from $14 million to $39 million. Overall, this meant three and a half times as much income.

These figures are a reminder that California agriculture is responsive to the market and that even the tree-borne part of its output can be stepped up by more intensive cultivation, application of more water and plant food, and more thorough harvesting. The total realized, $1.744 billion in 1944 as against $625 million in 1939, was almost a threefold increase and only less startling than the strides being made in industry. Furthermore, while California had climbed only to eighth or ninth among the states in manufacturing, in agriculture she was in first place.

The Manhattan Project

With far less fanfare California scientists applied their talents to the problems of the war. At Stanford, Berkeley, and Los Angeles, area training programs were started for those who might be assigned responsibilities of military government in occupied countries. At the Institute of Technology and UCLA there were elaborate programs of training in meteorology. A variety of other specialized training programs were conducted at the colleges and universities. Conventional civilian instruction continued alongside these programs except at the Davis campus of the university, which was turned over to the Air Force for the duration.

Capitalizing on the reservoir of researchers assembled in the state, the national authorities turned to them for a variety of services. Some went into the field with the armed forces, as for example a geologist, who advised on problems of terrain that would be encountered in the island-to-island progression in the Pacific. Others were asked to participate in research studies at laboratories set up by the armed forces, such as the sonar laboratory on Point Loma or the Naval Research Center at Inyokern. Still others, with contracted support from federal funds, were encouraged to stay on in their laboratories and work on a specified problem critical in the war effort. The emphasis was upon science that could be applied as in the search for a better drug to cope with malaria. Some scientists expressed concern that there would be an exhaustion of the pure or theoretical science waiting application, yet the range of assignments was broad and basic research was involved. The dimensions of this activity are suggested by the total of $57 million in research contracts entered into by the University of California. Other institutions in the state had proportionate shares.

The most spectacular of these projects was in atomic research. At the Radiation Laboratory in Berkeley, Dr. E. O. Lawrence had built the first cyclotron and thus paved the way for the production of U-235 and the atomic bomb. The discovery of two other elements, neptunium and plutonium, also took place at the Radiation Laboratory. Under the Manhattan Project, the University of California accepted responsibility for setting up and exercising managerial supervision over the facility at Los Alamos in New Mexico where further atomic research was conducted and the first atomic bombs were actually produced. Selection of the University of California to conduct the enterprise at Los Alamos was a tribute to the state's high attainment in scientific study and in managerial skill.

Like many of the other wartime projects, that at Los Alamos was shrouded in secrecy, and many facts about it were kept confidential after the war. Only a limited number of persons knew that the university's involvement was not just in research but in the production of the atomic bombs that would be dropped on Hiroshima and Nagasaki. They did not challenge this participation, and the university went on after the war at another installation to make the key contribution to development of the hydrogen bomb and to supervise production of these bombs.

Quickly, after the atomic bombs were dropped, Americans were appalled at what their country had done. Feverishly the government began to get as many nations as possible to covenant not to use this fearsome weapon and, in order to deter, raced to stockpile as many bigger and better nuclear bombs as possible. Among Americans there is widespread remorse that, besides making the bomb, the United States was the one nation that used it.

Many years went by before anyone faced up to the question whether war-serving research was a legitimate or condonable university function. Clearly there were basic researches that might be applicable in the service of mankind or in the destruction of mankind. For instance, the identification of the germ or virus causing a particular disease could serve the ends of preventive medicine or of germ or virus warfare. That basic research, however, is to be encouraged. University participation in munition making, however, the ultimate reached in the University of California's supportive role in the fashioning of the atomic bombs, is now seen as irreconcilable with a university's reason for being.

Troop Training and Staging Area

It is notorious and, at least to a degree, understandable that wars are fought without any sparing of the cost. Except for a strong effort to curb inflation, the United States made no pretense of economizing on the Second World War. There were times, however, when factors quite extraneous led to provident decisions. One was the selection of California as a major area for troop training. Continuing the process begun before American involvement as a belligerent, the Army developed huge training camps near Monterey, Paso Robles, San Luis Obispo, and Santa Maria. The Marines opened a west coast Quantico near Oceanside, the Navy built up its facilities at San Diego, and the Air Force added major training fields near Victorville, Merced, and Santa Ana. These training centers amounted to more than 10 per cent of the national total. Much of the construction was routine; barracks, for example, were built according to blueprints left over from the First World War, yet there was some accommodation to the environment and some use of its particular features. At Oceanside, for example, the Marines had an ideal setting for practice landings, and on the desert beyond Palm Springs General Patton's Third Army found plenty of heat and sand in which to prepare for the African campaign.

In addition to housing, this many-sided training program California was the principal staging area for the Pacific War. For its part in this work the Navy enlarged and improved its facilities at Mare Island, San Francisco, and San Diego. It also took over Treasure Island and converted it into a naval station, acquired Terminal Island in Los Angeles harbor, and, at a cost of $78 million, converted it into a base, and by comparable work developed Port Hueneme as an efficient working port. Most of the troops sent out into the Pacific embarked at San Francisco or Los Angeles. In cargo loading for the Pacific convoys Port Hueneme had a substantial share.

Relocation of the Japanese

Californians in 1941 had not entirely escaped from the heritage of anti-Japanese sentiment built up earlier in the century. The Japanese seemed inscrutable. Many had not sufficiently Americanized themselves in language and looks. In several lines of business they were formidable competitors. Their imperial homeland, too, had roused general apprehensions by its aggressions in China.

In this setting it was perhaps natural that horror-fiction anecdotes circulated widely about what the Japanese Americans would do if war came. This fisherman, it was said, would put on his uniform as an officer of the Imperial Navy and lead the Japanese fleet into Los Angeles Harbor. That gardener would signal in a landing party. Another was to dynamite the Los Angeles Aqueduct, others would demolish the San Francisco bridges, while the maid in the Beverly Hills mansion was to assassinate her mistress. Those who retailed these stories did not always believe them; nevertheless, there was at least a suspicion that some of these scare stories might come true.

Against this background the news from Pearl Harbor had particular impact. The losses officially admitted were heavy enough; rumor multiplied them, and the popular supposition was that, with the Pacific fleet and the Hawaiian bastion knocked out, the west coast was wide open to attack. Except through limited submarine action, the sinking of a tanker off Crescent City, and the lobbing of a few shells into the Goleta oil fields, the attack did not come. The general belief, however, was that it could have happened.

On December 7 the Department of Justice took prompt action to restrain enemy aliens. It imposed contraband rules, travel restrictions, and inspections and moved in quickly to arrest aliens known or suspected to be dangerous to the public safety. On December 7 some 736 Japanese aliens were arrested; by February, 1942, more than 2,000 were being detained. This work seemed thoroughly efficacious. A difference of opinion developed, however, between the Department of Justice and General John L. DeWitt, head of the Western Defense Command, about what further steps should be taken. At his urging, the Department stepped up its rules and raids, but, without more specific evidence than he presented, it was unwilling to go as far as he wanted. By mid-February an impasse had developed between the General and the Department. In part, and perhaps in very large part, DeWitt's demands for more drastic measures were the outgrowth of heavy pressures exerted by west coast civilians.

The first loud voice in this campaign was that of radio commentator John B. Hughes, who on January 5 took up the theme that all the Japanese ought to be removed. His cry drew an immediate echo from groups habitually anti-Japanese, including the California Joint Immigration Committee, the Native Sons, and the American Legion. Agricultural and marketing organizations and certain labor unions joined the chorus, and practically all the newspapers agreed that "the Japs must go." Public officials and politicians were equally clamorous. The west coast delegations in Congress were unanimous on the issue, while on the scene the most active official spokesmen were State Attorney General Earl Warren and Mayor Fletcher Bowron of Los Angeles. In speaking to the district attorneys and sheriffs of the state, Warren interpreted the total absence of fifth column and sabotage activity as "a studied effort" on the part of the Japanese to hold any such action until the zero hour. Bowron saw to it that all Japanese were removed from city jobs, pressed the issue in Washington, and declaimed over the radio that the Japanese in California were "a hotbed and a nerve center for spying and sabotage." Both Warren and Bowron carried their urgings direct to DeWitt. After the war Bowron publicly expressed profound regret for his part in this agitation.

From early January to early February DeWitt's requests to the Justice Department were solely for more vigorous controls on enemy aliens. On February 5 his office gave out a statement that "military judgment" called for the removal of all Japanese. Subsequently this demand was laid more categorically before the Department of Justice. That Department pleaded lack of authority to carry out such a removal, lack of facilities for any such undertaking, and lack of evidence submitted to demonstrate that removal was called for. It was not in a position to deny the military necessity alleged by DeWitt. Higher authority would have to decide.

The most simplistic explanation of the indiscriminate removal of all persons of Japanese ancestry is to blame General DeWitt. Research in military records pinpoints Colonel Karl R. Bendetson as the man who drew up the detailed plan and defended it vigorously. Further research suggests that he was not much more than an active and willing emissary, with the decision making centered more in Assistant Secretary of War John J. McCloy and Secretary Henry L. Stimson, with minimal resistance by Francis Biddle, the head of the Department of Justice. They could recommend, but the ultimate decision to issue Presidential Order 9066 was Franklin D. Roosevelt's. As Harry Truman understood so well, the buck stopped there. Yet the impetus for all these actions is traceable to the west coast agitators and the groundswell of public clamor, especially in California.

On February 19 President Roosevelt took the fateful step of transferring control of enemy aliens to the War Department. Through a series of public proclamations General DeWitt then ordered "voluntary" departure of Japanese from designated coastal areas, an 8:00 P.M. to 6:00 A.M. curfew, other restrictions, and, on March 27, evacuation of all Japanese, citizens and aliens alike. Some 110,000 persons were subject to this order, two thirds of them American citizens. The Japanese Americans of western Washington and Oregon and southern Arizona were included but the main body to be evacuated was from California.

In an age when almost that many persons turned out for a football game and several times as many flocked to the beaches on a holiday or to the Tournament of Roses parade, it might seem that the removal could have been accomplished overnight. Actually it took from April to August. Assembly centers were improvised at racetracks and fairgrounds. Summoned to register and then to report on specified dates, the Japanese were taken to these centers. At best there was little time to wind up business affairs, dispose of property, and get ready to leave. From these makeshift camps the evacuees were transferred to more distant relocation centers, two of them on the eastern margin of California, the other eight scattered as far east as Arkansas.

Although the terminology was polite—these were called relocation rather than concentration camps—barbed-wire fences and armed guards gave the opposite impression. Without the goodwill of the administrators headed

Assembly for Relocation

War Relocation Authority

by Dillon Myer the lot of the evacuees would have been much worse. Even so, the uprooting and the detention were enough to impose a severe psychological strain. To the more sensitive the inescapable imputation of disloyalty and inferiority before the law was the hardest cross to bear. All felt the stigma of being sentenced to sit out the war idle and unproductive. In time, to be sure, some of them were released from the centers. Through enlistment or the draft many of the young men went off to the battlefields in Europe and later in the Pacific where they performed with extraordinary valor. Others were released to go to guaranteed jobs outside General DeWitt's proscribed area. Late in the war a few were permitted to come back into California. Most were kept in camp until after V-J Day and the centers were not closed until January 1, 1946.

The cause of this wholesale removal cannot in its entirety be weighed in the balance. Since, fortunately, there was no Japanese assault on the mainland, the question of military necessity was not tested. Several of the arguments for relocation, for example, the citing of sabotage in Hawaii, have been proven altogether false. In marshaling arguments DeWitt showed great indebtedness to the civilian agitators for removal and an equal degree of dominance by these pressure groups. Some of the pressure groups, in turn, made no bones about their ulterior motives. The fundamental force thus can be clearly identified as lying in these elements in the California population, nurtured on the accumulated spirit of opposition to Orientals, and quickened by considerations of economic or political advantage. The clamor and the hysteria were none the less genuine. There was a measure of accuracy in the claim that relocation was to protect the evacuees from mob violence—certainly no compliment to the law-abiding character of the Caucasian Californians.

Most of the sympathy for the removed Japanese came long after the fact. A few Californians at the time questioned the propriety of the removal and did what they could to ensure good treatment of the evacuees and considerate provisions for their ultimate return. Their principal agency was the Fair Play Committee, headed by Galen M. Fisher and including a number of prominent businessmen and educators. Among them President Robert G. Sproul of the University of California was one of the most active, especially in persuading the heads of other colleges and universities to welcome students from the detention camps. Mere civilians, no matter how distinguished, were not in position in 1942 to challenge the asserted military necessity for removal.

That justification, on the other hand, was rendered suspect by the contrast of Hawaii. There, a larger number of Japanese, less Americanized than those on the mainland, were not removed. The area was at least as critical as the west coast, but the general in charge was quite a different man from DeWitt and the community was far less prone to racist extremism.

In California the Japanese were sorely missed. The decline in the quality of fruits and vegetables in the local market was a token of the loss sustained. At a time when production for the war effort was at a premium the retirement of these thousands of competent enterprisers and workers was economically unsound. To the Japanese it meant a more direct loss, which by one calculation amounted to $365 million. What scars it would leave on their regard for America could not be forecast.

There was an inescapable consequence, too, for the constitutional system of the United States. Except for the weaker parallel of Indian removal in Jackson's day there was no American precedent for a mass internment of aliens and citizens alike, without evidence of disloyalty and with race as the sole basis of determining who should be interned. Prior to 1942 most Americans assumed that the Constitution was a safeguard against such arbitrary treatment. Belatedly, the issue was taken to court and, about the time the war ended, there were rulings that the color of military necessity had been sufficient, but that the federal government had a limited liability for damages. Thereby a most unfortunate precedent of group proscription had been set, which would stand as a legacy of the hysteria which led to the expulsion of the Japanese Americans.

The Population Spiral

In addition to the incarceration of the Japanese, the Second World War transferred more than 700,000 Californians into the armed services. It also brought about major changes in employment and a flood tide of migration to

the state that exceeded any rate previously attained. The population move-
ments in the gold rush and the boom of the eighties were small by comparison.
That in the booming twenties was more grandiose, but the war years' increase,
1,916,000 between 1940 and 1945, was almost as large as that for the entire
decade of the twenties, 2,251,000.

The tremendous increase in industrial activity required expansion
of the industrial labor force. In 1939 there had been 381,000 thus employed.
In 1943 almost three times as many, 1,121,200, were at work. Over the same
four years the personnel employed in agriculture increased by 31,000, in utilities
and transportation by 58,000, in trade by 54,000, and in government by 188,000.
Thus, the aircraft and shipbuilding plants, which boosted their labor force by
462,000, were not the only elements active in increasing employment.

In many instances the workers moving into these expanding fields
of employment came by shift-over from other going elements in the state's
economy. Bakers became riveters, gas-station attendants turned welders, clerks
took hold of factory tools, and so on down the line. In the overall picture the
statistics show clearly where the extra workers did and did not come from. The
service trades released a net total of 55,000; mining, 15,000; construction, 8,000;
printing, 1,400; and automobile making, 1,300. Those were the only lines of
employment reporting a net decrease, and, with a million new jobs to fill and
half that many servicemen and Japanese to replace, these transfers left about
95 per cent of the new jobs unfilled.

The new recruits included some young people going to work a year
or two earlier than they normally would have. They included thousands of
women who in peacetime would have stayed at home. They included a few
men who had other work but took on a war job in addition. A much larger
number were new arrivals pulled in from all the outlying states by the war's
requirements and the prevailing good wages. Some Mexican nationals joined
the trek. The vast majority, however, were from other parts of the Union. They
were a reasonably accurate cross section of America, drawn, however, more from
the South and West than from the industrialized Northeast, much more concentrated in the working-age bracket than had been true in the eighties or the
twenties, and including many more Negroes than had been present in California.

Even without the complications of war such an influx of new inhabitants would have created a serious housing problem. True enough, the curtailment of nonessential construction released certain materials. Highway building,
for example, was practically called off for the duration. On the other hand, the
priorities exercised by the military and the defense plants hampered the building program. The most effective solution in meeting the immediate emergency
was the company construction of temporary housing units as an adjunct to the
war plants. On hills above Vallejo and Marin City, on the flats at Richmond,
and at various locations in southern California, seried ranks of these structures
took shape. Built without much benefit of architecture, intended to provide only
minimum shelter, and that only for the duration, these buildings did not adorn
the landscape or provide for California living at its best. A limited amount of
private dwelling construction went on, most of it held to unpretentious small

homes and some to even starker prefabricated houses. Many of the newcomers substituted a trailer for a home. Trailer camps blossomed as a new variety of real-estate subdivision.

The added throng strained other facilities. Utilities—water, electricity, gas, telephone, and sewer—were hard put to achieve the sudden expansion that was necessary. The same was true of the public transportation companies, streetcar and bus. School districts in the vicinity of the war plants were confronted with a sudden enrollment jump far above previous expectations, and the problem of what to do about it was complicated by the thought that at war's end the workers might all depart and the school population revert to what had been normal. The state program of equalizing school costs helped greatly, though the system of allotment on the basis of average daily attendance in the preceding year did not fit the emergency. The answer on the school problem in some instances was to erect and staff a new school. Often it was to crowd more pupils into the existing buildings and often to make these schools and teachers do double duty through half-day sessions.

The problem of accommodating the newcomers was broader than housing, utilities, transportation, and schools. Involved also were all the matters of governmental service, such as police and fire protection, garbage collection, and public health; all the matters of shopping centers and the supply of groceries, drugs, clothing, and furniture; all the matters of social provision, churches, theaters, public parks, and the like. In earlier stages of growth such elements had tagged along or had seemed to come automatically as population grew. The war did not repeal the natural impulses to try to fill these needs, but shortages and priorities made it difficult, if not impossible, to do so. These difficulties were not peculiar to California but they were present only in other suddenly congested areas. A fixed impression of the period is one of standing in line to board a crowded bus, standing in line to buy vegetables, taking a number and waiting one's turn at the meat counter, queueing up at Christmas time to buy a box of candy. A penalty for California's very rapid growth was that shortages were more acute, the ration point system therefore subjected to more strain, and its abuses more of a temptation than in more normal parts of the country. The temptation being greater, black market and under-the-counter transactions were worse.

One element of shortage and rationing certainly came home to California with special force. In the more compact eastern communities, where public transportation was convenient and cheap and the private automobile something of a luxury, gasoline rationing was just an incident. The average Californian, however, was as dependent on his car as an Eskimo on his snowshoes, the full gasoline tank was a more compelling symbol than the full dinner pail had ever been, and to qualify for a B ration book was an achievement supreme. Streets and parking lots had good business-hour patronage, but the open highways were strangely deserted. The fact was that pleasure driving all but disappeared. To avoid being grounded most people had to confine their driving to business and essential shopping.

Another respect in which California was unusual was in its presumed

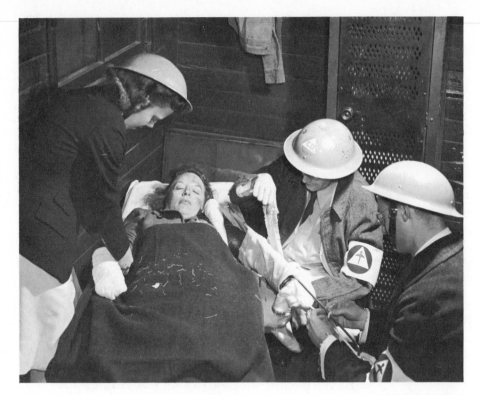

Civil Defense Drill

Rollem, Office of War Information

exposure to attack. At continent's end, and with its population massed near the coast, it was in position to catch the first blows of a Japanese assault on the mainland. Furthermore, its war plants and military installations seemed to set it up as a target worth striking. Accordingly, there was concern about this exposure. Some individuals were fatalists enough to take the hazard lightly; others built private bomb shelters and kept their cars stocked for a flight to the desert.

Also, California was a flourishing area for civilian defense. House-holders were encouraged to lay in a supply of primitive fire-fighting equipment —ladders, rope, axes, and sand. Enrolled as air-raid wardens, they were issued stirrup pumps, helmets, armbands, and stickers for their cars. They took first-aid courses and learned to apply traction splints. To fire and temblor drills the schools added air raid exercises. Neighborhoods organized telephone chains to spread warnings quickly, and wardens stood watches at the communications centers. Perhaps more usefully, many citizens worked as airplane spotters. In prospect of air raids the defense authorities designated bomb shelters, de-creed blackout preparations, and followed with several alerts.

Barrage balloons, radar emplacements, searchlights, and anti-aircraft batteries provided the similitude of war. On one occasion, which went down in history as the "Battle of Los Angeles," the guns were actually unlimbered.

Whether the target was a cloud, an escaped balloon, the successive shell bursts, a strayed plane, or enemy aircraft was not announced. Rumors quickly encompassed all conceivable explanations, and the authorities did not bother to clear up the mystery. Seemingly the "battle" involved much warlike exercise and no casualties.

In retrospect the activity of civilian defense seems to have been mostly waste motion though perhaps worthwhile as a morale builder. It did knit communities together to a degree seldom achieved before or since. As in other parts of the nation Californians quickened their patriotism by inserting the national anthem in theater programs and church services. They expressed their loyalty, too, as was done throughout the country, by giving blood to the Red Cross, buying defense bonds, and working with the USO. The Hollywood professionals made special contributions to morale building and entertainment of troops at home and abroad.

The more solid achievement of California's war effort was in its men who entered the services, the troop training program centered in the state, and the production of the sinews of war. In these accomplishments California could take real pride. In them, too, her people reaped very substantial profits. During the war years their annual income advanced from a gross of just over $5 billion to almost $13 billion, while the holdings in liquid assets increased from $4.5 billion to $15.25 billion. Even with allowance for inflation estimated at 30 per cent, this was a remarkable prospering. Although proprietors and labor each had a threefold increase in cash income, it was not shared evenly. White-collar workers lagged behind, farmers ran ahead of everyone else in the gains in cash income, and many industrialists had capital gains not yet converted into cash. The most striking features were the general sharing in the gains and the fact that California had built a complex and high-powered economic machine which in time of war, at least, could produce at a prodigious rate.

For Further Reading

CAREY McWILLIAMS, *California, The Great Exception* (1949).

KATHERINE ARCHIBALD, *Wartime Shipyard* (1947).

WILLIAM G. CUNNINGHAM, *The Aircraft Industry, A Study in Industrial Location* (1951).

FRANK J. TAYLOR and LAWTON WRIGHT, *Democracy's Air Arsenal* (1947).

EWALD T. GRETHER, *The Steel-Using Industries of California* (1946).

NORRIS HUNDLEY, *Dividing the Waters: A Century of Controversy between the United States and Mexico* (1966).

MORTON GRODZINS, *Americans Betrayed: Politics and the Japanese Evacuation* (1949).

ALLAN R. BOSWORTH, *America's Concentration Camps* (1967).

BRADFORD SMITH, *Americans from Japan* (1948).

EUGENE V. ROSTOW, *The Sovereign Prerogative and the Quest for Law* (1962).

CAUGHEY, *California Heritage*, 466–70.

chapter thirty

A Touch of Midas

What will happen when California is filled by fifty millions of people, and its valuation is five times what it is now, and the wealth will be so great that you will find it difficult to know what to do with it? The day will, after all, have only twenty-four hours. Each man will have only one mouth, one pair of ears, and one pair of eyes. There will be more people—as many perhaps as the country can support—and the real question will be not about making more wealth or having more people, but whether the people will then be happier or better.

Lord James Bryce,
in a speech at Berkeley in 1909

Elements of Growth

1945 and after

In the immediate postwar years the California economy stumbled slightly, not for lack of demand, but because of shortages in various lines of merchandise, building materials, and film for the movie-makers. Nationwide there was a similar hesitation before the re-adjustment to peacetime pursuits was achieved; then followed a long stretch of prosperity, occasionally slacking off slightly but generally continuing strong through the fifties and sixties.

California had always flourished best in times of national prosperity, as in the boom of the eighties, the bigger boom of the twenties, and the still greater acceleration of the war years. The correlation was logical: the state's chances of drawing visitors and new residents were best when they could afford to make the trip, and many California products, fruits and films, for instance, were at most borderline necessities selling best in a strong market. In this greatest

Tract Housing, Daly City

Rondal Partridge

of American prosperities thus far California surpassed the national average, not just because its technical position was favorable but because many of its enterprisers showed extraordinary initiative.

Throughout this long period the state's population increased at a formidable rate. Newcomers poured in from every state in the union but particularly from Texas, Illinois, and New York. They came from the Deep South and from foreign lands, notably Mexico and Canada. Part of the migration consisted of elderly men and women whose intention was merely to spend their last years in a mild climate. A few of these people would be active. Most of the newcomers were young, capable, and immediate additions to the work force. They brought children with them and also contributed to an explosion of babies, ultimately a second wave of workers and immediately an addition to the roster of consumers. With migration as the main source, population growth averaged more than 500,000 a year for 25 years.

The tourist business grew correspondingly. Californians are such ardent vacationers that it is difficult to strike a balance on the flow of the tourist dollar. California license plates are in the lead at Las Vegas and Reno, the Grand Canyon and Yellowstone, and commonplace on all the national arteries. But out-of-state visitors by the millions mingled with Californians at Yosemite and Sequoia, at the desert and coastal resorts, Hearst's Castle and Disneyland. Over its first 10 years Disneyland averaged 8 million admissions a year. A number of cities entered the bidding for conventions. By the sixties the State Chamber of Commerce listed the tourist industry as third in dollar volume in the state.

Both public and private construction boomed. Industry also faced formidable challenge to retool and refit. Although many had assumed that the steel mill at Fontana was solely for the war effort, Kaiser Steel enlarged it in 1952. In the aircraft plants the wartime models rapidly became obsolete, and the companies had to reprogram for more advanced designs or for the civilian market. Electronic firms turned from military communications systems to radio, television, and sound systems.

The railroads reequipped elaborately. In the 1930's the Southern Pacific had used articulated, lightweight streamliners—the Daylights and the Lark—between San Francisco and Los Angeles. The Santa Fe had a streamliner on the San Joaquin Valley run and the Chief and El Capitan to Chicago, to which it added the diesel-powered Super Chief in 1937. The Union Pacific was pioneering even more venturesomely with the diesel-powered City of San Francisco and City of Los Angeles from Chicago. By the time of the war all the railroads were turning gradually to diesels for freight hauling and for switching.

In the postwar era the trend toward diesels and streamliners culminated. The Santa Fe converted practically all its operations to streamliners and diesels; the Union Pacific moved in the same direction. The Southern Pacific put new Daylights on the San Joaquin and Cascade runs and shiny new trains on the Golden State and Sunset routes to Chicago and New Orleans. The Western Pacific, in cooperation with eastern affiliates, launched the California Zephyr on the Feather River–Moffat Tunnel route to Chicago. Even the most casual observer could see that California railroading had entered a new day.

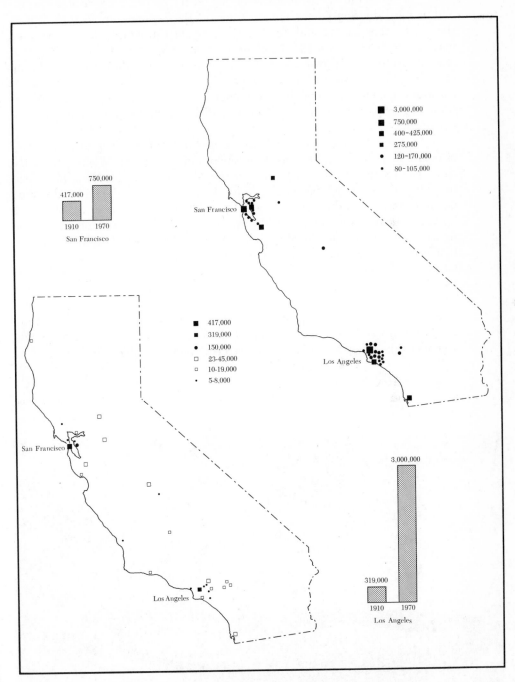

Population Concentrations, 1970

With diesels the roads could lay off the servicing crews at every second or third division point. The operators of the Zephyr combined showmanship with labor saving and ran the whole train through a window-washing machine at Denver. On the mountain runs, whereas every helper steam locomotive had to have its own engineer and fireman, a set of diesels operated from one control and required only one crew. The unions insisted that a fireman or substitute engineer accompany every engineer. The unions sought to prevent train lengthening and other economizing in labor costs, yet step by step a number of such changes were made.

For a brief time railroading to and in California was at its pinnacle of convenience and comfort, thanks to smooth diesel power and air-conditioned cars. The companies sought business, using their boxcars as rolling billboards to advertise their crack passenger trains. In the sixties this part of railroading ran into its private depression. Patronage shifted to the airlines. Pointing to losses by the passenger divisions, the railroads began to cut back on service and to withdraw these trains as rapidly as possible. The Southern Pacific in particular used every device to discourage anyone from boarding a train. The Post Office cooperated by cancelling the mail contracts, and, by the centennial of the Pacific Railroad, passengers were almost as ghostly as the Irish paddies and the Chinese who long ago had joined the rails.

Meanwhile the railroads boosted their freight business. They put better springs and shock absorbers on boxcars and could promise dead freight a gentler ride. They replaced the old iced fruit and vegetable cars with mechan-

On the Tehachapi Loop

Southern Pacific Railroad

ically cooled cars. They offered special cars for special cargoes, such as the many-tiered automobile carriers and the flatcars for piggyback or containerized freight. With vast sorting yards the companies speeded up the assembling of trains. They advertised faster freight schedules and kept track of every boxcar by computer. The pride of the Santa Fe was a big-hopper ore train carrying trainloads of coal from Raton to the steel mill at Fontana.

In the course of these decades Californians wore out and discarded millions of automobiles, of which some were crushed into scrap and fed back into the mills, a few were dropped into the ocean to encourage marine life, and others were left stranded in fields and junk yards. By the close of the sixties 20 million Californians operated more than 10 million cars representing an original investment of at least $25 billion. These cars, for which the feeding, shoeing, and care cost a tidy sum each year, represented a large element in the economy.

A tenth of the autos were imports from Germany, England, or Japan. A much larger number were put together in the California plants of General Motors, Ford, or Chrysler, mostly out of components designed and ordered by the eastern management and directors and shipped in. Others came from Detroit.

California contributes to design and development mainly through small teams engaged in building and tuning racing cars, working their way up toward the Indianapolis 500. Of Americans, Californians own the most cars, spend the most time in them, and roll up the most man-and-car miles, yet California has almost no standing as a creator, even for its own gigantic market.

In airplane building the state developed a large stake. Operationally the dependence in the main was on eastern owned and managed lines such as United, American, TWA, and Pan American. Only Western and a few smaller carriers have been California based, something of a contrast to railroading in which two of the four major carriers, the Southern Pacific and the Western Pacific, had their headquarters in San Francisco.

In sheer volume of air traffic, Los Angeles Airport became the busiest in the world and the Los Angeles–San Francisco run, the most patronized air route. Whatever the company ownership, California was assured of large payrolls for pilots, copilots, stewardesses, and ground crews and a large outlay for fuel and supplies. The state saw flying machines earlier, but most of the volume was delayed until the sixties. The carrying of mail, express, and freight also rose spectacularly. At certain seasons, planes take off with full loads of cut flowers and carry away half the strawberries going out of the state.

Military Procurement Continues

As a peacetime growth record the California achievement after 1945 requires a Roger Maris asterisk because the period turned out not to be so peaceful after all.

Some Americans distrusted Russia even in the midst of the defense of Stalingrad. After 1945 it soon became apparent that the Soviets intended to challenge the United States on many fronts. In short order the United States moved to stiffen its defenses, at first with the idea of containing the Soviet Union and then of intimidating her through open preparedness to retaliate in greater force.

The rivalry escalated after 1949 when the Russians exploded an atomic bomb. In 1950, when Chinese Communists poured into Korea, the United States on behalf of the United Nations took up the fighting, technically a police action but with every similitude to war. In 1957 Russia scored with Sputnik, whereupon the United States redoubled its commitment to rocket launching and missile development. The emergency suggested a new dedication to mathematics and science. Four years later President John F. Kennedy promised that the United States would put a man on the moon by 1970, a feat duly accomplished on July 20, 1969, at a quoted cost of $24 billion. Meanwhile, following earlier commitment of technical advisers, the United States embarked on undeclared war in Vietnam in 1964. This war grew and intensified, rose in costs to about $80 billion a year, became the United States' most unpopular war, but seemingly defied all efforts at resolution.

American involvement in the cold war, in the hot wars in Korea and Vietnam, and in the intensely competitive space race had momentous repercussions on the California economy. Adversely it resulted in a larger draw-off of income and excise and special tax payments to the federal government and in required expenditures by California agencies in support of war-related activities. Some of the outlay for the buildup of the colleges and universities, for example, was to equip them to support the kinds of teaching and research that would contribute to the military and space efforts. Nevertheless, the reverse flow of money and credits to California was ever so much greater. For military and space procurement and for development and delivery of what would be needed in these interrelated endeavors, the federal government looked particularly to this state. California led the states in the dollar value of military and space contracts. Its share was several times more than its ratio in population or in taxes paid in would indicate.

Through its schools, particularly the University of California and California Institute of Technology, the state participated in contracted research on nuclear energy, rocket fuel, guidance systems, remote controls, navigation in space, problems of weightlessness, biological hazards and protections, improved missile launchers and warheads, methods of detection and interception, and many other problems in basic or applied science. Through these schools or the Rand Corporation came contracts to measure the effectiveness of a propaganda device, the cost of achieving a political result, or the methods best calculated to ensure the fall of a particular ruling faction.

California firms received contracts to produce planes or helicopters for use in Korea or Vietnam, napalm for the fire bombings in Vietnam, first- and second-stage boosters for spaceflights, landing gear for the moonflight, control systems for satellites, camera controls for the fly-by of Mars, and a good fraction of the communications equipment for the first landing on the moon.

Vandenberg Air Force Base was the launching pad for many un-manned satellites and space probes. More prosaically Port Chicago was the principal loading point for munitions for the Korean and Vietnamese wars. California was a staging area, through San Francisco Bay, Port Hueneme, Los Angeles, San Diego, and the California airfields, for these later wars in the Pacific.

To many Americans it was inconceivable that California, the great vacationland, the home of orange groves and make-believe, of Sinclair's Epic and the Townsend Plan, should rise to prominence in the most sophisticated military hardware and the greatest extrapolation of scientific technology. East-ern universities and technical schools had a long headstart on those of California. The industrial might of the Northeast dwarfed that of the Pacific coast not only in production but in research and development as well. Had the task been mass production of hundred-ton tanks, Pittsburgh and Detroit would have won hands down, but for the requirements of the space and nuclear age California was prepared.

The state's aircraft industry, specializing in designing airframes and fitting them to fly, readily moved ahead to supersonic jet planes and the prob-lems of outer space. It had no fixation for the piston engine such as harnessed the automobile industry. The universities, already heavily oriented toward science, thrived on contract research and were congenial to practical applica-tions. From short courses for farmers it was an easy transition to degree pro-grams appropriate to the new shape of industry and to extension courses to train or upgrade the skills of scientists and technicians employable in California laboratories and plants.

Still First in Agriculture

California entered the postwar period as the leading farm state, widest by far in range of crops and at the top in total value. She had achieved that rank with the vast majority of her people busy in their urban and suburban pursuits, with no commodity accounting for as much as a tenth of the total, and with far less than a tenth of her land under cultivation.

In the decades that followed, urban and industrial expansion relent-lessly challenged agriculture's hold on much of the best land in the state. Some-times it was by condemnation of a wide swath for a freeway or by polluting the air and thus foreclosing successful crop production. More often it was by urban sprawl, the proliferation of housing tracts, airport runways, industrial sites, and new school campuses.

In 1969 almost a square mile of prime cropland west of Bakersfield was dedicated to the new state college. The Santa Clara Valley, once 200 square miles of prune, peach, and pear orchards, is so decimated by the subdividers that not a single square mile remains intact. In San Diego County avocado groves have proved a lodestone for housing developers well aware of the avocado's penchant for good soil, level or slightly rolling land, and benign climate. In Orange County the assaults on farmland have been so relentless that the name should be changed. And Los Angeles, for many years the nation's number one farm county, was violated to such an extent that it barely held on in the first ten.

Year by year land became too valuable to farm. Each year the number of active farmers dropped, as did the number of farms and the number of farmworkers. The cost of implements and supplies rose more rapidly than farm prices. Nevertheless, over these years the state's farmers so adjusted their methods that they substantially increased production. They have kept California first in agriculture, with annual output approaching $5 billion in value.

Redeployment was one necessary tactic. Poinsettia growing had to retreat from Los Angeles to new and larger fields near San Diego. Major milk producers in the San Fernando Valley and Norwalk had to move out. But orange growers could not relocate so readily. In most instances they had to go to poorer soils and greater exposure to frost, yet some were able to compensate with larger acreage, which promised greater efficiency. The wise farmer protected himself with a soil test, a report on the microclimate, and expert advice on the most suitable planting. Some of the farms swallowed up by the subdividers were more country residences than genuine producers. Redeployment in some instances helped to bring the units of farm operation up to the size conducive to efficiency.

For a long time the state's farmers had been benefiting from advice from federal agents and University of California researchers and teachers. Scientists developed or identified new varieties better adapted for particular districts. They worked out improvements in fertilizers and pest control. On their recommendation some two million acres of new grazing land was opened by controlled burning of the brush and seeding and fertilizing for better forage.

These scientists also cooperated with mechanization. To meet the requirements of the tomato-picking machine they developed a tomato with slightly tougher skin and ripening all at once rather than progressively. Giant lettuce pickers now move through the field with rubber hands that by the feel determine whether a head shall be picked. The long dry harvest season that favored the California wheat harvests a century ago similarly favors cotton picking by machine, the California way and a major reason why cotton rose to be the most valuable field crop. Mechanization extended to many operations once done by hoe, cultivator, or pruning shears. Packing sheds were now equipped with electronic fruit sorters and automatic box movers. Because of such advances the number of year-round workers on the farms dropped from 100,000 in 1955 to 92,000 in 1965, though over that same period production doubled.

By the sixties the Central Valley water project was sufficiently advanced to provide for considerably more irrigation in the upper part of the San Joaquin Valley. Funded originally with a bond authorization of $170 million, the project moved slowly until the federal government became a participant. By the end of the sixties on the order of $1 billion had been invested, resulting in much additional irrigated farming in Tulare, Fresno, and Kern

Vineyard near Sebastopol

Philip Hyde

counties. Elsewhere, irrigation was extended as in the upper Salinas Valley by Nacimiento Dam and in Santa Barbara County by the Cachuma project.

Experiences in the grape industries illustrate the kinds of readjustment necessary. This industry has an aristocratic nucleus centered in the Napa, Sonoma, Livermore, and Santa Clara valleys and is famous for its fine varietal wines such as Cabernet Sauvignon, Chardonnay, and Pinot Noir. Table grapes, raisin grapes, and grapes for volume production of dessert and table wines come mainly from the San Joaquin Valley and southern California. The San Joaquin and southern California branch of the industry was able to adjust territorially to urban sprawl. That in the northern valleys was threatened with virtual extinction.

Two defenses were set up. Growers persuaded the legislature to enact an agricultural reserve system which assured for a period of years agricultural zoning and resultant tax saving. Through its operation subdividers' bulldozers were restrained from tearing out prizewinning vines. Science, particularly as represented by enologists and vinologists of the Davis Campus of the University of California, helped the growers locate additional sites with the

517

qualities needed for fine wine grapes, gave them several promising new varieties, and devised cheaper and quicker methods of wine making.

Still another modification assisted this branch of the industry. Substantial parts of the industry passed into the hands of national companies such as Schenley, which recognized the general sales advantage of perpetuating and expanding the production of fine wines. That in the long run may have been more fortifying than the Agricultural Reserve Act.

As before, California agriculture capitalized upon a remarkable endowment for farm production. This natural endowment features a long growing season of nine months or more, making possible many cuttings of alfalfa, successive plantings of row crops, and, taking advantage of the state as a whole, a table-grape harvest that can stretch from May to October and similar extended seasons for many fruits and vegetables. The long growing season applies to livestock too; at the feedlots cattle convert the carefully selected feed into beef more rapidly than they would in a harsher climate. The long dry season, coupled with irrigation, sets up much of the state as one great hothouse or assembly line over which moves almost the entire national commercial supply of pears, plums, prunes, garlic, grapes, apricots, lemons, lettuce, carrots, asparagus, dates, and walnuts, and almost that fraction of many other foods. California leads the nation in beef production, tomatoes, sugar beets, strawberries, and turkeys. It is second only to Texas in cotton and third to Wisconsin and New York in milk. California agriculture looks to 20 million California consumers, selectively to another 180 million consumers across the nation, and to others elsewhere.

The process is not an unmitigated social success. Its methods lead some to question whether it is a work of farmers or of extractive industry. As a production it is a marvel, and all the more so because it has come about in a state of very few farmers and very few farm-minded people.

Diversified Industry

Since midway in World War II, Californians have been told that their economy is so heavily weighted to military purchasing that, if peace were to break out, the state would be a shambles. The involvement is real. At its peak in the early sixties, with NASA contracts piled on the Pentagon's, southern California had 40 per cent of its manufacturing workers so employed and traced about that same fraction of its personal income to military and space work. But with the passage of time, panic over the pending cutback proved difficult to sustain. There was skepticism that peace would terminate the federal programs and, besides, much of the state's economy was not visibly aimed at Vietnam or the moon. Agriculture, the tourist trade, the oil companies, and the construction industry had independent justification. Even in transportation equipment and electrical machinery, which bracketed most of the military and space projects, the companies engaged had a substantial civilian business or potentials of good promise. Even the engaged part of the economy might not be vulnerable to peace.

Californians, to be sure, had before them evidence that flourishing industries could go into quick decline. A San Francisco bank failed and a Los Angeles savings and loan company went into bankruptcy. Ice companies had fallen in the face of new technology. Monterey's Cannery Row and the sardine fishery had been wiped out by the virtual disappearance of the sardines. More disconcerting, the Hollywood movie industry dropped far below the peak of prosperity it had reached in 1945–47. Other recreational opportunities cut down the box office and, at the same time, California's vaunted advantages for film making—open climate, clear skies, and locations that would pass for the Sahara, the Alps, Sherwood Forest, or small-town America—disappeared, depreciated, or turned out not to be unique. Cost factors prompted shooting in France, Italy, Mexico, or anywhere but Hollywood. The industry still saw Hollywood as its center but dropped many points in the total economy of the state and suffered a decline in volume.

Other industries flourished. Food processing, for instance, rose proportionately to the increase in farm output. Principal elements included large-volume canning and quick freezing of fruits and vegetables, wine making, and dehydrating and packing raisins, prunes, figs, dates, and apricots. In all these industries California leads the nation. Its meat companies convert shipped-in animals and the end-product of its massive feedlots into the cuts here consumed. Most of the milk produced in the state is consumed fresh, but a substantial part is condensed or powdered or used in ice cream and cheese making. Of the cotton raised a much smaller fraction is processed in the state; a third or more is compressed and shipped to Japan.

High-Octane Refinery of the Vintage Coinciding with the
Incidence of Smog in Los Angeles

Los Angeles Chamber of Commerce

A miscellany of other manufacturing flourishes with products as diverse as tires, buses, trailers, small boats, plastics, toys, drugs, furniture, and leisure wear. To these may be added the roll out of planes, radios, television sets, tapedecks and record players, computing and copying machines, and many other such commodities for the market in and out of the state.

In recent decades California has acquired branch offices of many national or international firms in banking, insurance, publishing, and merchandising. It has the corporate offices of other firms with far-flung activities such as Litton and Occidental Petroleum and of other firms as specialized as Global Marine whose only interest is offshore drilling.

A feature of the period has been the launching of many new companies. Some of them, despite the advantages offered to small businesses, failed or are candidates for liquidation. One company much publicized was to produce Watts Wallopers to compete with Louisville Sluggers. Through no fault of the workers at the lathes or of the advertising manager, this company ran into grief because the formula for hardening California oak was faulty. Another fraction of the new companies survived and a few shot up rapidly.

Yet the overall trend has been to bigger and fewer companies. Giants such as Standard Oil of California and Lockheed simply grew bigger. Or growth has been by merger, North American acquiring Rockwell, Security–First National Bank taking in Pacific, and the Los Angeles *Times* annexing a map company, a book bindery, a timber company, and a land company. Signal and Litton pursued the popular route of the conglomerates. Amalgamations could have the effect of making a major California company subordinate to out-of-state management and control, as happened to Douglas in the merger with McDonnell and to Richfield in the merger with Atlantic. Many other big businesses moved into the state, among them Standard Oil of New Jersey as Humble Oil, Standard of Ohio as American Oil, Phillips 66, Xerox, and IBM. With the federal government relaxing its objections to mergers and acquisitions, the trend nationally and in California has been increasingly toward big business. This trend has run strong both in urban and rural California.

Internal Growth and the GSP

Implied in the description of these various factors in the great recent upsurge of the California economy is the involvement of a far larger number of persons. That indeed is the case and, further, the continuing upswing of population has been itself a major stimulant to this burgeoning economy.

Translated into purchasing power, and with due notice of the sustained prosperity, these added millions necessitated great activity in construction, sales, and services. Increased local demand was a major factor stimulating production, for instance, of nurseries in Los Angeles County agriculture. Local demand boomed the building of pleasure craft and surfboards at Costa Mesa and Newport. California continues to buy far more than its share of automobiles. It supports more than its share of stockbrokers and has a particularly active real-estate market.

In fact, as Henry George would have appraised it, the present net worth of California rests in substantial part on appreciation in the value of land and improvements. Higher valuations affected much of the urban area, most of suburbia, much of the near-in agricultural and vacant land, most of the resort locations, and some of the farther-out unused and agricultural land. Improvements appreciated because the cost of construction and of land preparation had risen. The rest of the appreciation may be attributed to the onward surge of the economy, the wisdom of the speculators, and in particular to the tremendous population increase. Purchasers, lenders, and the tax assessor recognized this reality. The appreciated property values are basic to the resplendently flourishing economy.

At the end of the sixties California reached a plateau where its Gross State Product (GSP) approximated $100 billion, on a per capita basis far above the average in what is the most prosperous nation in the world. The credit for this achievement must be widely divided between government and private enterprise, management and workers, war and peace, agriculture, minerals, industry, business, and other pursuits.

The magnitude may be better grasped by thinking of California as, in its economy, a nation. Its Gross National Product (GNP), so considered, would weigh in at sixth in the Free World, surpassed only by Russia, Britain, West Germany, France, Japan, and the rest of the United States. California has no wish to be a separate nation nor, for that matter, could it afford to be outside the American Common Market. But it has grown to the dimensions of a nation more populous than Canada, an area equal to that of eight or nine of the original 13 states, and an economy more productive than that of any nation on the Asian, African, or American continents and of most nations of Europe.

For Further Reading

NEIL MORGAN, *The California Syndrome* (1969).
EARL S. POMEROY, *The Pacific Slope* (1965).
R. L. DUFFUS, *Queen Calafia's Island* (1965).
REMI NADEAU, *California, the New Society* (1963).
REMI NADEAU, *Los Angeles, from Mission* [sic] *to Modern City* (1960).
"California, the Nation within a Nation," special issue of the *Saturday Review*
         (September 23, 1967).
ERNEST A. ENGELBERT, *Metropolitan California* (1961).
University of California, *The Metropolitan Future* (1965).
H. O. STEKLER, *The Structure and Performance of the Aerospace Industry* (1965).
EDMUND G. BROWN and others, *California, the Dynamic State* (1966).
CAUGHEY, *California Heritage*, 486–504, 515–18.

chapter thirty-one

Great Constructions

Smile, Los Angeles, you're the center of the world. Sooner or later it had to happen. After all, who's got a better climate? Or an easier life-style? Just look at our population. By the mid-1970's we'll be the biggest city in the world. Where are all the new trends in music and art coming from? Where are all the athletic teams moving? Look at all the big companies building L.A. offices. We deserve to be the center of the world.

TWA ad,
November 4, 1969

1945
and
after
During the Second World War patriotism and priorities diverted the construction industry from its usual pursuits to war-related activities such as shipbuilding, airplane making, and erecting rows of training-camp barracks. Throughout the war years California's population continued to mount, with the result that in 1945 there were accumulated needs for housing and the utilities to match, shops and stores, school buildings, other public buildings, and repair and extension of streets and highways.

Capacity to buy also rose sharply through wartime earnings and profits, austerities enforced by rationing, and frugalities imposed on corporations, the state government, and its subdivisions. Therefore a construction boom was one of the first manifestations of peace. The boom started jerkily because of shortages of building

Construction Detail, University of California, Riverside

Ansel Adams, Fiat Lux

materials and skilled workmen. Once under way, it spun out far into the post-war era. At the 25-year mark, having assisted and benefited from a population spurt to more than two and a half times the 1945 figure, postwar construction overshadowed the prewar by considerably more than that ratio would indicate.

Housing

A major element in this building activity was the erection of housing for the new Californians, whose number had increased more than 13 million in 25 years. The task was accomplished with single-family residences, alone and in tracts; apartments, small, medium, and high rise; rentals, condominia, and separate ownership; occasionally with all cash on the escrow line, but primarily with mortgages and time payments. Of prime importance is the sheer magnitude of this statewide housing development. Secondary features involved substantial departures from the patterns that had prevailed.

The first postwar housing starts were small apartments and single-family dwellings on city lots left over from earlier promotions. Pent-up and spiraling demand then suggested mass production. That is the way most of the postwar housing construction came into being, most flamboyantly in tract housing. Examples had been set in Los Angeles' Westchester district and in the Levittowns of New Jersey and Long Island.

In the boom of the eighties the promoters did little more than flag the corners of the lots. By the twenties the practice was to survey, lay out streets, and even pave and bring in utilities, but the emphasis still was on sale of lots. The postwar tract developer did much more. Acquiring a sizable piece of raw or agricultural land, he marked it off, put in improvements, and erected a house on every lot. To the prospective purchaser he offered immediate occupancy, the house complete even to the financing.

Economically much can be said for tract housing. It saves substantially on the cost of components and particularly of labor. In its ultimate form the assembly line is brought to the site. Advance crews put in paved streets and utility lines, a machine quickly digs the foundation trenches, and other specialist crews pour the concrete, raise the pre-cut and perhaps prefabricated frame, shingle the roof, plaster, hang doors and windows, paint, and clean up. Selling of the first houses is in full swing while the construction crews are approaching other parts of the tract.

Some tracts were laid out on a conventional grid of streets. Others used the curved line and a maze of streets out of reach of through traffic. Some tracts endlessly repeated one house plan; others used two or more plans and broke the monotony by varying placement and ornamentation. The habit of the tract house is to sidle close to its neighbors. When tract adjoins tract, as they characteristically do, this compactness seems appropriate. But where a tract stands apart from any other habitations, as occurs south of Laguna, on the road to Castaic, and on the road to Palmdale, the crowding seems incongruous.

Urban Sprawl, Los Angeles, 1954

William A. Garnett

Tract housing has its traducers, as in Malvina Reynold's ballad, "Ticky-Tacky Houses," inspired by the view from the Bayshore Highway south of San Francisco. Examined more closely, the tract house is seen to be true to the central precept of individual ownership, most especially in the fenced-in back yards giving at least the illusion of privacy.

Tract housing is the major element in the urban sprawl that is predicted to spread continuously from San Diego to San Bernardino and Santa Barbara and from San Jose to Santa Rosa and Sacramento. It is particularly in evidence in San Diego, Orange County, Lakewood and Downey, Torrance and Hawthorne, south of Los Angeles, and all across San Fernando Valley. It proliferates in Santa Clara County, the East Bay and North Bay, and Sacramento. In fact, it may be inspected roundabout every California city.

A more incidental element in housing development is the trailer court or park. Initially these were ports of call for those who wanted to be footloose to follow the seasons or to move on whim. Mobile homes are so used, as can be seen at the beaches and at mountain and desert resorts, but the new feature is the trailer home that has taken root and sprouted ramada and patio and even a small garden. It amounts to an individually owned residence but on leased ground. Some of the inhabitants are, in fact, two-trailer families, using one as a home base and the other for travel.

Apartment building advanced at a more rapid rate and by the sixties accounted for more than half of the new units. The start was with two- or three-story structures occupying a single or double lot, some on virgin ground but many owing their existence to bungalow or mansion clearance. In West Hollywood apartment projects repeatedly threatened an architectural treasure, the Dodge House by Irving Gill. Aroused admirers stayed the wrecking crew, but only temporarily. In 1970 Gill's Dodge House was demolished to be replaced by the Dodge House Apartments! In many a residential area the apartment invasion has changed the character of an entire neighborhood.

More impressive are the complexes that occupy the equivalent of several city blocks, the units generously spaced and with a parklike environment made part of the development. Often the builder was content with two-story design and the trees could outreach the roofs. Other examples include the ten-story Park La Brea Towers in Los Angeles, convenient to the Farmers' Market, the Miracle Mile stores, the Tar Pits, and the Los Angeles Museum of Art. Considerably higher apartment complexes have risen in San Francisco, as well as those built where Los Angeles' Bunker Hill once stood, and those lining Wilshire Boulevard to the west.

To many of these multiple-unit residences condominium or participatory co-ownership has been applied. Condominia are bought rather than leased, making possible a more predictable set of residents. Maintenance and services are centralized, and tax savings may result.

The condominium principle is also applied in many of the more elaborate tract developments with varying restrictions as to pets, children, age, and celibacy. Cooperatives may have communal facilities such as lawns, swimming pool, hobby rooms, a restaurant, shops, and access to a golf course. They range up to self-contained communities, some of which are actually unincorporated towns as a further tax shelter.

Notwithstanding the economies in construction and in land requirements and the exemptions from responsibility for care and upkeep which condominia and apartments offer, many Californians of the postwar epoch have made substantial investments in individually constructed residences. None is as grandiose as Hearst's Castle or the mansions of Nob Hill, the Peninsula, Oak Knoll, or early Bel Air. Many are distinguishable from the better tract houses mainly in the higher cost per foot. A great many lend themselves to comfortable living, and a sprinkling are triumphs in design to fit a particular site and to suit a given family.

This branch of architecture, though small in its dividends as compared to the design of monumental structures, has benefited from the attention of highly talented designers. Although he is best known for his Wisconsin, Chicago, and Arizona houses, Frank Lloyd Wright planned several for California. Richard Neutra was responsible for a much larger number, some on grand scale, others, much more modest, including his own residence, a demonstration of the spaciousness that could be achieved on a very small lot.

In their *Guide to Architecture in Southern California* (1965) David Gebhard and Robert Winter picture dozens of dramatically successful houses designed by Wright, Neutra, Craig Ellwood, Charles Eames, Eero Saarinen, Raphael S. Soriano, and others. Similar collections could be assembled for San Diego, Santa Barbara, and the San Francisco area. There is, in fact, no dearth of such designs for display in the architectural and better homes magazines.

Some designers more consciously draw on the historical heritage. Cliff May's ranch houses, for instance, use resawed beams and boards for texture, slump stone with the feel of adobe, an occasional grilled window, and Spanish or Mexican doors. From patios or terraces the outdoors flows indoors.

In 1969 the American Institute of Architecture awarded its gold medal to William Wurster of Berkeley for his contributions to residential as well as public building design and its architectural firm award to A. Quincy Jones and Frederick Emmons of Los Angeles for their achievements in residences as well as in churches and college buildings.

A California Ranch House by Cliff May

Maynard L. Parker

Commercial and Industrial Buildings

Queues of customers at stores and theaters in the summer of 1945 demonstrated the state's need for commercial construction. In that sector there also was a revival, with new suburban shopping centers a most prominent feature. Such centers sprang up facing existing streets, as happened in Beverly Hills, Westchester, and Crenshaw in the Los Angeles area. The preferred pattern made the center an island to itself, near an artery but not right on it, with inviting turnoff and accommodation for the car as well as the customer. The typical center offered food and drink, clothing, barbering and beauty applications, cleaning and laundry, appliances, furniture, and all other vital needs. The more ambitious boasted major department stores as well as supermarkets. In Los Angeles the bulk of the trade shifted from downtown to the satellites. Smaller cities felt similar pull; Santa Barbara shared its business with Montecito on the east and two new centers to the west. Small towns also were affected, as by the Five Cities center, so called, south of Pismo Beach.

The satellite shopping centers accelerated urban sprawl. So popular did the new merchandizing centers become that tract developers increasingly included them in their plans. So heavily did they compete with the older shopping districts that renovation at the city cores appeared the only way to survive. Not every city attempted it. Not every effort succeeded. The Fresno Mall is a showplace. That of Hillsdale draws visitors. Santa Monica's has been criticized for its shortage of specialty shops.

The new building in San Francisco was primarily for financial institutions, law and corporation offices, and hotels. In Los Angeles banks, oil companies, and office buildings dominate the scene together with the cluster of new city, county, state, and federal buildings. The urban renewal constructions include a few display performances in architectural design and occasionally a notable restoration, as of the Bradbury Building in Los Angeles. Downtown survives, but without slowing the satellite cash registers.

Postwar California added a number of new hotels such as the San Francisco and Beverly Hiltons and the Statler, Century City, and Sheraton Universal in Los Angeles. Accommodations many times more numerous were added in the motels that festoon every highway. Most of this growth is represented by chains with repetitive plans and services at scores of locations throughout the state. Others have an individuality of name and sometimes of management. The larger look more and more like hotels and do not hesitate to invade the inner city, as for instance the Jack Tar and Del Webb's in San Francisco. The California motels en masse represent a tremendous investment and a major layout in construction. Their primacy is suggested in that whereas Richard Nixon campaigned for the Presidency from a hotel suite in New York, he located his California presidential office in one of the state's five-star motels, the Newporter.

Industry also engaged in a large amount of new construction, which on the whole has been much less conspicuous. The oil industry made its presence felt in catastrophies such as the Standard tank fire at El Segundo that blazed and smoked for more than a month in 1967 and the Union oil leak off Santa Barbara in 1969 that did more to popularize conservation than a thousand homilies. In refinery construction the industry kept pace with the rapidly expanding market. At Richmond and Oleum in the north and at El Segundo and Los Angeles Harbor in the south mammoth tank farms and intricate breaking plants are spread out and uplifted for all to see.

The enlarged output of electric power is impressively represented by the huge steam plants at Moss Landing, Morro Bay, Redondo, and Seal Beach. Several nuclear generators are in operation and plans have been made but postponed for a much larger one on an island to be constructed south of the Los Angeles–Long Beach harbor. California now burns several times as much natural gas as it did in 1945. The pipelines that bring it in were major constructions, but now are out of sight and taken for granted. Cement plants, already formidable at the time of building Boulder Dam, have been further expanded. Other plant development has occurred in chemical industries, drug making, toy manufacturing, steel making, and various other lines.

On the San Francisco peninsula, at Livermore, along the coast from Santa Monica to Redondo, in Pasadena, and again in Orange and San Diego counties the state bristles with buildings about the size of a bank or bakery or country club but which are laboratories, workshops, computer housings, and the like, in which the devising, improvement, and production of electronic, missile, and space-age devices occur. Individually these structures do not loom large, but the gear they contain often represents a high investment. The number of stations also runs high. Los Angeles Airport, for instance, is ringed with hundreds of plants thus engaged. Others are located in San Fernando Valley, Ventura and Santa Barbara counties, in the vicinity of Stanford University, and around Sacramento, a distribution of industry not earlier expected.

Public Structures

In Sacramento the traditional gold-domed Capitol still symbolizes state government, though in 1969 there was talk of demolishing it and building anew. Internally it is somewhat changed, particularly the Senate Chamber which was redecorated in 1967 in the finest Victorian splendor. That same year the Governor's Mansion fell into disrepute. Governor Reagan moved in and as promptly moved out. Public plans for replacing the obsolete, combustible, and noise-assaulted structure had been abortive. Private money-raising for an elegant new building on the banks of the American River, nine miles away, also aborted. The funds thus raised were diverted to buying the residence that the governor had leased. Along the mall that leads westward from the Capitol a battery of new state buildings suggests the enlarged role of state government. In San Francisco, Los Angeles, and elsewhere there are other reminders of state government—offices of the Department of Motor Vehicles, the Board of Equalization (collector of the sales tax), and the Franchise Board (income tax). San Quentin looks its familiar self, but more modern correctional facilities are seen at Vacaville, Soledad, San Luis Obispo, and elsewhere.

The decommissioning of Alcatraz suggests a lessening of federal operations and plant requirements in the state. On the contrary, federal activities grew and called for additional building and investment in Los Angeles and San Francisco and at Vandenberg, Port Hueneme, China Lake, and elsewhere. Cities and counties were responsible for a larger volume of construction. There is a showing in magnitude at Los Angeles Civic Center with a Water and Power building, a county administrative building, a county courthouse, a music center and theater, a parking structure, and an enlarged jail. Los Angeles county has also erected satellite courthouses in Van Nuys, Santa Monica, Long Beach, and on the eastside.

Much more money has gone into school construction. The University of California entered the postwar period with projects for $170 million in new construction. Existing campuses expected large increases in enrollment and the opening of new campuses at Santa Cruz, Irvine, and San Diego raised the sights substantially. The university also undertook to provide dormitories, of which there had been a few at Berkeley and Davis. In the postwar years living quarters for a significant fraction of the students were erected at every one of the eight general instruction campuses. These constructions were facilitated by loans that could be paid off by the charges for room and board. Similarly, parking fees provided the means to amortize the cost of the parking structures without which no campus could be up to date.

At the insistence of the private colleges the university authorities, though unwilling to call it tuition, raised the "incidental fee" to several hundred dollars a year. The funds thus accumulated made possible lavish outlay for noninstructional purposes such as student unions, recreation centers, and athletic fields. For classroom buildings, laboratories, libraries, and office structures, the university had depended on legislative appropriations or special bond issues. It seldom received all it asked, but through the first 23 postwar years was generously supported. Statewide, the university's plant is mostly postwar construction.

The state college system grew from six colleges in 1945 to 21 much larger institutions a quarter century later. Since the responsibilities for graduate and professional training were less than in the university, the construction needs were somewhat more modest, but because of the tremendous number of students involved they too were substantial. Junior colleges new and old participated in the building boom, as did the majority of the private universities and colleges.

Using local revenues and bond issues, with some help from the state, the hundreds of school districts in the course of the same years trebled their classroom capacity. The new construction of this period could have accommodated the entire public school enrollment of any state in the union except New York.

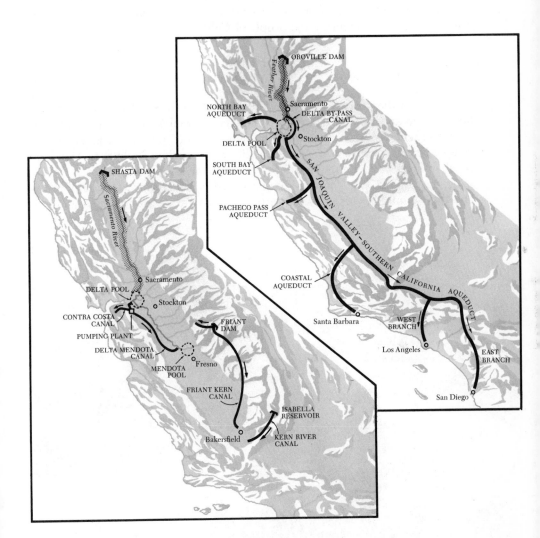

Central Valley Water Project and California Water Project

In esthetic quality some of these buildings were far more pleasing than others, though not necessarily more so than the little one-room red schoolhouse still functioning at Ballard. The architects in many instances undertook to attune to the environment. Thanks to the post-earthquake Field Act of 1935 these later schools conform to more rigorous safety standards. In sum they represent a large investment by the people of California.

Water Projects

In the postwar years work continued on the Central Valley project. Shasta Dam and Friant Dam were completed, as well as the canal from Friant to Bakersfield. Several years went by before the pumping plant at Tracy was completed, where Shasta power could lift water to flow "uphill" to Mendota. A subordinate project impounded the waters of the Kern at Kernville.

In 1947–48 a severe drought called a halt to the watering of lawns and the washing of cars at Santa Barbara and catalyzed the community to pro-

Friant-Kern Canal

B. G. Glaha, *Bureau of Reclamation*

ceed with damming the Santa Ynez at Cachuma and tunneling through the unstable mountain range to refill the reservoirs and revive the community.

Other communities were precariously near to running out of water. In the summer of 1948 the County of Los Angeles was asked to consider measures that would arrest any further population growth in Flintridge and La Canada because, it was calculated, a 10 per cent increase in population would parch the area.

Los Angeles, though eligible for Colorado River water through the Metropolitan Aqueduct, looked again to Owens Valley and the Mono Basin to the north. Without fanfare, its Department of Water and Power proceeded with a second aqueduct paralleling Mulholland's 1913 tube, with completion scheduled for 1970.

Meanwhile state water engineers looked ahead to the time when needs in the arid south would exceed the yield from local rainfall and streams, Owens Valley, and the Colorado. Eyes were cast on the Snake, the Columbia, and even the Yukon. A science writer proposed towing icebergs from the Antarctic to the lee of Catalina Island and ladling out the melt. Scientists forecast desalting ocean water. The engineers, more conservatively, looked to northern California's surplus waters in the Feather and the Eel. They drafted what they called the California Water Project, the gist of which was to impound the waters of these two rivers and move its surplus all the way to southern California. The plan in its entirety, subject to amendment, recalculation, and inflation, might run to $12 billion or more. An initial authorization of $1.75 billion was asked by Governor Brown and was approved by the voters in 1960.

The first authorization was expected to pay for an earthfill dam, higher than any other in the world (735 feet) at Oroville on the Feather, a mammoth pumping plant at the Delta, an aqueduct skirting the western San Joaquin Valley, and tunneling and more aqueduct through the mountains and on to the thirsty cities south of the Tehachapi. Delivery of the first water was scheduled for 1972.

State water executives, army engineers, and reclamation officers projected a dam across the Eel at Round Valley and a diversion eastward to replenish the Sacramento with more water for southern California. The Round Valley inhabitants, white and Indian, expostulated against the ruination of the best agricultural land along the Eel, their displacement, and the drowning of the Round Valley Indian Reservation. Conservationists entered their objections. Governor Reagan, who had shown minimal interest in saving the redwoods, intervened in 1969 to quash this particular plan. At the close of the sixties, therefore, the waters of the Feather, no mean stream, were the only additional waters known to be destined for southern California.

The constructions thus far mentioned—residential, commercial, industrial, educational, and for the management and movement of water—do not exhaust the postwar achievements. Mention should also be made of marinas and airports, harbor improvements, Disneyland, and the stadia at Candlestick, South Oakland, Chavez Ravine, Anaheim, and San Diego. The greatest constructions of all, in bulk, cost, man-hours of use, and influence, were the freeways.

The Freeway Explosion

On December 30, 1940, Mayor Fletcher Bowron of Los Angeles snipped a tape and opened the Arroyo Seco Parkway, more commonly known as the Pasadena Freeway. This 8.9 mile, six-lane divided roadway had evolved from suggestions of an access road to picnic grounds in Arroyo Seco Park. As an artery the road needed approval by the cities of Pasadena, South Pasadena, and Los Angeles, not to mention the businessmen of Highland Park. It needed designation as part of the state highway system and state participation. With the right of way transferred from the park and free fill obtained from the flood-control work in progress in the Arroyo Seco, the construction still cost $560,000 a mile, and that in depression dollars.

As Marshall Goodwin, the chief authority on this and all the California freeways, has pointed out, by modern standards the Pasadena Freeway was too narrow, too sharp in curvature, insufficiently banked, deficient in turn-outs, too abrupt in its entrances and exits, and too stingy in its center divider. But thanks to studies made by the Automobile Club of Southern California, the Los Angeles city engineer, and the state highway engineer, there was awareness of the central concept in Germany's Autobahns and the parkways being developed in New York, Connecticut, and Pennsylvania. All cross traffic was eliminated, and that is the essence of a freeway. Traffic began to flow at the speed for which this freeway was designed—45 miles an hour, at the time the posted speed limit throughout the state.

Then came the war and a moratorium on nonmilitary projects. The Pasadena Freeway was a thrill and a boon to motorists. It whetted the appetite for more roadways free of cross traffic and left-hand turns. This first California freeway also served as a laboratory for improving design. Accidents so trivial as a flat tire or running out of gas brought home the need for turnouts. Bottlenecks at stop-signed entrances and exits underlined the advisability of merging in motion. Speeders who jumped the divider into oncoming traffic illustrated the wisdom of more width or deterrence in the divider.

In 1911 the legislature entrusted supervision of the highway program to the Highway Commission. The agencies under its direction have undergone changes in designation and function but without breaking the administrative continuity. Through the 1950's and 1960's Senator Randolph Collier of Siskiyou, long-time chairman of the Senate Committee on Transportation, sedulously protected the gas tax against raids and the Highway Commission against challenges to its authority to determine where and how and what freeways should be built. In administering the program the Highway Commission has been more autonomous than the regents of the university. In 1923 the legislature endowed the highway program by initiating the gas tax, thus providing an allocated income which by the late sixties amounted to $800 million a year, "bubbling up," as one critic put it, from the "sacrosanct fountain" of the gas tax.

In 1946, when the number of licensed cars had risen to 3 million, the Highway Commission could point to 14,000 miles of highways in use, some of them prodigiously difficult in construction, for instance the Feather River Canyon route and the coast road from Carmel to San Simeon. Because both maintenance and construction were in arrears, the commission asked for more money. The legislature first investigated and then in 1947 voted the Collier–Burns Act, raising the gas tax, revising the formula for sharing with counties, accepting state responsibility for highway construction through cities, and authorizing a statewide freeway and expressway system. This measure was the enabling act for freeway construction.

Other modifications followed, including further increases in the gas tax, authorization for earlier letting of contracts, improved auditing of expenditures, and partial correction of a sectional inequity under which for many years southern California motorists paid well over half the tax but northern California received well over half the construction. But the same guiding principles continued—financing through the gas tax rather than by bonding, decision making by the Highway Commission rather than by the more political legislature, emphasis on freeways, and freeways that would be free rather than toll roads. Senator Collier, perennial chairman of the Transportation Committee, is to be credited more than any other one man with holding California to this line.

In the fifties and sixties the freeway builders addressed themselves first of all to the problem of easing, speeding, and making safer long distance driving. Where traffic snarled or slowed on the great arteries such as 99 and 101, a section of multilane divided freeway was built.

The tortuous Ridge Route was one such candidate. The Grapevine ascent was widened and straightened and an entirely new route was opened replacing the twisting ridge. In the late sixties what seemed to be an almost perfect divided highway from Lebec to Gorman was replaced by a wider and slightly faster freeway. As an added dividend, the grading at the summit finally got rid of the "Impeach Earl Warren" billboard placed there by his detractors shortly after the Supreme Court ruling in *Brown* vs. *Board of Education.*

Bypassing of cities was another standard device. On 101, Ventura, which had been a horrendous bottleneck, was avoided by swerving the freeway a little farther to the south. San Luis Obispo was negotiated by a depressed freeway with several overpasses. The freeway circled San Jose, and the Bay Shore section on toward San Francisco was one long bypass of the Peninsula cities. Bypasses were thrown around Santa Maria, Salinas, Carpinteria, and King City, in approximately that order, and even around so small a community as Buellton. Some of these communities must miss the revenue that once came from gas, lunch, and coffee breaks. The dire prediction of doom for Buellton fictionized in Eugene Burdick's *The Ninth Wave* did not come to pass, perhaps because the novelist underestimated the consistency of pea soup.

In certain localities the freeway planners have been rebuffed. The Monterey–Carmel community vigorously protested a plan to cut through the scene as they love it and push on to Hearst's Castle. To date this opposition prevails. Santa Barbara and the Highway Commission are at loggerheads over which should go underground where State Street and 101 intersect. Whichever does will plunge slightly below sea level, and neither side has perfect confi-

Los Angeles Freeway Interchange

Ansel Adams, Fiat Lux

dence in pumps and drains. Therefore, the motorist on 101 encounters in rapid succession four grade crossings with traffic lights, cross traffic, and left turns. Once those are negotiated, the southbound driver can proceed without another such interference all the way to the state line at Blythe.

Conservationists have objected strenuously to proposals for a freeway through the redwoods, additional routes across the Sierra, and a freeway that would disfigure the beach or waterfront or the mountains from Santa Monica to Point Mugu. Another school of conservationists regrets the retirement of a wide swath of agricultural land for the full length of 99 through the Central Valley. The freeway program encounters more spirited resistance and astronomical expense when it penetrates urban areas. The citizens of Beverly Hills want no freeway invasion. If it must come, they want it underground and with no exits or entrances.

Entering urban areas, the freeway builders found their problems compounded. Acquiring right of way can be extremely expensive, and all the country problems are complicated by the mass of urbanites who crowd onto the freeway just to go to work or to shop or to a ball game. The urban sections of the freeway system are by all odds the most heavily traveled. They are the samples by which the freeways are most often judged. That is not quite fair. To be sure of being able to cruise along at 60 to 70 miles an hour on any of the freeways in metropolitan Los Angeles, a motorist has to choose carefully the day and the hour. For any stretch of 101 between Santa Barbara and San Jose or of 99 between San Fernando and Stockton, that is not so.

The freeways represent endless lessons learned in curvatures and gradients permissible, the proper width of lanes and center dividers, the optimum angle of approach for on-ramps with due regard to visibility and appropriate merging speed, the ways of insuring outflow at off-ramps, and the optimum size, shape, lettering, and placement of signs. The state abides by the national standard of lettering in capitals but knows that there is quicker recognition of words printed in capitals and small letters. Lane markings have advanced from painted lines to buttons to reflector buttons. Center barriers have gone from solid steel and concrete to bend and break fencing and to curved concrete designed to steer an angling wayward car back into its proper lane.

A few of these lessons may have been figured out on the drawing-board. A few are the result of freeway building elsewhere in the nation or the world. A great many have emerged through trial and error. The pedestrian pass will illustrate. Underpasses were found to be an invitation to flooding, obscene inscriptions, and child molestation. Open overpasses presented the hazards of youngsters dropping objects or falling on cars below. Wire fences were a temptation for climbing over, and a wire overlay was an inviting trampoline. The best answer to date is an overpass fenced high with a frame that bends in toward the walkway. There are stretches of freeway where these successive experiments may be viewed. Trial and error also yielded the answers on lane width, curvature, gradients, entrances and exits, signposting, structural elements, landscaping for erosion control, light screening, esthetics, and visibility.

California's network of freeways, still in process of elaboration, is the most visible, pervasive, and massive monument raised in the great postwar building boom. Millions of Californians use the freeways every day of their lives. The freeways greatly affect other transportation options, the livelihood of many persons, and the life of the entire society.

For Further Reading

REMI NADEAU, *Los Angeles, from Mission to Modern City* (1960).

MEL SCOTT, *The San Francisco Bay Area: A Metropolis in Perspective* (1959).

LAWRENCE KINNAIRD, *History of the Greater San Francisco Bay Area*, three volumes (1967).

WINSTON W. CROUCH and BEATRICE DINERMAN, *Southern California Metropolis: A Study in Development of Government for a Metropolitan Area* (1964).

JOHN ANSON FORD, *Thirty Explosive Years in Los Angeles County* (1961).

SAMUEL E. WOOD and ALFRED E. HELLER, *The Phantom Cities of California* (1963).

MARSHALL KAPLAN, *The Community Builders* (1967), developers of new towns.

California Water Resources Board, *The California Water Plan* (1957).

H. MARSHALL GOODWIN, California's Growing Freeway System (UCLA dissertation, 1969).

CAUGHEY, *California Heritage*, 435–39, 449–52, 489–504.

chapter thirty-two

Politics and Government

"What," James Reston asked me, "does California have to give to the nation?"

Well, I said, for one thing it offers the example of a large number of people who have scrapped the party system in its orthodox American form, and have got along fairly well nevertheless.

Gladwin Hill,
Dancing Bear (1968)

The Warren Years

1945
and
after

In the 1930's and for some time thereafter Californians gave the impression of being most erratic voters. From 1934 on, Democratic registrations were in the majority and in presidential elections up to Eisenhower's the state went Democratic. In the alternating gubernatorial elections, however, except in 1938 when Olson slipped in, these same voters chose Republicans. This behavior led pundits such as Gladwin Hill to call California "the state that swings and sways" and, more engagingly, the "Dancing Bear."

Many things made California politics erratic. The reformers of the Hiram Johnson era, intent on precluding machine control such as had plagued the state for 40 years, deemphasized party politics. They saw to it that elections of all city and county

The Stanford House in Modern Sacramento

Department of Water Resources

538

officers, school boards, and judges were nonpartisan races. The initiatives and referendums that filled most of the ballot space also were nonpartisan. Only in voting for state and national offices did party labels appear. The electorate was also unstable, what with Californians exhibiting high mobility and new voters by the tens or hundreds of thousands showing up at each election. It was easy for voters to cross party line by reregistering; still easier by cross-voting. Candidates could cross-file and without much ado could switch parties.

With the state changing so rapidly, the issues also changed, another factor contributing to political volatility. Rolfe, Sinclair, Merriam, and Olson, and Franklin D. Roosevelt for that matter, had trouble sailing these seas. Earl Warren was the first to combine a technique and a personality resulting in their mastery.

A native of Los Angeles and a graduate of the University of California Law School, Warren was in private practice briefly and then in uniform during World War I. In 1919 he was appointed deputy city attorney of Oakland, in 1920 shifted to deputy district attorney of Alameda County, and in 1925 was promoted to district attorney. In that nonpartisan office he made a reputation as a vigorous enforcer of the laws. Most publicized was his prosecution of three labor officials charged with sending thugs to beat up the engineer of the ship *Port Lobos*. The engineer having died, Warren won convictions for second-degree murder. Alongside this nonpartisan work as district attorney, he was active in party politics, rising in 1934 to Republican state chairman.

In 1938, with encouragement from Joseph Knowland, Oakland publisher and a power in the Republican party, and from Robert Kenny, a leader among the Democrats, Warren announced for state attorney general. After nine terms in office Ulysses S. Webb was retiring. Because of his position in

Earl Warren

Howard M. Smith, California State Library

the party, Warren could count on Republican support. But knowing full well that his party was a poor second in registrations, he cross-filed in the Democratic and Progressive primaries and in his campaign quoted none other than FDR on the good citizenship of splitting the ticket and voting for the best candidate for each office rather than by party emblem. The opposition was not formidable and Warren won the Democratic as well as the Republican nomination. He thus was an entrenched bystander the following November when Olson and the others followed him into office.

As attorney general Warren showed the same vigor he had as district attorney. One of his first steps was to challenge a county judge recently appointed by outgoing Governor Merriam. The evidence justified this judge's conviction as a bribe-taker. As his chief assistant Warren appointed William Sweigert, a highly capable attorney and a Democrat. He made other appointments on merit rather than party affiliation, and he made changes and reassignments in the 50-man staff that substantially improved its efficiency. Dramatizing his role in cleaning up the state, Warren personally headed the process servers on Tony Carnero on his gambling ship beyond the three-mile limit in Santa Monica Bay.

Under the California system the elected head of the Department of Justice has substantial independence of the governor. Their functions, however, intermesh. On two noteworthy occasions Warren and Olson clashed head-on. When, after a visit to San Quentin, Olson questioned the incarceration of the union officials in the "Ship Murder Case," Warren responded tartly, "These men are assassins—proved to be so." Again when Olson nominated Max Radin, distinguished law professor, to the state supreme court, Warren cited Radin's letters urging clemency in certain contempt-of-the-legislature cases and blocked his appointment.

In his third most remembered action as attorney general Warren had no opposition from Olson. That was in beseeching the federal government to collect all Japanese Americans, citizens as well as aliens, and move them to remote concentration camps for the duration of the war.

As the 1942 election approached, with the Olson administration a shambles, the signs were that anyone but Olson could win. If the Democrats put up Robert Kenny, that would mean a different kind of race. To neutralize that possibility, Kyle Palmer of the Los Angeles *Times* ran up a trial balloon on Warren for governor and Kenny for attorney general. Logic prevailed. Warren, the one prominent Republican in state office and popular for his stands against corruption, crime, and the Japanese, won easily over Olson. And Kenny, not having to oppose Warren, walked into the Department of Justice.

Warren's campaign was emphatically nonpartisan. The exigencies of war made it fashionable to set aside party politics for the duration. To some extent this truce prevailed in Washington where there were Republicans in the Cabinet and bipartisan support for the war effort. Warren knew that in 1934 the Republicans had had to attract a large bloc of Democratic votes to defeat Sinclair. Even more transparently, in his own election as attorney general he had won on Democratic votes added to Republican. Emphasizing independence of party, Warren had his own well-financed campaign organization and did not allow it to be merged with the party effort. He retained public relations expert Clem Whitaker of Whitaker and Baxter to manage his campaign. His candidacy was aided by Olson's refusal to cross-file and by his tardiness about active campaigning. That combination meant that Warren had opportunity for several valuable weeks to concentrate on cultivating Democratic voters. Several well-known persons announced themselves as "Democrats for Warren." The end result was that he came into office with what appeared to be a bipartisan mandate.

The California that Warren began governing in 1943 was bustling with war industries, troops training for the European war and the war in the Pacific, and forwarding men and materiel to the Pacific front. War industry employment was close to its peak. The biggest problems in accommodating the influx of war workers and in arranging for food, shelter, and other necessities had been met. The war imposed a shutdown on several activities which stood high in state budgets, notably street and highway construction and expansion of school facilities and other public building. The state could economize. Warren proposed and achieved a program to lower taxes and at the same time accumulate reserves for postwar catch-up on building needs.

All Californians applauded these good housekeeping elements in Warren's administration. Democrats took it in stride that his keynote address at the Republican national convention in 1944 was stridently partisan, and even, in 1945, that he named to the United States Senate a comparative unknown, William Knowland, son of his champion, Joseph Knowland. Republicans expressed reservations about Warren's penchant for nonpartisan appointments. He ran into bipartisan opposition when he advocated employee–employer financed medical insurance—in modern parlance, medicare. Conservative legislators blocked his health-insurance programs, and in 1945 Whitaker and Baxter turned against him as managers of the California Medical Association's campaign to defeat an initiative for, as they called it, socialized medicine.

The voters, nevertheless, recognized rectitude, efficiency, and commitment to the best interests of Californians. In 1946 they reelected Warren in the primaries, giving him a majority in the Democratic as well as in the Republican balloting. As to the governorship, that was unprecedented and continues unmatched.

In 1948 Warren headed the delegation to the Republican national convention and emerged as the vice-presidential candidate. Harry Truman's "give-'em-hell" campaigning, which confounded the experts and won a narrow victory, was mostly directed at the Republican presidential nominee, Thomas E. Dewey. Truman had one bon mot for Warren: "He's a Democrat—and doesn't know it."

In 1950 the Democrats fielded an active campaigner for governor in James Roosevelt, but Warren won by more than a million votes. His total approximated the Democratic registration; Roosevelt's approximated the Republican registration—which suggests the ultimate in nonpartisanship. Part of the margin may be attributed to the outbreak of war in Korea. Without that assist Warren would still have won handily.

Two years later, although recalcitrant Republicans put up an opposition slate, a Warren-pledged delegation went to the Republican convention. This time Warren appeared to be the most logical contender for president should a deadlock develop between the supporters of Robert Taft and Dwight D. Eisenhower. California's junior Senator, Richard Nixon, after arming himself with a poll of Californians on their preference for Republican nominee, spread the word on the train ride to Chicago that Eisenhower would win on the first ballot. This work promoted Nixon toward the vice-presidency. But Eisenhower's winning of the nomination was more precisely in the seating of disputed delegations, and on these motions Warren directed the California votes to pro-Eisenhower delegations. Eisenhower acknowledged that Warren, more than any other man, clinched his nomination.

In September, 1953, Eisenhower announced Warren's appointment as Chief Justice of the Supreme Court. Unofficial testimony has it that prior to the election there was conversation about an appointment to the Court. Still more tantalizing are statements that at a luncheon meeting with Attorney General Herbert Brownell in the summer of 1953, Eisenhower promised to name Warren to the first vacancy. That report is substantiated by Warren's announcement on September 3 that he would not seek a fourth term as governor. On September 8 Chief Justice Fred M. Vinson died. Allegedly Eisenhower and Brownell then proposed an associate justiceship, but Warren held out for what he had been promised—the first vacancy. Be that as it may, on October 4, 1953, Warren terminated California's longest governorship and moved to Washington for a longer and highly productive period of service as head of the Supreme Court.

Propositions Unlimited

If on reassessment Warren's high repute as governor seems to rest on capable administration rather than on leading the state into ambitious new programs, it may be because the California system puts much of the opportunity for innovations elsewhere. One place is in direct legislation.

Today's California voter takes for granted a long ballot encrusted with a spate of proposed statutes and constitutional amendments. The drafters of the 1879 constitution are partly to blame. They made it too long and too legislative, thereby inviting amendment. The Lincoln–Roosevelt reformers, in their zeal to thwart special interest or pressure group influence on the legislature, added the options of initiative and referendum. The legislature may put proposed statutes or amendments on the ballot. Or, by registering sufficient signatures within a specified time, the voters can invalidate an enacted law, impose a new law, or amend the constitution. The presence of this option stimulates more referrals to the voters, that being the only way in which initiated statutes or amendments can be modified or repealed. Politicians also have used referral as a means of escaping the political consequences of being for or against a controversial proposal.

The 1911 legislature laid 23 amendments before the electorate, a substantial quantity to digest. Yet they stood as a package central to the reform program evolved by the Lincoln–Roosevelt League and further developed in legislative debate. The conservative press attacked some of the proposals but not the referral to popular vote.

In subsequent decades wilder assortments of measures have been thrust before the voters, some confusingly complex, some heatedly controversial, some misleadingly labeled, some so far out that their consequences were unpredictable. Political scientists see many of these measures as much more appropriate for consideration in the legislature where they would be subject to hearings, debate, and revision before enactment.

The sponsors of the direct legislating methods may have presumed that a groundswell of public opinion would produce the signatures on the petitions. In a few instances that is what happened. Far more often a special interest or pressure group has mustered the signatures. There are groups large enough to do it, among them the state employees, the unions, and church members. More commonly the method has been to hire the signature gathering.

Early in the twenties Joseph Robinson went into the business of qualifying petitions. Initially he could afford to do it for a few cents a signature. With inflation the unit cost rose, while the number of valid signatures needed continued to mount. By 1967 it had passed half a million. Allowing a 20 to 25 per cent cushion for invalid or irregular signatures, that pushed the cost of qualifying a petitioned initiative to well over a quarter of a million dollars in cash or volunteered soliciting.

The pattern came to be that most of the more drastic initiatives, the more forward looking or the more backward looking, and the ones that would have most effect, were put on the ballot by special interests or pressure groups. Among them were several very expensive pension plans, a proposal for a state lottery from which 13 per cent of the profits would go to the promoters of the plan, the real-estate association's proposition to prohibit state or local fair-housing legislation, and one to prohibit pay television.

Often it seemed that the initiative and referendum were more a nuisance than a check on the people's representatives in government. These devices have the untoward effect of transferring responsibility from the duly elected representatives. A governor or a legislator may come out strongly for or against a proposition, but an astute politician can avoid that merely by saying, "Let the people decide." There have been campaigns in which the burning issues were in the propositions, and most candidates were safely encapsulated from them.

The mechanism of direct decision making by the people somewhat reduces the role of the governor. Only indirectly can he initiate any such vote. His opportunities to control are hemmed in further by his limited appointing power, limitations on his power to pardon or reprieve, the many elements of government assigned to semi-independent boards and commissions, and prior commitment of the greater part of the state's annual revenue to functions beyond his effective reach.

The initiative is more of an impingement on the status of the legislature, which up to 1966 had the further handicap of a most unrepresentative upper house. This combination of circumstances, debilitating to the legislature, played into the hands of what is sometimes called the third house, the professional lobbyists.

The Lobbyists

Lobbying is not quite the oldest profession. In California it did not appear in the constitutional convention of 1849, and in the first legislature it was present only in the mild form of Senator Green's private bar and his ready motion to adjourn and drink. By 1907 it was in full flower, though with the peculiarity that the control was frankly in the hands of a machine run by the one business that was big, the Southern Pacific Railroad. The Lincoln–Roosevelters broke this machine. They were accused of substituting a machine of their own, but at most it was one of politics and patronage.

By the twenties conditions were ripe for lobbyists to rise again. The unrepresentative character of the legislature, especially after 1926, made that body particularly susceptible. The torrent of migration delivered a voting majority with no knowledge of the old machine and the fight against it. The overnight growth of many corporations and combines as formidable as the Octopus of old, and each with a special interest to be served, gave incentive for a rebirth of lobbying.

In the thirties, in particular, with the return of legalized liquor, racing, and gambling, the new style of lobbying forged ahead. In 1939 some of its details were itemized in detective H. R. Philbrick's report to the Sacramento grand jury. This report spelled out in detail how influence had been brought to bear on certain legislators by retainers, donations, and campaign contributions, and how large a part of this influence was funneled and directed by professional lobbyists. Through the accounts of one such man, Arthur H. Samish, Philbrick had traced $496,138.26 in 1935–38, all provided by individuals and organizations with a direct interest in legislation.

The Philbrick report created little stir at the time, though some of the legislators named failed to be reelected. Any general concern about "government by lobbyists" was postponed until 1949 when Carey McWilliams in the *Nation* of July 9 and Lester Velie in the August 13 and 20 issues of *Collier's* offered candid exposés of Samish and his methods. Velie quoted Governor Warren as saying, "On matters that affect his clients, Artie unquestionably has more power than the governor." Samish freely admitted that the legislature did his bidding. A posed photograph with a puppet "Mr. Legislature" held on his knee did not exaggerate.

The beauty of Samish's system was that it was within the law, and part of it through the law. As public relations counselor for the brewers, the liquor wholesalers, the motor carriers, and other clients, Samish worked through front organizations which carried on public-relations drives, donated to campaigns, entertained influential persons, and retained a surprising number of lawyers, especially legislator–lawyers. The reciprocal favors asked were limited. Usually they seemed to concern mere details in the grand total of legislation and in many instances details remote from the interests of a particular legislator's constituents.

On the state as a whole the weight of lobbyist control was most felt through the welter of "fair trade and practices" codes of the sort popularized under the NIRA of the early New Deal. These codes enlisted the police power of the state to curb competition and, by corollary, to award special privilege to established elements in business and the professions. The Alcoholic Beverage Control Act of 1934, for instance, was deliberately made so complicated that it was almost impossible for a retailer to avoid violating it. The kind of violation most rigorously policed was price cutting.

In many other lines state law moved in to prevent competition. It became a crime to sell milk below the fixed price or above a specified cream content. In a price regulating system of all floor and no ceiling, the consumer would seem to be the forgotten man. There was a gimmick, however, that ensured that the lobbyist would not be forgotten by his clients. Even after a law to the advantage of such a client was passed and in force, it was comparatively simple to point to agitation against it or to a proposed amending act and thus to get a continuing retainer for "the man who gets things done."

For his bragging Samish was barred from the floor of the 1949 legislature. That legislature also voted to require an accounting of expenditures by each lobbyist, which proved only mildly informative. In 1953 Samish was convicted of income-tax evasion. That and the conviction of one speaker of the assembly for bribe-taking and the indictment of another led to more circumspect behavior. An investigator in the late fifties concluded that campaign contributions by individual lobbyists were spread thin and for the typical assemblyman amounted to only a small fraction of his expenditures. A similar study by another political scientist led to the conclusion that, although interest groups in the Samish era "did purchase legislation," subsequent contributors "carefully refrain from demanding a specific quid pro quo." In other words, the third house, which outnumbers the legislators three or four to one, still operated, but circumspectly.

The legislature in 1966 enacted a conflict-of-interest law said to be the toughest in the nation. Its impact was more on state officers than on members of the legislature. In 1969 when two members of the state senate assertedly gained extraordinary profits in insurance deals, the ethics committee of the senate showed no interest in investigating. Jess W. Unruh at the same time was pushing legislation to require every officeholder to make full disclosure of his investment holdings.

Lobbying the Electorate

Prevalence of direct legislation called for another breed of lobbyists to work upon that other body of lawmakers, the voters. Specialists soon arose, much as Joseph Robinson had moved into the business of qualifying initiatives.

In 1930 the barbers of California wanted a state board set up to regulate their business. They could not stir legislators to act, but a young newsman, Clem Whitaker, offered to do the job for a fee of $4,000. Instead of going to assemblymen, he carried the message to the people, stirred attention and interest, and the desired measure soon became law.

Three years later Whitaker and Leone Baxter collaborated in defeating the Pacific Gas and Electric Company's referendum against the enactment of the Central Valley water project. The next year they masterminded and staged the defeat of Sinclair's candidacy for governor, thereby solidifying the role of public-relations expertise in California politics. In 1936 the limelight was on Don Francisco, an advertiser temporarily on leave from his regular work to defeat the initiative for a graduated chain-store tax.

The methods used were akin to advertising, since they consisted of ad writing, slogan devising, endorsements, and display through billboards, leaflets, planted stories, sky writing, moving-picture trailers, radio messages, and, in time, television commercials. The experts decided what image a candidate should have; Whitaker and Baxter are credited with teaching Warren to smile. Operating on a fee basis, they had more power of decision than in most of their commercial accounts.

From the thirties on it became almost the rule to rely on a public-relations firm to sway the electorate on every significant proposition and wherever possible to bring in such a firm for every major candidacy. The tendency carried over into other semipublic activities. When a group of professors faced the problem of suing the university regents in the oath controversy, one of the first suggestions was that a public relations expert be retained.

Within 20 years Whitaker and Baxter, operating part of the time as Campaigns, Inc., masterminded and conducted close to a hundred campaigns. Thus, by courtesy of this team, California voters twice rejected health-insurance proposals. In 1948 the firm won approval of an antifeatherbedding initiative and persuaded a majority of the voters to approve continuation of malapportionment which meant less than their fair share of representation at Sacramento. On the basis of these performances Whitaker and Baxter were retained by the American Medical Association to stage a nationwide fight against medicare.

Murray Chotiner handled Nixon's campaign for Congress in 1946. Baus and Ross were consulted but not given full charge in the California part of Adlai Stevenson's races in 1952 and 1956 and in Brown's campaign in 1966. In 1964 they had a winner in Goldwater's bid in the California primary.

Stuart Spencer, recreation director, and Bill Roberts, television dealer, entered the field of image-making in 1960 and soon headed the list. They began with Alphonso Bell, a middle-of-the-road Republican, and John Rousselot, a Birch Society Republican, and piloted the two of them into the House of Representatives. In 1962 they helped Senator Thomas Kuchel survive his reactionary foes and critics. In 1964 they piloted Nelson Rockefeller to a near miss in the Republican primary, delivering in passing a few aspersions at Ronald Reagan among the Goldwater forces. Then in 1966 they earned a $150,000 fee by managing Reagan's bid for the governorship. Spencer and Roberts thus have a certain elasticity but serve only Republicans.

One hesitates to say that any image-maker could be more sophisticated than Whitaker and Baxter of the 1930's through the early 1950's. They demonstrated superlative knowledge of human nature and familiarity with California politics. Several of their campaigns were classics, the one against Sinclair so much so that Whitaker later expressed regret over having gone so far. Spencer and Roberts may be no closer to omniscience, but this firm has the advantage of the computer, stockpiles of data about voting behavior, opinion surveys, and other such aids in determining when and where to make what push in behalf of the current candidate.

There also are free-lancers, including one who prefers absolute simplicity on a formula such as "Three Cheers for ———" or "Anybody but ———," and another who in the movies would be called a stunt man. He is credited with putting the attractive young lady aboard the Goldwater train to hand out anti-Goldwater literature and with arranging for an oversize banner in Chinese characters for Nixon's parade through Chinatown in Los Angeles in 1962. Its legend asked, "What about the Hughes loan?"

From "the guy who gets things done" in the legislature, lobbying has expanded to the public-relations "guys who get things done" with the electorate. That California has pioneered in managed campaigns is due partly to the initiative and partly to the pattern of highly personalized campaigning and the many millions of voters to reach. The nation and some other states are following the example. The label "image-makers" implies a rebuke. Others would say that numbers and the media make something of the sort inevitable, yet it is disconcerting to observe a candidate for the Senate or for governor peddled like a bar of soap.

Knight and the Musical Chairs

On Warren's departure for Washington, Goodwin J. Knight acceded to the governorship. In the undemanding role of lieutenant governor he had been waiting out Warren's long tenure as governor. A man of abundant energy, Knight had improved his time by travel up and down the state making countless public appearances. Gregarious by nature, he seemed to delight in the ribbon cuttings, service club luncheons, and public festivals. On that circuit it is not easy to appear profound, but on a number of issues, among them the university loyalty oath, Knight pointedly disagreed with Warren. On his accession as

Goodwin J. Knight

A. Jonniaux, California State Library

governor most alert Californians took for granted a considerably different leadership, more Republican and more conservative.

Knight proved more astute. He understood the secret of Warren's popularity. He had no intention of narrowing his support to Republican registrants, nor would he petulantly antagonize a major block of constituents. Recognizing that California was well served by the Warren methods, he had no wish to jeopardize a continuation.

Labor leaders, however, found him far more cooperative. He backed increases in workmen's compensation and in unemployment insurance, boosting the latter from $25 to $40 a week. He signed into law measures designed to protect pension and union welfare funds.

He was easily elected to a full term in 1954 and the prospects were bright for reelection four years later, notwithstanding the Democratic bulge of close to a million in registrations.

There was one cloud on the horizon. In 1953 a gathering of Democrats, distraught at the inept campaigning of their party, organized to try to bring unity out of chaos. They launched the California Democratic Council (CDC), modeled in part after the California Republican Assembly, but backed by 100 clubs, eventually 500, in which enthusiasts could buoy their spirits, raise a little money, organize for precinct work, develop candidates, and hopefully see some of them into office. Adlai Stevenson was in a way the patron saint of the CDC. Its touchstone was preprimary endorsements, a way of breaking through the advantage to incumbents that was built into cross-filing.

Lightning struck Knight from another quarter. In January, 1957, Senator William Knowland announced that he would not seek reelection but would return to California to be with his family. No matter how uxorial he was, it strained belief that an able-bodied politician, leader of his party in the Senate, would break off in midcareer. The explanation was soon forthcoming; Knowland would run for governor and then be strongly based for mounting to the presidency.

Had Knowland been California's only prominent Republican, this maneuver might have been as graceful as it was calculated. But Knight was not one to be cavalierly set aside, and Nixon, as Eisenhower's choice for vice-president, could see himself as closer to the presidency than either Knowland or Knight. Only the year before, the three had to be taken into account in the delegation to the Republican national convention—supporters of each were made equal in number, plus one spot for Senator Thomas Kuchel, a neutral.

Nixon is credited with suggesting how to avoid a knockdown primary between Knowland and Knight. Knight should be persuaded to step aside and run for Knowland's vacated Senate seat. Knight refused, and advisedly when it became clear that Knowland planned to run on "right-to-work," that is, on an antiunion, antilabor plank. With the support he could count on from labor, Knight measured his chances as good and so stated. But a month later he dolefully announced that his "most constructive course" would be to run for the Senate; a Knight–Knowland battle was too likely to split the party and turn California over to the Democrats. Later Knight was more explicit, saying that he had been notified that if he fought on for the governorship the big campaign contributors would find their conservative way to Knowland. "Standing on the burning deck in midocean," as Knight later soliloquized, "I had no choice."

Although on his last time around Knowland had won handily, he was a bumbling campaigner. Labor baiting, even brightly packaged as the "right to work" or the "American way," had the feel of a return to the nineteenth century or at least to Herbert Hoover. Knowland's wife circulated statements that made him seem a more arch reactionary than he was. Native son though he was, he came back for this race as an outlander. That was held against him, and so with greater vehemence was the shunting of Goody Knight out of his earned position and into an inferior one. To the voters it all appeared too manipulated.

On the countdown Knowland lost by 3,140,000 to 2,111,000, and Knight by 2,927,000 to 2,204,000. In the races for Congress and the legislature the landslide was more moderate, but the end result was an across-the-board Republican defeat. For the first time in many a year they would be a minority (14 to 16) in the House delegation, for the first time since 1942 a minority (33 to 47) in the assembly, and for the first time since 1890 an outright minority (13 to 27) in the state senate.

The general opinion was that Knowland got the comeuppance he deserved. Almost as widespread was the sentiment that Knight deserved a better fate, though not necessarily the Senate seat. The consensus was that Knowland and Nixon and Knight had played musical chairs, for which Robert

Kenny sagely remarked that, when the music stopped, Nixon was sitting in both chairs. That oversimplifies. So far as influence went, Knowland was cut down to one newspaper and one vote. Knight was retired. Nixon's ploy had not really saved the Republicans from splitting. And there was another way to read the election returns. With Edmund G. (Pat) Brown moving into the governor's seat and Clair Engle into the Senate, the election was a Democratic victory, not just a Republican defeat.

Governor Pat Brown

A native of San Francisco, Brown grew up in its Mission district and worked his way through law school. He also worked his way up to the post of district attorney, attained in 1944. Initially he was a Republican, natural enough for an admirer of Hiram Johnson, but in 1934, prompted by FDR and the New Deal rather than by Sinclair and Epic, he changed his registration to Democratic. An open, warm-hearted man, he also displayed unmistakable integrity. In a much publicized case, on the verge of getting a conviction, he learned that a key witness had lied. Unhesitatingly he asked for dismissal. In 1950 he won election as attorney general.

That Brown could have defeated Knight is open to question. Against Knowland his campaign could capitalize on the selfish conniving of the opposition, imply less radical departure from the good features of the Warren and Knight regimes, and count on union support. Brown came out flatly against Knowland's pet antiunion initiative. Invoking the tradition of Hiram Johnson and Warren, he announced that as governor he would call on the most able Californians regardless of party. His road to the governor's mansion thus closely paralleled Warren's.

In his first message to the legislature Brown emphasized the need to combat racial discrimination. The legislature responded with a Fair Employment Practices Act and a Civil Rights Act authored by the new speaker of the assembly, Jess W. Unruh. Attorney General Stanley Mosk was congenial to these same purposes. His staff was soon exerting itself to persuade businessmen in many lines to avoid discriminatory practices.

Well aware of the way in which cross-filing had inured to the benefit of the Republicans, the new legislature joyfully abolished this practice. Brown asked and got an increase in unemployment benefits, improved compensation to injured workmen, and an increase in state aid to local school districts. He did not succeed in having the minimum-wage law extended to agricultural workers. He appointed a dedicated humanitarian as consumers' counsel, essentially to help buyers beware, but for lack of anything more than a very short hat pin her work was not highly effective. In 1959 Brown appointed a new state economic planning board, and he set the legislature to thinking about the program and support that higher education should have in the years to come.

From his predecessors Brown inherited a deficit and a need for state services that was growing in step with the rapid rise in population. He

recommended a budget approaching $2.5 billion and increases in income, inheritance, corporation, and excise taxes to bring it into balance. The legislature voted approximately what he requested; indeed, for the session, of 40 measures which he urged, 35 were made laws. And alongside the laws passed, Brown was laying the basis for a much larger achievement.

Eight years earlier the legislature had approved a Warren-recommended plan for capturing the water of the Feather River and conducting it to the Bay cities, the parched west side of San Joaquin Valley, and southern California. Funding the project hung fire. Northern Californians were reluctant to see a natural resource of their section siphoned off to Los Angeles, and the Senate had the votes to prevent a commitment. On January 22, 1959, midway in his first month in office, Brown urged the legislature to take action to bring into use 3 billion acre-feet of water that was going to waste each year.

Brown made several very practical suggestions. One was to give prospective water purchasers commitments by contracts with the state rather than by more cumbersome constitutional amendment. Another was to allocate the state's Investment Fund (tideland oil royalties) to this resource project, with water bonds accepted in exchange. This feature would later come in for criticism as robbing the schools to pay for water. To make the project manageable Brown proposed leaving until later the $11.8 billion package for the projected needs of the year 2050 and an immediate commitment to $1.75 billion which should suffice for the seventies and early eighties.

As a practical politician Brown decided to crack the harder nut first, the senate. Debate, hearings, buttonholing, and off-the-floor consultations began, with the governor most active in trying to persuade reluctant senators. During the luncheon recess on May 29 he was in touch with several senators and that afternoon the senate voted to put the bond issue on the ballot. The assembly was sufficiently committed to the project that it approved the Burns–Porter bill without amendment, thereby obviating necessity for conference where the bill might have died. All told, the 1959 legislative achievement was even more lustrous than that of the famous legislature of Hiram Johnson and the Lincoln–Roosevelt reformers in 1911.

Throughout the next year and a half Brown continued to plead for his water bonds at every opportunity throughout the state. He met opposition from conservatives who questioned the investment, and from liberals who were critical of the escape from the 160-acre limitation, one consequence of state sponsorship rather than federal. In November, 1960, the voters validated this largest of all state bond issues.

In other respects the year was less gratifying to Brown than 1959. The Chessman case, as described in another chapter, came after much anguish to the end that Brown deeply regretted. The legislature rejected his request that the death penalty be abolished. He headed the California delegation to the Democratic convention in Los Angeles and swung most of its votes to John Kennedy, even though the gallery was madly for Stevenson and a third of the delegation so voted. At the polls in November Kennedy edged Nixon but, when the absentee ballots were counted, California ended up in the other column, though nationally Kennedy prevailed. That meant that California might not be quite so influential in Washington as hoped. Brown, however, had maintained good liaison with the state's representatives and with the Eisenhower administration, a relationship that improved when Kennedy came into office.

Politically the prime development in 1961 was the exposure of the Birch Society by Thomas M. Storke in his Santa Barbara *News-Press* and then by the Los Angeles *Times*. What set Storke off was a covertly backed student essay contest on impeaching Earl Warren. Now wealthy reactionaries could know where to put their money to work against the income tax, the UN, school integration, social security, medicare, and fluoridation. "Bircher" entered the lexicon signifying an extremist of the right, all out for private enterprise as opposed to reliance on government or government regulation. In southern California in particular the Birch Society visibly flourished.

In 1962 Nixon attempted a comeback by running for governor. Knight started to enter the race but illness forced his withdrawal and Nixon was nominated. Conscious that he must woo middle-of-the-road Democrats, Nixon pointedly rejected Bircher support. That probably cost him no votes but it did reduce campaign contributions. Brown cited his record as governor, made much of Nixon's long absence from the state, and accused his opponent of intending to use the governorship as a stepping-stone for another try at the Presidency in 1964. To the surprise of many Brown won by some 300,000. The next morning Nixon called in the press, berated them for the way his campaign had been reported, and told them that they would not have him to kick around any more. Then he left California to join a New York law firm.

Brown's second term began auspiciously with the Rumford Act, banning discrimination in sale or rental except in owner-occupied housing of two to four units. The realtors immediately reacted with Proposition 14, an elaborate ban on any such legislation past, present, or future. That proposition shared the limelight with the campaign, helped mightily by California and the Birchers, in which Goldwater won the Republican nomination. That fall Berkeley seethed with the Free Speech Movement. Lyndon Johnson carried California handily in 1964, but the state Democratic clubs had hard going, in part because of the reactionary resurgence and in part because the stands of the clubs on such issues as recognition of Red China were an embarrassment to incumbents such as the governor and to candidates such as Alan Cranston and Pierre Salinger. Reactionary posture did not prevent song and dance man George Murphy from making his way to the Senate.

Inspired by Murphy's victory, a group of Goldwater supporters reached into late-evening television for a candidate for governor. After many a starring role in the movies, Ronald Reagan had presided over the Death Valley television serial and barnstormed for General Electric with a speech extolling conservatism. Magnetic and marvelously adept before camera and microphone, he was able to belabor Brown and the Democrats for all sorts of alleged failures and malfeasances while at the same time retaining for himself the "good guy" image.

The flaws that Reagan and his supporters stressed were mostly in areas outside the governor's jurisdiction, among them the Free Speech and Dirty Speech convulsions at Berkeley, the Los Angeles riot, the running fight between Superintendent Max Rafferty and the state board of education, and an adverse court decision on the recently adopted anti–fair-housing proposition. Reagan had much to say about the need for better government, but little that was specific in criticism of the actual Brown administration.

Mayor Sam Yorty of Los Angeles, an on-and-off Democrat, ran interference for Reagan by forcing Brown into a factional fight for the Democratic nomination. Democratic disunity hurt in other ways. A factional fight arose over the second spot on the ticket; Unruh's support was invisible until almost the last moment, and the clubs gave indifferent help. In the face of the well-oiled Spencer–Roberts campaign, the voters seemed to tire of Brown and no longer remembered the noteworthy program enacted under his leadership. In what was almost an identical recount of the Proposition 14 vote, Reagan claimed the governorship in 1966.

Brown left an excellently administered state and a code of laws better for his presence. Relations with Washington were efficient and productive. The California Water Project was on schedule; in fact, the half-completed dirt dam at Oroville held back Feather River floodwaters in 1964 that would have caused a disaster, and in 1968 this great dam, larger than Boulder Dam, would be ready for dedication. Brown also had made extraordinarily good appointments. By the luck of the draw, Warren had named no one to the state supreme court and Knight but one. Brown had opportunity to name six and by his choices endowed the state with an outstanding bench. Reagan was critical of almost everything handed over from the Brown administration, but he made no complaints about Chief Justice Roger Traynor and his associates.

There was yet another legacy of the Brown era. Curiously it came from Warren in a Supreme Court ruling that representation in state legislatures must be on the formula of one man, one vote. The case could well have arisen from California where each resident of Alpine, Mono, and Inyo counties had 40,000 per cent more voice in the state senate than a resident of Los Angeles County. Warren as governor had not pushed for reapportionment but, in the opinion he wrote for the court in June, 1964, rising out of a Tennessee case, he held that the equal protection clause of the Fourteenth Amendment was violated by malapportionment of representation. Californians had shown no disposition to make this reform. Even Los Angeles voters seemed content with the status quo. But in 1965 the legislature had to comply. The senate in particular held back, not relishing that several members would have to leave the club. There was also some muttering about state division, but under threat of a court-administered reapportionment the legislature finally acted and the 1966 election was on the new and constitutional basis.

Republican Take-over

Showmanship called for Reagan to be sworn in at the earliest possible moment so as to lose no time in correcting Brown's alleged errors. Accordingly, shortly after the first midnight of the new year, Reagan launched into his inaugural speech. It included irrelevancies about federal issues such

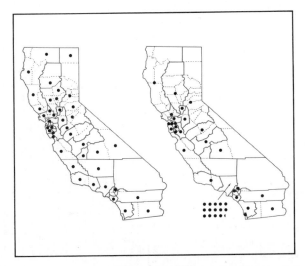

Representation in the State Senate, 1927–66 and 1967–

as social security and the 160-acre limitation, then concentrated on the econo-mizing—"We are going to squeeze and cut and trim."

Reagan's relations with the legislature and with those who worked for the state were much stormier than expected from a governor who had just proven himself so popular. The legislature, though only by a hairline, was Democratic; Unruh could say with some bite that the legislature would give the governor on-the-job training.

Alleging a financial crisis, most of which was merely the seasonal wait for the income-tax payments which, with no withholding, poured in in April, Reagan began to make cuts and promised more. Because the state operates with many fixed charges such as the disbursements to local school districts, the places where he could cut and trim came down essentially to welfare and higher education. He put a freeze on new appointments to the university and the state colleges and began to shift institutions for the mentally ill toward purely cus-todial functions. Despite cutbacks, the budget as it eventually shaped up approximated $5 billion. To match it he asked that the state sales tax be raised 33⅓ per cent and the income tax by 100 per cent or more, depending on the bracket. The eventual result was a surplus.

Population Growth

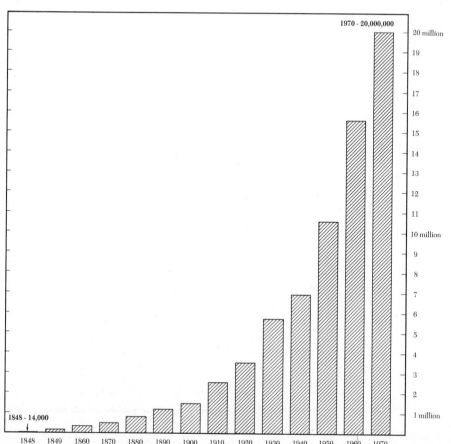

"Promise mother you'll run only in the far right lane, Ronnie."

Dennis Renault, Frontier, September, 1965

In appointments Reagan departed abruptly from the nonpartisan tradition of Warren, Knight, and Brown. Even more consistently he was intent on redressing liberalism. These actions along with his pronouncements encouraged his California backers and a similar coterie from Texas to raise their sights to the presidency. It was a natural impulse. Reagan had instant attention as the dramatic new governor of the number one state. His fund-raising appearances at party gatherings were received enthusiastically in all parts of the country. He projected himself as sincere, alert, determined, and well meaning. Many who flocked to hear him were convinced that the polls erred in putting him back of Nixon and Rockefeller. Yet other Californians thought seriously of initiating a recall.

More than any governor before him, Reagan took a domineering role as a university regent and a state college trustee. His predecessors had not thought that the administration of higher education required that much of their personal attention or had not thought it appropriate to risk intruding politics into the administration of the university and the state colleges.

Reagan came into office with several set ideas about higher education —that its costs were outrageously high, that students would take college more seriously if they paid a part of their way, and that stiff discipline was needed to control student and faculty activists. In his campaign he made these points vigorously, and even without an applause meter it was evident that no other issue brought more popular support. To push hard was clearly good politics.

As governor he could exert the budgetary pressure. Tight budgets strengthened his repeated pitch for requiring tuition in the university and, by implication, in the state colleges. On the disciplinary front Reagan wanted tightened rules, much more vigorous enforcement, total rejection of demands, and more immediate police action whenever emergency threatened. Personalizing this campaign, as soon as his appointments gave him a majority in the board of regents, Reagan saw to the firing of University President Clark Kerr. Reagan also precipitated the action in the summer of 1969 to reward disciplinarian S. I. Hayakawa by elevating him to the presidency of beleaguered San Francisco State College.

Almost every regents' or trustees' meeting provided publicity, either in the business discussed or transacted or in confrontation with angry students and sometimes professors eagerly volunteering for walk-in roles in tableaus in which the governor could star.

To the Republican national convention in 1968 Reagan headed California's favorite-son delegation. Nixon, however, had laid thorough groundwork with the party faithful and his nomination was almost automatic. California was a battleground for the Eugene McCarthy and Robert Kennedy forces protesting the war in Vietnam. The appearance was that a coalition of the two groups could carry the state. All such calculations went by the board with Kennedy's assassination in Los Angeles on election night, and in November, though the voters sent Cranston rather than Rafferty to the Senate, they sent Nixon to the White House.

The election of 1968 and interim elections that followed gave the Republicans control of both houses of the legislature in 1969. Reagan was not able to capitalize on that advantage. Because he obstinately held out against withholding, no program of tax reform was achieved; because the executive branch's projections of state income and balance were so unreliable, nothing more than stopgap provision was made for increased support of local school districts and for easing the burden of the property tax.

Political opinion as of the close of the sixties was better gauged in the Los Angeles city election of that year. In the primary Councilman Thomas Bradley had a substantial plurality over Mayor Sam Yorty, who was seeking a third term. In the runoff, the white backlash was whipped up by allegations that the e would be mass resignations from the police force if Bradley were elected and by spurious bumper stickers linking Bradley and Black Power. This scurrilous attack flourished so well in the Mexican precincts as well as in the lily-white westside and San Fernando Valley that, in spite of the scandals in his appointed commissions, Yorty retained the scepter as mayor.

In 1970 Senator Murphy began his campaign for reelection with a suggestion that Supreme Court rulings should be subject to review and reversal by some kind of higher authority vaguely described. Asked how that jibed with the position of the Marshall Court, he showed complete ignorance. Much more damaging was a disclosure that all the time he had been Senator he had been on retainer by Technicolor, a firm controlled by the arch-reactionary, William A. Frawley. The retainer was in the amount of $20,000 a year plus half the rental of an apartment in Washington and a credit card for air travel. In the opinion of the Los Angeles *Times*, by accepting this retainer Murphy had forfeited his eligibility to represent the people of California.

That Reagan allowed a group of wealthy admirers to buy the house he wanted to live in in Sacramento and become his landlords and that he accepted another $40,000 worth of furniture donated or loaned by other admirers caused

Thomas Bradley

Mary Leipziger

some raised eyebrows. As candidate for reelection in 1970, while barnstorming from one confrontation to another, he could promise a hard line against student and radical violence, tighter budgets for higher education and welfare, and selective tax increases including, of all things, withholding. Unruh entered the race, and so did Yorty with the likelihood of repeating his 1966 performance. With the Democrats maintaining their lead in registrations and the Republicans in the polls, California continued to be politically, in Gladwin Hill's phrase, the "Dancing Bear," or in Carey McWilliams' "the state that swings, spins and turns."

For Further Reading

GLADWIN HILL, *Dancing Bear, An Inside Look at California Politics* (1968).

LEO KATCHER, *Earl Warren: A Political Biography* (1967).

JOHN D. WEAVER, *Warren: The Man, the Court, the Era* (1967).

DEAN R. CRESAP, *Party Politics in the Golden State* (1954).

LESTER VELIE, "The Secret Boss of California," *Collier's* (August 13, 20, 1949).

TREVOR AMBRISTER, "The Octopus in the State House," *Saturday Evening Post* (February 12, 1966).

CAREY MCWILLIAMS, "Government by Whitaker and Baxter," *Nation* (April 14, 21, May 5, 1951).

FRANCIS CARNEY, *The Rise of the Democratic Clubs in California* (1958).

JAMES Q. WILSON, *The Amateur Democrat* (1962).

LEONARD C. ROWE, *Pre-primary Endorsements in California Politics* (1962).

HERBERT L. PHILLIPS, "A Bucketful of Smoke," in *California, The Dynamic State* (1966).

EUGENE BURDICK, *The Ninth Wave* (1956), a novel.

CAUGHEY, *California Heritage*, 443–48, 455–59, 515–21.

chapter thirty-three

Challenging Injustice

We believe that in California we have the greatest scientific and engineering community in the world. Its members have created and built machines to land on the moon, photograph Mars and circle the sun, explore the bottom of the oceans and very soon, perhaps, decipher the genetic code of life.

Yet at the same time, the rest of us in California are still struggling to solve economic and social problems as old, in many cases, as civilization itself.

Edmund G. (Pat) Brown

1945
and
after

The First World War, which President Wilson persuasively insisted was "to make the world safe for democracy," was followed in the United States by a Red Scare in which there was violent suppression of radicals and mass arrests and deportation of aliens classified as undesirables. The hysteria did not last long, but it left monuments, among them the harshly restrictive immigration control act of 1924.

After the Second World War a second Red Scare of far greater proportions swept the land. America and its allies were under great obligation to the Russians for their heroic stand against Hitler's war machine through the long period when there was no western front. That gratitude evaporated almost at once as Soviet obstructions in the United Nations, aggressions in Europe and Asia, espionage, and, in 1949, achievement of an atomic bomb set up the Soviet

School Integration in Berkeley

Helen Nestor

Union as the prime threat to American interests and security. For decades to come the main thrust of American foreign policy would be to contain Soviet and Communist expansion, a goal also pursued by American military spending and engagement. The wars in Korea and Vietnam intensified fear of Russia and hatred of Communism.

That same combination of fear and hatred carried over into the internal affairs of the nation, the more so because to many Americans the words "bolshevik," "red," "communist," and "socialist" were at the heart of what Martin Dies had labeled un-American. The late forties and fifties witnessed a massive hunt-down of loyalty suspects or security risks, the ruling definition being Communists and Communist supporters, sympathizers, dupes, or associates.

The House Un-American Activities Committee seized most of the headlines with its hearings, ostensibly to prepare for legislation but concentrating on exposing alleged participants in Communist causes. President Truman contributed substantially with his program for a loyalty check on every federal employee, as did Attorney General Tom Clark with his list of subversive organizations. The FBI and other governmental agencies, through informers and otherwise, built files and indexes on the memberships and associations of literally millions of Americans. The committee developed a technique of exposure through questioning that would lead witnesses to take refuge in the Fifth Amendment, from which followed loss of public employment and blacklisting from many forms of private employment.

In the stormier climate of the Korean War, Senator Joseph McCarthy brought the machinery of character assassination to climax. Operating with immunity as a congressional committeeman, he blazoned charges against librarians and cleaning women, saw to the defeat of two senators who opposed him, intimidated the Senate, forced the hand of the State Department, put the Army into retreat, and pressured the President into toning down a speech that would have been offensive to him. Anticommunism thus pursued embarrassed officials. Harassing, persecuting, intimidating, it bore down more heavily on liberals and thereby was a strong discouragement to progressivism. Although McCarthy lost luster in the Army–McCarthy hearings in 1954, many of his practices continued long after that date.

The Tenney Committee

California had much more than its pro rata share of this hysteria about security. In 1941, on motion of Sam Yorty and Jack B. Tenney, the legislature created a "little Dies Committee," the Tenney Committee. After brief attention to right-wing extremists and warnings against the return of the Japanese from Manzanar, the committee turned almost exclusively to the Communist menace. It hired counsel and investigators. Using and expanding the attorney general's list and an index compiled by the House committee and relying heavily on the *People's Daily World*, the committee developed an ever-growing card index of sponsors and participants in organizations and events allegedly part of the Communist apparatus. The committee hearings, which Tenney dominated, were used as a platform for pillorying unfriendly witnesses. The committee reports continued the process.

Tenney might have gone on indefinitely had he not committed the indiscretion of hiring Edward H. Gibbon of the smear sheet *Alert* to write the 1949 committee report. Gibbon made it more lurid than the average and listed half a dozen Democratic legislators along with other alleged Communist dupes and well-wishers. Tenney had already antagonized a powerful segment of organized labor. The farcical methods of fact finding and a sheaf of bills he introduced early in 1949 alarmed others. Nevertheless, it was the attack on respected legislators that led to his downfall. Colleagues could rally to their defense, as did lobbyist Artie Samish, who had had much to do with Tenney's election to the legislature. Tenney's bills failed, he was forced to resign his chairmanship, and the legislature reconstituted the committee with the intention that it should be conducted more sensibly.

By the summer of 1949, with Tenney deposed, there was reason to think that the California frenzy against political dissenters had run its course. Yet, even in his blundering way, Tenney had demonstrated how damaging to liberalism a legislative inquisition could be. Senator Hugh Burns picked up the role, played it more discreetly, and used it as his power base for another 20 years.

Tenney contributed one other institution. R. E. Combs, whom he retained as committee counsel, proved highly adept in maintaining close rapport with the FBI, the military, and other related agencies. He dedicated himself to the study of Communist method and apparatus, and he was equally diligent in building up for the committee and for himself arsenals of evidence and testimony on a great many persons involved in organizations which at some point in place and time came in touch with a part of the Communist operation. Combs continued as chief counsel for the Burns Committee.

The Hollywood Ten

In 1947 Parnell Thomas led the House Un-American Activities Committee in its famous safari into Hollywood. The complaint was that the Communist line had penetrated what might be the most insidious of all channels for propaganda, the movies. Brought down to cases, the committee cited *Mission to Moscow* (1942), which Jack Warner defended as true to Ambassador Davies' book and a picture intended to aid the war effort; *Song of Russia* (1942), a Tchaikovsky musical which Louis B. Mayer said of course was friendly to our Russian ally; and *None but the Lonely Heart*, in which Ginger Rogers' mother saw Communist infection.

From its failure as film critic, the committee turned to exposing subversives. It brought to the stand a distinguished cast of Hollywood writers, directors, and actors. John Howard Lawson, the first witness called, asked permission to read a statement and was refused. Asked if he was a member of the Screen Writers Guild, he challenged the authority of the committee to ask such a question. Asked, "Are you now or have you ever been a member of the Communist party in the United States?" he objected that the question was an invasion of his privacy. He alluded to the Bill of Rights but did not specifically rest his refusal on the Fifth Amendment or any other. Lawson similarly refused to answer other personal and political questions.

After a sharp exchange of unpleasantries with the committee and its counsel, Lawson was removed from the stand. One of the committee staff then read into the record a representation of Lawson's Communist-related activities and associations. The most concrete assertion was that his party registration card for 1944 bore the number 47275. In *The Time of the Toad,* Dalton Trumbo, another of the Hollywood Ten, argued that the committee was given nothing more than "the alleged office record of an alleged card." The impression conveyed, however, was of proved membership. The testimony trailed off to such subjective assertions as that Lawson had hailed "the rise of the revolutionary theater."

Over the next three days the committee went through the same routine with ten other witnesses, one of whom proved friendly, which is to say, cooperative, while the other nine reacted as Lawson had. After each such performance the committee voted unanimously to cite the witness for contempt. Chairman Thomas announced that there were 68 more witnesses to be heard, but for reasons not stated he adjourned the hearings.

The Hollywood Ten had their day in court. Not having invoked the Fifth Amendment at the time they refused to answer, they lacked its protection against required self-incrimination. Not until many years later was the freedom of speech clause in the First Amendment interpreted as covering also the right to remain silent. Accordingly, they were found guilty of contempt and sentenced to fine and imprisonment. Eric Johnson, successor to Will Hays as czar of movie-industry public relations, pronounced a more far-reaching penalty. Until the ten purged themselves by disavowing communism, they would not be employed in any shape or form in the movie industry. Thus originated the Hollywood Blacklist by which hundreds of writers, actors, and artists were barred from the studios. A few were smuggled back in, including one who won an Oscar anonymously, but for the group as a whole this was a long-lasting blacklist.

Loyalty by Oath

In the forties Californians reached about for other ways of combatting Communism. In Los Angeles in 1948 the Board of Supervisors ordered that Communist books be removed from the county library. In the face of strong protests the supervisors reconsidered. In Burbank it was proposed that every Communist book be branded. At the University of California, where invited speakers were carefully scrutinized, the regents were miffed that so radical a thinker as Harold J. Laski had slipped through. When the innovative texts in the *Building America* series were attacked as though they were unpatriotic, the state board removed them from the state-approved list. In 1952, the Los Angeles school board was similarly persuaded to dismantle the study program on the United Nations and UNESCO.

There was experiment also with required oaths of denial, or, more engagingly, "loyalty oaths." Los Angeles County in 1947 demanded such an oath from every employee together with a check off of affiliations in a long list of organizations. The City of Los Angeles installed a loyalty oath in 1948. Radio station KFI put its 200 employees to such a test. In 1949 the University of California set up an oath requirement and the state followed suit in 1950. Before long millions of Californians had faced the necessity by one agency or several to swear, "I am not now nor have I been a member of . . ." These oaths came with or without mention of the Communist party by name, with or without a list of organizations to check, and with or without a time limit on how far back into the past one must look, but the essence was a denial of Communist party membership or affiliation. As the Tenney Committee had been the foremost symbol of anticommunism in California from 1941 to 1949, the loyalty oath claimed that role from 1949 through 1967.

As a fitting gesture in 1949, as the mantle of chief tribune against communism was slipping from his shoulders, Tenney gave a boost to the new enforcer of loyalty, the oath. Early in that year's legislative session he had introduced a proposal to empower the legislature to ensure the loyalty of university personnel. University lobbyist James M. Corley asked Tenney to drop the proposal in expectation that the regents would require a loyalty oath. In March, in secret session, President Robert G. Sproul asked the regents to "strengthen his hand" by instituting such an oath. They agreed to do so.

In the days of Gilman or Wheeler, presidential authority was so taken for granted in the university that a test oath requirement probably would have met little opposition. By 1949 there was a strong tradition of 25 years' standing of faculty determination of courses of instruction and of faculty appointments. The university operated with a long period of apprenticeship—eight years was regarded as normal—during which the option of not reappointing was wide open. With advancement to associate or full professor, however, a faculty member gained tenure and could be dismissed only for cause and after review by his peers. An oath of denial as an added condition of employment ran counter to rights under tenure. The ideological aspect of these oaths presented a further intrusion on freedom to teach and to learn or, as the professors put it, on academic freedom. These were circumstances about which some of the proponents of the oath knew little or nothing.

Though voted in March, the oath was not made known to the faculty until the close of the spring semester. At the last faculty meetings of the year at Berkeley and Los Angeles the wisdom of asking for oaths was questioned and the wording criticized. Late in June the oaths were mailed out with a cover letter from the president requesting their execution. Gradually it became apparent that without an oath no contract for the ensuing year would be issued. Salary payments were made on July 31 and August 31, but classes started in September with no assurance that nonsigners would be allowed to continue.

Thus began the first year of the test oath. The faculty, most of whom had signed, undertook to persuade the regents to rescind the requirement. Regent John Francis Neylan, initially critical of the oath, became its staunchest supporter. Other regents, their convictions intensified by a feeling that the board's authority was being challenged, held firm. President Sproul, the original proponent, became convinced that the requirement should be dropped. Several other regents, among them Governor Warren, joined him. In February, 1950, however, these regents were not numerous enough to defeat a sign-or-be-fired ultimatum.

At that point, with faculty–regent negotiations at an impasse, an alumni committee developed a compromise whereby nonsigners might request a hearing by the faculty committee on privilege and tenure. A hundred elected to do so, only to find in August that a majority of the regents intended to apply a rule of be-heard-and-be-fired. By July the number of professors seeking retention by the hearing's route had shrunk to 46 and by August to 31. A substantial number of researchers, teaching assistants, and junior faculty had been denied reappointment, and a number of professors had resigned. On August 25 the regents fired the last of the nonsigners.

By resolution, the faculty rebuked the regents who had voted these dismissals. Faculty committees raised money for the relief of their colleagues. Several of the fired professors, headed by Edward C. Tolman of the psychology department at Berkeley, brought suit against the regents.

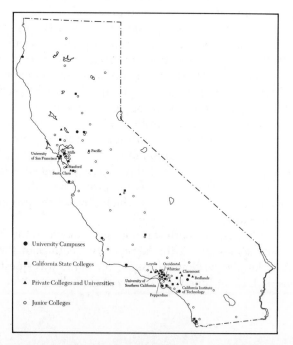

Colleges and Universities

University Campuses

California State Colleges

Private Colleges and Universities

Junior Colleges

Their counsel, Stanley A. Weigel, criticized the test oath as a violation of the spirit, if not the letter, of the national and state constitutions and as hostile to the respect for minority and dissenting opinion which is necessary to the safe functioning of American democracy. He deplored the silencing of criticism as a disservice to the sovereign people who need to hear a rounded discussion of vital issues. As applied to school and university personnel, he held that oaths of conformity were a blow to academic freedom, an interference with the objective pursuit of truth, and a constraint upon opportunity to learn.

The Third District Court, in an eloquent opinion by Justice Paul Peek, ruled in April, 1951, that the university oath was a violation of tenure, destructive of true scholarship, and unconstitutional.

This decision, along with the question of the validity of a subsequently enacted test oath for all state employees, passed under the scrutiny of the state supreme court. Meanwhile the various elements of the test-oath program had full effect. The 26 professors dismissed, allegedly for insubordination, were still kept out, even though the university's special oath was abolished six months after the District Court decision.

Another year later, in October, 1952, on the ground that the legislature years earlier had occupied the field of spelling out oath requirements, the Supreme Court ruled the university's special loyalty rules invalid and ordered that the men dismissed be restored to their regular posts in the faculty. The university complied to the extent of offering new appointments for the spring semester of 1953, but left the matter of the intervening two and a half years to later determination. On the basis of this limited restoration, half a dozen of those dismissed resumed teaching in February, 1953. One of them was astonished to find that, in the calculation of what his salary should be, a merit increase as of the middle of his enforced absence had been figured in.

Those who came back soon discovered, however, that the regents had no intention of paying back salaries or patching up rights to sabbaticals or retirement income. Another round of litigation thus became necessary on behalf of tenure. The case moved slowly. Finally, toward the close of the seventh year of the oath, the regents agreed to settle. They were on notice that the American Association of University Professors had before it a recommendation to censure the administration of the University of California for its persistent flouting of academic freedom and tenure.

Meanwhile, loyalty oaths had proliferated. In the fall of 1950, shortly after the university firings, Governor Warren had instigated a loyalty-oath requirement affecting every employee of the state or any of its branches. This measure, the Levering Act, would answer a criticism of the university oath—that it singled out one small group of public servants. The Levering Act was ridiculed because it extended the oath requirement to everyone who drew wages or a fee from the state or any of its branches, including out-of-state consultants and infants employed as models in art classes. At least one university professor who had signed the regents' oath balked at signing one more and was fired. A scattering of state employees, including a number of state college professors, refused to sign and were cut off. A group of these people took the issue to court. Their case, *Pockman* vs. *Leonard* came before the State Supreme Court along with *Tolman* vs. *Underhill*.

On that same decision day in October, 1952, when it declared the regents' oath illegal and void, the court upheld the Levering oath. To reconcile it with the constitutional specification, after setting forth the positive oath of office ("And no other oath, declaration, or test, shall be required as qualification for any office or public trust"), the court had to contend that the oath of denial was identical to the affirmative pledge to support the Constitution and therefore was not an additional requirement. Justice Jesse W. Carter, in a blistering dissent, emphatically rejected this sophistry. The voters, a few weeks later, incorporated the Levering oath into the state constitution.

A multitude of further oath and loyalty laws were passed. One made every tax exemption to veterans or to churches subject to the registering of a test oath. Most churches complied, some only after much soul-searching. On appeal, the Supreme Court declared this requirement unconstitutional. The Luckel Act (1953) and the Dilworth Act (1953) gave state and local school boards power of dismissal for refusal to respond to questions about affiliations.

The Burns Committee, in addition to its hearings and reports, offered to assist colleges and universities in the screening of loyalty and security risks. In 1953 Counsel Combs told a committee of the United States Senate that his committee had liaison with specially designated officers on many California campuses and that "100 faculty members have been removed." The heads of several private colleges and universities denied any such tie-up; the presidents of public institutions confirmed the relationship or were much less explicit in their denials.

That these so-called loyalty programs really protected the state is dubious. Although the test oaths were of the perjury type, in all the years they were in force not one of all the millions who swore to them was tried and convicted of perjury. The required denials and the probing into associations discouraged speaking out on controversial issues or supporting any organization that might be considered radical, leftist, or liberal. These programs cost the state some excellent public servants and contributed to the reticence of the silent generation.

In 1967 the Levering oath, the centerpole of this entire apparatus, was condemned and removed. Taxpayer Robert Vogel went to court with support from the American Civil Liberties Union to complain that part of the taxes he paid was being improperly spent in enforcement of the Levering oath amendment to the state constitution. Judge Robert Kenny, taking into consideration the outlay for printing the oath forms, the paper on which they were printed, the files in which they were stored, and the time and energy of the notaries before whom they were executed, issued a temporary injunction, which was promptly appealed to the state supreme court. On December 21, 1967, that court, with wry comment on how much wiser it had become in 15 years, upheld Judge Kenny's action and declared the California oath requirement an infringement of First Amendment rights and therefore invalid.

In the summer of 1969 the issue of loyalty as measured by a membership test came back to haunt the University of California. Learning that a recently appointed member of the UCLA faculty was a member of Che Lumumba, identified to them as a black cell of the Communist party, a majority of the regents forthwith voted to fire this person, Professor Angela Davis. The action was purely and simply on the basis of this party membership. The firing was consistent with the "loyalty oath" firings of 1950, in which the insubordination charged was refusal to certify nonmembership in the Communist party.

The regents' rule of 1940 that no Communist be employed had been weakened or perhaps superseded by a 1968 pronouncement that no political test would ever be applied. By 1969 there also was new case law that was applicable. In addition to the decisions of the state supreme court in *Tolman* (1952) and *Vogel* (1967) there were rulings in federal cases, such as *Elfbrandt* (1966) and *Keyishian* (1967), holding that, in itself, membership in an organization is not sufficient ground for dismissal.

At the time they voted, the regents were advised that their action was illegal. At least one regent who voted to fire did so with the rationalization that the courts might reverse their position. At a subsequent meeting the regents backed off slightly, allowing Professor Davis temporarily to continue on the salary roll and even to teach, provided it was not for credit, a strange splitting of a hair.

The faculty at UCLA strongly protested application of a political test or a judgment based simply on an association or membership rather than on the broader basis of personal qualifications, character, and performance. The faculty also objected to the regents' interference with decision making on courses of study and credit toward degrees. Judge Jerry Pacht, to whom the issue was carried, ruled that the dismissal on the grounds stated was contrary to law. The regents appealed this decision and the judge's earlier ruling against a change of venue to their "home base" in Alameda County. On the latter point the appellate court agreed with the regents, opening the door for plaintiff to appeal to the state supreme court. The decision itself may travel the same repeal route. In December the statewide faculty of the university notified the regents that, in and of itself, being a Communist was not a disqualification for membership in the faculty.

Meanwhile, black leaders on campus interpreted the action against Angela Davis as the firing of a black and a blow to the whole program of minority recruitment and Afro-American studies. That almost certainly was not the regents' intention, but these side effects have a measure of reality, and the more so because, in the black community, the charge of Communist party membership is regarded as totally irrelevant.

Capital Punishment

When Edmund G. Brown became governor in 1959 he faced a dilemma. As chief executive he was under obligation to enforce the law. Yet his lifelong experience in law enforcement convinced him that capital punishment was a mistake. He issued several reprieves and asked the legislature to reconsider the death penalty. When it did not act, he called a special session for this particular business, but again without avail. He suggested a moratorium on executions and a thorough study of the place of capital punishment in modern scientific penology. The issue was at fever point in California because Caryl Chessman was then in his eleventh year on Death Row.

In 1948, with a record of earlier burglaries and armed robbery, Chessman was arrested in a stolen car. He was brought to trial as a Hollywood Lovers' Lane bandit and charged among other things with having forced a girl to move to another car with intent of sexual assault. The moving of the girl met the recently extended definition of kidnapping and led to a death sentence. Irregularities in the proceedings and glaring deficiencies in the trial record that was available for appeal led to several postponements of execution and to grave doubt that Chessman received full protection of the law.

Chessman strengthened his cause by reading up on law while in prison and acting as his own counsel and also by being most articulate in letters, interviews, and in his book *Cell 2455, Death Row*. He became San Quentin's best-known resident and his case a cause célèbre. As with Tom Mooney there was an arrogance about him which contributed to his case being malignantly sensationalized by the California press. Yet, although Death Row is not designed for the purpose, Chessman rehabilitated himself, some said not enough, but substantially. And he endured the torture of over 11 years on Death Row.

The case roused serious questioning of the death penalty. Many European nations, most of Latin America, and several American states had abolished it. Wardens testified that the penalty was a severe handicap to the overall program of prison operation. Experts denied that it deterred crime. Sociologists maintained that by this ultimate use of force the state set a most unfortunate example in violence. Yet public opinion still seemed to be that certain crimes called for capital punishment and that lawmen needed the backing of this extreme penalty.

Session after session, Assemblyman Lester A. McMillan introduced bills for abolishment, but the legislature did not act. In 1955, in fact, California led the nation in number of executions. A series of court decisions, however, put in doubt several matters of procedure, such as exclusion from juries of opponents of capital punishment. In the much agitated Chessman case, after exhausting all other options, Brown asked the chief justice of the state supreme court to sound out the justices on a commutation of sentence to life imprisonment. Since Chessman had an earlier felony conviction, the governor could not commute without consent of the court. Four of the justices strongly opposed. Brown did not make a public issue of it and in 1960 with regret allowed the execution to take place. Permitting the execution disappointed the foes of capital punishment; the postponements had infuriated those who wanted Chessman to die.

Later in 1960 the American Civil Liberties Union of Southern California pioneered with the argument that, in the light of modern knowledge, capital punishment is a relic of barbarism and violative of the Eighth Amendment ban on "cruel and unusual punishments." Other arguments advanced by the ACLU were that the death penalty is not an effective deterrent or an asset in penal administration, that on the record it is imposed disproportionately on minorities and the poor, and that, when applied to a defendant later proved innocent, society is left powerless to make amends. An unproclaimed moratorium arose and the last several years of Brown's administration saw no executions. In December, 1967, after hearing argument on the familiar grounds and on the additional one that California's laws are defective in providing no standard by which judge and jury are to decide whether to impose the death penalty, the state supreme court came within one vote of abolishing death sentences.

In September, 1969, the state supreme court narrowed the application of capital punishment by making more reasonable its definition of kidnapping, for which the "Little Lindbergh Act" set the death penalty. By the law as expounded in 1969 Chessman would not have been executed.

Ronald Reagan, in his first two years as governor, permitted one execution. Thereafter the unofficial moratorium continued with some 100 persons on Death Row. The assassination of Robert Kennedy in Los Angeles in 1968 and the death sentence of his killer complicated the problem. The Kennedy family made known that it did not ask or want Sirhan Sirhan put to death. Meanwhile, throughout the nation capital punishment was very seldom invoked.

Toward Equal Opportunity

For the entire nation midcentury was a time of quickening awareness of discriminations by race and color that stood in the way of equal opportunity. In 1947 California-born Jackie Robinson became the first Negro in organized baseball, brought in by Branch Rickey of the Brooklyn Dodgers. California had to wait several years for discovery by major league football, baseball and basketball. When the big leaguers came, it was with Negro stars as a standard feature.

In 1948, in *Shelley* vs. *Kraemer,* the Supreme Court struck down racial covenants, a device by which a group of property owners tied every title in a tract to nonminority ownership and occupancy. California supplied an important follow-up case that put restrictive covenant permanently to rest. In *Barrow* vs. *Jackson,* the Supreme Court held that a damage suit by neighbor against seller was not to be tolerated as an indirect means of continuing such a covenant in force.

With the Korean War, effective integration began in the armed services. In 1954 the Supreme Court, with Californian Earl Warren presiding, demolished the "separate but equal" sham as window dressing for school segregation. In 1955 came the Montgomery bus boycott, from which Martin Luther King emerged with his gospel of nonviolence as the means of gaining equal opportunity.

Meanwhile many Japanese moved ahead in school, business, and the professions as did Negroes and Mexicans, though proportionately fewer. Embarrassments about access to housing, restaurants, and barbershops continued. Committees of the YWCA and the Associated Students of UCLA undertook to persuade the Westwood Village merchants to open their doors. Yet as late as the fifties a Negro girl could make reservation by mail at the UCLA dormitory and be told on arrival that there was no room.

In California the year 1959 marks a recognizable new era in the curbing of discriminations, with the Unruh Civil Rights Act, the Fair Employment Act, and a newly created constitutional rights division in the Department of Justice. In 1963 the legislature approved a measure introduced by Assemblyman W. Byron Rumford which banned racial discrimination in the rental or sale of any housing publicly assisted and of owner-occupied housing of more than four units. Neither the Unruh Act nor the Rumford Act had automatic or full enforcement. For some years the Congress of Racial Equality was busy picketing noncomplying businesses and real-estate firms.

The California Real Estate Association (CREA) decided to roll back this whole invasion of what it considered its prerogatives. Going over the head of the legislature to the people, the CREA drafted a constitutional amendment, commissioned the gathering of the necessary signatures to put it on the ballot in 1964, and mounted a clamorous campaign. Long and complicated, Proposition 14 in essence made illegal any denial, past, present, or future, of the right of any owner of real property to choose to whom he would rent, lease, or sell.

The arguments for Proposition 14 were that it would protect the "God-given right" of the owner and that without it property rights and values

"A White Man's Home Is His Castle and, by God, This Is Mine!"

Dennis Renault, Ventura Star–Free Press, April 16, 1967

were not safe. The arguments against were that it was maliciously reactionary, an affront to minorities, an infringement on the right to buy, and in all likelihood unconstitutional. To the last of these criticisms the realtors retorted that they had retained high-salaried lawyers to draft the amendment. The campaign for Proposition 14 was professional and well financed; the campaign against it, volunteer and inevitably more diffused.

In what could be interpreted as a referendum on property rights above human rights, on faith in Republican program rather than Democratic, and on continuation of racial discriminations, the voters approved by a landslide of better than two to one. As law, Proposition 14 was shortlived. The state supreme court in May, 1966, saw it as denying the equal protection of the laws spelled out in the Fourteenth Amendment, a ruling which the Supreme Court upheld in May, 1967. Yet the vote on Proposition 14 had profound and lasting effect. Negroes and other minorities could not read it as anything other than a true revelation of where white California stood on equalizing opportunity and ending discriminatory practices.

The Attack on School Segregation

Although news of the 1954 decision banning school segregation penetrated the West, it was taken to refer only to the outright designation of certain schools for whites and others for Negroes. In California, with school assignment by residence, families in theory had complete freedom to move into another attendance area and send their children to another school. In 1946 suit was brought in Orange County alleging inequity to Mexican pupils segregated in the schools of four districts. The federal judge hearing the case rendered judgment for the plaintiffs, but on appeal the district court upheld in such a fashion that the ruling was inoperable. No useful precedent resulted. In El Centro, where the school authorities were more blatant about gerrymandering Negro and Mexican pupils into separate schools, the NAACP and the Alianza Hispano-Americana went to court and procured a promise in 1956 that that kind of separation would cease. Not until the 1960's was there serious challenge to de facto as distinguished from de jure segregation, with an alert sounded that the vast majority of Negro, Mexican, and Oriental pupils were assigned to schools apart and inferior in opportunity.

In most counties, minority representatives were few. In the cities, where most were concentrated, there was awareness of Negro and Mexican workers and voters but much less of Negro and Mexican schools, because the latter were within the confines of the ghetto where few whites had reason to go. As late as 1968–69, had the people of Los Angeles been told that their district consisted of 333 predominantly white schools and 222 predominantly minority schools and that most schools in each group were in the range of 90 to 100 per cent concentration, they would have been astounded.

In Los Angeles in June, 1962, representatives of ACLU, CORE, and NAACP discovered to the school board that school segregation existed in that

Earl Walter, President of Los Angeles CORE, leading a march
protesting the setting of the dogs on the Birmingham demonstrators

far-flung system. The board set up a committee to investigate, but not until the
following May did this committee confirm that there was indeed a substantial
amount of segregation and that the educational process was not working well
in the Negro and Mexican schools. The committee proposed a few changes, but
its emphasis was on compensatory programs as the means to bring these Negro
and Mexican schools up to par.

In 1963, in a rally at Wrigley Field, Martin Luther King roused many
Los Angeles Negroes to be more active for civil rights. The newly organized
and Negro-led United Civil Rights Council (UCRC) took command of the drive
for school integration as well as for minority gains in employment, housing, and
treatment by the police. For two years UCRC backed up its requests to the
board of education with marches, picketing, a study-in at board headquarters,
a hunger strike, and other such devices. Demonstrations prompted counter-
demonstrations.

From the outset the ACLU asked for a school-by-school report on
racial enrollment on the basis of an impersonal visual census. The board refused
until ordered four years later by the state board of education. The census for
1967–68 showed an increase and that for 1968–69 a further increase. As of
1968–69 some 266,000 pupils were assigned to segregated minority schools with
their built-in handicaps.

In 1968 the ACLU brought suit to end the discriminatory practice
of school segregation in Los Angeles. On the basis of the evidence adduced in
70 days in court, volunteer counsel Bayard F. Berman contended that "with full

574

knowledge of the consequences" the board had maintained and perpetuated a system in which there were 222 segregated minority schools, demonstrably unequal and inferior, causing incalculable harm in achievement, good citizenship, democratic values, and racial strife, and that the damage inured to white pupils as well as to Negro and Mexican-American. He asked the court to take note that these baleful effects are the same whether the segregation is de facto or de jure and that the board had never had an integration policy, never made an integration study, and never formulated an integration plan.

The board conceded that integration probably would enable minority pupils to improve their scholarly achievement, but argued that this improvement would be at the expense of lessened total learning by the pupils of the district as a whole—in other words, that white pupils would learn less. The board made it clear that it intended to leave pupils where they were and concentrate on upgrading the quality of education in the segregated ghetto schools. On that note, strongly reminiscent of the "separate but equal" doctrine which the Supreme Court discarded in 1954, the case of *Crawford* vs. *Los Angeles Board of Education* was submitted.

On February 11, 1970, Judge Alfred Gitelson rendered his decision. He found that massive segregation existed, that this segregation had been maintained and increased under the administration of the Board of Education, that the Board had acted knowingly and in bad faith, that the segregation therefore was de jure rather than merely de facto, that educational opportunity is defective in segregated schools, and that the Los Angeles segregation was violative of state and federal law, including provisions of the state and federal constitutions. Judge Gitelson therefore ordered that by June 1 the Board submit a plan for integrating the schools, that by September it start putting the plan into operation, and that by September, 1971, all schools be integrated.

Judge Alfred Gitelson

The Board immediately announced that it would appeal and, as further demonstration of bad faith, sought to generate revulsion against the decision. Board spokesmen falsely insinuated that the Court had ordered daily busing of 240,000 pupils. The cost they represented to be $40 million the first year and $20 million thereafter, or $180 million over an eight-year period, and they predicted disastrous consequences to education.

Mayor Yorty, State Superintendent Rafferty, Governor Reagan, President Nixon, Secretary Robert Finch, and many other notables declaimed against forced busing. The State Board of Education, up to that date a staunch advocate of integrated schooling, took emergency action to repeal all sections of the State Education Code that contained any commitment to or instructions on integration.

President Nixon on March 24 issued a white paper on school desegregation in which he undertook to interpret the law of the land. Given the American system of judicial review, such a treatise, even by the President, must have something of the quality of a schoolboy exercise. Because it contained scathing criticism of the Gitelson decision, the presiding judge of the Los Angeles Superior Court sharply criticized Nixon as a lawyer for commenting thus on a case still in litigation. Attempting to placate Negroes and integrationists, Nixon asserted that the law must be enforced against de jure school segregation. Attempting to placate southern whites, wherever they are, he postulated that this part of the Constitution should have its support from the state governments rather than from the Nixon administration. As to de facto segregation, he recommended leaving it be, but that this kind of separate schooling should be made equal by injecting half a billion dollars in the current budget and $1.5 billion thereafter. Neither scholarly analysis nor experience gives reason to believe that, in segregated schooling, separate can be made equal in opportunity.

Berkeley, with a Negro enrollment just a few points below 50 per cent, began early in the sixties to integrate its schools. It enlarged its high school rather than build a second which would have been segregated. It changed a segregated junior high school into a 9th grade school for the entire community and thereby kept integrated the other two schools, each serving 7th and 8th grade pupils. Action accelerated when Neil Sullivan arrived as superintendent. In Prince Edward County, Virginia, he had headed a display performance with a special private school program attempting to help Negro pupils catch up after three years during which the integration-defying county had shut down all public schools. Under his leadership, in the fall of 1968, Berkeley converted the elementary schools in the hills (residentially white) into schools for the first three grades, and the schools in West Berkeley (residentially Negro and Oriental) into schools for grades four to six. Buses shuttled back and forth, taking younger children up into the hills and older ones down toward the Bay. Concentration of these schools on half the elementary program made possible many elements of enrichment. Great care was taken also to achieve parent involvement and, indeed, community involvement.

Other California school districts also integrated. In Sacramento a key step was not to rebuild a segregated junior high school. Its pupils were redistributed where they would help to integrate. Riverside with moderate use of busing was able to integrate. San Bernardino responded to urging by minority parents and rescued a considerable number of pupils from segregated schooling.

In Pasadena a Negro boy was plaintiff in a suit asking permission to enroll in an integrated school rather than having to go farther to a predominantly Negro school. In 1963 the state supreme court ruled in his favor (*Jackson* vs. *Pasadena*) and went on to hold that school boards were under obligation to take positive steps to bring about integration where it did not exist.

In 1968 in another Pasadena suit in which, among others, white students asserted that they were entitled to integrated schooling, the federal department of justice under Attorney General Ramsey Clark intervened as an additional litigant. In 1969 the state attorney general brought suit against the school boards of Bakersfield and San Diego as flagrantly derelict in allowing segregated schooling to persist.

In the Bakersfield and San Diego cases the court, without dismissing the cases, ruled that insufficient evidence had been presented. In the Pasadena case in mid-January, 1970, Judge Manuel Real brushed aside the defense argument that the segregation was de facto rather than de jure and ordered the district to submit a plan for complete integration by mid-February and to put it into effect by September. The school board, convinced of the educational necessity for integration, voted not to appeal and instructed staff to bring the schools into compliance with the court order.

By the end of the decade discriminatory practices had been eliminated or greatly reduced elsewhere in the public sector: in the right to vote and hold office, in public employment, in the administration of justice, in public housing, and in access to public service and accommodations. In the public sector the schools were the laggards.

For Further Reading

EDWARD L. BARRETT, JR., *The Tenney Committee* (1961).

GORDON KAHN, *Hollywood on Trial* (1948).

JOHN COPLEY, *Report on Blacklisting*, two volumes (1956).

ABRAHAM POLONSKY, *A Season of Fear* (1956).

SEYMOUR KERN, *The Golden Scalpel* (1960).

GEORGE R. STEWART, JR., *The Year of the Oath* (1950).

DAVID P. GARDNER, *The California Oath Controversy* (1967).

JOHN W. CAUGHEY, "Farewell to California's 'Loyalty' Oath," *PHR*, 38 (1969), 123–28.

DAVID HULBURD, *This Happened in Pasadena* (1951).

GERALD GOTTLIEB, *Capital Punishment* (1967).

JOHN and LAREE CAUGHEY, *School Segregation on Our Doorstep: The Los Angeles Story* (1968).

IRVING HENDRICK, *The Development of a School Integration Plan in Riverside, California* (1968).

NEIL V. SULLIVAN and EVELYN S. STEWART, *Now Is the Time: Integration in the Berkeley Schools* (1969).

CAUGHEY, *California Heritage*, 443–59, 470–76, 521–29.

chapter thirty-four

A Time of Confrontations

Continue to express your dissent and your needs but remember to remain
civilized for you will sorely miss civilization if it is sacrificed in the
turbulence of change.

Will Durant

Alienation and Involvement

1945
and
after

When Kearney stirred the workingmen in the 1870's, it was to increase
their wages. The Wobblies battled for free speech, but what they
wanted to talk about was a better deal for workers. Sinclair, though
attacked as a wild-eyed radical, promised through state intervention
and operation to bring material benefits to the multitudes. Dr. Townsend wanted to extend the dividends of capitalism to the aged. And
Franklin Roosevelt, hated by the Union League, is now credited with
saving the capitalist system. Most of the criticism of the American
system until midtwentieth century, far from rejecting the material
products of capitalism, sought rather an increase and better distribution.

The View from Watts

Paul Conrad, The Los Angeles Times, 1965

579

The war years muted most protest, and the postwar pressures for conformity intensified the tendency. The age of McCarthyism was the period of the silent generation, when college students and their elders chose pragmatic goals and were circumspect to a fault about memberships and political activities. Then suddenly, alongside this pattern of noninvolvement out of complete dedication to the capitalist system, there arose another form of disengagement in the formula of Sam Goldwin's famous phrase, "Include me out."

The beatniks and after them the hippies expressed their contempt of the prevailing mores by being deliberately unkempt and by declining to participate. They were young; they were numerous. They clustered in select parts of the state: Carmel and the Big Sur, Venice, and along San Francisco's Columbus Avenue. Some had jobs and earnings. Some allegedly were bank clerks during the week and hippies over the weekend. The generation gap was real, but not such a chasm as to prevent many of these young people from living on remittances from their parents left behind in the world of the squares. These nonconformists prevailed on a number of points. Their sideburns and long and

Early stage in hosing the protesting students down the steps of City Hall, San Francisco, May, 1960. All the students staging the sit-down on the balcony are still to be hosed down.

San Francisco Chronicle

deliberately ragged hair style spread to young workers and across the generation gap to many oldsters. By the sixties many of the disaffected had turned to marijuana, LSD, or heroin as part of their of society.

Another change was a new eagerness to be involved. In May, 1960, students from many campuses came to City Hall in San Francisco to show their disapproval of the House Un-American Activities Committee. Finding that passes to the auditorium were given exclusively to "friendly" spectators, they filled the corridor to chant and sing until the police drove them out with clubs and firehosed them down the steps of the building.

Later in the year many students found a cause in John Kennedy's candidacy against Nixon. In 1961, when Kennedy as President issued invitations to the Peace Corps, California students were among the most numerous volunteers. They found another cause in the sit-ins in Mississippi and Alabama, designed to break the hold of Jim Crow. Others went to the Old South as volunteer teachers and to help in voter registration drives. By easy extension came participation in California in picketing, marches, sit-ins, and other demonstrations for an end to discriminations in employment and housing. In 1964 many students entered the campaign against Proposition 14.

The Free Speech Movement

In that climate of active concern about problems of the day students assembled at Berkeley for the fall semester. At Sather Gate some of them undertook to enlist supporters and participants for off-campus activism. They found an old rule brought out and enforced against such solicitations. They protested and were rebuffed, whereupon other students, not originally interested in going off to picket or to sit-in against a nonemployer of Negroes in San Francisco or Oakland, insisted on the right of university students to participate in politics.

This issue triggered the Free Speech Movement—the proposition that, although the university must stay clear of partisan politics, its students (most of whom at Berkeley were over 21) need not be political neuters. The protesting students, aided tremendously by the charismatic appeal of quick-witted Mario Savio, gained many supporters among the faculty as well as among the students.

Savio and his collaborators broadened the issue. They wanted the university made more relevant to the times and to student needs. They called for a different deployment of professors' attention, less to contract research and off-campus employment and more to the teaching function. They proposed overhaul of courses and degree programs and that students have more voice in decision making. Nothing in the past experience of half the professors and most of the administrators and regents conditioned them favorably to these proposals. Concessions came haltingly.

The Free Speech Movement then degenerated into the Filthy Speech movement. The activists used the tactics they had learned in off-campus protest and brought them to climax in a sit-in in Sproul Hall, nominally the administrative nerve center of the university. On request of President Clark Kerr, Governor Brown sent state police to clear the building. Some 700 persons, not all of them registered students, were forcibly evicted, and some 578 were eventually convicted of trespassing or resisting arrest.

Although many classes went on as usual and credits were earned, degrees awarded, and researches continued, the sound and fury of the Free Speech Movement dominated the scene through the 1964–65 academic year. The faculty and many students saw merit in the political action issue and need for educational reconsideration. By year's end there was a relaxing of some rules, a change in chancellors, and moves toward more student participation in educational planning. In time there would be experimental programs, student initiated courses, less emphasis on grades, and other modifications. The university emerged intact from the year's buffeting, but there was question how much more it could stand.

A Minority Reconstituted

American California started off with a holdover minority from the former regime, almost at once reinforced by Mexican and Chilean gold seekers. In the diggings these Spanish-speaking miners, including the "native foreign-born," were subjected to harassment. There followed over the next half century what Leonard Pitt has called "the decline of the Californios," the fading of this minority from view, in part because many were assimilated and with some honorable recognition into the general population.

Early in the twentieth century the railroads began to look to Mexico for track laborers, as did California agriculture in the twenties for its labor gangs. A Mexican-American minority began to rebuild, enumerated at 120,000 in 1920 and 368,000 in 1930, counting immigrants and children of immigrants. Fewer came in the thirties and, to lower the relief rolls, thousands were repatriated by Los Angeles County. Most of these newcomers congregated in metropolitan Los Angeles, which by 1945 had a Mexican population second only to Mexico City's.

In the forties the children of this immigration were showing the effects of their schizoid heritage. They were not entirely understood by their parents and they saw themselves discriminated against in the white community. They were targets for consistent abuse in the press, out of which came the overzealous and racist prosecution in the Sleepy Lagoon murder case in which 300 were arrested, 23 indicted, and 17 convicted, Mexicans all, an outcome which the appellate court reversed with a stinging rebuke to the judge. A year later anti-Mexican prejudice seethed again in the zoot-suit riots with mob action against the Mexicans, then called *pachucos*. For years thereafter the police enforced a curfew harshly and selectively against *pachucos*.

Before the end of the sixties the Mexican minority passed the 2 million mark, still heavily southern and urban. Always there was the paradox that the Mexican Americans who succeeded in business or the professions had no social barrier to surmount, but that the Mexican Americans as a group were almost without influence in politics or decision making.

César Chávez and the Grape Boycott

The nation's farmers, insisting that their labor requirements were inexorable (the cows had to be milked and the ripened crops had to be gathered in), won exemption from federal wage, hour, and organizational control. They also insisted that the relation between farmer and hired man was much more personal than in industry. In California with its industrialized farms, the latter argument lost most of its validity, but for every grape, pear, and melon there is a moment just right for the picking.

California growers were able to persuade federal and state officials to bring them low-wage laborers if necessary. Starting with a wartime emergency in 1942, the United States Department of Agriculture negotiated an agreement with Mexico for the importation of contract workers (*braceros*) to work for a season and then be returned to Mexico. Alongside them came many illegal entrants, the so-called wetbacks. In 1948 President Truman shifted the responsibility to the Labor Department, with some prospect that the volume of recruitment would be phased down. But with the Korean War as an excuse, Congress in 1951 revitalized the bracero program, which ran on through 1964 and with some concessions after that date.

In 1952 César Chávez opened a new chapter in California labor history by launching a drive to organize the migratory farm workers. He was one of them, born into and brought up in such a family. As a youngster he spent more time in the fields than in schools, and he continued in this shifting, sporadic, low-paid work, the only kind of employment he knew, until 1952. At that time he went to work in the AFL–CIO's Community Service Organization and its efforts among Mexican laborers. Having failed to persuade this organization to start a farm workers' union, Chávez decided in 1962 to try to do so himself.

From Delano as a base he launched the National Farm Workers Association (NFWA) and began soliciting members. In this union he set up a death-benefit plan, a credit union, and a newssheet, *El Malcriado*. The appeal was primarily to Mexicans. By August, 1964, membership was a phenomenal 50,000.

This new union scored several victories. It won a suit against a grower who was paying less than the $1.25 an hour then required by the country-cousin clause of the federal minimum wage law. It won a court order that Tulare County improve the housing at two labor camps. In May, 1965, with a four-day strike it won a substantial wage increase for rose grafters.

In September, 1965, as the grape harvest shifted from Coachella Valley to the San Joaquin, a group of Filipino grape pickers came to Delano,

César Chávez
The Los Angeles Times

bringing with them a union organization under the AFL–CIO. They struck for pay equal to what the growers were paying imported pickers. On September 16 a quickly called meeting of Chávez' union faced the issue of joining the strike. The fervor of Mexico's Independence Day rally readily transferred to the cause. "Viva Mexico!" transmuted to "Viva la Huelga [the strike]! Viva la Union!" Chávez soon became the guiding spirit in the collaborating unions and eventually they coalesced.

Because table grapes had to be picked with special care, Chávez focused on this most vulnerable part of the industry. In 1966 a major grower, Schenley Industries, agreed to a contract and the DiGiorgio workers voted to be represented by Chávez' union, the NFWA. These gains proved illusory because both companies disposed of their table-grape interests. Chávez next struck the Guimarra Vineyards, the largest grower, and as added pressure he called for a boycott against Guimarra grapes. Guimarra frustrated that effort by selling its grapes under other labels, and that led to a boycott against all table grapes.

Boycotts by definition are against producers or marketers and by brand rather than by commodity. That one could succeed against so mouth-watering a morsel as the grape goes contrary to nature. Yet the state's monopoly is such that any table grape other than Concords in any market in high probability is from California.

The strike already had the attention of many well-wishers. Students, churchmen, and other volunteers went to the San Joaquin to teach the migratory children and to offer other help. Many were eager to do something to counteract what they saw as a clear injustice in the chain of foodhandling. They enthusiastically joined the boycott. Robert Kennedy, Jess Unruh, Eugene McCarthy, and Mayor Daley gave it support. The boycott took hold in Chicago, New York, Great Britain, and Sweden, but not in the Pentagon, which increased its purchases. Boycott-breakers announced that they were tasting "the Forbidden Fruit," but a surprising number of persons, including children who thus far in their lives had never tasted a grape, took this pledge and kept it. In 1968 receipts for table grapes were down 12 per cent and in early 1969 were down 15 per cent. It is unreasonable to think, however, that this strike can go on forever.

La Huelga benefits from a carryover of remorse about exploitation of migratory workers in earlier California and as "stoop labor" elsewhere. The remorse is strengthened by remembrance of Steinbeck's Grapes of Wrath and by the inspiration of the Montgomery, Alabama, bus boycott. Chávez ties the strike to Catholic endorsements of social reform and, for the strikers, with the resurgent pride in being Mexican. Dedication to nonviolence and the self-sacrificing commitment of Chávez, Dolores Huerta, and other NFWA leaders have been fundamental to the initial successes in this movement to upgrade the agricultural branch of California labor.

A New Minority, The Negroes

California Negro history extends back almost to the Spanish entrance in 1769. One scholar, Jack D. Forbes, interprets the rosters to signify that a quarter of Anza's reinforcement and more than half of Los Angeles' founding settlers were Negro or mulatto. Unquestionably Negroes and mulattos were present. For some unexplained reason the population whitened, and by the late Mexican period the tabulations show only a small sprinkling of Negroes. Of one Mexican governor it was said retrospectively that he was pretty dark, but he was not typed as a Negro.

The written record identifies a few Negroes, a storekeeper in Yerba Buena before it was renamed San Francisco, a majordomo on a southern rancho, a barber in early Los Angeles, and a pioneer stage driver into Yosemite. The pictorial record shows more Negroes in the diggings than are mentioned in the forty-niner writings. Nevertheless, for almost another hundred years Negro participation was as scattered individuals, seldom in position of influence or leadership, and not nearly as numerous or visible as the Chinese or Japanese.

The census of 1900 found only 11,045 Negroes in the state, 0.7 per cent of the population. Into Los Angeles, however, a small-scale migration was under way, resulting in a "Pullman porter" neighborhood, then a larger concentration on Central Avenue, and by 1920 other clusters at Watts, Budlong, and Temple Street. None of these neighborhoods was solidly Negro, and there were other Negroes interspersed in other districts. Negro employment opportunity was inferior—very few had jobs in industry or as salesmen—and there were discriminations against them in theaters and restaurants, though not by segregation of schools. To visitors from other parts of the country, however, their residential area did not look like a slum. A correspondent of *Crisis* reported that the Los Angeles Negroes were "without doubt the most beautifully housed group of colored people in the United States."

After 1919, with restrictive covenants upheld by the courts, the ghetto walls began to rise, though at first only on selective fronts. Migration increased, particularly from southern states. By 1940 Negroes had risen to 1.8 per cent of the state total, and of these some 75,000, or better than two thirds, were in Los Angeles County. Negroes were making their mark, among them Walt Gordon as coach and respected resident in Berkeley, Carlotta Bass of the *Eagle*, and Loren Miller as journalist and attorney in Los Angeles.

With war work as the magnet a much larger migration poured in during the early forties, mostly from Texas and its neighbors, in largest numbers to Los Angeles, but for the first time with heavy attention also to the Bay area and its war plants. After the war the Negro population growth continued at about twice the rate of the rest of the population. At the end of the sixties the Negro total was approaching that of the Mexican Americans, and it was considerably more concentrated in the cities and in the Negro ghettos of these cities. In Compton and Richmond Negroes were well over 50 per cent of the population, in Oakland and Berkeley over 40 per cent, in San Francisco approximately 30 per cent, and in Los Angeles, with the largest contingent, approaching 20 per cent.

In the nation Negroes have long been recognized as the largest and most significant minority. They did not precede the Indians, but a history of the Negro in America is entitled *Before the Mayflower*, and with accuracy because the Dutch slaver checked in at Jamestown a year before the Pilgrims reached Plymouth. By midpoint in the colonial period the Negro was the foremost minority and would continue to be so.

The California branch of Negro history is in sharp contrast. True enough, Negroes arrived early and thereafter Negroes made at least a pro rata contribution in the ranks of California workers. Some of them scored creditable achievements. They did so, however, as scattered individuals. Following the Second World War they were numerous enough, yet it was white leadership that spearheaded the drive for civil rights and fair employment legislation in 1959 and the agitation for desegregated housing and schools.

With the sixties Negro participation became much more effective, as evidenced by the winning of seats in Congress and in both houses of the legislature, judgeships, school board posts, city council seats, and other positions of influence. In the late sixties more revolutionary leadership raised the pitch of demands. Not until this decade did Negroes make their presence really felt and claim recognition as a new minority to be reckoned with, active and vigorous.

The Los Angeles Riot

The white community was more aware of these gains than of the continued inequities and discriminations and consequently was startled in mid-

Interlude in the Watts Riot

The Los Angeles Times

August, 1965, when violence erupted in Los Angeles' Negro ghetto. A police incident with the appearance of unnecessary harshness touched it off. Once started, the striking back at police spread to an attack on "Whitey" wherever he showed. Windows were smashed, especially of those businesses blamed for exploiting ghetto customers. Fires were set, again selectively, and the firemen answering the calls were turned back. Many Negroes who committed no other violence joined in the looting of supermarts, clothing stores, liquor shops, and appliance shops. They did so with the rationalization that they were collecting something white society had been owing them for a long time.

At first Police Chief William Parker was confident that his men could restore order. By the second day he was ready to ask for the national guard. Lieutenant Governor Glenn Anderson, powerless to act up to that time, issued the order and within hours guardsmen reached the riot area. The riot turned into a six-day shoot-out, snipers on one side and police and guardsmen on the other. It affected an area of 50 square miles, almost the entire ghetto, with added flare-ups in Venice and the harbor area. The toll mounted to 34 killed, 31 of them Negroes; 1,032 injured; 3,952 arrested; 3,411 charged with felony or misdemeanor; and property damage of $40 million. By several measures it was the largest race riot ever.

Agitators had nothing to do with starting this riot. Frustrations over unemployment and poor schools, irritation over police practices, and resentment of white segregationist attitude manifested so clearly in the vote for Proposition 14 motivated this outburst.

The state-appointed McCone Commission conducted a post mortem on the riot, exculpating the police, making Anderson the scapegoat for alleged delay in bringing in the national guard, and calling for improvements in ghetto employment, housing, and education. The riot called attention to the plight of the ghetto dwellers. On the negative side it prompted race fear, as evidenced by a rash of gun buying, and it stimulated white backlash.

In the later sixties, although Los Angeles did not repeat the Watts riot, there were many violent confrontations up and down the state. On earlier occasions the Los Angeles police had maintained aggressive surveillance over the Black Muslims, including an unprovoked shoot-up of their headquarters. In 1969 the mayor of Vallejo was aghast at what his police had done to the local Black Panther headquarters and commissary for school lunches. In Oakland, San Francisco, and San Diego there were clashes between Negroes and police. In Los Angeles and Fresno there were incidents involving Mexicans.

On December 8, 1969, the Los Angeles police moved to make a predawn arrest of two Panther leaders. They cordoned off the streets in all directions, then made simultaneous demands for surrender at Panther headquarters and two lesser stations. Firing broke out, each side later maintaining that the other had fired first. The shoot-out lasted long enough for television cameramen to reach the scene and record the climactic barrage, the tear gasing, and the bringing out of the men, women, and infants who had been besieged. Eleven were held without bail; for others bail was set at $10,000 to $110,000.

The elected legislators from this part of town objected strenuously, and at the scene later in the day Senator Mervyn Dymally was clubbed by the police. Many whites were of the opinion that the police had chosen a violent way to make an arrest. The mayor of Seattle later stated that federal officials asked his cooperation, which he refused, for a raid in Seattle on that same date. Because other lawmen carried out like raids in Chicago, Philadelphia, and elsewhere there was the appearance of coordination, enough so to generate charges of intended genocide and to call forth several investigations. In addition to official inquiries, the black congressmen banded together to investigate, and another nationwide inquiry was launched by a group of lawyers and law school deans headed by Arthur Goldberg, Roy Wilkins, and Ramsey Clark.

The Black Separatists

This half decade also witnessed an intensification of black separatism. The movement had its surface manifestations in natural hair styles, beads and amulets, African print blouses and dresses, Swahili names, and soul food. Picking up where Malcolm X and Elijah Muhammed left off, the Black Panthers, an organization calling itself US, the Black Student Union, the national leadership of CORE, and the southern California leadership of the NAACP put forth successive demands for black control of relief and welfare programs, black business, ghetto schools, and black studies. They demanded, among other things, that the colleges provide black scholarships, and preferential admissions, appointments, and space assignments. In support of the black separatist movement in Los Angeles a Texas millionaire made a six-figure grant.

This new leadership scoffed at Martin Luther King's technique of nonviolence and at what it calls yesterday's goals of an integrated America. It has drawn off many once strong workers for that reform. It was a Californian who organized the threatened black boycott of the Olympic Games in 1968, and another Californian who saluted there with black-gloved fist. The spokesmen for separatism proclaim violence if necessary. Going beyond James Baldwin's warning of "the fire next time," some of them threaten a holocaust.

To some extent, at least, they go beyond threats. At Los Angeles City College, after breaking up an awards luncheon, the black intruders sat down and ate the lunch. At San Fernando Valley State College administrators charge that they were forced to negotiate at knife point. At UCLA, one of the less disturbed campuses, two Black Panther leaders were "executed." The suspects, three of whom were arrested and subsequently convicted, were members of a rival organization seeking control of the campus Afro-American studies program.

Mexican Americans stirred with similar ethnic pride, raised the banner of *Raza* (race), demanded control of their eastside Los Angeles schools, tacos and tortillas on the school menus, more attention to recent Mexican achievements in California, and Chicanos to teach this history. Perhaps because of the lamentably small number of Mexican Americans in the colleges, the center of this agitation has been in the high schools but with some attention to selected colleges.

The Indians, a much smaller minority which, even with a large ingathering from other parts of the country, numbers only about 0.2 per cent of the population of the state, are also on the warpath for recognition and equal opportunity. In the *Indian Historian*, published in San Francisco by Rupert and Jeannette Costo, this group speaks up vigorously. Late in 1969 a war party made headlines by occupying Alcatraz Island, which they offered to buy for $24 in baubles and beads. On intercession by Jane Fonda, early in 1970, the state assembly adopted a resolution urging assignment of Alcatraz to this group. Decision however, rests with the Great White Father in Washington.

Protesting the War

Alongside the escapism of the hippies and psychedelics, the student unrest, and the insistent minorities, there rose a groundswell of dissatisfaction

War Is Not Healthy

Another Mother for Peace

with the war in Vietnam. The war increasingly took on the aspect of a ghastly mistake, and the draft an unwarranted imposition on American youth. Antiwar sentiment knew no age limitation, but it was natural that young people should be most active.

Opposition to this war took many forms. Harold Willens' Business Executives for Peace hoped for a man-to-man talk with the President. The volunteer group that called itself Another Mother for Peace set out through greeting cards and letters to bring into being a Department of Peace and an end to the war. Others pinned their hopes on teach-ins and marches, on picketing induction centers, and demonstrating at munitions factories and loading points. The Eugene McCarthy campaign in 1968, which many saw as a crusade for peace, did not end the war but led to the retirement of the officer who had been its champion.

A year earlier, when President Johnson came to Los Angeles to speak at a $100-a-plate dinner for Democratic bigwigs, thousands of nonviolent marchers for peace approached the Century Plaza Hotel hoping for a confrontation. The President was whisked in and out by the back door. Meanwhile, in the full glare of television the police broke up the demonstration, whacking away with their "batons"on the skulls and bodies of the demonstrators, in this instance all of them white, and followed up with wholesale arrests and prosecutions.

In 1968 agitation for peace was not immediately respectable, but it drew more and more supporters and was a momentous issue in the presidential campaign. The assassination of Martin Luther King in Memphis and of Robert Kennedy in Los Angeles intensified this concern.

On October 15, 1969, Californians participated in the nationwide moratorium for peace. In the course of it a businessman said reprovingly to a Stanford freshman, "My country right or wrong." "You didn't finish it, sir," came the answer, "The rest is: 'When it's right, keep it right; when it's wrong, make it right.'" The businessman muttered, "Traitor." There were many other shades of opinion about the moratorium and the war, among them Art Buchwald's constructive suggestion a few days later that a San Francisco Bay incident should be arranged, whereupon the President could ask and the Senate authorize immediate assignment of 500,000 seasoned fighting men to defend California until the Californians themselves could man the defenses.

Impelled by their consciences, Californians also have resisted the draft. For some that meant alternate service in the medical corps, an option open to those who could prove that their objection stemmed from long inculcation in a church-supported pacifism. Jehovah's Witnesses by the hundreds, though basing their objection on religion, rejected that alternative as too participatory in the war and went to jail. Then there were those, of whom Joseph Maizlish is representative, who also went to jail. They might be equally religious but were not enrolled in any of the pacifist sects. For them the objection to this war was a matter of personal conscience. In a few instances judges saw conscience as a valid objection. More often they sentenced to prison, the variable being merely in assigning the five-year maximum or some shorter term. In a nation committed to separation of church and state, the acceptance of religious scruples but not personal scruples is a contradiction or at least an enigma.

Embattled Campuses

In the late sixties the alienated and addicted took over the Haight-Ashbury district in San Francisco and a large sector of Berkeley. The peace advocates redoubled their efforts and far more than redoubled their numbers. They won token concessions as to the draft in the retirement of General Lewis B. Hershey as well as the promise that none but 19 year olds would be called up. They also won predictions, if not hard promises, of a gradual phaseout from Vietnam. Black separatists gained the ascendancy over integrationists as spokesmen for their minority and there were similar pulsations in the Mexican-American community.

These several drives not only climaxed, they drew together on the campuses to create a series of more formidable crises. It was happening all across the nation—at Columbia, Wisconsin, Brandeis, Harvard, Howard, Cornell, and countless other schools. It happened at half a dozen campuses of the University of California, at Stanford, Mills, San Jose State, San Francisco State, San Fernando Valley State, and in Los Angeles at City College, four or five high schools, and at least one junior high school.

The issues raised included several that were quite beyond the jurisdiction of any faculty, administration, or board of governors. The list began with stopping the war, ending the draft, eliminating ROTC, banning military recruiting, closing the University of California's Livermore Laboratory or the Stanford Research Institute, introducing black or brown studies, making exceptions in favor of minority students, revamping course offerings and degree requirements, and bringing students in on all decision making.

Characteristically these issues were raised as nonnegotiable demands, backed up by open or implied threats of bodily harm, sabotage, or arson. At Stanford the ROTC building was burned and the president's office ransacked and vandalized. There was a token bombing at UCLA which scorched a door. At the University of California in Santa Barbara what was perhaps intended as a token bombing killed a custodian. At San Francisco State, in one of many explosions, the young man responsible was severely injured. The tabulation of property damage and of hazard to persons is long and distressing. It is small wonder, therefore, that those who make demands feel that they are negotiating from strength.

Furthermore, many school people were troubled in conscience that reforms had been so long delayed. They were determined, therefore, to make compensatory adjustments, to approve a course in modern Mexican history in California without requiring a demonstration that there is sufficient content, to set up "benevolent quotas" which exclude better qualified applicants, and to revise course offerings and requirements to comport with relevance as defined by current students.

Throughout two school years San Francisco State College was in the most turmoil. A succession of demands related to the black students and the black studies program. Many professors were equally disturbed by what they saw as arbitrary governance by the state board and chancellor. With the police called in repeatedly because of marches, sit-ins, break-ins, and bombings, confrontation was almost perpetual. Presidential heads rolled. Acting President S. I. Hayakawa, noted semanticist, had so much exposure as a tough exponent of law and order that he led the polls as a possible candidate for senator or for superintendent of instruction.

Across the Bay at Berkeley confrontation multiplied on issues less germane to higher education than those of the Free Speech Movement. Berkeley's "street people," in demeanor indistinguishable from the inhabitants of Haight-Ashbury in San Francisco or those who took over and depreciated Sunset Strip in Los Angeles, intermingled with insurgent students still intent on curricular reform, relaxation of disciplinary rules, peace, pot, and black power. In the 1968–69 school year this amalgam of young people found an issue in a vacant lot where they had set up camp but where the university now proposed to build. When the squatters resisted eviction, the police used force and put many under arrest.

Although squatters' rights has not been a good rallying cry for a hundred years, students and others came from far and near to protest the eviction. The establishment responded with counterviolence, with blasts of Double-O buckshot, fatal to one rooftop observer, and a helicopter overflight spraying the campus with tear gas. This excess roused still more opposition, made visible in a still larger demonstration.

The dissidents, meanwhile, had discovered another half block of university land at Bowditch and Haste, south of the campus. Descending on it with rented grader, which one of the hippies expertly operated, they leveled it artistically and moved in to improve it as they had their earlier People's Park. The city fathers wrestled with the question whether to accept the loan of this land as a city park. Then it was the regents' turn to refuse to make any such offer. Resolution of what is intrinsically a phony issue was held over for later consideration.

Professors and administrators have not found the ideal way to deal with all the problems germane to institutions of learning. Their difficulties are much greater when issues essentially external to the schools are added to the demands. Violence seems endemic; for instance, at Devonshire Downs in 1969 many young people invoked it for no higher purpose than to crash the gate to a rock-and-roll concert. Early in 1970 at Ysla Vista, a bedroom suburb adjacent to the university campus at Santa Barbara, demonstrators burned down the branch of the Bank of America, allegedly as a gesture against the Establishment. Subsequently, in an outburst of even great insanity, arsonists attempted to destroy California's greatest cultural asset, the library of the University of California at Berkeley.

Violence can be the undoing of a university, and so can counterviolence. Every school should be protected by a gun law, a knife law, a bomb law, a Molotov cocktail law. There is general agreement that no university should be a sanctuary for law breakers. A university or college should thrive on dissent and constructive criticism, but the nature of the institution presupposes a clientele willing to be civilized.

For Further Reading

Lawrence Lipton, *The Holy Barbarians* (1959).

Seymour M. Lipset, and Sheldon S. Wolin, *The Berkeley Student Revolt* (1965).

Lloyd S. Fisher, *The Harvest Market in California* (1953).

Leo Gebler, *Mexican Immigration to the United States* (1966).

Ernest Galarza, *Merchants of Labor: The Mexican Bracero Story* (1964).

Truman E. Moore, *The Slaves We Rent* (1965).

W. Willard Wirtz, *Year of Transition: Seasonal Farm Labor, 1965* (1966).

John Gregory Dunne, *Delano: The Anatomy of the Great California Grapeworkers' Strike* (1967).

McCone Commission, *Violence in the City* (1965).

Robert Conot, *Rivers of Blood, Years of Darkness* (1967).

Jack Jones, *The View from Watts Today* (1967).

Carey McWilliams, *The California Revolution* (1968).

Denis Hale and Jonathan Eisen, *The California Dream* (1968).

Caughey, *California Heritage,* 505–15, 521–29.

chapter thirty-five

Impact of Massive Growth

> Mankind has reached the point of his greatest knowledge and power and has come to a dialectical turning point when, if he is to become greater, he has to become smaller.
>
> Gary Snyder

Influence from Washington and by Science

1945 and after

California's fantastic growth in the 1940's through the 1960's produced radical change. With population almost trebled, most Californians were comparative strangers in the land. Since they poured into the cities, forcing them to bulge outward and upward, massed living became characteristic. Economic production soared out of proportion to population increase and with it came greatly increased purchasing power.

In these same years the state found itself part of the world's richest, most powerful, and most domineering nation. The federal government provided new services such as social security, safeguarding of commercial flights, and vastly increased aid for interstate highways. The federal income tax, which had been nom-

Girl and Redwood

Wynn Bullock

inal, was boosted and reboosted. Federal regulation accompanied these actions. In addition, through the Pentagon and NASA, the federal government became California's best customer, buying food, fuel, and munitions for the routine needs of the servicemen at home and in Korea and Vietnam and contracting in the state for a large fraction of the development of improved weapons and space vehicles.

Under Spanish rule the key decisions about developments and the level of activity in this distant province were made by the monarch or by his officials in Mexico. In the 1860's, although Judah and others clamored for action, the decision to build a railroad to the Pacific was made in Washington. The Boulder Dam project could not move ahead until Congress and the President approved. Nevertheless, although Californians were concerned about national policies on money management, tariffs, and transportation, local initiative and performance appeared to be much more determinative among the miners, wheat farmers, real-estate promoters, orange growers, oil men, the Johnsonian reformers, and the builders of Stanford University, the University of California, and the public school system.

During the Second World War and thereafter much of the most crucial decision making shifted to Washington. What should be the prime interest rate? At what level should the income tax and the corporation tax be set, and with or without a surtax? What overseas commitments and what outlay for research and development in the ongoing nuclear and space competitions should the United States make? In the long run it may be more important to the state that Governor Brown in 1960 persuaded the voters to approve the $1.75 billion commitment for the first stage of the California Water Project, but in the decade of the sixties it was of much greater consequence that our Presidents step by step committed us to the $80 billion a year war in Vietnam. Californians, in their alter ego as American citizens, of course exert some influence in national decision making. That does not contradict the reality that today much of California's fate is determined externally.

These recent decades present another significant innovation in the ways in which scientists and technologists have reshaped destiny. It was a Californian who pioneered in splitting the atom; appropriately, one of the new elements discovered is called californium. In the scientific revolution the state's personnel and laboratories made their share of contributions. The impingement on the state, however, was from discoveries and fabrications by the whole world of scientists. By their courtesy Californians were emancipated from many tasks, took on new habits, and gained new categories of businesses and employment resting on the new science and the new technology.

The Prevailing Culture

What Neil Morgan has called the Pyramids of Los Angeles, the new Music Center with its Chandler Pavilion, Taper Forum, and Ahmanson Theater, provided elegant setting for music and theater. These structures, however, were not entirely a net gain for the arts since they supplanted the old Philharmonic Auditorium, repossessed by Temple Baptist Church, and the Biltmore Theater, razed for a parking lot. The number of listeners to classical music has grown only moderately. Such radio programs as the Standard Hour and the Metropolitan Opera gave exposure not matched today. The disc jockeys continue to stress the popular, as do the tape and record makers. The peak turnout for music in the sixties was for the Monterey Rock festivals and for a corresponding jamboree at Devonshire Downs until eclipsed by the Rolling Stones in a field near Livermore. The greatest cry of anguish when the 1969 summer television programs closed was that Johnny Cash and his country music were dropped from the tube.

Live theater, even on Broadway, had a hard time sustaining itself in this period. That was true in California. Television for a time promised to be a lively substitute, with Hollywood and New York sharing productions, but the style changed, serious theater was relegated to the educational channels, and more superficial entertainment took over.

As they had done for the Music Center, private donors made possible the new Los Angeles County Art Museum at the tar pits on Wilshire. The core collection of works of art moved over from its old quarters in Exposition Park making room there for more display of bones from the tar pits. Oakland built a new museum dedicated to California ecology, history, and art. San Francisco added a wing to the De Young Museum to accommodate the Brundage collection of Oriental art. Chancellor Franklin D. Murphy brought into being a noteworthy sculpture garden at UCLA. San Francisco's Benny Bufano flooded his area with strong and whimsical figures in Chinatown, at the longshoremen's union hall, at the Hillsdale shopping center, the airport auto park, and many other unexpected places. Rescuing massive pieces of driftwood and still larger redwood boles, J. V. Blunk created impressive sculptures for the University of California at Santa Cruz and the Oakland Museum.

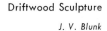

Driftwood Sculpture

J. V. Blunk

Edward Kienholz's "constructions" are experiments in less conventional media and are noteworthy for the social message conveyed. Lee Mullican, a master in space control and an Indiophile, is an experimenter in spontaneous painting, in which, though with utmost concentration, impulses felt but not coldly calculated are transmitted to the canvas. Among other painters of special merit Rico LeBrun and Arnold Mesches stand out for their conviction that the central function of an artist is to serve society in a critical capacity.

The Sierra Club, particularly through its exhibit format picture books, has encouraged a noble tribe of California landscape and seascape photographers. Edward Weston, Cedric Wright, and Ansel Adams begin the list, which goes on to include Philip Hyde, Eliot Porter, William Garnett, Cole and Brett Weston, Steve Crouch, and Wynn Bullock.

The state abounded in capable and industrious writers. It may be that the tracts of Bronson and Dasmann will rate on a par with those of Sinclair and Steffens, and the commentaries of Morgan and Gladwin Hill with those of McWilliams. No novelist and no poet matches the stature of Steinbeck and Jeffers. Nor has magazine publishing held its own. *Sunset*, widest in circulation, is the western home and campout magazine. *Westways* is geared to the membership and interests of the giant Automobile Club of Southern California. *Ramparts* since 1962 has pushed its exposés, most notably that of the CIA. *Pacific Spectator*, which aspired to be a western outpost of belles lettres, expired in 1956, and *Frontier*, a western journal of opinion, fell silent in 1967. Shrinkage of the continent and almost instantaneous delivery from New York or from the western edition printery gave advantage to the national publishing center in New York. The enlarged and rejuvenated Los Angeles *Times* with cartoonists Paul Conrad and Frank Interlandi and its staff of special writers flourishes through excellence. In writings that find publication Californians exceed the tenth that is their population quota. The state's writers, however, do not attain the higher percentile achieved by their brethren in science, aerospace, or athletics.

In the postwar decades the churches grew in membership though modestly. Churchmen were less prominently in the news than had been Bob Shuler, J. Whitcomb Brougher, and Aimee Semple McPherson. Episcopalian Bishop James Pike came closest, most often in relation to a social or moral issue rather than one strictly religious. Billy Graham brought his revival to the state occasionally and in 1969 struck a modern note by saying on opening night that the tent would have been filled except for a freeway tie-up. Two issues particularly stirred churchmen, the plight of César Chávez' farm workers and the war in Vietnam. Church groups supported what were virtually missions to the farm laborers in the San Joaquin Valley and marched in Chávez' processions. In the peace movement church people were concerned, active, and outspoken.

The Pilgrimage Play, a hardy perennial in an amphitheater near the Hollywood Bowl, broke off its run in the mid-sixties. A neighboring institution, Forest Lawn, registered as a religious force, if not exactly as a sect, with a theology and doctrine widely accepted in southern California. It clearly would continue for a long time to come. The following report is excerpted from the San Francisco *Chronicle* of September 27, 1966, for what it has to say about the prevailing culture.

> Dr. Hubert L. Eaton, founder of the vast Forest Lawn Memorial Parks, was entombed yesterday in an elaborately grandiose ceremony climaxed by his formal induction as an immortal of Forest Lawn Memorial Court of Honor.
>
> The spectacle was attended by some 1000 business and cultural leaders and was reminiscent in its sweep and grandeur of some of the funerals for screen stars held at Forest Lawn in years past.
>
> The invited guests included Richard Nixon, Ezra Taft Benson, George Randolph Hearst, Jr., Joe E. Brown, Greer Garson, Ronald Reagan, Conrad Hilton, and opera singer Mary Costa.
>
> The honorary casket bearers included Herbert Hoover, Jr., Walt Disney, Norman Chandler, president of the Los Angeles Times Mirror Company, and such prominent businessmen as Leonard K. Firestone, A. C. Rubel, and Asa V. Call....
>
> The ceremony began with an organ rendition of "March Romaine." Brian Sullivan, the operatic tenor, then sang "Ah Sweet Mystery of Life" accompanied by the Roger Wagner Chorale.
>
> After readings from the Scriptures and a eulogy delivered by former Governor Goodwin Knight, Eaton's name was formally submitted by W. Turney Fox, a retired judge of the Court of Appeals, as an immortal of the Memorial Court of Honor.

Reacting to the Pupil Explosion

In 1940 California could claim an excellent school system. Typical of the West it was in the main a system of public schools and colleges, though a quarter of San Francisco's elementary pupils were in parochial schools and a sixth of the state's college students were in private schools. Investment per pupil was among the highest in the nation. Colleges and universities attracted out-of-state students and President Sproul boasted that as a place to study the University of California at Berkeley was unsurpassed, on a par with Harvard and bigger.

Beginning in 1945 a pupil explosion struck the state's schools. Junior college enrollment doubled in five years; elementary and secondary doubled in 10, and in another 15 years doubled again. From 1.2 million in 1945 the school population in 25 years vaulted to 5 million, advancing from 6 per cent of the national total to 12 per cent.

To provide school buildings, facilities, and teachers for such a multitude was a gargantuan task. Los Angeles, with much expertness, needed two to four years after site acquisition and funding to plan, build, and outfit a new school. To get enough teachers the school districts had to send recruiters to the Midwest, the South, and the east coast. Financing such a rapidly expanding operation called for expenditures far above the national average.

To put a floor under school support California was operating under a formula for state payments from sales, income, and corporation taxes and local support from the locally set property tax. On the average the state was supposed to contribute 50 per cent but, as needs and costs rose, the remittances fell to 35 per cent or less. Local taxpayers were called on to make up the difference. Before long, taxpayer resistance was showing itself in defeat of bond and tax-rise proposals. Expenditure per pupil fell several notches in the national standings. In the national test scores in reading and arithmetic achievement California fell back even farther.

Since the time of Marvin and Swett public education in California has been seen as a state function. Elected district boards have a role, but state educational policy takes priority. The constitution contains certain specifics. The legislature has added to the educational code, as in the Fisher Act of 1961, a main purpose of which was to stress subject matter in the credentialing of teachers. The state board of education more directly sets standards on length of school year, pupil–teacher ratios, basic program of instruction, and instructional materials for grades 1–8. Through the sixties the board encouraged consolidation of ineffectively small districts and blocked redistricting that would increase or perpetuate segregation. The state program is an equalizing force in an upward direction and also serves as a protection against the more extremist pressures.

One such instance occurred in the mid-sixties. In 1964 the board asked for texts for the great introductory eighth grade course in United States history that would, among other things, give balanced coverage of the contributions by Americans of all backgrounds. Of the books submitted, the board was advised that a new book, *Land of the Free*, best met the requirements. In May, 1966, the board voted the adoption.

What had been a small rumbling of criticism now became an angry attack manifested in representations to the board, letters to the editor, fliers, phone calls, radio and television talk shows, sermons, political speeches, pamphlets, and a film strip. This book, so the critics said, was too attentive to Negroes, too frank in reporting American mistakes, insufficient in its praise of captains of industry and Republican presidents, critical of atomic warfare, and calculated to break down pride in America. The Birch Society actively circulated these materials, and a small group of Republican legislators held up the general appropriation bill for 1966–67 because it included purchase of *Land of the Free*. The Junior Chamber of Commerce, the vast majority of whose members had never opened the book, by statewide referendum condemned it. Not since *The Grapes of Wrath* had any book stirred up so much hatred.

The board stood by the adoption, the necessary 400,000 copies were printed and delivered, and in September, 1967, this text along with a wealth of

"It's Slanted toward CIVIL RIGHTS!"

Bastian, San Francisco Chronicle, May 13, 1966

supplementary readings came into use. Two pairs of parents who went to court to protest exposure of their children to this book got no satisfaction. The Downey school board also resisted, broadening the issue to an attack on the whole procedure of state selection of texts.

In 1962 Max Rafferty campaigned vigorously for the office of state superintendent of instruction, with sweeping attack on progressive education and promises of taking the schools back to fundamentals. Elected by a very comfortable majority, Rafferty found that any drastic change of policy was blocked by the board, then under the presidency of newspaperman Thomas Braden. Verbal clashes between the superintendent and board members featured most board meetings, *Land of the Free* fueled more of this debate, and it spilled over into more public forums, especially in 1966 when Braden sought nomination as lieutenant governor.

Reagan's and Rafferty's triumph at the polls in 1966 was followed by appointments that reconstituted the board. The new board, however, proved jealous of its authority. Rafferty in 1968 put much of his energy into winning nomination and then running unsuccessfully for the Senate. The board remained the major power center and pushed on to an ultraprogressive experiment with research and discovery as the method in lower elementary social studies.

In 1969 the board moved the battle to sex education and evolution. As to sex the action was that parental requests for shielding from such instruction must be honored. The board still further dumbfounded its educational advisers by rejecting a recommended science text for the earliest grades because of its matter-of-fact language on evolution. The board then went on to amend a meticulously prepared guideline on the teaching of science. It inserted a requirement that, along with "the theory of evolution," teachers must present the Biblical "view of special creation." The official position, as a reporter put it, of "giving God equal time" is as to religion as fundamentalist as Tennessee's in the 1920's. The board also seems blissfully unaware that, on the relationship and origin of species, evolution is considerably more than a mere theory.

Teaching and learning went on with some difficulty into the seventies. The metropolitan schools were constantly inundated with pupils transferring in, many with far less adequate preparation than the California schools provided. Crowding and teacher shortages were inevitable. Race confrontations increased, and segregation, as previously described, continued to doom many thousands of pupils to substandard educational opportunity.

Colleges in Ferment

Higher education proliferated at a comparable rate. By the late sixties 79 junior colleges had an enrollment of half a million students, 19 state colleges had 200,000, the state university on its 10 campuses had more than 100,000, and private schools had almost another 100,000. This growth necessitated a vast construction program and the appointment of many more professors. Increased attention to graduate and professional programs greatly augmented the cost factor.

In 1959 Governor Brown called for a master plan for higher education in the state. The educators who undertook the task endorsed the existing arrangements with slight modifications. They took as their premise that private colleges could be only slightly expanded, therefore the additional students of the future would have to be in public colleges. The junior colleges should continue their dual function, preparing some students to continue academic studies and others for a vocation. The state colleges each should have well-rounded programs, be primarily teaching institutions, and, where resources permitted, give limited graduate work. The university should continue four-year undergraduate programs but have special responsibility for graduate and professional programs. One defect in the allocations is that the junior colleges are typed simply as teaching institutions, and the state college faculties are thought of in almost the same way, with research and contributions to knowledge left almost exclusively to the university.

The Donohue Act of 1960 incorporated the gist of this master plan, set up a board of trustees for the state colleges, and prepared the way for a state board of trustees for the junior colleges which was created in 1967. The junior colleges retained substantial autonomy but made little use of it. The state colleges had far less autonomy in budget, selection of administrators, or educational planning, with acrimonious controversy as the result. By internal decision the university permitted local option on many such matters, with UCLA striving for distinction in sciences, medicine, and engineering, Santa Cruz becoming a cluster of small self-contained colleges, and the other new campuses developing their own special identities.

In the early postwar years a wave of older, more experienced students subsidized under the GI Bill vitalized college and university programs. Then came the silent generation of the McCarthy era, a procession of students and faculty wary of involvement in challenge or change of established ways. The prolonged controversy over the University of California oath requirement had this setting. Those in authority tried to keep the lid on; in 1960 a group of students were disciplined for riding to a rally at the Hollywood Bowl in a bus displaying a banner "UCLA Republicans for Nixon."

Understandably, the unrest on the campuses stirred a formidable backlash, of which some can be laid to the generation gap, some to resentment of criticism of an ongoing war, some to the race issue, and some to the flaunting of law and order. There are, of course, many Californians who were not privileged to go to college and who do not see any real prospect of having that experience. They are not automatically convinced that great outlays for colleges and universities should have priority.

There was a time when the university's great contributions to agriculture ensured strong support from the highly influential farm bloc. The California schools of higher education have been performing at least comparable services for the most sophisticated and most prosperous branches of industry. To all appearances, however, these great corporations are not comparable protectors. Or perhaps management in these industries has its own backlash against campus protest.

At the same time that they were struggling to adjust to student militancy and to provide better educational opportunity for minority students, the university and the state colleges were under particular pressures from Governor Reagan. Although more and more young people wished to enroll, budgets were cut back sharply, building programs were curtailed, and the university was forced to use up its reserves. In 1970, in most questionable economizing and with hardly any thought to educational policy, the summer quarters were abolished at Berkeley and UCLA. In budgeting for 1970–71 both the university and the state colleges were instructed to identify 20 per cent of the total in order of the "fat" contained, that is, in order of nonessentiality.

Although for 99 years the University of California had functioned as a school open to the best qualified sons and daughters of the poor as well as of the rich, Reagan was adamant on changing it into a tuition-charging institution. The regents resisted but wavered to the extent of boosting fees for purposes other than instruction. They boggled at the word "tuition," but in 1970 gave in and set tuition rates exceeded by only one state university, that of Vermont. The domino theory prevailing, the state college trustees two months later voted to collect tuition from their 200,000 enrollees. The junior colleges stand next in line and the logic may be extended to high school, elementary, and kindergarten. With a means test for enrollment, students from the lower and middle income brackets inexorably will find it more difficult to achieve higher education. The university and the state colleges will have a more elitist clientele and will be less representative of a true cross section of the people of the state.

A Premium on Mobility

Emerging from the travel restrictions of the war years, Californians as soon as possible resumed their high mobility. As the transportation revolution continued, old standbys became obsolete. Once the troops were brought home from the Pacific most of the transports were decommissioned. For the Korean War some were taken out of the mothball fleet but only temporarily. Passenger ships on the Pacific routes soon gave way to jets. The state's most publicized ship came to be the *Queen Mary*, purchased by Long Beach with part of its oil royalties and refitted as a stationary tourist attraction. Freight shipping continued and the most efficient working ships were the giant tankers and the container carriers. The railroads in the immediate postwar era rose to their most splendid performance and then abruptly declined as passengers and mail shifted to the jets.

In these same years Californians completed their divorce from public transportation. San Francisco Bay ferries disappeared. The Elkhorn Sacramento ferry and San Diego's Coronado ferry made their last runs in 1969. The electric interurbans, once the great carriers in and out of San Francisco and in Metropolitan Los Angeles, dwindled and died. For a brief period they ran over the Bay Bridge to a San Francisco terminal, only to be replaced by buses. Streetcars also lost out. Out of sentiment San Francisco held on to the cable cars. Elsewhere the surrender to the bus, or rather to the bus and the automobile, was universal.

In Los Angeles, it is true, a Rapid Transit District existed on paper and periodically was rebuffed by the voters when it asked funding for subways to Century City, the harbor, San Fernando Valley, and eastward. The trouble was that Angeleños were not that clustered along these corridors and not that eager to go downtown. In contrast, San Francisco and the East Bay counties voted in 1962 for BART (no relation to Black Bart, the famous rhyming bandit). For the next several years the Bay Area Rapid Transit was busy burrowing under Market Street and under the bay for tubes to bring in the East Bay commuters.

On the positive side, Californians embraced the jet plane with tremendous enthusiasm. Flying is the most favored avenue to Las Vegas, the Union Pacific's Sun Valley, New York and Washington, Mexico, Hawaii, Alaska, Europe, and Asia. The flyway between San Francisco and Los Angeles is the most traveled air route in the world. The thoroughness of the switch-over is evident in the contrast between Los Angeles Union Station, an architectural gem now silent and cavernous which probably should be converted into a mausoleum, and International Airport, bustling, crowded, overflowing with cars, its noise increasingly a blight to the neighborhood and its added runways forcing the closing of nearby schools.

Jet schedules shrank the travel time between the major California terminals and their counterparts throughout the world. Way points such as San Luis Obispo, Colton, and Dunsmuir found themselves passed by, and the options of how to go to Tucson, El Paso, or Colorado Springs were reduced. It became possible to commute between San Francisco and San Diego or Los Angeles and New York, and some individuals allegedly do so. Business adjusted to the air age. Hotels with conference facilities sprang up near the major airports, and at Los Angeles an office building offered office-away-from-the-office facilities. The airplane repatterned California life.

Airborne though many of them often are, it was to the automobile that Californians became really dedicated. Motor vehicle registrations passed 5 million in 1950, 10 million in 1963, and 13 million in 1969. By 1969 that meant one car for almost every person old enough to drive.

To drive one's own car fitted in with residential sprawl, decentralized business, scattered employment, and the open climate. The freeways, especially their urban sections, accentuated this tendency. Freeway off-ramps pointed to ideal locations for businesses and factories. In California, perhaps more than anywhere else in the world, this interaction of forces culminated in a people on wheels.

Cry California in 1969 published an illustrated documentary on a "freeway family," whose home was a camper. The day began with a drive out the Hollywood Freeway, with breakfast cooking en route and the husband dropped off at a Burbank factory, then by the Golden State and the San Bernardino Freeways to Azusa where the baby was left with his grandmother. The mother and camper backtracked to a half-day job, then picked up the baby, then the father, and home again to a downtown parking lot—128 miles a day. The father was quoted as saying, "One day is about the same as another; about ten gallons of gas a day. We're beginning to feel that the freeways, particularly the Hollywood Freeway, belong to us." Author William Bronson later reported that the story was a hoax, "as anyone should have known." But to Californians it seemed plausible enough.

So many cars snarl and clog even the freeways, especially during commuting hours. So many cars, most of them concentrated in the urban areas, poison the air. They are blamed for 90 per cent of the contaminants (13,500 tons daily) poured into the Los Angeles air. Yet the major complaints are about the cost and shortage of parking. It is the parking rather than the freeways that accounts for the downtown pave-over.

The freeways do have spectacular accidents. In the spring of 1969 jackknifing trucks in Los Angeles spilled live cattle, a load of red wine, a tanker of vegetable oil, and a sprinkling of 300-pound napalm bombs destined for Vietnam. The cattle were rounded up, the wine sustained only 15 per cent breakage, the vegetable oil was flushed away, and the bombs by good fortune were without detonators. All of which accords with the statistics that freeway driving has a phenomenally low accident rate per man-mile and should have a preferential insurance rate. Drivers are told they would be happier going home from work by rapid transit, but they are not persuaded. The psychological explanation is that to ask a Californian to give up his car is like asking an old-time cowboy to give up his horse.

Public transit may return, BART for sure. The more wishful thinking is that the gasoline-exploding engine with its inferior combustion will turn into an electric motor, or a gas burner, or a steam engine. Meanwhile, the Division of Highways races ahead with more freeways, trying to catch up with the demands of more than 13 million auto addicts.

Paul Conrad, The Los Angeles Times, June 24, 1968

Preservation of Nature

Within 20 or 30 years the poachers killed off the sea otter. The beaver trappers in even less time exterminated their quarry. The grizzly, once the monarch, no longer survives in California except in the zoos. In the 1930's the seining fleet disposed of the sardine. Compared to what man has been doing to Nature in the latter part of the twentieth century, these, however, were minor forays.

The modern blows come from man and the machine. Bulldozers and paving machines eat up the farmland. A drilling rig off Santa Barbara triggered the massive oil leak. The internal combustion motor with its appalling inefficiency makes most of the smog. The jet and the supersonic air bus in motion blight the entire surroundings of our airports.

Science also is to blame. The industrial wastes of applied science killed off all marine life in Los Angeles harbor. The predictable consequences of outfall from the projected nuclear power plant at Bodega Bay induced cancellation of that project. The blighting of sea birds and marine life by DDT and the threatened engulfing of the entire state in nonreturnable but indestructible containers are other illustrations of the power of science.

Nevertheless, the population explosion is the major pressure on the land. The hazard to the California environment rises, and more than just arithmetically, with the increase in population. In December, 1969, Lee DuBridge, the head of California Institute of Technology and President Nixon's science adviser, urged the imperative of halting population increase and holding the line right where it is. He had reference to the nation as a whole but undoubtedly particularly to California.

John Muir almost a hundred years ago insisted that there was an obligation to preserve for posterity the magnificent beauties of nature with which California was endowed. The program then proposed was simply to ban destructive exploitation, and much was achieved by designating state parks and national parks, monuments, wildlife refuges, and forests. Preservation of wilderness is a continuing cause. In 1963 a Point Reyes National Seashore Park was proclaimed and in 1968 a Redwoods National Park. These victories may have been celebrated prematurely because the funds voted were by no means sufficient for buying the privately held properties.

Now population presses hard on these "protected" reserves. Vacationers and tourists go by the thousands to look at the redwoods, the tread of their feet damaging the root structure. They crowd by the millions into Yosemite Valley. That park registered 2,781,000 visitors in 1968; Kings Canyon had 1,064,000, Sequoia 874,000, and Lassen 442,800.

If Californians were simply spectators, the pressure of numbers might be tolerable. On the less than 640 acres that he was allowed to homestead in Chavez Ravine and with a season only slightly longer than Yosemite's, Walter O'Malley has accommodated 2 million customers at Dodger Stadium. But California invites participation. It is used as one vast playground. Residents and tourists have a passion for camping, fishing, hunting, hiking, climbing, swimming, skiing, boating, sailing, surfing, skindiving, off-the-road motorcycling, and dune buggying. True enough, many Californians are not all that athletic, but on a Fourth of July or a Labor Day weekend 2 million may swarm to the Los Angeles beaches. When the fishing season opens, Lake Crowley is ringed and covered with fishermen. Throughout the summer most of the public campgrounds, of which there are many, have turnaway crowds. At the summit of Mt. Whitney, which has had as many as 500 visitors in one day, the Park Service had to airlift in two steel gray outhouses.

The vacationers, setting out innocently enough to rekindle their spirits through communing with Nature at its best, create a traffic jam at Yosemite and a smoke haze if not outright smog in its valley. It is a question whether the park can survive such volume of attention. And there are schemes to drum up much more mountain resort business.

When Walt Disney died in 1968 he left a legacy of two great projects. One was to construct a greater Disney World in Florida—a survey had revealed that 100 million Americans had no expectation of ever coming to Disneyland. The other project was to construct a mammoth winter playground for a projected million visitors a year in the fastness of Mineral King in the Sequoia back country. The roads, facilities, lodges, shops, lifts, and ski slopes could be counted on to denature a large virgin area. The Sierra Club, carrying on in the Muir tradition, entered objections to the proposed invasion.

Pollution

Belatedly Californians came to realize that saving the redwoods, saving the condors, and safeguarding Yosemite would not be enough. The whole sta e and the whole way of life were in danger. If the washout of DDT threatened to extinguish the brown pelican, some people could take that in stride. Some might agree with Secretary of the Interior Walter Hickel that the way to protect against another blowout of oil into the Santa Barbara Channel was to step up the drilling and relieve the pressure. It was said also that, after the Union Oil clean-up crews had done their work, the beaches had never been so clean. The news that Lake Tahoe was about to turn into an open cesspool like Lake Erie was more alarming. An energetic pressure group exposed the shrinkage of San Francisco Bay through municipal and industrial dumping and fill, which if continued could destroy that once noble expanse of water. This group won state endorsement of a Bay Conservation and Development Commission to act as brake on further damage to this natural asset.

Trash and garbage were a more immediate threat. San Francisco, which had been dumping in the Bay, was desperate enough to consider running a daily garbage train to Lassen County, which allegedly had aspirations to be the garbage capital of the world. That run was not put into operation but remains a possibility. Los Angeles used to burn its refuse but, out of consideration for

Berkeley from the Bay

Rondal Partridge

smog, changed to cut and fill. The west side of Los Angeles contributes to a vast project in the Santa Monica Mountains which in another 30 or 40 years is scheduled to produce parklands adequate for 15 or 20 golf courses in, as the saying goes, the Santa Garbage Mountains.

Trash disposal is a problem compounded by the ever-increasing per capita discard, the resistance of the new synthetics to breakdown, and the perpetual issue of methane gas and other contaminants from these trash burials.

Air pollution is the number one problem. The harbor management may maintain that polluted water is fine because it discourages the worms that otherwise eat into the pilings, but no one has a good word to say for smog. Los Angeles smog gained visibility as far east as the state line and was killing more than a million pines in the San Bernardino Mountains. Growers of leafy vegetables learned to flee its presence. Doctors have certified smog as a cause of death and increasingly they prescribe a life-saving or health-saving flight from Los Angeles. In 1969 the coroner, after an autopsy, could certify that a murder victim had recently come to Los Angeles because there was no trace of smog in the victim's lungs.

In the summer of 1969 the health authorities began broadcasting smog alerts for the various parts of the Los Angeles basin. The incidence is expected to be 1 or 2 days a year on the west side, 7 in the San Fernando Valley, 24 in east San Gabriel Valley, 28 or 29 in west San Gabriel Valley, and 20 or 21 in Pomona. These warnings are beamed to school children; adults presumably are to gasp and choke at their own discretion. The instructions to school children are: "During heavy smog conditions do not exercise strenuously and do not breathe deeply!"

Smog of course is only a temporary disaster. One of these days we shall have burned up the last of the world's oil, and smog as we know it will no longer exist. In the meantime, for California's most besmogged areas, electrically powered rapid transit seems a very remote possibility. Steam automobiles have more plausibility because they would allow each driver his independent mobility. The other option, to give up so much moving about, gets no consideration, even

Paul Conrad, The Los Angeles Times, October 20, 1969

Interlandi, *The Los Angeles Times*, 1969

though, as Assemblyman Robert Monagan said, "Cars kill cities just as surely as they kill people. It could be that we are building the world's biggest freeway system to serve the world's biggest ghost town."

The Sierra Club has broadened its program from saving the Sierra to saving California. In this broader effort the Sierra Club has many allies, among them California Tomorrow, publisher of *Cry California*, a jeremiad against willful and thoughtless damages 20 million Californians do their state. Raymond F. Dasmann hit hard on this theme in his *The Destruction of California* (1965) and William Bronson underlined the warning in *How to Kill a Golden State* (1968). In *Eden in Jeopardy* (1966), Richard Lillard excoriated man's prodigal meddling with the southern California environment.

Throughout most of the modern scientific and technological revolution there were assurances that the Earth had an abundance of resources on which man was making only a modest draft, that if one fuel were exhausted there were others we could turn to, and that if there were undesirable side effects to particular applications of science, science itself could design remedies or controls. Rachel Carson's *Silent Spring* (1962) evoked more nostalgia than alarm, and Linus Pauling's warnings on the damage that unseen fallout was doing to mankind's genes had at least partial rebuttal from other scientists.

Belatedly a few naturalists and scientists alerted us to side effects and aftereffects, often invisible, that came with many of these applications of science. They pointed out the domino theory as a reality in the DDT passing from field and garden to plankton and fish and to food animals, and accumulating in brown pelicans to the point of eliminating any hatchable eggs and in human beings to the point of poisoning mothers' milk.

611

Ecologists cite example after example in which the elimination of one life form disrupts a balance and does heavy damage to associated life forms. Others point to geometrically increased damages from mere arithmetical increase in population or cropping or water use.

On the more occult side are the doomsday predictions that the littering of the outermost atmosphere by smoke, gases, and the contrails of superjets may rob the Earth of much of its ration of solar heat, and that overproduction of carbon dioxide and decimation of the vegetation which performs photosynthesis may bring about a heating that will melt the polar icecaps and bring on a Noah's flood raised to the nth dimension. The environmental scientists say convincingly that we are moving headlong toward making ours a dead planet. The activities that these scientists complain about are the very ones in which Californians are doing far more than their per capita share. Californians thus are leading in this race toward destruction.

Continuities

Big, bustling, only a phone call away from any city in the world, and a leader in the most advanced sciences, how does today's California relate to the traditional one or to any of the state's pasts? Most of its people do not know any of these pasts and, furthermore, the modernizing influences are strong.

The early reports of California were of a Lotus Land. Visitors still get that impression and multitudes of Californians achieve such experiences. California for health, another part of the reputation, was at its peak in the late nineteenth century. It is still true today that, with some discrimination as to location, a fragile person or a convalescent should be better off here than in a harsher climate.

Much used to be made of California's natural bounty, particularly the wide range of fruits and vegetables and other crops. The commercial crop list still reaches beyond that of the rest of the nation. The potential, except in the millions of acres paved over, built over, or blighted by smog, is as great as ever. As a gesture of patriotism during the Second World War a UCLA professor took over the lot next door and made it yield a prodigious quantity of garden produce. With a small plot and water anyone almost anywhere in the populated area can achieve a bountiful subsistence with tree crops, row crops, flowers, and social security.

In pastoral California everyone was on horseback, the forty-niners were footloose, and Californians from then on have enjoyed high mobility. That certainly prevails, though there are exceptions. Watts, it is said, has many youngsters who have never seen the ocean only 10 miles away.

The percentage of absentee ownership, though somewhat reduced as the state has prospered, remains substantial, and the percentage of anonymous control is greater than ever. The warning is up: "Right now some committee is deciding your fate."

The Torrey Pine, A Threatened Species

Marc Myton

Modern California is a complex of private enterprise and government projects, federal and state regulations and the profit motive, labor–management tensions, supply and demand, computerized planning and trial and error. Superficially the sum total seems a most uncoordinated way of meeting the needs and meshing the activities of a tenth of the nation. Parts of the process are not working right: the educational machinery sputters; minorities have much less than equal oportunity; the land takes an unnecessary and devastating beating; and unearned increment all too often passes as incentive pay. That the process as a whole works as well as it does stems in part from California's superlative natural endowment and in part from lessons learned in the earlier stages of this state's history. The force of continuity runs strong in spite of the avalanche of new residents and new ideas.

Where Have All the Heroes Gone?

Historic California is rich in heroes: Serra, Portolá, Anza, Lasuén, Smith, Bidwell, Coleman, Judah, Huntington, Swett, Bancroft, Muir, Jordon, Chaffey. The motto inscribed on the Capitol, "Give me men to match my mountains," was not just an aspiration but something realized.

Suddenly, on the modern scene, where have all the heroes gone? There are churchmen better versed in theology than was Serra, test pilots carrying on in the Anza tradition, engineers ushering in the new developments in transportation, school men with more power than was granted to Swett, and historians better trained than Bancroft. A few individuals stand out. David Brower, as the long-time executive secretary and director of publication for the Sierra Club, spearheaded the fight for conservation. A. L. Wirin through 50 active years symbolized the cause of civil liberties. Otis Chandler, who has presided over the transforming of the Los Angeles *Times* into just about the best American newspaper, has made himself a force for the state's well-being.

A few other individuals are identifiable: Pauley of Pauley Petroleum, Kaiser of Kaiser Industries, and Colonel Sanders of Kentucky Fried Chicken. In their day Huntington and his partners were the Southern Pacific Railroad. But who can name the president of North American, Lockheed, Standard Oil, Victorville Cement, Bank of America, Occidental Life, or Almaden winery? Who is chairman of the board at Wells Fargo, Union Oil, Foremost–McKesson, California Packing, or Safeway?

As long ago as the thirties when the first gigantic dam was to be built on the Colorado, no individual builder or corporation was big enough for the task, and the bid had to be made by the Six Companies. The Central Valley project had to be a coalition effort. In 1970, significantly, the second tube paralleling Mulholland's Los Angeles Aqueduct was known merely as a construction by the Department of Water and Power, and the nuclear power plants on the drawing boards belonged to PG & E and Southern California Edison. The motto now should read, "Give me corporations to match my problems."

This shift from emphasis on the individual to the group flows naturally from the tremendous increase in all California magnitudes. Certain tasks are so large, the California Water Project, for instance, that only the federal government or the state can handle them. Many undertakings can be taken care of in the private sector only by a pooling of resources. Most require more on-going attention than any one man could give.

Outlook

For the future, many Californians have the darkest forebodings. They do not see how the state can endure another doubling of the population and perhaps a redoubling. Realtors at this writing are puffing a tract near the center of Los Sandiegeles, the metropolis to be, from which by some quirk of selfishness Santa Barbara has been omitted. It is not certain that the lessons of the past, the expertness gained about California potentials, will meet the challenge of 80 million or even 40 million souls.

Californians, however, are long experienced in urban–suburban living. Current employment and current housing fit this pattern. The more modern the industry, the cleaner it tends to be, and the more high-rising and cooperative the housing, the more moderate the per capita demands for water and acreage. Some impulses toward less violence to the natural resources do not have to be legislated, but there must be forethought. Eternal vigilance is the price of livability. Parks, greenbelts, and public beaches must be expanded. Californians now make out with public beaches that provide 1/4 inch of frontage per capita. It is unreasonable to think that future generations could manage with only 1/8 inch or 1/16 inch.

As to smog, pollution, and mobility, and living equably together, more drastic readjustment is necessary. Concerning pollution, the best suggestion is that we do not create so much of it, that we demand returnable bottles and refuse the plastic toy with its almost immediate obsolescence built in. On mobility, the solution may be that we cultivate immobility, by reaching for a cluster-type living arrangement in which shops, schools, playgrounds, and employment are within walking distance. San Francisco, with an assist from the cable cars, was like that, and so was Berkeley for its students and faculty in the 1920's. Many present-day colleges and universities seem designed to give this experience and to cultivate the taste. The press of numbers can be counted on to generate some of this wisdom, though along with it there will be demand for transportation improved in mechanics and consistent with clean air.

Thus far Californians can boast that, except at Sonoma, San Pascual, the Mesa, Cahuenga Pass, the Lava Beds, and Gaviota, they have not allowed war to mar this beautiful country. Their record of living together equably is much spottier, possibly because there was always elbowroom enough to make the resolution of all disputes unnecessary. For all concerned, the most privileged as well as the least advantaged, California now faces the imperative that handicaps to equal opportunity be removed and that the assets of the state be conserved and used for the best interests of all present and future Californians.

For Further Reading

NEIL MORGAN, *The California Syndrome* (1969).

EDMUND G. BROWN and others, *California, the Dynamic State* (1966).

ARTHUR BLOOMFIELD, *The San Francisco Opera, 1923–1961* (1961).

ESTHER McCOY, *Richard Neutra* (1960).

ESTHER McCOY, *Five California Architects* (1960).

THOMAS W. STORKE, *I Write for Freedom* (1963).

RAYMOND McHUGH, *Land of the Free and Its Critics* (1967).

LIBBIE BLOCK, *The Hills of Beverly* (1957).

CYNTHIA LINDSAY, *The Natives Are Restless* (1960).

ELIOT PORTER, *The Place No One Knew: Glen Canyon on the Colorado* (1963).

PHILIP HYDE and FRANCOIS LEYDET, *The Last Redwoods* (1963).

RICHARD KAUFMANN, *Gentle Wilderness: The Sierra Nevada* (1964).

SAMUEL E. WOOD, *California, Going, Going...* (1962).

RAYMOND F. DASMANN, *The Destruction of California* (1965).

RICHARD G. LILLARD, *Eden in Jeopardy* (1966).

WILLIAM BRONSON, *How to Kill a Golden State* (1968).

CAUGHEY, *California Heritage*, 489–502, 515–18, 530–43.

Selected
References

In 1933 the noted bookman, Robert E. Cowan, published a select bibliography of California history that ran to three oversize volumes. A complete library would include tens of thousands of books that bear directly on the subject, countless papers published separately or in widely scattered periodicals, and other works in great number, broader in scope, but with essential information relating to this state. The stockpile of available material continues to grow in serials such as the *CHSQ* (*California Historical Society Quarterly*, 1922 on), the *PHR* (*Pacific Historical Society Quarterly*, 1932 on), and the *SCQ* (*Southern California Quarterly*, 1935 on) and in book publication by Dawson, Clark, Westernlore, Talisman, Howell-North, the Huntington Library, Stanford, University of California, and publishers at large.

The Bancroft Library and the Huntington Library in San Marino are the two major assemblages and research centers. Each is rich in manuscripts, and the Bancroft has made a point of stocking microfilm copies of relevant documents found in the archives of Spain, Mexico, and the United States. The State Library, the California Historical Society, Stanford, UCLA, USC, Library of Congress, and

Yale have important holdings, each possessing some that are unique, and in and out of the state there are dozens of noteworthy private and public collections.

What follows is a selected sampling with emphasis on books and some concession to availability. After a section on general works, the arrangement follows the chapters in this book.

General Works

First in dimensions and in significance are the 39 stout volumes of the *Works* (1884–90) of Hubert Howe Bancroft. Bancroft and his staff amassed and presented a tremendous amount of data on the history of the western half of North America. Seven of the volumes are labeled *History of California*, another four are purely Californian, and most of the rest tie in closely. They are the foundation for much subsequent work in the field. Theodore H. Hittell, *History of California* (4 vols., 1885–97) is especially rich on the early American period. Zoeth S. Eldredge, ed., *History of California* (5 vols., 1915) is a fluent narrative. In 1929–31 the Powell Publishing Company issued a nine-volume set entitled *California*, individual volumes of which will be cited. In 1960 Richard F. Pourade began issuance of a spritely and richly illustrated *History of San Diego,* which by 1967 had reached the sixth volume and the 1930's; in the process this set recites a substantial part of the history of the state.

The first authoritative survey in shorter compass was in the companion volumes, Charles E. Chapman, *A History of California, The Spanish Period* (1921), the first general work using the results of research in the archives of Spain and Mexico, and Robert G. Cleland, *A History of California, The American Period* (1922), which emphasizes the processes leading to acquisition by the United States. Single-volume treatments preceded and followed, e.g., those by McGroarty (1911), Norton (1913), Atherton (1914), Tinkham (1915), Hunt and Sanchez (1929), Caughey (1940), Rolle (1963), and Bean (1968).

The Cowan bibliography is the most useful research aid, even though its annotations are addressed to the collector rather than to the scholar. Useful specialized bibliographies include: Ethel Blumann and Mabel W. Thomas, *California Local History* (1950); Henry R. Wagner, *The Spanish Southwest* (1924, revised 1937) and *The Plains and the Rockies* (1920; revised 1937); and Oscar O. Winther, *The Trans-Mississippi West, A Guide to Its Periodical Literature, 1811–1957* (1961). *Libros Californianos* (1931; 1958) and *The Zamorano Eighty* (1945) are booklovers' choices of outstanding books. Glen Dawson, *California* (1943) and *West and Pacific* (1947) are cumulative dealer catalogues. Information on new publications is available in the book review sections of *CHSQ, SCQ,* and *PHR.*

Robert W. Durrenberger, *Patterns on the Land* (1965) and *Hammond's California Atlas* (1969) offer descriptive maps, many of them historical. William J. Miller, *California through the Ages* (1957) is a summary of geological history. Clifford M. Zierer, ed., *California and the Southwest* (1956) and David W. Lantix, Rodney Steiner, and Arthur E. Karinen, *California, Land of Contrast* (1963) are geographical analyses. Peveril Meigs, III, *Climates of Cali-*

fornia (1938) and Ernest L. Felton, *California's Many Climates* (1965) deal with one of the most important features of the environment.

Piecemeal descriptions abound in topical studies such as William L. Dawson, *The Birds of California* (4 vols., 1921); Willis L. Jepson, *The Trees of California* (1909) and *A Manual of the Flowering Plants of California* (1925); Howard E. McMinn, *An Illustrated Manual of California Shrubs* (1939); Edith S. Clements, *Flowers of Coast and Sierra* (1928); Francis M. Fultz, *The Elfin-Forest of California* (1923); and Tracy I. Storer and Lloyd P. Tevis, Jr., *California Grizzly* (1955); and in regional studies such as François E. Matthes, *The Incomparable Valley, A Geologic Interpretation of the Yosemite* (1950) and *Sequoia National Park, A Geological Album* (1950); John Muir, *The Mountains of California* (1894) and *The Yosemite* (1912); Roderick Peattie, *The Sierra Nevada* (1947) and *The Pacific Coast Ranges* (1946); Godfrey Sykes, *The Colorado Delta* (1937); E. C. Jaeger, *The California Deserts* (1933); George Wharton James, *The Wonders of the Colorado Desert* (1906); Edwin Corle, *Desert Country* (1941); Mary Austin, *The Land of Little Rain* (1903); Anne B. Fisher, *The Salinas, Upside-down River* (1945); and J. Smeaton Chase, *California Coast Trails* (1913).

Rhapsodic description had early representation in such titles as Charles Nordhoff, *California for Health, Pleasure, and Residence* (1872); Sutton Palmer and Mary Austin, *California, The Land of the Sun* (1914); and George Wharton James, *California, Romantic and Beautiful* (1914). This message is better documented in photographically enriched books such as Edward Weston, *California and the West* (1940); Ansel Adams, *The Eloquent Light* (1963); Richard Kaufmann, *Gentle Wilderness, The Sierra Nevada* (1964); Philip Hyde and Francois Leydet, *The Last Redwoods* (1963); and David Brower, *Not Man Apart* (1965).

1. The First Californians

Recording of data on the California Indians began with the early Spaniards, the most illuminating record being Gerónimo Boscana's "Chinig-chinich" on the Juaneño and Gabrielino. Alfred Robinson included an English translation in his *Life in California* (1846). Hugo Reid's notes on the Gabrielino, written for the Los Angeles *Star* in 1852, were reprinted as *The Indians of Los Angeles County* (1926). Similarly, John Caughey, ed., *The Indians of Southern California in 1852* (1952) makes available the B. D. Wilson report, serialized in the Los Angeles *Star* in 1868. To the *California Farmer*, in many installments, 1860–63, Alexander S. Taylor contributed "Indianology of California," a vast miscellany on all aspects of Indian history, some of it otherwise lost to memory. Stephen Powers, *Tribes of California* (1877) is based on observation and empathy for the Indians. In that same decade Bancroft and his staff were combing the written and published records and compiling *The Native Races* (5 vols., 1874–75), which took stock of pre-Columbian culture in the whole of western America.

Scientific study of the Indians came later. Its results are set forth in many formidable monographs, particularly in the University of California, *Publications in American Archaeology and Ethnology* and the series *Ibero-*

Americana. Robert F. Heizer and M. A. Whipple, eds., *The California Indians, A Source Book* (1951) is made up of selections from this scholarship. More cyclopedic but most readable is A. L. Kroeber, *Handbook of the Indians of California* (1925). Robert F. Heizer, "The California Indians: Archaeology, Variety of Culture, Arts of Life," *CHSQ*, 41 (1962), 1–28, and *Languages, Territories, and Names of California Indian Tribes* (1966); and C. Hart Merriam, *Studies of California Indians* (1955) have broad range. Lorraine M. Sherer, *The Clan System of the Fort Mojave Indians* (1965); David P. Barrows, *The Ethno-Botany of the Coahuilla Indians of Southern California* (1900); Harry C. James, *The Cahuilla Indians* (1960); Bernice Eastman Johnston, *California's Gabrielino Indians* (1962); Campbell Grant, *The Rock Paintings of the Chumash* (1965); Annie R. Mitchell, *Jim Savage and the Tulareño Indians* (1957); and Robert F. Heizer and John E. Mills, *The Four Ages of Tsurai* [Trinidad Bay] (1952) are scholarly analyses of particular Indian groups.

A. L. Kroeber, *Cultural and Natural Areas of Native North America* (1939); Ruth M. Underhill, *Red Man's America* (1953); and Harold E. Driver, *Indians of North America* (1961) put the Californians in the context of the continent.

George Wharton James, *Indian Basketry* (1904) deals with one culture trait. Another, the Indians' traditive literature, is sampled in Edward W. Gifford and Gwendoline H. Block, *Californian Indian Nights Entertainments* (1930); Jaime d'Angulo, *Indian Tales* (1953), stories collected from the Pit River Indians; and Theodora Kroeber, *The Inland Whale* (1959).

Theodora Kroeber, *Ishi in Two Worlds: A Biography of the Last Wild Indian in North America* (1961) and *Ishi, Last of His Tribe* (1964); W. W. Waterman, "Ishi, The Last Wild Indian," *Southern Workman*, 46 (1917), 528–37; Florence C. Shipek, ed., *The Autobiography of Delfina Cuero* (1968), which is about a twentieth century Diegueno; Burt W. and Ethel G. Aginsky, *Deep Valley* (1967), based on field work with the Pomo; and Charles L. McNichols, *Crazy Weather* (1944), a novel about the Mojave, reach into modern times. *The Indian Historian* (1968 on), a San Francisco publication, is alert to current issues as well as past experiences.

2. Explorers

Excellent brief narratives of the first Spanish activities in America are I. B. Richman, *The Spanish Conquerors* (1919) and E. G. Bourne, *Spain in America* (1904). S. E. Morison, *Admiral of the Ocean Sea* (1942) is a masterpiece on Columbus and the early exploration. On the campaign against the Aztecs two works stand out: *The Conquest of Mexico* (3 vols., 1843) by W. H. Prescott, one of the first great American historians, and *Historia verdadera de la conquista de México*, by one of Cortés' men, Bernal Díaz del Castillo. Díaz' *True History* is available in many translations, notably a five-volume edition by A. P. Maudslay (1908–16) and a poetic paraphrase by Archibald MacLeish, *Conquistador* (1932). On these and subsequent phases of imperial development consult C. H. Haring, *The Spanish Empire in America* (1947) and, if desirous of more emphasis on colonial life, H. I. Priestley, *The Coming of the White Man* (1929) and Bailey W. Diffie, *Latin American Civilization* (1945). See also H. E. Bolton,

Wider Horizons of American History (1939) and, on the post-conquest stabilization in Mexico, A. S. Aiton, *Antonio de Mendoza, First Viceroy of New Spain* (1927).

The whole sweep of northward searching is sketched in H. E. Bolton, *The Spanish Borderlands* (1921). Much is available on individual expeditions and explorers from Ponce de León across country to Coronado. Examples are: Morris Bishop, *The Odyssey of Cabeza de Vaca* (1933); Haniel Long, *The Power within Us* (1944); Cleve Hallenbeck, *Alvar Núñez Cabeza de Vaca* (1933) and *The Journey of Fray Marcos de Niza* (1949); Carl Saur, *The Road to Cíbola* (1932); A. Grove Day, *Coronado's Quest* (1940); H. E. Bolton, *Coronado* (1949); G. P. Hammond and Agapito Rey, eds., *Narratives of the Coronado Expedition* (1940).

On west coast exploration the most prolific scholar is Henry Raup Wagner. See his *Spanish Voyages to the Northwest Coast* (1929), consisting of Spanish texts, translations, and annotations, *Cartography of the Northwest Coast of America to the Year 1800* (2 vols., 1937), *Juan Rodríguez Cabrillo, Discoverer of the Coast of California* (1941), and *Sir Francis Drake's Voyage around the World* (1926). See also Donald C. Cutter, ed., *The California Coast* (1969) and Michael Mathes, ed., *California: Documentos para la historia de la demarcación comercial de California, 1583–1632* (1965). In 1937 and 1938 the California Historical Society brought out two special publications, *Drake's Plate of Brass,* including excerpts from the sources, and *Drake's Plate of Brass Authenticated,* the report of electrochemist Colin G. Fink. Debate on the location of Drake's landing resumed in *CHSQ* in 1957, 1962, and 1964. Archaeological exploration of the vicinity of Cermeño's landing is reported by Robert F. Heizer and Clement W. Meighan in *CHSQ,* 20 (1941), 315–28, and 31 (1952), 99–108.

J. Lloyd Mecham, *Francisco de Ibarra and Nueva Vizcaya* (1927) and Philip W. Powell, *Soldiers, Indians and Silver* (1952) deal with the northward advance of New Spain in the late sixteenth century. W. L. Schurz, *The Manila Galleon* (1939) is the first book on the Philippine-Mexican trade. Wagner's *Spanish Voyages* is the most informative on the Unamuno, Cermeño, and Vizcaíno voyages. Several volumes in the Quivira Society publications and in the Coronado Cuarto-Centennial series, both edited by G. P. Hammond, relate to the renewed interest in New Mexico and include Gilberto Espinosa's translation (1933) of a metrical history of the conquest, composed by one of Oñate's men, Gaspar Pérez de Villagrá, published at Alcalá in 1610. On the companion activities on the coast see W. Michael Mathes, *Vizcaíno and Spanish Expansion in the Pacific Ocean, 1580–1630* (1968).

3. Spanish Approaches

For perspective on the northern frontier of New Spain in the seventeenth and eighteenth centuries Herbert E. Bolton's essays in *Wider Horizons in American History* (1939) and his *Spanish Borderlands* (1921) are valuable. See also two collections of studies in his honor, *New Spain and the Anglo-American West* (2 vols., 1932) and *Greater America* (1945).

The soldiers and civilians who helped advance the frontier are known mainly through the efforts of the Jesuits, who were indefatigable chroniclers. Modern members of the order have been active in studying this history. For the advance into Sinaloa and beyond, Peter M. Dunne is the principal historian, represented by his *Pioneer Black Robes on the West Coast* (1940), *Pioneer Jesuits in Northern Mexico* (1944), and *Early Jesuit Missions in Tarahumara* (1948). William E. Shiels, *Gonzalo de Tapia, 1561–1594* (1934) is a biography of the earliest missionary on the Pacific slope. Andrés Pérez de Ribas, *Historia de los triumphos de Nuestra Santa Fee* (1645) continues the narrative.

On Kino the basic work is his own "Celestial Favors," translated by Herbert E. Bolton as *Kino's Historical Memoir of Pimería Alta* (2 vols., 1919). Bolton's *The Padre on Horseback* (1932) is an admiring sketch of Kino's career. R. K. Wyllys, *Pioneer Padre* (1935) gives more detail, but in turn is surpassed by Bolton, *The Rim of Christendom* (1936), a full-length, lifelike portrait of this most remarkable man.

On the Sonora frontier after Kino's time see Theodore E. Treutlein, *Pfefferkorn's Description of Sonora* (1949); George P. Hammond, "Pimería Alta after Kino's Time," *NMHR (New Mexico Historical Review)*, 4 (1929), 220–38; R. K. Wyllys, "Padre Luis Velarde's Relación of Pimería Alta," *NMHR*, 6 (1931), 111–57; Peter M. Dunne, *Juan Antonio Balthasar, Padre Visitador to the Sonora Frontier, 1744–1745* (1957); and Theodore E. Treutlein, *Missionary in Sonora: The Travel Reports of Joseph Och, 1755–1767* (1965).

Peter Gerhard, "Pearl Diving in Lower California, 1533–1830," *PHR*, 25 (1956), 239–49; Sanford Mosk, "The Cardona Company and the Pearl Fisheries of Lower California," *PHR*, 3 (1934), 50–61; and Peter Gerhard, *Pirates on the West Coast of New Spain* (1960) report intermittent activities. Charles N. Rudkin, *Father Kino at La Paz* (1952) relates to the Atondo expedition.

Miguel Venegas, *Noticia de la California* (3 vols., 1757) is the standard record of the peninsula missions; the actual writing is credited to another Jesuit, Andrés Marcos Burriel. Other general accounts are Francisco Javier Clavigero, *Storia della Callifornia* (1789), translated into English by Sara E. Lake and A. A. Gray, *The History of [Lower] California* (1937) and Constantino Bayle, *Historia de los descubrimientos y colonización de los padres de la Companía de Jesús de la Baja California* (1933).

Miguel Venegas' laudatory biography of the founder of the first peninsular missions, *Juan María de Salvatierra* (1754) has been translated by Marguerite Eyer Wilbur (1929). Francisco María Pícolo, *Informe del estado de la nueva christianidad de California* (1702) is a report on the first five years of the missions. Juan José Villavicencio, *Vida y virtudes de el venerable y apostólico padre Juan de Ugarte* (1852) eulogizes Salvatierra's successor. Sigismundo Taraval, *The Indian Uprising of Lower California, 1734–1737*, translated by Marguerite Eyer Wilbur, centers on a hectic period. The closing years of the Jesuit period are best described in Jacob Baegert, *Nachrichten von de amerikanischen Halbinsel californien* (1772), which is available in Spanish translation by Pedro R. Hendrichs (1942), and in English by M. M. Brandenburg and Carl L. Baumann (1952). The melancholy facts of declining Indian population are set forth in S. F. Cook, *The Extent and Significance of Disease among the Indians of Baja California, 1687–1733* (1937). For an overall view of the Jesuit period see Peter M. Dunne, *Black Robes in Lower California* (1952).

Dominican labors are reported in Luis Sales, *Noticias de la provincia de California* (1794) and an anthropogeographic study by Peveril Meigs, III, *The Dominican Mission Frontier of Lower California* (1935).

J. Ross Browne, *Sketch of the Settlement and Exploration of Lower California* (1869) and Albert W. North, *The Mother of California* (1908) and *Camp and Camino in Lower California* (1910) are popular descriptions. A more vivid picture of life in the peninsula after the mission period is Antonio de Fierro Blanco [Walter Nordhoff], *The Journey of the Flame* (1933, 1955), which purports to be reminiscence but rests on field work and recent research.

On the adjudication of the Pious Fund see *Transcript of Record of Proceedings* (1902) and *United States* vs. *Mexico, Report of Jackson H. Ralston* (1902). Kenneth M. Johnson, *The Pious Fund* (1963) is a summary analysis.

4. Outpost of Spain

The immediate background for the occupation of Alta California is delineated in Herbert I. Priestley, *José de Gálvez, Visitador-General of New Spain* (1916). Charles E. Chapman, *The Founding of Spanish California* (1916) analyzes the problems of frontier advance from the 1680's to the 1770's. See also I. B. Richman, *California under Spain and Mexico* (1911). These volumes were pioneers in drawing on the resources of the Spanish and Mexican archives. Original narratives of 1769–70 written by Portolá, Costansó, Vilá, and Fages appear in the *Publications* of the Academy of Pacific Coast History, 1–2 (1910–11). Herbert E. Bolton, *Fray Juan Crespi, Missionary Explorer* (1927) and Douglas E. Watson, *The Spanish Occupation of California* (1934) are mainly documentary. The Canizares diary of the Rivera party from Velicatá to San Diego in 1769, trans. by Virginia E. Thickens and Margaret Mollins, appeared serially in *CHSQ*, 31 (1952), 109–24, 261–70, 343–54. Theodore E. Treutlein reassesses the evidence in "The Portolá Expedition of 1769–1770," *CHSQ*, 47 (1968), 291–314, and *San Francisco Bay, Discovery and Colonization, 1769–1776* (1968).

Francisco Palóu, *Noticias de la Nueva California* is the major compendium of primary material on the first dozen years of Spanish California. Completed in 1783, it was published in Spanish in 1857 and 1874 and in English translation by Herbert E. Bolton as *Historical Memoirs of New California* (4 vols., 1926). Palóu's *Junípero Serra* (1787), translated by C. S. Williams (1913) and by Maynard J. Geiger (1955), is the earliest California biography. The story of Serra's life has been capably sketched in Abigail H. Fitch, *Junípero Serra* (1914); Agnes Repplier, *Junípero Serra, Pioneer Colonist of California* (1933); Theodore Maynard, *The Long Road of Father Serra* (1954); and 'Omer Engelbert, *The Last of the Conquistadors* (1956). Far more detailed are Charles J. G. Maximin Piette, *Evocation de Junípero Serra, fondateur de la Californie* (1946) and *Le Secret de Junípero Serra* (2 vols.,

1949). The most satisfactory, though doubtless not the ultimate biography of Serra is Maynard J. Geiger, *The Life and Times of Fray Junípero Serra* (2 vols., 1959). On the mission beginnings and on every phase of their history see Zephyrin Engelhardt, *The Missions and Missionaries of California* (4 vols., 1908–15). Engelhardt also wrote separate volumes on most of the individual missions.

5. Strengthening the Colony

Several of the works cited in the preceding section are rich in materials for the ensuing years, particularly Palou's *Noticias* and *Serra,* and Chapman's *Founding of Spanish California* and *History of California*. Bernard E. Bobb, *The Viceregency of Antonio María Bucareli in New Spain* (1962) takes issue with Chapman's high praise of Bucareli as a positive force. *La administración de D. Frey Antonio María de Bucareli y Ursúa* (2 vols., 1936) is a documentary. Michael E. Thurman, *The Naval Department of San Blas* (1967) follows up one of Bucareli's contributions. John Galvin, *The Coming of Justice to California* (1963) and Sidney B. Brinckerhoff and Odie B. Faulk, *Lancers for the King* (1965) reproduce the rules and regulations for frontier presidios issued in 1772.

Herbert E. Bolton, *Anza's California Expeditions* (5 vols., 1930) is the complete record of the opening and use of the trail from Sonora. The first volume, reprinted as *Outpost of Empire* (1931), narrates the two expeditions and the founding of San Francisco. Alan K. Brown, "Rivera at San Francisco," *CHSQ,* 41 (1962), 325–41, reproduces the journal of Rivera's exploration in 1774. Z. S. Eldredge, *The Beginnings of San Francisco* (2 vols., 1912) is an older work. Elliott Coues, *On the Trail of a Spanish Pioneer* (2 vols., 1900) and John Galvin, *A Record of Travels in Arizona and California, 1775–1776* (1967) center on Francisco Garcés. Alfred B. Thomas, *Forgotten Frontiers* (1932) and J. N. Bowman and Robert F. Heizer, *Anza and the Northwest Frontier of New Spain* (1967) follow Anza's career after his departure from California.

On the province in 1775 see Herbert I. Priestley, *A Historical, Political and Natural Description of California by Pedro Fages* (1937). Benito de la Sierra, "The Hezeta Expedition to the Northwest Coast in 1775," *CHSQ,* 9 (1930), 201–42, and Francisco Antonio Maurelle, *Journal of a Voyage in 1775 To Explore the Coast of America Northward of California* (1781) concern what was then thought of as an extension of California. Alfred B. Thomas, *Teodoro de Croix* (1941) supplies background on the Yuma Massacre. Herbert I. Priestley, "The Colorado River Campaign, 1781–1782," *Publications* of the Academy of Pacific Coast History, 3 (1913), translates a Fages diary on the aftermath.

A minimum has been written about the work of Felipe de Neve, but the 1931 *Publication* of the Historical Society of Southern California contains the basic materials on the founding of the pueblo of Los Angeles. See also Laurance L. Hill, *La Reina: Los Angeles in Three Centuries* (1929) and W. W. Robinson, *Los Angeles from the Days of the Pueblo* (1959).

6. Local Annals

Bancroft deals generously with these latter years of Spanish control, devoting to them half of the first volume and the entire second volume of his *History of California*, a full thousand pages. Engelhardt's account is almost as voluminous. Chapman, *History of California* and Richman, *California under Spain and Mexico* are detailed. Bancroft, *California Pastoral* (1888) plays up the romance of the period, as do Nellie V. Sánchez, *Spanish Arcadia* (1929) and Alberta Johnson Denis, *Spanish Alta California* (1927). Of dozens of rhapsodic tributes to the missions George Wharton James, *In and Out of the Old Missions of California* (1916); Charles Francis Saunders and J. Smeaton Chase, *The California Padres and Their Missions* (1915); John A. Berger, *The Franciscan Missions of California* (1948); Will Connell, *The Missions of California* (1941); and Paul C. Johnson, *The California Missions: A Pictorial History* (1964) are representative. Kurt Baer, *Architecture of the California Missions* (1958) and *Paintings and Sculpture at Mission Santa Barbara* (1955) and Ruth Mahood, *A Gallery of California Mission Paintings* [by Edwin Deakin] (1966) concentrate on the structures.

Descriptions by visitors to the province are found in Jean Francois Galaup de la Pérouse, *Voyage de la Pérouse autour du monde* (4 vols., 1797); Gilbert Chinard, *Le voyage de Lapérouse sur les côtes de l'Alaska et la Californie* (1937); Donald Cutter, *Malaspina in California* (1960); George Vancouver, *A Voyage of Discovery to the North Pacific Ocean* (3 vols., 1798); Marguerite Eyer Wilbur, *Vancouver in California* (1954); William Shaler, *Journal of a Voyage* (ed. Lindley Bynum, 1935); and Louis Choris, *Voyage pittoresque autour du monde* (1822), translated with some additions in August C. Mahr, *The Visit of the* Rurik *to San Francisco in 1816* (1932).

The new stirrings of activities to the north are related in Henry R. Wagner, *Spanish Explorations in Juan de Fuca Strait* (1933) and W. R. Manning, *The Nootka Sound Controversy* (1905). T. C. Russell, *The Rezanov Voyage to Nueva California in 1806* (1926) and *Langsdorff's Narrative of the Rezanov Voyage to Nueva California in 1806* (1927), Gertrude Atherton, *Rezanov* (1906), and Hector Chevigny, *Lost Empire, The Life and Adventures of Nikiolai Petrovich Rezanov* (1937) concern the first Russian visits to California. The Russian establishment above Bodega Bay is dealt with in a special issue of *CHSQ* for September, 1933.

Jeanne Van Nostrand, *Monterey, Adobe Capital of California* (1968) is a pictorial, complemented in the south by Richard F. Pourade, *Time of the Bells* (1961). On rancho beginnings see W. W. Robinson, *Land in California* (1948) and Robert H. Becker, *Diseños of California Ranchos* (1964). The third civilian settlement is described in Florian Guest, "The Establishment of the Villa de Branciforte," *CHSQ*, 41 (1962), 29–50.

On the Bouchard episode, Peter Corney, *Voyages in the Northern Pacific* (1896), though by a participant, is not altogether accurate. More circumstantial accounts are Ricardo Caillet-Bois, *Nuestros corsarios: Brown y Bouchard en el Pacífico, 1815–1816* (1930) and Lewis Bealer, "Bouchard in the Islands of the Pacific," *PHR*, 4 (1935), 328–42.

7. A Mexican Province

The works of Bancroft, Sánchez, Denis, Richman, and Chapman, earlier cited, apply also to the Mexican regime. Gertrude Atherton, *The Splendid Idle Forties* (1902) is another glowing description. Alexander Forbes, *California, A History of Upper and Lower California* (1839), the first book on California written in English, reported on the province from the author's vantage point in Mexico. Visitors to California became more numerous. Their reports include A. Duhaut-Cilly, *Voyage autour du monde* (2 vols., 1834–35) [its California portion is translated by Charles F. Carter in *CHSQ*, 8–9 (1929–30)]; Frederick W. Beechey, *Narrative of a Voyage to the Pacific* (2 vols., 1831); George Simpson, *Narrative of a Journey Round the World* (2 vols., 1847); the California portion of Abel du Petit Thouars' narrative translated by Charles N. Rudkin, *Voyage of the Venus: Sojourn in California* (1956); Marguerite Eyer Wilbur's translation, *Duflot de Mofras' Travels on the Pacific Coast* (2 vols., 1937); and Charles Wilkes, *Narrative of the United States Exploring Expedition* (5 vols., 1844). Foreigners who came to trade or to settle also contributed important descriptions. Richard Henry Dana, *Two Years Before the Mast* (1840) and Alfred Robinson, *Life in California* (1846) head this class; many others are mentioned in the next two sections of this bibliography.

The most thorough exposition is an unpublished dissertation by George Tays, "Revolutionary California: The Political History of California during the Mexican Period" (Berkeley, 1932). See also his "Mariano Guadalupe Vallejo and Sonoma—a Biography and a History," six installments in *CHSQ*, 16–17 (1937–38); Marion L. Lothrop, "The Indian Campaigns of General M. G. Vallejo," *Quarterly of the Society of California Pioneers,* 9 (1932), 161–205; Myrtle M. McKittrick, *Vallejo, Son of California* (1944); Guadalupe Vallejo, "Ranch and Mission Days in Alta California," *Century,* 41 (1890–91), 183–92; Terry E. Stephenson, *Don Bernardo de Yorba* (1941); George L. Harding, *Agustín V. Zamorano, Statesman, Soldier, Craftsman, and California's First Printer* (1934); José Arnaz, "Memoirs of a Merchant," *Touring Topics,* 20 (Sept.–Oct. 1928); Charles F. Lummis, *Flowers of Our Lost Romance* (1929); Robert G. Cleland, *The Place Called Sespe* (1940) and *The Cattle on a Thousand Hills* (1941).

J. N. Bowman, "The Resident Neophytes of the California Missions, 1769–1834," *SCQ*, 40 (1958), 138–48 and "The Number of California Indians Baptised during the Mission Period," *SCQ*, 42 (1960), 273–77, present statistical tables. Sherbourne F. Cook, *The Conflict between the California Indian and White Civilization* (1943) is an analysis of population decline. Gerald J. Geary, *The Secularization of the California Missions* (1934) is a fair statement from the viewpoint of the churchmen. Manuel P. Servín, "The Secularization of the California Missions: A Reappraisal," *SCQ*, 47 (1965), 133–49 is considerably more critical of the missionary program, and Martha Voght, "Shamans and Padres, The Religion of the Southern California Mission Indians," *PHR*, 36 (1967), 363–73, finds that the religious impact of the missions was ephemeral. C. Alan Hutchinson, *Frontier Settlement in Mexican California* (1969) centers on the Padrés-Híjar colonization project but is informative on much else.

8. Hide Traders and Mountain Men

The classics on the hide trade are Richard Henry Dana, *Two Years Before the Mast* (1840), edited, with passages restored and other additions, by John H. Kemble (2 vols., 1964), and Alfred Robinson, *Life in California* (1846). William D. Phelps, *Fore and Aft* (1871) is by another sailor; Doyce B. Nunis, Jr., ed., *The California Diary of Faxon Dean Atherton, 1836–1839* (1964) is by another of the agents ashore. George P. Hammond, ed., *The Larkin Papers* (10 vols., 1951–66) is a great collection of documents on trade and other topics.

Adele Ogden deals with several parts of the hide trade in "Hides and Tallow: McCulloch, Hartnell and Company, 1822–1828," *CHSQ*, 6 (1927), 254–64; "Boston Hide Droghers along the California Shores," *CHSQ*, 8 (1929), 289–305; "Alfred Robinson, New England Merchant in Mexican California," *CHSQ*, 23 (1944), 193–218; and "Business Letters of Alfred Robinson," *CHSQ*, 23 (1944), 301–34. Californians tell of the trade in José Arnaz, "Memoirs of a Merchant," *Touring Topics*, 20 (Sept.–Oct. 1928) and Prudencia Higuera, "Trading with the Americans," *Century*, 41 (1890), 192–93. Susanna B. Dakin, *The Lives of William Hartnell* (1949) and William Heath Davis, *Sixty Years in California* (1899), reissued as *Seventy-five Years in California* (1929) with editing by Harold A. Small (1967), are broadly informative. More specialized is D. Mackenzie Brown, ed., *China Trade Days in California, Selected Letters from the Thompson Papers* (1947). On the trade with Mexico see Eleanor Lawrence, "Mexican Trade between Santa Fe and Los Angeles, 1830–1848," *CHSQ*, 10 (1931), 27–39; J. J. Hill, "The Old Spanish Trail," *HAHR*, 4 (1921), 444–73; and B. D. Wilson, "Observations on Early Days in California and New Mexico," *HSSCP*, 16 (1934), 74–150.

Of the general works on the fur trade, the one most relevant to California is Robert G. Cleland, *This Reckless Breed of Men* (1950). First-hand material on the earliest entrances are H. C. Dale, *The Ashley-Smith Explorations* (1918); Maurice S. Sullivan, *The Travels of Jedediah Smith* (1934); and *The Personal Narrative of James O. Pattie* (1831), a vivid adventure tale, not always to be taken literally. Charles L. Camp, *George C. Yount and His Chronicles of the West* (1966) describes a later entry from New Mexico. Two members of the Walker party left accounts: *Narratives of the Adventures of Zenas Leonard* (1839; ed. John C. Ewers, 1959) and William H. Ellison, ed., *The Life and Adventures of George Nidever* (1937).

Biographies include: Dale L. Morgan, *Jedediah Smith and the Opening of the West* (1953); Maurice S. Sullivan, *The Life of Jedediah Smith* (1936); Stanley Vestal, *Kit Carson: The Happy Warrior of the Old West* (1928); John E. Sunder, *Bill Sublette, Mountain Man* (1959); LeRoy R. Hafen and W. J. Ghent, *Broken Hand, The Life Story of Thomas Fitzpatrick* (1931); Douglas S. Watson, *West Wind, The Life Story of Joseph Reddeford Walker* (1934); T. D. Bonner, *The Life and Adventures of James P. Beckwourth* (1856); Charles Kelly, *Old Greenwood* (1936; 1965); and Joseph J. Hill, "Ewing Young in the Fur Trade of the American Southwest," *OHQ*, 24 (1923), 1–35. Francis P. Farquhar, "Explorations of the Sierra Nevada," *CHSQ*, 4 (1925),

3–58 traces the Sierra crossings. Alice B. Maloney, ed., *Fur Brigade to the Bonaventura* (1945) and John S. Galbraith, *The Hudson's Bay Company as an Imperial Factor, 1821–1869* (1957) bear on British activities.

9. Pioneer Settlers

As an appendix to volumes 2 to 5 of his *History of California*, Hubert Howe Bancroft inserted a "Pioneer Register," a Who's Who of Californians to 1848, with an almost complete roll call and thumbnail sketches of many persons. Glen and Muir Dawson in 1964 reissued this *Register of Pioneer Inhabitants of California* as a book. Many of these individuals appear in *The Larkin Papers*.

Reuben L. Underhill, *From Cowhides to Golden Fleece* (1939) is a biography of Larkin intended for the general reader. Robert J. Parker, *Chapters in the Early Life of Thomas Oliver Larkin* (1939) is fragmentary. Susanna B. Dakin does considerably better by two other residents in *The Lives of William Hartnell* (1949) and *Scotch Paisano, Hugo Reid's Life in California* (1939), Pearl P. Stamps, "Abel Stearns, California Pioneer," *Grizzly Bear* (May–August, 1926) and Robert G. Cleland, *The Cattle on a Thousand Hills* touch more lightly on the life of Abel Stearns. Andrew F. Rolle, *An American in California* (1956) covers the life of William Heath Davis. William H. Ellison and Francis Price, *The Life and Adventures in California of Don Agustin Janssens, 1834–1856* (1953) is the narrative of a Belgian who came with the Híjar-Padrés expedition. J. J. Hill, *History of Warner's Ranch and Its Environs* (1927) is, in passing, a life of a former fur man, J. J. Warner. Camp performed a similar service to George Young, and Ellison to George Nidever.

There are several books on Sutter: Douglas S. Watson's edition of his *Diary* (1932); Edwin G. Gudde's editing of his dictation to Bancroft (1936); Julian Dana's journalistic *Sutter of California* (1936); and James P. Zollinger, *Sutter, The Man and His Empire* (1939). George D. Lyman, *John Marsh, Pioneer* (1930) is a well-rounded biography.

On the overland pioneers there is general coverage in W. J. Ghent, *The Road to Oregon* (1929); Owen C. Coy, *The Great Trek* (1931); and much detail in tracing the routes in Irene D. Paden, *In the Wake of the Prairie Schooner* (1943) and *Prairie Schooner Detours* (1949). John Bidwell, *A Journey to California in 1841* (1842), ed. Francis P. Farquhar (1964), is supplemented by Nicholas "Cheyenne" Dawson, *California in '41, Texas in '51* (1894) and Rockwell D. Hunt's scholarly and laudatory *John Bidwell, Prince of California Pioneers* (1942).

On the promotional literature see Thomas Jefferson Farnham, *Travels in the Californias, and Scenes in the Pacific Ocean* (1844); Lansford W. Hastings, *The Emigrant's Guide to Oregon and California* (1845); and Thomas F. Andrews, "The Controversial Hastings Overland Guide: A Reassessment," *PHR*, 37 (1968), 21–34. Other pioneer settlers are presented in Charles L. Camp, ed., *James Clyman, American Frontiersman* (1928; enlarged edition, 1960); Ruby Swartzlow, "Peter Lassen, Northern California's Trail-blazer," *CHSQ*, 18 (1939), 291–314; and John Caughey, "Don Benito Wilson," *HLQ*, II (1939), 285–300.

Edwin Bryant, *What I Saw in California* (1848); J. Q. Thornton, *Ore-*

gon and California (2 vols., 1849); and Heinrich Lienhard, From St. Louis to Sutter's Fort, 1846, trans. by Erwin G. and Elisabeth K. Gudde (1961), report on successful overland expeditions in 1846, a year covered in detail, in Dale L. Morgan, Overland in 1846 (2 vols., 1963) and Bernard De Voto, The Year of Decision, 1846 (1943). For the migration of 1847 see Douglas M. McMurtrie, ed., Overland to California in 1847, Letters . . . by Chester Ingersoll (1937) and Charles L. Camp, "William Alexander Trubody and the Overland Pioneers of 1847," CHSQ, 16 (1937), 122–43.

The stark tragedy of the Donner party dominates. Charles F. McGlashan, History of the Donner Party (1879) is the product of a patient assembling of information; George R. Stewart, Jr., Ordeal by Hunger (1936; 1960) is superior. Eliza P. Houghton, The Expedition of the Donner Party and Its Tragic Fate (1911) is by one of the Donner children who, as a four-year-old survived the ordeal. It is based on traditive material more than on her own recollections. Original testimony includes "Diary of Patrick Breen," APCHP, I (1910), 269–84; George McKinstry, Jr., Thrilling and Tragic Journal (1917); and Virginia Murphy Reed, "Across the Plains in the Donner Party," Century, 42 (1891), 409–26.

10. American Take-over

Robert G. Cleland, "The Early Sentiment for Annexation of California," SHQ, 8 (1915) may be read in association with John A. Hawgood, "The Pattern of Yankee Infiltration in Mexican Alta California," PHR, 27 (1958), 27–38 and First and Last Consul: Thomas Oliver Larkin and the Americanization of California (1962); Norman A. Graebner, Empire on the Pacific (1955); E. I. McCormac, James K. Polk (1922); and Charles G. Sellers, James K. Polk, Continentalist (1966). George B. Brooke, "The Vest Pocket War of Commodore Jones," PHR, 31 (1962), 217–33 describes the abortive first effort. Rival aspirations are treated in E. D. Adams, "British Interest in California," AHR, 14 (1919), 744–63 and A. P. Nasatir, "The French Consulate in California," CHSQ, 11–13 (1932–34), passim.

Frémont's expeditions are well represented in his Report of the Exploring Expedition . . . to Oregon and North California (1846); Allan Nevins, ed., Narratives of Exploration and Adventure (1956); Charles Preuss, Exploring with Frémont, trans. by Erwin G. and Elisabeth K. Gudde (1958); Charles H. Carey, ed., The Journals of Theodore Talbot (1931); S. N. Carvalho, Incidents of Travel and Adventure in the Far West (1857); and Frederic S. Dellenbaugh, Frémont and '49 (1914). His role in the conquest of California has been the subject of a many-sided debate. With the exception of Cardinal L. Goodwin in his John Charles Frémont, An Explanation of His Career (1930), biographers have been lavish in praise. Smucker, Upham, and Bigelow set the pattern in their campaign biographies in 1856; Herbert Bashford and Harr Wagner used the title A Man Unafraid (1927); and Allan Nevins' titles were Frémont, The West's Greatest Adventurer (2 vols., 1928) and Frémont, Pathmarker of the West (1939). Irving Stone reflected the same enthusiasm in his book on Jessie Frémont, Immortal Wife (1944). Frémont's Memoirs of My Life (1887) and Jessie Benton Frémont, Souvenirs of My Time (1887) and Far West Sketches (1890) were perhaps unconsciously self-justificatory. Beginning with John S. Hittell, A History of the

City of San Francisco and Incidentally of the State of California (1878), Bancroft, Theodore H. Hittell, and Josiah Royce, *California* (1886), historians have been less entranced with his performance in California. See also *Proceedings of the Court Martial in the Trial of Frémont* (1848).

On the Bear Flag revolt see Werner H. Marti, *Messenger of Destiny: The California Adventures, 1846–1847, of Archibald H. Gillespie* (1960); William B. Ide, *Who Conquered California?* (1880); Fred B. Rogers, *Bear Flag Lieutenant: The Life Story of Henry L. Ford* (1951) and *William Brown Ide, Bear Flagger* (1962); John A. Hussey, "New Light on the Original Bear Flag," *CHSQ*, 31 (1952), 205–17; and John A. Hawgood, "John C. Fremont and the Bear Flag Revolution," *University of Birmingham Journal,* 7 (1959), 80–100 and *SCQ*, 44 (1963), 67–96.

The general histories of the war with Mexico say little about the California campaigns. The Navy's operations are represented in Fred B. Rogers, ed., *A Navy Surgeon in California* [Marius Duvall] (1956), *Filings from an Old Saw* [Joseph T. Downey] (1956), and *Montgomery and the Portsmouth* (1958); Howard Lamar, ed., *The Cruise of the Portsmouth* [Joseph T. Downey] (1958); John H. Kemble, ed., "Lieutenant Tunis A. M. Craven's Journal on the *Dale*," *CHSQ*, 20 (1941), 193–234; Thomas C. Lancey, "The Cruise of the *Dale*," serialized in the San Jose *Pioneer* (1879–81); and 28 sketches by William H. Meyers, gunner on the *Dale*, in *Naval Sketches of the War in California* (1939). William H. Ellison, "San Juan to Cahuenga," *PHR*, 27 (1958), 245–61 covers the experiences of Frémont's Battalion.

On the progress of Kearny's Army of the West, see Dwight L. Clarke, *Stephen Watts Kearny, Soldier of the West* (1961); Ross Calvin, *Lieutenant Emory Reports* (1951), reproduced from William H. Emory, *Notes of a Military Reconnaissance* (1848); George W. Ames, Jr., ed., *A Doctor Comes to California, The Diary of John S. Griffin* (1943); and Arthur Woodward, *Lances at San Pascual* (1948). Daniel Tyler, *A Concise History of the Mormon Battalion* (1881); Henry Standage, *The March of the Mormon Battalion* (1928); and Francis D. Clark, *The First Regiment of New York Volunteers* (1882) account for the reinforcements. Peter Gerhard, "Baja California in the Mexican War," *PHR*, 15 (1946), 418–24 and Eugene Keith Chamberlin, "Nicholas Trist and Baja California," *PHR*, 32 (1963), 49–63 discuss the peninsula during the war and the peace.

11. Gold

Materials on the gold rush are abundant, and almost all of them are specialized. The most comprehensive account is John W. Caughey, *Gold Is the Cornerstone* (1948). Joseph Henry Jackson, *Gold Rush Album* (1949) is a picture book viewing the subject in the round. Hubert Howe Bancroft, *California Inter Pocula* (1888), inspired in title, deals with most phases, as do Stewart Edward White, *The Forty-niners* (1918); Valeska Bari, ed., *The Course of Empire* (1931); and John W. Caughey, ed., *Rushing for Gold* (1949).

California Gold Discovery, Centennial Papers on the Time, the Site, and Artifacts (1947), a special publication of the California Historical Society, assembles reports ranging from contemporary to archaeological; Rodman W.

Paul, *The California Gold Discovery* (1966) is a meticulous analysis of the evidence. Theressa Gay, *James W. Marshall* (1967) is a study in depth of the discoverer. Records of 1848 include E. Gould Buffum, *Six Months in the Gold Mines* (1850; 1959); James H. Carson, *Early Recollections of the Mines* (1852); William McCollum, *California as I Saw It* (1850; 1960); William R. Ryan, *Personal Adventures in Upper and Lower California* (2 vols., 1851); and Erwin G. Gudde, *Bigler's Chronicle of the West* (1962). Elizabeth L. Egenhoff, *The Elephant as They Saw It* (1949) features contemporary statements and pictures on gold mining.

Joseph E. Ware, *The Emigrants' Guide to California* (1849; ed. John W. Caughey, 1932) is the best of the two dozen guidebooks prepared for the forty-niners.

Octavius T. Howe, *Argonauts of '49* (1923), though limited to companies from Massachusetts, is the nearest approach to a monograph on the Cape Horn argonauts. For briefer treatments see Oscar Lewis, *Sea Routes to the Gold Fields* (1949) and the appropriate chapter in Rydell, *Cape Horn to the Pacific*. Carolyn Hale Ross, ed., *The Log of a Forty-niner* (1923); Franklin A. Buck, *A Yankee Trader in the Gold Rush* (1930); Enos Christman, *One Man's Gold* (1930); and Robert S. Fletcher, *Eureka: From Cleveland by Ship to California* (1959) are representative accounts.

On the Panama route see Bayard Taylor, *Eldorado, or Adventures in the Path of Empire* (2 vols., 1850); Carl Meyer, *Nach dem Sacramento* (1855; trans. by Ruth Frey Axe, 1938); Charles A. Barker, ed., *Memoirs of Elisha Oscar Crosby* (1945); and John W. Caughey, ed., *Seeing the Elephant, Letters of R. R. Taylor, Forty-niner* (1951). John H. Kemble, *The Panama Route* (1943) is authoritative on the steamers.

The saga of the overland march of the gold seekers is best read in some of their journals, notably, Alonzo Delano, *Life on the Plains and among the Diggings* (1854); Georgia Willis Read and Ruth Gaines, eds., *Gold Rush: The Journals, Drawings, and Other Papers of J. Goldsborough Bruff* (2 vols., 1944); David M. Potter, ed., *Trail to California: The Overland Journal of Vincent Geiger and Wakeman Bryarly* (1945); *Autobiography of Isaac J. Wistar* (2 vols., 1914); Sarah Royce, *A Frontier Lady* (1932); Walker D. Wyman, *California Emigrant Letters* (1952); Howard L. Scamehorn, *The Buckeye Rovers in the Gold Rush* (1965); Elisha D. Perkins, *Gold Rush Diary* (1967), ed. Thomas D. Clark; and Dale L. Morgan, ed., *The Overland Diary of James Avery Pritchard* (1959). With the Pritchard diary Morgan supplies a table of 100 forty-niner diarists passing waypoints along the trail. Excellent recent studies are Irene D. Paden, *The Wake of the Prairie Schooner* (1943) and *Prairie Schooner Detours* (1947); Owen C. Coy, *The Great Trek* (1931); and, with exaggerated drama, Archer B. Hulbert, *Forty-niners* (1931).

Southwestern offshoots from the main trail are described in W. L. Manly, *Death Valley in '49* (1894); John W. Caughey, "Southwest from Salt Lake in 1849," *PHR*, 6 (1937), 143–81; John G. Ellenbecker, *The Jayhawkers of Death Valley* (1938); and Carl I. Wheat, "Trailing the Forty-niners through Death Valley," *SCB*, 24 (1939), 74–108. Still more southerly routes are described in Ralph P. Bieber, *Southern Trails to California in 1849* (1937); Grant Foreman, *Marcy and the Gold Seekers* (1939); H. M. T. Powell, *The Santa Fe Trail to California* (1931); Charles Pancoast, *A Quaker Forty-niner* (1930); John W.

Audubon, *Audubon's Western Journal* (1906); and George W. B. Evans, *Mexican Gold Trail* (1945).

Rodman W. Paul, *California Gold* (1947) is a masterly analysis of the miner at work. Chauncey L. Canfield, *The Diary of a Forty-niner* (1906), though fictional in plot, is graphic on mining methods. "How We Get Gold in California," *Harper's*, 20 (1860), 598–616 is amplified and extended by Otis E. Young, Jr., *How They Dug the Gold* (1967). See also Buffum, Delano, Buck, and Christman, and a few other travel accounts that carry on into the diggings, and J. D. Borthwick, *Three Years in California* (1857); Vicente Pérez de Rosales, *Recuerdos del pasado* (1890), trans. by Edwin S. Morby as *California Adventure* (1947); John Steele, *In Camp and Cabin* (1928); Frank Marryat, *Mountains and Molehills* (1855); John W. Caughey, ed., "Life in California in 1849, as Described in the Journal of George F. Kent," *CHSQ*, 20 (1941), 26–46; Dale L. Morgan and James R. Scobie, eds., *William Perkins' Journal of Life at Sonora, 1849–1852* (1964); Friedrich Gerstäcker, *Scenes of Life in California*, trans. by George Cosgrave (1942); and Carvel Collins, *Sam Ward in the Gold Rush* (1949). The classic description is in the "Shirley Letters," contributed to the *Pioneer* in 1854 by Louisa Amelia Knapp Smith Clapp and several times reissued in book form. Rodman W. Paul, "In Search of 'Dame Shirley,'" *PHR*, 33 (1964), 127–46 draws together the fugitive details about the author. G. Ezra Dane, *Ghost Town* (1941) is a capital recounting of the foibles of the gold miners.

Charles H. Shinn, *Mining Camps* (1885) emphasizes the development of law and government. Richard Henry Morefield, "Mexicans in the California Mines, 1848–53," *CHSQ*, 35 (1956), 37–46 and David V. DuFault, "The Chinese in the Mining Camps of California, 1848–1870," *SCQ*, 41 (1959), 155–70 relate to two minorities. Shirley H. Weber, *Schliemann's First Visit to America, 1850–1851* (1942) and George P. Hammond, ed., *Digging for Gold without a Shovel: The Letters of Daniel Wadsworth Coit* (1967) describe the experiences of two gold buyers.

12. Mushrooming Economy

The first six chapters of the final volume of Bancroft's *History of California* pertain to this economic transformation. See also Robert G. Cleland and Osgood Hardy, *March of Industry* (1929). There are excellent local histories, among them Owen C. Coy, *The Humboldt Bay Region, 1850–1875* (1929) and George W. and Helen P. Beattie, *Heritage of the Valley* [San Bernardino] (1939). See also the county histories, such as those published by Thompson and West about 1880.

Of the volumes compiled expressly to describe California's economy, the most successful was John S. Hittell, *The Resources of California* (1863), which ran through seven editions. Hittell also assembled a handbook on *Mining in the Pacific States of North America* (1868). Titus Fey Cronise, *The Natural Wealth of California* (1868), even bulkier than Hittell's *Resources*, rivaled it in popularity, while on the West in general, J. Ross Browne, *Resources of the Pacific Slope* (1869) was an alternative choice.

The state's banking history is detailed in Ira B. Cross, *Financing an Empire* (4 vols., 1927), while biographies of William Ralston by Cecil J. Tilton (1935), Julian Dana (1936), and George D. Lyman (1937) summarize the problems and progress of San Francisco. See also Frank Soulé, John H. Gihon, and James Nisbet, *The Annals of San Francisco* (1855).

On Los Angeles there is information in Harris Newmark, *Sixty Years in Southern California* (1916); Benjamin Hayes, *Pioneer Notes* (1922); Horace Bell, *Reminiscences of a Ranger* (1881) and *On the Old West Coast* (1930); J. J. Warner, Benjamin Hayes, and J. P. Widney, *An Historical Sketch of Los Angeles County* (1876); and particularly in William B. Rice, *The Los Angeles Star, 1851–1864* (1947).

Kenneth M. Johnson, *The New Almaden Quicksilver Mine* (1963); Robert L. Kelley, "Forgotten Giant: The Hydraulic Gold Mining Industry in California," *PHR*, 32 (1954), 343–56 and *Gold vs. Grain: The Hydraulic Mining Controversy in California's Sacramento Valley* (1960); H. Brett Melendy, "Two Men and a Mill: John Dolbeer, William Carson, and the Redwood Lumber Industry of California," *CHSQ*, 38 (1959), 59–71; John E. Baur, "Early Days and California Years of John Percival Jones," *SHQ*, 44 (1962), 97–131; Patricia M. Bauer, "The Beginnings of Tanning in California," *CHSQ*, 33 (1954), 59–72; and Lloyd C. Miltare, *Salted Tories: The Story of the Whaling Fleets of San Francisco* (1960) follow the rise of selected industries.

On the agricultural development in the first American decades see the summary chapter by Frank Adams in C. B. Hutchison, ed., *California Agriculture* (1946); Paul W. Gates, *California Ranchos and Farms, 1846–1862* (1967); E. T. Treadwell's rather superficial biography of Henry Miller, *The Cattle King* (1931); Vincent P. Carosso, *The California Wine Industry, 1830–1895* (1951); Walton Bean, "James Warren and the Beginnings of Agricultural Institutions in California," *PHR*, 13 (1944), 361–75; John W. Caughey, "Don Benito Wilson," *HLQ*, II (1939), 285–300; and Robert G. Cleland, *The Cattle on a Thousand Hills*. Less typical activities are the subjects of Richard H. Dillon, *California Trail Herd, The 1850 Missouri-to-California Journal of Cyrus C. Loveland* (1961) and Nelson Klose, "California's Experimentation in Sericulture," *PHR*, 30 (1961), 213–27 and "Louis Prevost and the Silk Industry at San Jose," *CHSQ*, 43 (1964), 309–17. Rodman W. Paul deals with a more substantial subject in "The Great California Grain War: The Grangers Challenge the Wheat King," *PHR*, 27 (1958), 331–49 and "The Wheat Trade between California and the United Kingdom," *MVHR*, 45 (1958), 391–412.

The glories of the Comstock are recorded in Mark Twain, *Roughing It* (1872); by his crony William Wright, who wrote under the pen name Dan DeQuille, in *The Big Bonanza* (1876) and *A History of the Comstock Mines* (1889); and in Charles H. Shinn, *The Story of the Mine* (1896). A later flood of writing includes Swift Paine, *The Big Bonanza* (1931); George D. Lyman, *The Saga of the Comstock Lode* (1934); Wells Drury, *An Editor on the Comstock Lode* (1939); Grant H. Smith, *The History of the Comstock Lode* (1943); Oscar Lewis, *Silver Kings* (1947); Duncan Emrich, ed., *Comstock Bonanza* (1950); Lucius Beebe and Charles Clegg, *Legends of the Comstock Lode* (1950); and Zeke Daniels and Ben Christy, *The Life and Death of Julia C. Bulette* (1958).

13. Political Experiment

For broad views of politics in this formative period see Josiah Royce, *California, from the Conquest in 1846 to the Second Vigilance Committee* (1886) and Earl Pomeroy, "California, 1846–1860: Politics of a Representative Frontier State," *CHSQ*, 32 (1953), 391–402. Theodore Grivas, *Military Governments in California* (1962) is the principal reference on its topic. Contemporary comment is available in Walter Colton, *Three Years in California* (1850); Lawrence Clark Powell, *Philosopher Pickett* (1942); and Samuel H. Willey, *The Transition Period of California* (1901).

The road to statehood is followed in Cardinal L. Goodwin, *The Establishment of State Government in California* (1914); Joseph Ellison, "The Struggle for Civil Government in California," *CHSQ*, 10 (1931), three installments; and James A. B. Scherer, *Thirty-first Star* (1942). See also William E. Franklin, "Peter H. Burnett and the Provisional Government Movement," *CHSQ*, 40 (1961), 123–36; Rockwell D. Hunt, *The Genesis of California's First Constitution* (1895); Bayrd Still, "California's First Constitution, A Reflection of the Political Philosophy of the Frontier," *PHR*, 4 (1935), 22–34; Grace E. Tower, "Sentiment in California for Admission into the Union," *HSSCP*, 13 (1925), 149–227; and J. Ross Browne's official *Record of the Debates in the Convention of California on the Formation of the State Constitution* (1850).

William H. Ellison, *A Self-governing Dominion* (1950) follows politics through the fifties; Joseph Ellison, *California and the Nation* (1927) deals with federal relations through another decade. Bancroft, Hittell, and Royce have much to say about politics in this period. William H. Ellison, ed., "Memoirs of Hon. William M. Gwin," *CHSQ*, 19 (1940), four installments, is an important source. See also James O'Meara, *Broderick and Gwin* (1881); Jeremiah Lynch, *A Senator of the Fifties, David C. Broderick* (1911); David A. Williams, *David C. Broderick: A Political Portrait* (1970); A. Russell Buchanan, *David S. Terry of California, Dueling Judge* (1956); A. E. Wagstaff, *Life of David S. Terry* (1892); Peyton Hurt, *The Know Nothing Party in California* (1930); and William H. Ellison, "The Movement for State Division in California, 1849–1860," *TSHQ*, 17 (1914), 101–39.

Benjamin Franklin Gilbert, in "California and the Civil War: A Bibliographical Essay," *CHSQ*, 40 (1961), 289–307, goes beyond his subtitle and summarizes this history, for instance, in challenging the suggestion that California was in reality a border state. The December, 1961, issue which it leads, is devoted to California and the Civil War. W. D. Simonds, *Starr King in California* (1917) and Charles W. Wendte, *Thomas Starr King, Patriot and Preacher* (1921) have the defect of going overboard in praising King for saving California for the Union, while E. R. Kennedy, *The Contest for California in 1861* (1912) is comparably fulsome for E. D. Baker. Nor is G. T. Clark, *Leland Stanford* (1931) adequately critical. Cornelius Cole, *Memoirs* (1908) and Stephen J. Field, *Personal Reminiscences* (1880) are pertinent.

Milton H. Shutes, *Lincoln and California* (1943) addresses itself to the problems of California support of the Union. Benjamin F. Gilbert, "The

Confederate Minority in California," *CHSQ*, 20 (1941), 154–70 and Clarence C. Clendenen, "Don Showalter, California Secessionist," *CHSQ*, 35 (1953), 41–53 put a more conservative estimate on the opposition. Russell M. Posner, "Thomas Starr King and the Mercy Million," *CHSQ*, 43 (1964), 291–308 tells of a major contribution. Harold M. Hyman, "Oroville's Reputation Redeemed: A Loyalty Investigation in California, 1862," *PHR*, 25 (1956), 173–78 and "New Light on *Cohen* vs. *Wright*, California's First Loyalty Oath Case," *PHR*, 28 (1959), 131–40 have twentieth century overtones. On the California troops sent into New Mexico and Utah see Aurora Hunt, *The Army of the Pacific* (1951) and *Major General James Henry Carleton* (1958) and Fred B. Rogers, *Soldiers of the Overland* (1938).

14. Vigilantes and Filibusters

Hubert Howe Bancroft, *Popular Tribunals* (2 vols., 1887) has a wealth of detail on the California vigilantes, both urban and rural. In his *California*, Josiah Royce addressed himself seriously to this phenomenon. Charles H. Shinn, *Mining Camps* (1885) has much to say about people's courts in the diggings, as do many of the forty-niner narratives. Mary Floyd Williams edited *Papers of the San Francisco Vigilance Committee of Vigilance of 1851* (1929) and wrote *History of the San Francisco Committee of Vigilance of 1851* (1921), to which is added George R. Stewart, Jr., *Committee of Vigilance, Revolution in San Francisco, 1851* (1964). James A. B. Scherer, *The Lion of the Vigilantes* (1939) is about William T. Coleman and his work in 1851, 1856, and 1877.

The case for the second committee is stated in moderation in Frank M. Smith, *The San Francisco Vigilance Committee of 1856* (1883) and with less restraint in Stanton A. Coblentz, *Villains and Vigilantes* (1936) and Alan Valentine, *Vigilante Justice* (1955). For a sidelight see, Richard H. Dillon, "Rejoice Ye Thieves and Harlots! The Vigilance Editorials of James King of William," *CHSQ*, 37 (1958), 137–69. Herbert G. Florcken, "The Law and Order View of the San Francisco Vigilance Committee of 1856," *CHSQ*, 14–15 (1935–36), in several installments, selects from the correspondence of Governor J. Neely Johnson. The law and order viewpoint is reflected in James O'Meara, *The Vigilance Committee of 1856* (1887); William Tecumseh Sherman, *Memoirs* (2 vols., 1875) and in his article in *Century*, 43 (1891), 296–309; and bluntly in Isaac J. Wistar, *Autobiography* (2 vols., 1914). A. Russell Buchanan, *David S. Terry of California* (1956); William H. Ellison, *A Self-governing Dominion* (1950) and John W. Caughey, *Their Majesties the Mob* (1960) are more critical, as is Walter Tilburg Clark in his novel *The Ox Bow Incident* (1942).

Rufus K. Wyllys, *The French in Sonora, 1850–1854* (1932) is the prime authority on California-based filibustering. See also his "The Republic of Lower California, 1853–54," *PHR*, II (1933), 194–214; "An Expansionist in Baja California, 1855," *PHR*, I (1932), 477–82; and "Henry A. Crabb, A Tragedy of the Sonora Frontier," *PHR*, 9 (1940), 183–94. On a Sam Brannan venture see Andrew F. Rolle, "California Filibustering and the Hawaiian Kingdom," *PHR*, 19 (1950), 251–63. Works less germane to California include William

O. Scroggs, *Filibusters and Financiers* (1916), William V. Wells, *Walker's Expedition to Nicaragua* (1856), and William Walker, *The War in Nicaragua* (1860).

15. Challenge to Land Ownership

The resolvement of hold-over land titles in newly acquired California is a principal subject in W. W. Robinson, *Land in California* (1948), useful because it describes the setting as well as the processes. John W. Dwinelle, *Colonial History of San Francisco* (1863, and enriched in subsequent printings), though it deals with an irregular claimant, is informative. Henry W. Halleck, *Report on Land Titles in California* (1850) and William Carey Jones, *Land Titles in California* (1850) present the findings of two assigned investigators. These works are embalmed in the Executive Documents series of Congress. Ogden Hoffman, *Report of Land Cases Determined in the United States District Court of the Northern District of California* (1862) and California Surveyor-General, *Reports, 1879–80* are useful government records. Robert H. Becker, *Diseños of California Ranchos* (1964) illuminates one detail. Rancho histories, such as J. J. Hill, *History of Warner Ranch* and Robert Gillingham, *The Rancho San Pedro* (1961), usually have a chapter on the adjudication of the title. There is a 4-volume printing of the proceedings in the litigation that exposed Limantour's fraudulent claim to half of San Francisco, *United States* vs. *José Yves Limantour* (1858), well summarized in Kenneth M. Johnson, *José Yves Limantour* vs. *the United States* (1961).

Early and descriptive references include: Josiah Royce, "The Squatter Riot of '50 in Sacramento," *Overland*, n.s. 6, (1885), 225–46; Henry George, *Our Land Policy, National and State* (1874); William M. Gwin, *Private Land Titles in California* (1851); Albert Wheeler, *Land Titles in San Francisco* (1852); *Report of the Attorney-General ... on the Resolutions of the Legislature of California* (1860); *Letters of William Carey Jones in Review of Attorney-General Black's Report* (1860); John Curry, *Treaty of Guadalupe Hidalgo and Private Land Claims* (1891); and W. W. Morrow, *Spanish and Mexican Land Grants* (1923).

Bancroft and Hittell in their histories, John S. Hittell in his *Resources of California*, Royce, George, and several others of these writers sharply criticize the program applied. Alston G. Field, "Attorney-General Black and the California Land Claims," *PHR*, 4 (1935), 235–45 supports the thesis that Black rendered a great service in fighting fraudulent claims. In a series of articles ["The Adjudication of Spanish-Mexican Land Claims in California," *HLQ*, 21 (1958), 213–26; "California's Embattled Settlers," *CHSQ*, 41 (1962), 99–130; and "Pre-Henry George Land Warfare in California," *CHSQ*, 46 (1967), 121–48], Paul W. Gates insists that the United States was only doing what it had done in earlier acquired territories. Gerald D. Nash, "Problems and Projects in the History of Nineteenth-Century California Land Policy," *A&W*, 2, (1960), 327–40 looks beyond these disputes, as does Paul W. Gates in his "California's Agricultural College Lands," *PHR*, 30 (1961), 103–22.

16. A White Man's Country

Bancroft castigates the treatment of the Indians in his *History of California and California Inter Pocula*. William H. Ellison, "The Federal Indian Policy in California, 1846–1860," *MVHR*, 9 (1922), 37–67 is to the point, as are his "The California Indian Frontier," *GB* (March 1922) and "Rejection of California Indian Treaties, A Study of Local Influence on National Policy," *GB* (May–July 1925). Alban W. Hoopes, *Indian Affairs and Their Administration, with Special Reference to the Far West, 1849–1860* (1932) notes the spread of the reservation system. Edward E. Dale, *The Indians of the Southwest* (1949) has greater breadth. See also Charles C. Royce, *Indian Land Cessions in the United States* (1899) and Stephen Bonsal, *Edward Fitzgerald Beale, A Pioneer in the Path of Empire, 1822–1903* (1912), a biography of the originator of the reservation system.

Indian experiences in this period are described in John W. Caughey, ed., *The Indians of Southern California in 1852* (1952); J. Ross Browne's caustic *The Indians of California* (1864) and "The Indian Reservations in California," *Harper's* (August 1861); William R. Benson, "The Stone and Kelsey 'Massacre' on the Shores of Clear Lake in 1849—The Indian Viewpoint," *CHSQ*, 11 (1932), 266–73; Lafayette Bunnell, *The Discovery of the Yosemite and the Indian War of 1851* (1881); Annie Mitchell, *Jim Savage and the Tulareño Indians* (1957); C. Gregory Crampton, ed., *The Mariposa Indian War, 1850–1851: Diaries of Edward Eccleston* (1958); William Edward Evans, "The Garrá Uprising: Conflict between San Diego Indians and Settlers in 1851," *CHSQ*, 45 (1966), 339–49; Richard E. Crouter and Andrew F. Rolle, "Edward Fitzgerald Beale and the Indian Peace Commissioners in California, 1851–1854," *SCQ*, 42 (1960), 107–32; Helen S. Giffen and Arthur Woodward, *The Story of El Tejon* (1942); and Theodora Kroeber, *Ishi in Two Worlds* (1961).

Keith A. Murray, *The Modocs and Their War* (1959) is the account of a resistance against formidable odds. In *The Indian History of the Modoc War*, by Jeff C. Riddle (1914), the adjective in the title is at least partly justified. A. B. Meacham, *Wigwam and War-path, or, The Royal Chief in Chains* (1875) is the melodramatic account of an Indian agent. The military are represented in LaFayette Grover, *Modoc War* (1874); Alvan Gillem, *Final Report of the Operation of Troops in the Modoc Country* (1877); and Max Heyman, *Prudent Soldier* (1960), a biography of E. R. S. Canby.

Reports on the mission Indians of southern California by John G. Ames and C. A. Wetmore were printed as government documents in 1873 and 1875. The pleas for a just and more generous treatment voiced by Helen Hunt Jackson in *A Century of Dishonor* (1881) and *Ramona* (1884) and, with the collaboration of Abbot Kinney, in *Report on the Conditions and Needs of the Mission Indians* (1883) were continued and reinvigorated by Charles F. Lummis in the columns of *Land of Sunshine* and *Out West*. Of Helen Hunt Jackson's life, there is a thorough study by Ruth Odell (1939). Twentieth century review of the dispossession of the California Indians and their claims for compensation are described in Robert W. Kenny, *History and Proposed Settlement of Claims of California Indians* (1944) and Kenneth M. Johnson, *K–344, or the Indians of California vs. the United States* (1966).

The problems of minorities in the early American decades are touched on in Ferdinand F. Fernandez, "Except a California Indian: A Study in Legal Discrimination," *SCQ*, 50 (1968), 161–75; Rudolph M. Lapp, "Negro Rights Activities in Gold Rush California," *CHSQ*, 45 (1966), 3–20; William E. Franklin, "The Archy Case," *PHR*, 33 (1963), 137–54; Robert Seager, II, "Some Denominational Reactions to Chinese Immigration to California, 1856–1892," *PHR*, 28 (1959), 49–66; Elmer Sandmeyer, *The Anti-Chinese Movement in California* (1939); Ping Chiu, *Chinese Labor in California, 1850–1880* (1963); Gunther Barth, *Bitter Strength: A History of the Chinese in the United States, 1850–1870* (1964); and Leonard M. Pitt, *The Decline of the Californios* (1966).

17. Cultural Awakening

Pauline Jacobsen, *City of the Golden 'Fifties* (1941) pictures the life of San Francisco and, to a degree, that of the state. Other works, such as T. A. Barry and B. A. Patten, *Men and Memories of San Francisco* (1873); Idwal Jones, *Ark of Empire, San Francisco's Montgomery Block* (1951); and Robert E. Cowan, *Forgotten Characters of Old San Francisco* (1938) support this description. William H. Brewer, *Up and Down California in 1860–1864* (1930) is an important source on the interior.

William W. Ferrier, *Ninety Years of Education in California* (1937) is the basic reference on educational beginnings. David F. Ferris, *Judge Marvin and the Founding of the California Public School System* (1962); John Swett, *History of the Public School System of California* (1876) and *Public Education in California* (1911); William G. Carr, *John Swett, The Biography of an Educational Pioneer* (1933); and Nicholas C. Polos, "A Yankee Patriot: John Swett, The Horace Mann of the Pacific," *History of Education Quarterly*, 4 (1964), 17–32 chart the growth of public schooling. On higher education, see William W. Ferrier, *Origin and Development of the University of California* (1930) and *Henry Durant, First President of the University of California* (1942); and Abraham Flexner, *Daniel Coit Gilman* (1946).

William Hanchett, "The Question of Religion and the Taming of California, 1849–1854," *CHSQ*, 32 (1953), 49–56, 119–44 and his "The Blue Law Gospel in Gold Rush California," *PHR*, 24 (1955), 361–68 introduce some of the Protestant churchmen. John B. McGloin, *California's First Archbishop: The Life of Joseph Sadoc Alemany, O. P.* (1966) and Francis J. Weber, *California's Reluctant Prelate: The Life and Times of Right Reverend Thaddeus Amat, C. M.* (1964) are biographies of San Francisco's first Catholic archbishop and Los Angeles' first bishop.

Constance Rourke, *Troupers of the Gold Coast* (1928) is a light-hearted volume with most applause for Lotta Crabtree. G. R. MacMinn, *The Theater of the Golden Era* (1941) and Edmond M. Gagey, *The San Francisco Stage* (1950) are supplemented by a series of articles by Lois Foster Rodecape in the *CHSQ*.

Early journalism is described in E. C. Kemble, *A History of California Newspapers, 1846–1858* (1858, 1927, and, with annotations by Helen Harding Bretnor, 1962); John P. Young, *Journalism in California* (1915); and John Bruce, *Gaudy Century, The Story of San Francisco's Hundred Years of Robust Journalism* (1948). William B. Rice, *The Los Angeles Star, 1851–1864* (1947) covers the beginnings of journalism in southern California. Francis P. Weisenburger, *Idol of the West* (1965) follows the western career of journalist Rollin M. Daggett. Benjamin S. Harrison, *Fortune Favors the Brave* (1953) describes, among many other adventures, Horace Bell's editorship of the *Porcupine.*

Franklin Walker, *San Francisco's Literary Frontier* (1939) is a sheaf of sketches of early California writers with much sage comment on their works and on the society in which they moved. His *A Literary History of Southern California* (1950) has a longer time span and likewise is social as well as literary history. Ella Sterling Cummins [Mighels], *The Story of the Files* (1893) is a useful general survey. Hubert Howe Bancroft has a long chapter on the subject in *Essays and Miscellany* (1890). Much of the writing of the period is available in the collected works of Mark Twain and Bret Harte, in the volumes of Delano, Derby, Mulford, Stoddard, Miller, et al., and in anthologies beginning with Mary Wentworth, *Poets of the Pacific* (1865); Bret Harte, *Outcroppings* (1866); and Oscar T. Shuck, *California Anthology* (1880). Among biographies may be mentioned George R. Stewart, Jr., *Bret Harte, Argonaut and Exile* (1931); Bernard De Voto, *Mark Twain's America* (1932); Ivan Benson, *Mark Twain's Western Years* (1938); Edgar M. Branch, *The Literary Apprenticeship of Mark Twain* (1950); Henry Nash Smith, ed., *Mark Twain of the Enterprise* (1957); Bernard Taper, ed., *Mark Twain's San Francisco* (1963); Stewart, *John Phoenix, Esq., the Veritable Squibob* (1937); Rodman W. Paul, "In Search of Dame Shirley," *PHR*, 33 (1964), 127–46; Thurman Wilkins, *Clarence King* (1958); Martin S. Peterson, *Joaquin Miller, Literary Frontiersman* (1937); M. M. Marberry, *Splendid Poseur: Joaquin Miller* (1953); and David Michael Goodman, *A Western Panorama, 1849–1875, The Travels, Writings, and Influence of J. Ross Browne* (1966).

18. Stages and Steamers

The start of public transportation in California is described in Ernest A. Wiltsee, *The Pioneer Miner and the Pack Mule Express* (1931). Oscar O. Winther, *Express and Stagecoach Days in California* (1936) and the highly graphic *Six Horses,* by William and George Banning (1930), describe western staging with special reference to James Birch and the California developments. Maymie Krythe, *Port Admiral, Phineas Banning* (1957) is a biography of southern California's most enterprising stage operator. Two representative secondary operations are dealt with in William Harland Boyd, "The Stagecoach in the Southern San Joaquin Valley," *PHR*, 26 (1957), 365–71 and Franklin Hoyt, "The Bradshaw Road," *PHR*, 21 (1952), 243–54. The rise of riverboats and ferries on San Francisco Bay is the subject of Jerry MacMullen, *Paddlewheel Days in California* (1944). Jack McNairn and Jerry MacMullen, *Ships of the Redwood Coast* (1945) is a companion book on the coast trade north of San Francisco.

John H. Kemble, *The Panama Route, 1848–1869* (1943) is a masterly account of the mail steamers and their runs. A. H. Clark, *The Clipper Ship Era, 1843–1869* (1910) relates largely to California voyages. There are pertinent chapters in Morison, *The Maritime History of Massachusetts;* Rydell, *Cape Horn to the Pacific;* and Robert G. Albion, *The Rise of the Port of New York, 1815–1860* (1939). Victor M. Berthold, *The Pioneer Steamer "California,"*

1848–1849 (1932) is the biography of the first steamer on the Panama run. On the isthmian link see F. N. Otis, *Illustrated History of the Panama Railroad* (1861). John H. Kemble, *San Francisco Bay, A Pictorial Maritime History* (1957) is a rich compilation on ships and shipping in and out of the great bay. Much of the maritime history of the period is covered in Felix Rosenberg, Jr., *Golden Gate, The Story of San Francisco Harbor* (1940) and William M. Camp, *San Francisco, Port of Gold* (1947).

Lewis B. Lesley, *Uncle Sam's Camels* (1929) and Harlan D. Fowler, *Camels to California* (1950) are book-length studies of one of the more fanciful experiments in transcontinental travel. W. Turrentine Jackson, *Wagon Roads West* (1952) reports western demands for federal aid and subsidy for road improvement to California. LeRoy R. Hafen, *The Overland Mail, 1849–1869* (1926) is a solid reference on its topic. Roscoe P. and Margaret B. Conkling, *The Butterfield Overland Mail, 1857–1869* (3 vols., 1948) goes into much more voluminous detail. There are popular histories of Wells Fargo by Neill C. Wilson (1936), Edward Hungerland (1949), and Lucius Beebe and Charles Clegg (1949), the latter largely in pictures. Alexander Majors, *Seventy Years on the Frontier* (1893) contains one of the few accounts of wagon freighting, also prominent in Raymond W. and Mary Lund Settle, *War Drums and Wagon Wheels* (1966), a history of the firm of Russell, Majors, and Waddell. The dashing but brief episode of the Pony Express has half a dozen histories: William L. Visscher, *A Thrilling and Truthful History of the Pony Express* (1908); Glenn D. Bradley, *The Story of the Pony Express* (1913); Arthur Chapman, *The Pony Express* (1932); Raymond W. and Mary Lund Settle, *Saddles and Spurs* (1955); Roy S. Bloss, *Pony Express—the Great Gamble* (1959); Waddell Smith, *The Story of the Pony Express* (1960); and Waddell Smith, *Pony Express versus Wells Fargo Express* (1966), a rebuttal of W. Turrentine Jackson, "A New Look at Wells Fargo Stagecoaches and the Pony Express," *CHSQ,* 45 (1966), 291–324. Smith's contention is that Wells Fargo was one of the travel agents or ticket agents for the Pony but not its operator. The conqueror of the Pony is the subject of Robert Luther Thompson, *Wiring a Continent* (1947).

Vivid narratives of the transcontinental journey by stage include Waterman L. Ormsby's account as the one through passenger on the first westbound stage. It is available in Walter B. Lang, ed., *The First Overland Mail* (2 vols., 1940, 1945) and Lyle H. Wright and Josephine M. Bynum, eds., *The Butterfield Overland Mail* (1942). An eastbound report with expressive subtitle is William B. Tallack, *The California Overland Express, the Longest Stage Ride in the World* (1935). "Parson's Progress to California," *SCQ,* 21 (1939), 45–78 is by a passenger from Texas in 1859. The central route is represented by Horace Greeley, *An Overland Journey* (1860); Samuel Bowles, *Across the Continent, A Summer's Journey* (1865); Demas Barnes, *From the Atlantic to the Pacific, Overland* (1866); Albert D. Richardson, *Beyond the Mississippi* (1867); and, most widely read, Mark Twain, *Roughing It* (1872).

19. Rails Over the Sierra

The *Pacific Railroad Reports,* 13 quarto volumes with numerous maps, plates, and colored plates (1855), were of little practical assistance to the builders but are concrete evidence of governmental interest. George L. Albright attempted, without entire success, to reduce the meat of these reports to one slender narrative, *Official Explorations for Pacific Railroads, 1853–1855* (1921). Grant Foreman, *A Pathfinder in the Southwest* (1941) reproduces Whipple's report of the survey along the 35th parallel.

E. L. Sabin, *Building the Pacific Railway* (1919); Robert L. Fulton, *Epic of the Overland* (1924); John D. Galloway, *The First Transcontinental Railroad* (1950); Robert West Howard, *The Giant Iron Trail: The Story of the First Transcontinental Railroad* (1963); and Wesley S. Griswold, *A Work of Giants: Building the First Transcontinental Railway* (1963) range from sketchy to detailed and from matter of fact to vibrant in telling the story of this epoch-making construction project. Briefer presentations are in Robert E. Riegel, *The Story of the Western Railroads* (1926); John Moody, *The Railroad Builders* (1921); and Glenn C. Quiett, *They Built the West* (1934).

Chief engineer Grenville M. Dodge committed to print his memoirs on *How We Built the Union Pacific Railway* (1903). This narrative is expanded and made more effective in J. R. Perkins, *Trails, Rails and War* (1929). Belatedly, in 1960, economist Robert William Fogel ran an economic analysis which led him to the conclusion that, if just a few more years of patience had reigned, the road could have been built without the need for a great federal subsidy.

Carl I. Wheat, "A Sketch of the Life of Theodore D. Judah," *CHSQ*, 4 (1925), 219–71 is the first required reading on the building of the Central Pacific. See also Judah's pamphlet, *A Practical Plan for Building the Pacific Railroad* (1857). George T. Clark, *Leland Stanford* is less critical than it should be, and Cerinda W. Evans, *Collis Potter Huntington* (2 vols., 1954) is unrelieved adulation. Oscar Lewis, *The Big Four* (1938) sees the magnitude of the achievement yet deplores some of the methods employed. Harry J. Carman and Charles H. Mueller, "The Contract and Finance Company and the Central Pacific Railroad," *MVHR*, 14 (1927), 326–41 goes about as far as the meager records permit. Alexander Saxton, "The Army of Canton in the High Sierra," *PHR*, 35 (1966), 141–52 is an aside on the prevalent attitude of white superiority. Hubert Howe Bancroft, *Chronicles of the Builders* (8 vols., 1891-92) pays special attention to the railroad men.

For vivacious descriptions of travel on the early trains, one may turn to Samuel Bowles, *Our New West* (1969) and Robert Louis Stevenson, *Across the Plains* (1892). A trip on a Southern Pacific emigrant train is described feelingly in "California in the Eighties, as Pictured in the Letters of Anna Seward," *CHSQ*, 16 (1937), 391–403.

20. Social Unrest

Doris M. Wright, "The Making of Cosmopolitan California," *CHSQ*, 19 (1940), 323–43, and 20 (1941), 65–79 takes stock of the elements that had gone into the California population by 1870. On rural population and problems, see Paul S. Taylor, "Foundations of California Rural Society," *CHSQ*, 24 (1945), 139–61 and Ezra S. Carr, *The Patrons of Husbandry on the Pacific Coast* (1875).

On the eve of completion of the Pacific Railway, Henry George issued a warning, "What the Railroad Will Bring Us," *Overland,* 1 (1868), 297–304. The rising resentment against the railroad is described in several of the titles in the section above, particularly in the latter part of Lewis, *The Big Four.* See also Stuart Daggett, *Chapters on the History of the Southern Pacific* (1922) and, as sidelights on the corporation's unpopularity, C. B. Glasscock, *Bandits and the Southern Pacific* (1929) and Wallace Smith, *Prodigal Sons, The Adventures of Christopher Evans and John Sontag* (1951).

Mary R. Coolidge, *Chinese Immigration* (1909) is a standard reference on California's first Orientals. On special phases consult Charles Morley, "The Chinese in California as Reported by Henryk Sienkiewicz," *CHSQ,* 34 (1955), 301–16; Rodman W. Paul, "The Origin of the Chinese Issue in California," *MVHR,* 25 (1938), 181–96; and Elmer C. Sandmeyer, *The Anti-Chinese Movement in California* (1939). Paul M. De Falla, "Lantern in the Western Sky," *SCQ,* 42 (1960), 57–88, 161–85 and William R. Locklear, "The Celestials and the Angels: A Study of the Anti-Chinese Movement in Los Angeles to 1882," *SCQ,* 42 (1960), 239–56 describe the Los Angeles Massacre.

Henry George contributed an article on "The Kearney Agitation in California" to *Popular Science Monthly,* 17 (1880), 433–53; James Bryce devoted a chapter to "Kearneyism in California," in his *The American Commonwealth* (2 vols., 1888). Ralph Kauer, "The Workingmen's Party of California," *PHR,* 13 (1944), 278–91; Gerald D. Nash, "The Influence of Labor on State Policy, 1860–1920, The Experience of California," *CHSQ,* 42 (1963), 241–57; "The California Railroad Commission, 1876–1911," *SCQ,* 44 (1962), 287–305 and "Henry George Reexamined: William S. Chapman's Views on Land Speculation in Nineteenth Century California," *AH,* 33 (1959), 133–37; Ira B. Cross, *A History of the Labor Movement in California* (1935); and Frank B. Roney, *Irish Rebel and California Labor Leader: An Autobiography* (1931) relate to this political unrest.

On the new constitution see Winfield J. Davis, *History of Political Conventions in California* (1893) and Carl Brent Swisher, *Motivation and Political Technique in the California Constitutional Convention, 1878–1879* (1930).

21. Health Seekers and Speculators

There are background references such as George W. Groh, *Gold Fever, Being a True Account, Both Horrifying and Hilarious, of the Art of Healing (so-called) During the California Gold Rush* (1966) and John E. Baur, "The Health Factor in the Gold Rush Era," *PHR,* 18 (1949), 97–108, which attest that California exerted an earlier attraction to health seekers. On the health rush at its height the principal authority is John E. Baur, *Health Seekers of Southern California 1870–1900* (1959). See also Oscar O. Winther, "The Use of Climate as a Means of Promoting Migration to Southern California," *MVHR,* 33 (1946), 411–24; Charles Nordhoff, *California for Health, Pleasure, and Residence* (1873); William A. Edwards and Beatrice Harraden, *Two Health-Seekers in Southern California* (1897); and F. C. S. Sanders, *California as a Health Resort* (1916).

The general setting is charted in J. J. Warner, Benjamin Hayes, and J. P. Widney, *An Historical Sketch of Los Angeles County* (1876); Sarah Bixby Smith, *Adobe Days* (1925); Ludwig L. Salvator, *Eine Blume aus dem goldenen Lande oder Los Angeles* (1878), trans. by Marguerite Eyer Wilbur as *Los Angeles in the Sunny Seventies* (1929); and John Albert Wilson, *History of Los Angeles County* (1880). Richard F. Pourade gives an overview of San Diego in *The Glory Years* (1964); Remi A. Nadeau furnishes a more searching analysis in *City-makers, The Men Who Transformed Los Angeles from Village to Metropolis, 1868–1876* (1948). See also Robert M. Fogelson, *The Fragmented Metropolis: Los Angeles, 1850–1930* (1967); Oscar O. Winther, "The Rise of Metropolitan Los Angeles, 1870–1900," *HLQ*, 10 (1947), 391–405, "Los Angeles: Its Aquatic Life Lines," *Journal of Geography*, 49 (1950), 45–56, and "The Colony System of Southern California," *AH*, 27 (1963), 94–103; Robert V. Hine, *William Andrew Spalding, Los Angeles Newspaperman* (1961); and, more offbeat, Robert V. Hine, *California's Utopian Colonies* (1953).

On railroad development Quiett, *They Built the West* and Daggett, *Chapters in the History of the Southern Pacific* are supplemented by Neill C. Wilson and Frank J. Taylor, *Southern Pacific, The Roaring Story of a Fighting Railroad* (1952); Glenn D. Bradley, *Story of the Santa Fe* (1920); James Marshall, *Santa Fe, The Railroad That Built an Empire* (1949); and L. L. Waters, *Steel Trails to Santa Fe* (1950).

The promotional literature that contributed to the boom may be sampled in California Immigrant Union, *All About California and the Inducements to Settle There* (1870); Jerome Madden, *The Lands of the Southern Pacific Railroad Company* (1876); Benjamin F. Taylor, *Between the Gates* (1878); William H. Bishop, *Old Mexico and Her Lost Provinces* (1883); Ben C. Truman, *Homes and Happiness in the Golden State of California* (1883); T. S. Van Dyke, *Southern California* (1886); and Walter Lindley and J. P. Widney, *California of the South* (1888). Further information is afforded by Newmark, *Sixty Years in Southern California;* Guinn, *Los Angeles and Its Environs;* Charles Dudley Warner, *Our Italy* (1891); Laurance L. Hill, *La Reina, Los Angeles in Three Centuries* (1929); and W. W. Robinson, *Panorama: A Picture-History of Southern California* (1953).

Glenn S. Dumke, *The Boom of the Eighties in Southern California* (1944) and T. S. Van Dyke, *Millionaires of a Day* (1890) offer, respectively, a serious assessment and a hilarious lampoon. Edna M. Parker, "The Southern Pacific Railroad and Settlement in Southern California," *PHR*, 6 (1937), 103–19 deals with one aspect of the promotion. Walker, *A Literary History of Southern California* takes stock of the cultural consequences.

22. Broadening the Base

Cleland and Hardy, *March of Industry* charts the economic development through these decades. Gerald D. Nash, *State Government and Economic Development: A History of Administrative Policies in California, 1849–1933* (1964) is an important supplement. On agriculture there is general coverage in Hutchison, *California Agriculture.* Wallace Smith, *Garden of the*

Sun (1939) and Joseph A. McGowan, *History of the Sacramento Valley* (3 vols., 1961) pay much attention to agriculture. Scattered papers discuss limited phases; among these papers are Arpad Haraszthy, *California Wines and Vines* (1883); Idwal Jones, *Vines in the Sun* (1949), a novel; F. A. Magnuson, "History of the Beet Sugar Industry in California." *HSSCP*, 11 (1918), 68–79; L. T. Burcham, *California Range Land* (1957) and "Cattle and Range Forage in California, 1770–1880," *AH*, 35 (1961), 140–49.

Rahno Mabel McCurdy, *The History of the California Fruit Growers' Exchange* (1925) and Kelsey B. Gardner and A. W. McKay, *The California Fruit Growers Exchange System* (1950) tell the basic facts. The genius displayed in marketing is brought to light in Josephine Kingsbury Jacobs, "Sunkist Advertising" (UCLA dissertation, 1966). See also Charles C. Teague, *Fifty Years a Rancher* (1944); Sidney Burchell, *Jacob Peek, Orange Grower* (1915); H. E. Erdman, "The Development and Significance of California Cooperatives, 1900–1915," *AH*, 32 (1958), 179–84; and E. Kraemer and H. E. Erdman, *History of Cooperation in Marketing California Fresh Deciduous Fruits* (1933).

William H. Hall, *Irrigation in California* (1888) is an inventory of operative projects. Samuel C. Weyl, *Water Rights in the Western States* (1905); Elwood Mead, *Irrigation Institutions* (1903); and W. E. Smythe, *The Conquest of Arid America* (1905) provide background. J. A. Alexander, *The Life of George Chaffey* (1928) is a brief biography of the leading irrigator of his time. On particulars see R. Louis Gentilcore, "Ontario and the Agricultural Boom of the 1880's," *AH*, 34 (1960), 77–87; Frederick D. Kershner, Jr., "George Chaffey and the Irrigation Frontier," *AH*, 27 (1953), 115–22; Margaret Darsie Morrison, "Charles Robinson Rockwood, Developer of the Imperial Valley," *SCQ*, 44 (1962), 307–30; H. T. Cory, *The Imperial Valley and the Salton Sea* (1915); E. F. Howe and W. J. Hall, *The Story of the First Decade in Imperial Valley* (1910); Otis B. Tout, *The First Thirty Years* (n.d.); and George Kennan, *The Salton Sea: An Account of Harriman's Fight with the Colorado River* (2 vols., 1917).

Robert L. Kelley, "Taming the Sacramento: Hamiltonianism in Action," *PHR*, 34 (1965), 21–49 outlines a major victory in reclamation scored by cooperative effort and federal aid. On the background conditions see Kenneth Thompson, "Historic Flooding in the Sacramento Valley," *PHR*, 29 (1960), 349–60 and *Sacramento River Basin*, Bulletin No. 26 of the California Department of Public Works (1931).

On town and city development see Robert M. Fogelson, *The Fragmented Metropolis, Los Angeles, 1850-1930* (1967); James M. Guinn, *A History of California and an Extended History of Los Angeles and Environs* (3 vols., 1915); H. L. Sherman, *History of Newport Beach* (1931); Mildred Yorba MacArthur, *Anaheim: The Mother Colony* (1959); H. F. Raup, *The German Colonization of Anaheim* (1932) and *San Bernardino: Settlement and Growth of a Pass-Site City* (1940); Merlin Stonehouse, *John Wesley North and the Reform Frontier* (1965); Donald H. Pflueger, *Glendora: The Annals of a Southern California Community* (1951) and *Covina: Sunflowers, Citrus, Subdivisions* (1964); Clara H. Hisken, *Tehama: Little City of the Big Trees* (1948); Chester G. Murphy, *The People of the Pueblo, or, The Story of Sonoma* (1937); and Lawrence Kinnaird, *History of Greater San Francisco Bay Region* (3 vols., 1967).

John R. Spears, *Illustrated Sketches of Death Valley* (1892); Ruth

C. Woodman, *The Story of the Pacific Coast Borax Company* (1951); W. A. Chalfant, *Death Valley, The Facts* (1930); and Scherer, *The Lion of the Vigilantes* provide glimpses of the borax mining. On the oil industry see Gerald T. White, *Formative Years in the Far West* (1962), on Standard Oil of California through 1919; Frank J. Taylor and Earl M. Welty, *Black Bonanza* (1950), on Union Oil; and Frank Latta, *Black Gold in the Joaquin* (1949). The flowering of other industries is touched upon in C. B. Glasscock, *Lucky Baldwin* (1935); H. Austin Adams, *John D. Spreckels* (1924); Gilson Gardner, *Lusty Scripps* (1932); William H. B. Kilner, *Arthur Letts* (1927); Robert O. Schad, "Henry E. Huntington," *Huntington Library Bulletin*, 1 (1931), 3–32; John H. Kemble, "The Big Four at Sea: The History of the Occidental and Oriental Steamship Company," *HLQ*, 3 (1940), 339–58; L. J. Rose, Jr., *L. J. Rose of Sunny Slope, 1827–1899* (1958); and Ruth Waldo Newhall, *The Story of the Newhall Land and Farming Company* (1958).

Remi A. Nadeau, *The Water Seekers* (1950) contains a good account of Los Angeles' Owens Valley project. On the valley before Los Angeles took a hand see Mary Austin, *The Land of Little Rain* (1903). *Report of the Aqueduct Investigating Board* (1912) tells of the inception of the project; *Final Report of Construction of the Los Angeles Aqueduct* (1916) describes the building. W. A. Chalfant, *The Story of Inyo* (1922); Morrow Mayo, *Los Angeles* (1933); and Carey McWilliams, *Southern California Country* (1946) comment scathingly on the methods of getting the water.

23. Strong Individualists

Reminiscences of end-of-the-century San Francisco are both numerous and glowing. The tone is set by Will Irwin's nostalgic essay, *The City That Was* (1906). Evelyn Wells, *Champagne Days of San Francisco* (1939) is an effective dramatization incorporating a multitude of authentic details. Oscar Lewis and Carroll D. Hall, *Bonanza Inn, America's First Luxury Hotel* (1939) throws a similar halo around the city's chief showplace, Ralston's Palace. Charles C. Dobie, *San Francisco's Chinatown* (1936) is a tribute to a most picturesque quarter; other writers have dwelt on the less distinctive but more notorious Barbary Coast, while more genteel memoirs are embodied in Amelia R. Neville, *The Fantastic City* (1932). Other sidelights are Irving McKee, "The Shooting of Charles DeYoung," *PHR*, 16 (1937), 271–84 and M. M. Marberry, *The Golden Voice, A Biography of Isaac Kalloch* (1947). See also Edgar M. Kahn, *Cable Car Days in San Francisco* (1940); Frank Parker, *Anatomy of the San Francisco Cable Car* (1946); and Lucius Beebe and Charles Clegg, *Cable Car Carnival* (1951).

Arthur Miller, "Growth of Art in California," in Frank J. Taylor, *Land of Homes* (1929), 311–41, is an introduction to a neglected topic. Eugene Neuhaus, *William Keith, The Man and the Artist* (1938) is a sketch of the best-known painter of the generation. Harold Kirker, *California's Architectural Frontier* (1960) discusses style and tradition in nineteenth century design. To it a useful supplement is Porter Garnett, *Stately Homes of California* (1915).

Joseph Henry Jackson, *Continent's End: A Collection of California Writing* (1944) stresses the writers of this period, as does George Sterling's anthology of poetry, *Continent's End* (1925). Walker's *San Francisco's Literary Frontier* and *A Literary History of Southern California* appraise many of these writers. Although his third volume is incomplete, Vernon L. Parrington, *Main Currents in American Thought* (3 vols., 1927–30), comments at length on Norris, London, and George. Direct appraisal of the writings of this period is the best approach and, although first editions command a stiff premium, is feasible.

On individual authors see, Gertrude Atherton, *Adventures of a Novelist* (1932); Mary Austin, *Earth Horizon* (1932); Franklin Walker, *Frank Norris* (1932); Ruth Odell, *Helen Hunt Jackson* (1939); Irving Stone, *Sailor on Horseback, The Biography of Jack London* (1938); and Joan London, *Jack London and His Times* (1939). For perspective on Robert Louis Stevenson's California experiences see J. C. Furnas, *Journey to Windward* (1951). On local events see Henry M. Bland, *Stevenson's California* (1924); Anne Roller Issler, *Stevenson at Silverado* (1939) and *Our Mountain Heritage, Silverado and Robert Louis Stevenson* (1950); Anne Fisher, *No More a Stranger* (1946); James D. Hart, ed., *From Scotland to Silverado* (1966); and Edwin R. Bingham, *Charles F. Lummis, Editor of the Southwest* (1955).

John W. Caughey, *Hubert Howe Bancroft, Historian of the West* (1946) is a full-length study of an unusual man. On his technique of production see Bancroft's *Literary Industries* (1890) and William A. Morris, "The Origin and Authorship of the Bancroft Pacific States Publications," *CHQ*, 4 (1903), 287–364. Of the myriad works on George, Charles A. Barker, *Henry George* (1955) is superior; Henry George, Jr., *Life of Henry George* (1900) and Arthur N. Young, *The Single Tax Movement in the United States* (1916) supplement. Ambrose Bierce is on display in his *Collected Works* (12 vols., 1909–12), a badly planned and poorly edited set. Of numerous short appraisals, Wilson Follett, "Ambrose, Son of Marcus Aurelius," *Atlantic Monthly*, 140 (1937), 32–42 and Paul Fatout, *Ambrose Bierce, The Devil's Lexicographer* (1951) stand out. Chief item in a substantial body of writing on William Randolph Hearst is W. A. Swanberg, *Citizen Hearst* (1961), which suggests Orson Welles' remarkable film, *Citizen Kane* (1940). Useful also is John Tebbel, *The Life and Good Times of William Randolph Hearst* (1952).

Linnie M. Wolfe's biography, *Son of the Wilderness: The Life of John Muir* (1950) was preceded by her *John of the Mountains* (1938), drawing freely on his writings, which also have been given much currency in Sierra Club picture books. Holway R. Jones, *John Muir and the Sierra Club: The Battle for Yosemite* (1966) concentrates on the intersection of the man and the institution. Related titles include Joseph LeConte, *Journal of Ramblings* (1875); Hans Huth, "Yosemite, the Story of an Idea," *SCB*, 33 (1948), 47–78; Elmo Richardson, "The Struggle for the Valley: California's Hetch Hetchy Controversy, 1905–1913," *CHSQ*, 38 (1959), 249–58; M. M. O'Shaughnessy, *The Hetch Hetchy Water Supply of San Francisco* (1916); Ray W. Taylor, *Hetch Hetchy* (1926); and Samuel P. Hays, *Conservation and the Gospel of Efficiency: The Progressive Conservation Movement, 1890–1920* (1959).

Ferrier's books on education in California are supplemented for the south by Laurance L. Hill, *Six Collegiate Decades* (1929). David Starr Jordan's educational theories are set forth in his voluminous writings, especially *The Voice of the Scholar* (1903) and *The Days of a Man* (2 vols., 1922), as are Benjamin Ide Wheeler's in his *The Abundant Life* (1926). See also Edward M. Burns, *David Starr Jordan, Prophet of Freedom* (1953) and Benjamin P. Kurtz, *Charles Mills Gayley* (1943). For the California stay of another strong individualist, see R. L. Duffus, *The Innocents at Cedro* (1944).

24. Political Housecleaning

W. H. Hutchinson, *Oil, Land, and Politics, The California Career of Thomas Robert Bard* (2 vols., 1965) and Edith Dobie, *Political Career of Stephen M. White* (1927) dip into the politics of the eighties and nineties. Beyond them scattered articles such as C. C. Plehn, "The Taxation of Mortgages in California," *Yale Review*, 8 (1899), 35; Alexander Callow, Jr., "San Francisco's Blind Boss," *PHR*, 25 (1956), 261–80; Donald E. Walters, "California Populist T. V. Cator and Democrats James Maguire and James Barry," *PHR*, 37 (1958), 281–98; Alexander Saxton, "San Francisco Labor and the Populist and Progressive Insurgencies," *PHR*, 34 (1965), 421–38; Howard H. Quint, "Gaylord Wilshire and Socialism's First Congressional Campaign," *PHR*, 26 (1957), 327–40; and W. H. Hutchinson, "Prologue to Reform: The California Anti-Railroad Republicans, 1899–1905," *SCQ*, 44 (1962), 175–218 are the main resources.

Complaints against the Southern Pacific are represented in James L. Brown, *The Mussel Slough Tragedy* (1958); Irving McKee, "Notable Memorials to Mussel Slough," *PHR*, 17 (1948), 19–27; Gordon W. Clarke, "Significant Memorials to Mussel Slough," *PHR*, 18 (1949), 501–04; and *Letters of Collis P. Huntington to David D. Colton, 1874–1878*.

Charles D. Willard, *The Free Harbor Contest at Los Angeles* (1899) may be supplemented by Franklyn Hoyt, "Influence of the Railroads in the Development of Los Angeles Harbor," *SCQ*, 35 (1933), 195–212; Richard W. Barsness, "Railroads and Los Angeles: The Quest for a Deepwater Port," *SCQ*, 47 (1965), 379–94; Barsness, "Iron Horses and an Inner Harbor at San Pedro," *PHR*, 34 (1965), 289–304; Ella A. Ludwig, *History of the Harbor District of Los Angeles* (1928); Charles H. Matson, *The Story of Los Angeles Harbor* (1935); and a series of brochures issued by the Harbor Commissioners.

Walton Bean, *Boss Ruef's San Francisco* (1952) is definitive on the San Francisco graft prosecution. Earlier references include Franklin Hichborn, *"The System," as Uncovered by the San Francisco Graft Protection* (1915); Fremont Older, *My Own Story* (1919), Evelyn Wells, *Fremont Older* (1936), Lincoln Steffens' *Autobiography* (2 vols., 1931); and Robert Davenport, "San Francisco Journalism in the Time of Fremont Older" (UCLA dissertation, 1969). Lately Thomas, *A Debonair Scoundrel* (1962) centers on Ruef. On reform drives in southern California the best study is Albert H. Clodius, "The Quest for Good Government in Los Angeles, 1890–1910" (Claremont dissertation, 1953).

Three recent works approach San Francisco's great earthquake pictorially, breezily, and technically: William Bronson, *The Earth Shook, The Sky Burned* (1959), Monica Sutherland, *The Damndest Finest Ruins* (1959), and Robert Jacopi, *Earthquake Country: How, Why and Where Earthquakes Strike in California* (1964). Trumbull White, *Complete Story of the San Francisco Horror* (1906) and an anonymous work, *San Francisco Earthquake Horror* (1906) gave immediate sensational coverage. Adolphus W. Greely (1906),

David Starr Jordan (1906), and A. C. Lawson (1908), responded with technical reports.

For the Lincoln–Roosevelt League and its work there is basic material in Franklin Hichborn, *Story of the Session of the California Legislature of 1909* (1909) and similar volumes for 1911 and 1913. See also the files of the League's organs, *The California Weekly*, 1908–1910, and *The California Outlook*, 1911–1912. J. Gregg Layne, *The Lincoln–Roosevelt League* (1943) is important mainly for the documents quoted. Alice Rose, "The Rise of California Insurgency" (Stanford dissertation, 1942) is more fundamental. George E. Mowry, *The California Progressives* (1951) is a thorough analytical study. Discussion continues in Spencer C. Olin, Jr., *California's Prodigal Sons* (1968); Irving McKee, "The Background and Early Career of Hiram Johnson," *PHR*, 19 (1950), 17–30; Helene Hooker Brewer, "A Man and Two Books" [Francis J. Heney], *PHR*, 32 (1963), 221–34; H. Brett Melendy, "California's Cross-filing Nightmare: The 1918 Gubernatorial Election," *PHR*, 64 (1965), 317–30; Franklin Hichborn, "The Party, the Machine, and the Vote; The Story of Cross-filing and the Progressive Movement in California Politics," *CHSQ*, 38 (1959), 349–57, and 39 (1960), 19–34; James C. Findley, "Cross-filing and the Progressive Movement in California Politics," *WPQ*, 12 (1961), 699–711; and Jackson K. Putnam, "The Persistence of Progressivism in the 1920's," *PHR*, 35 (1966), 395–411.

25. Race Prejudice and Labor Conflict

Roger Daniels, *The Politics of Prejudice* (1962) is a concise review of the anti-Japanese movement in California to 1924. Carey McWilliams, *Prejudice: Japanese-Americans, Symbol of Racial Intolerance* (1945); Yamato Ichihashi, *Japanese in the United States* (1932); T. Iyenaga and Kenoske Sato, *Japan and the California Problem* (1921); K. K. Kawakami, *The Real Japanese Question* (1921); and Thomas A. Bailey, *Theodore Roosevelt and the Japanese-American Crisis* (1934) may also be consulted. The periodical literature is also extensive. Examples are: Raymond L. Buell, "The Development of the Anti-Japanese Agitation in the United States," *Political Science Quarterly*, 37 (1922), 605–38; Roger Daniels and Eric F. Petersen, "California's Grandfather Clause: The 'Literacy in English' Amendment of 1894," *SCQ*, 50 (1968), 51–58; Robert E. Hennings, "James D. Phelan and the Woodrow Wilson Anti-Oriental Statement of May 3, 1912," *CHSQ*, 42 (1963), 291–300; Thomas A. Bailey, "California, Japan and the Alien Land Legislation of 1913," *PHR*, 1 (1932), 36–59; and Paolo E. Coletta, "'The Most Thankless Task': Bryan and the California Alien Land Legislation," *PHR*, 36 (1967), 163–87.

On other minorities in farm labor see *Facts about Filipino Immigration into California* and *Mexicans in California*, issued by the California Department of Industrial Relations (1930); Bruno Lasker, *Filipino Immigration to Continental United States and Hawaii* (1931); Dhan Gopal Mukerji, *Caste and Outcast* (1923); Rajani Kanta Das, *Hindustani Workers on the Pacific Coast* (1923); Paul S. Taylor, *Mexican Labor in the United States* (1929); and Carey McWilliams, *North from Mexico* (1949) and *Factories in the Field* (1939).

California labor relations are seen in the large in Cross, *History of the Labor Movement in California* and, more rapidly, in Carey McWilliams, *California, The Great Exception* (1949) and David F. Selvin, *Sky Full of Storm* (1966). On San Francisco-centered labor problems see Robert E. L. Knight, *Industrial Relations in the San Francisco Bay Area 1900–1918* (1960); Bernard C. Cronin, *Father Yorke and the Labor Movement in San Francisco, 1900–1910* (1943); Frederick L. Ryan, *Industrial Relations in the San Francisco Building Trades* (1936); Paul S. Taylor, *The Sailors' Union of the Pacific* (1923); and Hyman G. Weintraub, *Andrew Furuseth, Emancipator of the Seamen* (1959).

Grace Heilman Stimson, *Rise of the Labor Movement in Los Angeles* (1955) and Louis B. and Richard S. Perry, *A History of the Los Angeles Labor Movement, 1911–1941* (1963) provide a comprehensive account. Supplementary works include Richard C. Miller, "Otis and His *Times*" (Berkeley dissertation, 1961); Louis Adamic, *Dynamite* (1929); *The Forty Years War*, a Los Angeles *Times* brochure, October 1, 1929; William J. Burns, *The Masked War* (1913); Ortie McManigal, *The National Dynamite Plot* (1913); *Autobiography of Lincoln Steffens;* and Clarence Darrow, *The Story of My Life* (1932).

Paul F. Brissenden, *The IWW, A Study of American Syndicalism* (1920); Patrick Renshaw, *The Wobblies* (1967); and Martin Dubofsky, *We Shall Be All: A History of the Industrial Workers of the World* (1969) survey the movement as a whole. Carleton Parker, *The Casual Laborer and Other Essays* (1920) and Cornelia S. Parker, *An American Idyll, Carleton H. Parker* (1919) are of interest. Hyman G. Weintraub, "The IWW in California, 1905–1931" (UCLA thesis, 1947) is the most complete on its subject. Thinly disguised as fiction, part of the story appears in Wallace Stegner, *The Preacher and the Slave* (1950). On another episode see Woodrow C. Whitten, "The Wheatland Episode," *PHR*, 17 (1948), 37–42. Robert H. Frost, *The Mooney Case* (1968) is the most thorough follow-through on its subject. Other useful works are Curt Gentry, *Frame-up* (1967) and Ernest J. Hopkins, *What Happened in the Mooney Case* (1932). Eldredge F. Dowell, *A History of Criminal Syndicalism Legislation in the United States* (1939) trains the spotlight on a disgraceful injustice. See also Franklin Hichborn, *The Case of Charlotte Anita Whitney* (1920) and Woodrow C. Whitten, "Trial of Charlotte Anita Whitney," *PHR*, 15 (1946), 286–94.

26. The Boom of the Twenties

Cleland and Hardy, *March of Industry* reaches into the twenties. Its tables and maps are a valuable adjunct. Useful also are the reports of the Bureau of the Census and such state issues as *California Crop Reports, Economic Resources and Extractive Industries of California,* and *California Mineral Production.* Julian Dana, *A. P. Giannini, Giant in the West* (1947) deals with a key figure and Joe S. Bain, *Economics of the Pacific Coast Petroleum Industry* (3 vols., 1944–47), with a key industry. John O. Pohlmann, "Alphonzo E. Bell: A Biography," *SCQ*, 46 (1964), 197–217, 315–50 tells of a fortune made in oil and real estate. Other businesses are represented in William C. Odisho, "Salt Lake to Oakland: The Western Pacific" (Berkeley dissertation, 1941); Latta, *Black Gold in the Joaquin;* Dwight L. Clarke, "'The Big Silver,' California's Greatest Silver Mine," *CHSQ*, 32 (1963), 1–41; Giles T. Brown, *Ships That Sail No More: Marine Transportation from San Diego to Puget Sound, 1910–1940* (1966); and Josephine Kingsbury Jacobs, Sunkist Advertising. Anton Wagner, *Los Angeles: Werden, Leben und Gestalt der Zweimillionenstadt in Südkalifornien* (1935) is a geographer's analysis of the factors that contributed to the rise of the state's largest city.

The growing addition to the automobile can be followed in *Touring Topics* and its successor *Westways*, particularly in the December, 1950, issue marking the 50th anniversary of the Automobile Club of Southern California. See also Ben Blow, *California Highways* (1920); Frederic L. Paxson, "The Highway Movement, 1916–1935," *AHR*, 51 (1946), 236–53; Ashleigh E. Brilliant, "Some Aspects of Mass Motorization in Southern California, 1919–1929," *SCQ*, 47 (1965), 191–208; John C. Burnham, "The Gasoline Tax and the Automobile Revolution," *MVHR*, 48 (1961), 435–59; and Earl S. Pomeroy, *In Search of the Golden West, The Tourist in Western America* (1957).

Lewis Jacobs, *The Rise of the American Film, A Critical History* (1939) and Leo Rosten, *Hollywood, the Movie Colony, the Movie Makers* (1939) analyze economic growth, artistic development, and social impact. Later appraisals include Arthur Knight, *The Liveliest Art* (1957) and A. R. Fulton, *Motion Pictures: The Development of an Art from Silent Films to the Age of Television* (1960). Bosley Crowther writes authoritatively in *The Lion's Share* (1957), a history of Metro-Goldwyn-Mayer, and in *Hollywood Rajah, The Life and Times of Louis B. Mayer* (1960). There is a vast amount of writing about the movie makers. Among the most readable are Nathanael West's novel, *The Day of the Locust* (1939); F. Scott Fitzgerald's *The Last Tycoon* (1941); and Lillian Ross, *Picture* (1952), a *New Yorker* report on the filming of *The Red Badge of Courage*.

In McWilliams, *Southern California Country* C. C. Julian and Aimee Semple McPherson are viewed as sociological phenomena. Nancy Barr Mavity, *Sister Aimee* (1931) does justice to the most widely heralded southern Californian of the twenties. Various bits of social and political history are presented in Norris C. Hundley, Jr., "Katherine Phillips Edson and the Fight for the California Minimum Wage, 1912–1913," *PHR*, 29 (1960), 271–86; Abe Hoffman, "A Look at Llano: Experiment in Economic Socialism," *CHSQ*, 40 (1961), 215–36; Paul K. Conkin, *Two Paths to Utopia* (1964), 103–96; Gilman M. Ostrander, *The Prohibition Movement in California* (1957); and Wendell E. Harmon, "The Bootlegger Era in Southern California," *SCQ*, 37 (1955), 335–46.

27. The Great Depression

Dixon Wecter, *The Age of the Great Depression* (1948) portrays the nationwide impact of hard times after 1929. There is no comparable study for California, though Paul N. Woolf, *Economic Trends in California, 1929–1934* (1935); Leigh Athearn, *The California State Relief Administration, 1935–1939* (1939), and the California State Chamber of Commerce, *Economic Survey of California and Its Counties, 1942* (1943) inform on certain aspects. Carey McWilliams, *California, The Great Exception* (1949); Robert G. Cleland, in his historical summation, *California in Our Time, 1900–1940* (1947); and Oliver Carlson, more bitingly, in *A Mirror for Californians* (1941) offer analysis and commentary.

The labor problems of this decade are discussed in Camp, *San Francisco, Port of Gold*, and McWilliams, *California, The Great Exception*. On the San Francisco general strike see Paul Eliel, *The Waterfront and General Strikes* (1934); William F. Dunne, *The Great San Francisco General Strike* (1934); and Mike Quin, *The Big Strike* (1949). Another element in labor history is discussed in Manuel P. Servin, "The Pre–World War II Mexican American: An Interpretation," *CHSQ*, 44 (1966), 325–32.

On the plight of the migratory farm workers a quick introduction is Dorothea Lange and Paul S. Taylor, *American Exodus* (1939; enlarged and reprinted, 1969). Varden Fuller, "The Supply of Agricultural Labor as a Factor in the Evolution of Farm Organization in California" (Berkeley dissertation, 1939) was published in a United States Senate Committee on Education and Labor report, *Violations of Free Speech and Rights of Labor*, part 54 (1940), 19, 777–819, 898. Other studies include Walter Goldschmidt, *As You Sow* (1947), a sociological analysis of two San Joaquin Valley communities; Carlton Beals, *The American Earth* (1939); Clarke Chambers, *California Farm Organizations, 1929–1941* (1952); and Carey McWilliams, *Factories in the Field* (1939). John Steinbeck communicated the message far more effectively in *In Dubious Battle* (1936) and *The Grapes of Wrath* (1939).

The cults and "isms" are admirably handled in McWilliams, *Southern California Country* (1946) and in the Cleland and Carlson volumes cited above. See particularly Luther Whiteman and Samuel L. Lewis, *Glory Roads: The Psychological State of California* (1936); Abraham Holtzman, *The Townsend Movement, A Political Study* (1963); and Winston and Marian Moore's aptly titled book on Ham and Eggs, *Out of the Frying Pan* (1939). Upton Sinclair, *I, Governor of California and How I Ended Poverty* (1933) and *I, Candidate for Governor, and How I Got Licked* (1934) are key documents on Epic. A mainstay of the campaign, the *Epic News*, suddenly became a rarity. See also *The Autobiography of Upton Sinclair* (1962); George Creel, *Rebel at Large* (1947); Charles E. Larsen, "The Epic Campaign of 1934," *PHR*, 27 (1958), 127–48; and Russell M. Posner, "A. P. Giannini and the 1934 Campaign in California," *SCQ*, 39 (1957), 190–201. Robert E. Burke, *Olson's New Deal for California* (1953) is an admirable study. The issue central in Frost's *The Mooney Case* continued important in California politics. Thomas S. Barclay writes on another piece of unfinished business left until the thirties in "Reapportionment in California," *PHR*, 4 (1936), 93–129.

Remi A. Nadeau, *The Water Seekers* (1950) and Vincent Ostrom,

Water and Politics: A Study of Water Policies and Administration in the Development of Los Angeles (1953) have much on the Boulder Canyon project. G. Bailey, *Water Resources of California* (1927); the Los Angeles Department of Water and Power, *Data on Available Water Supply and Future Requirements of Los Angeles and the Metropolitan Area* (1928); and Ernest L. Bogart, *The Water Problem of Southern California* (1934) assess the needs. David O. Woodbury, *The Colorado Conquest* (1941); Reuel Olson, *The Colorado River Compact* (1926); and F. E. Weymouth, *Summary of Metropolitan Aqueduct Situation* (1931) address themselves to the preliminaries. Federal decision making that a high dam should be built is best presented in Beverley R. Moeller, "Phil Swing and the Boulder Canyon Project" (UCLA dissertation, 1969). Frank Waters, *The Colorado* (1946) is particularly informing on the construction, also stressed in Ray L. Wilbur and Elwood Mead, *Construction of Hoover Dam* (1935); George A. Pettitt, *So Boulder Dam Was Built* (1935); and Paul L. Kleinsorge, *The Boulder Canyon Project* (1941). International competition for the flow of the Colorado is the subject of Norris Hundley, Jr., *Dividing the Waters: A Century of Controversy Between the United States and Mexico* (1966). On the delivery system see Metropolitan Water District, *The Colorado Aqueduct* (1939) and *The Great Aqueduct* (1941).

Robert De Roos, *The Thirsty Land, The Story of the Central Valley Project* (1948) is a popular prospectus but less elementary than *The Central Valley Project* (1942), compiled by the Writers' Program. Marion Clawson, *Acreage Limitation in the Central Valley* (1944), *The Effect of the Central Valley Project on the Agricultural and Industrial Economy and on the Social Character of California* (1945), and *History of Legislation and Policy Formation of the Central Valley Project* (1946) are expository and supportive of the policies of the Bureau of Reclamation. Senator Sheridan Downey's *They Would Rule the Valley* (1947) abominates the 160-acre limitation. For antidote see Paul S. Taylor, "Excess Land Law: Pressure versus Principle," *California Law Review*, 47 (1959), 499–541. In a different vein see Viola P. May, *Shasta Dam and Its Builders* (1945).

28. A Distinctive Culture

Rediscovery of the environment is represented in guidebooks such as those by Aubrey Drury (1935, 1947) and the Federal Writers' Project (1939), in the publications of the automobile clubs, and in photographic albums such as Edward Weston, *California and the West* (1940), and Ansel Adams, *The Sierra Nevada* (1938) and *My Camera in Yosemite Valley* (1949). There also was a new round of nature writing in the series devoted to regions, rivers, mountains, and lakes. Edwin Corle, *Desert Country* (1941); Carey McWilliams, *Southern California Country* (1946); Anne B. Fisher, *The Salinas, Upside-down River* (1945); Roderick Peattie, *The Pacific Coast Ranges* (1946) and *The Sierra Nevada* (1947); and George and Bliss Hinkle, *Sierra-Nevada Lakes* (1949) are examples. François E. Matthes, *Geologic History of the Yosemite Valley* (1930), *The Incomparable Valley, A Geologic Interpretation of the Yosemite* (1950), and *Sequoia National Park, A Geological Album* (1950) go back to the geological beginnings. Carl P. Russell, *One Hundred Years in Yosemite* (1931, 1947) recites the human history.

The writings of this period are available in libraries and, in varying degree, can still be bought. They can be sampled generously in George Sterling, ed., *Continent's End, An Anthology of Contemporary California Poets* (1925); Joseph Henry Jackson, ed., *Continent's End, A Collection of California Writing* (1944); J. H. Jackson, *The Western Gate, A San Francisco Reader* (1952); and in Caughey, *California Heritage,* 379–426, 435–59.

Edmund Wilson, *The Boys in the Back Room* (1941) is a rapid glance at several of the writers of this time. Appraisals of Steinbeck include: Harry T. Moore, *The Novels of John Steinbeck* (1939); E. W. Tedlock, Jr., and C. V. Wicker, *Steinbeck and His Critics, A Record of Twenty-five Years* (1957); Warren French, *John Steinbeck* (1961); and Joseph Fontenrose, *John Steinbeck, An Introduction and Interpretation* (1964). Lawrence Clark Powell wrote the first book on Jeffers in 1932, *Robinson Jeffers, The Man and His Work* (revised, 1940). Radcliffe Squires, *The Loyalties of Robinson Jeffers* (1956); Frederic L. Carpenter, *Robinson Jeffers* (1962); and Melba Berry Bennett, *The Stone Mason of Tor House: The Life and Times of Robinson Jeffers* (1966) are supplemented by Ann N. Ridgeway, ed., *The Selected Letters of Robinson Jeffers* (1969) and *The Selected Poetry of Robinson Jeffers* (1938).

The astronomy story is detailed in G. Edward Pendray, *Men, Mirrors, and Stars* (1935) and in David O. Woodbury, *The Glass Giant of Palomar* (1946). Palomar and other phases of scientific advancement are noted in Mc-Williams, *California, The Great Exception.* On the directions in historical scholarship there are hints in Oscar Lewis, *I Remember Christine* (1942) and more concrete data in *New Spain and the Anglo-American West* (2 vols., 1932) and *Greater America: Essays in Honor of Herbert Eugene Bolton* (1945). See also Lawrence Kinnaird, "Bolton of California," *CHSQ,* 32 (1953), 97–103 and John W. Caughey, "Herbert Eugene Bolton," *AW,* 1 (1964), 36–39, 79.

29. Wartime Upsurge

McWilliams, *California, The Great Exception,* though broader in scope, is the closest approach to a survey of California during the war years. The reports of the Bureau of the Census and of various state agencies provide statistics. Particularly useful is the California State Chamber of Commerce, "Economic Survey of California and Its Counties," *California Blue Book, 1946,* pp. 409–772. Davis McEntire, *The Population of California* (1946) and Marion Clawson, "What It Means to Be a Californian," *CHSQ,* 24 (1945), 139–61 deal with characteristics as well as numbers.

Katherine Archibald, *Wartime Shipyard* (1947); William G. Cun-

ningham, *The Aircraft Industry, A Study in Industrial Location* (1951); Frank
J. Taylor and Lawton Wright, *Democracy's Air Arsenal* (1947); and Ewald
T. Grether, *The Steel-using Industries of California* (1946) deal selectively
with war industries.

Morton Grodzins, *Americans Betrayed* (1949) is an analysis of the
motivation for the removal of the Japanese. Western Defense Command,
Japanese Evacuation from the West Coast (1943) is General De Witt's apologia.
In Kent Robert Greenfield, *Command Decisions* (1960), Stetson Conn concentrates on the decision to evacuate. Allan R. Bosworth makes a most effective
summation in *America's Concentration Camps* (1967). Carey McWilliams,
Prejudice: Japanese-Americans, Symbols of Racial Intolerance (1944) and
Bradford Smith, *Americans from Japan* (1948) are sharply critical. War Re-
location Authority, *A Story of Human Conservation* (1946) is the formal report
of the administrators. Ansel Adams, *Born Free and Equal: The Story of
Manzanar* (1944) and Mine Okubo, *Citizen 31660* (1946) are pictorial; the
latter by one of the evacuees. The sociological consequences are meticulously
reported in Dorothy S. Thomas and Richard Nishimoto, *The Spoilage* (1946);
Thomas, with Charles Kikuchi and James Sakoda, *The Salvage* (1952); Jacobus
TenBroek, Edward N. Barnhart, and Floyd W. Matson, *Prejudice, War and the
Constitution* (1954); Leonard Bloom and Ruth Riemer, *Removal and Return*
(1949); Leonard Broom and John I. Kitsuse, *The Managed Casualty* (1956);
and Leonard J. Arrington, *The Price of Prejudice* (1962). On the law see
Eugene V. Rostow, *The Sovereign Prerogative and the Quest for Law* (1962).
On neglected features see Edward N. Barnhart, "The Individual Exclusion of
Japanese Americans in World War II," *PHR*, 29 (1960), 111–30; and "Japanese
Internees from Peru," *PHR*, 31 (1962), 169–78. James Edmiston, *Home Again*
(1955) is a novel which personalizes the enormity of the injustice.

30. A Touch of Midas

A number of references cited in this chapter are also relevant to
the content of the other five chapters, 31–35, which concern California since
the Second World War. Among them are: Neil Morgan, *The California Syndrome* (1969); R. L. Duffus, *Queen Calafia's Island* (1965); Earl S. Pomeroy,
The Pacific Slope (1965); Remi Nadeau, *California, the New Society* (1963)
and *Los Angeles, from Mission to Modern City* (1960); Edmund G. Brown
and others, *California, the Dynamic State* (1966); Carey McWilliams, *The
California Revolution* (1968); "California, the Nation within a Nation," special
number of the *Saturday Review* (September 23, 1967); and "California, Where
the Land Ends," *Harper's* (December 1969).

Reports of the Bureau of the Census are useful, as are the successive
issues of *California Statistical Abstract*, by the California Economic Development Agency. Specialized studies include Warren S. Thompson, *Growth and
Changes in California's Population* (1955); Margaret S. Gordon, *Employment*

Expansion and Population Growth, The California Experience, 1900–1950 (1954); and Davis McEntire, *The Labor Force in California, 1900–1950* (1952). *Fortnight,* launched in 1946, and *Frontier* (1949–67) are broadly informative.

Ernest A. Engelbert, *Metropolitan California* (1961) and a University of California publication, *The Metropolitan Future* (1965), may be supplemented by Winston W. Crouch and Beatrice Dinerman, *Southern California Metropolis: A Study in Development of Government for a Metropolitan Area* (1964); Mel Scott, *The San Francisco Bay Area: A Metropolis in Perspective* (1959); Kingsley Davis and Eleanor Langlois, *Future Demographic Growth of the San Francisco Bay Area* (1959); Thomas J. Kent, Jr., *City and Regional Planning for the Metropolitan San Francisco Bay Area* (1963); and Lawrence Kinnaird, *History of the Greater San Francisco Bay Region* (3 vols., 1967). H. O. Stekler, *Structure and Performance of the Aerospace Industry* (1965) has much about California. Seymour Chapin, "Garrett and Pressurized Flight: A Business Built on Thin Air," *PHR,* 35 (1966), 329–43 is a capsule history of one company.

31. Great Constructions

Many of the works cited for chapter 30 carry over. Nadeau, *Los Angeles, from Mission to Modern City* is most vivid on the tract-housing assembly line. See in addition Samuel E. Wood and Alfred E. Heller, *The Phantom Cities of California* (1963); Marshall Kaplan, *The Community Builders* (1967); and John Anson Ford, *Thirty Explosive Years in Los Angeles County* (1961). California Water Resources Board, *The California Water Plan* (1957) outlines that most ambitious project. H. Marshall Goodwin, Jr., "The Arroyo Seco: From Dry Gulch to Freeway," *SCQ,* 47 (1965), 73–102 is the history of the first California freeway. His "California's Growing Freeway System" (UCLA dissertation, 1969) is a detailed account of almost every phase of freeway development.

32. Politics and Government

By all odds the best introduction to recent California politics is Gladwin Hill, *Dancing Bear, An Inside Look at California Politics* (1968). For many years Hill has been California correspondent for the New York *Times.* There are handbooks on California government and politics by Henry A. Turner and John A. Vieg; Winston W. Crouch, Dean E. McHenry, John Bollens, and Stanley Scott; and Bernard L. Hyink, Seyom Brown, and Ernest W. Thacker, political scientists all. Dean R. Cresap, *Party Politics in the Golden State* (1954) is an earlier treatment. Don A. Allen, *Legislative Sourcebook, 1849–1965* (1965) is a useful reference.

Leo Katcher, *Earl Warren: A Political Biography* (1967) and John

D. Weaver, *Warren: The Man, the Court, the Era* (1967) are salutes to a Californian who went on to a noteworthy term as Chief Justice of the United States. Lester Velie, "The Secret Boss of California," *Collier's* (August 13 and 20, 1949) and Carey McWilliams, in *Nation* (July 9, 1949), report the lobbying prowess of Art Samish. Trevor Ambrister, "The Octopus in the State House," *Saturday Evening Post* (Feb. 12, 1966) tells of Samish's tribe of successors. McWilliams, "Government by Whitaker and Baxter," *Nation* (April 14 and 21, and May 5, 1951) and Irwin Ross, "The Supersalesmen of California Politics: Whitaker and Baxter," *Harper's*, 219 (July 1959) inform on a potent agency.

Ernest R. Bartley, *The Tidelands Oil Controversy* (1953) discusses a matter pressed in court and politically. Winston W. Crouch, *The Initiative and Referendum in California* (1950) measures the effectiveness of these techniques of direct democracy.

On one of the peculiarities in California politics see Markell C. Baer, *Story of the California Republican Assembly* (1955); Francis Carney, *The Rise of the Democratic Clubs in California* (1958); James Q. Wilson, *The Amateur Democrat* (1962); and Leonard C. Rowe, *Pre-primary Endorsements in California Politics* (1962). As long ago as 1956 Eugene Burdick set his political novel *The Ninth Wave* in California.

Malcolm E. Jewell, ed., *The Politics of Reapportionment* (1962) came too soon to report success. Helen Fuller, "The Man to See in California," *Harper's*, 226 (January 1963) and Ed Cray, "Jesse Unruh, 'Big Daddy' of California," *Nation* (March 9, 1963) relate to the same individual. Raymond E. Wolfinger and Fred I. Greenstein, *The Political Cultures of California* (1966) and Herbert L. Phillips, "A Bucketful of Smoke," in *California, The Dynamic State* (1966) use contrasting titles to approach the same subject. Journals of opinion, such as *Frontier* and the *Nation*, have given much attention to California politics.

Ronald Reagan has been much written about in the local and national press and magazines and in Bill Boyarsky, *The Rise of Ronald Reagan* (1968) and Joseph Lewis, *What Makes Reagan Run?* (1968). More revealing would be a book on *What Makes Henry* [Salvatori] *Make Ronnie Run?*

33. Challenging Injustice

Edward L. Barrett, Jr., *The Tenney Committee* (1961) is a judiciously restrained study. On the Hollywood Ten and what followed see Gordon Kahn, *Hollywood on Trial* (1948) and John Cogley, *Report on Blacklisting* (2 vols., 1956). With an engineer as protagonist, Abraham Polonsky, *A Season of Fear* (1956) measures the impact of inquisition by so-called loyalty oaths. Seymour Kern, *The Golden Scalpel* (1960) similarly explores the collision course of the Hippocratic Oath and the one imposed by the state. On the exit of the test oath for all state employees see John W. Caughey, "Farewell to California's 'Loyalty' Oath." *PHR*, 38 (1969), 123–28. On the University's oath experience see George R. Stewart, Jr., *The Year of the Oath* (1950); David P.

Gardner, *The California Oath Controversy* (1967); and John W. Caughey, "A Battlefield Revisited," *Law in Transition*, 4 (1967), 172–78.

The Berkeley pathway to school integration is charted in Redmond C. Staats, *Interracial Problems and Their Effect on Education in the Public Schools of Berkeley, California* (1959); *De Facto Segregation in the Berkeley Public Schools* (1963), report of a citizens committee; Neil Sullivan, *Integration, A Plan for Berkeley* (1968); Virginia T. Hadsell and Grethel C. Newcom. *Equal Start: A New School, A New Chance* (1969); and Neil Sullivan and Evelyn S. Stewart, *Now Is the Time: Integration in the Berkeley Schools* (1969). Another success story is Irving Hendrick, *The Development of a School Integration Plan in Riverside, California* (1968). John and LaRee Caughey, *School Segregation on Our Doorstep: The Los Angeles Story* (1966) and *Segregation Blights Our Schools* (1967) and John W. Caughey, "Segregation Increases in Los Angeles," *California Teachers Association Journal*, 64 (1968), 39–41 describe an effort largely unsuccessful. Beginning in the fall of 1966, the State Board of Education mandated racial and ethnic surveys, school by school, throughout the state. The first summary report on distributions of pupils, that for the fall of 1966, was issued in 1967. The Los Angeles City Schools published their figures under the title *Racial and Ethnic Survey*, starting with the fall of 1966, as did certain other districts.

On related matters see David Hulburd, *This Happened in Pasadena* (1951); J. Allen Broyles, *The John Birch Society: Anatomy of a Protest* (1964); Thomas W. Storke, *I Write for Freedom* (1963), featuring his tiff with the Birch Society; and Gerald Gottlieb, *Capital Punishment* (1967). *Open Forum* (1941 on), the periodical of the ACLU of Southern California, reports occasionally at length on violations of civil liberties and efforts in and out of court to prevent repetitions. *The Dixon Line* (1963 on) is a monthly commentary issuing from Los Alamitos in Orange County.

34. A Time of Confrontations

In *The Holy Barbarians* (1959) Lawrence Lipton gives an avuncular view of the hippies. Albert T. Anderson and Bernice P. Biggs, *A Focus on Rebellion* (1962) is a documentary on the San Francisco City Hall incident of May, 1960. A perceptive account of the Free Speech Movement at Berkeley is Seymour M. Lipset and Sheldon S. Wolin, *The Berkeley Student Revolt* (1965). *The Muscatine Report*, an approximate forecast of changes in educational program and governance, appeared under the title *Education at Berkeley* (1967). Art Seidenbaum, *Confrontation on Campus* (1969) is a revealing report after in-depth observing and interviewing at nine California campuses.

Leo Gebler, *Mexican Immigration to the United States* (1966); Fernando Penalosa, "The Changing Mexican-American in Southern California," *Sociology and Social Research*, 51 (1967), 405–17; and *Education in the Mexican American Community in Los Angeles County* (1968), Report of the California State Advisory Committee to the U.S. Commission on Civil Rights, are introductory to the Mexican minority, prominent also in Lloyd S. Fisher, *The Harvest Labor Market in California* (1953). On the braceros see Ernest Galarza, *Merchants of Labor: The Mexican Bracero Story* (1964); Truman E. Moore, *The Slaves We Rent* (1965); and W. Willard Wirtz, *Year of Transition; Seasonal*

Farm Labor, 1965 (1966), a report on the termination of the bracero program. César Chávez' efforts on behalf of California harvest workers have been described in many newspaper and magazine stories. The principal book is John Gregory Dunne, *Delano: The Anatomy of the Great California Grapeworkers' Strike* (1967).

Though based on elaborate and well-financed hearings, the McCone Commission report, *Violence in the City* (1965), is a far from convincing analysis of the Los Angeles Riot. Valuable supplements are Robert Conot, *Rivers of Blood, View Years of Darkness* (1967) and Jack Jones, *The Voice from Watts* (1967). Budd Schulberg, *From the Ashes, Voices from Watts* (1967) is an anthology of writers in the workshop he organized in Watts after the riot. See also Denis Hale and Jonathon Eisen, *The California Dream* (1968).

In *American Racism: Exploration of the Nature of Prejudice* (1970), a historian and a social psychologist, Roger Daniels and Harry H. L. Kitano, use California as an exhibit for a resumé of race prejudice operative up to and including the present generation.

35. Impact of Massive Growth

Morgan, *The California Syndrome*; Brown, *California, the Dynamic State*; Nadeau, *California, the New Society*; Duffus, *Queen Calafia's Island*; and Hill, *Dancing Bear* inventory many of the consequences of the hyperthyroid growth of the forties, fifties, and sixties. Engelbert, *Metropolitan California*; Crouch and Dinerman, *Southern California Metropolis*; Nadeau, *Los Angeles*; Scott, *San Francisco Bay Area*; and Kinnaird, *History of the Greater San Francisco Bay Area* focus on the two principal concentrations of population and activity. Libbie Block, *The Hills of Beverly* (1957) and Cynthia Lindsay, *The Natives Are Restless* (1960) exercise the novelist's opportunity to appraise a culture. Richard M. Elman, *Ill at Ease in Compton* (1968) accomplishes something similar for another segment of society.

Mel Scott, *Partnership in the Arts: Public and Private Support of Cultural Activities in the San Francisco Bay Area* (1963); Arthur Bloomfield, *The San Francisco Opera, 1923–1961* (1961) and *The Arts in California* (1966) and Howard Taubman, "Arts on the West Coast: Challenge to the East," New York *Times*, January 3, 1967, are introductory. Douglas Honnold, *Southern California Architecture, 1769–1956* (1956); Esther McCoy, *Five California Architects* (1960), *Richard Neutra* (1960), and *Modern California Houses: Case Study Houses, 1945–1962* (1962); and Harold Gilliam and Phil Palmer, *The Face of San Francisco* (1960) concentrate on one art form.

James C. Stone, *California's Commitment to Public Education* (1961); Merton E. Hill, *The Junior College Movement in California, 1907–1948* (1949); and Theodore L. Reller, *Problems of Public Education in the San Francisco Bay Area* (1963) extend into the recent past. Glenn S. Dumke, "Higher Education in California," *CHSQ*, 42 (1963), 99–110 and Arthur G. Coons, *Crises in California Education* (1968) are much concerned with the master plan for higher education. On a much controverted issue see Raymond McHugh, *Land of the Free and Its Critics* (1967).

Eliot Porter, *The Place No One Knew: Glen Canyon on the Colorado*

(1963); Philip Hyde and Francois Leydet, *The Last Redwoods* (1963); and Richard Kaufmann, *Gentle Wilderness: The Sierra Nevada* (1964) are pleadings for conservation of natural beauties. *Cry California* (1965 on) is a periodical dedicated to the fight against pollution in all its forms. By their titles Raymond F. Dasmann, *The Destruction of California* (1965); Samuel E. Wood, *California, Going, Going . . .* (1962); Richard G. Lillard, *Eden in Jeopardy* (1966); and William Bronson, *How To Kill a Golden State* (1968) proclaim this same concern. In the opening issue of the Los Angeles *Times* for 1967, Art Seidenbaum's question and Jim Murray's answer—"Onward California's Millions—And Upward?" and "I'll Get Off Here If You Don't Mind"—state the fundamental problem and underline its gravity. The apocalyptic message that exploding population and runaway science are on the verge of sounding Doomsday for life on this planet is expounded in Rachel Carson, *Silent Spring* (1962) and Paul R. Ehrlich, *The Population Bomb* (1968). John G. Burke, "Technology and Values," *The Great Ideas Today* (1969), part 2, pp. 190–235 is a telling resumé of the rise of the problem of existing with mushrooming science and technology and with the accompanying necessary changes in our national value system.

Index